Essays in American Intellectual History

Essays in American Intellectual History

Edited by

Wilson Smith

The Dryden Press
Hinsdale, Illinois

A division of Holt, Rinehart and Winston

Library of Congress Catalog Card Number: 74-2804
ISBN: 0-03-079415-3
Printed in the United States of America
56789 081 987654321

Preface

Like obtrusive framing around a great painting, a lengthy introduction to a collection of good essays is unnecessary. Each of these thirty-nine essays is a display piece. Each creates its own setting and defines, at least implicitly, its own perception of intellectual history. Most of the essays are already well known to students of American thought. Some are the only pieces written on particular themes; others are memorable discussions of topics that historians will always be reexamining. All of the essays are addressed to important problems in the history of ideas, broadly conceived. Their durability and excellence are reason enough for making them available to students in one volume.

The essays represent a distinct era in studying the history of ideas in America. I do not suggest that this era, which reaches from the 1930s to the 1960s, has passed, only that its style is being modified. The leading intellectual historians of the era, measured by their insights and the comprehensiveness of their discussions, as well as by the universal classroom acceptance of their work, are Vernon L. Parrington, Perry Miller, Merle Curti, Ralph Henry Gabriel, and Herbert W. Schneider. Men from different academic specialties have long been attracted to intellectual history: Parrington and Miller were professors of literature; Schneider is a professor of philosophy; Curti and Gabriel are historians.

Though this collection includes only representative pieces by four of these men, and none by Parrington, whose writing in this field was confined mainly to his three-volume study of American democratic thought, these five men were the master historians of American ideas in the twentieth century. Their textbooks and large-scale studies established the boundaries of intellectual history for historians who came of age intellectually throughout the years of the Great Depression and the Second World War. Some of the other authors in this book were their students; others were their committed readers, as I have been.

Like other veterans of World War II who returned to the graduate study of history, I looked to their writings as dependable and illuminating guides into the history of ideas. Of course, my generation of graduate students also admired earlier writers, like George Santayana, John Dewey, and Arthur O. Lovejoy, whose essays are included here (just as we were taught or influenced by a slightly later group of leading historians whose major works in intellectual history did not appear until the

1950s: Henry Steele Commager, Richard Hofstadter, and Stow Persons), but it was Parrington, Miller, Curti, Gabriel, and Schneider who, for me and for many other students of that era, furnished the expository models of intellectual history. We were grateful to them then. We continue to admire their Emersonian zeal for ideas and their Jamesian dedication to the pragmatic search for historical truths in human experience.

In keeping with this introduction, most of the headnotes preceding each selection also are brief. They try to remind the reader of the essays' significance for intellectual history and, where pertinent, point out some of the largest themes in the history of ideas, such as the problems of man's perception of God, of nature, and of himself as a free or limited individual and as a member of society. Since I believe that students will be better informed through their classroom experiences and wider reading than by lengthy editor's comments, each headnote suggests several additional readings relevant to the essay. Citations of paperbound books are preceded by an asterisk (*). Most footnotes have been omitted in order to save space in this volume and in the expectation that students who want the citations will be able to find the original essays in any good library.

My thanks go to the authors who graciously permitted me to reprint their writings, and to Thomas H. Bender, who gave me the benefit of his good judgment in helping to choose this particular group of essays.

Wilson Smith

Contents

Part I
Colonial Ideas in America **1**

1 *Alan Simpson* The Puritan Tradition **3**
2 *Perry Miller* The Marrow of Puritan Divinity **12**
3 *Herbert W. Schneider* A Review of "The New England Mind: The Seventeenth Century" by Perry Miller **45**
4 *Edmund S. Morgan* Miller's Williams **50**
5 *Roland Bainton* Jonathan Edwards: "The Great Awakening" **58**
6 *Edwin S. Gaustad* The Theological Effects of the Great Awakening in New England **66**

Part II
Ideas in the Revolutionary Republic **83**

7 *Edmund S. Morgan* The Puritan Ethic and the American Revolution **85**
8 *I. B. Cohen* The Empirical Temper of Benjamin Franklin **98**
9 *Douglas Adair* "Experience Must Be Our Only Guide": History, Democratic Theory, and the United States Constitution **107**
10 *Arthur O. Lovejoy* The Theory of Human Nature in the American Constitution and the Method of Counterpoise **119**
11 *Adrienne Koch* Philosopher-Statesmen of the Republic **132**
12 *Clinton Rossiter* Hamilton's Political Science: Man and Society **142**
13 *John Ryerson* On John Adams **153**
14 *Julian P. Boyd* Thomas Jefferson Survives **159**

Part III
Ideas for a Constitutional Democracy **169**

15 *Merle Curti* The Great Mr. Locke: America's Philosopher, 1783-1861 **171**
16 *Clarence H. Faust* The Background of the Unitarian Opposition to Transcendentalism **192**
17 *Perry Miller* Theodore Parker: Apostasy within Liberalism **208**
18 *Stephen E. Whicher* Emerson's Tragic Sense **223**
19 *Ralph H. Gabriel* Constitutional Democracy: A Nineteenth-Century Faith **229**
20 *Louis Hartz* The Reactionary Enlightenment **238**

Part IV
Ideas in a Darwinian Age **251**

21 *Conrad Wright* The Religion of Geology **253**
22 *Stow Persons* Darwinism and American Culture **264**
23 *John Dewey* The Influence of Darwinism on Philosophy **272**
24 *Max H. Fisch* Evolution in American Philosophy **281**
25 *Robert B. Notestein* The Moralist Rigorism of W. G. Sumner **293**
26 *Henry S. Kariel* The Limits of Social Science: Henry Adams' Quest for Order **303**

Part V
Ideas in the Progressive Era **317**

27 *George Santayana* The Genteel Tradition in American Philosophy **319**
28 *David W. Noble* Veblen and Progress: The American Climate of Opinion **334**
29 *John Higham* Toward Racism: The History of an Idea **350**
30 *Henry F. May* The Rebellion of the Intellectuals, 1912-1917 **370**

Part VI
Ideas for the Twentieth Century **381**

31 *Alfred Kazin* The Freudian Revolution Analyzed **383**
32 *Charles Frankel* John Dewey's Legacy **389**
33 *Robert Goedecke* Holmes, Brandeis, and Frankfurter: Differences in Pragmatic Jurisprudence **402**
34 *Walter M. Horton* The New Orthodoxy **415**
35 *Clarke A. Chambers* The Belief in Progress in Twentieth-Century America **422**
36 *William G. Carleton* American Intellectuals and American Democracy **438**
37 *Harvey Brooks* Scientific Concepts and Cultural Change **452**
38 *Merle Curti* Human Nature in American Thought: Retreat from Reason in the Age of Science **463**
39 *John E. Smith* The Spirit of American Philosophy **473**

Essays in American Intellectual History

Part I
Colonial Ideas in America

1
The Puritan Tradition

Alan Simpson

How do we most perceptively view American Puritanism today? Where do we find its influences or its remnants in the nineteenth- and twentieth-century English-speaking world? These questions are posed and answered here by Alan Simpson without cudgeling the reader with pleas for the "relevance" of Puritanism. In an overview of his subject that only one deeply immersed in it can present, Simpson explores the life span of "Puritan consciousness" from the mid-sixteenth-century English reformers through English and American Victorianism of the nineteenth century. Along the way he emphasizes the Anglo-American tie in education through Puritanism, the development of Puritan attitudes toward self-government, and the questionable legacy of the Puritan sense of righteousness toward political affairs. Though American Puritanism was rooted in Calvinism, the reader can understand through this essay (and through the next one, by Perry Miller) how unique the Puritanism of England and America became in its theology and in its lasting secular overtones.

For further reading: Michael Walzer, "Puritanism as a Revolutionary Ideology," *History and Theory*, 3 (1961), 59-90, reprinted in *Paul Goodman (ed.), *Essays in American Colonial History* (1967), pp. 33-67; Richard Schlatter, "The Puritan Strain," in *John Higham (ed.), *The Reconstruction of American History* (1962), pp. 25-45; *Perry Miller, *Errand into the Wilderness* (1956); *Ralph Barton Perry, *Puritanism and Democracy* (1944); *H. Richard Niebuhr, *The Kingdom of God in America* (1937); H. Shelton Smith, *Changing Conceptions of Original Sin* (1955).

How does one assess the influence of some profound experience on the subsequent history of a people? The effort of [the] Puritan saints to seize and dominate the life of English-speaking people in the seventeenth century was obviously such an experience, and everyone who inspects the national consciousness of Englishmen and Americans today finds Puritanism a part of its makeup, whether the inspection is

Puritanism in Old and New England (Chicago: University of Chicago Press, 1955), pp. 99-114. Reprinted by permission of the author and The University of Chicago Press. Footnotes have been omitted.

made by ourselves or by strangers who look at us with the incredulity—sometimes kindly, sometimes irritated—of visitors from another world. But what is this Puritanism which has a continuing history? Obviously, it is not the Puritanism which I have been discussing in this book. That is a historical movement with a beginning and an end. It does not repeat itself. Nor is the Puritanism with a continuing history the sum total of the connections which can be traced to Puritanism. Unitarianism can be traced to Puritanism and Transcendentalism to Unitarianism, but is Emerson to be regarded as part of the Puritan tradition? I should say "Yes" only if it could be shown that Emerson was attempting to solve his problems as he believed that Puritans tried to solve theirs or if his solutions bore some direct resemblance to Puritan solutions. Let me foreshorten this type of question and make it more extreme. There were Puritans in the seventeenth century who telescoped into their own lives a history which might take fifty years to work itself out in a dissenting congregation; that is to say, they began as dogmatic Puritans with an intense conviction of their election and ended as lukewarm deists with a few Puritan inhibitions. Is such a man to be considered a Puritan after he has worked his passage from the ages of faith into the ages of reason? I should say not, if the term is to have any meaning at all. Similarly, I should say that the continuing history of Puritanism, if it is to have any useful meaning, must be the continuing history of attempts to solve problems in a Puritan spirit.

To limit it to this is still to leave it sufficiently ambiguous, for it is in the nature of such attempts that they represent selections and adaptations of the original experience. Let me give an example. When the statue of Oliver Cromwell, with his Bible and his sword, which stands in the shadow of the House of Commons, was unveiled toward the close of the last century, the address was given by the Earl of Roseberry. It was a symbolic occasion: the final touch in the adoption of Cromwell as a national hero. After vindicating his essential honesty from all the old charges of ambition and hypocrisy and explaining that the secret of his strength lay in the fact that he was a practical mystic, Roseberry continues: "We could find employment for a few Cromwells now. . . . The Cromwell of the nineteenth or the twentieth centuries would not naturally be the Cromwell of the seventeenth. . . . He would not decapitate; he would not rise in revolution or speak the Puritan language. But he would retain his essential qualities as general, as ruler, as statesman. He would be strenuous. He would be sincere. He would not compromise with principles. His faith would be in God and in freedom, and in the influence of Great Britain as promoting both. . . . I know there are some individuals to whom this theory is cant. . . . I know it and I am sorry for them. I believe that the vast majority of our people are inspired by a nobler creed; that their Imperialism, as it is called, is not the lust of dominion or the pride of power, but rather the ideal of Oliver."

Victorian England is making its own appropriation of the Puritan tradition. Puritan itself, it derives strength and purpose from its Puritan past, but it takes what it can use and transforms it in the taking.

Thomas Carlyle might serve as another example. He came from a Calvinist home where he learned the same lessons as the Puritans from the same sacred Book. Like them, he encountered the unbelief and false belief of his generation. He passed through an experience of conversion and discovered his mission in a prophetic ministry. His overpowering sense of divinity, of moral law, of human sin, and of the duty of man to save himself through strenuous self-denial is the same as theirs. He writes their history with an insight into the Puritan soul which few people have ever equaled and trumpets to the modern world that only in deep-hearted believing spirits like Oliver Cromwell will they find the true saviors of society. However, he belongs to no church; he cannot believe that Scripture is literally true; he buries, in what he calls a wise silence, all sorts of questions to which the Puritans had dogmatic answers; and he has enlarged the fraternity of believers to include a pantheon of pagans which would have stupefied his Calvinist ancestors.

But, when all this has been said, the fact remains that the gulf between them is theological rather than moral. If the life of man begins in darkness and ends in darkness, the lesson is to cling all the more passionately to the feeling that there is some kind of order behind the mystery and that this order reveals itself most clearly in the moral sense. And the moral sense to which Carlyle appeals is indestructibly Puritan.

Here, then, is another appropriation of the Puritan tradition. Occasionally the appropriator has some idea of what Puritanism originally stood for and of the kind of selection he is making. No one needed to tell either Roseberry or Carlyle that the Puritan's zeal for freedom was always being overcome by his passion for righteousness and that, if that meant knocking Irish priests over the head or governing Englishmen through major generals, he could do it with a good conscience. Roseberry rejected that side of the Puritan; Carlyle kept it. He was fond of saying that Oliver Cromwell was the best friend poor Ireland ever had. But the appropriator is not usually as familiar with the original Puritans as either Roseberry or Carlyle, and he endows them with all sorts of qualities that they never possessed. However, to say this is only to say that we are dealing with a creative tradition: something which performs its operational function of directing responses to changing situations and which is entitled to bear the original name so long as it shows some correspondence with the original spirit.

If one is looking for the broadest definition of the original Puritanism, it obviously falls into the category of religious revivals. This has been a recurring rhythm in the history of Christian culture, and a more general view than I am taking in these essays would relate Puritanism to earlier revivals. However, if one is to ignore this previous history, and to start with Puritanism, one finds that it has certain drive and that it goes through the typical history of self-discovery, enthusiasm, organization, and decay. It derives its drive from its view of the human predicament. When the Puritan surveys the world within the terms laid down by Christian tradition, he is struck by the profundity of human sin, by the necessity for a work of grace in his own soul to redeem him from the lot of fallen humanity, and by the demand for a disciplined warfare against sin which God makes on those he has saved. His pilgrimage is therefore a search for regeneration, which is usually achieved through an experience of conversion, and for the development of the type of character which is appropriate to the regenerate—a character marked by an intense sense of personal responsibility to God and his moral law, which expresses itself in a strenuous life or self-examination and self-denial. So much for the drive. As for the typical history, it takes rather more than a century to work itself out. The origins of English Puritanism are to be found among the Protestant Reformers of the mid-sixteenth century; it takes shape in the reign of Elizabeth; produces thrust after thrust of energy in the seventeenth century, until the final thrust throws up the Quakers; and then ebbs away.

This revival is clearly followed by another, working within the same tradition, having a similar drive, and much the same scope in time. The low-water mark between the two is obviously in the first half of the eighteenth century. If I may take an arbitrary symbol for the state of religious life in England—something which is suggestive without pretending to be representative—I would use a casual pleasantry from one of the witty letter-writers of the period, the Lady Mary Wortley Montagu. "I was told," she said, "by a very good author, who is deep in the secret, that at this very minute there is a bill cooking up at a hunting seat in Norfolk, to have *not* taken out of the commandments and clapped into the creed, the ensuing session of Parliament . . . honour, virtue, reputation, etc., which we used to hear of in our nursery, is as much laid aside and forgotten as crumpled ribbons." I need hardly say that Massachusetts never fell as low as that. But if, in this period, New England has an established Puritan church, with the flag of the Covenant pinned firmly to the masthead of the community, the Puritanism which exists there has been diluted and confused by the same forces which have had a freer field in the country where Puritanism failed to capture the community.

Now turn from the Lady Mary, who wrote her letter in 1723, to John Wesley's *Journal* of May 24, 1738. "I went," he writes, "very unwillingly to a society in Aldersgate Street, where one was reading Luther's Preface to the Epistle to the Romans. About a quarter before nine, while he was describing the change which God works in the heart through faith in Christ, I felt my heart strangely warmed. I felt I did trust in Christ, Christ alone, for my salvation. And an assurance was given me that he had taken away *my* sins, even *mine*, and saved *me* from the law of sin and death." Three days before, his brother Charles Wesley had also been converted, in his case through Luther's Commentary on the Epistle to the Galatians, which had been the instrument of John Bunyan's conversion. Add to this experience of conversion this glimpse of the life of the converted, which is taken from Wesley's rules for the communion of saints and which might be described as the Puritan's version of the priesthood of all believers:

The design of our meeting is, to obey that command of God, "Confess your faults one to another, and pray for one another that ye may be healed." . . . Do you desire to be told of all your faults and that plain and home? Consider! Do you desire we should tell you whatsoever we think, whatsoever we fear, whatsoever we hear, concerning you? Do you desire that, in doing this, we should come as close as possible, that we should cut to the quick, and search your heart to the bottom? . . . You are supposed to have the faith that overcometh the world.

This has a familiar ring. Equally familiar are the series of sermons which Jonathan Edwards had delivered in Massachusetts a few years before and the Great Awakening which followed them. On both sides of the Atlantic the same symptoms have appeared; they quickly reinforce each other, and they form the beginning of an evangelical movement which continues to pulse through the English-speaking people until it reaches a climax of influence in the second half of the nineteenth century, and then once again ebbs away. In America it is the chief means through which the Protestant churches undertake the enormous task of Christianizing a continent. In Britain there is the same problem of impressing religion and morality on an expanding population both at home and overseas.

I have already touched on some of the contrasts between this second revival and the first. Let me make some of them more explicit.

One contrast lies in the relationship between the Puritan and the intellect of his age. Though I have said . . . that I think the picture of the Puritan as an intellectual has been overdrawn, to the extent that Puritanism was always more an affair of the heart than of the head, the fact remains that the earlier Puritan did not have to maintain his faith in spite of or against the evidences of philosophy or science. Many Puritans, in my definition, which includes the anti-intellectuals as well as the intellectuals, were neither interested in these evidences nor capable of judging them, but those who were could feel that the truths of Scripture were in harmony with all learning and experience. There was much in the philosophic tradition to support the Puritan. There was little in historical science to shake his faith in Scripture or his conception of human history as the field in which God gathers his elect. There was nothing in the older physical science to cause him great concern: no mechanistic theory of the universe, no displacement of this planet from its central place, no doctrine of evolution. His use of the prophetic books of the Bible to interpret human history, his doctrine of special providences in which God was constantly setting aside the ordinary operations of nature to achieve his purposes, seemed eminently reasonable to him. The result was that among the Puritan scholastics—the last representatives of the medieval ambition to synthesize all experience—it was possible to achieve a fusion of intellect and emotion that was less and less possible for their descendants. Increasingly, it becomes necessary to bury difficult questions in a wise silence or to compromise with them in a way which robs the Puritan impulse of some of its otherworldliness or to shunt them aside. On the whole, evangelism has chosen either to bury or to shunt. Although it has been able to impart its ethical impulse to almost all classes of society, so that even the high aristocrat in Victorian England cultivates a sense of duty and the agnostic himself is a very earnest moralist, it has been less and less able to sound intellectually respectable. And in its extremer forms it becomes a religion of feeling without any intellectual structure at all.

The second contrast lies in the relationship between the Puritan and the religious organization of his society. When the first revival began, his society had a dogmatic religious commitment, and no such thing as toleration existed, apart from the concessions which politicians have always made to expediency. Working within this tradition, the first impulse of the Puritan was to turn his community into a rigorous theocracy. Government of the people, by and for the saints, might be described as his idea of good government. However, partly as a result of divisions among the saints, and of the genuine theory of religious liberty which some saints developed, and partly as the result of developments for which the saints can claim no credit, what emerged from that enterprise was not a theocracy but a regime of toleration. The second revival begins under that regime. In America it is turned into a regime of religious liberty, with the state separated from the church. The diversity of religions left no alternative so far as the federal government was concerned, and the rationalists combined with the evangelicals to get the state churches disestablished. In Britain, religious toleration is turned into a system where no religion is discriminated against, but an established church remains. All this means that the second revival is working within either a liberal or a democratic community. But its theocratic impulse dies hard. The converted soul is likely to cling to its conviction that it has a superior insight into God's design for the social order—a conviction which irritates the unconverted and which is not based on any experience. The belief of Roger Williams that the state should be left to the natural reason which God has bestowed on all his creatures, with the Christian only playing his part as one witness, would seem to be more appropriate. However, if political leaders, like Lincoln, are sometimes afflicted by preachers who insist that God demands the immediate abolition of slavery, these reformers are no longer in a position to use any force but argument.

So much for the obvious contrasts. As for the comparisons, there is the conversion experience, which I have chosen as the central feature of the original Puritanism. There is the fission process, the endless splintering, the Babel of heresies, or the flowering of the sects, whichever you prefer to call it—a process which demonstrates once again how fundamental the individualism of the Protestant Reformation has proved to be compared with its superficial collectivism. There is, furthermore, the same bewildering variety of consequences which the search for regeneration can have; the same variety as it had during the Puritan Revolution. Some activities no doubt tend to be shared: an educational mission, a philanthropic mission, a mission to preserve Sabbatarianism or to promote the adoption of Puritan morals, an evangelical impulse which prompts the converted to adopt causes of one description or another. But in this last category it is noticeable that the southern churches feel little disposition to adopt the antislavery cause and that the conversion experience is compatible with every kind of social outlook. John Wesley is a Tory, but the movement he starts will produce liberals, chartists, and socialists. English nonconformity, smarting under the legal privileges and social snobberies of parsons and squires, is either middle or lower class; but English evangelicalism will make as many converts within the privileged classes as outside. Jacksonian democrats like Orestes Brownson are in the tradition of seventeenth-century Levellers, and they are resisted by Puritans in the tradition of seventeenth-century Brahmins. Evangelicalism can mean an individualistic search for salvation or a social gospel. It can reinforce capitalism or produce experiments in communism. It can sustain the privileged or rally the underprivileged. The insights of the converted, as they survey the social scene, are simply not to be marshaled under any single formula.

The final similarity is, of course, in the character. I have said enough in this book about the heroic virtues. The defects have often been made the subject of jibes, and I shall try to restrain myself.

The Puritan has a very limited sense of humor, as one can see from a glance at his portrait. I am thinking not of Grant Wood's "American Gothic" but of seventeenth-century portraits. The corners of the mouths in the divines, at least, are almost invariably pulled down. Emerson has a good phrase for his ancestors. He calls them "the great grim earnest men who solemnized the heyday of their strength by planting New England." I will only add that life seldom struck them as funny. I know that the historian of New England can produce one humorist in Nathaniel

Ward; but I have not been so fortunate with the English Puritans. The nearest I came to it was in a Puritan diary, where the author admits he cannot repress his desire to tell a good story, but he tries to keep the account straight by capping every joke with what he calls "a savoury morsel" of divinity. Cromwell's characteristic humor is a sort of horseplay; this is the Cromwell who throws cushions at his officers, who is said to have spattered an officer's face with ink while they were signing the king's death warrant, or who gets a good laugh watching a soldier tip a pail of milk over another soldier's head. Perhaps it is a relief from tension with a touch of hysteria about it; or perhaps it is just the bucolic antics of a plain russet-coated captain. Later in the history of Puritanism a certain humor develops, but it is naturally rather wry—or it has to be indulged when the great Taskmaster is not looking. Of course I do not want to imply that the Puritan, while he is being a Puritan, cannot make a good remark. I have always liked the reply of the revivalist preacher who had not much grammar and was one day ridiculed for it. "That's all right, brother; what little I have I use for the Lord. What do you do with yours?" But you see he is keeping his eye on the main business. Of all the gifts of humor, the only one which blends naturally with the Puritan's purpose is satire: the sort of satire which Carlyle used to such effect in producing conversions.

The other defects of the Puritan character all spring from the fact that he has stripped himself of nonessentials for the struggle and finds it grim. He makes very little contribution to literature outside the didactic sphere. He is likely to regard the arts as the trimmings of life. And he can degenerate into a kill-joy. Macaulay's jibe about the reason why the Puritans suppressed bear-baiting has a grain of symbolic truth in it. They suppressed it, not because it gave pain to the bear, but because it gave pleasure to the spectators.

In conclusion, let us return to the Puritan's impact on politics. Among his virtues I would list:

1. *His contribution to our system of limited government*.—The original Puritans had a genuine basis for their distrust of arbitrary power in addition to their experience of arbitrary government. They thought that man was too sinful to be trusted with too much power. They were likely to make an exception of the saint, but, once saints were prevented from ruling, they have kept their conviction that nobody else should be trusted. The Puritan tradition, with its everlasting insistence that only God is worthy of worship, is one insurance among Anglo-Saxon people that the state has no claim to worship. Fortunately, there are many other securities, but no one will undervalue the stubbornness of this one. They have defended, in season and out of season, the right to preach, to criticize, and to judge. A shrewd observer of the English scene after the Puritan Revolution was struck by the difference it had made to the power of authority to procure respect for its pronouncements:

> *He* [*the author*] *thinketh that the Liberty of the late times gave men so much Light, and diffused it so universally amongst the people, that they are not now to be dealt with, as they might have been in Ages of less enquiry; and therefore tho in some well chosen and dearly beloved Auditories, good resolute Nonsense back'd with Authority may prevail, yet generally Men are become so good Judges of what they hear, that the Clergy ought to be very wary how they go about to impose upon their Understandings, which are grown less humble than they were in former times,*

when the Men in black had made Learning such a sin in the Laity, that for fear of offending, they made a Conscience of being able to read; but now the World is grown sawcy, and expecteth Reasons, and good ones too, before they give up their own Opinions to other Mens Dictates, tho never so Magisterially deliver'd to them.

2. *His contribution to self-government–to the development of initiative and self-reliance in the body of the community.*—The Puritan pilgrimage has been a perpetual pilgrimage in self-help. The significance of the dissenting chapel as a training ground for working-class leadership in English history has often been emphasized, and much the same services have been performed by the free church tradition in America. Nor should we forget, in the nineteenth century as in the seventeenth, the direct transfer from church affairs to political affairs of certain techniques of action. The political meeting of the nineteenth century owes an obvious, if not wholly healthy, debt to the camp meeting of the revivalist preacher.

3. *His contribution to education.*—The most anti-intellectual Puritan has been obliged to master at least one book—and that a great one. The most intellectual Puritans, in their desire to promote saving knowledge, have thrown up academy after academy, college after college, until their influence has been writ large over the history of education in England and America.

4. *His contribution to morality.*—The Puritan code has its repellent features, but it is no bad thing to have habits of honesty, sobriety, responsibility, and hard work impressed on a community. It seems probable that the acquisitive energy of the nineteenth century would have created far more havoc than it did without the restraining influence of this evangelical spirit.

Finally, there is the contribution which Puritanism, within the religious tradition of Anglo-Saxon peoples, has made to "the class peace." Almost the worst thing that can happen to the politics of a modern society is to have them polarized around social classes. Any force which works across these divisions, and either conceals or cements them, has a permanent claim on our gratitude.

As the limitations of Puritanism have been sufficiently stressed . . . I shall quote only one passage which seems to sum them up. I might have chosen for censure the *cri de cœur* of the nonconformist conscience in nineteenth-century English politics as it appears in the protest of the famous preacher Hugh Price Hughes: "What is morally wrong can never be politically right." Instead, I shall take a passage from an American sermon called "Puritan Principles and the Modern World," which was delivered in 1897:

Puritanism stands for reality; for character; for clean living as a condition of public service; for recognition of responsibility to God; for the supremacy of the spirit. When Oliver Cromwell entered Parliament in 1653, and said, pointing to one member, "There sits a taker of bribes"; to another, "There sits a man whose religion is a farce"; to another, using the hardest name possible, which I soften, "There sits a man whose personal conduct is impure and foul"; and then in the name of Almighty God broke up the Parliament, he was the impersonation of Puritanism; and for one, I wish he would rise from his grave and in the same spirit enter some of our halls of legislation, both state and national.

That passage, with its conviction that righteousness ought to prevail, with its tendency to make the Puritan's own moral character a test of political fitness, and with its pressure to turn politics, which ought to be the art of reconciliation, into a moral crusade, reminds us of the darkest blot on his political record.

2

The Marrow of Puritan Divinity

Perry Miller

Serious study of the Puritan mind cannot be made without going to the writings of Perry Miller (1905-1963). His analyses of Puritan theology and his explications of Puritan texts stand unmatched for clarity and insight. One is hard put to single out one piece by Miller on Puritan thought. He wrote several essays, as well as books, that have become classics of modern American scholarship. Beyond the essay reprinted here, his " 'Preparation for Salvation' in Seventeenth-Century New England" can, for example, carry the reader confidently into the perplexing situation of changing yet consistent Puritanism in its last regnant years. But the essay I choose here, whose title comes from a sermon preached by William Ames in 1643, "The Marrow of Sacred Divinity," explains the unique view of early New England Puritans that enabled them to depart from "the absolute dogmatism of original Calvinism" and to work the wedge of "rationalism" or simple reasonableness into their religion." The brunt of Miller's argument rests upon the "federal" or covenant idea; it is the touchstone of New England-style Congregationalism, and has contributed in very general but tangible ways to later American attitudes toward the individual and his community. Though Miller unraveled or expanded the simple but awesome Calvinist beliefs about the predicament of man held by the Puritans—the concepts of an omnipotent and inscrutable God and of man's miserable place beneath Him—he was unwilling to let it go at that. Through this essay, and others, he was discovering that the covenant theology was an "idiom" for the Puritan mind (as he explained in a preface to this essay in 1956), which sometimes ironically "took such mastery over the [*Calvinist*] creed as in effect to pervert it." By revealing each layer of Puritan logic and rationale, Miller was paying the greatest tribute of the historian to men of another time and faith. He was taking, seriously and compassionately, the thought of Puritan leaders in an effort to understand them in all their intellectual complexity and peculiar brilliance. In so doing, he left us the work of an intellectual historian of the first rank, but even more the gift of a humane man of letters who believed that "the mind of man is the basic factor in human history."

Publications of the Colonial Society of Massachusetts, 32 (1937), 247-271, 273-295, 299-300. Reprinted by kind permission of the Colonial Society of Massachusetts. Footnotes have been omitted.

For further reading: Perry Miller, " 'Preparation For Salvation' in Seventeenth-Century New England," *Journal of the History of Ideas*, 4 (June, 1943), 253-286, reprinted in *Paul Goodman (ed.), *Essays in American Colonial History* (1967), pp. 152-183; *Edmund S. Morgan, *Visible Saints* (1963); Larzer Ziff, "The Social Bond of the Church Covenant," *American Quarterly*, 10 (Winter 1948), 454-462; L. J. Trinterud, "The Origins of Puritanism," *Church History*, 20 (March 1951), 37-57; *William Haller, *The Rise of Puritanism* (1938).

We invariably think of the original settlers of New England as "Calvinists." So indeed they were, if we mean that in general terms they conceived of man and the universe much as did John Calvin. But when we call them Calvinists, we are apt to imply that they were so close in time and temperament to the author of the *Institutes* that they carried to America his thought and system inviolate, and to suppose that their intellectual life consisted only in reiterating this volume. Yet students of technical theology have long since realized that Calvinism was in the process of modification by the year 1630. There had come to be numerous departures from or developments within the pristine creed, and "Calvinism" in the seventeenth century covered almost as many shades of opinion as does "socialism" in the twentieth. The New England leaders did not stem directly from Calvin; they learned the Calvinist theology only after it had been improved, embellished, and in many respects transformed by a host of hard-thinking expounders and critics. The system had been thoroughly gone over by Dutchmen and Scotchmen, and nothing ever left the hands of these shrewd peoples precisely as it came to them; furthermore, for seventy years or more English theologians had been mulling it over, tinkering and remodelling, rearranging emphases, and, in the course of adapting it to Anglo-Saxon requirements, generally blurring its Gallic clarity and incisiveness.

Much of this adaptation was necessitated because, to a later and more critical generation, there were many conundrums which Calvin, and all the first Reformers for that matter, had not answered in sufficient detail. He had left too many loopholes, too many openings for Papist disputants to thrust in embarrassing questions. His object had been to compose a sublime synthesis of theology; he sketched out the main design, the architectural framework, in broad and free strokes. He did not fill in details, he did not pretend to solve the metaphysical riddles inherent in the doctrine. He wrote in the heyday of Protestant faith and crusading zeal, and it is not too much to say that he was so carried along by the ecstasy of belief that an assertion of the true doctrine was for him sufficient in and for itself. There was no need then for elaborate props and buttresses, for cautious logic and fine-spun argumentation.

Hence the history of Reformed thought in the late sixteenth and early seventeenth centuries reveals the poignant inability of Calvin's disciples to bear up under the exaction he had laid upon them. He demanded that they contemplate, with steady, unblinking resolution, the absolute, incomprehensible, and transcendent sovereignty of God; he required men to stare fixedly and without relief into the very center of the blazing sun of glory. God is not to be understood but to be adored. This supreme and awful essence can never be delineated in such a way that He seems even momentarily to take on any shape, contour, or feature recognizable in the terms of human discourse, nor may His activities be subjected to the laws of human reason or natural plausibility. He is simply the sum of all perfections, that being who is at one and the same time the embodiment of perfect goodness and justice, perfect power and mercy, absolute righteousness and knowledge. Of course, man will never understand how these qualities in unmitigated fullness exist side by side in one being without conflict or inconsistency; though man were to speculate and argue to the end of time, he can never conceivably reconcile plenary forgiveness with implacable righteousness. Calvin said that it is not man's function to attempt such speculation. Man has only to discover the specific laws, the positive injunctions which God has laid down in His written word, to take God's statements as recorded, and to accept them through faith. "To desire any other knowledge of predestination than what is unfolded in the word of God, indicates as great folly, as a wish to walk through unpassable roads, or to see in the dark." There does not have to be any necessary or discernible reason for these decrees, they do not have to form any comprehensive and consistent system; Calvin may with titanic effort marshal them in the form of a coherent logical pattern, but each individual item rests, in the final analysis, not upon the logic of its place in the system, but upon the specific and arbitrary enactment of God. The object of our faith, as far as His personal character is concerned, is an utter blank to human comprehension; He is a realm of mystery, in whom we are sure that all dilemmas and contradictions are ultimately resolved, though just how, we shall never in this world even remotely fathom.

It is of the essence of this theology that God, the force, the power, the life of the universe, remains to men hidden, unknowable, unpredictable. He is the ultimate secret, the awful mystery. God's nature "is capable properly of no definition," so that all that one can say is that "God is an incomprehensible, first, and absolute Being." He cannot be approached directly; man cannot stand face to face with Him, "for in doing so, what do we else but draw neere to God, as the stubble or the waxe should draw neer to the fire? . . . He is a consuming fire to the sonnes of men, if they come to him immediately." The English Puritans may be called Calvinists primarily because they held this central conception, though the thought is older in Christian history than Calvin, and they did not necessarily come to it only under Calvin's own tuition. "Now, sayth the Lord, my thoughts go beyond your thought as much as the distance is betweene heaven and earth." William Ames, whose *Medulla Sacrae Theologiae* was the standard text-book of theology in New England, lays it down at the very beginning that "what God is, none can perfectly define, but that hath the Logicke of God himselfe," and argues that therefore our observance of His will can never be based upon God's "secret will," but only upon His explicitly revealed command. William Perkins, from whom Ames and English Puritans in general drew a great share of their inspiration, asserted squarely once and for all that even the virtues of reasonableness or justice, as human beings conceive them, could not be predicated of God, for God's will "it selfe is an absolute rule both of justice and reason"; and that nothing could therefore be reasonable and just intrinsically, "but it is first of all willed by God, and thereupon becomes reasonable and just." The glory of God no man or angel shall know, preached Thomas Shepard; "their cockle shell can never comprehend this sea"; we can only apprehend Him by knowing that we cannot comprehend Him at all, "as we admire the luster of the sun the more in that it is so great we can not behold it."

This system of thought rests, in the final analysis, upon something that cannot really be systematized at all, upon an unchained force, an incalculable essence. For the period of Protestant beginnings, for the years of pure faith and battle with Babylon, this doctrine, as Calvin expressed it, was entirely adequate. It took the mind off speculation, economized energies that might have been dissipated in fruitless questionings, simplified the intellectual life, and concentrated attention on action. The warriors of the Lord were certain that in the innermost being of God all the cosmic enigmas which the Scholastics had argued and debated to the point of exhaustion were settled, that they need not bother with ultimate truth in the metaphysical sense, because in faith and revelation they had clear and explicit truth once and for all. But by the beginning of the seventeenth century Protestant schools and lectureships had been established; the warfare with Rome had become a matter of debate as well as of arms, and logic had become as important a weapon as the sword. Calvinism could no longer remain the relatively simple dogmatism of its founder. It needed amplification, it required concise explication, syllogistic proof, intellectual as well as spiritual focus. It needed, in short, the one thing which, at bottom, it could not admit—a rationale. The difference between Calvin and the so-called Calvinists of the early seventeenth century cannot be more vividly illustrated than by a comparison of the *Institutes* with such a representative book as Ames's *Medulla* (1623). Where the *Institutes* has the majestic sweep of untrammeled confidence, the *Medulla*, though no less confident, is meticulously made up of heads and subheads, objections and answers, argument and demonstration. The preface admits that some readers may condemn the author's care for "Method, and Logicall form" as being "curious and troublesome," but such persons would "remove the art of understanding, judgement, and memory from those things, which doe almost onely deserve to bee understood, known, and committed to memory." Even if the specific doctrines of Calvinism were unchanged at the time of the migration to New England, they were already removed from pure Calvinism by the difference of tone and of method. It was no longer a question of blocking in the outlines; it was a question of filling in chinks and gaps, of intellectualizing the faith, of exonerating it from the charge of despotic dogmatism, of adding demonstration to assertion—of making it capable of being "understood, known, and committed to memory."

The history of theology in this period indicates that the process of development was accomplished in many guises. Learned doctors wrote gigantic tomes on the Trinity or the Incarnation, and soon were creating for Protestantism a literature of apologetics that rivalled the Scholastic, not only in bulk, but in subtlety, ingenuity, and logic-chopping. For our purposes it is possible to distinguish three important issues which particularly occupied the attention of Dutch and English Calvinists. These are not the only points of controversy or development, but they may be said to be the major preoccupations in the theology of early New England. Calvinism had already by 1630 been subjected to attack for what seemed to Catholic, Lutheran, and Anglican critics its tendency toward self-righteousness at the expense of morality; in spite of Calvin's insistence that the elect person must strive to subject himself to the moral law—"Away, then," he cried, "with such corrupt and sacrilegious perversions of the whole order of election"—there was always the danger that the doctrine of predestination would lead in practice to the attitude: "If I am elected, I am elected, there is nothing I can do about it." If man must wait upon God for grace, and grace is irrespective of works, simple folk might very well ask, why worry about works at all? Calvinist preachers were often able to answer this question only with a mere assertion. Calvin simply brushed aside all objection and roundly declared: "Man, being taught that he has nothing good left in his possession, and being surrounded on every side with the most miserable necessity, should, nevertheless, be instructed to aspire to the good of which he is destitute." Perkins taught that the will of man before it receives grace is impotent and in the reception is purely passive: "by it selfe it can neither beginne that conuersion, or any other inward and sound obedience due to Gods law"; he distinctly said that God's predestination is regardless of any quality or merit in the individual, and that man can achieve any sort of obedience only after being elected. Ames restated this doctrine; yet at whatever cost to consistency, he had to assert that though without faith man can do nothing acceptable to God, he still has to perform certain duties because the duties "are in themselves good." The divines were acutely conscious that this was demanding what their own theory had made impossible, and they were struggling to find some possible grounds for proving the necessity of "works" without curtailing the absolute freedom of God to choose and reject regardless of man's achievement.

Along with this problem came another which Calvin had not completely resolved, that of individual assurance, of when and how a man might reach some working conviction that he was of the regenerate. The decrees of election and reprobation were, according to Calvin, inscrutable secrets locked deep in the fastness of the transcendent Will:

Let them remember that when they inquire into predestination, they penetrate the inmost recesses of Divine wisdom, where the careless and confident intruder will obtain no satisfaction to his curiosity, but will enter a labyrinth from which he will find no way to depart. For it is unreasonable that man should scrutinize with impunity those things which the Lord has determined to be hidden in himself; and investigate, even from eternity, that sublimity of wisdom which God would have us to adore and not comprehend, to promote our admiration of his glory.

This was sufficient for men of 1550, but men of 1600 wished to ascertain something more definite about their own predicament. The curve of religious intensity was beginning to droop, and preachers knew that a more precise form of stimulation had to be invoked to arrest the decline; men wished to know what there was in it for them, they could not forever be incited to faith or persuaded to obey if some tangible reward could not be placed before them. Yet to say roundly that all the elect would be immediately satisfied by God of their promotion was to say that God was bound to satisfy human curiosity. The theologians could only rest in another inconsistency that was becoming exceedingly glaring in the light of a more minute analysis. Assurance is sealed to all believers, said Ames, yet the perceiving of it "is not always present to all"; this uncertainty, he was forced to admit, is a detriment to "that consolation and peace which Christ hath left to believers."

In both these discussions the attempt to arrive at bases for certainty led directly to the fundamental problem: no grounds for moral obligation or individual assurance could be devised as long as God was held to act in ways that utterly disregarded human necessities or human logic. In order to know that God will unquestionably save him under such and such circumstances, man must know that God is in reality the sort of being who would, or even who will have to, abide by these conditions, and none other. He must ascertain the whys and wherefores of the divine activity. In some fashion the transcendent God had to be chained, made less inscrutable, less mysterious, less unpredictable—He had to be made, again, understandable in human terms. If the sway of the moral law over men were to be maintained, men must know what part it played in their gaining assurance of salvation; if men were to know the conditions upon which they could found an assurance, they must be convinced that God would be bound by those conditions, that He would not at any moment ride roughshod over them, act suddenly from an abrupt whimsy or from caprice, that salvation was not the irrational bestowal of favor according to the passing mood of a lawless tyrant.

The endeavor to give laws for God's behavior was attended with apparently insuperable obstacles, for it was clear that such principles as men might formulate would be derived from reason or from nature, and Calvin had made short work of all rational and natural knowledge in the opening chapters of the *Institutes*. Not only does God transcend reason and nature, but the corruption of the universe which followed the sin of Adam has vitiated whatever of value once existed in them. Reason was originally endowed with an inherent knowledge of God, which is now hopelessly extinguished by ignorance and wickedness; the knowledge of God may be conspicuous in the formation of the world, but we cannot see it or profit by it. We may still have the light of nature and the light of reason, but we have them in vain. "Some sparks, indeed, are kindled, but smothered before they have emitted any great degree of light." Ames went as far as he dared toward bringing order into God's character by saying that since God is obviously perfect, He must be perfectly rational; that in His mind must preexist a plan of the world as the plan of a house preexists in the mind of an architect; that God does not work rashly, "but with greatest perfection of reason." But we can never in our discourse attain to that reason. The principles of other arts may be polished and perfected "by sense, observation, experience, and induction," but the principles of theology must be revealed to us, and "how ever they may be brought to perfection by study and industry, yet they are not in us from Nature." Divinity may utilize "Intelligence, Science, Sapience, Art or Prudence," but it cannot be the product of these natural faculties, but only of "divine revelation and institution." Knowledge and rational conviction may be prized by the theologian, and may be preached by him as much as doctrine, but in the final analysis he must declare that reason is not faith, that it is not necessary to justification, and that in itself it cannot produce the effects of grace. He may also study nature and natural philosophy, but his knowledge will always be vain and useless; his faculties are too corrupted to observe correctly; nature is under God's providence, and God's ways are past finding out; and, finally, the works of nature "are all subject to corruption."

Here, then, was the task which seventeenth-century Calvinists faced: the task of bringing God to time and to reason, of justifying His ways to man in conceptions meaningful to the intellect, of caging and confining the transcendent Force, the inexpressible and unfathomable Being, by the laws of ethics, and of doing this somehow without losing the sense of the hidden God, without reducing the Divinity to a mechanism, without depriving Him of unpredictability, absolute power, fearfulness, and mystery. In the final analysis this task came down to ascertaining the reliability of human reason and the trustworthiness of human experience as measurements of the divine character—in short, to the problem of human comprehension of this mysterious thing which we today call the universe.

The Arminian movement in Holland (and the "Arminian" theology in the Church of England) represented one Calvinist attempt to supply a reasonable explanation of the relation of God to man. But Arminians went too far; they jeopardized the foundations of Calvinism, and were stigmatized as heretics at the Synod of Dort. In the seventeenth century Arminianism stood as a ghastly warning to all Calvinists. It was an admonition to stay well inside the structure of the creed, whatever redecorations they undertook. The orthodox soon perceived that the basic error in Arminianism was not any one of its "five points" formulated at Dort, but its exaltation of the human reason and consequently its reconstruction of God after the human image. William Ames said that grace, as conceived by the Arminians, "may be the effect of a good dinner sometimes"; and Thomas Shepard pointed out that by their putting into the unregenerate will and the natural reason an ability to undertake moral duties and to work out assurance without the impetus of grace, they became no better than heathen philosophers and Roman Stoics.

. . . I heard an Arminian once say, If faith will not work it, then set reason a-work, and we know how men have been kings and lords over their own passions by improving reason, and from some experience of the power of nature men have come to write large volumes in defence of it; and . . . the Arminians, though they ascribe somewhat to grace . . . yet, indeed, they lay the main stress of the work upon a man's own will, and the royalty and sovereignty of that liberty.

The Arminians yielded too far to the pressure for construing theology in a more rational fashion and so succumbed to the temptation of smuggling too much human freedom into the ethics of predestination. A more promising, if less spectacular, mode of satisfying these importunities without falling into heresy was suggested in the work of the great Cambridge theologian, William Perkins, fellow of Christ College, who died in 1602. Anyone who reads much in the writings of early New Englanders learns that Perkins was a towering figure in Puritan eyes. Nor were English and American divines alone in their veneration for him. His works were translated into many languages and circulated in all Reformed communities; he was one of the outstanding pulpit orators of the day, and the seventeenth century, Catholic as well as Protestant, ranked him with Calvin. He was one of the first to smell out the Arminian heresy—"a new devised doctrine of Predestination," he called it—and his works were assailed by the Arminians as being the very citadel of the doctrine he opposed. As I read Perkins today, it seems to me that the secret of his fame is primarily the fact that he was a superb popularizer. His books were eminently practical in character. He was typically English in that he was bored by too intricate speculation on a purely theoretical plane, and that he wanted results. Thomas Fuller hit him off with his customary facility when he said that Perkins "brought the schools into the pulpit, and, unshelling their controversies out of their hard schoolterms, made thereof plain and wholesome meat for his people." I cannot find that in making wholesome meat out of controversy Perkins added any new doctrines to theology; he is in every respect a meticulously sound and orthodox Calvinist. What he did contribute was an energetic evangelical emphasis; he set out to arouse and inflame his hearers. Consequently, one of his constant refrains was that the minutest, most microscopic element of faith in the soul is sufficient to be accounted the work of God's spirit. Man can start the labor or regeneration as soon as he begins to feel the merest desire to be saved. Instead of conceiving of grace as some cataclysmic, soul-transforming experience, he whittles it down almost, but not quite, to the vanishing point; he says that it is a tiny seed planted in the soul, that it is up to the soul to water and cultivate it, to nourish it into growth.

This idea was palliative; it lessened the area of human inability and gave the preacher a prod for use on those already, though not too obviously, regenerate. In Perkin's works appear also the rudiments of another idea, which he did not stress particularly, but which in the hands of his students was to be enormously extended. He occasionally speaks of the relationship between God and man as resting on "the Covenant of Grace," and defines this as God's "contract with man, concerning the obtaining of life eternall, upon a certaine condition." He uscs the covenant to reinforce his doctrine of the duty that man owes to God of cultivating the slightest seed of grace that he may receive.

The most eminent of Perkin's many disciples was Dr. William Ames, who in 1610 was so prominent a Puritan that he found it advisable to flee to Holland, where he became professor of theology at the University of Franeker. He was the friend and often the master of many of the New England divines, and I have elsewhere claimed for him that he, more than any other one individual, is the father of the New England church polity. Like Perkins, Ames was an orthodox Calvinist. His was a more logical and disciplined mind than that of his teacher, and his great works, the *Medulla Sacrae Theologiae* (1623) and *De Conscientia* (1630), became important text-books on the Continent, in England, and in New England because of their compact systematization of theology. There is very little difference between his thought and Perkins's, except that he accords much more space to the covenant. He sets forth its nature more elaborately, sharply distinguishes the Covenants of Works and of Grace, and provides an outline of the history of the Covenant of Grace from the time, not of Christ, but of Abraham.

In 1622, John Preston became Master of Emmanuel College, Cambridge. Preston was the statesman, the politician among Puritan divines. He was that Puritan upon whom the Duke of Buckingham showered his favor while fondly endeavoring to delude the Puritans into rallying about his very un-Puritanical banner. Preston had been converted in 1611 by a sermon of John Cotton, and was a close friend of Cotton, Davenport, and Hooker; his works, like those of Perkins, were a mainstay of New England libraries. Like Perkins, he was a magnificent preacher, but he was so active a man that he published little before his death in 1628. His works were issued posthumously, one of the editors being John Davenport. Thomas Goodwin, later the great Independent leader, was another editor, and in the preface to one volume says that Preston spent his living thoughts and breath "in unfolding and applying, the most proper and peculiar Characters of Grace, which is Gods Image; whereby Beleevers came to be assured, that God is their God, and they in covenant with him." This passage reveals the great contribution of Preston to the development of Calvinist thought, for in the elaborate exegesis which Preston devoted to unfolding and expounding the philosophy of the covenant, which he held to be "one of the main points in Divinitie," he contrived the seeming solution of the problems which then beset his colleagues. His greatest work on this subject (though all his many books deal with it to some extent) was entitled *The New Covenant, or The Saints Portion* (London, 1629). This work is prerequisite to an understanding of thought and theology in seventeenth-century New England.

Another friend of Preston, probably his closest, was Richard Sibbes, preacher at Gray's Inn from 1617 until his death in 1635, and Master of St. Catherine's Hall, Cambridge, from 1626. He, too, was an editor of Preston's work; it was to a sermon of his that John Cotton owed his own conversion, and Davenport and Goodwin edited many volumes of Sibbes's writings after 1635. Throughout these writings the covenant is expounded and all the theology reshaped in the light of this doctrine. One of the fascinating aspects of the history of this idea is the intimate connection that seems to exist among most of its exponents; they form a group bound together by personal ties, and the completed theology is the work of all rather than of any one man. Sibbes was associated with Gouge in the "feofees" scheme; he was the friend and correspondent of Bishop Ussher. He edited a work of John Ball, and one of his students at St. Catherine's was William Strong, who died in 1654, and whose treatise *Of the Covenant* was prepared for the press by Sibbes's friend Lady Elizabeth Rich in 1678. In the work of all these authors the covenant plays a conspicuous part. Furthermore, this group seems to coincide frequently with the coherent group who formulated the peculiar philosophy of Non-Separating Congregationalism. They were students or friends of Ames, whose works they quote frequently. Sibbes owed his conversion to a sermon of Paul Baynes, and he edited Baynes's *Exposition of Ephesians*. There are many ascertainable relations of almost all the school with one or more of the New England divines; their works were read in New England, and Perkins, Ames, Preston, and Sibbes are clearly the most quoted, most respected, and most influential of contemporary authors in the writings and sermons of early Massachusetts. Sibbes revealed his awareness of the great migration in the year 1630 when he said in *The Bruised Reed*: "The gospel's course hath hitherto been as that of the sun, from east to west, and so in God's time may proceed yet further west." Both in the works of all these men, including Cotton, Hooker, Shepard, and Bulkley, and in their lives there is evidence for asserting that they constituted a particular school, that they worked out a special and peculiar version of theology which has a marked individuality and which differentiates them considerably from the followers of unadulterated Calvinism. And the central conception in their thought is the elaborated doctrine of the covenant.

The word "covenant" as it appears in the Bible presents for the modern scholar a variety of meanings. Possibly suspecting or intuitively sensing these confusions, Luther and Calvin made hardly any mention of the covenant, and the great confessions of sixteenth-century Protestantism avoided it entirely. But with Preston and his friends the word seemed to suggest one simple connotation: a bargain, a contract, a mutual agreement, a document binding upon both signatories, drawn up in the presence of witnesses and sealed by a notary public. Taking "covenant" to mean only this sort of commitment under oath, Preston proceeded, with an audacity which must have caused John Calvin to turn in his grave, to make it the foundation for the whole history and structure of Christian theology. He says:

> . . . *we will labour to open to you now more clearely, and distinctly, this Couenant; though a difficult thing it is, to deliuer to you cleerely what it is, and those that belong to it; yet you must know it, for it is the ground of all you hope for, it is that that euery man is built vpon, you haue no other ground but this, God hath made a Couenant with you, and you are in Couenant with him.*

For all the members of this school, the doctrine of the covenant becomes the scaffolding and the framework for the whole edifice of theology; it is the essence of the program of salvation. As Peter Bulkley phrases it, "Whatsoever salvation and deliverance God gives unto his people, his setting them free from this misery, he doth it by vertue of, and according to his Covenant."

The theology of the Covenant of Grace, invested with such importance by these authors, proceeds upon a theory of history. It holds that man has not only been in relation to God as creature to creator, subject to lord, but more definitely through a succession of explicit agreements or contracts, as between two partners in a business enterprise. God entered into such a bond with man as soon as He created him. He stipulated that if Adam performed certain things He would pledge Himself to reward Adam and Adam's posterity with eternal life. In order that man might know what was required of him, Adam was given specific injunctions in the form of the moral law. In addition, the law was implanted in his heart, built into his very being, so that he might perform his duties naturally and instinctively. The original Covenant of Works, therefore, is the Law of Nature, that which uncorrupted man would naturally know and by which he would naturally regulate his life. Of course, Adam failed to keep this covenant, and by breaking the bond incurred the just penalties. But God did not rest there. Beginning with Abraham, He made a new covenant, and the seventeenth chapter of Genesis, which describes the new bargain, becomes thereby the basic text for the school. The new covenant is just as much an agreement as its predecessor, stipulating terms on both sides to which the contracting parties are bound.

> . . . *these words containe the* Covenant *on both sides, sayth the* Lord, *this is the* Covenant *that I will make on my part,* I will be thy God . . . *you shall haue all things in me that your hearts can desire: The* Covenant *againe, that I require on your part, is, that you be* perfect with me, *that you be* upright, *that you be without* hypocrisie.

The idea of a mutual obligation, of both sides bound and committed by the terms of the document, is fundamental to the whole thought.

It has pleased the great God to enter into a treaty and covenant of agreement with us his poor creatures, the articles of which agreement are here comprised. God, for his part, undertakes to convey all that concerns our happiness, upon our receiving of them, by believing on him. Every one in particular that recites these articles from a spirit of faith makes good this condition.

Furthermore, in form at least, a bargain between two persons with duties on both sides is an arrangement between equals.

. . . *he takes* Abraham *as a friend for ever, and* Abraham *takes God as his friend for ever; and this league of friendship implyes not only preservation of affection, but it requires a kinde of secret communication one to another, and a doing one for another.*

In the Covenannt of Grace, God, observing the form, contracts with man as with a peer. But since the Fall man is actually unable to fulfil the law or to *do* anything on his own initiative. Therefore God demands of him now not a deed but a belief, a simple faith in Christ the mediator. And on His own side, God voluntarily undertakes, not only to save those who believe, but to supply the power of belief, to provide the grace that will make possible man's fulfilling the terms of this new and easier covenant. "In the Covenant of works a man is left to himselfe, to stand by his own strength; But in the Covenant of grace, God undertakes for us, to keep us through faith." Man has only to pledge that, when it is given him, he will avail himself of the assistance which makes belief possible. If he can believe, he has fulfilled the compact; God then must redeem him and glorify him.

The covenant which God made with Abraham is the Covenant of Grace, the same in which we are now bound. The only difference is that Abraham was required to believe that Christ would come to be mediator for the covenant and compensate God for the failure of Adam; since Christ we have merely to believe that He has come and that He is the "surety" for the new covenant. But from Abraham to Peter Bulkley the covenant between God and man is one and the same. "We are the children of *Abraham;* and therefore we are under *Abrahams* covenant." This arrangement between the two is not simply a promise on God's part, it is a definite commitment. These authors, in fact, practically do away with the conception of God as merely promising, and substitute a legal theory of God's delivering to man a signed and sealed bond. "It is impertinent to put a difference betweene the promise and the Covenant. . . . The promise of God and his Covenant . . . are ordinarily put one for another." The covenant, therefore, is the only method by which God deals with man at all. Salvation is not conveyed by simple election, influence, promise, or choice; it comes only through the covenant and only to those who are in the covenant with God.

God conveys his salvation by way of covenant, and he doth it to those onely that are in covenant with him . . . this covenant must every soule enter into, every particular soul must enter into a particular covenant with God; out of this way there is no life.

This legalized version of Biblical history may at first sight seem to offer nothing toward a solution of the problems of Calvinism. It may even appear an unnecessarily complicated posing of the same issues, for the grace which gives salvation even in the covenant comes only from God and is at His disposing. But in the hands of these expert dialecticians the account leads to gratifying conclusions. In their view it succeeded in reconciling all contradictions, smoothing out all inconsistencies, securing a basis for moral obligation and for assurance of salvation while yet not subtracting from God's absolute power or imposing upon Him any limitations prescribed by merely human requirements.

Because a definition of the divine nature must be preliminary to deductions concerning assurance and morality, the problems enumerated may be considered in reverse order. The first effect of the doctrine was to remove the practical difficulty of conceiving of the Deity as a definite character. He might still remain in essence anything or everything, incomprehensible and transcendent. That no longer need concern mankind, for in His contacts with man He has, voluntarily, of His own sovereign will and choice, consented to be bound and delimited by a specific programme. He has promised to abide by certain procedures comprehensible to the human intellect. He has not, it is true, sacrificed His sovereignty by so doing; He has not been compelled by any force of reason or necessity. He has merely consented willingly to conform in certain respects to stated methods. For all ordinary purposes He has transformed Himself in the covenant into a God vastly different from the inscrutable Divinity of pure Calvinism. He has become a God chained—by His own consent, it is true, but nevertheless a God restricted and circumscribed—a God who can be counted upon, a God who can be lived with. Man can always know where God is and what He intends. Thus Preston represents the Almighty speaking as He lays down the terms of the covenant:

. . . I will not onely tell thee what I am able to doe, I will not onely expresse to thee in generall, that I will deale well with thee, that I haue a willingnesse and ability to recompence thee, if thou walke before mee and serue me, and bee perfect; but I am willing to enter into Couenant with thee, that is, I will binde my selfe, I will ingage my selfe, I will enter into bond, as it were, I will not bee at liberty any more, but I am willing euen to make a Couenant, a compact and agreement with thee.

If God speaks to us thus, we then have His own authorization for ceasing to be concerned about His hidden character, His essence, and instead are warranted in assuming that in our experience we will find Him abiding by definite regulations. He will no longer do all the unimaginable things that He can do, but He "will do all things which he hath promised to doe," because the covenant is a mutual bond, and by consenting to it God has committed Himself—"by which God binds us to himselfe, as well as he binds himselfe to us." He is no longer an unpredictable fury that strikes like the lightning without warning or reason—at any rate not in the business of salvation. John Cotton said, professing that he spoke with all reverence, that since the establishment of the covenant, God has become "muffled" as though with a cloak, so that "he cannot strike as he would . . . he is so compassed about with his nature and property, and Covenant, that he hath no liberty to strike."

As soon as the theologians of this school had explained what a covenant involved, they realized that they had come upon an invaluable opportunity to present the hitherto stern Deity in a new light. The very fact that God allows Himself to become committed to His creature must be in itself some indication of His essential disposition. Hence, if God condescends to treat with fallen man as with an equal, God must be a kindly and solicitous being:

. . . how great a mercie it is, that the glorious God of Heauen and Earth should be willing to enter into Couenant, *that he should be willing to indent with vs, as it were, that he should be willing to make himselfe a debtor to vs. If we consider it, it is an exceeding great mercie, when wee thinke thus with our selues, he is in heauen, and wee are on earth; hee the glorious God, we dust and ashes; he the Creator, and we but creatures; and yet he is willing to enter into Couenant, which implyes a kinde of equality betweene vs.*

We need no longer torture ourselves trying to imagine a being made up at once of both justice and mercy, because in stooping to the covenant the Lord has shown that His mercy takes command of His justice. He is bearing in mind the frailties and desires of man, He is endeavoring to bind His will and His requirements to suit man's abilities. He tried the Covenant of Works with Adam, and it failed; He knew, says Preston, that it would fail if He tried it again. "There was no other way to make mankinde partaker of the Couenant of Grace, but onely by faith." He is not aiming directly at His own glory, regardless of man's suffering, but is exerting Himself to secure man's happiness at the same time; His commandments to men "are for their good, and not for his profit." "He stoops to all conditions of men," says Sibbes. "It is a most sweet sign of God's great love, that he will stoop so low as to make a covenant with us." In the same terms the New England ministers expatiated upon God's mercy and condescension as proved by the existence of the covenant. He might easily have dealt with men "without binding himselfe in the bond of Covenant," said Thomas Shepard, "but the Lords heart is so full of love . . . that it cannot be contained so long within the bounds of secrecy." Therefore Shepard rhapsodized upon the covenant thus:

On the depth of Gods grace herein . . . that when he [man] *deserves nothing else but separation from God, and to be driven up and downe the world, as a Vagabond, or as dryed leaves, fallen from our God, that yet the Almighty God cannot be content with it, but must make himselfe to us, and us to himselfe more sure and neer then ever before!*

Naturally the burden of these reflections was that man should respond in kind: seeing God no longer harsh and cruel, but full of compassion, man's heart "melts toward the Lord, it relents, it comes to be a soft heart, that is easie and tractable."

Certainly the implacable mystery celebrated in the *Institutes* has been materially transformed by the time He appears as the God of the covenant. He may still be essentially unknowable, but He has told enough about Himself, and betrayed enough of His character, so that He is not an utter blank. His eternal purposes are still "sealed secrets," but in the covenant He has given us more than a glimpse of their direction. "In Gods Covenant and promise we see with open face Gods secret purpose for time past. Gods purposes toward his people being as it were nothing else but promises concealed, & Gods promises in the Covenant being nothing else but his purposes revealed."

Some of the deductions which followed these premises carry us still further from the conventional notion of the Puritan Jehovah. For one thing, the terms of the contract are decidedly reasonable. God has not only limited Himself to specific propositions, but to propositions that approve themselves to the intellect. "All the Commandments of God, are grounded upon cleare reason, if we were able to finde it out." By propounding the covenant He has enabled us to find out the clear reason for salvation or reprobation. We do not have to do with "a confused God," Cotton says, one "that vanisheth away in a general imagination, but God distinctly considered," and it is as such that "the Lord giveth himself to Abraham and his seed." Upon this basis these theologians thought that they could avoid the inconveniences of resting reason and justice upon the fiat of His arbitrary will. An eloquent section in Shepard's *Theses Sabbaticae* is devoted to proving that the particular laws which God has established are also the very laws of reason. Though by virtue of His absolute sovereignty God might have promulgated any laws He chose, those which He has voluntarily invested with moral significance are exactly the same laws which reason finds ethical, precisely as the terms to which He has voluntarily consented in the covenant are humanly understandable ones. "It is his will and good pleasure to make all laws that are moral to be first good in themselves for all men, before he will impose them upon all men." Goodness is consequently discoverable by right reason; the goodness of a moral law "is nothing else but that comely suitableness and meetness in the thing commanded unto human nature as rational, or unto man as rational, and consequently unto every man." Theoretically God is above and beyond all morality as we formulate it; yet by committing Himself to the covenant God has sanctioned as His law not just any absurdity, but things which are in their own nature suitable, good, and fitting. The difficulty of reconciling God's will with reason vanishes in this interpretation; reasonable justice and His sovereign power of enactment "may kiss each other, and are not to be opposed one to another."

A God who conforms thus cheerfully to reasonable terms must obviously be all-excellent, "and therefore reasonable, he must have the most excellent faculties," and would therefore be such a one as would endeavor also to abide by reason the ordering and governing of nature. Probably no other tenet reveals so clearly how earnestly these writers were striving to bring Calvinism into harmony with the temper of the seventeenth century. They made their gesture of obedience to the unconfined Deity of Calvinism. They prefaced their remarks with the statement that He always *could* interrupt the normal course of nature if He wished to, but they said that a God who voluntarily consented to a covenant would generally, as a matter of choice, prefer to work through the prevailing rules. The realm of natural law, the field of scientific study, and the conception of mathematical principle presented few terrors to this variety of Calvinist. Preston declares: "*God* alters no Law of nature"; nature is not to be feared, it is "to be observed and regarded." One and all, they insisted that God's dignity as ruler of the material universe is not curtailed if He be held to operate whenever possible through secondary causes rather than through miracles. He will appear even more admirable if He accomplishes His will by conspiring with nature, governing not the events themselves but the causes of events, without interrupting or jarring the normal processes. "We must know, God's manner of guiding things is without prejudice to the proper working of the things themselves. He guideth them sweetly according to the instincts he hath put into them." He may come to the aid of His people by direct interposition in moments of crisis, as in the passing of the Red Sea; more often He will contrive that assistance come by guiding the natural causes, and when He has arranged "a course of means, we must not expect that God should alter his ordinary course of providence for us."

Dr. Ames defined the Law of Nature as "that order in naturall things . . . common to all things of the very nature of things." Preston stressed still more the inviolability of this order, and on such matters could quote Aristotle as easily as could Thomas Aquinas: "Nature, it cannot be altered againe, for that is the property of Nature, it still stickes by us, and will not be changed, but, as Aristotle observes, throw a stone up a thousand times, it will returne againe, because it is the nature of it to returne." Ames was willing to carry his veneration for law almost to the point of relinquishing miracles. He replies to the "atheist" theory of pure mechanism, not by stressing Biblical marvels, but by insisting that there is more religious inspiration in the daily operations of Providence than in special acts, and that God's power is better demonstrated by His controlling nature without going contrary to it than in turning its course: "The things that are ordinary amongst us, wherein there is no such swarving, but they are constant in their course, doth not *God* guide them and dispose of them as he pleaseth?" So in the government of man, God does not boot him about like a football, but leads him by persuasion and demonstration: "As God hath made man a free agent, so he guides him, and preserves that free manner of working which is agreeable to man's nature." Even in dispensing grace, God does not thrust it abruptly or rudely into the soul. He does not act upon man with unnatural violence, but conveys grace along the ordinary channels; He contrives that it come to man in the regular course of events.

> . . . *for he doth in the worke of grace, as he doth in the worke of nature. . . .* God *carries all things to their end, by giving them a nature suitable to that end. An Archer makes an impression vpon an Arrow, but it is a violent impression;* God *carries every thing to that end, to which he hath appointed it; but with this difference, that he makes not a violent impression . . . & therefore he doth it not by an onely immediate hand of his owne, as we doe, but he causeth the Creature to goe on of it selfe, to this or to that purpose, to this or that end. And so he doth in the worke of grace; he doth not carry a man on to the wayes of righteousnesse, leaving him in the state of nature, taking him as he is, but he takes away that heart of his, and imprints the habits of grace in it, & he changeth a mans heart, so that he is carried willingly to the wayes of* God, *as the Creature is carried by a naturall instinct to its owne place, or to the thing it desires.*

Normally the instruments by which He engenders faith in an individual are the sermons of ministers and the sacraments of the church. These ordinances, it should be noted, are not in themselves the causes of faith, they are simply the "means." Though God is at perfect liberty to summon a man by a direct call, in the vast majority of cases He will work upon him through these secondary causes. When the sound of the preacher's voice comes to the ear, and the sense of his words to the mind, then by that means the Spirit comes into the soul, "either to convert thee, or to confound thee." The physical impressions are not to be confused with grace itself. Nevertheless they are almost always the indispensable vehicles of grace: ". . . they are meanes to convey grace, mercy and comfort from Christ to our Soules. Though they are not meat, yet they are as dishes that bring the meat. . . . These are the conduits to convey this water of life." Therefore Cotton expressed the theory of sermonizing in New England when he said: "While we are thus speaking to you, God many times conveys such a spirit of grace into us, as gives us power to receive Christ. . . . The word that we speake conveyes spirit and life unto . . . [you]." The grace of God is still theoretically free as the wind to blow where it listeth, but in most instances it is channelized in a sequence of causes that are understandable on a natural—we might almost say, in the jargon of today—"behavioristic" plane.

The historical theory of the Covenant of Grace, its progressive unfolding from Abraham to the Christian era, permitted these theologians to add the final touches to their portrait of the divine character. God did not simply present the covenant point-blank to fallen man, but introduced it by degrees, unfolding it gradually as men could be educated up to it. The beginnings of this conception are to be found in Ames, and it was probably his chief contribution to the system. He said that though from the time of Abraham there has been one and the same covenant, "yet the manner . . . of administring this new Covenant, hath not alwayes beene one and the same, but divers according to the ages in which the Church hath been gathered" While other writers in the school sometimes drew up charts of the stages different from Ames's, all agreed that God has allowed the covenant to grow with time. He first administered it through conscience, then through the prophets and ceremonies, now through Christ, preaching of the Word, and the sacraments. He has done this, the writers agreed, out of solicitous consideration for man's limitations; had the whole thing been enunciated to Abraham, it would have put too great a strain upon his faith, already overburdened as it was in the effort to believe that Sarah would conceive. "Dr. *Ames* saith well," Bulkley wrote, "the Church was then considered . . . Partly as an heire, and partly as an infant." By the long period of tuition in the covenant in its Old Testament form, the Church was educated up to grasping it clearly and distinctly.

. . . the nature of man is so exceeding opposite to the doctrine of Christ and the Gospel, that if it had not been long framed by the tutoring of many hundred yeers by the Law, it had never been convinced of the necessitie of salvation by Christ, and the Gospel.

The effect of this theory was to introduce an element of historical relativity into the absolute dogmatism of original Calvinism. God is seen deliberately refraining from putting His decisions fully into effect until man can cope with them and profit by them. He is not so much a mail-clad seigneur as a skillful teacher, and He contrives on every hand that men may be brought to truth, not by compulsion, but by conviction. For these reasons theologians of this complexion were eagerly disposed to prize knowledge, logic, metaphysics, and history. They were prepared to go as far as their age could go in the study of Biblical history and commentary, for truth to them resided in the history as well as in the doctrine. Preston confesses that intellectual persuasion and historical research are not in themselves sufficient for absolute faith in the Scriptures unless God also "infuseth an inward light by his Spirit to worke this faith." Yet even so he holds that sufficient testimonies exist in the Scriptures "to give evidence of themselves." Knowledge is not to be despised because faith also is necessary: "Wisedome is the best of all vaine things under the Sunne." Knowledge and faith must go hand in hand:

I deny not but a man may haue much knowledge, and want Grace; but, on the other side, looke how much Grace a man hath, so much knowledge he must haue of necessity. . . . You cannot haue more Grace than you haue knowledge.

It is a significant indication of the bent of his mind that Preston argues for the reliability of Scripture because heathen histories corroborate Old Testament chronology.

To describe this theology as "rationalism" would be very much to overstate the case; before the triumph of Newtonian science reason did not have the rigid connotation it was later to carry. Preston drew back from out-and-out mechanism, and he never doubted that even where God was steering events by the rudder of causation, He was charting the course according to His own pleasure. But in this way of thought appears an entering wedge of what must be called, if not rationalism, then reasonableness. It is a philosophy that put a high valuation upon intellect. Its tendency is invariably in the direction of harmonizing theology with natural, comprehensible processes. The authors were prepared to welcome the scientific advance of the century with open arms, until some of their successors in the next century were to realize too late that they had let the wooden horse of rationalism into the Trojan citadel of theology. But thus early there were few misgivings; the Puritans were so secure in their faith that they could with perfect serenity make it as understandable as possible. If we today insist upon supposing that their philosophy was an absolute authoritarianism, we ought to be very much disconcerted by their continual appeals to experience and reason, appeals which, from our point of view, imply assumptions altogether at variance with those of the creed. John Winthrop, in his manuscript debate with Vane in 1637, took it as axiomatic that man is a reasonable creature, and his statement of political theory in these papers owes more to logic than to the Word of God. Thomas Hooker constantly reinforced a dogma by such statements as that it "hath reason and common sense to put it beyond gainsaying," or that to deny it "is to go against the experience of all ages, the common sense of all men"; and Samuel Stone eulogized his colleague because "He made truth appear by light of reason." Professor Morison has found that Elnathan Chauncy, while an undergraduate at Harvard in the 1660s, copied into his commonplace book the remark, "Truth and the rational soule are twins." According to the conventional notions of New England Calvinism this would seem to be somewhat startling. In view, however, of the disposition of the covenant theology, this truism was as appropriate to young Chauncy's background as some admonition concerning the integration of complexes might be to the undergraduate of today. Such passages make it increasingly clear that our notions of the Puritan philosophy, derived in the main from a casual acquaintance with "Calvinism," are in need of drastic reconsideration. . . .

The covenant theory admitted into the official theology many ideas that bade fair to undermine it entirely, and this idea, that man can by fulfilling terms extort salvation from God, might well seem the most incongruous. But at the moment the authors were confident that they had skillfully incorporated the new device into the old orthodoxy. Their account does not deny that God and God alone elects or rejects according to His mere pleasure; the grace which enables us to fulfil the covenant still comes from above, and only God knows whether we have it or not. But in practical life the dogmatic rigors of absolute predestination are materially softened. A juridical relationship is slyly substituted for the divine decree. Men cannot trace the private thought of God, but since God has agreed to manifest what He thinks concerning certain persons in an explicit bond, the individual has a way of knowing that much of the divine determination: "Now we can never know the things which are given unto us of God, but by knowing of the covenant which conveys all the blessings which God doth impart unto his people." Stating the theory of predestination within this frame shifts the point of view from that maintained by Calvin. We no longer contemplate the decrees in the abstract, as though they were relentlessly grinding cosmic forces, crushing or exalting souls without regard for virtue or excellence; instead we are free to concentrate our attention upon what immediately concerns us. We do not have to ask whether God be ours; we need ask only whether we be God's. . . .

The covenant made it possible to argue that while God elects whom He pleases, He is pleased to elect those who catch Him in His plighted word, and that it is up to fallen man to do so. The subtle casuistry of this dialectic is altogether obvious. Yet the spectacle of these men struggling in the coils of their doctrine, desperately striving on the one hand to maintain the subordination of humanity to God without unduly abasing human values, and on the other hand to vaunt the powers of the human intellect without losing the sense of divine transcendence, vividly recreates what might be called the central problem of the seventeenth century as it was confronted by the Puritan mind.

These considerations as to the grounds of assurance paved the way for the supreme triumph of the school—the establishment of a code of ethics and of moral obligation. In two respects they could achieve this end: first, by partial rehabilitation of natural man, and second, by incorporating moral effort into the terms of the covenant. For in this theory man as well as God is no longer left in precisely the state decreed by original Calvinism. God is seen condescending to behave by reason because in man there exists at least a potential rationality. Calvin himself had admitted that in depraved man lingered some remnants of the divine image in which Adam had been created, but, as we have seen, he held them too feeble to be of any use. The Federal theologians also held that these remains, in the form of natural reason or "the light of nature," were exceedingly unreliable, but they rescued them from the rubbish heap where Calvin had cast them. Perkins remained fairly close to Calvin on this question, but in Ames there were signs of the development. While repeating the usual dictum upon the deterioration of human nature, he points out that in all men some knowledge of truth is written in the heart, that a rudimentary inclination to goodness is found in the will, so that men pursue at least "shadows" of virtue, and that we can learn enough from contemplating the natural universe to conclude, without the aid of revelation, that God exists and is to be worshipped. In the work of Preston the importance of these "remains" is considerably accentuated. This achievement was greeted with hosannas by some of his contemporaries, one of his editors boasting that while his *Life Eternall* emblazons the glory of the Divine Essence, at the same time it delineates "the most noble dispositions of the Divine Nature in us, which are the prints and imitations of those his attributes." Preston's sermons frequently remind his hearers that the soul, though fallen, "is the Image of the Essence of God," that it possesses both understanding (which in these discussions is used synonymously with "reason") and will, so that man "understands all things, and wils whatsoever he pleaseth." The speculative faculty he defines as "that by which we know and judge aright concerning God and morall vertues," and its decisions are corroborated by the natural conscience and an innate inclination in the will:

There is in naturall men not onely a light to know that this is good, or not good, and a Conscience to dictate; this you must doe, or not doe, but there is even an Inclination in the will and affections, whereby men are provoked to doe good, and to oppose the Evill. And therefore the proposition is true, that naturall men have some truths, because they have this Inclination remaining, even in the worst of them.

As a matter of fact, Preston comes startlingly close to agreeing at times with Lord Herbert of Cherbury; all that the *De Veritate* says man may know by the unassisted use of reason the Puritan author would admit; he differs from the father of English Deism only in feeling that these conclusions are not quite enough in themselves for a religious man to live by.

. . . when such a man knowes there is an almighty power, by his naturall wit, hee is able to deduce, if there be a God, I must behave my selfe well towards him, I must feare him as God, I must be affected to him as God, I must worship him with all reverence as God; but the most ignorant man confesses there is a God, no Nation denyes it.

Even when he insists that something more is necessary to man than the deductions of natural wit, Preston does not view them as antagonistic to faith. Imperfect as they are, they do not run contrary to supernatural illumination. Within the sphere of demonstration, for instance, the evidence of the senses is sound, Calvin to the contrary notwithstanding:

Of all demonstrations of reason that we have to prove things, nothing is so firme as that which is taken from sense: to prove the fire is hot, we feele it hot, or honey to be sweet, when we taste it to be sweet: There is no reason in the world makes it so firme as sense: As it is true in these cases, so it is an undoubted truth in Divinity, that in all matters of sense, sense is a competent judge.

Faith may be above reason, but since reason comes as directly from God as does revelation, there can be no conflict between them:

But, you will say, faith is beyond sense and reason, it is true, it is beyond both, but it is not contrary to both; faith teacheth nothing contrary to reason, for sense and reason are Gods workes as well as grace, now one worke of God doth not destroy another.

Seen in this light, the imperfections of the human mind are not so much a vitiation resulting from sin, as simply the limitations under which a finite being inevitably labors. Confined in time and space, we cannot conceivably "see all the wheeles, that are in every business," or if we do see them, we are "not able to turne euery wheele." In these purely physical terms Preston occasionally interprets original sin, and ideas of this sort can be matched in all the writings upon the covenant. Sibbes declares that "the soul of man, being an understanding essence, will not be satisfied and settled without sound reason"; and Thomas Hooker defines man as "a living creature indued with a reasonable soul." Thomas Shepard interpreted the Law of Nature as "all that which is agreeable and suitable to natural reason, and that from a natural innate equity in the thing," and taught that it is made known "either by divine instruction or human wisdom." If rightly managed, the results of research, logic, and demonstration will therefore coincide with the teaching of Scripture, and should be held in almost as great esteem by Christians.

If traces of the image of God are still to be found in the soul, they should even more clearly be manifested in the material universe, where all can decipher them if they will. "The heavens are the worke of his hands, and they declare it, and every man understands their language." "When a man lookes on the great volume of the world, there those things which God will have known, are written in capital letters." "Quite apart from faith, therefore, there are two important sources of truth to which man has immediate access: himself and his experience of the world. Hence, secular knowledge—science, history, eloquence, wisdom (purely natural wisdom) is doubly important for these Puritans; for knowledge is not only useful, it is a part of theology. Of course, the writers are always careful to stipulate, we must have Scripture to supplement the discovery of God in nature and providence, but having made that concession, they go on valiantly to exonerate the study of nature from the charge of obscuring the religious goal, and confidently press it into the service of theology. They insist that we can reach God through science as well as through revelation:

For, though I said before, that Divinity was revealed by the Holy Ghost, *yet there is this difference in the points of* Theologie: *Some truths are wholly revealed, and have no foot-steps in the creatures, no prints in the creation, or in the works of* God, *to discerne them by, and such are all the mysteries of the* Gospell, *and of the* Trinitie: *other truths there are, that have some* vestigia, *some characters stamped upon the creature, whereby wee may discerne them, and such is this which we now have in hand, that,* There is a God.

"The workes of Nature are not in vaine," and it behooves us to study them with as much care and precision as the Bible:

Can we, when we behold the stately theater of heaven and earth, conclude other but that the finger, arms, and wisdom of God hath been here, although we see him not that is invisible, and although we know not the time when he began to build? Every creature in heaven and earth is a loud preacher of this truth. Who set those candles, those torches of heaven, on the table? Who hung out those lanterns in heaven to enlighten a dark world? . . . Who taught the birds to build their nests, and the bees to set up and order their commonwealth?

Shepard pronounced a flat condemnation upon those who would cast the Law of Nature from the domain of theology merely because it is not so perfect today as at the Creation; these, he said, "do unwarily pull down one of the strongest bulwarks."

The theologians were treading on dangerous ground at this point; they were perilously close to talking Arminianism. But in their own opinion they were still safe. They were carrying the frontiers of reason to the very boundaries of faith, yet they were not allowing them to encroach. They were careful to point out that regeneration cannot come by the intellect without the inspiration of grace, at the same time adding that the road to grace is also the highway of knowledge. They denied that faith imparts any new doctrines or enlarges the scope of the understanding; the doctrine, as such, can be grasped by anyone. "They may be enlightened to understand all the truths of God; there is no Truth we deliver to you, but an unregenerate man may understand it wholly, and distinctly, and may come to some measure of approbation." Consequently, though by understanding alone no man may achieve salvation, any man does by nature learn so much of God's law that he cannot plead ignorance as an excuse for not obeying it. Here was indeed a triumph in the justifying of God's ways to man! Natural knowledge, such as all men can attain, cannot make a man holy, but it can at least render him inexcusable, and God is exculpated from the charge of injustice in His condemnations. An individual may not be able to deliver himself from the bondage of sin, but in the meantime he can be held personally responsible for doing what the light of nature teaches him is wrong.

. . . It is true, a man hath not power to performe these, but yet withall, I say, he hath power to doe those things, upon the neglect of which, God denyes him ability to beleeve and repent: So that, it is true, though a man cannot beleeve and repent, and neverthelesse for this is condemned; yet withall take this with you, there be many precedent Acts, which a man hath in his liberty to doe, or not to doe, by which he tyes God, and deserves this Iustly, that God should leave him to himselfe, and deny him ability of beleeving and repenting.

Because man still has reason, and reason is not utterly decayed, he has the power to recognize the good, to know when he sins, and to desire a better life. By thus reasserting a distinct validity for the natural reason, the Federal theologians took a long stride forward, entailing an obligation upon natural man to aspire toward moral perfection.

> *But when a reasonable creature lookes on a thing as* Eligible *or* non Eligible, *and not only so, but is able to reason on both sides, is able to see arguments for both, that makes it differ from Spontaneity, when there is no outer impediment, when you may take or refuse it, when you have Arguments to reason, and see the commodity and discommodity of it, your will is now free, so that I may truly affirme every man hath a free-will to doe that, for the not doing of which he is condemned.*

In accordance with their disposition to enlarge the sphere and opportunities of natural reason, the authors redefined, or rather redescribed the nature of grace itself. They did not forget that grace is an influx from the supernatural, but they preferred to concentrate upon its practical operations in the individual, and to conceive of it, not as a flash of supernal light that blinded the recipient, but as a reinvigoration of slumbering capacities already existing in the unregenerate soul. As in the ruins of a palace, so runs one of their favorite metaphors, the materials still exist, but the "order" is taken away, grace reestablishes the order by rebuilding with the same materials. Or as another image has it, natural promptings, passions, and desires are like the wind; holiness is the rudder. "So Nature, the strength of nature, affections, or whatsoever they be, are like the wind to drive the ship, thou mayst retaine them, only godliness must sit at the Sterne." Grace, once infused into the soul, becomes itself "natural," just as when a man has learned to play a lute, the instrument becomes second nature to him; "so is this, it is planted in the heart, as the senses are, it is infused into the Soule, and then we exercise the operations of it; so that it is another Nature, it is just as the thing that is naturall." Hence the faith preached in early New England was not the violent convulsion of the camp-meeting, but the exercise, under divine guidance, of reason and virtue. Thomas Hooker conceived that "the main principall cause of faith is rather an assisting power working upon, than any inward principall put into the soule to worke of its self." In this description, faith emerges, not as prostration on the road to Damascus, but as reason elevated. It enables us to see existing truths exactly as a telescope reveals new stars. . . . According to this theology, the regenerate life is the life of reason.

This line of argument indicates a predisposition in the minds of early New England theologians to minimize the power of original sin, so that by pointing out the advantages which all men inherently possess, they could at least hold the unregenerate responsible for their own damnation. As far as we have followed them at this point, their conclusions concerning what remains of God's image in man since the Fall resulted simply from their strong bent toward making the most of what reasonable elements they could find in the original doctrine of Calvin, and thus far did not necessarily involve the covenant theory. But from the theory they were able to derive an ingenious support for their contentions, to construct a theoretical basis for maintaining that the image of God in man was not so hopelessly debauched as Calvin had imagined. For by conceiving the relationship between man and God as a contract, the sin of Adam appeared in a new light. Adam in his disobedience had broken a bond, had violated a lease. The punishment which he received as a consequence was not deterioration so much as it was the infliction of a judicial sentence; it was expulsion for non-payment, it was not inherent pollution. It was just such a disability as a man would suffer who was under sentence for embezzlement or defalcation. Adam had stood as the agent, the representative of all men, the "federal" head of the race. When he, as the spokesman for man in the covenant, broke it and incurred the penalty for disobedience, it was imputed to his constituents as a legal responsibility, not as an inherent disease. These writers did not openly deny that all men were by birth partners in Adam's guilt, as Augustine had said and Calvin had repeated after him, but they were very much inclined to give lip-service to this historic theory of transmission and then concentrate upon their own version of legal imputation. Both theories at once are outlined by Ames, and amplified by Preston, who argues that men are corrupted first because they, as the heirs of Adam, have imputed to them the blame for breach of covenant.

There being a compact and covenant betweene God and him, that if Adam stood, all his seed should stand with him; but if he fell, then that all that were borne of him should by vertue of that covenant, compact, or agreement have his sinne imputed to them, and so should be corrupted, as hee was, and die the death.

Hooker in turn preached the double doctrine that men inherit a fallen nature from Adam but also incur the legal penalty for his failure as their agent: "Adam in innocencie represented all mankind, he stood (as a Parliament man doth for the whole country) for all that should be born of him." Shepard taught that this was justice itself, "it being just, that as if he standing, all had stood, by imputation of his righteousness, so he falling, all should fall, by the imputation of his sin." Original sin in this version becomes something like the poverty and disgrace a young man might suffer if his father were executed for treason and the estate confiscated. Such an explanation for the persistence of original sin seemed to these lawyerlike theologians more intelligent, more in keeping with the manners of a God who dealt with men through legal covenants. Man is born owing God a debt; his creditor compounds with him, making a new agreement out of consideration for his bankrupt state. When man fulfils the new and easier terms, the debt is cancelled. Though the debt is a serious hindrance to man's freedom of action, it is not an utterly crushing burden, and it does not entirely obliterate the qualities of reason and intelligence he possessed before he acquired it. So something of these qualities remains in him, enough to make him inexcusable for a neglect of God's law, enough to leave him no defence if he fails in moral effort, particularly since God in the covenant has condescended to deal with him by appealing to precisely these qualities and ordering the scheme of salvation in just such a fashion as he can understand by virtue of them.

Thus the Federal theory, freeing man from the absolute moral impotence of the strict doctrine, first made possible an enlargement of his innate capacities. Secondly, it provided a logical device for immediately enlisting these capacities in the service of morality, even before they had been further invigorated by divine grace. It had been with these considerations in mind that God framed the covenant precisely as He did, and thereby demonstrated His cleverness by devising a scheme to insure the continuation of moral obligation even in a covenant of forgiveness. He did not discard the Covenant of Works after Adam's fall; He included it within the Covenant of Grace. "For the Morall Law, the Law of the ten Commandments, we are dead also to the covenant of that law, though not to the command of it." But in this arrangement it exists no longer as a command, the literal fulfilment of which is required of man, but as a description of the goal of conduct toward which the saint incessantly strives. The Law, which no man can perfectly fulfil any more, exists as a "schoole-master"; it teaches us what we should do, whether we can or no, and as soon as we realize that we cannot, we flee to Christ for the assistance of grace. And since Christ has satisfied God by fulfilling the Law, there is no necessity that we do it also. It is only necessary that we attempt it. God's agreement in the second covenant is that if a man will believe, he will receive the grace enabling him to approximate a holy life, but his failure to reach perfection will not be held against him. "We ought not to thinke, because we are not exact in keeping all the Commandements of *God* . . . that therefore *God* rejects vs." The regeneration of any man, as long as he is in the body, will be imperfect at best. It will manifest itself in a perpetual struggle to an unattainable end, and according to the Covenant of Grace God will accept the intention and the effort for the deed.

. . . *there will bee impuritie in the heart wherein there is faith, but yet where there is faith, there is a continuall purging out of impuritie, as it manifesteth it selfe. You may conceive it by a similtude, if a pot be boyling upon the fire, there will a scum arise, but yet they that are good house-wives, and cleanly, and neat, they watch it, and as the scum riseth up, they take it off and throw it away, happily more scum will arise, but still as it riseth they scum it off.*

The demand made upon benighted human nature in the Covenant of Grace is not exorbitant, and demonstrates again how solicitous God appears as He is pictured by this school. It is indeed a little surprising to the modern student to find how large a part of Puritan sermons was devoted to proving to people that they need not be weighed down with too great a sense of sin. The ministers seem to have been fully aware that the stark predestination of early Calvinism was too often driving sincere Christians to distraction, and that it needed to be softened, humanized. Hence they said again and again that there need be very little difference between the performances of a saint and the acts of a sinner; the difference will be in the aims and aspirations of the saint and in the sincerity of his effort. The proof of election will be in the trying, not the achieving. "God accepts at our hands a willing minde, and of childe-like indeavours; if we come with childe-like service, God will spare us; a father will accept the poor indeavours of his childe for the thing it selfe."

Yet while our endeavors will be satisfactory though poor, they must still be real endeavors. Since the conception of grace in this theory is not so much that of rapture as of the reawakening of dormant powers, grace is by definition the beginning of a moral life. It is a strengthening of the remains of the Law that still exist in the natural heart, in unregenerate reason, and in conscience. Saints are not able to do all they should, "yet this they doe . . . they carry a constant purpose of heart to doe it. . . . They never come to give over striving to doe it." The regenerate, by the very fact of being regenerate, exert themselves to become sanctified:

. . . by the same faith whereby we receive Christ to dwell in us, we receive the holy Spirit also, to work from Christ and through Christ, all the power of godlinesse which a Christian life holds forth, and from that day forward.

Conversely, it follows as night the day that sanctification is a very handy evidence of justification, and that we may even receive grace first in the form of a moral ability before we have any inward experience of regeneration. God's predestination is of course absolute, He picks and chooses without regard to merit. But in the covenant He has consented to bestow His favor upon those who fulfil the conditions, and to guarantee to those who do so the assurance of their salvation. In this devious fashion the Puritans avoided the Arminian heresy of conditional election, but gained almost all that the Arminians sought by preaching a "conditional" covenant, which entailed the obligations of morality as thoroughly as did the erroneous doctrine, and yet did not bind the Lord to attend upon human performance. . . .

Armed by this logic at every point, the theologians were prepared to concentrate their attack upon the question of passivity. They were equipped to counteract the danger of lassitude which threatened to result from the fatalistic doctrine of predestination. They could show that men are responsible for a great deal, even though God alone bestows grace, and in more ways than one they could prove that a sinner brings reprobation upon himself. All those who live within the hearing of Christian doctrine—particularly of covenant doctrine—are offered the opportunity of taking up the covenant, because to them its terms are made clear. An offer of the covenant from God includes also an offer of enabling grace, because God is under obligation to supply grace when He presents the contract to men. Therefore, when the covenant is presented, through the sermon of a minister, to a particular individual, and the individual does not then and there embrace it, or attempt to embrace it, then he must be resisting it. Though faith comes from God, yet because it is not forced upon any, but is presented through reasonable inducements, and is conveyed by "means," by sermons, and by sacraments, men have of themselves the power to turn their backs upon it, to refuse to be convinced by the most unanswerable demonstrations, to sneer at the minister, and to pay no attention to the sermon. Thereafter the onus is entirely on their own shoulders:

Take heede of refusing the acceptable time . . . Beloued, there is a certaine acceptable time, when God offers Grace, and after that hee offers it no more . . . there are certaine secret times, that God *reserues to himselfe, that none knowes but himselfe, and when that time is past ouer, he offers it no more.*

Consequently, men must be constantly in readiness to take up the convenant, so that they will not fail to respond when the acceptable time comes to them individually.

The covenant theory, then, was an extremely strategic device for the arousing of human activity: it permitted divine grace to be conceived as an opportunity to strike a bargain, a chance to make an important move, an occasion that comes at a specific moment in time through the agency of the ministry. If an individual does not close the deal when he has the chance, he certainly cannot blame God because it gets away from him. "The Lord is a suitor to many a man," said Shepard, "that never gives himself to him." The heathen, indeed, might have some grounds for complaint, but not those who live under a ministry, because to them the preaching of the Word is *ipso facto* the presentation of the covenant.

. . . they that live under such meanes, that are ever learning, and never come to the knowledge of the Truth, and so have brought a sottishnesse on themselves, they are inexcusable, because themselves are the cause of their not profiting, as a man that is drunke, though he is not able to understand the commands of his Master, yet because he was the first author of the drunkennesse, (which caused such sottishnesse), he is inexcuseable. . . . So . . . God requires no more of any man, than either he doth know, or might have knowne.

Of course, God must give the faith; but by these agencies He is, as a matter of fact, giving it, and giving it thus out of respect for the intelligence of men. "Hee will not doe it without us, because wee are reasonable men and women, and God affords us meanes." Consequently, the duty of any man in a Christian community is to use the means to the end for which they are intended:

. . . howsoever God promiseth to enable his people to doe all he commandeth, yet this shutteth not out their endeavour. His promise of enabling them is upon this supposition, that they doe indeavour in the use of the meanes he shall appoint them. The Lord in promising doth not meane that they should be idle, and look that he should doe all; but his promising includeth their endeavouring, and upon their endeavouring in the use of the meanes that God hath appointed, he hath promised to enable them to doe what he hath commanded.

Hooker says that if persons have lived under a "powerful ministry" a halfdozen years or so and have not profited therefrom, "It is no absolute conclusion, but . . . it is a shrewd suspicion, I say, that God will send them downe to hell." Consequently, it behooves us all not to lie back until the Lord comes to us, but to exert ourselves at once in accordance with the instructions of our pastor.

On these grounds the school carried on Perkins's tendency to reduce the actual intrusion of grace to a very minute point. They not only insisted that the tiniest particle is sufficient to start a man on the road to salvation, they even argued that before any faith is generated, a man can at least "prepare" himself for it. He can put himself in an attitude of receptivity, can resolve with himself not to turn down the covenant when it seems to be offered to him. God may decree, but a man must find out whether the decree applies to himself; "the kingdom of heaven is taken with violence." "You must not thinke to goe to heaven on a feather-bed; if you will be Christs disciples, you must take up his crosse, and it will make you sweat." If any man excuse himself by the sophistry that Christ must work for him and that he cannot under his own power "bring forth fruit to him," that man despises Christ's honor, and in that act rejects the Covenant of Grace.

In this respect, as in others, the covenant doctrine did not intend to depart from essential Calvinism; it did not openly inculcate free-will. But by conceiving of grace as the readiness of God to join in covenant with any man who does not actively refuse Him, this theory declared in effect that God has taken the initiative, that man can have only himself to blame if he does not accede to the divine proposal. This was indeed a marvellous stratagem for getting around a thorny difficulty in theology, a hazard which Calvin had simply taken in stride by asserting roundly that though God elects or rejects according to His pleasure, the responsibility for damnation is man's own. The generation of Peter Bulkley could no longer accept so brusque or unsophisticated an account as this. They were under greater compulsion to clear God of the charge of arbitrary condemnation and to place the responsibility for success or failure squarely on human shoulders. The result was the conception, not of conditional election, but of conditional covenant, according to which the absolute decree of God is defended, and yet the necessity of activity by man is asserted:

The Lord doth not absolutely promise life unto any; he doth not say to any soule, I will save you and bring you to life, though you continue impenitent & unbelieving; but commands and works us to repent and believe, and then promises that in the way of faith and repentance, he will save us. He prescribes a way of life for us to walk in, that so wee may obtaine the salvation which he hath promised.

The covenant involved ethics in the very stuff of grace itself:

. . . we must for our part assent unto the Covenant, not onely accepting the promise of it, but also submit to the duty required in it; or else there is no Covenant established betwixt God and us; we must as well accept of the condition as of the promise, if we will be in Covenant with God.

The final outcome of the intricate system was a shamelessly pragmatic injunction. It permitted the minister to inform his congregation that if any man can fulfil the covenant, he is elected. The way for him to find out is to try and see: "Therefore goe on boldly, God hath promised to heare you, hee cannot deny you." Whatever the differences among the various writers, there is a marvellous unanimity among them on the ultimate moral: "The way to grow in any grace is the exercise of that grace," said Preston. "It is not so much the having of grace, as grace in exercise, that preserves the soul," said Sibbes. And John Cotton said in Boston: "If thou hast but a thirsty soule, and longest for grace under sense of thine owne droughtinesse, then God will not deny the holy Ghost to them that aske him."

The conclusion toward which the doctrine of the covenant shapes is always the practical one that activity is the essence of a Christian life, that deeds are not merely the concomitants of faith, but can even be in themselves the beginning of faith. Some kind of revision of Calvinism seemed absolutely inevitable if the doctrine of justification by faith were not to eventuate in a complete disregard of moral performance. The covenant theology was the form that that revision took among this particular group of thinkers. It was the preliminary to their proving that faith without performance is an impossibility, a contradiction in terms, and that that which must be performed is the moral law, the law which reason and common sense know to be good in itself. In dogmatic Calvinism morality could exist only as a series of divine commands. It had no other basis, and to Calvin it needed no other.

The covenant theology is a recognition on the part of a subsequent generation that this basis was inadequate, that it reduced morality to an arbitrary fiat, that it presented no inducement to men other than the whip and lash of an angry God. Consequently, in New England morality was first of all the specific terms of a compact between God and man, and rested, therfore, not upon mere injunction but upon a mutual covenant in which man plays the positive role of a cooperator with the Lord. In the second place morality was also that which can be considered good and just.

This conception was of tremendous value to the leaders of Massachusetts, not only in the realm of faith and personal conduct, but just as much in the realm of politics and society. The sphere of moral conduct includes more than such matters as individual honesty or chastity; it includes participation in the corporate organization and the regulation of men in the body politic. The covenant theology becomes, therefore, the theoretical foundation both for metaphysics and for the State and the Church in New England. An exhaustive study of the social theory would lead too far afield for the purposes of this paper, but a brief indication of the connection between it and the theology will demonstrate that without understanding this background we shall misread even such a familiar classic as Winthrop's speech of 1645 on liberty. That address is not what it is most often described as being—an expression of pure Calvinism. All that strictly Calvinistic political theory needs to contain is in the fourth book of the *Institutes*. It amounts in effect to the mandate that men must submit to magistrates because God orders them to submit, to the assertion that the power of the governor is of God, never of the people. But Winthrop outlines a much more subtle conception in his account, and by invoking the covenant theory secures the sway of morality in the State in precisely the same fashion in which the theologians secured it in the religious life. He distinguishes between the liberty all men have in the state of nature, the liberty to do anything they wish, which generally means something bad, and the liberty men exercise in society:

> *The other kind of liberty I call civil or federal, it may also be termed moral, in reference to the covenant between God and man, in the moral law, and the politic covenants and constitutions, amongst men themselves. This liberty is the proper end and object of authority, and cannot subsist without it; and it is a liberty to that only which is good, just, and honest.*

I do not believe that the real connotation of Winthrop's words has been altogether recognized in modern accounts. He is saying that just as the covenant between God and man is a coming to terms, and as the validity of that which is by its nature good, just, and honest rests not upon its intrinsic quality but upon its being agreed to by the contractors, so also in the State, the rule of law rests upon a similar agreement among the participants. The covenant theory cannot claim for that which is inherently good the force of a cosmic law, because the universe and man are corrupted; it cannot identify the good completely with the thought of God, because God transcends all systematic formulations. But being arrived at by compact, the good then acquires the power to compel obedience from those who have covenanted to observe it, be they gods or men. The personal covenant of the soul with God is impaled on the same axis as the social, like a small circle within a larger. Before entering into both the personal and social covenants men have a liberty to go their own gait; afterwards they have renounced their liberty to do anything but that which has been agreed upon. The mutual consenting involved in a covenant, says Hooker, is the "sement" which solders together all societies, political or ecclesiastical; "for there is no man constrained to enter into such a condition, unlesse he will: and he that will enter, must also willingly binde and ingage himself to each member of that society to promote the good of the whole, or else a member actually he is not." The implanting of grace, being by definition an acceptance of the covenant, produces by the same token a people prepared and ready to be disciplined in a holy society. "The same Spirit quickneth us unto holy duties; so that . . . the Spirit sanctifying draweth us into an holy Confederacy to serve God in family, Church, & Common-wealth."Peter Bulkley illustrates the paralleling of the social and political covenants which is characteristic of New England theory by insisting that he who accepts the covenant must obey its terms, exactly "as in a Common-wealth or Kingdome, none hath the benefit of the Law, but those that subject themselves to the Law: none have the protection of authority, but those that obey it." Since grace takes the form of enabling men to embrace the covenant, the regenerate automatically obey the law of God both in personal life and in social relations:

. . . *Where the Lord sets himselfe over a people, he frames them unto a willing and voluntary subjection unto him, that they desire nothing more then to be under his government. . . . when the Lord is in Covenant with a people, they follow him not forcedly, but as farre as they are sanctified by grace, they submit willingly to his regiment.*

The covenant upon which a Congregational church was founded was viewed by the theologians in the same light as the political compact. It was held to be a miniature edition of the divine covenant. The saints come together and formally agree to carry out in ecclesiastical life the obligations to which they stand individually bound by their covenant with God. The duties and requirements are those determined in the Covenant of Grace. The church compact is the agreement of the people in a body to constitute an institution which will facilitate the achievement of these ends. "The rule bindes such to the duties of their places and relations, yet it is certain, it requires that they should *first freely ingage* themselves in such covenants, and *then* be carefull to fulfill such duties." The creation of a church by the saints is necessary, furthermore, because the church makes possible the machinery of "means." The argument from the covenant, therefore, clinched the theoretical justification for the existence of a formal ecclesiastical order, for the dispensing of sacraments, and for the applicaiton of such regulatory measures as censure and excommunication, while at the same time protecting the liberty of God to enter into covenant with anyone He chose, inside or outside the church. Yet as long as it seemed that God would normally work through the regular means, He would therefore generally dispense grace through the ordinances of the church. Consequently the children of the saints should be baptized as a means toward their conversion, and should be taken into the church covenant:

> The Covenant of Grace *is to be considered, either according to the* benefits *of saving grace* given *in it, or according to the* means *of grace* offered. . . . [*The church covenant*] *is not the Covenant of the Gospel in the first sense; but it is within the verge, and contained within the compasse of the Covenant in the second sense.*

In this distinction between the covenant as faith and the covenant as the provision of means for the engendering of faith were contained the seeds of the difficulties which later produced the Half-Way Covenant. But in the first decades of New England history no difficulties were anticipated because the theologians were so supremely confident that grace would almost inevitably accompany the means. "God delights in us, when we are in his Covenant, his Covenant reacheth to his Church, and wee being members of that Church: Hence it comes to passe, that we partake of all the pleasant springs of Gods love."

Thus the sign of true faith is not only a desire on the part of the regenerate individual to fulfil the moral law, but it is also a determination to join in the setting up of the one and only polity which Christ has outlined in Scripture. For this reason New England was settled: "When faith is stirring, it longs and desires much after the strongest, purest, and liveliest Ministery, and every Ordinance in the greatest purity."

I have not attempted in this account of the covenant theology to give more than a rapid survey; the summary of each point could easily be amplified, and revealing quotations multiplied indefinitely. But in even as compressed a treatment as this, the bent of the thought becomes clear. In every position there is a remarkable consistency of tone, a resolute determination to solve the riddles of Calvinist theology, as far as may be possible by the ingenuity of man or the subterfuges of metaphysics, in a reasonable, comprehensible fashion, and yet at the same time to preserve, in form at least, the essential structure of Calvinism. To understand why these men should have been driven by this urgency, it is necessary to remember what was taking place in the intellectual life of Europe at the time, in science, in politics, in the work of Bacon, of Descartes, and of Hobbes. Within the limits of their particular theology, within the framework of their creed, these Puritans were responding to the same impulses as their philosophical contemporaries. They were seeking to understand, to draw up explicable laws, to form clear and distinct ideas, to bring order and logic into the universe. They could not interpret it as extension and movement as did Descartes. They could not reduce it to atoms as did Hobbes. They could not deify its natural construction as did the Newtonians. But oddly enough they could take many steps in the same direction once they had seized upon their fundamental discovery that God has voluntarily engaged Himself to regular, ascertainable procedures. The rest followed surely and easily from this premise: the validity of reason in man, the regularity of secondary causes in nature, the harmony of knowledge and faith, the coincidence of the arbitrary with inherent goodness, the intimate connection between grace and the incitements that generate grace, the necessity for moral responsibility and activity. Everywhere along the line the method of the divine dispensation, while authorized only by God and remaining under His constant control, is actually synchronized with a completely scientific account. God works grace in the soul, not by compulsion, but by persuasion and reasonable inducements, by the sermon of the minister which penetrates the sinner's mind. Was the real cause God working through the sermon, or was it the sermon itself? The authors have no hesitancy in saying that the sermon was simply the efficient cause and that God was the final cause, but they were delighted to find that God's activity could take the form of a natural stimulus. This seemed to make religion doubly secure and to enhance it by the addition of comprehensibility.

Yet there is a caution to be observed before we rest in this conclusion. By marshaling from the works of Cotton and Hooker passages which deal only with the covenant and its implications, an impression could easily be created that New England thought had ceased to have any affinities with Calvinism, that there was really no difference between the Puritans of the covenant school and the rational theologians of the century who, like John Smith listening to the Arminians at Dort, had bidden Calvin good-night. To imply that there is an essential unanimity between Preston and Chillingworth, Cotton and Whichcote, would be to misread the whole history of Puritanism. For reasonable as this system was, coherent and uniform as was its cosmology, sequential as was its theory of causation, in the final analysis the basis of every contention, the goal of every proposition, was still the transcendent, omnipotent Divinity.

The achievement of this theology was that it did everything that could be done to confine the unconfinable God in human terms. It transformed the revealed Word from an exaction arbitrarily imposed by a conqueror into a treaty of mutual obligation. But it never forgot that at the long last God is not to be fathomed, understood, or described with absolute certainty. Such certainty as we do have is temporary, the result of an agreement, of God's having consented to be bound in the main by such and such conditions, of His condescending for the moment to speak the language of men. There is no absolute guarantee that *all* His manifestations will appear within the scope of the covenant. The essence of Calvinism and the essence of Puritanism is the hidden God, the unknowable, the unpredictable. In this sense the Puritans were indeed Calvinists. They hedged the undiscoverable Essence about with a much more elaborate frame than did Calvin. They muffled it and cloaked it (to borrow Cotton's phrase), they cabined it and circumscribed it up to a point; and though the point was far beyond anything Calvin would have allowed, there was still a limit beyond which even the Federal theologians could not go. They could not say that natural law was immutable and eternal, though they might say it was generally reliable. They might say that God's justice was for all intents and purposes the same as human justice, but they could not say that it was invariably the same. Always they had to leave a loophole, they had to be wary and circumspect; for behind the panorama of the world, behind the covenant and behind the Scriptures there loomed an inconceivable being about whom no man could confidently predict anything, who might day in and day out deal with man in stated forms and then suddenly strike without warning and scatter the world into bits. There was no telling with unqualified certitude what He might do; there was only the rule of thumb, the working agreement that by and large He would save and reject according to reason and justice as we understand the words. For ordinary purposes this was enough; we could feel fairly secure, we need not be too distraught. But the Puritan, as long as he remained a Puritan, could never banish entirely from his mind the sense of something mysterious and terrible, of something that leaped when least expected, something that upset all regularizations and defied all logic, something behind appearances that could not be tamed and brought to heel by men. The covenant thought kept this divine liberty at several removes, placed it on a theoretical place, robbed it of much of its terror, but it could not do away with it entirely. . . .

. . . The Puritan wished to bring his theology into harmony with science and reason wherever they might be made to coincide, but he could never lose his hunger for the inward exultation that came from a union with God which, though it might be brought about by natural causes, was yet something supernatural, something different from the causes, something which was bestowed only at the pleasure of God. Faith adds no new doctrine, teaches us no new facts, is not an addition to the contents of the mind. It is a glow of inspiration that quickens knowledge, and for that reason is all the more valuable and indispensable:

There is indeed a common faith, which the others may have, and thou mayest have, but the strong faith ariseth from the Spirit, God *dispenseth it where he pleaseth; this infused faith is not gotten by strength of argument, or perspicuitie of the understanding; it is not brought in by custome, but* God *doth worke it; it is not all the antecedent preparation that will doe it, but* God *must first worke it, and then you are able to beleeve these principles of faith, and able to beleeve them to the purpose.*

Morality and God's decree may, as we have seen Shepard saying, kiss each other and agree, but the Puritan could never forget that the agreement comes of God's own choice, and Shepard must add that the agreement is not always perfect, that the will of God remains superior to the demands of human equity. "When they [moral precepts] are called perpetual and unchangeable, we must understand them in respect of God's ordinary dispensation; for he who is the great Lawgiver may, and doth sometimes extraordinarily dispense with moral laws." The Puritan temperament is nowhere so well illustrated as in the contrast between the tenor of these passages and the tendency of the Puritan metaphysic. As far as possible Puritans would explain, draw diagrams, plot the course of God's will, and generalize upon His character. But it would be the end of Puritanism if they ever succeeded completely in penetrating the ultimate secret, if they could reach the point of saying that thus and so is not simply the way God does behave, but the way in which He must behave for these and those reasons. If the covenant theology is, as I think it is, a characteristic product of the Puritan mind, then we are perhaps justified in describing Puritanism as a willingness to follow nature and reason as far as possible, but not completely; for though Puritanism will use reason and enjoy nature, it can never overcome a fundamental distrust. . . .

To be wise unto sobriety was the purpose of this theology, to elucidate the laws of God's universe, but to keep a wary eye upon the unpredictability, the mystery of God. The evidence of subsequent history, both in England and in New England, would seem to be that it failed. Eventually the ideas which it introduced into the creed, reinforced by the triumph of Newtonian physics, displaced the theology in the estimation of such men as Charles Chauncy. The moral of this episode in the story is, I think, that the Calvinism to which the Puritans were ostensibly dedicated was already in the process of far-reaching modification at the hands of English theologians before it was transported to Massachusetts. The men who directed the intellectual life of seventeenth-century New England left Cambridge and London when their tradition was in the first flush of transformation. They did not depart until into that tradition, under the guise of a doctrine of covenants made by God with man, there had been injected many ideas which derived, not from theology and revelation, but from law, from the study of nature, from the principles of reason and common sense. As time went on, the incompatibility of these ideas with the official confession was bound to become more apparent. Seen in this light, the development of rationalism in eighteenth-century New England is not a phenomenon produced entirely by the stimulation of imported ideas. The intellectual life of American Puritans in the seventeenth century was by no means so sparse and monotonous as it has sometimes been accused of being. The pristine doctrine was not rigorous, iron-clad, and inflexible; it had in it the elements of complexity, the seeds of future growth, making for diversity and contradiction. That period which is sometimes spoken of as the "glacial age" was not an era of intellectual dearth and philosophical sterility, but one of slow progression toward the ultimate separation of the diverse attitudes which had somehow been awkwardly and unwittingly put together in the covenant theology of Ames, Preston, and Sibbes. It was, therefore, no accident, no violent break in the course of New England thought, that John Wise should shift the grounds for defending Congregationalism from the Bible to the laws of reason and nature and to the character of the social compact. It is also not surprising to find that when Jonathan Edwards came to feel that rationalism and ethics had stifled the doctrine of God's sovereignty and dethroned the doctrine of grace, he threw over the whole covenant scheme, repudiated the conception of transmission of sin by judicial imputation, declared God unfettered by any agreement or obligation, made grace irresistible, and annihilated the natural ability of man. It was Jonathan Edwards who went back to the doctrine from which the tradition had started; went back, not to what the first generation of New Englanders had held, but to Calvin, and who became, therefore, the first consistent and authentic Calvinist in New England.

3
A Review of "The New England Mind: The Seventeenth Century"

Herbert W. Schneider

Appreciative yet critical in the best sense, this review of Perry Miller's third book on early New England thought appeared in the opening issue of the *Journal of the History of Ideas,* a scholarly quarterly that has become synonymous with the study of intellectual history in the United States. Herbert Schneider had earlier published his own book, *The Puritan Mind,* wherein he emphasized the symptoms of waning Puritanism in the eighteenth century, and by 1946 he had published his comprehensive *History of American Philosophy,* now the standard work on that subject. When, in this review, Schneider calls for further explanation from Miller of "the practical meanings embedded in the theological arguments" and for a clearer picture of what was done about what was said, he is speaking for the pragmatic tradition in American academic philosophy that had been nurtured for many years by John Dewey in the Department of Philosophy at Columbia University, where Professor Schneider also became a teacher. Moreover, the temper of looking for what is done about what is said has been shared—then and now—by most American historians. But though Perry Miller came from the Harvard of Charles Sanders Peirce and William James, as Schneider notes here, I think Miller owed no apologies to the founders of pragmatism for his treatment of the Puritans. The pragmatic test of faith, for the Puritan, was not action but more faith. Put another way, right action was a correct but not a conclusive sign of regeneration. Or again, what was done about what was said was often, for the Puritan, what was further said. The world of communication among Puritan true believers was one in which "mere talk" and "genuine thought" were the same. Their world was indeed, as Miller insists, based upon abstract theology. If this is not an adequate picture of colonial New England for all historians, it is the most telling image for the intellectual historian.

Miller's focus upon the Scholasticism of early New England thought, his reminder that the Copernican Revolution was late in reaching America, and his description of the Puritans' defense of their intellectualism against what we today would call the anti-intellectualism of William Dell in England are the contributions of *The*

The Journal of the History of Ideas, 1 (January 1940), 119-122. Reprinted by permission of the author and *The Journal of the History of Ideas*.

New England Mind that Schneider applauds. Where he again significantly differs with Miller is over the philosophic background or lineage of American Transcendentalism and its connection, if any, with Puritanism. For Schneider, Puritan Platonism is best located in a philosophic line that later produced Scottish "common sense" realism, against which the Transcendentalists revolted. The Transcendentalist temper, in Schneider's view, is much closer to a different kind of Platonism, the "intuitional" kind as illustrated by the antinomian individualism of Anne Hutchinson. Although intellectual historians now fairly well agree upon the eclectic makeup of Transcendentalist thought, there is still some disagreement over the degree and kind of Platonism within it.

For further reading: *Herbert W. Schneider, *The Puritan Mind* (1930); *Perry Miller, *The New England Mind: The Seventeenth Century* (1939); *Perry Miller, *The New England Mind: From Colony to Province* (1953); *Edmund S. Morgan, *The Puritan Dilemma* (1958); Michael McGiffert, "American Puritan Studies in the 1960s," *William and Mary Quarterly,* 27 (January 1970), 36-67.

This volume is the most substantial contribution that has yet been made to the critical history of philosophy in America, and if its projected successors, dealing with the eighteenth and nineteenth centuries, continue to present a corresponding wealth of fresh material and erudition, the work itself will certainly be one of the most distinguished products of the New England mind. This first volume of the series makes no attempt to write a general history of the ways of Puritan thought in early New England; it is rather a composite portrait of the Puritan mind, revealing the traits and concerns that dominated philosophical thinking in New England throughout the seventeenth century. Its value as a history lies chiefly in its exposition of the European origins of New England thought; in fact, the volume applies to a certain branch of Puritanism in general and there is very little that is exclusively "New England" about it.

Professor Miller states very well his chief aim:

Recent writers on New England history have tended to minimize the importance of abstract theology and of the pulpit, to point out that, whatever the theology, Puritan conduct can be explained without it. This conclusion has the advantages of appealing to an age that has no relish for theology, and of making the task of writing about New England appreciably simpler. It would perhaps be unkind to suggest that historians, particularly those known as "social and economic," are not prone to be themselves conspicuous examples of the Augustinian piety and are therefore the more inclined to discount spiritual motives. Whatever the reason, many students of Puritan journals and behavior, finding both preoccupied with "cases of conscience," conclude that the essence of Puritanism was its morality and that its theology was no more than an unnecessarily elaborate rationalization. If such a view is entirely correct the story of thought and expression in New England should pass over the abstract ideas more hurriedly than the present work is disposed to do. [P. 47.]

The volume is a proof that Puritan theology was philosophical; and in his interest in the theology, Professor Miller pays only scant attention to the political and economic institutions in which this theology lived. As a reaction against the negligence of other historians this emphasis is intelligible and useful, but a complete history still awaits writing, which would show the interrelations of New England thinking and doing. Professor Miller confesses that his interest is "not to judge what was done but to narrate what was thought and said" (p. 60). It would clarify the meaning of what was thought and said if the reader knew what was done about what was said; or, which is more and ought not need saying at the Harvard of Peirce and James, it is difficult for the reader to tell whether the theology of the Puritans is merely "talk" or genuine "thought" until he sees the application they made of what they said to what they did. Fortunately the volume contains so many scattered references to what Puritans did, that the discerning reader readily gets a sense of the practical meanings embedded in the theological arguments. This is particularly true of the last chapters on the Covenants of Grace, Society, and Church, in which the social implications of the Congregational theory of grace become evident. It is in these chapters, too, that the more distinctively New England themes emerge. In England and on the Continent the Congregationalists had to contend chiefly against "papists" and Anglicans, and they were relatively on the left wing of the Protestant revolt; but in New England, with the Roman and English churches at a safer distance, the Puritan divines were faced increasingly with antinomianism, illuminism, Arminianism, and similar movements still further to the left. The story of the transformation of Puritanism in New England from a defense mechanism to a working theocracy is distinctively American history, and though it can be read between the lines of Professor Miller's volume, it might well have been given more prominence. However, there is still room for this story in his volume on the eighteenth century.

The chief theme of the present volume is the exposition of the theory of "Augustinian piety." Professor Miller, on what seems to me rather meager evidence, thinks that the Puritans were conscious of their indebtedness to St. Augustine and even to Plato. If they were, they certainly made little use of this heritage. They were not familiar even with the great Protestant pioneers; Beza they knew a little better than they did Calvin. In general they were content with the academic treatises and compendia based on the Protestant scholasticism of Peter Ramus. Puritan philosophy is, technically, dialectical pietism, or, still more technically, the application of dichotomical method to the technology of the covenant of grace. This theory was elaborated by Dutch Calvinists and then imported to Cambridge, England, where it led to a vigorous polemic against the Aristotelianism entrenched at Oxford. Out of this polemic came most of the treatises used by the New England clergy and taught as philosophy at Harvard: those of Richardson, Ames, Perkins and Preston. Underlying these English works were the Latin treatises of Alsted, Wollebius, Burgersdicius, Beurhusius, Keckermann, Talon, to say nothing of Peter Ramus himself. Professor Miller has made the first comprehensive study of this whole body of writings, and has made it available to historians of philosophy and literature in a form that is intelligible. It is an important branch of late Scholasticism that has gone largely unnoticed and is indispensable for an understanding of Cambridge Platonism and its relations to Puritanism.

To most students of American history it will be a surprise, if not a shock, to learn that New England thought was thoroughly Scholastic until 1700. Though anti-Thomist and anti-Aristotelian, the framework, terminology, and problems of Puritan theology were essentially Scholastic. The physics taught in New England, for example, was largely Peripatetic and Ptolemaic until late in the seventeenth century, and it was not until the news gradually spread to Cambridge, Massachusetts, that in Cambridge, England, the Newtonian mathematics had supplanted the Scholastic cosmologies as an adequate account of "the ordinary power of God" (*i.e.,* nature), that the Copernican Revolution took place in academic circles and theological quarters. It may also surprise many readers to learn that the Puritans read and thought much that was not in the Bible. Especially during the seventeenth century there was a vigorous cultivation of "natural theology," or philosophy, with all the technical apparatus of Scholasticism and the encyclopedic interests of dialectical systems. When writers like Dell and Webster began to protest because the divines " 'speak in the words which *man's wisdom* teacheth, and so mingle *Philosophy* with *Divinity,* and think to *credit* the Gospel with Termes of Art' " (p. 81), the Puritans defended their Scholasticism wholeheartedly, though not very consistently. They believed in "sanctifying and saving *knowledge*." It turned out later that Dell and Webster were speaking not merely in behalf of illiterate pietism or Muggletonianism (as it was then called), but in the hope of encouraging a new philosophy by discrediting the old learning. Especially in New England the Puritans defended tenaciously their intellectualism both in the pulpit and the classroom, because they feared more than any other danger the spread of irresponsible "revelations and dreams." Puritan philosophy, as Professor Miller repeatedly points out, was caught in a serious dilemma: though its own inspiration came from Augustinian piety and the fruits of grace in the inner depths of the individual soul, it was forced to make a social order out of this faith and to transform "election" into a church covenant.

In this connection Professor Miller makes an interesting comment on the relation of New England Transcendentalism to its Puritan predecessor:

> *Transcendentalism might be called a remote outcropping of the same vein which in Puritanism took the form of technologia, but Transcendentalists could not go back to Richardson and Ames. Hence they resorted to Swedenborg, Plotinus, and the wonders of Oriental philosophy. These doctrines, or something like them, had been in part asserted by Puritans, and had played an important part in the intellectual life of the seventeenth century, but they had been kept in check by a psychological theory that only in one particular permitted innatism to flourish or intuition to become self-reliant. Of course, by the time of Emerson the eighteenth century had intervened, and the generation of 1830 could not reach across a whole century to recapture seventeenth-century terms; even had they been able to understand fully the language of their forebears, they would have found it of little use so long as what had been asserted in technologia was contradicted in physics.* [*Pp. 278-279.*]

On the contrary, I think the intuitional type of Platonism in which Transcendentalism abounded was an eruption of that individualism which the Puritans feared ever since the days of Anne Hutchinson, and that Puritan Platonism as it became established in New England was more similar to the Edinburgh type of Platonism, moralized and socialized by a strong tincture of "sensational psychology" and "common sense," against which the Transcendentalists revolted. The Scottish Platonists appealed to common sense for the same reasons for which the Puritan Yankees chose the "common course" amid "revelations and dreams."

While we are speculating on later American history we ought to add that there is a real connection between the later political Federalism of New England and the "federal theology" of the Puritans. In his admirable exposition Professor Miller makes it clear that the "federal" theory of sin and redemption was the theological form of the growing republican conscience. According to the federal interpretation of the covenant of grace, a regenerated sinner could claim grace as a contractual right. The ethics of covenanting had Platonic roots and developed both a secular and a sacred myth.

4
Miller's Williams

Edmund S. Morgan

Though outside the mainstream of Puritan New England thought, Roger Williams continues to fascinate us. His devotion to independence of mind and complete intellectual honesty, even when these traits challenged the roots of Congregationalist belief, have made his life and ideas subjects for historical reappraisals in our day. The two outstanding books on Williams in recent years have been one by Perry Miller, which is described in this review, and one by the reviewer, (Miller's student) Edmund S. Morgan, who has brilliantly carried on Miller's interest in the life of the Puritan mind. Morgan here recounts the three major themes in Miller's book: (1) Williams was a religious, not a political, thinker, (2) Williams' thinking was based upon a method of Biblical exegesis called "typology," and (3) Williams, by using typology, broke away from the Puritan consensus and became skeptical of all establishments, whether church or state connected. It is the last point that has especially attracted historians to Williams in their search for the antecedents of modern intellectual liberalism. Building upon Miller's suggestion, Morgan here explains the "subversive" and consistently unorthodox aspects of Williams' thought. His discussion strikes at the heart of several pressing late twentieth-century questions concerning individuality, the sources of its expression, and the place of the private person within the public conformity of the democratic community.

For further reading: *Edmund S. Morgan, *Roger Williams: The Church and the State* (1967); *Perry Miller, *Roger Williams* (1953); Alan Simpson, "How Democratic Was Roger Williams?" *William and Mary Quarterly,* 13 (1956), 53-67; Sidney Mead, *The Lively Experiment* (1963).

In 1953 an ambitious publisher launched a series of books called "Makers of the American Tradition." It proposed to "combine the best and most characteristic of the original written and recorded spoken words of outstanding American figures

The New England Quarterly, 38 (December 1965), 513-523. Reprinted by permission of the author and *The New England Quarterly*.

with thoughtful and incisive interpretations by the distinguished scholars chosen to put these books together." Roger Williams was one of the first, in time at least, of outstanding Americans; and Perry Miller was the distinguished scholar who undertook for the new series to collect and interpret selections from Williams' writings. The interpretations were both thoughtful and incisive, and the approach was genuinely new. In *Roger Williams: His Contribution to the American Tradition*, Miller said, in effect, that Williams contributed virtually nothing to the American tradition. "Although," Miller wrote, "Williams is celebrated as the prophet of religious freedom, he actually exerted little or no influence on institutional developments in America; only after the conception of liberty for all denominations had triumphed on wholly other grounds did Americans look back on Williams and invest him with his ill-fitting halo."

In the remainder of the book Miller argued that Williams was indeed a great man and a great thinker but not for the reasons usually assigned. His ideas had been misunderstood and distorted by well-meaning nineteenth-century liberals, who had made him over in their own image. Actually, said Miller, Williams could speak to the twentieth century more pertinently than to the eighteenth or nineteenth. But in 1953 the twentieth century still preferred the nineteenth-century Williams, who continued in the schoolbooks to lead the American march toward liberty and democracy, while the "Makers of the American Tradition" series quietly expired. But Miller's Williams was not forgotten by scholars. Now a nearly complete edition of Williams' writings has been brought out by another publisher.

Six of the seven volumes in the new edition are simply facsimiles of the Narragansett Club series published from 1866 to 1874, with the introductions and annotations of the nineteenth-century editors. The seventh volume, edited by Miller, contains tracts by Williams that were not included by the Narragansett Club (it does not contain, however, several of Williams' letters that have been discovered since 1874). Professor Miller provided brief introductions for each of the new tracts (but did not annotate them) and also a general introduction ("An Essay in Interpretation") which rehearses the points he had made earlier.

It must be confessed that neither this essay nor the earlier version constitutes one of Perry Miller's major efforts. But even Miller's minor efforts have brought about major reorientations in intellectual history, and this is no exception. In brief, he presented three contentions. The first and most general is that Williams' thought received its force and direction from religious, not political, ideas, and that accordingly Parrington and other liberals have wholly misconstrued him. The separation of church and state, in Williams' view, was not designed to protect the state from control by the church but vice versa.

The source of Williams' thinking on this and other subjects—and this is Miller's second and most original point—may be found in the method of Biblical exegesis known as typology. To the typologist, events chronicled in the Old Testament were symbols, prefigurations of events to follow in the New. For example, Joseph's descent into the pit and Jonah's into the belly of the whale prefigured Christ's descent into hell. Joseph and Jonah were "types" of Christ, and Christ was the "antitype" of Joseph and Jonah. With the coming of Christ the events recorded in the Old Testament acquired or retained their typological significance for the instruction of future generations of Christians, but the literal significance of many of those events departed. Christians were called upon to imitate not Joseph or Jonah but Christ. Christ thus wrought a break in the continuity of history that could be bridged only by typology.

Not everything in the Old Testament was typological: the Ten Commandments, for example, were as binding on Christians as they had been on Jews. But theologians disagreed about precisely which events or institutions were to be interpreted literally and which typologically. Roger Williams had a special view of the matter. Williams maintained that Israel itself was a type of the Christian church and retained only a typological significance for Christians. Israel was, as Williams put it, a "nonesuch," combining two things that could never be combined again: God's church and a national state. With the coming of Christ the combination was destroyed, never to be restored, and the Jews became simply a nation like other nations. The ecclesiastical character of the old Israel passed to spiritual associations, to groups of believers who gathered to worship God and his Son, wholly divorced from any national state or government. Christian churches were the antitype of Israel, and in the antitype the temporal powers of the government of Israel were transformed into the purely spiritual powers of church discipline.

The churches of Massachusetts came close to Williams' view of what a church should be. But he thought that the civil government, in attempting to maintain and protect the churches, overstepped its bounds and adopted an archaic character. Because Israel's significance was typological rather than literal, it was wrong of Massachusetts (and of every other modern state) to imitate Israel literally, by linking church and state in a union that allowed the state to exercise temporal powers in spiritual matters. Thus to follow the example of Israel was the equivalent of imitating Joseph or Jonah rather than Christ. Since the coming of Christ the church must operate entirely as a spiritual association withdrawn from the world and unconnected with government. For the state to direct religious matters in any way at all was to assume powers granted only to Israel and defunct since the coming of Christ, powers which inevitably corrupted and destroyed the very church they sought to support.

Miller's third point, in which he sought to restore Williams to the twentieth century, was closely related to the second. Williams, Miller maintained, by following typology to new conclusions broke the historical continuity on which orthodox Puritanism and every other creed or system of thought ultimately rested its claims to authority. The point is somewhat obscurely made in the earlier version and amplified only a little in the present essay. What it apppears to do, however, is to give back to Williams, in another form, the rationalism which in its eighteenth-century and nineteenth-century guise Miller had taken from him. Williams the typologist is the Williams who denies anyone the authority to dictate thought, the Williams who menaces every orthodoxy, the Williams who in Miller's view was and is a subversive character. "Few realize," Miller writes in the new essay, "that he is today, if he be listened to, as serious a threat to any sort of 'establishment' as he was visibly to that constructed by the Puritans in Massachusetts Bay." It was not, of course, the doctrine of typology itself that gave him this modernity but the scepticism with which that doctrine furnished him about all projects designed to enlist government in crusades for righteousness.

Even in this brief summary can be seen, I hope, some of the force and originality of Miller's argument. Anyone who has the patience to read the volumes it accompanies will find that they amply support what Miller says. He will also perceive the full extent of Williams' subversiveness and thus perhaps grasp the import of Miller's third point. Although Williams writes in a prose that is often awkward and occasionally opaque—he could make a sentence stretch out for several paragraphs before reaching a predicate—the reader who perseveres will discover a man who had the nerve to trust his own mind. Most of his ideas originated in assumptions that were shared by his contemporaries in New England. But Williams was never content to leave the implications of an assumption unexplored. He pushed every thought to its outer limits and accepted its consequences, however unwelcome. He must have been an alarming man to confront in argument. His friends John Cotton and John Winthrop tried to talk him out of his heresies by demonstrating the absurd conclusions that must follow from them. Williams' answer was to examine the absurdities closely and pronounce them to be the simple truth.

What must have given Williams assurance was the fact that his ideas, thus pushed to the extreme, proved consistent with one another. Taken as a whole his writings, though mainly polemical, offer an almost systematic set of propositions about the church and about the state, the two great subjects to which he devoted himself. The reissue of his writings, if it achieves nothing else, should make possible a wider appreciation of Williams' thought taken as a whole. Miller by explaining Williams' use of typology has furnished the most important clue to understanding the structure of that thought. The typological argument is present in nearly everything Williams wrote. It was usually his first line of attack in every dispute. (Its effectiveness is apparent from the fact that his opponents did not venture to deny, as Calvin might have, that typology held any validity. Instead, they generally admitted Williams' premise, that Israel was a type of the church, and sought only to stop his reasoning somewhere short of the conclusion that Israel could therefore be no model for the state.) But in his thinking about church and state, Williams by no means confined himself to typology. And to appreciate the way the different elements of his thought meshed together, one must follow him not only in his typological reasoning but also along the other avenues by which he traveled from accepted premises to unaccepted and unacceptable conclusions. Although his extant writings, except for a few letters, were written after his thought had reached maturity, they all embody the conventional premises from which he began as well as the novel conclusions at which he arrived. One can therefore reconstruct with some confidence the logical, if not the chronological, progression of his thought.

One line of progression, apart from the typological one, began with the accepted Puritan definition of the church as a company of visible saints. The definition had become common in the sixteenth century, and the ecclesiastical history of Puritanism may be read as the history of successive efforts to make the definition come true by excluding all but saints from the church. While Puritans remained within the Church of England, they urged a voluntary withdrawal from the sacraments by persons who could not discern the movements of God's grace in their souls. The Separatists who left the Church of England to set up churches of their own were able to approach closer to the ideal: only persons of proved good behavior and orthodox belief were admitted to their churches. When the Puritans arrived in New England, they were able without formal separation to establish churches with admission standards even more strict than the Separatists had employed. In order to be admitted to a church in Massachusetts, a candidate had to show not only that he lived a decent life and held orthodox views, but also that he had undergone the religious experiences that gave promise of his being a true saint, one of God's elect.

Williams shared with other Puritans the desire for a pure church; even before his arrival in New England he had become a Separatist. In Massachusetts he made himself troublesome by insisting that the churches there should disavow the Church of England, a formality that struck other Puritans as both unwise and uncharitable. Williams did not quarrel with the new, strict admissions standards of the Massachusetts churches. What he found wrong was that they were not strict enough: he believed that anyone who failed to denounce the Church of England had thereby failed fully to repent of past sins and was therefore no true saint. The idea of a pure church, a church composed only of saints, led Williams in the end to reject all the churches of Massachusetts except that of Salem, and finally to reject Salem too. After he departed for Rhode Island, accompanied by a few choice spirits, he presumably set up a church there, but within a couple of years, if we may believe Winthrop's report, he found the other members of that church unworthy too and would worship only with his wife.

Williams thus pursued the ideal of a pure church to the point where he could find none but his wife to make a church with. The seeming absurdity of this conclusion might have led another man to question the validity of the idea that a church could be composed only of saints, but Williams did not shrink from the conclusion. Instead, he went on to the ultimate absurdity, that there could be no church at all. And here he drew abreast of another line of reasoning from another accepted premise.

Protestants in the sixteenth and seventeenth centuries knew that the Pope was Antichrist. In their eagerness to discover how long his reign would endure and when they could expect the second coming of Christ, they gave their days and nights to the book of Revelation. Wishful thinking made most Englishmen look for the millennium to arrive soon; others were doubtful. What they agreed on, Puritan and Anglican alike, was that Antichrist had dominated the church of Christ for some time before the light of the gospel broke out in the successive holy rebellions against the Pope led by Wycliff, Hus, Luther, and Calvin.

Williams too was sure that the Pope was Antichrist and that the Reformation marked the beginning of his downfall, but his thinking on the subject was characteristic: nowhere in history or Revelation could he find evidence of an Antichrist who was less than wholly successful. The Pope had not only dominated the church, he had snuffed it out. It was impossible to think of the church of Christ with Antichrist at its head. And if the church of Christ had expired, how could it be restored?

Williams evidently had not thought this question through before his departure from Massachusetts. He had accepted a post as teacher of the church at Salem, and he must at the time have considered it a true church. But before he published his first book, he had decided that there was no way of restoring the church short of Christ's return and the total destruction of Antichrist. Williams believed that the church, being the church of Christ, must rest itself on the commission He gave to

His apostles. A church could not be self-created; it must be summoned into existence by a minister of Christ, who could trace his appointment through a succession of other minsters back to the first apostles. The minister must precede the church. Since Antichrist had broken the succession, there could be no ministers until Christ himself should return to appoint them in person. Meanwhile, without ministers, there could be no churches.

Other Puritans avoided this stunning conclusion by arguing that the church did not become wholly extinct under the Pope. In various corners of the world, they said, for example in England, it retained an existence, however tenuous. Moreover, they denied that a minister must trace his commission directly to Christ: a group of saints, agreeing to worship together, became a church with full powers to appoint a ministry. Neither of these positions was easy to defend, and Puritans were especially uneasy in arguing the second one. In affirming that a church could start itself, they always advised that wherever possible an existing, ordained minister should be on hand. By the eighteenth century they were reaffirming the necessity of an apostolic succession, and resting the validity of existing churches entirely on the precarious continuity of the church throughout the reign of Antichrist.

No Puritan longed to be a minister more than Williams. He particularly yearned to bring the gospel to the Indians of New England and labored hard to that end, handicapped more than a little by the fact that he could not regard himself as a minister and could not start churches among his converts. But he accepted meekly the conclusion to which his reasoning had brought him. In *The Bloudly Tenent,* he had Peace declare to her companion, Truth: "this doctrine of a Ministry before the Church, is harsh and deep, yet most true, most sweet." Only a Williams could have found sweet a doctrine that frustrated his deepest yearnings.

Williams did not despair of finding a way out of his impasse. His thinking had undergone many changes in what he called "these wonderful searching, disputing and dissenting times" and he hoped that further thought would reveal a way of restoring the church. He did not cease to write and think about the way it should be organized and run, if it did exist. But he never discovered a valid way to resume it. Both his zeal for a pure church and his reading of Revelation and history led always to the same conclusion: there could be no church of Christ in the existing state of the world.

Williams' thinking about the state was closely linked to his thinking about the church, and here his willingness to follow where reason led resulted, not in an annihilation of the institution, but in a new and daring conception of government. In denying the possibility of a self-created church, formed by an agreement or covenant among believers, Williams had been moved by a strong sense of the distance between God and man. Men, he believed, could not make God a party to an agreement simply by saying that they were doing so. God acted upon men, not men upon God. Hence the covenants by which New Englanders began their churches were at best a delusion and at worst a kind of blasphemy.

But if men could not form churches by agreement, nothing prevented them from forming civil governments that way; indeed this was the only way other than mere force to form a government. What people could not do was to bring God into the process. To be sure, God approved of government in a general way, just as He approved of marriage, but He did not participate in it. Government was a good thing for men in the same way that houses and clothes were good: it protected lives and property. But there was nothing sacred about it. It was a creation of men and it could rise no higher than its source.

The implications of this idea were immense. At the time Roger Williams conceived it, his fellow New Englanders thought themselves in covenant with the Almighty, commissioned to plant true churches in the New World. John Winthrop had explained to them that they were a special people, and that God had ratified his covenant with them by bringing them safely to New England. It was up to them to carry out their part of the bargain by keeping out or stamping out false gods and false worship. Williams scorned such a thought. The God he knew did not deal so lightly with men as to be imperceptible in his operations. If He had made an agreement with New Englanders or any other people, the fact would be recorded plainly for all the world to see and would require no John Winthrop to explain it to them. But in fact God had made a covenant with only one people in history, with Israel (here Williams' sociology joined his typology), and to look for a repetition of his dealings in that case was to pull down Christ and restore Moses.

Since God did not make agreements with any people as a people, no people could claim an obligation or a right to enforce his religion. And since men had no authority to create churches by agreement among themselves, they certainly had no authority to decree that churches be created or for that matter to enforce any kind of religious worship. But even if the church of Christ had still existed, government could not properly have supported it, except by preventing others from persecuting it. God had specifically forbidden force in religion when He sent Christ into the world. Christianity, by Christ's own injunction, was to be propagated by the spirit, and the church's demise had begun when Constantine made Christianity the imperial religion. An imperial Christianity, a state Christianity, an enforced Christianity —these were all contradictions in terms.

Williams' opponents charged that by depriving government of its divine mission, he undermined its authority. He responded convincingly that his was the conservative doctrine and theirs the seditious one. Rebellions were usually undertaken on the pretext of some religious failing. By Williams' view, people had no business overthrowing governments on behalf of God or righteousness. Orthodox Puritans had always maintained that rulers should be overthrown if they commanded a false worship. This, Williams suggested, was better than Cardinal Bellarmine's doctrine, which allowed the Pope, as vicar of God, a power to withdraw the allegiance of a heretical ruler's subjects. If it was the business of government to enforce true religion, then a man who believed his ruler's religion to be untrue would be justified in rebellion.

Williams' position was a strong one, and he buttressed his claim to conservatism by social and political views that were highly authoritarian. He applauded the Roman Emperor's censure of Ovid for writing *De Arte Amandi;* he called upon the civil government to forbid men to wear long hair; and even while asking toleration for Catholics, he suggested that they be disarmed and required to wear identifying badges on their clothes. Williams believed that government was an instrument of civilization, a means by which men were elevated from barbarism, and that without it they would quickly revert to every kind of wickedness. Government saved them from murder, theft, adultery, and uncleanness. Williams had no patience with any claims to exemption from governmental supervision of morals. Morality, he evidently believed, was entirely separable from religion, and it was only in religious matters that government had no authority.

From the vantage point of the twentieth century, Williams' views, at first sight, seem far from seditious: the authority of government in the United States has not been weakened by its exclusion from ecclesiastical affairs, and Williams in demanding such an exclusion seems to have been asking for no more than we have now achieved. The appearance is deceptive. On further consideration one senses the connection between Miller's two observations that Williams contributed nothing to the American tradition and that he is a threat to every establishment. The United States was born in a rebellion which, in its invocation of Nature's God, would scarcely have won Williams' approval. And in its history ever since, the country has retained some sense of the divine mission that Winthrop had originally assigned to New England and that Williams had rejected. In spite of the fact that the United States has separated church and state, Americans continue to think of their government as embodying some sort of righteousness. By Williams' view, all governments were useful, but none enjoyed an access to divinity. They all gained their authority simply from the agreement of the people who established them, and as long as a government could claim such an origin, it was entitled not only to the obedience of its citizens but to the respect of other governments. The governments of Indians and Turks, papists and pagans were as valid, as useful to those who created them, as the governments conducted by so-called Christians.

The seditious character of such a belief lay less in its substance than in the relentless rationality with which Williams applied it. He was quite willing to support the governments of New England when they were attacked by the Indians, but he was unwilling to support them when they were the attackers. He was deaf to all claims by his countrymen that theirs was a holy cause, that they were the people of God, that their armies were the armies of God. Reason applied to government, or for that matter to any institution, is not only the most constructive but also the most subversive instrument at man's command. If it supports government in one instance, it may undermine it in the next. In the last analysis, Williams' claim to conservatism breaks down. His rationality, even as applied to forgotten controversies of the seventeenth century, even as couched in his obscure, involved, and awkward prose, remains thrilling, noble, and seditious. Perry Miller and John Winthrop were both right in considering him a dangerous man.

5
Jonathan Edwards: "The Great Awakening"

Roland H. Bainton

Jonathan Edwards has been recognized (with Ralph Waldo Emerson and William James) as one of the three most original and profound minds that America has produced. An examination of his thought has inspired many modern scholars, particularly in the "post modern" age since the Second World War. Edwards' Christian insights into the human tendency to sin have given his ideas powerful appeal to contemporary neo-orthodox theologians and "realistic" public men who have rediscovered the human propensity for evil. Edwards belongs to the small group of American thinkers, which includes Herman Melville, Josiah Royce, and Reinhold Niebuhr, who have addressed themselves squarely to the problem of human evil, and have been unable to accept an optimistic view of human nature.

Peter Gay, historian of the European Enlightenment, sees Edwards as "the last medieval American" among intellectuals. Perry Miller, author of an intellectual biography of Edwards, viewed Edwards as "a man of his century, though his thought was in the forefront of it," and as one who "dealt with the primary intellectual achievements of modernism." If nothing else, these differing perspectives demonstrate how strongly intellectual historians can feel that past ideas must speak to present circumstances. Gay reflects the modern liberal intellectual's confidence in human reason, his heritage from the Enlightenment; Miller, though coming out of the same tradition, insisted that Edwards, whose thought stands outside the American cult of progress, has much to say to twentieth-century man in his present crisis.

From all the writing on Jonathan Edwards I have chosen this essay by Roland Bainton, an outstanding scholar of the Protestant Reformation, for two reasons. It briefly states the chief intellectual influences upon Edwards, and it depicts Edwards' thought as effectively centered in his preaching. The reader is reminded that, widespread though his ideas became, Edwards' first concern was the salvation of his flock in the little Connecticut River Valley town of Northampton, Massachusetts.

For further reading: *Perry Miller, *Jonathan Edwards* (1949); Conrad Wright, "Edwards and the Arminians on the Freedom of the Will," *Harvard Theological Review,* 25 (October 1942), 241-261; Paul Ramsey (ed.), *The Works of Jonathan Edwards* (1957), vol. 1, introduction; Vincent Tomas, "The Modernity of Jonathan Edwards," *New England Quarterly,* 25 (March 1952), 60-84; *Peter Gay, *A Loss of Mastery* (1966), chap. 4; Vincent Buranelli, "Colonial Philosophy," *William and Mary Quarterly,* 16 (July 1959), 343-362.

Jonathan Edwards inherited the problems of his grandfather Solomon Stoddard, who had lowered the standards as to baptism and the Lord's Supper and sought to retrieve the holy commonwealth by consolidating the churches, educating the clergy, and reviving the community. The first two points were covered by the Saybrook Platform and the third by the successive harvests in his parish, but the last had occurred in 1718 and during the ensuing nine years there had been no further ripening of the grain. The veteran evangelist might well attribute the failure to his diminishing powers, and rejoice that the church at Northampton invited his grandson, Jonathan Edwards, to become his colleague.

The young man had had his schooling at Yale in the turbulent days when the seat of the school was as yet indeterminate. He had shared in a secession to Weathersfield. Returning to New Haven in 1721, he reported, "Monstrous impieties. . . . In the Colledge, Particularly stealing of Hens, Geese, turkies, piggs, Meat, Wood, &c,—Unseasonable Nightwalking, Breaking People's windows, playing at Cards, Cursing, Swearing, and Damning, and Using all manner of Ill Language, which never were at such a pitch in the Colledge as they Now are." The first week in New Haven was marked by despondencies. "I have now," he said, "abundant Reason to be convinced, of the Troublesomeness and Vexation of the World, and that it will never be another Kind of World."

Yale taught Jonathan Edwards to know the depravity of man, but yet at Yale came his own awakening, the new sense of the glory of divine things. On the completion of his graduate study he was for two years in a pastorate, then for another two years a tutor at Yale. In 1727 he became a colleague of his grandfather. As the two men sat behind the pulpit, the generations were met. The one was eighty-four, the other twenty-three. Both were patricians, Solomon Stoddard, "the Pope of the Great River," a venerable figure; Jonathan Edwards, slight of frame, with a finely chiseled face, and a voice somewhat languid with a note of pathos. Within three years the great Elijah was gathered to his fathers, and the young Elisha, then twenty-six, assumed the mantle.

The problems confronting the young minister were: How might Northampton be quickened? How might Yale College be touched? How might New England be revived? To a generation emancipated from Calvinism such questions appear unanswerable on the basis of Calvinist presuppositions. If God at Creation had predetermined the number of the elect, no human effort would alter the quota. And if conversion is a condition of election, and the election is absolutely fixed, then God must will to convert those whom He has chosen; and man can in no way contribute. Yet, manifestly, Calvinists never acted on this assumption; the very survival of the holy commonwealths depended on winning the stranger within the gates and the children within the portals. Moreover, efforts to that end did appear to have been efficacious. God would seem to have ordained not only that there should be conversions but that there should also be preparation for conversion.

But what sort of preparation could man make? Recognizing that he has no claim on God he can only subject himself to those disciplines and influences through which God has been known commoead the Scriptures, observe the Sabbath, engage in self-examination. All this the seeker can do. The shepherd of souls, however, can do much more. Grace is never bestowed without knowledge, not mere theoretical knowledge but "the sense of the heart." The information that honey is sweet differs from the tasting of it. The role of the minister, then, is to preach theology: to let man know where he stands, to make him acutely sensible of God's majesty, of the wonder of His mercy and the terror of His wrath, of man's dire sin and perilous plight, of Christ's proffered redemption.

There was nothing new in the content of this message. The new note appeared in the exceptional manner in which Edwards presented his theology. In southern New England of his day he was the supreme exemplar of a unique combination of elements from the Renaissance, the Reformation, the Enlightenment, and Pietism. Edwards communicated a Calvinistic theology enriched with Pietistic fervor. His aim was so to impart knowledge as to cause his hearers not simply to assent to a fact but to be swayed by a conviction. His forcefulness sprang from his ability to communicate his own experience. In his seventeenth year during his graduate study at Yale, he had experienced "a new sense of things." According to his own narrative, the "inward sweet delight in God" came to him on the reading of the words I Timothy 1:17, "Now unto the King eternal, immortal, invisible, the only wise God, be honor and glory for ever and ever. Amen."

As I read the words, there came into my soul, and was as it were diffused through it, a sense of the glory of the Divine Being; a new sense, quite different from anything I ever experienced before. . . . I thought with myself, how excellent a Being that was, and how happy I should be, if I might enjoy that God, and be rapt up to him in heaven, and be as it were swallowed up in him forever!

The sense I had of divine things, would often of a sudden kindle up, as it were, a sweet burning in my heart; and ardor of soul. . . . I walked abroad alone, in a solitary place in my father's pasture, for contemplation. And as I was walking there, and looking up on the sky and clouds, there came into my mind so sweet a sense of the glorious majesty *and* grace *of God, that I know not how to express.*

The appearance of everything was altered; there seemed to be, as it were, a calm, sweet cast, or appearance of divine glory, in almost everything. God's excellency, his wisdom, his purity and love, seemed to appear in everything; in the sun, moon . . . and all nature. . . . I often used to sit and view the moon for continuance; and in the day, spent much time in viewing the clouds and sky, to behold the sweet glory of God in these things; in the meantime, singing forth, with a low voice, my contemplations of the Creator and Redeemer. And scarce anything, among all the works of nature, was so sweet to me as thunder and lightning; formerly, nothing had been so terrible to me. . . . But now, on the contrary, it rejoiced me. I felt God, so to speak, at the first appearance of a thunderstorm; and used to take the opportunity, at such times, to fix myself in order to view the clouds, and the lightnings play, and hear the majestic and awful voice of God's thunder, which often times was exceedingly entertaining, leading me to sweet contemplations of my great and glorious God. While thus engaged, it always seemed natural to me to sing.

He who had been thus so singularly lifted up was greatly exercised to know what "contrivance" God had ordained for promoting harvests among others. He marveled at the coldness of men's hearts. The need, he concluded, was not that men should "have their heads stored, so much as to have their hearts touched." How should it be done?

Edwards found the clue in John Locke's *Essay Concerning Human Understanding,* where the mind is said not to be endowed with any innate ideas but to receive everything by sensation from without. For that reason, Edwards argued, the preacher must be "sensational," literally creating a "sensation." However, Edwards' interpretation differed from Locke's. For the latter, sensations result from the impact of things material upon the senses; for Edwards, the only reality is idea, sensations being therefore ideas resulting from the impact of God upon the mind. The sensation which results from preaching is then nothing other than God at work. Can the preacher prepare those conditions which are favorable to the working of God? The answer is that the preacher can impart only the truth. The natural man may thereby be given a view of God's natural perfections, the heinousness of sin, and the frightfulness of the punishments denounced against sin. The spiritual man may gain a sense of the excellency, beauty, and sweetness of divine things. God, His glory and excellency; man, his capacities, depravity, and peril; Christ, his compassion and the work of redemption—these are the truths to be declared. The manner of the declaration should be matter-of-fact because these are matters of fact. Yet the voice, though subdued, must be surcharged with emotion like that of the judge who pronounces sentence of death or reprieve to life.

The first word is about God. Here Edwards fused two traditions and thereby made God more accessible. The first came directly from John Calvin, the second from Cudworth, the Cambridge Platonist. The Calvinist strain, derived mainly from the Old Testament, pictures God in personal terms as the great Sovereign of the universe, the King of Kings, the Potentate of time and eternity, who shows forth His glory in the creation and government of the world, and elaborates His purpose in the course of history. His justice is displayed in consigning the rebellious to the fate which they deserve and His mercy by granting to some the compassion which they in no way have merited. All of this is in Edwards, and this is the reason why he is rightly regarded as a Calvinist. It is a formidable picture.

At the same time, there is a more approachable view interfused with Neoplatonic strains of God conceived less as a person than as a being with an inner necessity of self-diffusion, a fountain gushing streams or a radiance emitting shafts of light. This is the reason for the elaboration within the being of God of the Trinitarian structure. This self-diffusion of God issues in the creation of the world which is pervaded by the effulgence of His glory. God's end in creation was the "infinitely perfect union of the creature with himself." This is the point at which God becomes more approachable. If He be the sovereign, man can only bow and obey. But if He be self-diffusive being, there is then the possibility of the return to God of that which came from God, so that man can be united with God and share in the excellency of His nature.

The picture of God affects the picture of man. In accord with this Neoplatonic strain, long since appropriated by Christian mysticism, Edwards held that the end of religion is the participation on the part of man in the divine nature. The very reason for the incarnation was that as God became man, so man might become God. The pledge of such union was the combination of human and divine in Christ so that in communion with him the believer might partake of divinity.

This type of thinkng, completely alien to John Calvin, was characteristic of his great opponent, Michael Servetus, who thought not to degrade God but to elevate man by union with God. To Calvin any such fusion must demean deity. Odd that New England's greatest Calvinist at this point sided with one whom Calvin regarded as a monstrous blasphemer!

Yet Edwards actually combined this view, so repulsive to Calvin, with Calvin's own picture of man. The result was that for Edwards the depravity of man was heightened by the capacities of man. If he be capable of union with the divine and rejects his opportunity, how much the more is he vile! Such defection is not to be considered merely the negation of good in Neoplatonic terms. Rather like a Hebrew prophet, Edwards portrayed sin as rebellion, malice, venomous hate, warranting the comparison of man to a poisonous insect. Sin is a fire as intense as the fires of hell, and the wicked will have no principle of corruption in hell save that which they take with them. This fire may be smothered or restrained, but given an opportunity it will flare forth. Man hates God. He hates His very mercy because it is holy and puts man to shame. If man does not hate God, it is only because he has constructed for himself a God whom he does not need to hate. If man continues God's enemy until death, he will always remain an enemy. "When you come to be a firebrand of hell . . . you will be all on fire, full of the fire of God's wrath: and you will be all on a blaze with spite and malice towards God. You will be as full of the fire of malice, as of the fire of vengeance. . . . Then you will appear as you are, a viper," no longer disguised.

All men so behave, granted the opportunity, because owing to the fall of Adam, they are venomous by nature. The reason is not so much a hereditary taint as a solidarity of the human race with itself and with its progenitor. This theory of social cohesion is only one example of Edwards' theory of identity in the midst of change. From Newton he had learned that physics has an unsolved problem in that the atoms of a particular object adhere instead of flying apart. Edwards' answer was that they are held in cohesion by an unceasing act of God. Likewise the persistent identity of a changing individual is a work of God, who by continuous creation preserves continuity in the context of change whether from the acorn to the oak or from the infant to the aged. Just as the atoms of any particular object are held from flying apart by divine power, just as the successive moments in an individual existence are held in cohesion by an ongoing creation, similarly individual men adhere within the entity of humanity through God's embracing activity. For God is really the only substance in whom and through whom all things subsist. Thus in Him humanity is one.

But humanity is sinful. If, then, any men are capable of union with God it can only be because they have been extricated from this nexus of corruption and their very nature has been transformed. The conversion which turns a viper into a saint must be drastic. The language of the new birth is therefore more than a metaphor. It is a description of the sheer miracle of religion. It consists in a pure and disinterested delight in the excellency of God as He is in Himself. True saints are "inexpressibly pleased and delighted with the sweet ideas of the glorious and amiable nature of the things of God. And this is the spring of all their delights, and the cream of all their pleasures . . . [a] ravishing entertainment . . . in view of the beautiful and delightful nature of divine things."

But once again, how shall they, who are without relish, taste and see that the Lord is good? Not directly. Herein lies the necessity for the self-disclosure of God in Jesus Christ. The preacher is not to dwell unduly on the majesty of God but is to disclose the excellency of Christ.

A sight of the greatness of God, in His attributes, may overwhelm men, and be more than they can endure; but the enmity and opposition of the heart may remain in its full strength, and the will remain inflexible, whereas one glimpse of the moral and spiritual glory of God, and the supreme amiablness of Jesus Christ, shining into the heart, overcomes and abolishes this opposition, and inclines the soul to Christ, as it were, by an omnipotent power; so that now, not only the understanding, but the will, and the whole soul, receives and embraces the Savior. . . . [*And*] *the sight of the glory of God, in the face of Jesus Christ, works true supreme love to God."*

Here again mere information does not suffice. There must be an apprehension by the sense of the heart. At the same time, "holy affections are not heat without light, but evermore arise from an information of the understanding." When Christ caused hearts to burn, it was through the opening of the Scriptures, and it is only by the discovery of the beauty of the moral perfection of Christ that the believer is led into the knowledge of the excellency of his person.

Therefore, it is well to begin by a contemplation of him who is both the lion and the lamb, infinite in elevation and infinite in condescension, infinite in justice and infinite in grace, infinite in glory and infinite in humility, infinite in majesty and transcendent in meekness. "His infinite condescension marvellously appeared in the manner of his birth." There was no room for him in the inn because none would give up a room. The squalor of his birth was a foretaste of the agony of his cross, where he was tormented in his love and pity by the fire of our sins which he so took to himself as to feel himself forsaken by God. "This was infinitely terrible to Christ." And in all this he continued to exercise dying love to his enemies.

Thus did Christ consume our sins upon the cross. Our redemption consists in being joined with him as he is joined with us. Justification by faith has reference to no mere belief, nor even acceptance. We must be one with Christ as the members with the head, as the branches with the stock, which is the ground of their partaking of the sap, as the wife with the husband, which is the ground of her joint interest in his estate. Because of the union of the believer with Christ, God deems it meet that the merits and benefits of the Redeemer should be conferred on the redeemed. As there is solidarity with Adam in corruption, so is there also with Christ in newness of life.

Why then are not all saved? Why should the law of solidarity be more potent for the lost than for the found? Depravity follows the principle of social cohesion but regeneration is individualistic and atomistic. No doubt one reason for Edwards' view was that he retained the traditional Calvinist scheme. But to say this is only to push the problem back to Calvin and his predecessors. The final reason is a rugged realism with regard to the tougher facts of life. So far as we can see, all are not saved. "How insensible and unmoved are most men!" cries Edwards.

"How they can sit and hear of the infinite height, and depth, and length, and breadth of the love of God in Christ Jesus, of his giving his infinitely dear Son, to be offered up a sacrifice for the sins of men, and of the unparalleled love of the innocent, and holy, and tender Lamb of God, manifested in his dying agonies, his bloody sweat, his loud and bitter cries, and bleeding heart, and all this for enemies, to redeem them from deserved, eternal burnings, and to bring [*them*] *to . . . everlasting joy and glory; and yet be cold, and heavy, insensible, and regardless!*

But the plain fact is that they are.

Nor are we to suppose that God is subject to any sentimental leniency in dealing with the rebellious; rather, as a lion He breaks our bones. It is all very well to talk of death as a benefit to wean us from the world, but what shall we say of the deaths of infants which exceed in number those of any other age (that was true in Edwards' day), and why should children before dying be tortured by disease? These things happen, and God does not stop them. Harriet Beecher Stowe well said that "Nature . . . is a more inexorable Calvinist than the Cambridge Platform," and the Puritans were too ruthlessly honest to dilute the vinegar of life. One wonders only why they felt constrained to project the tragedies and the inequalities of the temporal into the eternal.

On this point Edwards was clear: grace is available to some, and they are free to accept it. His "Treatise on the Freedom of the Will" undertook to vindicate freedom, though at the same time to conserve God's all-sufficiency without which man would be plunged into cosmic insecurity. God is in control but man is free. The reconciliation is effected by a subtle distinction between the will as choice and the will as inclination. Man is free to choose though he will choose in accord with his inclination and the inclination is determined by his very nature. The inclination to choose the good can result only from a change of nature and this is effected by the Holy Spirit infusing whom it will. All then comes back to God's arbitrary and immutable determination to damn some according to their desert and to save others according to His mercy, and Edwards said it plainly enough on occasion. But at the same time he exhibited again the paradox of Calvinism that it should be both predestinarian and revivalist. Ardent pleas were addressed to the congregation on the assumption that they could accept the proffered grace.

That was the whole point of the celebrated sermon on *Sinners in the Hands of an Angry God.* It was a revival sermon, designed to create a sensation in Edwards' sense by placing before men the fact of their condition, for

the bow of God's wrath is bent, and the arrow made ready on the string, and justice bends the arrow at your heart. . . . The God that holds you over the pit of hell, much as one holds a spider, or some loathsome insect over the fire, abhors you. . . . He is of purer eyes than to bear to have you in his sight; you are ten thousand times so abominable in his eyes, as the most hateful and venomous serpent is in ours. You have offended him infinitely more than ever a stubborn rebel did his prince: And yet, it is nothing but his hand that holds you from falling into the fire every moment.

This is the point. God is holding back. He is giving you another chance, "O sinner!"

Consider the fearful danger you are in: It is a great furnace of wrath, a wide and bottomless pit, full of the fire of wrath, that you are held over in the hand of God. . . . How dreadful is the state of those that are daily and hourly in danger of this great wrath and infinite misery! But this is the dismal case of every soul in this congregation that has not been born again. . . . O that you would consider it, whether you be young or old! . . . And it would be no wonder if some persons, that now sit here in some seats of this meeting-house in health, and quiet and secure, should be in hell before tomorrow morning.

Before the close of that sermon "there was a great moaning & crying out through ye whole House . . . ye shrieks & crys were piercing & Amazing. . . . Several Souls were hopefully wrought upon yt night. & oh ye cheerfulness and pleasantness of their countenances yt receivd comfort." The Great Awakening was under way in New England. . . .

6
The Theological Effects of the Great Awakening in New England

Edwin S. Gaustad

Religious beliefs continued to form part of the mainstream of intellectual history in America long after the Puritan age. Edwin S. Gaustad describes how the fragmentation of once solid Puritan dogma during the Great Awakening from the mid-1730s through the 1740s resulted in theological factions that foreshadowed nineteenth-century American denominational ideas. These factions modified or altered seventeenth-century beliefs about the total authority of God, human predestination, and the freedom of man's will. In so doing, some of the theological parties furnished strength for independent thinking and for an enlightened and critical, if not empirical, challenging of old creeds. Others became anti-intellectual in their insistence upon emotion and revelation as the rock of faith.

Readers may want to question the author's conclusion that the theology of the Great Awakening was dead by the end of the eighteenth century. The recurring revivals of the first half of the nineteenth century, though lacking the "old Calvinist" view of God from the Great Awakening, still preached to the same basic issues of man's sinfulness and the glory of finding divine grace. Nor was the force of the Great Awakening felt only in orthodox religion. Both religious liberalism, which it opposed, and the popular enthusiasm for ideological conformity that it engendered became ingredients of pre-Revolutionary thought.

For further reading: *Edwin S. Gaustad, *The Great Awakening in New England* (1957); Perry Miller, "Jonathan Edwards and the Great Awakening," in his **Errand into the Wilderness* (1956), pp. 153-166; Alan Heimert, *Religion and the American Mind* (1966); *William G. McLoughlin, *Isaac Backus and the American Pietistic Tradition* (1967); Frank Hugh Foster, *A Genetic History of the New England Theology* (1907).

On Sunday, September 14, 1740, a stodgy young man set foot for the first time on New England's soil. Debarking at Newport, he greeted the town's elderly Anglican

Mississippi Valley Historical Review, 40 (March 1954), 681-683, 685-706. Reprinted by permission of the author and The Organization of American Historians. All footnotes but one have been omitted.

minister and proceeded to wrest from him permission to preach in his pulpit the next day. With reluctance and misgivings, the minister agreed. The new arrival, George Whitefield, showing no reluctance himself, mounted the pulpit on Monday morning to preach a simple, vigorous, and extemporaneous gospel to "Persons of all Denominations." Speaking with "much Flame, Clearness and Power," as he confessed with typical candor, Whitefield observed that the people were "exceedingly attentive," while "Tears trickled down their cheeks." On Wednesday, this bustling Boanerges ferried to Bristol, preached there, and the next day urged his horse on to Boston. Whitefield's first tour of New England had begun. Before the end of October the tour was finished; but when the "Grand Itinerant" departed for New York, he left the countryside rocking.

New England's epochal revival of 1741-1742, the "Great Awakening," is not to be explained, of course, solely in terms of the impassioned rhetoric of this twenty-six-year-old Anglican clergyman. The way was prepared for him in many important respects. The decline of Puritanism, of which the Half-Way Covenant (allowing children of unregenerate parents to be baptized) and Stoddardeanism (admitting those without an experience of grace to the service of communion) are partial evidences, had evoked a guilty awareness that the earlier, sterner faith had been diluted. Diversity in and indifference toward church services had brought about a more rigid ecclesiastical control, compromising the autonomy of the local congregation and creating entangling alliances with the legislature—of which Connecticut's Saybrook Platform was the prime example. Calvinism, moreover, had been adulterated by the covenant theology which—whatever its modifications and rationalizations—vastly altered the creature-Creator relationship as it had been conceived by men of Augustine's and Calvin's stamp. Under the contractual arrangement of covenant theology, grace tended to become hereditary while Puritanism, with its disdain for the "mixed multitudes," faded into religious snobbery. God and the covenanters understood each other; the latter were a chosen people in a sense more literal and provincial than had been true since the days of Ezra. Religion had become more institutional and less personal; more formal and less spontaneous; more inclusive and less demanding. When, at the beginning of the eighteenth century, Boston's new Brattle Street Church declared that a public relation of one's conversion experience was no longer a prerequisite to full church membership, the decline of Puritanism was in full view. On election days and fast days, the clergy repeatedly noted and as often bemoaned the "many and great Impieties" of the day. Finally, the influx of rationalism and an improved economy brought new ideas and sinful pride. God, if still a despot, was an enlightened one, and men, if still depraved, found depravity no cause for anxiety nor any hindrance to social respectability.

A more immediate preparation for Whitefield, however, was the Northampton revival of 1734-1735, which began under the pastoral leadership of Jonathan Edwards and moved in a southerly direction along both sides of the Connecticut River Valley. Edwards' popular and moving report of this frontier awakening, *A Faithful Narrative of Surprising Conversions,* drew attention to New England's religious potential in a time generally regarded as one of "extraordinary dullness in religion." The harvest of converts was the more surprising because there was "no Earthquake, no Inundation of Water, no Desolation by Fire, no Pestilence or any other sweeping Distemper, nor any cruel Invasion by their Indian Neighbors, that might force the Inhabitants into a serious Thoughtfulness, and a religious Temper by the Fears of approaching Death and Judgment." A continuity between this revival and the more intense and much more pervasive one of 1741-1742 was provided in the person of Jonathan Edwards, who was an amazed spectator and reporter of the first upheaval, and of the latter a vigorous apologist and leading theologian. By 1737, revivalism was "very much at a Stop" in New England, though it was still to be found among Presbyterians of New York and New Jersey. In these evangelistic successes of the Middle Colonies as well as in the early activities of the distant Whitefield, the clergy of New England demonstrated keen interest. In Boston in 1739, as many as seven items by Gilbert Tennent, enthusiastic Presbyterian evangelist from New Brunswick, were published. And the Boston newspapers in 1739 and 1740 carried extensive notices of books and tracts by or about the astounding work of the astounding young English preacher. By September, when Whitefield landed at Newport, New England was a field ready for harvest.

And the harvest was without parallel. The Great Awakening of New England was not a series of isolated revival meetings, held over a period of several decades—as was the case in the Middle and Southern colonies. It was a rushing flood that swept over all the land, recognizing no boundaries, whether social, civil, or ecclesiastical, leaving no inhabited area untouched, and receding as suddenly as it had come. . . .

But the ebb was almost as sudden as the flow. By the end of 1742, some two years after the arrival of Whitefield, Edwards reported of his Northampton parish that "People's Engagedness in Religion and the Liveliness of their Affections have been on the Decline." It was true everywhere. Opposition to the revival which earlier had been sporadic and disorganized was by 1743 more vocal and more systematic. Taking antagonistic positions among themselves, the clergy held conflicting conventions, issued contrasting testimonies, and launched a prolonged "paper war." Charles Chauncy of the First (Old Brick) Church, Boston, led the "Opposers" with a prodigious writing and editing of anti-revivalist materials. Bitter pronouncements were leveled against the itinerants who wrecked ecclesiastical order, entered parishes without permission, and often split churches into irreconcilable factions. The friends of the Awakening, styled New Lights, were set against its foes, the Old Lights; the former were denounced as enthusiastic and antinomian, the latter as Pharisaic and Arminian. "Such distinguishing names of reproach," wrote Edwards, "do as it were divide us into two armies, separated, and drawn up in battle array, ready to fight one with another; which greatly hinders the work of God." When this stage had been reached, the revival was passed; only the post-mortem remained. By 1744, even the turbulent Tennent was preaching on "The necessity of studying to be quiet and doing our own Business."

Although the revival itself was short-lived, its effects were lasting. Into the nineteenth century, the shaping of Connecticut's political parties was determined by the Awakening. From it, a democratic, evangelistic ministry for the frontier areas emerged. Congregational churches were multiplied, if only through the division of the older ones. The Baptists, falling heir to many of the unchurched New Lights or Separates, greatly accelerated their denominational growth. The Presbyterianizing of New England's established churches, particularly in Connecticut, was halted, while religious liberties were gradually increased. Dartmouth College and Brown University in New England, as well as Princeton University in the Middle Colonies, were direct outgrowths of this "extraordinary outpouring of the Spirit." These effects and others in the realm of institutional life are the more readily discernible and familiar ones. There were, however, important effects also in the realm of ideas, and it is with these effects that we are here chiefly concerned.

To a significant degree, any account of New England theology must be rendered in terms of movements first distinctly appearing in the generation following the Great Awakening. This generation, poised between an epochal revival and an epochal revolution, saw a more self-conscious theological development than had heretofore been visible in New England. "Calvinistical Schemes" were deliberately defended, while Arminianism was boldly espoused. Arianism, Unitarianism, and Universalism found advocates in eastern Massachusetts. Within the lifetime of many of the principals of the Awakening the central issues of an evangelical Christianity—general or particular atonement, a human or divine Christ, reason or revelation, reform or regeneration, free or earned grace—were subjected to severe testing.

In theology as within the churches and the ministry, the immediate effect of the Awakening was divisive. But in theology, more than in any other area, that schism tended more toward divorce than to temporary alienation. In an election sermon before the Connecticut legislature in 1758, Benjamin Throop of Norwich sadly observed the manner in which "the fear of God is amazingly cast off in this day." He further observed:

While some are disputing the Personality of the Godhead, and denying the Lord that brought them; others are ridiculing the important Doctrine of Atonement, and casting contempt upon the efficacious Merits of a Glorious Redeemer; many are exploding the Doctrine of a free and Sovereign Grace, and exalting human Nature under all its Depravity to a situation equal to all its Necessities; thereby perverting the Designs of the Gospel, and frustrating, as far as may be, the Means of our Salvation.

Many of these points had long been controversial, but now it was possible to identify factions because it was fashionable to take sides. The great revival had destroyed the fetish of an undivided ministry. Before 1740, church disputes could generally be settled by calling a council of churches. Now, however, the practicality of this device was nearly obviated when the decision of a council called by one faction of a church might be reversed by a later council called by the other faction. And so with heterodoxy. Heresy was more difficult to define and to extirpate. When, as in the case of John Bass of Ashford, a minister was deposed for Arminianism, it was because he was opposed by a majority sufficient to pack the council and to insure that no counter-council would be called.

Even catechetical instruction was no longer feasible. Samuel Niles complained that the ministers were telling the people "(practically at least, if not verbally) that the Catechism is corrupt, containing false Points of Doctrine." Parents as a result do not instruct their children and the minister "dare not teach the Children what he himself does not believe." A committee defending Lemuel Briant of Braintree against charges of heresy acknowledged that "tho' Mr. Briant has too much neglected Catechising, yet he is now ready to teach our Children such Parts of the Catechism as he apprehends agreeable to the Scriptures." The last clause is particularly significant. Rationalists did not now feel under the necessity of waiting until the orthodox could keep pace with them. Open schism was the order of the day; theologians campaigned boldly, crystallized their ideology, and organized their forces.

The Awakening, moreover, by its extravagances in belief and behavior, pushed many of the normally orthodox into strongly anti-Calvinist positions. The countless accusations and defenses, the endless searching of the Scriptures, made men long for roomier, calmer meadows. Some, like William Hooper and Ebenezer Turell, overshot Congregational liberalism and landed in Anglicanism. Others, like Charles Chauncy, deliberately abandoned the theology which the revival espoused. Though certainly disposed by temperament toward a religion rather of the head than of the heart, Chauncy in 1741 displayed a healthy Calvinism. In his published works he did not return to specifically theological matters until 1758 when he abandoned the doctrine of original sin. But in the years when ecclesiastical and doctrinal disorders were at their height, Chauncy's adamant opposition to the New Light party was accompanied by an opposition to the Calvinism in which that party lived. His *Seasonable Thoughts* was, Wheelock reported with disdain, "never vendible, except among Arminians in the colony of Connecticut."

The theological divisions which followed in the wake of the revival were more complex than the familiar Old Light versus New Light dichotomy. Four parties may be distinguished. The extremists, least important of the four, were hyperzealous New Lights whose beliefs were characterized either by theological novelty or by theological vacuity. The traditional orthodoxy, which had existed before the Awakening and which tried desperately to maintain itself thereafter, came to be known as "Old Calvinism." A third party, the Liberals or rationalists—a left wing within the older orthodoxy—spoke with new vigor and clarity. Finally, the Strict Calvinists or New Divinity men fully displayed and effectively extended the theological bias of the revival.

The breathless quality of an inspired evangelism, too busy propagating a faith to inquire into the nature of that faith, continued to characterize extremist elements of the New England clergy long after 1742. Whitefield, whose sole theological effort was a letter reproving John Wesley for his Arminianism, was a perfect pattern for those who lacked the time or other requirements for making theology an essential part of their religion. How impressive was his example? It was certainly followed by many of the New Lights: Samuel Buell, Andrew Croswell, James Davenport, John Moorhead, John Cleaveland, Elisha Paine, and even Eleazar Wheelock—to mention but a few. Laymen who suddenly felt an impulse or call saw no great incongruity in their proceeding, without benefit of theological education, to exhort sinners to repentance and faith. It was not difficult to reach the intellectual level of Whitefieldian sermonizing. A Boston newspaper advertised for a runaway slave who could be identified because he is "very forward to mimick some of the strangers that have of late been preaching among us."

Within this extreme faction, a minority of the New Light party, "human learning" was assigned a low value; it was noted that often a minister had zeal in inverse proportion to his knowledge. The precedent established in these years together with this prejudice against erudition made more probable the growth of an unlearned, untrained ministry. Congregationalists and the main body of the Presbyterian church, however, refused to yield to these obscurantist pressures. An additional pressure from the frontier, where no educated ministry was available, inclined Baptists and Methodists to utilize such leadership as there was, making possible their phenomenal expansion in America. To what extent the Awakening was responsible for a theological vacuum in given segments of American religion is problematic. That it demonstrated the feasibility of and made fashionable a fervent evangelism without intellectual discipline seems probable. It was evident to all, moreover, that those who talked most of the value of reason adhered least to the dogmas of religion.

The extremists, when they did become theological, sometimes produced doctrinal novelties. Enthusiasm and antinomianism, each with its several connotations, were extended by those whose "new light" was truly a will-o'-the-wisp. Beyond contributing to the rapid decline of the Awakening their perversions of dogma had little significance, though to some they occasionally served as convenient examples of the outcome of an unchecked Calvinism. One theological bypath of special interest led to a consideration of the imminent end of the world. It is surprising, not that millennial prophecies were a feature of this as of all periods of religious excitement, but that they occupied so minor a place in the popular preaching of the time. The court proceedings at the trial of James Davenport afford one of the few examples of their use. It was charged that Davenport affected and terrified his hearers by pretending to revelations regarding the approaching end of the world. Millennialism was not confined to the extremists, however. Edwards' concern with the future kingdom of Christ on earth is particularly evident in his *Humble Attempt*, written in an effort to establish a "concert of prayer" for the revival of religion and return of Christ. Samuel Hopkins, according to William Ellery Channing, was possessed by the subject: "The millenium was more than a belief to him. It had the freshness of visible things. He was at home in it." Yet there is no evidence that any but extremists adopted millennialism as a lever to force conversion; it was hell, not Armageddon, which for most New Lights constituted the greater threat.

The "Old Calvinists," who continued to espouse a theology that gradually and painlessly adapted itself to cultural change, were made up of theological conservatives of both Old and New Light parties. These were the middle-of-the-road travelers. To many of this group the thunderous, turgid doctrinal battles that were waged around their heads seemed obstructive and unnecessary. They saw the wrangling between Strict Calvinists and Liberals as the result of an overconcern for "metaphysical niceties," and advocated a "large measure of charity" on abstruse doctrinal matters. In 1760, Ezra Stiles viewed the conflict between Arminians and Calvinists as, in fact, only a verbal dispute. Interrogating so-called Arminians, he found that they believed in the redemptive grace of Christ; inquiring of so-called Calvinists, he learned that they did not deny the importance of good works. On the whole, he concluded, "I cannot perceive any very essential real difference in their opinions respecting the fundamental principles of religion."

In this discourse Stiles deliberately minimized all differences because he was trying to unify New England's tottering ecclesiastical structure. And with good reason. Old Calvinists, losing adherents both to liberalism and to a more consistent Calvinism, enjoyed ever fewer fellow travelers on their judicious middle path. Men of great piety or ability abandoned the theology of compromise for the "New Divinity," while men of outstanding intellect or daring forsook the genial orthodoxy for a cautious testing of rationalism's full force. Conscious of this depletion of their ranks, though somewhat mystified by it, even the Old Calvinists were on occasion aware that in current theological opinion there were some "very essential real differences." Braintree, whose ministers were as voluble as those of Boston, affords in the decade following the Awakening an instructive instance of the reaction of Old Calvinism to some real differences.

In 1749, Lemuel Briant, the Liberal minister of the First Church in Braintree, preached in Jonathan Mayhew's pulpit (West Church) in Boston a sermon belligerently entitled *The Absurdity and Blasphemy of Depreciating Moral Virtue*. With Isaiah 64:6, the proof-text of the Calvinists, as his own text, Briant set out to demonstrate "that neither all, nor any part of our Righteousness when true and genuine, sincere and universal, can possible, consistent with Reason, Revelation, or indeed so much as common Sense, deserve this odious Character of filthy Rags." To deprecate righteousness was to reflect dishonor on Christ, for "Our Savior was the great Preacher of Righteousness: For this End was he born, and on this grand design came he into the World, to propagate Truth and Vertue among Mankind." Though Christ was still "our Savior" the plan of salvation was no longer in evidence. The reduction of religion to morality by Briant lacked even the advantage of subtlety and finesse. Righteousness, he declared, is "that which the Son of God thought worth his coming down from Heaven to establish on Earth, that which is the Basis and in short the whole Superstructure of this his divine Religion." Divine grace, honored above all else by the Edwardean party and not at all forgotten by the Old Calvinists, was completely ignored by this Braintree liberal. "It is the Righteousness of the Saints that renders them amiable in God's Sight, that is the Condition of all his Favours to them, and the sole Rule he will proceed by in judging of them; and dispensing eternal Rewards to them." Upon this same righteousness "the general Good of all Mankind essentially depends."

This sort of preaching, Briant acknowledged, is "not calculated for the general Taste of the present Age. . . . It may not, at present, be the Way to popular Applause." He was right. Such a wholesale abandonment of orthodoxy would bestir Calvinists of any degree to a defense of the ancient faith. Upon the same text John Porter, who did not share Briant's views on righteousness, preached to the South Society in Braintree on *The Absurdity and Blasphemy of Substituting the Personal Righteousness of Men in the Room of the Surety-Righteousness of Christ*. It is most proper and correct, Porter affirmed, to style the personal righteousness of the best of men as filthy rags in certain instances: viz., when that righteousness is viewed in comparison with the righteousness of God, or when it is viewed in "Point of Justification before God." There can be no faith in Scripture nor semblance of orthodoxy that does not "include these two Things . . . (1) Renunciation of our own Righteousness as to Dependence—having no Confidence in the Flesh . . . (2) Appropriation of Christ's Righteousness to ourselves, and resting on it alone for Justification and Life." Most Calvinists were quick to recognize that a moral reform was no substitute for a spiritual regeneration, and that true righteousness was the result, not the cause, of justification. In his seventy-eighth year, Samuel Niles of the Second Church, Braintree, also moved to counteract the tendencies of Briant's heresy. After waiting to see if Briant would make any respectable reply to Porter's sermon, Niles finally published in 1752 *A Vindication of Divers Important Gospel-Doctrines*. Here he contended, not for novel doctrine or strange theology, but "for the Faith once delivered to the Saints; even that Faith, which the Churches of the Saints in New-England have been in the Possession and Profession of, now to the third Generation down from our renowned Ancestors." Briant, on the other hand, had denied and destroyed that faith, making "the whole Doctrine of Christ but a mere refined System of Morality." In Braintree liberalism had proceeded with such haste and indiscretion that even Old Calvinists were roused from a slumber of easy orthodoxy, rudely awakened by doctrinal differences both real and essential. To allow, as old orthodoxy had, the respectable unregenerate to come into the churches or even to partake of communion was one thing. It was quite another thing to admit these unregenerate into heaven.

Although this residual orthodoxy known as Old Calvinism spent some energy refuting the excesses of a strict Calvinism, it was the Liberal party which caused the greatest concern. The Liberals had been tampering with rationalism even before the Awakening, but then it was less obtrusive and much less divisive. In the turbulence of 1741-1742, Liberals had found both incentive and justification for more emphatic declarations of their position. Jonathan Mayhew, for example, while an undergraduate at Harvard had visited York, Maine, in the midst of its spiritual convulsions. Though his criticism of the revival there was reserved, it indicated an independent and skeptical mind. He later referred to the intellectual side of the Awakening with less reserve:

. . . it is the manner of vain enthusiasts, when the absurdity of their doctrine is laid open, to fall a railing, telling their opposers that they are in a carnal state, blind, and unable to judge; but that themselves are spiritually illuminated. Thus they endeavor to palm the grossest absurdities on their neighbors, under a notion of their being divine and holy mysteries. . . . Whatever is reasonable, is with them carnal; and nothing is worthy of belief, but what is impossible and absurd in the eye of human reason.

To men like Samuel Niles, however, who complained of doctrinal disloyalty to the ancient and pious forefathers of New England, Mayhew had sharp words: "Nothing is more unworthy a reasonable creature, than to value principles by their age, as some men do their wines"; or, "No man in his senses will allow himself to be in error, because he cannot get as many hands held up in favor of his tenet, as another."

The reaction against Calvinism, intensified by the prestige and prolixity of the revival party, was accelerated; and the "hardest" doctrines of Calvin were ridiculed and pronounced inhuman, unreasonable, and indefensible. The doctrine of original sin was treated in terms of thousands of innocent infants burning in hell. Predestination was viewed from the point of the reprobate, not of the regenerate, while the doctrine of free and irresistible grace was made to appear inimical to good works and all moral effort. If, furthermore, man's will was not free, then all men were simply automatons, victims of an impersonal and inexorable fate. To be sure, Christ's death provided an atonement, but that atonement was not *ex opere operato*. Mayhew warned that the "one grand capital error" was to believe "that the merits of Christ's obedience and sufferings, may be so applied or imputed to sinners, as to be available to their justification and salvation, altho' they are destitute of all personal inherent goodness." When this "grand mistake" is "cloathed in scripture language, it is expressed thus; that we are saved by grace." Since the theological system of the early New Divinity men grew out of the doctrine of an unearned and allpowerful grace, the Liberals were striking at the root.

Along with this attention to divine grace, there was a meticulous examination of the person of Christ, the instrument and manifestation of that grace. To what extent did the Christocentric preaching and writing of the revival provoke a liberal reaction against the Son? There had been instances of New Light preaching that treated Christ with an intimacy that must have repelled the more staid. Yet the Arianism which Mayhew cautiously voiced in 1755 seems rather a reflection of the growth of that movement in England than a direct effect of the revival. Like the fourth-century Arians, some of New England's theologians sought to remove all mystery from religion, to eliminate that which defied the noble reason of man. And nothing was more mysterious or irrational than the dogmatic assertion of Jesus' equality with God. Rationalism in general, not the Great Awakening in particular, was responsible for New England's humanizing of Jesus.

This growing confidence in the powers and potentialities of human reason was not the possession alone of the Liberal party. Among the Liberals, however, reason found its happiest home and some of its ablest exponents. Arminians and Arians began by quoting from the Bible to offset Calvinist texts, but before the argument was over there was sure to be some appeal, usually explicit, to Reason or mere Common Sense. Calvinists, particularly the less able among them, found it necessary to take refuge in revelation, depending "not upon human Tradition or Antiquity . . . But on the pure and unerring Word of God." Whereas the Awakening provoked on the one hand a rapidly increased devotion to the dictates of reason, it resulted on the other hand in a dogged reaffirmation of the divine origin and infallible nature of the Bible. All three major parties, Old Calvinists, Liberals, and Strict Calvinists, imbibed enough of rationalism, however, to be aware of the fact that dogmatism and authority were not perfect persuaders. In their efforts to explain as well as to declare their doctrines, these parties developed into theological schools, a new and important phenomenon in New England's religious history.

From this standpoint, i.e., of a theological school, the party of New or Strict Calvinists was the most significant. Its relationship to the Great Awakening was, moreover, the closest; indeed, this school of "The New England Theology" was the monument of the Awakening. Old Calvinism had prevailed before the revival, and a liberal faction would surely have risen within its fold whether or not the religious storm had swept New England. But that there would have ever been a powerful, vigorous Edwardean party apart from the Awakening is highly improbable. In order to appreciate the connection between that party and the revival, it is necessary to examine more closely the theology of the Awakening itself.

Edwards' series of sermons in 1734 on the doctrine of justification by faith was a major cause of the Northampton revival of 1734-1735. In 1738, Edwards noted that the "Beginning of the late Work of God . . . was so circumstanced, that I could not but look upon it as a remarkable Testimony of God's Approbation of the Doctrine of Justification by Faith alone." Many were beginning to doubt "that Way of Acceptance with God" and Edwards was even "greatly reproached for defending this Doctrine in the Pulpit," when "God's Work wonderfully broke forth." The validity of this teaching was thus confirmed. Thomas Foxcroft found a similar confirmation in the later general revival. In 1741 he observed in the preface to a primer of Calvinism by Jonathan Dickinson:

I'm persuaded, that few (or none) have to report any remarkable Fruits of their Ministry, in a prevailing Work of Conviction, and numerous effectual Conversions, where there has been either an open Opposition to the Doctrines of Grace, or a total Absence of them, or but a cold and unfrequent Glancing at them.—When there is an eminently successful Ministry, and when living practical Religion is restor'd to a flourishing State among a professing People in any Place, I believe it will very commonly . . . be found, there's a Proportionable Recovery of these Gospel-Principles [*i.e., Calvinsim*] *to their primitive Use and Esteem, Power and Influence.*

I frankly confess it is a pleasing Reflection to me . . . That this kind of Divinity, although run down by some as obsolete, jejune & insipid to the refin'd Taste of the present free and thinking Age, yet has of late in a happy Measure retriev'd its Reputation, & establish'd its value and Improvement with Multitudes among us. It has highly delighted me, to observe, with what a singular Gust this old-fashion'd mystical Divinity (so called) has been entertain'd by our awaken'd Congregations.

The close alliance between Calvinism and the Awakening is further revealed by a testimony "Professing the Ancient Faith," issued in September, 1745, by twenty New England ministers, apparently following a suggestion made the previous May. "We cannot but . . . observe," the group stated, "that the principal Means of the late Revival were the more than ordinary preaching of such Scripture and most important Doctrines as these"; and there follow one and one-half pages of what would have then been called "Solid Calvinism." Perfectly respectable and time-honored doctrines, they said, are often now ridiculed as New Light, "and they who Preach the same Truths of the Gospel and experimental Piety as those great Divines, Hooker, Cotton, Shepard, Goodwin, Owen, Flavel, the Mathers, Willard, Stoddard, are represented by some as New Light, Enthusiastical or Antinomian Preachers." The identification of the revival with Calvinism seemed complete. John Bass, removed from his pastoral office at Ashford because of his Arminianism, complained that "calvinistick Principles" were "at this Day a Clergyman's main Defence, the best he can hit upon to provide him Food and Raiment, and to fix him in the good Graces of the Populace." For those, on the one hand, to whom the revival was a time when "Multitudes were seriously, soberly and solemnly out of their wits," the Awakening was a discrediting of this "Ancient Faith." For those, however, to whom it was the occasion of "an extraordinary pouring out of the Spirit of God," the Awakening was the irrefragable argument which demonstrated the truth of Calvinist orthodoxy, and "retriev'd its Reputation."

In this respect, the religious upheaval brought about a revival of Calvinism. The preacher-theologians of the Strict Calvinist party, however, did not consciously promote John Calvin or peddle his *Institutes*. The frequency with which Calvinism is said to revive may suggest that there is a type of religious experience, and of theology interpreting that experience, which arises independently of external influences. The similarities between Augustine, Calvin, and Edwards are to be explained more in terms of a common experience than in terms of a common source. The personal piety of Edwards, added to the many instances of conversion experiences during the revival, made divine grace an immediate indwelling reality. The theology of this school, as suited to the pulpit as to the professorial desk, enjoyed a wide and effectual dispersion. Joseph Bellamy's *True Religion Delineated* was the *Pilgrim's Progress* of New England.

It is of course incorrect either to equate Edwardeanism with or to regard it as altogether the result of the Great Awakening. The revival had, however, very significant effects upon Edwards and upon his theological school. In the first place, any doubts which he might have entertained about the verity of Calvinism were effaced by the Northampton and New England revivals. The later and more pervasive revival, moreover, in calling attention to Edwards' theological position, forced him to conclusions he otherwise might not have reached. This is obviously so in the case of the *Treatise Concerning Religious Affections* and the *Humble Inquiry*.* It is likewise true, but in a less direct way, of his later theological works. Though he labored long upon a theological *summa,* the published portions of his system have a sequence that has order only in relation to the attacks which Calvinism was sustaining. His *Freedom of the Will,* published in 1754, was written in the recognition that

the decision of most of the points in controversy between Calvinists and Arminians, depends on the determination of this grand article concerning the freedom of the will, requisite to moral agency; and that by clearing and establishing the Calvinistic doctrines in general are supported, and the contrary doctrines demonstratively confirmed.

The treatise on *The Great Christian Doctrine of Original Sin,* prepared for publication just prior to his death in 1758, came out at a time when Samuel Webster, Peter Clark, Charles Chauncy, and Joseph Bellamy were engaged in a pamphlet war on that subject. Edwards' essay on *The Nature of True Virtue,* not published until 1765, was both the effect and the cause of continued controversy.

In addition to its direct effect on Edwards, the Awakening had a determinative influence on the fate of his theology by bringing to him his two earliest and most influential disciples, Joseph Bellamy (1719-1790) and Samuel Hopkins (1721-1803). Bellamy and Hopkins found in the Awakening the verification of, if not the impetus for, their theology, even as they found in Edwards their mentor and standard of excellence. Ordained only a few years before the Awakening, Bellamy gave strong and able support to the movement. The force of the Awakening temporarily took him from his parish, and he preached for some months in 1741 in both Connecticut and Massachusetts. Not wholly satisfied with the propriety of this method of evangelism, he returned to his church at Bethlehem which he pastored for fifty years. Bellamy, in whose home approximately sixty ministerial candidates were boarded, bedded, and instructed, extended to thousands through his teaching, his popular writing, and his even more popular preaching a faithful representation of Edwardean piety. Hopkins, while a senior at Yale, heard Edwards preach there his *Distinguishing Marks* in 1741 and thereupon decided that after graduation he would pursue his theological studies in Northampton. A powerful thinker, he propagated and modified Edwards' theology. Within a generation after the Awakening these three theologians had provided enough grist for the doctrinal mills to keep other theologians grinding for generations more.

Because it was Calvinistic, the New Divinity was concerned preeminently with the absolute sovereignty of God: God was almighty before he was loving, and perfect before he was pliable. Because it was closely associated with the Great Awakening, the New Divinity school saw the operation of that sovereignty chiefly in the redemption of mankind. "God's Sovereignty in Man's Salvation," that is to say, the doctrine of a divine, redeeming grace, was the heart of the Strict Calvinists' theology. The truth of that tenet above all else must be honored and protected, at whatever cost to human pride, at whatever odds with human reason. In the religious experience of the revival such theology found its stimulus. In 1743, Timothy Allen, leader of the ephemeral Shepherd's Tent at New London, rhapsodized that he had been led to "the most wonderfull, wonderfull, views of Richest, Richest, freest Grace of God; oh the Grace! oh the Grace! My Soul sees Oceans, boundless Oceans of Grace." This is not theology, but it is that which determines the direction theology shall take. This is the real clue to the revival's effect upon the New Divinity.

As the Liberals labored to reduce religion to morality, the New Calvinists made morality religious and dependent upon divine grace. The Liberals thought upon the habits of man who made choices regularly and freely, and attributed to him a free will. The New Calvinists thought upon the nature of God, and found free will inconsonant with divine sovereignty. Common sense spiced with just a pinch of Arminianism enabled one to see that good men were nearer to God than evil men, that filthy rags could be exchanged for better attire. Revelation and history read through the glasses of Calvinism and revival experience disclosed that man was, apart from the work of the Holy Spirit in him, wholly depraved and rightfully damned. Thus the Awakening set in sharpest relief the Strict Calvinists opposing and opposed by those who would "substitute Men's moral Attainments in the Room of the Righteousness of God, by Faith in Jesus Christ." An illustration of these diverging, irreconcilable theologies is provided in the controversy concerning original sin.

Here, too, the doctrine was first an experience. At New London, Allen wrote, "Christians have the most self-abasing Discoverise of their own Hearts, and the unspeakable Vileness of their Nature." But in the decade after the Great Awakening, a bitter and prolonged dispute arose concerning this "Calvinistical doctrine." In 1757, Samuel Webster of Salisbury, Massachusetts, published anonymously *A Winter-Evening's Conversation upon the Doctrine of Original Sin*. The brief tract was a calm, deliberate abandonment of the notion that the posterity of Adam is, by reason of Adam's sin alone, subject to an eternal damnation. Such doctrine was discarded as a palpable contradiction of the just and loving nature of God as we know it.

What doleful apprehensions must they have of this thine excellency and glory, who can suppose that thou shouldst pronounce a sentence by which myriads of infants, as blameless as helpless, were consign'd to the blackness of darkness to be tormented with fire and brimstone forever! Is this consistent with infinite goodness, nay with any general character of goodness? Impossible!

Sin, Webster contended, is as certainly a personal matter as is knowledge. In neither case can the sin or knowledge of another person—therefore not mine—be imputed to me as though it were mine. A person is punished for his own sins, and for no others. This applies similarly to Adam, who suffered punishment for his sin but did not pass that punishment on to his progeny. It was unreasonable to believe that Adam "should stand as a federal head or representative for all his posterity, so that if he sinned, he and all his posterity should be condemned to hell fire for his first transgression."

A twenty-eight-page pamphlet seemed innocuous enough, and indeed Webster spoke of the doctrine of original sin as a "very little Thing, compared with the great Fundamentals of Religion." To the Calvinist party, however, nothing was further from the truth. In an answer to Webster, published the following summer, Peter Clark maintained that "the Doctrine of the universal Apostacy of Mankind, I am sure, is fundamental to the Doctrine of Redemption by Christ." The beginning of that significant distinction between Christianity as a religion of salvation and Christianity as a religion of moral nurture is to be seen in camps dividing on the doctrine of original sin. That this division bore a relation to the parties of the Awakening is evident in the fact that Joseph Sewall, Thomas Prince, Samuel Phillips, Thomas Foxcroft, and Ebenezer Pemberton—all except Phillips ardent New Lights—wrote "A Recommendatory Preface" to Peter Clark's defense of the doctrine. One of the criticisms that these five ministers brought against the Liberals' attack upon original sin was that their arguments tended "to proselyte ignorant and unwary People by influencing their Passions." With tongue in cheek, New Lights now were charging their opponents with influencing men's passions.

The method used by Webster to raise men's passions and direct them against Calvinism was to describe the "Calvinistical scheme" by which innocent babes were condemned. Clark attempted to separate the issue of original sin from that of eternal torment. Webster had posed the question thus: "Whether We and all Adam's Posterity are charg'd by God with this first Sin of his, so as that Men, Women and Children, are exposed by this alone to the eternal Damnation of Hell?" Clark felt that this was an unfair presentation of the issue, because, he said: "Here are two questions, in one, of a distinct Nature: viz. 1st. Whether We, and all Adam's Posterity, are charg'd with that first Sin of his? And 2dly. Whether by this Sin alone, Men, Women and Children, are exposed to the eternal Damnation of Hell?" He waived the second question as not germane to the doctrine under discussion; but he did not concede it or desert it, as he later tried desperately to make clear to Chauncy. Through one hundred and thirty-two pages he labored to prove, mostly by Scripture, that God constituted Adam "the Grand Patriarch and Progenitor of all Mankind, and consequently their Natural Representative," and that since all men are "included in God's Covenant-Transaction with him" all men fell when Adam fell. Adam was carefully warned of the consequences of his sin. Yet he, and we through him, proceeded to sin. "This, I confess, is Matter of Humiliation and Lamentation to us, and to all Mankind; and we must all acknowledge, that herein there is no Unrighteousness with God." If proponents of "the Pelagian error" continued stubbornly to question the fate of unbaptized but innocent babes, Clark's considered advice to orthodox Christians was to "abide in your Intrenchment, viz., that secret Things belong to God."

Clark was not allowed, however, to abide in his entrenchment or blandly to waive the whole question of eternal damnation. In *The Opinion of One that Has Perused the Summer Morning's Conversation, Concerning Original Sin, Wrote by the Rev. Mr. Peter Clark,* attributed to Chauncy, Clark was rudely reminded that the fate of unregenerate infants was to the Calvinists no "secret Thing." The Westminster Confession, Chauncy pointed out, speaks only of elect infants being saved by Christ. Clark's attempt to dissociate the doctrine of original sin from the inevitable punishment of sin was fallacious if not dishonest. Chauncy cited the Westminster Confession and the longer catechism to show that "this Gentleman, tho' he wears the appearance of a friend to the Calvinistical doctrine of the imputation of Adam's guilt to his posterity, yet has deserted this doctrine, nay given it up." Clark refused to recognize, Chauncy continued, that by original sin is meant that all men sinned with Adam, and fell with him,

> *or, in other words, are so chargeable with his guilt, have it so imputed to them, as that they are, on that account, liable to, and deserving of, eternal damnation, the pains of hell-fire for ever; that it would be consistent with the justice and mercy of God eternally to damn them all; and that, if any of them are not thus damned, it is owing to nothing but grace, which grace might not have been shewed to any of them.*

This was a fair and adequate presentation of the Calvinist position, and, rationalize though he might, Clark could hardly escape the accusation of having abandoned a strict Calvinism for a depravity less ominous and less real.

While the controversy between Webster and Clark continued, another line of attack upon Webster was launched. Webster had presented his views in the form of a dialogue between a minister and "two neighbors." Clark had answered Webster by re-converting the First Neighbor to Calvinism. Now, in 1758, Joseph Bellamy posed as the Second Neighbor who, though convinced that Webster was right, happened to fall into the company of Calvinus who "beg'd Leave to ask a Question, or two." After many more than two questions by Calvinus, the Neighbor was in trouble. The argument, which is of considerable interest, may be summarized as follows: Assuming that it was necessary for a Savior to be sent by God, and God does nothing without a cause, the question arises: Why was a Savior necessary since God had already provided a Law whereby man could eternally live? There are only two possibilities: either the Law was imperfect, or man's nature was so depraved that it was impossible for him to obey the Law. Both from Scripture and from our knowledge of the Being of God we know that the law is holy, just, and good. Thus it is evident "that the Fault was not in God's Law, but in our own depraved Hearts." The only alternative is to deny the necessity of the sacrifice of Christ, "So I see no other Way, for a considerate, thinking Man, if he is resolved to be consistent with himself, but to become a Calvinist, or else a Deist." In suggesting deism as the alternative to Calvinism, Bellamy spoke better than he knew.

When Calvinus remarked that greater elaboration was unnecessary because these topics "have been sufficiently cleared up from the Press in some late writings," the Neighbor was eager to know of what writings he spoke. Calvinus replied:

I can heartily recommend to you two Sermons, one on Justification, and another on the Justice of God in the Damnation of Sinners, published by the Rev. Mr. Edwards, late President of New-Jersey College, about twenty Years ago. And there is now in the Press by the same Author, a Book on Original Sin, wherein all these Points are fully considered, and every Objection, of any Moment, answered.

Edwards' treatise, published in Boston in 1758, was the most exhaustive examination of the subject by either side; Bellamy warned potential readers not to "be at once disgusted at the Sight of an Octavo-Volume." If to the Liberals there was anything more absurd than the Calvinistic notion that man was not free, it was the equally Calvinistic notion that man was depraved. Though the Liberals might draw vivid pictures of suffering infants in order to convince men "by influencing their Passions," they had already decided that this point was only the most obvious absurdity in a doctrine wholly irrational and indefensible.

Jonathan Edwards endeavored to demonstrate that the doctrine of original sin was both rational and defensible, acknowledging like others of his camp that the doctrine was "of great Importance."

For, if the case be such indeed, that all Mankind are by Nature in a state of total Ruin, both with respect to the moral Evil they are subjects of, and the afflictive evil they are exposed to . . . then doubtless the great Salvation by Christ stands in direct Relation to this Ruin, as the remedy to the disease; and the whole Gospel, or Doctrine of Salvation, must suppose it; and all real belief, or true notion of that Gospel, must be built upon it.

Directing his treatise not so much against a mere twenty-eight-page tract as against the more extensive labors of the English Liberals, George Turnbull and John Taylor, Edwards appealed to experience and history to demonstrate the universality of sin. The fact that men of all times and in all circumstances do sin indicates there is a universal tendency to sin. This tendency or disposition to evil is what Edwards means by original sin.

. . . on the whole [he said], *it appears, all mankind have an infallibly effectual propensity to that moral evil, which infinitely outweighs the value of all the good that can be in them; and have such a disposition of heart, that the certain consequence of it is, their being . . . wicked men. And I leave all to judge, whether such a disposition be not in the eye of truth a depraved disposition.*

Not only is the sinfulness of man evident in his behavior, but the fact of death is irrefutable testimony to the universality of sin. The Scriptures, moreover, both Old and New Testaments, attest repeatedly to the fact that men are sinners, ungodly, and enemies to God. The redemptive act of Christ is itself a witness to human depravity; otherwise, man needed no Savior and "Christ's redemption is needless for the saving from sin, or its consequences."

Men are born with a propensity for sin, he wrote, not because God imparted that corrupt nature to man, but because upon Adam's sin the Holy Spirit was forced to withdraw from Adam and from mankind, leaving all to their natural, inferior principles.

When man sinned, and broke God's covenant, and fell under his curse, these superior principles left his heart: for indeed God then left him; that communion with God, on which these inhabitants depended, entirely ceased; the Holy Spirit, that divine inhabitant, forsook the house. . . . Only God's withdrawing, as it was highly proper and necessary that he should, from rebel man, being as it were driven away by his abominable wickedness, and men's natural principles being left to themselves, this is sufficient to account for his becoming entirely corrupt, and bent on sinning against God.

The real difficulty yet remained, Edwards continued. What justice was there in one man's suffering for another's evil doing? How was it possible that all mankind in Adam sinned and in Adam fell? With ingenuity and originality, he explained that this objection rests upon a "wrong notion of what we call sameness of oneness, among created things . . . created identity or oneness with past existence, in general, depends on the sovereign constitution and law of the Supreme Author and Disposer of the Universe." As personal identity is dependent solely on the will and agency of God, "so the derivation of the pollution and guilt of past sins in the same person, depends on an arbitrary divine constitution."

And I am persuaded [*he wrote*], *no solid reason can be given, why God who constituted all other created union or oneness, according to his pleasure . . . may not establish a constitution whereby the natural posterity of Adam, proceeding from him, much as the buds and branches from the stock or root of a tree, should be treated as one with him, for the derivation, either of righteousness, and communion in rewards, or of the loss of righteousness, and consequent corruption and guilt.*

There the argument rested until 1784, when Chauncy published *Five Dissertations on the Scipture Account of the Fall.* By that time, however, America had tired of both the British and the Calvinist yokes.

Few of the major issues debated by Liberals and Calvinists were ever really "settled." Rationalism steadily, relentlessly waxed stronger, while religion was made more comfortable, more intelligent, more unnecessary. As Christ became less divine, man balanced the scale by becoming more competent, independent, proud, and divine. And before the century had ended, the theology which the Awakening represented and promoted was dead. Yet it is hardly correct to say that Edwards was "a horrible example to his posterity," and that "with his death his ideas lost their vitality.'' It is true that the multitudes no longer thronged [to] ministers inquiring ''What must I do to be saved?'' nor sang of the ''Richest, Richest, freest Grace of God.'' It is no less true that Edwards' reflection in his popular biography of David Brainerd epitomized for a large segment of later American Protestantism the real nature of the religious life:

. . . there is indeed such a thing as true experimental religion, arising from an immediate divine influence, supernaturally enlightening and convincing the mind, and powerfully impressing, quickening, sanctifying, and governing the heart; which religion is indeed an amiable thing, of happy tendency, and of no hurtful consequence to human society.

Personal piety, the animating force of religion, was the legacy of the Great Awakening to those of its heirs who loved to ascribe absolute sovereignty, above all others, to God.

Part II
Ideas in the Revolutionary Republic

7 The Puritan Ethic and the American Revolution

Edmund S. Morgan

The path-breaking German social scientist Max Weber first published *The Protestant Ethic and the Spirit of Capitalism* in 1904 and 1905 as a series of essays. It was translated into English in 1930, and its central themes were recapitulated by the English scholar R. H. Tawney in 1926. Weber's general purposes were to challenge the Marxist thesis that human consciousness is determined by social class and to show some of the interrelationships between religious ideas and economic behavior. But his particular thesis, that Puritan ideas influenced (but did not cause) the development of Western capitalism, created widespread scholarly debate after his lifetime. Most historians tend to agree that Puritanism in America supported *some* of the impulses of modern capitalism, but there the matter has largely rested (though some economists and sociologists still push the Weber-Tawney thesis more dogmatically) for want of persuasive evidence that Protestantism was a greater force behind capitalism than other cultural drives, economic or urban developments, or even geographic setting. Aside from reminding us that the early Puritans shunned speculation and extravagance in their business dealings, American historians recently have not had much new to say about a connection between Puritan ideas and developing capitalism.

With the appearance of this essay by Edmund S. Morgan of Yale University, the theme of a "Puritan ethic" was pointed toward the larger question of its significance outside business life following the Puritan age. Morgan directs our attention to the ethic operating in a more secular (or less theological), revolutionary America. Modest though the claims of his essay are, they invite the reader to think of ways in which the historian can discover the course of a Puritan ethic in even the more recent American past.

For further reading: C. Vann Woodward, "The Southern Ethic in a Puritan World," *William and Mary Quarterly*, 25 (July 1968), 343-370; Perry Miller, "From the Covenant to the Revival," in James Ward Smith and A. Leland Jamison (eds.),

Reprinted by permission of the author from *The William and Mary Quarterly*, 3d series, 24 (January 1967), 3-43, with revisions by the author. Copyright 1967 by Edmund S. Morgan. Only one footnote has been retained.

The Shaping of American Religion (1961), pp. 332-368; *Max Weber, *The Protestant Ethic and the Spirit of Capitalism* (1930); *R. H. Tawney, *Religion and the Rise of Capitalism* (1926); Winthrop Hudson, "Puritanism and the Spirit of Capitalism," *Church History,* 18 (March 1949), 3-17.

The American Revolution, we have been told, was radical and conservative, a movement for home rule and a contest for rule at home, the product of a rising nationality and the cause of that nationality, the work of designing demagogues and a triumph of statesmanship. John Adams said it took place in the minds and hearts of the people before 1776; Benjamin Rush thought it had scarcely begun in 1787. There were evidently many revolutions, many contests, divisions, and developments that deserve to be considered as part of the American Revolution. This paper deals in a preliminary, exploratory way with an aspect of the subject that has hitherto received little attention. Without pretending to explain the whole exciting variety of the Revolution, I should like to suggest that the movement in all its phases, from the resistance against Parliamentary taxation in the 1760s to the establishment of a national government and national policies in the 1790s was affected, not to say guided, by a set of values inherited from the age of Puritanism.

These values or ideas, which I will call collectively the Puritan Ethic* were not unconscious or subconscious, but were deliberately and openly expressed by men of the time. The men who expressed them were not Puritans, and few of the ideas included in the Puritan Ethic were actually new. Many of them had existed in other intellectual contexts before Puritanism was heard of, and many of them continue to exist today, as they did in the Revolutionary period, without the support of Puritanism. But Puritanism wove them together in a single rational pattern, and Puritans planted the pattern in America. It may be instructive, therefore, to identify the ideas as the Puritans defined and explained them before going on to the way in which they were applied in Revolutionary America after they had emerged from the Puritan mesh.

The values, ideas, and attitudes of the Puritan Ethic, as the term will be used here, clustered around the familiar idea of "calling." God, the Puritans believed, called every man to serve Him by serving society and himself in some useful, productive occupation. Before entering on a trade or profession, a man must determine whether he had a calling to undertake it. If he had talents for it, if it was useful to society, if it was appropriate to his station in life, he could feel confident that God called him to it. God called no one to a life of prayer or to a life of ease or to any life that added nothing to the common good. It was a "foul disorder in any Commonwealth that there should be suffered rogues, beggars, vagabonds." The life of a monk or nun was no calling because prayer must be the daily exercise of every man, not a way for particular men to make a living. And perhaps most

*I have chosen this term rather than the familiar "Protestant Ethic" of Max Weber, partly because I mean something slightly different and partly because Weber confined his phrase to attitudes prevailing while the religious impulse was paramount. The attitudes that survived the decline of religion he designated as the "spirit of capitalism." In this essay I have not attempted to distinguish earlier from later, though I am concerned with a period when the attitudes were no longer dictated primarily by religion.

important, the life of the carefree aristocrat was no calling: "miserable and damnable is the estate of those that being enriched with great livings and revenues, do spend their days in eating and drinking, in sports and pastimes, not employing themselves in service for Church or Commonwealth."

Once called to an occupation, a man's duty to the Maker Who called him demanded that he labor assiduously at it. He must shun both idleness, or neglect of his calling, and sloth, or slackness in it. Recreation was legitimate, because body and mind sometimes needed a release in order to return to work with renewed vigor. But recreation must not become an end in itself. One of the Puritans' objections to the stage was that professional players made recreation an occupation and thereby robbed the commonwealth of productive labor. The emphasis throughout was on productivity for the benefit of society.

In addition to working diligently at productive tasks, a man was supposed to be thrifty and frugal. It was good to produce but bad to consume any more than necessity required. A man was but the steward of the possessions he accumulated. If he indulged himself in luxurious living, he would have that much less with which to support church and society. If he needlessly consumed his substance, either from carelessness or from sensuality, he failed to honor the God who furnished him with it.

In this atmosphere the tolerance accorded to merchants was grudging. The merchant was suspect because he tended to encourage unnecessary consumption and because he did not actually produce anything; he simply moved things about. It was formally recognized that making exchanges could be a useful service, but it was a less essential one than that performed by the farmer, the shoemaker, or the weaver. Moreover, the merchant sometimes demeaned his calling by practicing it to the detriment rather than the benefit of society: he took advantage of his position to collect more than the value of his services, to charge what the market would bear. In short, he sometimes engaged in what a later generation would call speculation.

As the Puritan Ethic induced a suspicion of prosperity, superficial readers of Max Weber have often leapt to the conclusion that Puritans viewed economic success as a sign of salvation. In fact, Puritans were always uncomfortable in the presence of prosperity. Although they constantly sought it, although hard work combined with frugality could scarcely fail in the New World to bring it, the Puritans always felt more at ease when adversity made them tighten their belts. They knew that they must be thankful for prosperity, that like everything good in the world it came from God. But they also knew that God could use it as a temptation, that it could lead to idleness, sloth, and extravagance. These were vices, not simply because they in turn led to poverty, but because God forbade them. Adversity, on the other hand, though a sign of God's temporary displeasure, and therefore a cause for worry, was also God's means of recalling a people to Him. When God showed anger man knew he must repent and do something about it. In times of drought, disease, and disaster a man could renew his faith by exercising frugality and industry, which were good not simply because they would lead to a restoration of prosperity, but because God demanded them.

The ambivalence of this attitude toward prosperity and adversity was characteristic of the Puritans: it was their lot to be forever improving the world, in full knowledge that every improvement would in the end prove illusory. While rejoicing at the superior purity of the churches they founded in New England, they had to tell themselves that they had often enjoyed more godliness while striving against heavy odds in England. The experience caused Nathaniel Ward, the "simple cobbler of Aggawam," to lament the declension that he was sure would overtake the Puritans in England after they gained the upper hand in the 1640s: "my heart hath mourned, and mine eyes wept in secret, to consider what will become of multitudes of my dear Country-men [in England], when they shall enjoy what they now covet." Human flesh was too proud to stand success; it needed the discipline of adversity to keep it in line. And Puritans accordingly relished every difficulty and worried over every success.

This thirst for adversity found expression in a special kind of sermon, the Jeremiad, which was a lament for the loss of virtue and a warning of divine displeasure and desolation to come. The Jeremiad was a rhetorical substitute for adversity, designed to stiffen the virtue of the prosperous and successful by assuring them that they had failed. Nowhere was the Puritan Ethic more assiduously inculcated than in these laments, and it accordingly became a characteristic of the virtues which that ethic demanded that they were always seen to be expiring, if not already dead. Industry and frugality in their full vigor belonged always to an earlier generation, which the existing one must learn to emulate if it would avoid the wrath of God.

These ideas and attitudes were not peculiar to Puritans. The voluminous critiques of the Weber thesis have shown that similar attitudes prevailed widely among many groups and at many times. But the Puritans did have them, and so did their descendants in the time of the Revolution and indeed for long after it. It matters little by what name we call them or where they came from. "The Puritan Ethic" is used here simply as an appropriate shorthand phrase to designate them, and should not be taken to imply that the American Revolutionists were Puritans.

The Puritan Ethic as it existed among the Revolutionary generation had in fact lost for most men the endorsement of an omnipresent angry God. The element of divinity had not entirely departed, but it was a good deal diluted. The values and precepts derived from it, however, remained intact and were reinforced by a reading of history that attributed the rise and fall of empires to the acquisition and loss of the same virtues that God had demanded of the founders of New England. Rome, it was learned, had risen while its citizens worked at their callings and led lives of simplicity and frugality. Success as usual had resulted in extravagance and luxury. "The ancient, regular, and laborious life was relaxed and sunk in Idleness," and the torrent of vices thus let loose had overwhelmed the empire. In modern times the frugal Dutch had overthrown the extravagant Spanish. The lesson of history carried the same imperatives that were intoned from the pulpit.

Whether they derived their ideas from history thus interpreted or from the Puritan tradition or elsewhere, Americans of the Revolutionary period in every colony and state paid tribute to the Puritan Ethic and repeated its injunctions. Although it was probably strongest among Presbyterians and Congregationalists like Benjamin Rush and Samuel Adams, it is evident enough among Anglicans like Henry Laurens and Richard Henry Lee and even among deists like Franklin and Jefferson. Jefferson's letters to his daughters sometimes sound as though they had been written by Cotton Mather: "It is your future happiness which interests me, and nothing can contribute more to it (moral rectitude always excepted) than the contracting a habit of industry and activity. Of all the cankers of human happiness, none corrodes it with so silent, yet so baneful a tooth, as indolence." "Determine never to be idle. No person will have occasion to complain of the want of time, who never loses any. It is wonderful how much may be done, if we are always doing." And Jefferson of course followed his own injunction: a more methodically industrious man never lived.

The Puritan Ethic, whether enjoined by God, by history, or by philosophy, called for diligence in a productive calling, beneficial both to society and to the individual. It encouraged frugality and frowned on extravagance. It viewed the merchant with suspicion and speculation with horror. It distrusted prosperity and gathered strength from adversity. It prevailed widely among Americans of different times and places, but those who urged it most vigorously always believed it to be on the point of expiring and in need of renewal.

The role of these ideas in the American Revolution—during the period, say, roughly from 1764 to 1789—was not explicitly causative. That is, the important events of the time can seldom be seen as the result of these ideas and never as the result solely of these ideas. Yet the major developments, the resistance to Great Britain, independence, the divisions among the successful Revolutionists, and the formulation of policies for the new nation, were all discussed and understood by men of the time in terms derived from the Puritan Ethic. And the way men understood and defined the issues before them frequently influenced their decisions.

In the first phase of the American Revolution, the period of agitation between the passage of the Sugar Act in 1764 and the outbreak of hostilities at Lexington in 1775, Americans were primarily concerned with finding ways to prevent British authority from infringing what they considered to be their rights. The principal point of contention was Parliament's attempt to tax them; and their efforts to prevent taxation, short of outright resistance, took two forms: economic pressure through boycotts and political pressure through the assertion of political and constitutional principles. Neither form of protest required the application of the Puritan Ethic, but both in the end were affected by it.

The boycott movements were a means of getting British merchants to bring their weight to bear on Parliament for the specific purpose of repealing tax laws. In each case the boycotts began with extralegal voluntary agreements among citizens not to consume British goods. In 1764-65, for instance, artisans agreed to wear only leather working clothes. Students forbore imported beer. Fire companies pledged themselves to eat no mutton in order to increase the supply of local wool. Backed by the nonconsumers, merchants of New York, Philadelphia, and Boston agreed to import no British goods until the repeal of the Stamp Act. The pressure had the desired effect: the Stamp Act was repealed and the Sugar Act revised. When the Townshend Acts and later the Coercive Acts were passed, new nonconsumption and nonimportation agreements were launched.

From the outset these colonial boycott movements were more than a means of bringing pressure on Parliament. That is to say, they were not simply negative in intent. They were also a positive end in themselves, a way of reaffirming and rehabilitating the virtues of the Puritan Ethic. Parliamentary taxation offered

Americans the prospect of poverty and adversity, and, as of old, adversity provided a spur to virtue. In 1764, when Richard Henry Lee got news of the Sugar Act, he wrote to a friend in London: "Possibly this step of the mother country, though intended to oppress and keep us low, in order to secure our dependence, may be subversive of this end. Poverty and oppression, among those whose minds are filled with ideas of British liberty, may introduce a virtuous industry, with a train of generous and manly sentiments." And so it proved in the years that followed: as their Puritan forefathers had met providential disasters with a renewal of the virtue that would restore God's favor, the Revolutionary generation met taxation with a self-denial and industry that would hopefully restore their accustomed freedom and simultaneously enable them to identify with their virtuous ancestors.

The advocates of nonconsumption and nonimportation, in urging austerity on their countrymen, made very little of the effect that self-denial would have on the British government. Nonimportation and nonconsumption were preached as means of renewing ancestral virtues. Americans were remided that they had been "of late years insensibly drawn into too great a degree of *luxury* and *dissipation*." Parliamentary taxation was a blessing in disguise, because it produced the nonimportation and nonconsumption agreements. "Luxury," the people of the colonies were told, "has taken deep root among us, and to cure a people of luxury were an Herculean task indeed; what perhaps no power on earth but a British Parliament, in the very method they are taking with us, could possibly execute." Parliamentary taxation, like an Indian attack in earlier years, was thus both a danger to be resisted and an act of providence to recall Americans from declension: "The Americans have plentifully enjoyed the delights and comforts, as well as the necessaries of life, and it is well known that an increase of wealth and affluence paves the way to an increase of luxury, immorality and profaneness, and here kind providence interposes; and as it were, obliges them to forsake the use of one of their delights, to preserve their liberty." The principal object of this last homily was tea, which, upon being subjected to a Parliamentary duty, became luxurious and enervating. Physicians even discovered that it was bad for the health. Importations, it now appeared, were mainly luxuries, "Baubles of Britain," "foreign trifles."

In these appeals for self-denial, the Puritan Ethic acquired a value that had been only loosely associated with it hitherto: it became an essential condition of political liberty. Americans, like Englishmen, had long associated liberty with property. They now concluded that both rested on virtue. An author who signed himself "Frugality" advised the readers of the *Newport Mercury* that "we may talk and boast of liberty; but after all, the industrious and frugal only will be free," free not merely because their self-denial would secure repeal of Parliamentary taxes, but because freedom was inseparable from virtue, and frugality and industry were the most conspicuous public virtues. Bostonians were told that "by consuming *less* of what we are not really in want of, and by industriously cultivating and improving the natural advantages of our own country, we might save our *substance, even our lands,* from becoming the property of others, and we might effectually preserve our *virtue* and our *liberty,* to the latest posterity," Liberty, virtue, and property offered a powerful rallying call to Americans. Each supported the others; but virtue was the sine qua non of the trio, for while liberty would expire without the support of property, property itself could not exist without industry and frugality. Expounding this point, the *Pennsylvania Journal* assured its readers that "our enemies very well know that dominion and property are closely connected; and that to impoverish us, is the surest way to enslave us. Therefore, if we mean still to be free, let us unanimously lay aside foreign superfluities, and encourage our own manufacture. "SAVE YOUR MONEY AND YOU WILL SAVE YOUR COUNTRY!"

There was one class of Americans who could take no comfort in this motto. The merchants, on whom nonimportation depended, stood to lose by the campaign for austerity, and it is not surprising that they showed less enthusiasm for it than the rest of the population. Their lukewarmness only served to heighten the suspicion with which their calling was still viewed. "Merchants have no country," Jefferson once remarked. "The mere spot they stand on does not constitute so strong an attachment as that from which they draw their gains." And John Adams at the Continental Congress was warned by his wife's uncle that merchants "have no Object but their own particular Interest and they must be Contrould or they will ruin any State under Heaven."

Such attitudes had been nourished by the merchants' behavior in the 1760s and 1770s. After repeal of the Stamp Act, Silas Downer, secretary of the Sons of Liberty in Providence, Rhode Island, wrote to the New York Sons of Liberty that "from many observations when the Stamp Act was new, I found that the Merchants in general would have quietly submitted, and many were zealous for it, always reciting the Difficulties their Trade would be cast into on Non Compliance, and never regarding the Interest of the whole Community." When the Townshend Acts were passed, it was not the merchants but the Boston town meeting that took the lead in promoting nonimportation, and after the repeal of the Acts the merchants broke down and began importing while the duty on tea still remained. Samuel Adams had expected their defection to come much sooner for he recognized that the nonimportation agreements had "pressed hard upon their private Interest" while the majority of consumers could participate under the "happy Consideration that while they are most effectually serving their Country they are adding to their private fortunes."

The merchants actually had more than a short-range interest at stake in their reluctance to undertake nonimportation. The movement, as we have seen, was not simply a means of securing repeal of the taxes to which merchants along with other colonists were opposed. The movement was in fact anticommercial, a repudiation of the merchant's calling. Merchants, it was said, encouraged men to go into debt. Merchants pandered to luxury. Since they made more on the sale of superfluous baubles than on necessities, they therefore pressed the sale of them to a weak and gullible public. What the advocates of nonimportation demanded was not merely an interruption of commerce but a permanent reduction, not to say elimination, of it. In its place they called for manufacturing, a palpably productive, useful calling.

The encouragement of manufacturing was an accompaniment to all the nonimportation, nonconsumption movements. New Yorkers organized a society specifically for that purpose, which offered bounties for the production of native textiles and other necessaries. The nonconsumption of mutton provided new supplies of wool, which housewives turned into thread in spinning matches (wheelwrights did a land-office business in spinning wheels). Stores began selling American cloth, and college students appeared at commencement in homespun. Tories ridiculed these efforts, and the total production was doubtless small, but it would be difficult to underestimate the importance of the attitude toward manufacturing that originated at this time. In a letter of Abigail Adams can be seen the way in which the Puritan Ethic was creating out of a Revolutionary protest movement the conception of a self-sufficient American economy. Abigail was writing to her husband, who was at the First Continental Congress, helping to frame the Continental Association for nonimportation, nonexportation, and nonconsumption:

If we expect to inherit the blessings of our Fathers, we should return a little more to their primitive Simplicity of Manners, and not sink into inglorious ease. We have too many high sounding words, and too few actions that correspond with them. I have spent one Sabbeth in Town since you left me. I saw no difference in respect to ornaments, etc. etc. but in the Country you must look for that virtue, of which you find but small Glimerings in the Metropolis. Indeed they have not the advantages, nor the resolution to encourage their own Manufactories which people in the country have. To the Mercatile part, tis considerd as throwing away their own Bread; but they must retrench their expenses and be content with a small share of gain for they will find but few who will wear their Livery. As for me I will seek wool and flax and work willingly with my Hands, and indeed their is occasion for all our industry and economy.

In 1774 manufacture retained its primitive meaning of something made by hand, and making things by hand seemed a fitting occupation for frugal country people who had always exhibited more of the Puritan Ethic than high-living city folk. Abigail's espousal of manufactures, with its defiant rejection of dependence on the merchants of the city, marks a step away from the traditional notion that America because of its empty lands and scarcity of people was unsuited to manufactures and must therefore obtain them from the Old World. Through the nonimportation movements the colonists discovered that manufacturing was a calling not beyond the capacities of a frugal, industrious people, however few in number, and that importation of British manfactures actually menaced frugality and industry. The result of the discovery was to make a connection with Britain seem neither wholly necessary nor wholly desirable, so that when the thought of independence at last came, it was greeted with less apprehension than it might otherwise have been.

Nonimportation had produced in effect a trial run in economic self-sufficiency. The trial was inconclusive as a demonstration of American economic capacity, but it carried immense significance intellectually, for it obliged the colonists to think about the possibility of an economy that would not be colonial. At the same time it confirmed them in the notion that liberty was the companion not only of property but of frugality and industry, two virtues that in turn fostered manufactures. By invoking the Puritan Ethic in behalf of a protest movement Americans had led themselves into affirmations of value in which can be seen the glimmerings of a future national economic policy.

While engaged in their campaign of patriotic frugality, Americans were also articulating the political principles that they thought should govern free countries and that should bar Parliament from taxing them. The front line of defense against Parliament was the ancient maxim that a man could not be taxed except by his own consent given in person or by his representative. The colonists believed this to be an acknowledged principle of free government, indelibly stamped on the British Constitution, and they wrote hundreds of pages affirming it. In those pages the Puritan Ethic was revealed at the very root of the constitutional principle when taxation without representation was condemned as an assault on every man's calling. To tax a man without his consent, Samuel Adams said, was "against the plain and obvious rule of equity, whereby the industrious man is entitled to the fruits of his industry." And the New York Assembly referred to the Puritan Ethic when it told Parliament that the effect of the sugar and stamp taxes would be to "dispirit the People, abate their Industry, discourage Trade, introduce Discord, Poverty, and Slavery." Slavery, of course, meant no liberty and no property, and without these, men had no motive for frugality and industry. In other words, the New York protest was pointing out that uncontrolled Parliamentary taxation, like luxury and extravagance, was an attack not merely on property but on industry and frugality, for which liberty and property must be the expected rewards. With every protest that British taxation was reducing them to slavery, Americans reaffirmed their devotion to industry and frugality and their readiness to defy the British threat to them. Students of the American Revolution have often found it difficult to believe that the colonists were willing to fight about an abstract principle and have sometimes dismissed the constitutional arguments of the time as mere rhetoric. But the constitutional principle on which the colonists rested their case was not the product either of abstract political philosophy or of the needs of the moment. In the colonists' view, the principle of no taxation without representation was a means, hallowed by history, of protecting property and of maintaining those virtues, associated with property, without which no people could be free. Through the rhetoric, if it may be called that, of the Puritan Ethic, the colonists reached behind the constitutional principle to the enduring human needs that had brought the principle into being.

We may perhaps understand better the urgency both of the constitutional argument and of the drive toward independence that it ultimately generated if we observe the growing suspicion among the colonists that the British government had betrayed its own constitution and the values which that constitution protected. In an earlier generation the colonists had vied with one another in praising the government of England. Englishmen, they believed, had suffered again and again from invasion and tyranny, had each time recovered control of their government, and in the course of centuries had developed unparalleled constitutional safeguards to keep rulers true to their callings. The calling of a ruler, as the colonists and their Puritan forebears saw it, was like any other calling: it must serve the common good; it must be useful, productive; and it must be assiduously pursued. After the Glorious Revolution of 1688, Englishmen had fashioned what seemed a nearly perfect instrument of government, a constitution that blended monarchy, aristocracy, and democracy in a mixture designed to avoid the defects and secure the benefits of each. But something had gone wrong. The human capacity for corruption had transformed the balanced government of King, Lords, and Commons into a single-minded body of rulers bent on their own enrichment and heedless of the public good.

A principal means of corruption had been the multiplication of officeholders who served no useful purpose but fattened on the labors of those who did the country's work. Even before the dispute over taxation began, few colonists who undertook trips to England failed to make unflattering comparisons between the simplicity, frugality, and industry that prevailed in the colonies and the extravagance, luxury, idleness, drunkenness, poverty, and crime that they saw in the mother country. To Americans bred on the values of the Puritan Ethic, England seemed to have fallen prey to her own opulence, and the government shared heavily in the corruption. In England, the most powerful country in the world, the visitors found the people laboring under a heavy load of taxes, levied by a government that swarmed with functionless placeholders and pensioners. The cost of government in the colonies, as Professor Gipson has shown, was vastly lower than in England, with the per capita burden of taxation only a fraction of that which Englishmen bore. And whatever the costs of maintaining the empire may have contributed to the British burden, it was clear that the English taxpayers supported a large band of men who lived well from offices that existed only to pay their holders. Even an American like George Croghan, who journeyed to London to promote dubious speculative schemes of his own, felt uncomfortable in the presence of English corruption: "I am Nott Sorry I Came hear," he wrote, "as it will Larn Me to be Contented on a Litle farm in amerrica. . . . I am Sick of London and harttily Tierd of the pride and pompe."

In the 1760s Americans were given the opportunity to gain the perspective of a Croghan without the need for a trip abroad. The Townshend Acts called for a reorganization of the customs service with a new set of higher officials, who would perforce be paid out of the duties they extracted from the colonists. In the establishment of this American Board of Customs Commissioners, Americans saw the extension of England's corrupt system of officeholding to America. As Professor Dickerson has shown, the Commissioners were indeed corrupt. They engaged in extensive "customs racketeering" and they were involved in many of the episodes that heightened the tension between England and the colonies: it was on their request that troops were sent to Boston; the Boston Massacre took place before their headquarters; the *Gaspée* was operating under their orders. But it was not merely the official actions of the Commissioners that offended Americans. Their very existence seemed to pose a threat both to the Puritan Ethic and to the conscientious, frugal kind of government that went with it. Hitherto colonial governments had been relatively free of the evils that had overtaken England. But now the horde of placeholders was descending on America.

From the time the Commissioners arrived in Boston in November 1767, the newspapers were filled with complaints that "there can be no such thing as common good or common cause where mens estates are ravaged at pleasure to lavish on parasitical minions." Samuel Adams remarked that the Commissioners were "a useless and very expensive set of officers" and that they had power to appoint "as many officers under them as they please, for whose Support it is said they may sink the whole revenue." American writers protested against the "legions of idle, lazy, and to say no worse, altogether useless customs house locusts, catterpillars, flies and lice." They were "a parcel of dependant tools of arbitrary power, sent hither to enrich themselves and their Masters, on the Spoil of the honest and industrious of these colonies." By 1774, when the debate between colonies and Parliament was moving into its final stages, town meetings could state it as an intolerable grievance "that so many unnecessary officers are supported by the earnings of honest industry, in a life of dissipation and ease; who, by being *properly* employed, might be useful members of society."

The coming of the Customs Commissioners showed the colonists that the ocean barrier which had hitherto isolated them from the corruption of Britain was no longer adequate. Eventually, perhaps, Englishmen would again arise, turn out the scoundrels, and recall their government to its proper tasks. And Americans did not fail to support Englishmen like John Wilkes whom they thought to be working toward this end. But meanwhile they could not ignore the dangers on their own shores. There would henceforth be in their midst a growing enclave of men whose lives and values denied the Puritan Ethic; and there would be an increasing number of lucrative offices to tempt Americans to desert ancestral standards and join the ranks of the "parasitical minions." No American was sure that his countrymen would be able to resist the temptation. In 1766, after repeal of the Stamp Act, George Mason had advised the merchants of London that Americans were "not yet debauched by wealth, luxury, venality and corruption." But who could say how long their virtue would withstand the closer subjection to British control that Whitehall seemed to be designing? Some Americans believed that the British were deliberately attempting to undermine the Puritan Ethic. In Boston Samuel Adams observed in 1771 that "the Conspirators against our Liberties are employing all their Influence to divide the people . . . introducing Levity Luxury and Indolence and assuring them that if they are quiet the Ministry will alter their Measures." And in 1772 Henry Marchant, a Rhode Island traveler in England, wrote to his friend Ezra Stiles: "You will often hear the following Language—Damn those Fellows we shall never do any Thing with Them till we root out that cursed puritanick Spirit—How is this to be done?—keep Soldiers amongst Them, not so much to awe Them, as to debauch their Morals—Toss off to them all the Toies and Baubles that genius can invent to weaken their Minds, fill Them with Pride and Vanity, and beget in them all possible Extravagance in Dress and Living, that They may be kept poor and made wretched."

By the time the First Continental Congress came together in 1774, large numbers of leading Americans had come to identify Great Britain with vice and America with virtue, yet with the fearful recognition that virtue stands in perennial danger from the onslaughts of vice. Patrick Henry gave voice to the feeling when he denounced Galloway's plan for an intercolonial American legislature that would stand between the colonies and Parliament. "We shall liberate our Constituents," he warned, "from a corrupt House of Commons, but thro[w] them into the Arms of an American Legislature that may be bribed by that Nation which avows in the Face of the World, that Bribery is a Part of her System of Government." A government that had succeeded in taxing seven million Englishmen (with the consent of their supposed representatives), to support an army of placeholders, would have no hesitation in using every means to corrupt the representatives of two and one-half million Americans.

When the Second Congress met in 1775, Benjamin Franklin, fresh from London, could assure the members that their contrast of England and America was justified. Writing back to Joseph Priestley, he said it would "scarce be credited in Britain, that men can be as diligent with us from zeal for the public good, as with you for thousands per annum. Such is the difference between uncorrupted new states, and corrupted old ones.'' Thomas Jefferson drew the contrast even more bluntly in an answer rejecting Lord North's Conciliatory Proposal of February 20, 1775, which had suggested that Parliament could make provisions for the government of the colonies. ''The provisions we have made,'' said Jefferson, ''are such as please our selves, and are agreeable to our own circumstances; they answer the substantial purposes of government and of justice, and other purposes than these should not be answered. We do not mean that our people shall be burthened with oppressive taxes to provide sinecures for the idle or the wicked.''

When Congress finally dissolved the political bands that had connected America with England, the act was rendered less painful by the colonial conviction that America and England were already separated as virtue is from vice. The British Constitution had foundered, and the British government had fallen into the hands of a luxurious and corrupt ruling class. There remained no way of preserving American virtue unless the connection with Britain was severed. The meaning of virtue in this context embraced somewhat more than the values of the Puritan Ethic, but those values were preeminent in it. In the eyes of many Americans the Revolution was a defense of industry and frugality, whether in rulers or people, from the assaults of British vice. It is unnecessary to assess the weight of the Puritan Ethic among the many factors that contributed to the Revolution. It is enough simply to recognize that the Puritan Ethic prepared the colonists, in their political as in their economic thinking, to consider the idea of independence. . . .

Who Should Rule at Home

Virtue, as everyone knew, was a fragile and probably fleeting possession. Even while defending it from the British, Americans worried about their own uneasy hold on it and eyed one another for signs of its departure. The war, of course, furnished the conditions of adversity in which virtue could be expected to flourish. On the day after Congress voted independence, John Adams wrote exultantly to Abigail of the difficulties ahead: ''It may be the Will of Heaven that America shall suffer Calamities still more wasting and Distresses yet more dreadfull. If this is to be the Case, it will have this good Effect, at least: it will inspire Us with many Virtues, which We have not, and correct many Errors, Follies, and Vices, which threaten to disturb, dishonour, and destroy Us.—The Furnace of Affliction produces Refinement, in States as well as Individuals.'' Thereafter, as afflictions came, Adams welcomed them in good Puritan fashion. But the war did not prove a sufficient spur to virtue, and by the fall of 1776 Adams was already observing that ''there is too much Corruption, even in this infant Age of our Republic. Virtue is not in Fashion. Vice is not infamous.'' Sitting with the Congress in Philadelphia, he privately yearned for General Howe to capture the town, because the ensuing hardship ''would cure Americans of their vicious and luxurious and effeminate Appetites, Passions and Habits, a more dangerous Army to American Liberty than Mr. Howes.''

Within a year or two Americans would begin to look back on 1775 and 1776 as a golden age, when vice had given way to heroic self-denial, and luxury and corruption had not yet raised their heads. In revolutionary America as in Puritan New

England the virtues of the Puritan Ethic must be quickened by laments for their loss.

Many of these eighteenth-century lamentations seem perfunctory—mere nostalgic ritual in which men purged their sins by confessing their inferiority to their fathers. But in the years after 1776 the laments were prompted by a genuine uneasiness among the Revolutionists about their own worthiness for the role they had undertaken. In the agitation against Britain they had repeatedly told themselves that liberty could not live without virtue. Having cast off the threat posed to both liberty and virtue by a corrupt monarchy, they recognized that the republican governments they had created must depend for their success on the virtue, not of king or of a few aristocrats, but of an entire people. Unless the virtue of Americans proved equal to its tasks, liberty would quickly give way once again to tyranny, and perhaps a worse tyranny than that of George III.

As Americans faced the problems of independence, the possibility of failure did not seem remote. By recalling the values that had inspired the resistance to British taxation they hoped to lend success to their venture in republican government. The Puritan Ethic thus continued to occupy their consciousness (and their letters, diaries, newspapers, and pamphlets) and to provide the framework within which alternatives were debated and sides taken. . . .

8
The Empirical Temper of Benjamin Franklin

I. B. Cohen

A unique American side to the eighteenth-century Enlightenment is clearly and fully displayed in the life and mind of Benjamin Franklin. Other men of enlightenment who followed Franklin into the famed American Philosophical Society at Philadelphia, some of them statesmen-scholars of the Revolutionary era like Thomas Jefferson, possessed more abstract minds or were more experienced in classical literature and the arts than was Franklin. But none, as I. Bernard Cohen reveals here, bespoke the central idea of the American Enlightenment better than Franklin. That idea was the working theme of Franklin's life. It was the empiricist's conviction that the results of original inquiry, like first concepts themselves, must be related to real experience. Professor Cohen, historian of science at Harvard University, traces this theme in Franklin's scientific thought. The same theme permeates Franklin's accomplishments in journalism, statecraft, city government, and diplomacy. His even-tempered and modest insistence upon the experiential test of ideas made him then, and ever after, a folk hero, one whom Americans have seen as the model "practical man." But, as Cohen emphasizes, Franklin's idea of usefulness is not the common idea of expedient practicality. Useful ideas must be tested not only by one's personal experience; they also must be consistent with the data of experience that make up one's external environment.

For further reading: *Alexandre Koyré, *From the Closed World to the Infinite Universe* (1957); *Herbert Butterfield, *The Origins of Modern Science* (rev. ed., 1957); I. B. Cohen, *Franklin and Newton* (1956); Harry Hayden Clark, "The Influence of Science on American Ideas," *Transactions of the Wisconsin Academy,* 35 (1944), 305-349; * Brooke Hindle, *The Pursuit of Science in Revolutionary America* (1956); Michael Kraus, "Scientific Relations between America and Europe in the Eighteenth Century," *Scientific Monthly,* 55 (1942), 259-272; John C. Greene, "American Science Comes of Age, 1780-1820," *Journal of American History,* 55 (June 1968), 22-41; *Richard H. Shyrock, *Medicine and Society in America: 1660-1860* (1960).

As an expression of the American character, Franklin spoke with the personality of his own genius, but the particular qualities of the American character that he represented were also the results of the time and place in which he lived. He was a product of the philosophies of the eighteenth century, but he also came out of an American background—in Boston and Philadelphia—that conditioned the way he thought and that gave him a view of man and nature that stamped his contributions to our American way of life with a mark of its own. To define exactly what Franklin was, and to grasp in its full integrity what it is that Franklin stands for, we must pause to examine the wellsprings of that blend of idealism and practicality that he displayed.

It is true, of course, that even when we emulate Franklin, or address ourselves to problems of business, government and society in the Franklinian manner, we do so from a motivation that is apt to be somewhat different from his. Yet, even though two centuries of time and culture intervene between him and us, there are elements in his general approach to the world that have appeared again and again in Americans from his day to ours. Franklin's orientation is most easily discernible in the field of action in which he made the most original contribution—science—and so we may best see him in his own terms by first exploring the qualities of mind he displayed in studying nature and only then seeing how these qualities illuminate his way through life.

It has become commonplace to say that Benjamin Franklin was a practical man and to imply that his standard of value was always the working usefulness of the end result rather than the means of obtaining it or the motivation. We think of Franklin as having been primarily a practical man because so many of his enterprises were successful and because he had a doctrine of "usefulness" that seems akin to practicality. But in thus limiting Benjamin Franklin, we fail to grasp his full dimensions and may even slight our own national character. For there is a sense in which practicality implies expediency, and ascription to the American character would rob our history of the lofty ideals and high purposes which have motivated so many of our leaders and our ordinary citizens; it would make a parody of Franklin as a guide through life.

As a man of the eighteenth century and an American, Benjamin Franklin was an empiricist. The America of his day was a young country in which a man's courage, faith, optimism or ability counted for nothing if he could not recognize and face up to the raw facts of life and nature. Franklin was not a product of the frontier in that he was an urban American, spending his boyhood in the city of Boston and his young manhood in the city of Philadelphia; he did not grow up in a log cabin in the wilderness, tilling fields with a flintlock by his side. But the spirit of the frontier certainly made its presence known in Philadelphia: the city itself was rough, unfinished and growing; there were Indian alarms not far away and a threat of pirates; and, in general, a spirit of building and material creation produced an atmosphere of close contact with the real world.

Nature, as Franklin realized, is both man's enemy and friend, providing fertile soil and rain and also plagues of insects and droughts. The only way to master nature is to understand her laws and to operate within her framework. Shaking a fist at the skies will neither make it rain nor stop the locusts, although in Franklin's day men believed that prayer and fasting might do both. But the men who had braved the wilderness, although placing their reliance on their prayer book and Bible knew that their faith in God needed to be buttressed by hard work and skill in shooting muskets. The Old World patterns of life, in which a man lived like his father and his father's father before him, could not long survive in the New World, where a man had to adapt himself to the realities of the situation in which he found himself, to find a way of life consistent with the data of experience that made up the external environment. It is this last quality which is the primary ingredient of empiricism: a respect for the data of experience and the application of reason to them.

In Benjamin Franklin this strain of empiricism enabled him to become a foremost scientist of that age, and it was a major factor in producing that special view of man, his needs, his rights and his works which has become so precious an element in our American heritage. Franklin stands in the American tradition for the proposition that reflections about society should produce useful institutions for the improvement of the conditions of life; considerations about the estate of man should yield more than eternal principles and noble concepts, and must be fruitful of a system of government and laws to safeguard man's rights; an understanding of the nature and character of man should lead to conduct that respects a man for what he is without regard to color or religion or economic and social origin. Many Americans have acted in accordance with these principles simply because they have become a part of our American pattern of behavior, but in Franklin they were a result of the brand of empiricism that marked his thought and conduct. To see Franklin's particular contribution to America, therefore, we must try to understand how being a good scientist and being a good neighbor, friend and citizen were but different aspects of a single fundamental quality of mind.

Empiricism is a philosophy which is of the eighteenth century and may be studied in Locke, whom Franklin respected, and Hume, whom Franklin knew and admired. One of its major tenets was the theory of how ideas originate in the mind by the action of sensations. Skeptical of any sort of metaphysics, Franklin was not a systematic philosopher, and doctrines of the origin of ideas held no great interest for him. Even so, throughout his writings we find a tendency to regard experience as the grand source of values and doctrines. He was certainly an empiricist in the sense that he considered an experiential test more important in evaluating the worth of concepts than their logical consistency or their mutual relatedness in a system.

Franklin's outlook demanded that concepts be founded on experience, whether that experience was the data of experiment in the laboratory or the observation of man's behavior. Reason, operating on these concepts, discovers laws of nature or rules of conduct, which must meet two important tests. First, these laws or rules or principles must be true—that is, they must be testable against that same experience of the laboratory or the world. But even if such an experiential test reveals the validity of the discovered generalization, the whole effort is not worthwhile unless it is productive of something new. It is this quality of productivity that gives man the final measure of the way in which the initial data and the reasoning process have led to the final conclusions.

Real works are thus, as Bacon put it, the fruits of knowledge and it is in this sense that he wrote that the roads to knowledge and to power are the same. For in the empiricist philosophy the end product can be no more divorced from real experience than the original concepts. In science, then, an empiricist begins by making experiments with his own hands, then constructing concepts that are related to the actual operations or manipulations he performs; next he applies his reason to generalize what he has observed into ground principles on which a logical theory can be built; then the final result is a new form of experience or at least a new view of some segment of experience.

One result of empirical science is a prediction, such as Newton made, of the tides; the time of tides was observable to anyone, but up until the time of Newton no one had understood the attractions of the sun and moon sufficiently well to explain how they might control the seas. Newton's predictions agreed so well with observation that the validity of his theory was assured. Newton's work led to predictions which were testable by experience and it contributed to an enlarged view of the world that we observe around us, thus being doubly productive. Sometimes the end product of empirical science is a new effect or phenomenon that the scientist can produce with his own hands in the laboratory, but often it is a new instrument or device which is itself the new experience that is the product or fruit of investigation.

As a scientist Franklin knew that the life of ideas in science is always controlled by experiment and observation and that a new theory such as he created is valuable in correlating phenomena that had not been thought related or in predicting new phenomena which, on being discovered, would prove the theory's usefulness. Applying his new concepts of electrical equilibrium and the states of electrification he called "plus" or "positive" and "minus" or "negative," Franklin discovered the first exact law of electricity: the law of conservation of charge. This occurred in the course of his experiments to analyze the charge in a condenser—the Leyden jar, consisting of a glass bottle coated on the outside with metal foil and filled with water or bird shot. Such an instrument, when charged, was capable of giving a noticeable shock to seven hundred men, but Franklin stated that there was no more "electricity" in a charged jar than an uncharged one and he proved it by the experiment of "electrical convection." He also found that the charge "resided" in the nonconducting glass rather than the metal coat or water. But this led immediately to the production of new experience, because if charge "resides" in glass because glass is a special kind of nonconductor, then a condenser need not have the shape of a bottle, but could be made of glass plates with metal sheets affixed to either side. To the nonscientist this example may appear trivial, but it marked the beginning of condenser design, and the condenser is one of the vital organs of every piece of electronic equipment ever made.

Furthermore, one of Franklin's greatest achievements was to show which electrical properties of bodies depend on their shape and which do not. Franklin never saw any practical use in the condenser, by which I mean that in his day the Leyden jar was never embodied in an instrument to serve man's needs or increase his fortune. Franklin's explanation of the condenser's action, we may note, was considered by his contemporaries to have been one of his major contributions to science; this discovery was useful because it increased man's understanding of nature's operations and it was productive because it led to new principles or laws of nature.

The distinction between productive usefulness and practicality may best be illustrated by Franklin's research on the lightning discharge. Having discovered that a pointed conductor will "draw off" the charge from an electrified body at a considerable distance, and having at last understood the role of grounding and insulation in electrostatic experiments, Franklin was in a position to make the grand experiment. If clouds are (as he thought) electrified, then an elevated vertical metal rod ending in a point will "draw off" some of the charge from low clouds though they are far away. This original experiment, described by Franklin and performed according to his specifications before he had thought of the kite experiment, established as an empirical fact the phenomenon that clouds are electrically charged and that lightning is therefore an electrical discharge. So the facts of experience and a theory based on correct reasoning had been productive of new experience; nature's artillery had been shown to be only a large-scale instance of a common laboratory phenomenon: the spark discharge. In this case, however, the research was not only productive, it was useful; it revealed the function of electricity in the "economy of nature" and it was applied by Franklin in an attempt to throw light on the whole process of cloud formation and rain.

But Franklin's research had led him to another conclusion, that a long vertical rod of metal, pointed at the top and set deep into the earth, would protect buildings from a stroke of lightning; the empirical test was to construct lightning rods in order to discover whether they would afford such protection (which Franklin, as an empiricist, never doubted), which is only another way of saying that the result of Franklin's research was a predicted new element of experience—a lightning rod—which had to be put to the trial of lightning.

This whole process of empirical science was beautifully described in the seventeenth century by Robert Hooke, who wrote:

> *So many are the links upon which the true philosophy depends, of which, if any one be loose, or weak, the whole chain is in danger of being dissolved; it is to begin with the hands and eyes, and to proceed on through the memory, to be continued by the reason; nor is it to stop there, but to come about to the hands and eyes again, and so, by a continual passage round from one faculty to another, it is to be maintained in life and strength, as much as the body of man is by the circulation of the blood through the several parts of the body.*

This is the sense in which Franklin's scientific research was productive and useful and fruitful. It was productive in that it led to a new theory of electrical action which was the source of a more profound understanding of nature, one which enabled men to predict (and for the first time) what would happen in many of their common electrical experiments in the laboratory, and it also led to many new physical phenomena that had never before been observed. It was useful in that it produced an instrument that enabled men (again for the first time) to protect their homes, barns, churches and ships from destruction by lightning. And the rod itself was fruitful in that it became an instrument that in Franklin's hands and ours has led to a deeper knowledge of the electrification of clouds and of the earth itself and the mechanism of the lightning discharge.

The doctrine of empiricism was always hospitable to the view of Bacon that "fruits and works" are "sponsors and sureties" for the truths of science. But we must keep in mind that Bacon had added that "works themselves are of greater value as pledges of truth than as contributing to the comforts of life." As an empirical scientist Franklin would have agreed, although, being Franklin, he might have questioned the word "greater." The empirical view of the scientist would be satisfied equally by the production of new experience, whether a phenomenon of importance or a device that embodied the newly discovered principles.

Franklin did not pursue the science of electricity because of a particular practical aim; had this been his intent he would hardly have chosen electricity as his major area of inquiry: in his day electrictiy was not a practical subject. The only supposedly practical application of electricity then was in a kind of medical therapy, but Franklin was convinced that the "cures" arose from the patient's desire to get well rather than from the electric shock. But once Franklin had reached the stage in his investigations where the new knowledge could be put to use in the service of man, he was quick to see an application. I believe that Franklin was convinced that pure science would always produce useful innovations, and here we may see him in the great scientific tradition that has only recently become a major feature of American civilization.

Throughout the nineteenth century, America was noted more for the applications of scientific discoveries that had been made in other lands than for the production of that fundamental scientific knowledge we applied so fruitfully. It is only in the last fifty years or so that America has risen to be a foremost scientific nation of the world. During the nineteenth century Franklin was considered by Americans to be an "applied scientist," the inventor of the lightning rod and the Franklin stove, and his whole contribution to pure science was reduced to the kite experiment. The great laboratory discoveries, the first unitary theory of electrical action—the research in pure science that made his contemporaries call him the Newton of their age—were ignored.

Today we are beginning to recognize that the applications of scientific discovery to the cure of disease, the improvement of our living conditions and the safeguarding of our national existence must depend on fundamental discoveries to apply. We may, therefore, in this new tradition look back on Franklin as our first scientist. We may see him as one of those pioneers who understood that empirical science must *always* produce new experience which enlarges our view of nature and our understanding of the processes going on in the world around us, and that it *sometimes* produces (along the way) practical innovations of inestimable value for our health and our economic security. Characteristically, Franklin's most eloquent defense of that research in science that has no particular practical consequence in view took the form of a witticism. Watching the first balloon ascent in Paris, he overheard the usual question: What good is it? His reply has never been equaled: "What good is a newborn baby?" Discussing the new element chlorine, discovered in 1810, and applied to the bleaching of cloth, Michael Faraday said in 1816:

Before leaving this substance, chlorine, I will point out its history, as an answer to those who are in the habit of saying to every new fact, "What is its use?" Dr. Franklin says to such, "What is the use of an infant?" The answer of the experimentalist would be, "Endeavor to make it useful." When Scheele discovered this substance it appeared to have no use, it was in its infantine and useless state; but having grown up to maturity, witness its powers, and see what endeavors to make it useful have done.

Franklin's scientific ideas and his conception of the potentialities of science have influenced Americans only indirectly, through the nineteenth-century European masters under whom our scientists studied. But, wholly apart from his personal influence or the effect of his discoveries and theories on the development of science as such, his empirical approach to the world of man produced qualities of concept and action that are embodied in great American institutions and that have become a precious American heritage.

Franklin was not a true philosopher in the sense that Jonathan Edwards was, but he was a natural philosopher—in that larger sense in which scientific learning and a general outlook on God, man, nature and the world were included within a single expression in a day when scientists were not merely physicists or chemists or astronomers or biologists. Franklin may be fairly described as an empirical Newtonian in the realms of science and of human affairs. In both realms, the principles and conclusions of reason applied to experiential data—the facts of nature and the facts of man—had to be embodied in experience or they were meaningless and irrelevant. Franklin's understanding of nature led him to control nature's operations just as his knowledge of men's actions made him a master of men and the affairs of the world. And just as in science his conclusions became elements of experience in new phenomena to be observed or new instruments to be put in use, so in society new elements of experience were created and put to the trial of use: new institutions (a hospital, school and fire company), new rules of conduct, a new form of government, a ta, or a simple act of kindness.

It is well known that the original rough draft of the Declaration of Independence contained Jefferson's statement that principles such as that all men are created equal were held to be "sacred and undeniable," and that in the manuscript these words are changed in Franklin's handwriting to make the statement read: "We hold these principles to be self-evident." Now historians usually interpret this alteration simply as a literary improvement, and certainly Franklin's cadence has a wonderful ring to it and is much more effective than Jefferson's. But the difference between the two phrases is much more profound than mere literary quality. Jefferson implied that the principles in question were holy, of divine origin, and were to be respected and guarded with reverence for that reason: to deny them would be sacrilege. But "self-evident" was a technical or scientific term applied to axioms, as John Harris' popular eighteenth-century *Dictionary of Arts and Sciences* defined it, and was exemplified in such propositions as: "That nothing can act where it is not; That a thing cannot be and not be at the same time; That the whole is greater than a part; That where there is no law, there is no transgression; etc." Such an axiom is "a generally received ground principle or rule in any art or science," and "it cannot be made more plain and evident by demonstration, because 'tis its self much better known than any thing that can be brought to prove it." This is the sense in which Franklin's phrase represents the summit of effectiveness.

Axioms or postulates are considered in our contemporary scientific language (mathematics, logic) to be propositions which are assumed without proof solely for the purpose of exploring the consequences or logical deductions which follow from them. But in Newtonian science, consequences were deduced from axioms because the axioms were true, which should imply that if the reasoning process or deduction were correct, the results would be equally true or verifiable in experience. In the *Principia Mathematica* Newton explored the logical or mathematical consequences of certain laws of force, notably the famous three laws of motion and the law of universal gravitation. Now, as Newton explained the matter in 1713, "experimental philosophy" or empirical science "proceeds only from phenomena" or the data provided by experience, and it "deduces general propositions from them only by induction." Thus anyone who wanted to take exception to the *Principia* would have to "draw his objection from some experiment or phenomenon." In this "experimental philosophy," Newton added, the "first principles or axiomes which I call the laws of motion" are "deduced from phenomena and made general by induction: which is the highest evidence that a proposition can have in this philosophy."

In other words, Newton's scientific outlook in the *Principia Mathematica* was that the whole system of dynamics was derived by reason (*i.e.*, mathematics) from self-evident principles, which were "self-evident" because they were based on phenomena or experience; the test of the reasoning process and the correctness of interpretation of the evidence from which these principles were "deduced" (we would rather say "induced") lay in the conformity of the final results with phenomena or further experience.

Franklin's revision of the Declaration of Independence placed the principle that all men are created equal in the category of an axiom, self-evident; like the laws of motion, it was a principle "deduced" from experience. Now the particular experience that Franklin had in mind was probably his own and that of his fellow Americans. The inequalities in men's material circumstances or position that could be observed in Europe must have been a product of the artificial circumstances of society, continued by the system of class structure and hereditary rights. Proof lay in America, where land was plentiful and where a man's fortune was apt to be determined by his industry, so that the differences between rich and poor tended to be less than in Europe. Franklin once compared American conditions to those in Ireland and Scotland, observing:

> *In those countries a small part of society are landlords, great noblemen, and gentlemen, extremely opulent, living in the highest affluence and magnificence; the bulk of the people tenants, living in the most sordid wretchedness in dirty hovels of mud and straw and clothed only in rags. I thought often of the happiness of New England, where every man is a freeholder, has a vote in public affairs, lives in a tidy, warm house, has plenty of good food and fuel, with whole clothes from head to foot, the manufacture perhaps of his own family. Long may they continue in this situation!*

The absence of great differences between rich and poor in a land of opportunity, America, surely was empirical justification that such inequality was not a result of man's innate character. Of course, some men are better endowed than others, just as some men are more virtuous than others. As Poor Richard put the matter in

"How to get riches"—"The art of getting riches consists very much in thrift. All men are not equally qualified for getting money, but it is in the power of every one alike to practise this virtue." This led to the conclusion that "Useful attainments in your minority will procure riches in maturity, of which writing and accounts are not the meanest." Hence the need for education: "Learning, whether speculative or practical, is, in popular or mixt governments, the natural source of wealth and honor."

We have already mentioned that Franklin was a confirmed abolitionist, but could he believe that Negroes were in any sense the equal of whites? Experience certainly showed that they were not, because anyone could observe that "negroes, who are free [and] live among the white people . . . are generally improvident and poor." But experience must always be interpreted by reason, and in this case reason, said Franklin, tells us that free Negroes are not by nature "deficient in natural understanding," but simply that Negroes "have not the advantage of education." Here we may see more than an example of the application of reason to explain the data of experience, the condition of free Negroes. In considering society, ideas must be just as productive as in the study of nature. Thus Franklin's analysis was fruitful in creating a new form of experience, a trade school for Negroes, and by its means the whole doctrine was put to the test: if Negroes are inferior because they lack education, he said in effect, let us educate them and see whether they will not then be able to do the work of whites.

Franklin was secure in his convictions about the natural equality of men despite their color, and so he had no fear about the outcome of the proposed test in experience. As a matter of fact, Franklin firmly believed that truth could, by his definition, survive every experiential test which falsehood would necessarily fail; so it is very much in keeping with his character of empiricist that he maintained the freedom of the press, the right of the printer to publish all views and to let truth combat error publicly and vanquish her on the field of experience. Over and over we see Franklin embodying his conclusions in acts rather than concepts. It is misleading to think of him as the enemy of the abstract and master of the concrete, however, because this description would rob his empiricism of the role of reason.

Reason produces concepts out of experience and these concepts are always abstract, like the mutuallly repelling invisible particles in the electric fluid which he supposed was transferred from one body to another in electrostatic experiments; or abstract generalizations about matter, like its inability to act where it is not, or about man, like equality or rights. But a wide gulf separated Franklin from those who professed equality, for example, but did not practice it universally. He was not necessarily more sincere than they were; he was motivated by a different philosophy which made each abstraction live in its productive effect upon society rather than live a life of its own. This may not be the dominant philosophy in our history, but Americans have often acted as if it were. Like Franklin, we have worked to found and support schools, hospitals, orphanages, homes for the aged, and we too have tried to improve our cities and towns and generally to make our habitation on earth pleasanter . . . .

9
"Experience Must Be Our Only Guide": History, Democratic Theory, and the United States Constitution

Douglass G. Adair

The thought of the Enlightenment is characterized by its appeals to human experience. But "experience" came to have different meanings in different fields of thought. Scientific inquiry built present experience on the observation of natural phenomena. To social thinkers like the men who drafted the American Constitution, some of whom were amateur scientists, experience meant something different. Douglass Adair (1912-1968) here explores the significance for these men of historical studies. Adair's first contribution is to show just how history minded the framers were. They wanted to shape the present and future experience of the new nation within what they believed to be the most dependable guidelines of human political experience as they read them through the precepts of history, especially the democratic experiments of the classical Greek republics. Adair's second and greater contribution is to reveal how the "enlightened" political theory of the framers was in its own way deterministic. A Newtonian world view supported their image of human reason. The mind of man, at its virtuous best and passionate worst, had always operated according to certain discoverable norms. The Golden Age of Greece, they thought, reveals man's wisest reasoning on political matters. Seeking to incorporate what they thought best in human experience into a blueprint for American government, the fathers were expressing the faith of the trans-Atlantic Enlightenment that application of the "laws" of human behavior will surely lead to improvement of the human condition. Their belief in the fixed relationship between human reason and conduct is in our eyes mechanical. A later age, influenced by Darwin, Freud, and Mannheim, has criticized it as "static." Yet hindsight need not lessen historical appreciation of the refreshing eighteenth-century conviction that the voice of experience, when heeded, could surely save the nation from the ancient pitfalls of superstition, dogma, and despotism.

For further reading: *Edward S. Corwin, *The "Higher Law" Background of*

Reprinted by permission of the Henry E. Huntington Library from Ray A. Billington (ed.), *The Reinterpretation of Early American History* (San Marino, Calif.: Henry E. Huntington Library, 1966), pp. 129-144. Footnotes have been omitted.

American Constitutional Law (1955); Bernard Bailyn, *The Ideological Origins of the American Revolution* (1967); *Gordon S. Wood, *The Creation of the American Republic, 1776-1787* (1969); *Caroline Robbins, *The Eighteenth-Century Commonwealthman* (1959); H. Trevor Colbourn, *The Lamp of Experience: Whig History and the Intellectual Origins of the American Revolution* (1965); Stow Persons, "The Cyclical Theory of History in Eighteenth-Century America," *American Quarterly,* 6 (Summer 1954), 147-163; Richard Buel, Jr., "Democracy and the American Revolution: A Frame of Reference," *William and Mary Quarterly,* 21 (April 1964), 165-190.

"The history of Greece," John Adams wrote in 1786, "should be to our countrymen what is called in many families on the Continent, a *boudoir,* an octagonal apartment in a house, with a full-length mirror on every side, and another in the ceiling. The use of it is, when any of the young ladies, or young gentlemen if you will, are at any time a little out of humour, they may retire to a place where, in whatever direction they turn their eyes, they see their own faces and figures multiplied without end. By thus beholding their own beautiful persons, and seeing, at the same time, the deformity brought upon them by their anger, they may recover their tempers and their charms together."

Adams' injunction that his countrymen should study the history of ancient Greece in order to amend their political behavior suggests two points for our consideration. First, John Adams assumed without question that history did offer lessons and precepts which statesmen could use in solving immediate problems. Secondly, Adams urged the study of the classical Greek republics as the particular history especially relevant, most full of useful lessons and precepts for Americans in 1787.

Adams, as is well known, practiced what he preached. Working at high speed between October 1786 and January 1787, in time stolen from his duties as United States Minister to Great Britain, he composed his *Defence of the Constitutions of the United States*—a 300-page book exhibiting for his countrymen the lessons of history. And though he included material from all periods of western civilization, a large part of his data was collected from the classical republics of antiquity.

Nor did his American audience who read Adams' work in the weeks immediately prior to the meeting of the Philadelphia Convention deny his assumptions or purposes in urging them to study the lessons of Greek history. Benjamin Rush, for example, reporting to the Reverend Richard Price in England on the attitude of the Pennsylvania delegation to the Convention, gave Adams' study the highest praise. "Mr. Adams' book," he wrote, "has diffused such excellent principles among us that there is little doubt of our adopting a vigorous and compounded federal legislature. Our illustrious Minister in this gift to his country has done us more service than if he had obtained alliances for us with all the nations of Europe."

Do Adams and Rush in their view on the utility of history for the constitutional reforms of 1787 represent the typical attitude of the members of the Convention? Did the fifty-five men gathered to create a more perfect union consciously turn to past history for lessons and precepts that were generalized into theories about the correct organization of the new government? Did lessons from the antique past, applied to their present situation, concretely affect their actions at Philadelphia? The evidence is overwhelming that they did, although the weight of modern commentary on the Constitution either ignores the Fathers' conscious and deliberate use of history and theory or denies that it played any important part in their deliberations.

Max Farrand, for example, after years of study of the debates in the Convention concluded that the members were anything but historically oriented. Almost all had served (Farrand noted) in the Continental Congress and had tried to govern under the impotent Articles of Confederation. There is little of importance in the Constitution (Farrand felt) that did not arise from the effort to correct specific defects of the Confederation.

Robert L. Schuyler, an able and careful student of the Constitution, goes even further in denying the Convention's dependence upon history.

The Fathers were practical men. They lived at a time when a decent respect for the proprieties of political discussion required at least occasional reference to Locke and Montesquieu . . . but . . . such excursions into political philosophy as were made are to be regarded rather as purple patches than as integral parts of the proceedings. The scholarly Madison had gone extensively into the subject of Greek federalism . . . but it was his experience in public life and his wide knowledge of the conditions of his day, not his classical lucubrations that bore fruit at Philadelphia. . . . The debate . . . did not proceed along theoretical lines. John Dickinson expressed the prevailing point of view when he said in the Convention: "Experience must be our only guide. Reason may mislead us."

Dickinson's statement on August 13th, "Experience must be our only guide," does indeed express the mood of the delegates; no word was used more often; time after time "experience" was appealed to as the clinching argument for a controverted opinion. But "experience" as used in the Convention, more often than not, referred to the precepts of history. This is Dickinson's sense of the word when he warned the Convention that "reason" might mislead. "It was not reason," Dickinson continued, "that discovered the singular and admirable mechanism of the English Constitution . . . [or the] mode of trial by jury. Accidents probably produced these discoveries, and experience has given a sanction to them." And then Dickinson, turning to James Wilson and Madison who had argued that vesting the power to initiate revenue bills exclusively in the lower house of the Legislature had proved "pregnant with altercation in every [American] State where the [revolutionary] Constitution had established it," denied that the short "experience" of the American States carried as weighty a sanction as the long historic "experience" of the English House of Commons. "Shall we oppose to this long [English] experience," Dickinson asked, "the short experience of 11 years which we had ourselves, on this subject[?]" Dickinson's words actually point to the fact that theories grounded in historical research are indeed integral parts of the debate on the Constitution.

For Dickinson is not alone in using "experience" in this dual fashion to refer both to political wisdom gained by participation in events and wisdom gained by studying past events. Franklin and Madison, Butler and Mason, Wilson and Hamilton all appeal to historical "experience" in exactly the same way. "Experience shows" or "history proves" are expressions that are used interchangeably throughout the Convention by members from all sections of the United States. Pure reason not verified by history might be a false guide; the mass of mankind might indeed be the slave of passion and unreason, but the fifty-five men who gathered at Philadelphia in 1787 labored in the faith of the enlightenment that experience-as-history provided "the least fallible guide of human opinions," that historical experience is "the oracle of truth, and where its responses are unequivocal they ought to be conclusive and sacred."

Schuyler's insistence that the Fathers were "practical men" who abhorred theory associates him with a standard theme of American anti-intellectualism that honors unsystematic "practicality" and distrusts systematic theoretical thought. His argument, undoubtedly too, reflects nineteenth-century theories of "progress-evolution" that assume the quantitative lapse in time between 400 B.C. and 1787 A.D. *a priori* makes the earlier period irrelevant for understanding a modern and different age. And, of course, what came to be called "sound history" after 1880, when the discipline came to roost in academic groves, is quite different itself from the "history" that eighteenth-century statesmen found most significant and useful. Modern historians have tended to insist that the unique and the particular is the essence of "real history"; in contrast the eighteenth-century historian was most concerned and put the highest value on what was universal and constant through time.

Eighteenth-century historians believed

that there is a great uniformity among the actions of men, in all nations and ages, and that human nature remains still the same, in its principles and operations. The same motives always produce the same actions; the same events follow from the same causes. Ambition, avarice, self-love, vanity, friendship, generosity, public spirit; these passions, mixed in various degrees, and distributed through society, have been from the beginning of the world, and still are the source of all the actions and enterprizes, which have ever been observed among mankind. Would you know the sentiments, inclinations, and course of life of the Greeks and Romans? Study well the temper and actions of the French and English.

Thus David Hume, distinguished eighteenth-century historian and philosopher.

The method of eighteenth-century history for those who would gain political wisdom from it followed from this primary assumption—it was historical-comparative synthesis. Again Hume speaks:

Mankind are so much the same, in all times and places, that history informs us of nothing new or strange, in this particular. Its chief use is only to discover the constant and universal principles of human nature, *by showing men in all varieties of circumstances and situations, and furnishing us with materials, from which we may form our observations and become acquainted with the regular springs of human action and behavior. These records . . . are so many collections of experiments, by which the politician or moral philosopher fixes the principles of his science, in the same manner as the physician or natural philosopher becomes acquainted with the nature of plants, minerals, and other external objects, by the experiments which he forms concerning them.*

John Adams would echo Hume's argument and use the identical metaphor in the preface to his *Defence*. "The systems of legislators are experiments made on human life, and manners, society and government. Zoroaster, Confucius, Mithras, Odin, Thor, Mohamet, Lycurgus, Solon, Romulus and a thousand others may be compared to philosophers making experiments on the elements." Adams was too discreet to list his own name with the Great Legislators of the past, but in his own mind, we know from his *Diary* and letters to his wife, he identified himself with Moses, Lycurgus, and Solon as the Lawgiver of his state, Massachusetts, whose republican constitution, based on his study of history, he had written almost singlehanded in October 1779. Now eight years later his *Defence* both justified the form of government he had prepared for his own state and "fixed the principles"—to use Hume's words—of the science of government that ought to be followed in modeling a more perfect union of the states. Adams' book, in complete accord with eighteenth-century canons, was a comparative-historical survey of constitutions reaching back to Minos, Lycurgus, and Solon.

History proved, Adams felt sure, "that there can be no free government without a democratical branch in the constitution." But he was equally sure that "democracy, simple democracy, never had a patron among men of letters." Rousseau, indeed, had argued, as Adams pointed out, that "a society of Gods would govern themselves democratically," but this is really an ironic admission by "the eloquent philosopher of Geneva that it is not practicable to govern *Men* in this way." For very short periods of time pure democracy had existed in antiquity, but "from the frightful pictures of a democratical city, drawn by the masterly pencils of ancient philosophers and historians, it may be conjectured that such governments existed in Greece and Italy . . . [only] for short spaces of time." Such is the nature of pure democracy, or simple democracy, that this form of government carries, in its very constitution, infirmities and vices that doom it to speedy disaster. Adams agreed completely with Jonathan Swift's pronouncement that if the populace of a country actually attempted to rule and establish a government by the people they would soon become their "own dupe, a mere underworker and a purchaser in trust for some single tyrant whose state and power they advance to their own ruin, with as blind an instinct as those worms that die with weaving magnificent habits for beings of a superior order to their own." It was not surprising then to Adams that when he surveyed contemporary Europe he found no functioning democracy. Indeed, governements that had even the slightest "democratical mixture" in their constitutions "are annihilated all over Europe, except on a barren rock, a paltry fen, an inaccessible mountain, or an impenetrable forest." The one great exception outside of the American states where a democratic element was part of the constitution was Britain, the great monarchical or regal republic. And as Adams contemplated the English Constitution, he felt it to be "the most stupendous fabric of human invention. . . . Not the formation of languages, not the whole art of navigation and shipbuilding does more honor to the human understanding than this system of government."

The problem for Americans in 1787 was to recognize the principles exemplified in

Britain, Adams thought, and to frame governments to give the people "a legal, constitutional" *share* in the process of government—it should operate through representation; there should be a balance in the legislature of lower house and upper house; and there should be a total separation of the executive from the legislative power, and of the judicial from both. Above all, if the popular principles of government were to be preserved in America it was necessary to maintain an independent and powerful executive:

If there is one certain truth to be collected from the history of all ages, it is this; that the people's rights and liberties, and the democratical mixture in a constitution, can never be preserved without a strong executive, or, in other words, without separating the executive from the legislative power. If the executive power . . . is left in the hands either of an aristocratical or democratical assembly, it will corrupt the legislature as necessarily as rust corrupts iron, or as arsenic poisons the human body; and when the legislature is corrupted, the people are undone.

And then John Adams took on the role of scientific prophet. If Americans learned the lessons that history taught, their properly limited democratic constitutions would last for ages. Only long in the future when "the present states become . . . rich, powerful, and luxurious, as well as numerous, [will] their . . . good sense . . . dictate to them what to do; they may [then] make transitions to a nearer resemblance of the British constitution," and presumably make their first magistrates and their senators hereditary.

But note the ambiguity which underlies Adams' historical thinking. Science, whether political or natural, traditionally has implied determinism—scientific prediction is possible only because what was, is, and ever shall be. Reason thus might be free to discover the fixed pattern of social phenomena, but the phenomena themselves follow a predestined course of development. The seventeenth-century reason of Isaac Newton discovered the laws of the solar system, but no man could change those laws or the pattern of the planets' orbits; Karl Marx might in the nineteenth century discover the scientific laws of economic institutions, but no man could reform them or change the pattern in which the feudal economy inevitably degenerated into bourgeois economy, which in its turn worked inexorably toward its predetermined and proletarian end.

In the same fashion Adams' scientific reading of history committed him and his contemporaries in varying degrees of rigidity to a species of *political determinism*. History showed, so they believed, that there were only three basic types of government: monarchy, aristocracy, and democracy, or government of the one, the few, or the many. Moreover history showed, so they believed, that each of these three types when once established had particular and terrible defects—"mortal diseases," Madison was to call these defects—that made each pure type quickly degenerate: Every monarchy tended to degenerate into a tyranny. Every aristocracy, or government of the few, by its very nature, was predestined to evolve into a corrupt and unjust oligarchy. And the democratic form, as past experience proved, inevitably worked toward anarchy, class conflict, and social disorder of such virulence that it normally ended in dictatorship.

On this deterministic theory of a uniform and constant human nature, inevitably operating inside a fixed pattern of limited political forms, producing a predictable series of evil political results, John Adams based his invitation to Americans to study the classical republics. This assumption of determinism explains the constant and reiterated appeal to Greek and Roman "experience," both during the Philadelphia Convention and in the State ratifying conventions. At the beginning of the Revolution Adams had invited his rebellious compatriots to study English history, for from 1765 to 1776 the immediate and pressing questions of practical politics related to the vices and corruption of the English monarchy. But after 1776, at which time Americans committed their political destinies to thirteen democratic frames of government loosely joined in a Confederation, English monarchical history became temporarily less relevant to American problems. The American States of 1776 in gambling on democratic republics stood alone in the political world. Nowhere in contemporary Europe or Asia could Americans turn for reassuring precedents showing functioning republican government. So, increasingly from 1776 to 1787, as Americans learned in practice the difficulties of making republican systems work, the leaders among the Revolutionary generation turned for counsel to classical history. They were *obliged* to study Greece and Rome if they would gain "experimental" wisdom on the dangers and potentialities of the republican form. Only in classical history could they observe the long-range predictable tendencies of those very "vices" of their democratic Confederacy that they were now enduring day by day.

It was these frightening lessons from classical history added to their own present difficulties under the Confederation that produced the total dimension of the crisis of 1787. Standing, as it were, in John Adams' hall of magic mirrors where past and present merged in a succession of terrifying images, the Founding Fathers could not conceal from themselves that republicanism in America might already be doomed. Was it indeed possible to maintain stable republican government in any of the thirteen American States? And even if some of the States units could maintain republicanism, could union be maintained in a republican confederation?

The answer of history to both of these questions seemed to be an emphatic no. As Alexander Hamilton reminded the Convention June 18th and later reminded the country speaking as Publius,

It is impossible to read the history of the petty Republics of Greece and Italy without feeling sensations of horror and disgust at the distractions with which they were continually agitated, and at the rapid succession of revolutions, by which they were kept in a state of perpetual vibration between the extremes of tyranny and anarchy. If they exhibit occasional calms, these only serve as shortlived contrasts to the furious storms that are to succeed. If now and then intervals of felicity open themselves to view, we behold them with a mixture of regret, arising from the reflection, that the pleasing scenes before us are soon to be overwhelmed by the tempestuous waves of sedition and party rage.

Hamilton along with Madison, Adams, Jefferson, and every educated eighteenth-century statesman thus knew from history that the mortal disease of democratical republics was and always would be the class struggle that had eventually destroyed very republican state in history. And *now* with the "desperate debtor'' Daniel Shays, an American Cataline—an American Alcibiades—proving only ten years after independence, the class struggle was raising monitory death's-heads among the barely united republican States of America. If potential class war was implicit in every republic, so too did war characterize the interstate relations of adjacent republics. The only union that proved adequate to unite Athens and Sparta, Thebes and Corinth in one functioning peaceful whole was the monarchical power of Philip of Macedon; Rome, after conquering her neighbor city-states, it is true, had maintained republican liberty for a relatively long period, in spite of internal conflict of plebes and patricians, but when the Empire increased in extent, when her geographical boundaries were enlarged, Roman liberty died and an Emperor displaced the Senate as the center of Roman authority. In 1787 the authority of scholars, philosophers, and statesmen was all but unanimous in arguing (from the experience of history) that no republic ever could be established for a moment, class war must eventually destroy every democratic republic.

These were the two lessons that Hamilton insisted in his great speech of June 18 the Constitutional Convention must remember. These were the lessons that were stressed in John Adams' morbid anatomy of fifty historic republican constitutions. This was the theme of Madison's arguments (which the Convention accepted) for junking entirely the feeble Articles of the Confederation in favor of a government that would, it was hoped, neutralize interstate conflict and class war. It was because these lessons were accepted by so many educated men in America that the commercial crisis of 1784-5 had become a political crisis by 1786, and a moral crisis by 1787.

Had the Revolution been a mistake from the beginning? Had the blood and treasure of Americans spent in seven years of war against England ironically produced republican systems in which rich and poor New Englanders must engage in bloody class war among themselves? Had independence merely guaranteed a structure in which Virginians and Pennsylvanians would cut each others' throats until one conquered the other or some foreign crown conquered both?

From our perspective, 179 years later, this may appear a hysterical and distorted analysis of the situation of the United States in 1787, but we, of course, are the beneficiaries of the Fathers' practical solution to this problem that *their* reading of history forced upon them. Americans today have the historic experience of living peacefully in the republic stabilized by their Constitution. History has reassured us concerning what only the wisest among them dared to hope in 1787: that the republican form could indeed be adapted to a continental territory. Priestley, a sympathetic friend of the American Revolution, was speaking the exact truth in 1791 when he said: ''It was taken for granted that the moment America had thrown off the yoke of Great Britain, the different states would go to war among themselves.''

When Hamilton presented his analysis of the vices of republicanism to his acceptant audience in Philadelphia, he also offered the traditional remedy which statesmen and philosophers from antiquity on had proposed as the *only* cure for the evils of the three types of pure government. This remedy was to ''mix'' or ''compound'' elements of monarchy, aristocracy, and democracy into one balanced structure. There was, Hamilton reasoned, little danger of class war in a state which had a king vested with more power than the political organs of government representing either the rich or the poor. The "size of the country" and the "amazing turbulence" of American democracy made him despair of republicanism in the United States, without an elective monarch who once in office could not be voted out by majority rule. The people, i.e., the multitudinous poor, would directly elect the lower house of the legislature; a Senate to represent the rich would be elected for life; and to guard against the poison of democracy in the separate States, they would be transformed into administrative districts with their governors appointed by the elected King.

We mistake the significance of Hamilton's proposal of an elective monarch as a solution of the crisis of 1787 if we think of his plan as either *original* or *unrepresentative* of the thought of important segments of American opinion in 1787. The strength of Hamilton's logical position lay in the fact that his proposal was the traditional, the standard, indeed, as history showed, the *only* solution for the specific dangers of interclass and interstate conflict that were destroying the imperfect Union. As early as 1776 Carter Braxton had offered almost his identical plan as the ideal constitution for Virginia. In May, 1782, reasoning parallel to Hamilton's had emboldened Colonel Lewis Nicola to invite Washington to use the Army to set himself up as a King. And after Shays' rebellion voices grew louder, particularly in the New England and the Middle States, proposing two cures for the ills of America. One cure was to divide the unwieldy Confederation into two or three small units; the other was the creation of an American throne. We have Washington's word for it that the most alarming feature of this revival of monarchical sentiment was its appearance among staunch "republican characters"—men who like Hamilton had favored independence in 1776 but who had become disillusioned about ever achieving order and security in a republic. Add to this group of new converts the large bloc of old Tories who had never forsaken their allegiance to monarchy, and it is easy to see why Washington, Madison, and other leaders were seriously alarmed that the Union would break up and that kings would reappear in the Balkanized segments.

Furthermore, at the very time the Philadelphia Convention was rejecting Hamilton's mixed monarchy as a present solution for the vices of American democracy, leading members of the Convention, most tenacious of republicanism, accepted the fact that an American monarchy was inevitable at some future date. As Mr. Williamson of North Carolina remarked, on July 24, "it was pretty certain . . . that we should at some time or other have a king; but he wished no precaution to be omitted that might postpone the event as long as possible." There is a curious statistical study of Madison's which points to his certainty also, along with the precise prophecy that the end of republicanism in the United States would come approximately 142 years after 1787—about the decade of the 1930s. John Adams' *Defence* contains the same sort of prophecy. "In future ages," Adams remarked, "if the present States become great nations, rich, powerful, and luxurious, as well as numerous, the "feelings and good sense" of Americans "will dictate to them" reform of their governments "to a nearer resemblance of the British Constitution," complete with a hereditary king and a hereditary Senate. Gouverneur Morris is reported to have argued during the Convention "we must have a Monarch sooner or later . . . and the sooner we take him while we are able to make a Bargain with him, the better." Nor did the actual functioning of the Constitution during its first decade of existence lighten Morris' pessimism; in 1804 he was arguing that the crisis would come sooner rather than later. Even Franklin, the least doctrinaire of the Fathers—perhaps with Jefferson the most hopeful among the whole Revolutionary generation regarding the potentialities of American democracy—accepted the long-range pessimism of the Hamiltonian analysis. Sadly the aged philosopher noted, June 2, "There is a natural inclination in mankind to kingly government. . . . I am apprehensive, therefore,—perhaps too apprehensive,—that the government of these States may in future times end in monarchy. But this catastrophe, I think may be long delayed."

The "precious advantage" that the United States had in 1787 that offered hope for a "republican remedy for the diseases most incident to republican government"—the circumstance which would delay the necessity of accepting Hamilton's favored form of mixed monarchy—lay in the predominance of small freehold farmers among the American population. Since the time of Aristotle, it had been recognized that yeoman farmers—a middle class between the greedy rich and the envious poor—provided the most stable foundation upon which to erect a popular government. This factor, commented on by Madison, Pinckney, Adams and others, helps explain why the Convention did not feel it necessary to sacrifice either majority rule or popular responsibility in their new Constitution.

Of equal importance was the factor of expedience. Less doctrinaire than Alexander Hamilton, the leaders of the Convention realized that a theoretical best—and member after member went on record praising the British Constitution as *the best* ever created by man—a theoretical best might be the enemy of a possible good. As Pierce Butler insisted, in a different context, "The people will not bear such innovations. . . . Supposing such an establishment to be useful, we must not venture on it. We must follow the example of Solon who gave the Athenians not the best government he could devise, but the best they would receive."

Consequently the Constitution that emerged from the Convention's debates was, as Madison described it, a "novelty in the political world"—a "fabric" of government which had "no model on the face of the globe." It was an attempt to approximate in a structure of balanced republican government the advantages of stability that such mixed governments as Great Britain's had derived from hereditary monarchy and a hereditary House of Lords.

It was an "experiment," as members of the Convention frankly admitted, but one about which most of the Fathers could be hopeful because it adapted to the concrete circumstances of the United States of 1787 the experience of mankind through all ages as revealed by history. Driven by the collapse of the Confederation, the depression of 1785-86, and Shays' Rebellion to take stock of their political situation six years after Yorktown had won for Americans the opportunity for self-government, the Fathers had turned to history, especially classical history, to help them analyze their current difficulties. Their reading of history, equally with their immediate experience, defined for them both the short-range and the long-range potentialities for evil inherent in a uniform human nature operating in a republican government. But their reading of history also suggested a specific type of government that would remedy the evils they already knew and those worse evils they expected to come. Utilizing this knowledge, building on the solid core of agreement which historical wisdom had helped supply, they created, by mutual concession and compromise, a governmental structure as nearly like mixed government as it was possible to approach while maintaining the republican principle of majority rule. And this they offered the American people *hoping* it would be ratified, *hoping* that after ratification their "experiment" with all its compromises of theory and interest would provide a more perfect union.

If there is substance in the argument offered in the foregoing paragraphs, it should throw some light, at least, on the intellectual confusion exhibited during the last half-century by many learned commentators in discussing the nature of our Constitution. This confused and confusing debate has focused in part on the question: "did the Fathers write a 'democratic' Constitution?" The answers given have been almost as "mixed" as the theory to which the framers subscribed.

Part of the bother lies in the lack of precision with which the word *democracy* was used then, and the even more unprecise way that we use it now. The more a word is used the less exact its meaning becomes, and in our day *democratic/democracy* has been extended to describe art, foreign policy, literature, etc., etc. Thus, from being a somewhat technical word of political discourse, in 1787, it has become a perfect sponge of squashy vagueness. Luckily, the context of formal theory that mixed government did imply in 1787 does allow us to recognize certain rather concrete and specific features usually associated, then, with the democratic form of government. In the first place, the very concept of "mixture" implies a relativism that modern doctrinaire democrats often forget: a political system, in 1787, was thought of as more or less democratic, as possessing few or many democratic features. Only in the pure form was democracy an either/or type of polity. In the second place, the simple democratic form was almost always thought of as appropriate only for a tiny territorial area—Madison in *Federalist 10,* for instance, would only equate the word with the direct democracy of the classical city-state. Thirdly, the functional advantages and disadvantages of the pure democratic form of government were almost universally agreed upon. A government *by* the people (so it was thought) always possessed *fidelity* to the common good; it was impossible for a people not to *desire* and to *intend* to promote the general welfare. However, the vices of democracy were that the people, collectively, were not *wise* about the correct measures to serve this great end and that the people could be easily duped by demagogues, who, flattering their good hearts and muddled heads, would worm their way to unlimited power. It was this well-meaning stupidity, the capacity for thoughtless injustice, the fickle instability of the popular will, that led the classical theorists, whom the Fathers were familiar with, to designate "pure democracy" as a form doomed to a short existence that tended to eventuate, with a pendulum swing, in the opposite extreme of tyranny and dictatorship.

In dark contrast to this *fidelity* of the democratic many was the vice afflicting both monarchy and aristocracy: an inveterate and incorrigible tendency to use the apparatus of government to serve the special selfish interests of the one or the few. However, the aristocratic form offered, so it was believed, the best possibility of *wisdom*, in planning public measures, while monarchy promised the necesssary *energy, secrecy,* and *dispatch* for executing policy.

It is in this ideological context that one can deduce some of the intentions of the authors of our Constitution. It is clear, I think, that the office and power of the President was consciously designed to provide the *energy, secrecy,* and *dispatch* traditionally associated with the monarchical form. Thus Patrick Henry, considering the proposed Chief Executive and recognizing that the President was not unlike an elective king, could cry with reason that the Constitution "squints toward monarchy." But it was equally possible for Richard Henry Lee, focusing on the Senate, to complain that the document had a "strong tendency to aristocracy." This was said by Lee six months before Madison, in *Federalists 62-63,* explicitly defended the Senate as providing the *wisdom* and the *stability*—"aristocratic virtues"—needed to check the fickle lack of wisdom that Madison predicted would characterize the people's branch of the new government, the Lower House. Nor were there other critics lacking who, recognizing that the Constitution ultimately rested on popular consent, who, seeing that despite the ingenuous apparatus designed to temper the popular will by introducing into the compound modified monarchical/aristocratic ingredients, could argue that the new Constitution was too democratic to operate effectively as a national government in a country as large and with a population as heterogeneous as the Americans'. One such was William Grayson, who doubted the need of *any* national government, but who felt, if one was to be established, it ought to provide a President and a Senate elected for life terms, these to be balanced by a House of Representatives elected triennially.

It is, thus, significant that if modern scholars are confused and disagreed about the nature of the Constitution today, so, too, in 1787-88, contemporary observers were also confused and also disagreed as to whether it was monarchical, aristocratic, or democratic in its essence.

My own opinion is that the Constitution of 1787 is probably best described in a term John Adams used in 1806. Writing to Benjamin Rush, September 19, 1806, Adams, disapproving strongly of Jefferson's style as President, bemoaned the fact that Jefferson and his gang had now made the national government "to all intents and purposes, in virtue, spirit, and effect a democracy." Alas! "I once thought," said Adams, "our Constitution was *quasi* or mixed government"—but alas!

"Quasi," or better still "quasi-mixed"—for, given the American people's antipathy to monarchy after 1776, and given the nonaristocratic nature (in a European sense) of the American upper class of 1787, the Constitution at best, or worst, could only be "*quasi*-mixed," since there were not "ingredients" available in the United States to compose a genuine mixture in the classic sense. So what the Fathers fashioned was a "quasi-mixed" Constitution that, given the "genius" of the American people, had a strong and inevitable tendency that "squinted" from the very beginning toward the national democracy that would finally develop in the nineteenth century.

10
The Theory of Human Nature in the American Constitution and the Method of Counterpoise

Arthur O. Lovejoy

At its most illuminating level, intellectual history has studied emerging democratic political theory not as a problem in the machinery of government but as a question of the essentially human character of citizenship and society. Some of the best essays on the thought of the Founding Fathers, such as the preceding by Douglass Adair and this one by Arthur Lovejoy (1873-1962), who was a distinguished professor of the history of ideas at the Johns Hopkins University, probe deeply into the themes of man and his freedom. They remind the reader that embryonic democratic thought, or the idea of popular representation in government (which must be distinguished from modern popular democracy), did not spring like Minerva from the brow of American statesmen-savants in 1787. Democratic thought has a remarkable history in seventeenth- and eighteenth-century English constitutional issues; it runs an even longer, although sporadic, course in the political thought of Western man since the Athenian age.

The framers of the Constitution were not concerned with creating a democracy; but they desired the kind of stable government that would be sufficiently responsive to the popular will to forestall irresponsible mob rule. The democratic republic they finally designed was, for them, a truly realistic form of government because it would balance the often competing interests of various groups or factions of citizens. Their deliberations over the ways in which men could perceive the sources of faction and erect checks upon the abuse of power were marked by probing testimony on human nature. They were sensitive to the best or most useful experiences of Western man, as Douglass Adair shows (Essay 9). Yet it does not follow from this that they believed human reason to have been infallible throughout history. These men of the Enlightenment wanted to discover and to remember, as Charles Frankel once wrote, where in history reason has overcome the inertia of human error. In other words, they celebrated human reason but did not assume that man is always governed by it. Man must always struggle to overcome his own irrationality and selfishness. It is this "realistic" appraisal of man that Arthur Lovejoy stresses here. His view of the Founding Fathers, and indeed of

Reprinted by permission of The Johns Hopkins Press from Arthur O. Lovejoy, *Reflections on Human Nature* (1961), pp. 37-63. All but three footnotes have been omitted.

intellectuals throughout the Age of Enlightenment, stands in contrast to Carl Becker's famous contention that in the "heavenly city" of the eighteenth-century philosophers "man in general is natively good."

For further reading: Douglass Adair, "The Tenth Federalist Revisited," *William and Mary Quarterly,* 13 (January 1951), 48-67; Cecilia M. Kenyon, "Men of Little Faith: The Anti-Federalists on the Nature of Representative Government," *William and Mary Quarterly,* 12 (January 1955), 3-46; Benjamin F. Wright, *American Interpretations of Natural Law* (1931); Ralph L. Ketcham, "James Madison and the Nature of Man," *Journal of the History of Ideas,* 19 (January 1958), 62-76; *John R. Howe, Jr. (ed.), *The Role of Ideology in the American Revolution* (1970).

In the late seventeenth and much of the eighteenth century man (as Vauvenargues put it) "was in disgrace with all thinking men" in the Western world—or at least with most of those who wrote disquisitions in prose or verse concerning him. He was described as a being actuated always by nonrational motives—by "passions," or arbitrary and unexamined prejudices, or vanity, or the quest of private economic advantage—and yet as always inwardly and incorrigibly assured that his motives *were* rational. When human nature was so conceived, it might naturally have been inferred that men were hopeless material for the construction of a peaceful, smoothly working, stable, and just political system, in which these diverse, conflicting, purely personal motivations would constantly be voluntarily subordinated to, and even made contributory to the general good." And such a view of human nature might well have appeared most of all incompatible with a scheme of government in which ultimate political power would be, through a wide (though still far from universal) extension of the franchise, placed in the hands of a multitude of individuals or groups prompted by such irrational and irreconcilable passions and prejudices. How could you build a safe, solid, and enduring structure out of bricks in which there were forces impelling them perpetually to push in different directions and to collide with one another? Yet it was precisely in the later eighteenth century that the scheme of "republican" government won the advocacy of political philosophers of immense influence in their time and made its first decisive advances; and (this is the particular fact relevant to our general subject which I wish to point out here) it was just at this time that the American Constitution was framed under the leadership of a group of extraordinarily able men who had few illusions about the rationality of the generality of mankind. . . .

This fact (for which I shall presently give some of the evidence) has the look of a paradox; but it is in large part (I do not say wholly) explained by the wide currency in the late seventeenth and the eighteenth century of two other conceptions, not hitherto mentioned, which implied that it is entirely possible to construct an ideal political society out of bad human materials—to frame a rational scheme of government, in which the general good will be realized, without presupposing that the individuals who exercise ultimate political power will be severally actuated in their use by rational motives, or primarily solicitous about the general good. Of these two conceptions, I shall try to elucidate and illustrate the first, which is the simpler and less far-reaching. . . .

Although philosophers of the seventeenth and eighteenth centuries, when discoursing on the divine government of the world, often declared it to be axiomatic that the Creator always accomplishes his ends by the simplest and most direct means, they also tended to assume that he is frequently under the necessity of employing what may be called the method of counterpoise—accomplishing desirable results by balancing harmful things against one another. This was illustrated in the admirable contrivance on which popular expositions of the Newtonian celestial mechanics liked to dwell, whereby the planets had within them a centrifugal force which alone would have made them fly off into space in straight lines, and a centripetal force, which alone would have caused them to fall into the sun; happily counterbalancing one another, these two otherwise mischievous forces cause these bodies to behave as they should, that is, to roll round in their proper orbits. And human nature was increasingly conceived after the analogy of such a mechanical system. Voltaire proposed to amend the famous dictum of Descartes: "God, whom he called the eternal geometer, and whom I call the eternal mechanician (*machiniste*); and the passions are the wheels which make all these machines go." The place of the method of counterpoise in the dynamics of human nature had been tersely pointed out by Pascal before 1660: "We do not sustain ourselves in a state of virtue by our own force, but by the counterpoise of two opposite faults, just as we stand upright between two contrary winds; remove one of these faults, we fall into the other." La Rochefoucauld used a different simile to express the same conception: "The vices enter into the composition of the virtues as poisons enter into the composition of remedies. Prudence assembles and tempers them and makes them serve usefully against the evils of life."

And the creator of a state, like the Creator of the universe and of man—and, in fact, as a *consequence* of his favorite method of the Author of Nature—must accomplish his lesser but beneficent design by pitting against one another forces (that is, human motives) which, taken separately, are disruptive or otherwise bad, or at the least nonmoral—since no other forces, no rational and virtuous motives, can be relied upon. He must harness together and counterbalance contrary defects and competing egoisms. It had been laid down by the judicious Hooker, in the earliest classic of English political thought, that

laws politic, ordained for external order, are never framed as they should be, unless, presuming the will of man to be inwardly obstinate, rebellious, and averse from all obedience unto the sacred laws of his nature; unless, in a word, presuming man to be in regard of his depraved mind little better than a wild beast, they do accordingly provide notwithstanding so to frame his outward actions that they be no hindrance unto the common good for which societies are instituted: unless they do this, they are not perfect.

This at least stated the problem: *how,* by means of what political device, could you bring creatures whose wills were always moved by irrational and "depraved" passions to behave in ways which would not be inconsistent with the "common good''? There were several proposed solutions to the problem; the one which here concerns us and which was to play an extremely influential part in eighteenth-century political thinking was the method of counterpoise. It was set forth in 1714 in doggerel verse by the very injudicious Mandeville. As was his custom, he put it in the most violently paradoxical form, describing a well-ordered state in which,

> Though every part was full of Vice,
> Yet the whole Mass a Paradise.
> Such were the Blessings of that State,
> Their Crimes conspired to make them great . . .
> The worst of all the Multitude
> Did something for the Common Good.
> This was the State's Craft that maintained
> The Whole of which each part complain'd:
> This, as in Musick Harmony,
> Made jarrings in the main agree.

But the textbook—though it was a very confused textbook—on the theory of human nature which was most widely read and admired in the middle decades of the eighteenth century was provided by Alexander Pope. Every well-educated Englishman of the period, in Britain and America, was acquainted with the *Essay on Man,* and many of them doubtless knew its most famous lines by heart. And one thesis concerning the *modus operandi* of volition and the motivation of all of men's actions which the poem set forth, especially in the Second Epistle, was essentially the same as that in the lines which I have quoted from *The Fable of the Bees,* though more elegantly expressed. For Pope, too, ''statecraft'' consisted in the recognition and application of the two premises underlying the political method of counterpoise: that men never act from disinterested and rational motives, but that it is possible, nonetheless, to fashion a good ''whole,'' a happy and harmonious State, by skillfully mixing and counterbalancing these refractory and separately antagonistic parts.

Since the *Essay on Man* is, I fear, much less familiar in the twentieth than it was in the eighteenth century, it is perhaps advisable to bring together here the principal passages illustrating the summary which I have just given. Men's actions, Pope declares, are always prompted by their passions, not by their reasons. The latter, it is true, has an important part as a factor in human behavior, but it is an ancillary part. It enables us to judge of the means by which the passions, which are all ''Modes of Self-Love,'' can be gratified, but it has not driving power.

> On life's vast ocean diversely we sail,
> Reason's the card, but Passion is the gale.

The card (i.e., compass) neither propels the ship nor determines the direction in which it is to sail; it merely enables the mariner to know in which direction it is moving, or in what direction to steer in order to reach the port he desires. And the passions, which thus provide the sole dynamic factor in human behavior, are not only diverse but antagonistic to one another. Every individual's will is dominated by some obsessing "Master Passion," which is the "mind's disease":

> Reason itself but gives it edge and pow'r,
> As Heaven's blest beam turns vinegar more sour.

That is one half of Pope's picture of the working of human motivations; but there is another half. Though these conflicting passions cannot be got rid of, they can be so combined and made to counteract one another than the total result will be social peace and order; and this was the purpose of the Creator in making man:

> Passions, like elements, tho' born to fight,
> Yet, mix'd and soften'd, in His work unite:
> These, 'tis enough to temper and employ;
> But what composes Man, can Man destroy? . . .
> Each individual seeks a sev'ral goal,
> But Heav'ns great view is one, and that the whole.
> That, counterworks each folly and caprice,
> That, disappoints th' effect of every vice.

Thus the statesman's task is to carry out this divine purpose by so adjusting the parts of "the whole" that "jarring interests" will

> of themselves create
> Th' according music of the well-mixed State.

By this means it will be possible for him to

> build on wants, and on defects of mind,
> The joy, the peace, the glory of mankind.

To achieve this great end, in short, it is not at all necessary to assume that man is controlled by his reason; it is, on the contrary, necessary to assume that he is not—since that is the fact about him.

Two decades later, probably borrowing some of these ideas from Pope, the poet laureate of the time, William Whitehead, included a syncopated version of them in his poem "The Enthusiast":

> [God] bids the tyrant passions rage,
> He bids them war eternal wage,
> And combat each his foe,
> Till from dissensions concords rise,
> And beauties from deformities,
> And happiness from woe.

Vauvenargues wrote in 1746: "If it is true that one cannot eliminate vice, the science of those who govern consists in making it contribute to the common good." And Helvetius, later in the century, more diffusely versifies a particular form of the same general conception: every man always pursues his private interest, but the art of government lies in contriving an artificial identification of private with public interest—or at least, in persuading men that the two are identical:

Le grand art de régner, l'Art du Législateur,
Veut que chaque mortel qui sous ses lois s'enchaíne,
En suivant le penchant oú son plaisir l'entraíne,
Ne puisse faire un pas qu'il ne marche à la fois
Vers le bonheur public, le chef-d'oeuvre des lois.
Selon qu'un Potentat est plus ou moins habile
A former, combiner cet Art si difficile,
D'unir et d'attacher, par un lien commun
A l'interêt de tous l'interêt de chacun,
Selon que bien ou mal il fonde la justice,
L'on chérit les vertus ou l'on se livre au vice.

Bearing in mind these earlier statements of the two presuppositions of the method of counterpoise, as applied to the problem of government, we are now ready to turn back to what happened in Philadelphia in 1787 and, I think, to understand somewhat better what it was that then happened. To any reader of *The Federalist* it should be evident—though apparently it sometimes has not been—that the chief framers of the Constitution of the United States, who had been reared in the climate of opinion of the mid-eighteenth century, accepted the same two presuppositions and sought to apply them, for the first time in modern history, in the actual and detailed planning of a system of government not yet in existence. The ablest members of the Constitutional Convention were well aware that *their* task—unlike that of the Continental Congress of 1776—was not to lay down abstract principles of political philosophy, not to rest the system they were constructing simply upon theorems about the "natural rights" of men or of States, though they postulated such rights. Their problem was not chiefly one of political ethics but of practical psychology, a need not so much to preach to Americans about what they *ought* to do, as to predict successfully what they *would* do, supposing certain governmental mechanisms were (or were not) established. Unless these predictions were in the main correct, the Constitution would fail to accomplish the ends for which it was designed. And the predictions could be expected to prove correct only if they were based upon what—in the eyes of the chief proponents and defenders of the Constitution—seemed a sound and realistic theory of human nature.

That theory was unmistakably set forth in what has come to be the most famous of the *Federalist* papers (No. X), written by James Madison, the member of the Convention who is, I suppose, now generally admitted to deserve, if any one member can be said to deserve, the title of "Father of the Constitution." Since, however, it would be unsafe to assume that the argument even of this celebrated essay is now familiar to most Americans, let me briefly summarize it, mostly in Madison's words. "The great menace," he writes, "to governments on the popular model" is "the spirit of faction." By a "faction," he explains he means "a number of citizens, whether amounting to a majority or a minority of the whole, who are united and actuated by some common impulse of passion or of interest adverse to the rights of other citizens, or to the permanent and aggregate interests of the community." There are two conceivable "methods of curing the mischiefs of faction: the one, by removing its causes, the other, by controlling its effects." The first method, however, is wholly inconsistent with popular government; you could abolish factions only by totally abolishing the "liberty" of individual citizens, i.e., their exercise, through the franchise, of the right severally to express and to seek to realize their own opinions and wishes with respect to the policies and acts of the government. But to expect that their exercise of that right will be, in general, determined by anything but what we now call "special interest"—which is what Madison chiefly meant by "the spirit of faction"[1]—is to expect an impossible transformation of human nature. "As long as the reason of man continues fallible, and he is at liberty to exercise it, different opinions will be formed." And "as long as the connection subsists between his reason and his self-love, his opinions and his passions will have a reciprocal influence upon each other. . . . A division of society into different interests and parties" will therefore be inevitable. Since, then, "the latent causes of faction are sown in the nature of man," the "indirect and remote considerations" which are necessary to "adjust these clashing interests and render them all subservient to the public good will rarely prevail over the immediate interest which one party has in disregarding the rights of another or the good of the whole."

But though the "causes" cannot be eliminated, the "effects" of the spirit of faction *can* be "controlled." How? By making sure, Madison answers, that the number and relative strength of the groups representing conflicting special interests will be such that they will effectually counterbalance one another. When they do so, no part will be able to dominate the whole, to use all the legislative and executive power of the government for its own purposes. Each faction will be unable to get a majority vote in favor of its special interest because all the other factions will be opposed to it, and thereby (Madison assumes) the "general good," or the nearest practicable approximation to it, will be realized.

In thus invoking the method of counterpoise as the solvent of the (for him) crucial problem of political theory, Madison was at the same time defending one of the chief practical contentions of the group in the Convention of which he was the leader. The question at issue, as he formulates it in *Federalist* No. X, was "whether small or extensive republics are most favorable to the public weal"; but this question did not imply that there was any conflict of opinion as to the number of states which it was desirable to include in the new Union. No one proposed the actual exclusion from membership of any of the former thirteen colonies which were willing to ratify the Constitution. The real issue concerned the apportionment of legislative authority between the national government and the States. And (at this time) Madison was an extreme advocate of "national supremacy"; the States should, of course, have power to make laws on strictly and obviously local concerns, but "in all cases to which the separate States are incompetent, or in which the harmony of the United States may be interrupted by individual legislation," that power (and adequate means to enforce its decisions) should be assigned to the Federal Congress. By an "extensive republic," then, Madison means one of this centralized sort.

As to the choice between "small" and "extensive" republics, Madison, in *Federalist* No. X, argues vigorously in favor of the latter, mainly on the ground that it alone would ensure an adequate counterbalancing of the political power of the groups representing regional (which, as he recognizes, were in America often also economic) special interests. "The smaller the society, the fewer probably will be the distinct parties and interests composing it; the fewer the distinct parties and interests,the more frequently will a majority be found of the same party, and . . . the more easily will they concert and execute their plans of oppression." But if all these clashing factions are pitted against one another in a *single* legislative body, it is unlikely that any one of them will be strong enough to carry through any such "oppressive" designs. "Extend the sphere, and you take in a greater variety of parties and interests; you make it less probable that a majority of the whole will have a common motive to invade the rights of other citizens." "Extending the sphere" meant for Madison, it is evident, increasing both the number of groups participating in the central legislative authority and the number of subjects (touching more than merely local interests) on which it may legislate. The more "extended" it is *de jur*, the more restricted will be its power *de facto*. The decisive "advantage," in short "of a large over a small republic" will "consist in the greater obstacles opposed to the concert and accomplishment of the secret wishes of an unjust and interested majority."

All this should be sufficient to justify the conclusion which I earlier propounded in advance of the proof of it, i.e., that the fundamental political philosophy of Madison (at this time) included two crucial propositions: (1) that the political opinions and activities of individuals will, with perhaps the rarest exceptions, always be determined by personal motives at variance with the general or "public" interest—in short, by bad motives; but (2) that, in framing a political constitution, you can construct a good whole out of bad parts, can make these conflicting private interests subservient to the public interest, simply by bringing all of them together upon a common political battleground where they will neutralize one another.

It has seemed to me worthwhile to present evidence for the first point at considerable length because there appears to be a still widely prevalent belief among Americans that the Founding Fathers were animated by a "faith in the people," a confidence in the wisdom of "the common man." This belief, to use the terminology of the logic books, is a grandiose example of the fallacy of division. For Madison, as we have seen—and in this he probably did not differ from the majority of his colleagues in the Convention—had *no* "faith in the people" *as individuals* acting in their political capacity. It is true that he recognized certain political *rights* of individual citizens—primarily the right to vote (with the large exceptions, *inter alia,* of women and Negroes) and to seek public office. It is also true that he sincerely believed, as apparently did many of his colleagues, that they themselves were disinterestedly constructing a scheme of government which would make for the good of the people as a whole and in the long run. But "the people" as voters, the total electorate, was made up wholly of "factions," i.e., of individuals combined into rival political groups or parties; and a faction always strives to accomplish ends "adverse to the rights of other citizens, or to the permanent and aggregate interests of the community." "Faith in the people" is plainly and vigorously repudiated in *Federalist* No. X. But what Madison did have faith in was the efficacy, and probable adequacy, of the method of counterpoise as a corrective of the evils otherwise inevitably resulting from "government on the popular model," a "republican remedy for the diseases most incident to republican government."

One fundamental thesis in this lecture, the learned reader will note, precisely contradicts a historical generalization set forth in a celebrated, learned and brilliantly written book by a recent American historian. Carl Becker's *The Heavenly City of the Eighteenth-Century Philosophers* offers an enumeration of "four essential articles of the religion of the Enlightenment"; two of these articles are: "(1) Man is not natively depraved; . . . (3) Man is capable, guided solely by the light of reason and experience, of perfecting the good life on earth. . . . The Philosophers . . . knew instinctively that 'man in general' is natively good, easily enlightened, disposed to follow reason and common sense, generous and humane and tolerant, easily led by persuasion more than compelled by force; above all, a good citizen and a man of virtue." That there were some writers in the eighteenth century who would have subscribed to these articles, and that a tendency to affirm them was increasing, especially in France in the later decades of the century, is true. That the conception of the character and dominant motives of "man in general" formulated by Becker in the sentences quoted was held by most, or even by the most typical and influential, "eighteenth-century philosophers" is not true; it is a radical historical error. To assume its truth is to fail to see the most striking feature of the most widely prevalent opinion about human nature current in the period and to misapprehend the nature of the peculiar problem with which the "enlightened" and innovating political and social theorists and statesmen of that age were dealing. The question here, of course, like all historical questions, is one to be settled chiefly by documentary evidence; and it is partly for that reason that I have cited the *ipsissima verba* of the designers of our own Constitution. To these let us now return.

It is not solely in his argument on the division of powers between the national and state government, in the tenth *Federalist* paper, that Madison rests his case upon the two propositions of which I have been speaking. In his defense of all the major provisions of the Constitution concerning the internal structure of the national government itself—its division into three departments (legislative, executive, and judicial), the division of the legislature into two houses, the whole scheme of "checks and balances"—the same two premises are fundamental and decisive. When Madison undertakes to justify the separation of the Federal government into three mutually independent departments, his distrust of human nature and his conception of the way to offset its defects in planning a system of government are even more sharply expressed than in No. X. I hope those who are familiar with the text of *The Federalist* will forgive me for quoting from it at some length, for the benefit of those to whom it is not familiar:

The great security against a gradual concentration of the several powers in the same department, consists in giving to those who administer each department the necessary means, and personal motives, to resist the encroachments of the others. *The provision for defence must in this case, as in all others, be made commensurate to the danger of attack.* Ambition must be made to counteract ambition. The interests of the man must be connected with the constitutional rights of the place. *It may be a reflection on human nature, that such devices should be necessary to control the abuses of government.* But what is government itself but the greatest of all reflections on human nature? . . . The policy of supplying, by opposite and rival interests, the defects of better motives *might be traced through the whole system of human affairs, private as well as public. We see it particularly displayed in all the subordinate distribution of power; where the constant aim is . . . that the private interest of every individual may be sentinel over the public interest.*

And this policy, Madison declares, is completely exemplified in the Constitution, which was then awaiting ratification.

In the Federal Republic of the United States, whilst all authority in it will be derived from, and dependent on the society, the society itself will be broken into so many parts, interests, and classes of citizens, that the rights of individuals, or of the minority, will be in little danger from interested combinations of the majority. In a free government, the security for civil rights must be the same as that for religious rights. It consists in the one case in the multiplicity of interests, and in the other in the multiplicity of sects. The degree of security in both cases will depend on the number of interests and sects; and this may be presumed to depend on the extent of country and the number of people comprehended under the same government.

In short, the bigger the country ("provided it lies within a practicable sphere"), the greater the assurance that "a coalition of the majority of the whole society could seldom take place upon any other principles than those of justice and the general good." It must be remembered that, in Madison's opinion, no coalition based upon *these* principles is likely except, perhaps, in times of grave national danger. Under such circumstances, there may be virtually universal agreement as to the measures necessary to avert the danger. But under normal conditions, the people will always be divided into factions, and it is essential that no faction—in other words, no *fraction* of the people—shall ever obtain a majority in the legislature. This, however, can easily be prevented by means of the counterposition of the factions to one another.

Madison's thesis here, then, may be summed up thus: The whole people has the sole right to rule, but no mere majority, *however large*, has that right. This seems a political paradox; but as actually applied—primarily, in the situation confronting the Convention itself—it resulted in the adoption of a series of compromises with which no faction was wholly satisfied, but which all, after much wrangling, were willing to accept, *faute de mieux.* Being under the practical necessity of arriving at *some* agreement, they reached a reluctant unanimity (barring a few irreconcilable individuals) made necessary by the approximate counterbalancing of the conflicting groups and interests represented. And when embodied in the Constitution, these compromises for a time—though with steadily increasing tensions—*worked*; they held the Union together for more than seventy years. In this sense, and to this extent, Madison's theoretical principles may be said to have been pragmatically vindicated.

Lest it be supposed that faith in the method of counterpoise was peculiar to Madison among the members of the Convention, let me cite one more example from a member very different in temperament and character and in many of his opinions on specific issues. In the discussion of the powers of the "second branch" of the Federal legislature—i.e., the Senate—Gouverneur Morris delivered a characteristic speech in which he declared that the essential function of such a second chamber is "to check the precipitation, changeableness and excesses of the first branch." But "what qualities are necessary to constitute a check in this case? . . . The checking branch must have a personal interest in checking the other branch. One interest must be opposed to another interest. Vices as they exist must be turned against each other." Morris regarded the Senate—whose members, he thought, should hold office for life—as representing the interest of the propertied class. Doubtless, "the rich will strive to establish their dominion and to enslave the rest. They always did; they always will. The proper security against them is to form them into a separate interest. The two forces will then control each other. By thus combining and setting apart the aristocratic interest, the popular interest will be combined against it. There will be a mutual check and a mutual security." As the body representative of those who have "great personal property," the Senate will "love to lord it through pride. Pride is indeed the great principle that actuates the poor and the rich. It is this principle which in the former resists, in the latter abuses, authority."

But though Morris here voiced the same opinion of human motives that we have seen expressed by Madison and also, in order to offset the absence of "better motives," relied upon the counterbalancing of bad ones, he was in fact employing partially identical premises to support a different conclusion. For Madison, when writing in *The Federalist*, assumed that there would always be a "multiplicity" of such special interests and that the numerical ratios of the groups severally supporting them, or of their representatives in Congress, would be such that no coalition of them could ever obtain a majority.[2] But Morris—at least when making this speech—recognized only two permanently opposed forces in politics, the rich and the poor. And he cannot, of course, have supposed that these two would usually, or indeed, ever, numerically counterbalance one another. They must therefore be *made* equal in legislative power—or, more precisely, in legislative impotence—by a specific constitutional provision; one of the Houses of Congress must be reserved for men having great wealth and the "aristocratic spirit," an American analogue of the House of Lords. True, Morris grants—human nature being what it is—such a body will always be inimical to the interests of "the rest," the nonpropertied classes. It is therefore necessary to have another chamber representative of the latter, to hold in check the former. But it is not in this latter consideration that Morris seems chiefly interested. What he wished to ensure was the protection of the vested interests of large property holders. And he saw that the method of counterpoise, especially in the form which he proposed, was perfectly adapted to the accomplishment of this end. For the effect of that method, when applied to a legislative body, would be—as Madison's arguments said—to prevent any one of the opposing factions from ever accomplishing its purpose. A Senate that was representative exclusively of one economic class would never concur in any measure affecting class interests passed by a House that was representative of other classes. And it followed that "the poor" could never get a law passed which would be unfavorable to the economic interests of "the rich."[3]

Thus the method of counterpoise could, without relinquishment of its two essential premises, be proposed as a means to the realization of quite different designs with respect to the distribution of legislative power. But, whatever the purpose for which it might be advocated, it obviously could have only negative effects. It was simply a way of *preventing* new proposals from being adopted. If it ever became completely effective (which, of course, it never quite did), it could result only in a deadlock, an equilibrium of forces in which no movement in any direction would be possible. It therefore tended to crystallize the *status quo* and was naturally favored by those who wished to keep the existing political and economic order unchanged—or as little changed as possible. It was a device of conservatives to block innovations. Yet it could hardly be openly argued for upon traditionally conservative grounds—e.g., upon the assumption that change is in itself a bad thing or that the "aristocratic" and propertied class is wiser than, and morally superior to, the "lower classes." For it rested, as we have seen, upon the generalization that (certainly in politics) the aims and motives of virtually all individuals, and therefore of all "factions," are equally irrational and "interested," equally indifferent to the "general good"; and it was *only* upon this assumption that the scheme of equipoise, of rendering all factions *equally* impotent, could be consistently defended.

But this generalization, though indispensable to the argument, had some awkward consequences. It implied that, in political discussion and agitation, appeals to purely ethical standards and rational disinterested ideals would be inappropriate and useless, since, by hypothesis, no such appeal could really influence the opinions and actions of the voters or legislators. But in practice such moral, or ostensibly moral, appeals were *not entirely* ineffective; and, once organized political parties were actually operating, their orators seldom, if ever, admitted that the policies they advocated were adverse "to the rights of others and the good of the whole"; on the contrary, they usually represented these policies as consistent with, or even required by, the highest moral principles, and they doubtless often believed this to be true. And though this usually was—and still is—simply "rationalization," even a rationalization is an admission that rational considerations, valid by criteria which are more than biases arising from private interests or from unexamined and unverifiable preconceptions, are relevant to the issue under discussion. However small the part which such considerations really play in the determination of individual opinions and individual behavior, as soon as you admit their relevance, and profess to justify your own contentions by them, you have accepted a change of venue to another and admittedly a higher court, in which the controversy must be fought out under the rules of that court, that is, rules of logical consistency and verifiable empirical evidence. Insofar as those who invoked the method of counterpoise implicitly denied even the possibility of such a change of venue, they ignored a real aspect of the workings of human nature in politics. But in saying this I am far from intending to imply that their assumptions about men's usual motivations, in their political opinions and actions, were false, or even that they were not the *more* pertinent and useful assumptions to apply to the immediate practical problems which confronted the Constitution makers in 1787.

In these comments on the latent implications, the degree of validity, and the practical effect of the theory of counterpoise which so powerfully influenced the framing of the American Constitution, I have deviated from the primarily historical purpose of the present lecture. That purpose was not to evaluate but to illustrate the wide prevalence, even in the later eighteenth century, of a highly unfavorable appraisal of the motives generally controlling men's political (and other) behavior, and to explain in part the seemingly paradoxical fact that, in the very same period, the American republic was founded, largely by men who accepted that appraisal. This purpose has, I hope, now been sufficiently accomplished. . . .

Notes

1. The "passion" which Madison regarded as the chief source of the "spirit of faction" is economic self-interest. He was a pioneer of the conception of political struggles as, often disguised, class conflicts, and of economic determinism. But (unlike Marx) he also (to borrow Mr. [Irving] Brant's summary on this point) "recognized the influence of differing opinions in religion, contrary theories of government, attachment to rival leaders, and many other points which stir the human passions and drive men into 'mutual animosities.' "

2. Why Madison made this assumption may seem at first hard to understand; he writes as if he, like Pope, accepted as evident beyond the need of proof the assumption that "jarring interests" will "*of themselves* create th' according music of the well-mix'd State"—though Madison adds, in substance, that they will not be well mixed unless the mixture comprises *all* of them, in an "extensive republic." As a generalization the assumption was certainly not self-evident, nor particularly probable. But in fact Madison had specific reasons for the assumption, which he set forth in his speech in the Convention on June 28, 1787. He was then arguing (unsuccessfully, as it turned out) in favor of giving to the larger states more Senators than to the small states. To the objection that this would enable the larger states to combine to dominate the smaller ones, he replied that this could happen only if the larger states had common "interests," which they did not have. The three largest were Massachusetts, Pennsylvania, and Virginia. These were remote from one another; they differed in "customs, manners, and religion"; and, still more important, their trade interests were entirely "diverse." "Where," then, "is the probability of a combination? What the inducements?" Thus, it will be seen, Madison was here asserting an *actual* existing counterpoise of political forces in the Federal Union: where there is no identity of economic and other interests, there can be no "coalition," and therefore no majority in Congress for any one group. But since the proposal of unequal state representation in the Senate failed to carry, he turned, in the *Federalist,* to another and less specific argument: be the states equally or unequally represented in the "second chamber," there would in any case be a natural counterbalancing of voting strength among such a "multiplicity" of sections and economic interests and religious sects. And though Madison now gave no definite or cogent reasons for believing this to be true, it *was* true, subject to the qualifications above noted.

3. Madison, in spite of his usual argument based upon the existing multiplicity of interests and factions, recognized, like Morris, that the most serious conflict within the Union was that between only two factions; but for him, this was not a conflict between "the rich" and "the poor," but between two major sections of the country. In a memorably prophetic speech on June 29 he warned the Convention that "the great danger to our general government is, the great southern and northern interests being opposed to each other. Look to the votes in Congress [i.e., of the Confederation], and most of them stand divided by the geography of the country, not according to the size of the States." This supreme danger he hoped and believed could be averted by means of a balance of power in Congress between the two sections. So long as, by various compromises, that balance seemed to remain approximately undisturbed, Madison's hope was realized. As soon as the balance was patently overthrown, the danger which he pointed out became a tragic reality.

11
Philosopher-Statesmen of the Republic

Adrienne Koch

Working with some of the broad themes set forth in the preceding essays by Douglass Adair and Arthur Lovejoy, Adrienne Koch (1912-1971) here pursues the idea of republicanism to its specific applications in the writings of John Adams, Alexander Hamilton, Thomas Jefferson, and James Madison. Her analysis of the political ideology of these four Founding Fathers, ranging from Jefferson's on the "left" to Hamilton's on the "right," is the conventional one. Yet her emphasis is less upon the relationship of these positions to modern "liberalism" and "conservatism" (at best a tricky connection for the historian to make) than upon the "double drive" of philosophy and leadership, thought and action shared by these four men. As working intellectuals whose thought shaped a national ideology, they helped to form a tradition of creative and critical intelligence applied to national councils, the tradition begun by Benjamin Franklin, and occasionally since their day reawakened to overcome that tendency to amiable democratic mediocrity in government that Alexis de Tocqueville so clearly perceived.

For further reading: *Adrienne Koch, *Jefferson and Madison* (1950); Edward S. Corwin, *John Marshall and the Constitution* (1919); *Carl L. Becker, *The Declaration of Independence* (1922); Henry Steele Commager, "Leadership in Eighteenth-Century America and Today," in his *Freedom and Order: A Commentary on the American Political Scene* (1966), pp. 149-170; James B. Conant, *Thomas Jefferson and the Development of American Public Education* (1962).

I

The founding fathers were men of remarkably broad interests with an uncanny aptitude for political analysis and for the adaptation of theories to practice. There are some who describe this phenomenon as no more than the heritage of humanism

The Sewanee Review, 55 (Summer 1947), 384-386, 392-405. Section 2 of the original essay has been omitted.

which the American enlightenment merely reembodied. Certainly the statesmen who shaped the Republic in its first form were confronting essentially the same issues as those formulated by the Renaissance humanists: the attempt to reconcile speculative thinking on the nature of man with the immediate task of creating a new political and social order. They differed from More, Erasmus, and their fellows in that these modern humanists were under more pressure to apply their theories to the urgent task at hand. But there is something breathtaking about the reembodiment of broad humanist principles in a struggling and relatively unsophisticated people, beset on every side by the problems of living. The "fathers" therefore deserve either spontaneous admiration or informed respect, whether we study their ideas and actions as we find them, or trace their intellectual heritage to another age.

Of the first statesmen of the Republic, four—Jefferson, Madison, John Adams, and Hamilton—trained their sights higher than did any others. Addressing themselves to more than practical considerations, they seemed to be genuinely inspired by the historical uniqueness of the experience open to them, to launch a new civilization on a large scale. In final outcome, they proved equal to the challenge of planning republican government, and they could only have become so because they tried to understand not only the buried sources of power, but the moral objectives of good government. In a sense they were, as Hamilton once contemptuously declared, "speculative" thinkers and "empirics." Even Hamilton himself belonged to the company he criticized, for he, with the others, assessed what he already found in existence as social habit and political tradition; he built upon that which was already "given"; and recommended, according to his lights, the best direction of change.

Jefferson, the greatest of them all, was conspicuously devoted to the theory and practice of good government. Further, he was actively critical of his own *methods* of establishing political judgments, and he was intellectually prepared to examine the logical, philosophical, scientific, or sentimental elements in his views of society. He learned to style himself an "ideologist," by which term he meant to identify himself with his friends, the French philosophers, who had founded a school of thought known as "Ideology" in the Napoleonic period. Hamilton, Madison, and Adams as well as Jefferson contributed characteristic ways of thought, individual tempers of belief which were to be important not only in the era of the Republic but for America thenceforth. The principles of the four philosopher-statesmen taken together almost define the range of our national ideology—our objectives, our character as a people, our economic and social patterns, our "Americanism."

The challenge of creating a new form of government gave rise to an atmosphere of intellectual adventure, in which the Platonic vision of the philosopher-king could for one brief period take on American reality. "Until philosophers take to government, or those who now govern become philosophers," Plato had boldly written, "so that government and philosophy unite, there will be no end to the miseries of states." In the timeless analogy of the cave in the *Republic*, the philosophers who struggle to free themselves from the chains of ignorance and superstition make their way to the light outside. They see the truth. Loving its clarity, they would bask in its light. But the thought of the chained multitude below gives them no rest, and they understand, as Platonic seekers of truth must, that they cannot fail to carry glimmerings of light to the poorer minds who inhabit the cave.

The four great philosopher-statesmen of the American "Enlightenment" conform admirably to the Platonic pattern. They grope in authentic Platonic fashion for the true principles of social order, accepting the responsibility of administering the affairs of their less far-sighted fellow men; yet they reject the Platonic ideal as an explicit inspiration. They are willing to exemplify it if they must; but justify it, direct from its ancient source, never. Plato, even for Jefferson who had the most developed philosophic predilections of the group, was too full of metaphysical flights and trances to prove sympathetic to the common-sense orientation of the new nation. In any event the double drive of philosophy and leadership, thought and action, vision and its fortifying concrete detail is heeded by Jefferson, Madison, Adams, and even Hamilton. From the time of Franklin to the present this double drive has dictated a double destiny for the American nation and a dualistic orientation for its literature. In the great period of American political literature, both forces were present without fatal conflict, and lend a peculiar divided charm and predictive importance to this body of writing. . . .

II

The ideology of American democracy began its career with a set of political principles termed "Republican." Although John Adams was quick to warn of the shifting meanings of the term "republic," it became a fixed pole of political reference in American political theory, directly contraposing that other pole, Monarchy, against which the Revolution had been waged. Adams himself believed in republican doctrine and, like the other political leaders of his day, made standard references to the ancient republics as the historical alternative to monarchy and to feudal hierarchic society. Almost everyone in early America agreed on the minimal connotation of the term, either explicitly or by implication. Like late eighteenth-century philosophers elsewhere, they understood that a republic was a government which derived its power from the people "originally," referred back to the people for an ultimate court of appeal in "crucial" questions transcending the ordinary affairs of legislation, and exercised its granted powers through representatives chosen by a majority of the voting citizens. In theory, at least, these voting citizens were further supposed to represent the "will of the people," and while they confided specific powers to their representatives, it was understood that a republic was essentially a government of laws rather than of men.

Were one to try to locate the maximum adherence to this republican ideal, one could project an imaginary political line with the left terminal point designating "maximum faith" and the right terminal point "minimum faith." We should then have to place Jefferson at the left and Hamilton at the right. John Adams accordingly must occupy the middle ground, to the left of Hamilton and the right of Jefferson; but he is also to the right of Madison, who is closer to Jefferson on most fundamental political matters—although it is important to note that Madison is sometimes closer to Hamilton in economic questions than is either Adams or Jefferson.

Had Jefferson written no more than the initial draft of the *Declaration of Independence* he would probably have earned his place on the radical left of our American political line. The achievement of the *Declaration*, if it proves nothing else, certainly established its author's title to the greatest pen in the patriotic cause. Certain contemporaries, either through faulty judgment or through jealousy of Jefferson's ability to fashion a line of fundamental national policy that could sing itself into the country's ears, challenged the author on the score of "originality." Madison was incensed for he knew that it was absurd to cavil thus. "The object," he protested, "was to assert not to discover truths, and to make them the basis of the Revolutionary Act. The merit of the Draught could only consist in a lucid communication of human Rights, a condensed enumeration of the reasons for such an exercise of them, and in a style and tone appropriate to the great occasion, and to the spirit of the American people." But if the content of the *Declaration* is not enough to establish Jefferson in his preeminence on the left, there is the *Notes on the State of Virginia* (1784), the first American book to become an accidental "expatriate," published in England and France in pirated versions before it reached print in the country of its origin. This series of informal essays ranges far and wide over disputed questions in philosophy, science, politics, and morals, and is the natural discourse of a born humanistic rationalist. Proud of his friend's prowess as a thinker, Madison once observed that Jefferson was "greatly eminent for the comprehensiveness and fertility of his genius, for the vast extent and rich variety of his acquirements; and particularly distinguished by the philosophic impress left on every subject which he touched." And then as if the *Notes* had come to mind, Madison hastened to add: "Nor was he less distinguished from an early and uniform devotion to the cause of liberty, and systematic preference of a form of Government squared in the strictest degree to the equal rights of man."

Indeed, although Madison had been a friend, follower, and co-worker of Jefferson's for many years when he wrote this tribute, it is notable that in all the advancing and receding waves of historical interpretation the residual significance of Jefferson's contribution to the American tradition has grown rather than diminished. Of American Presidents, this statesman of the "Enlightenment" most closely approximates the Platonic philosopher-king. No other incumbent of the presidency, and no other of the liberal philosophic spirits of his age—Many-sided men like Franklin, Benjamin Rush, and Thomas Cooper—could match Jefferson's happy union of learning, independence, and competent judgment in diverse fields such as social morality, government, education, natural science, agriculture, and the arts. What Washington began to do for the American personality by example and by the sheer weight of personal decency and leadership, Jefferson molded into an intellectualized ideal of social order. The entire development of American affairs, as the definition of our national ideology, is consequently more indebted to Jefferson than it is to any other single man.

This is not to say that Jefferson was an illustration of that *cliché*, the crusader of eighteenth-century enlightenment who preached the gross "goodness" of man and the inevitable rational progress of society. Jefferson, who never wearied of reading history—he knew excellently the classical and the best of modern historians—had come to recognize the hazards of evil in human as in social affairs. He had so acute an awareness of the consequences of entrenching evil men in public positions that he concluded no society would be safe without an informed, alert citizenry participating actively in government. Devoted to human possibilities of growth, he outdistanced the faith of the other philosopher-statesmen—although Madison and

Adams both had their areas of hope and solid, if less generous, funds of goodwill. Another way of viewing the difference between Jefferson and all others is to recognize his philosophy of education for what it was—a conscious "ideological" program to create rightthinking, tolerant citizens whose management of local affairs would be but a neighborly orientation for their wise judgment and activity in the affairs of the Union. It was a program fitted to practical needs and political responsibilities, and yet attuned to the highest cultivation of the arts, the sciences, and *belles lettres*.

If it was Jefferson who recommended the fullest participation in political control, just as he sustained the greatest confidence in the educability of the American people, it was Hamilton who had most concern for government as a *force*, who saw little to worry about in its suppressive intrusions upon local or personal "rights." It must be understood that the whole of the political "line" ranging from Jefferson to Madison to Adams and to Hamilton operated within *realistic* limits. Each statesman feared different contingencies, each phrased his hopes in typical or unique terms, each seized upon symbols of approbation or aversion sympathetic to his own personality and to the range of his ideational life. One might almost conclude: *therefore*, the Republic was made possible—through the very variety and divergence of the founders' visions, ideas, and wishes.

Hamilton, for instance, saw very clearly the vast economic potentialities of America if the government would ally itself on the side of those who possessed large fortunes and legislate in the direction of the expansion of financial and commercial activities. In the "people" Hamilton bought virtually no stock. He thought they might listen to a debate and repeat with fair accuracy another man's line of argument, but they were by and large susceptible to the flatteries and the manipulations of natural politicians. Indeed, when left to his own selfish and irrational devices, the "great beast" might actually retard the productive energy of the nation, rather than build it up.

It was some time after Hamilton's memorable project of the *Federalist* (1787-88)—that lucid exposition of constitutional republican government, not always consistent in its internal logic, but always impressive in its powerful defense of the need for national unity—that he began to voice his gloomiest thoughts about the survival of the republican experiment in self-government. "It is yet to be determined by experience whether it be consistent with that stability and order in government which are essential to public strength and private security and happiness," he wrote in 1792, having already tasted the strength of Jefferson's principled opposition. He seemed eager to give voice to his fear that republicanism might not "justify itself by its fruits." His progress tory-wise away from what he had called "the fair fabric of republicanism . . . modelled and decorated by the hand of federalism" was complete. In this short-sightedness Hamilton showed himself less of a philosopher and less of a statesman than one would desire. Were it not for the towering importance of certain of his administrative and governmental principles, Hamilton's temperament and the transparency of his self-interest would hardly qualify him as a philosopher-statesman. But there is great penetration in his theory that the extension of national prerogative is indispensable for achieving internal uniformity and efficiency in a genuinely "central" government. And there is undeniable truth in his perception that this is the first essential of defense against foreign powers. Another realistic principle of capitalist development appreciated by Hamilton early in the nation's life was that it was a direct obligation of the government to foster the development of the productive resources and activities of the nation—by whatever combination of interests might prove effective. The first of these principles figures in Hamilton's masterful *First Report on the Public Credit* (1790), when he unhesitatingly decides that "if the voice of humanity pleads more loudly in favor of some (classes of creditors) than of others, the voice of policy, no less than of justice, pleads in favor of all." The second principle is the key argument of Hamilton's classical treatise on protectionism, the *Report on Manufactures* (1791).

By a peculiar concentration of interest, Hamilton attained a definiteness in the body of his belief which sounds surprisingly modern in tone. Read today, his justification of strong efficient government comes close to a native American defense of totalitarian political management. But clever though his analysis was, it did not succeed in reconciling the two inseparable demands of prospering republicanism: national power, exercised to the full by an unimpeded, energetic central administration, and mature responsibility vested in the people of a free society.

The conservatism and legalism of John Adams and Madison explain almost as much about the success of the American republic as they do about the absence of these names from most of the emotional appraisals of the early American tradition. Adams was a testy man, given to incalculable fits of temper that could shake his soul and harden his behavior to the utmost expression of stubbornness. Madison was naturally prudent, neither commanding in person nor captivating in his imaginative vistas. He did not permit himself the occasional exaggerations of the genius which he himself detected in Jefferson, while Adams, unlike Hamilton, *never* lost sight of his high duty to guard the national interest and American republic. Adams was therefore saved from the extravagancies of Hamiltonian ambition. Since the "mean," in politics, is not golden, not, at any rate, in the "memory of the race," both Adams, the unorthodox federalist, and Madison, the conservative republican, paid the political price of hewing to the Aristotelian middle. Without Adams, the preservation of the dignified ideal of lawful, responsible government and a great example of Bolingbroke's ideal "Patriot King" who comes to guard like an "angel" destiny and the long-range interests of his country might not have been realized. Without Madison, the amelioration of factional (including "class") strife would not so early have been made a governmental objective, nor would the allocation of sovereign power in the federal and in state contexts have found so subtle an expositor.

The surety of republican foundations, one might say, depended upon the Jeffersonian "left," with its key insights that the preservation of individual freedom and the moral development of cooperative society were the ultimate objectives of free society. It depended upon the Hamiltonian "right" with its knowledge that governments need effective organization and the power which comes from having the substantial productive and financial forces in the nation solidly united behind the administration. The stability of the Republic and its true course depended much upon the labors of Madison, with his realistic conviction that the main purpose of a government is the protection of the many and diverse economic interests into which every country is divided—and with his belief that this protection can be accomplished through a limited, federal republic capable of preventing the monopolistic dictation of one faction or combine over the people of the nation. The experienced conclusion of the elder Adams, that republicanism would not dispel disparities of wealth and station and the aristocracies which there entail, was a grave note of warning. When Adams added that the chief function of wise governors would be to protect the separate but "balanced" powers delegated to them, by compact with the people, in order to prevent tyranny, chaos, or the anarchy of the impassioned mob, he further safeguarded the Republic from what the ancients had been pleased to characterize as the "inevitable" degeneration of the good society.

The main task of republican government, in the long view of John Adams, appeared to be the prevention of excessive power in the hands of any one group. Believing that "vice and folly are so interwoven in all human affairs that they could not, possibly, be wholly separated from them without tearing and rending the whole system of human nature and state," Adams had to put his trust in the rare statesmanlike leaders who would possess wisdom to formulate just laws, and discipline to abide by them. Adams thought the network of checks and balances would defeat the ambitious and power-hungry few who might design to capture government for their private ends, and would ensure fair representation of the interests of every region in the nation, thereby allowing the propertied and "responsible" citizens who were the mainstay of each region a voice in governmental affairs. By these devices, he thought he could make the most of fallible human nature. A republic, devoted to the interest of the people and operating through their own representatives, should be the outcome of these precautionary mechanisms. Adams accordingly thought his own republicanism as firm as that of anyone, including the leader of the Republican party, his good friend and occasional enemy, Thomas Jefferson, who, in Adams' opinion, differed from himself only in that he was for "liberty and straight hair. I thought curled hair was as republican as straight."

Madison's starting point was less psychological and more sociological. It began with the observed differences in group interests, differences which he took to calling "factions." Factions for Madison were special-interest groups arising out of the fundamental conflict present in every society between those who are rich and maintain their riches, and those who are poor and struggle to relieve their condition. "All civilized societies are divided into different interests and factions" he wrote in the interesting year of 1787, "as they happen to be creditors or debtors—rich or poor—husbandmen, merchants or manufacturers—members of different religious sects—followers of different political leaders—inhabitants of different districts—owners of different kinds of property, etc." The advantage of modern republicanism over other governments Madison expected to find in its ability to impede the full force of factional combinations, preventing them from controlling the state, and from usurping the rights of one or more minorities. Madison as a Virginian feared the added danger that the majority (the North) might suppress the rights of the minority (the South), contending in a letter to Jefferson that "where the real power in a government lies, there is the danger of oppression. In our Governments the real power lies in the majority of the Community, and the invasion of private rights is chiefly to be apprehended, not from acts of Government contrary to the sense of its constituents, but from acts in which the Government is the mere instrument of the major number of the constituents.'' Madison thus called to the attention of all men the inflexible requirement that democracies protect the civil rights of minorities from the real or reported ''will'' of the majority.

Madison and Adams made more of property rights than Jefferson did, but neither of them deserted the democratic theories of natural rights, popular sovereignty, limited government, anti-monarchism and anti-aristocracy. Nor did the two conservatives ever approach Hamilton's justification of plutocracy. Both Adams and Madison inclined to the ideal of a republic which was economically agrarian at base, but supplemented by mercantile and manufacturing interests. Madison perhaps a little more than Adams realized the vital role of credit and of government-financed expansion of the country's natural resources and communications—the role which John Adams' son, John Quincy Adams, was to develop fully in his program of ''Internal Improvement.'' Theoretically, therefore, it was Hamilton, of doubtful birth, who thought most exclusively of the moneyed interests of the country, partly because he saw in them the source of national strength, while Jefferson, graceful and learned ''landed esquire,'' cared most deeply about the widespread independent well-being of the ''people,'' farmers and laborers included. Adams and Madison, each aristocratic in taste in the typical styles of Massachusetts and Virginia, but far from dazzling in the family fortunes to which they were born, were actively promoting a scheme of society favorable to widespread middle-class prosperity and power.

III

The ethical theories of these men were influential factors upon the political and economic views they maintained. Save for the four philosopher-statesmen of the Republic, the American character might never have been given more than haphazard or perfunctory significance. Jefferson, Madison, and John Adams all understood the importance of character for those who would be leaders in a republic, and Hamilton sometimes did and sometimes paid only lip service to the ideal. Jefferson and Madison and Adams advocated that ''the purest and noblest characters'' (Madison's phrase) should serve as the people's representatives, since they alone would do so from the ''proper motives.'' Because these men dedicated themselves to the cause of their country before they consulted their immediate personal needs, the inceptive principles of the American republic betoken seekers of truth and wisdom, and good citizens in the Roman sense, rather than mere men of office.

Jefferson, perceiving that government was necessary for the release of man's fullest potentialities, liked to speak of it as of secondary or instrumental value—a habit which was later perversely construed to mean that government was ''evil.'' The range of realistic political choice for Jefferson lay entirely between repressive government and republicanism, and he identified the essence of republicanism as ''action by the citizens in person in affairs within their reach and competence, and in all others by representatives, chosen immediately, and removable by themselves.'' For this reason, a republic was the ''only form of government that is not eternally at open or secret war with the rights of mankind.'' To achieve republican freedom, citizens must pay a price, the wakefulness of "eternal vigilance," and, therefore, a citizenry trained in the principles of government, an *educated* citizenry, is the indispensable support of freedom.

Thus, subtly and indirectly, a moral climate had been postulated for the America in which republicanism was to be tried. Benevolence and moral sense, self-created will rather than coercive force, are the dynamic daily agents in free society as well as the purely *theoretical* factors of its ethics. "Natural" moralism is opposed to the reputed "natural" rule of force, which Jefferson saw as the breeder of authoritarian society, whether of "kings, hereditary nobles, and priests" or, in the language of our own day, of leaders, demagogues, and commissars. Jefferson's agrarianism, so often made the catchword for his variety of democracy, is in reality a by-product of an almost sentimental preference for the simplicity of classical republicanism joined to the supposed purity of "primitive" Christianity. Yet when Jefferson realized that the evolution of his nation demanded the self-sufficiency and expansion of her manufacture and trade—when he perceived that free society would be jeopardized if it were unable to defend itself on the high seas—he protested that "he . . . who is now against domestic manufacture, must be for reducing us either to dependence . . . or to be clothed in skins, and to live like wild beasts in dens and caverns. I am not one of these; experience has taught me that manufactures are now as necessary to our independence as to our comfort." Despite this, Jefferson's instinctive trust reposed in the fair and free interchange of nation with nation, as in citizen with citizen—which is to say that he was a man of peace, conceiving productive society basically as a peaceful society, an earnest judgment in which he was fully joined by James Madison.

Economically and politically, to Hamilton's expert eye the softer fringe of social morality was not a subject for enthusiasm nor even for *belief*. "The seeds of war are sown thickly in the human breast," Hamilton had written, and the rivalry that precipitated wars, in his view, stemmed partly from "the temper of societies," and partly from the human disposition to "prefer partial to general interest." Coming to terms with self-interested reality was accordingly Hamilton's basic preoccupation, whether that "reality" meant strong armies and navies for defense against foreign powers, or a strong system of national credit. In an ultimate separation of himself from his idealistic associates, whom he termed "political empirics," Hamilton, in an important unfinished paper called "Defence of the Funding System" (1795), identified the "true" politician as one who "takes human nature (and human society its aggregate) as he finds it, a compound of good and ill qualities, of good and ill tendencies, endued with powers and actuated by passions and propensities which blend enjoyment with suffering and make the causes of welfare the causes of misfortune." Afraid to warp this fundamental human complex by urging a happiness not suited to it, the true politician supposedly aims at the social measures designed to "make men happy according to their natural bent, which multiply the sources of individual enjoyment and increase national resources and strength." The great objective of the statesman should thus be to find the cement for compounding diverse elements of a state into a "rock" of national strength.

Governments would not need to be afraid to take power, Hamilton believed, could they strip themselves of false attitudes of modesty. In the logic of economic stability and national expansion, of credit and appropriations and "sound policy" versus the misguided pleadings of "common humanity," Hamilton saw an unanswerable imperative: to wit, that the "sacred" right of property must be defended by the laws and by the constitutions of the land and that even the nonpropertied groups in the community should protect property rights lest the "general principles of public order" be subverted.

John Adams, the self-styled "John Yankee" who could not bear to kowtow to "John Bull"—nor for that matter to any foreign power—seems more at home in Jefferson's and Madison's company than he is with Hamilton, the "boss" of his own party. Without Adams, the democratic precedent of the New England meeting hall, the training green, and the system of self-support for local schools, churches, and cultural institutions might have spoken only with muffled voice in the American tradition. The political "virtues" of Massachusetts even Jefferson commended, pointing to that state as the best exponent of the theme that knowledge is power. In Adams' championship of New England, there is a nucleus of national pride useful and perhaps necessary to a rising nation. To this Adams personally added the dignified appeal that however much republican government consisted of equal laws justly administered, it further required consistent benevolence and encouragement for the arts and sciences. Almost a humanist, but never quite freed of a Puritan sense of guilt and sin, Adams privately reveled in the classics just as Jefferson did. The late correspondence which flourished between Adams and Jefferson as the two aged statesmen with great *éclat* enacted the roles of sages in retirement is a phenomenon of tireless learning and peppery jest, joined in a correspondence the like of which is not known elsewhere in the annals of American statesmen.

IV

Such were the philosopher-kings of the American "Enlightenment." However often they may have erred—in description, in prognosis, in emphasis, and sometimes in behavior as statesmen—they seem to have possessed that rare wisdom about human and political affairs which never quite exhausts its power to suggest. On occasions, it restores its own original vitality and suffices to sanction an important change in national or international policy. We know that in the curious reversals of history, the truths of an age are likely to suffer sea-change. As Lincoln pointed out, the maxim "all men are created equal," once thought a self-evident truth, is termed a "self-evident lie" once we have "grown fat, and lost all dread of being slaves ourselves." So it may be with the far-ranging insights and veridical principles of the philosopher-statesmen of the Republic. Since the advent of the Jacksonian age—a "calamitous" presidency in Madison's prediction—the objectives of tempered democracy have been often ignored or ingeniously misinterpreted. As the letters and state papers of the Republican era again come under review, it is apparent that democratic ideology can still benefit by its own articulate original. The foundation of our national literature is present here, as well in the practical literature of ideas as in the imitative experiments of the deliberately "literary" work of the day.

12

Hamilton's Political Science: Man and Society

Clinton Rossiter

The ideas of American economic growth and business enterprise have not been easily incorporated into American intellectual history. The vigorous, spirited, and energetic entrepreneurial life that transformed an open continent into urban-industrial America has not readily been absorbed into the history of ideas. The reasons for this difficulty, if not sheer historical neglect, are twofold. Historians and academic men generally were for many years sympathetic to the Populist-Progressive view of business life, which usually saw businessmen as, at best, narrow in their thinking about social matters. Secondly, businessmen tended to be either fundamentalists in their support of "conservative Darwinist" (really Spencerian evolutionist) ideas or they were antagonized and placed on the defensive by charges of selfishness and social shortsightedness leveled against them by champions of the Populist-Progressive-New Deal tradition. Hence businessmen themselves were slow to search for and explain the intellectual contexts of their efforts. Only within the last decade have historians, following the lead of a few economic historians and even fewer businessmen, attempted a more searching appraisal of business life and corporate growth. Newer surveys underscore the business world's ideas of the prosperous community and national growth, of corporate responsibility and achievement, and of individual or group considerations behind corporate self-aggrandizement, social neutrality, or industrial welfare.

Going back to Alexander Hamilton does not locate the genesis of American business thought. If a prototypical American businessman ever existed, perhaps he can be found among early eighteenth-century Puritan merchants and traders. Yet the probing quality of Hamilton's ideas, his guarded and cautious view of human nature, his insistence upon accounting for man's instincts for self-gain and power, together with his brilliant efforts in the 1790s to place the new nation on a sound financial basis, all mark him, in this selection from a book by the political scientist Clinton Rossiter (1917-1970), as one of the most arresting American thinkers on the nature of economic man.

Reprinted by permission of Harcourt Brace Jovanovich from Clinton Rossiter, *Alexander Hamilton and the Constitution* (copyright 1964 by Clinton Rossiter), pp. 125-141. Footnotes have been omitted.

For further reading: Cecilia Kenyon, "Alexander Hamilton: Rousseau of the Right," *Political Science Quarterly*, 73 (June 1958), 161-178; Saul K. Padover, "The 'Singular' Mr. Hamilton," *Social Research*, 24 (1957), 157-190; *John C. Miller, *Alexander Hamilton: Portrait in Paradox* (1959), reprinted as **Alexander Hamilton and the Growth of the New Nation*; *Adrienne Koch, *Power, Morals, and the Founding Fathers: Essays in the Interpretation of the American Enlightenment* (1961), chap. 4.

Almost every political philosopher worth his salt is first of all a psychologist, a man who shapes his descriptions of social reality and prescriptions for political sanity to a core of assumptions about the urges, needs, habits, and capacities of men. Generalizations about something called "human nature" flow impulsively from his pen, and he seeks everywhere—in history, personal experience, tables of statistics, medical lore, even in the writings of poets and theologians—for evidence to support them.

Hamilton was no exception to this rule. Indeed, it would be hard to find a working and thinking politician in his generation, except perhaps John Adams, who talked more about principles of human behavior, or was more certain that these principles fixed the limits within which the arts of governing could be practiced. All his writings, from the most sober and public to the most passionate and private, are shot through with references to human nature—or, more exactly, with appeals to it for support of his schemes and arguments. "The science of policy," he told the members of the Philadelphia Convention, "is the knowledge of human nature" "All political speculation, to be just," he warned the citizens of New York, "must be founded" on a clear understanding of a "principle of human nature." No ruler of men, certainly no builder of a new political system, could be "ignorant of the most useful of all sciences—the science of human nature."

It may seem absurd to us, evidence of both his overconfidence as a politician and naiveté as a political thinker, that he should have described his own fund of knowledge and prejudice about human behavior and capacities as a "science." Yet, as a disciple of Hume, he seems to have believed sincerely that some "principles of human nature" were as "infallible as any mathematical calculations," and that some of his opponents were either weakly or willfully in contempt of the commands of these principles. . . .

If human nature was a science, Hamilton the tutor in human nature was hardly a scientist. His observations are scattered at random through his political and economic writings; never did he pause for long, not even in *The Federalist*, to elaborate on the earnest judgments about the motives and conduct of men that he tossed into the most severely practical arguments. He was not, as far as we can tell, a serious student of the psychological treatises of Locke, Rousseau, Hobbes, or even Hume; he was not a careful cataloguer of the range of emotions and traits he professed to have found at work in men; he did not even try to be precise in his definitions, often using quite different words to describe the same quality and the same word to describe quite different qualities. His convictions about human nature were, in truth, instruments of his political purposes, and the instruments were, even by the loose standards of those days, rather rudimentary in design.

Despite an occasional reference to the universality of the rules of human behavior, Hamilton was not interested in working out a set of abstract standards that applied to all men everywhere regardless of circumstance. When he talked of human nature, he seems to have meant the observed behavior of all men—or perhaps all but a few secular saints—in all situations of which he was cognizant. Natural man, man untouched by the influences of society, was a phenomenon, real or hypothetical, he could not imagine. His generalizations in psychology did not even range beyond the boundaries of Western society. Yet, despite the manifest inadequacies of Hamilton's psychology of politics, it is important for us to study his convictions for two reasons: first, because they were in fact convictions, articles of a faith strongly held, which did much to shape his approach to the practical business of making and manipulating constitutions; and, second, because many of them, however summarily arrived at and casually expressed, were among the first crude American models of more sophisticated and tested hypotheses about man that we use today in our political calculations. At the risk of bringing too much order to the most disordered area of Hamilton's political science, let me reduce the many convictions he held about human nature to five major themes.

The first is well known to all readers of *The Federalist:* the universal, enduring depravity and frailty of men. Even in the most sanguine days of his life, as an undergraduate enlisted in the glorious cause of the Revolution, he refused to be softheaded about his fellow men, and thus doused his audience with the cold water of Hume:

> "*Political writers (says a celebrated author) have established it as a maxim, that, in contriving any system of government, and fixing the several checks and controls of the constitution,* every man *ought to be supposed a* knave. . . . *It is therefore a just* political *maxim, that* every man must be supposed a knave."

Never in all his writings, never in all his doings, did Hamilton indulge in the Pelagian dream of the perfectibility of men, nor even in the Jeffersonian dream of amelioration. "The depravity of mankind, in all countries and at all times," was his relentless theme, and he did not even imagine that the improvement of social conditions might give a lasting boost upward to the general level of human conduct. Not "till the millenium comes," and perhaps not even then, would men break loose from the bonds of wickedness and weakness that nature had laid upon them in common.

Among the specific varieties of "natural depravity" that might occasionally take command of even the best of men, including presumably Alexander Hamilton and George Washington, were hatred, cruelty, envy, dishonesty, hypocrisy, treachery, avarice, and bellicosity. He was particularly insistent upon the power of the last of these unfortunate traits. As he demonstrated in *The Federalist,* he had a rather sophisticated grasp of the causes of war, but he always found the first cause to be the rapacious and vindictive nature of men. "The seeds of war are sown thickly in the human breast," he warned those of his countrymen who looked forward to enduring peace.

> *To judge from the history of mankind, we shall be compelled to conclude that the*

fiery and destructive passions of war reign in the human breast with much more powerful sway than the mild and beneficent sentiments of peace; and that to model our political system upon speculations of lasting tranquillity is to calculate on the weaker springs of the human character.

Among the varieties of "natural frailty" were fear, pride, vanity, ingratitude, fickleness, laziness, fallibility, intemperance, irresolution, narrowmindedness, obstinacy, and the capacity for self-delusion. While these evidences of human weakness did not disturb him as much as did cruelty or hatred or avarice, he thought of them as equally menacing hazards to social stability and political sanity.

Hamilton did not always paint his impressionistic pictures of human nature in dark and forbidding colors. "The supposition of universal venality in human nature," he wrote with feeling in *The Federalist,* "is little less an error in political reasoning than the supposition of universal rectitude." Depravity was a powerful but not omnipotent presence in the community. As he said in 1788 in defending the character of the future Congress of the United States against charges of easy corruptibility, "Human nature must be a much more weak and despicable thing than I apprehend it to be if two hundred of our fellow-citizens can be corrupted in two years." If this is not the most handsome compliment ever paid to the human race, it does show him in his usual frame of mind—"a man disposed to view human nature as it is, without either flattering its virtues or exaggerating its vices."

Like the implicitly loyal Whig he was, Hamilton found man a mixture of degrading vices, discouraging imperfections, and ennobling virtues. "Human conduct," he wrote, "reconciles the most glaring opposites." While the last of these categories was the weakest by far in the characters of all but a few extraordinary men, virtue did exist in most breasts, and it had a way of bursting forth at the most unexpected moments. At one point or another in his writings Hamilton spoke hopefully of honor, generosity, bravery, humaneness, love of liberty, desire for learning, and the sense of justice; and he knew from experience that there were situations in which "human nature" could be made to "rise above itself."

In those great revolutions which occasionally convulse society, human nature never fails to be brought forward in its brightest as well as in its blackest colors.

Yet if Hamilton had a Whiggish belief in the mixed nature of man, he was one of those Whigs like John Adams who found the mixture to be overloaded with vice and folly. Not only was wickedness more deeply planted than goodness in the human breast; it had a way of asserting itself with unusual vigor. "It is a common observation," Hamilton wrote as Phocion in 1784, "that men, bent upon mischief, are more active in the pursuit of their object than those who aim at doing good."

Unlike some of the men with whom he contested, Hamilton denied that Americans had any reason to think themselves "wiser, or better, than other men." In one of the most famous passages in *The Federalist,* he made clear his belief that Americans would bear the common burden of depravity and frailty.

What reason can we have to confide in those reveries which would seduce us into an expectation of peace and cordiality between the members of the present confederacy, in a state of separation? Have we not already seen enough of the fallacy and extravagance of those idle theories which have amused us with promises of an exemption from the imperfections, the weaknesses, and evils incident to society in every shape? Is it not time to awake from the deceitful dream of a golden age and to adopt as a practical maxim for the direction of our political conduct that we, as well as the other inhabitants of the globe, are yet remote from the happy empire of perfect wisdom and perfect virtue?

Although he attached great importance to the everlasting tension between well-armed vice and frail virtue in the character of men, Hamilton seems to have believed that three other traits or drives—of an essentially neutral moral nature—were dominant in directing social behavior. Borrowing alike from Hume's *Treatise of Human Nature* and Adam Smith's *Theory of Moral Sentiments,* and relying as always on the lessons he could draw from his own experience, he made much in his own writings of three consuming "loves"—of esteem, of gain, and of power.

The first of these Smith had called "emulation," a drive which ran the gamut of intensity from a simple need for respect to a prodigious thirst for glory. This was, of course, an urge whose power Hamilton could hardly have depreciated. As I wrote . . . fame was the spur that goaded him to his best efforts, and he had no reason to believe that he was an eccentric in this matter. If he was prompted by "the love of fame, the ruling passion of the noblest minds," to "plan and undertake extensive and arduous enterprises for the public benefit," men of every stripe could be roused to unaccustomed effort by the lure of "places, pensions, and honors." Hamilton agreed unreservedly with Hume that "a noble emulation is the source of every excellence," and with Smith that such a feeling of emulation was an "anxious desire."

Hamilton used the word "ambition" to describe a number of related drives, the most forceful of which was the desire of material gain. While he never spun out any elaborate theories of the universality and utility of the profit motive, he did recognize that in most men, if not in himself, it was at least as strong a drive as emulation, and that the operations of this motive in a well-ordered society could lead to happiness and prosperity on a broad scale. "Is not the love of wealth as domineering and enterprising a passion as that of power and glory?" he asked in a rhetorical passage in *The Federalist* that covered all three of the mightiest spurs to human endeavor. The behavior of his friend William Duer was proof enough of the force of this spring of human conduct.

The love of power was, of course, a favorite theme of the "approved writers" from whom Hamilton learned his lessons in political realism, and he never found anything in his own experience that gave him reason to dispute them. His comments on this tendency in the human spirit had force and feeling. "The love of power" was a major theme in his speech of June 18, 1787 to the Philadelphia Convention; it was restated with eloquent variations all through *The Federalist;* and he even managed to slip a sentence into the Farewell Address about the "love of power which predominates in . . . the human heart."

I have said that he seems to have looked upon these powerful drives as neither virtuous nor vicious in nature. They were facts of life that simply could not be placed into moral categories. Yet if they were neither good nor bad in essence, they could produce good or bad results. In a man held to paths of right behavior by the inner checks of reason and self-discipline and the outer checks of law and order these three "loves" could quite possibly work wonders of self-advancement and self-realization, and all society would be the gainer. Upon a man holding a license to behave as freely and arrogantly as he wished they would almost certainly bring down the sins of lust and corruption, and all society would be the loser.

Hamilton pointed clearly to the degenerate form of each of these mighty human urges. An overdose of emulation resulted in vanity, of ambition in avarice, of the love of power in the "lust of domination"—and, worse than that, in the abuse of power. Vanity, avarice, even the desire to play the tyrant were evidences of corruptibility which did not trouble Hamilton too deeply. The abuse of power, however, presented a stiff problem to a political scientist who put power at the center of his system, and it is important for us to know that, even in the midst of his campaigns for an energetic government, he held no illusions about the ultimately corrosive effects of power on all but the most saintly men, and perhaps even on them. One can imagine him as a young man nodding assent to Hobbes's awesome words about the "perpetual and restless desire of power after power, that ceaseth only in death." In 1775 he stated a belief from which he never wandered, and which lay at the core of his commitment to constitutionalism:

A fondness for power is implanted in most men, and it is natural to abuse it when acquired. This maxim drawn from the experience of all ages makes it the height of folly to entrust any set of men with power which is not under every possible control; perpetual strides are made after more as long as there is any part withheld.

And ten years later he stated the problem in terms that ought to have special meaning for this generation of Americans. "How easy it is for men," he wrote as Phocion,

to change their principles with their situations–to be zealous advocates for the rights of the citizens when they are invaded by others, and as soon as they have it in their power, to become the invaders themselves–to resist the encroachments of power, when it is in the hands of others, and the moment they get it into their own to make bolder strides than those they have resisted.

The third of Hamilton's major convictions about human nature centered upon the idea of "interest." He never tired of pointing out that every man was, in one important sense, a self-contained unit in the social structure whose first obligation was to himself. He described "self-preservation" respectfully as the "first principle of our nature," "self-love" ironically as an "indispensable duty," "self-interest" coldly as the "most powerful incentive of human actions." Every man had his "interests," whether in gain, esteem, power, pleasure, or simply survival, and there was not much point in telling him that he ought to pursue them in a spirit of moderation and with an eye out for the interests of others. "We may preach," he wrote, "till we are tired of the theme, the necessity of disinterestedness in republics, without making a single proselyte." Having noted already the young Hamilton's approving use of Hume's warning that "*every man* ought to be supposed a *knave,*'' we may now observe that Hume went on, still with Hamilton's approval, to describe his ''everyman'' as having ''no other end in all his actions, but private interest.'' While Hamilton, contrary to his own advice, did a fair share of preaching ''the necessity of disinterestedness,'' he based almost all his political calculations on the assumption that he had not made a ''single proselyte.''

I say ''almost'' because Hamilton occasionally relaxed the rigidity of his stance as political psychologist and acknowledged the existence of a handful of men to whom the laws of human nature seemed to apply imperfectly or not at all. Having admitted to his colleagues at Philadelphia that ''there may be in every government a few choice spirits'' who could rise above interest and passion and ''act from more worthy motives,'' he went on some months later in *The Federalist* to rest his case for a strong executive at least partly on the assumption that men of ''stern virtue,'' ''men who could neither be distressed nor won into a sacrifice of their duty,'' would be available for service. While such men were, to be sure, ''the growth of few soils,'' they did exist in sufficient numbers in the United States for the friends of ordered liberty to count upon their presence in the new government. They were evidence of the existence of a ''portion of virtue and honor among mankind''; they provided ''a reasonable foundation of confidence'' in the outcome of the American gamble in freedom. Hamilton did not pause to explain just how the voters, men laden with the average burden of fallibility and envy, could be persuaded to elect men of stern virtue to office. Yet he seemed to have confidence, not as strong as Jefferson's but strong enough to raise his hopes for liberty, that the machinery of election and appointment would throw up enough such men to give a tone of virtue and wisdom to the whole enterprise. As he wrote in an earlier number of *The Federalist:*

> *There are strong minds in every walk of life that will rise superior to the disadvantages of situation and will command the tribute due to their merit, not only from the classes to which they particularly belong, but from the society in general.*

And how could he have believed otherwise than in the existence of a ''few choice spirits,'' and in the possibility of their recognition by the community, when he had been a friend and servant of George Washington?

Another theme of Hamilton's political psychology was the unending war in the minds and hearts of men between ''reason'' and ''passion.'' This is one of those points at which Hamilton's meaning is especially hard to pin down because he was so casual in his use of words. We can excuse him for having made ''reason'' serve a half-dozen important purposes, for this is a word that all political thinkers call upon too easily and often. He could, however, have been more precise about ''passion,'' a word he called upon so easily and often that it gives a special flavor to all his writings on human nature. A favorite of many of the Founding Fathers, who would have come across it in Hobbes or Hume, or for that matter in Shakespeare or Pope or Adam Smith, it was used by Hamilton, often in the plural, as a shorthand term for each of the neutral drives or ''loves,'' and for all of them together; for each of the categories of wicked behavior, and for all of them together; for ''interests'' and ''prejudices''; for ''vanity,'' ''anger,'' ''pride,'' ''ambition,'' and ''caprice''; and, in company with most other men who found it useful, for what I can only describe as "unreason." In any case, Hamilton thought of every man, including himself, as a kind of grand prize in a perpetual "conflict between Reason and Passion"—reason being the faculty of thinking coolly, objectively, and broadly about problems of political allegiance and decision, passion being any trait or impulse from obstinacy to "rage and frenzy" (by way of ignorance and fear and prejudice) that corrupted reason and often drove it from the field. As he wrote to Bayard in 1802 in exasperation over the trend of events:

Nothing is more fallacious than to expect to produce any valuable or permanent results in political projects by relying merely on the reason of men. Men are rather reasoning than reasonable animals, for the most part governed by the impulse of passion.

Since reason is largely a product of nurture and passion a product of nature, the latter generally holds the upper hand—"Passion wrests the helm from reason"—and even "wise and good men" are led to the "wrong side of questions of the first magnitude to society" by the "numerous . . . and powerful causes which serve to give a false bias to the judgment." Like most men, including most famous political thinkers, Hamilton found himself to be a man of reason and his critics men of passion, yet this evidence of his own frailty should not obscure the essential candor of one of the constant themes of his declamations on mankind.

Finally, Hamilton insisted that the bad side of human nature, always in a position of natural superiority in its contests with the good, was put in an even more commanding position by the fact of human association. Men in groups, especially groups unrestrained by law or custom, behaved worse than men on their own. "There is a contagion in example," he noted sorrowfully in *The Federalist,* "which few men have sufficient force of mind to resist," and in the nature of things most examples of human behavior were sure to be degrading rather than uplifting. . . .

We may conclude this survey of Hamilton's psychology by noting that he listed a sound knowledge of human nature among the qualifications for lawgivers, especially those who set themselves the task of writing a fundamental law for free men. Somehow the vices of these free men must be brought under control, somehow their virtues must be encouraged, somehow their "loves" must be directed toward healthy ends, somehow their powers of reason must be fortified for the endless duel with prejudice and passion. Most important of all—and here we come close to the core of Hamilton's "science of policy"—their interest must be looked after, secured, if possible gratified, and thus enlisted in the service of the whole community. Again and again in the crucial debates of his public career Hamilton fell back upon this "axiom of political science," which taught him, even if it apparently did not teach men like Jefferson, that the interests of governors and governed alike could be made to "coincide with their duty." Writing in 1775 as A Sincere Friend to America, and also as a man unafraid to quote Hume, he said of "private interest":

By this interest, we must govern him, and by means of it, make him cooperate to public good, *notwithstanding his insatiable avarice and ambition. Without this, we shall in vain boast of the advantages of* any constitution, *and shall find in the end, that we have no security for our liberties and possessions, except the* good will *of our rulers; that is, we should have* no security at all.

. . . It must be acknowledged that Hamilton fell too easily into the assumption that the interests of "the moneyed men" were the most important to enlist in the service of the community. While he was by no means indifferent to the fact that the poor, too, have interests, and that these interests must be recognized and secured, he always showed special concern for the aspirations of the rich and would-be-rich, whether in his defense of the New York Tories, his plans for funding the debt, or his advocacy of the Bank of the United States. This concern, it has been argued, was altogether natural for a man who liked rich men better than poor men; his theory of interests was in fact nothing more than a cloak of verbiage to drape around his desire to give handouts to friends and neighbors. But this, I think, is unfair to Hamilton, a political realist who believed quite sincerely that some men had a great deal more power than others over the fortunes of the community, and that it was idle to make plans for the general welfare unless such men could be persuaded to support them. He also believed, as he told the Poughkeepsie Convention in a burst of candor, that the "vices" of "the wealthy" were "probably more favorable to the prosperity of the state than those of the indigent," and partook "less of moral depravity."

No accusation we can level against Hamilton for being a Samaritan toward the rich and a Levite toward the poor can detract from the authority of his message to all makers and manipulators of constitutions: men have interests; these interests govern their comings and goings; government must look to these interests and enlist them in the cause of order, prosperity, and progress. One may argue with Hamilton's identification of the principal interests of the community, or fault him for having enlisted them too lavishly, but one must admit that he put his finger on a fact of political life to which all successful American politicians have paid implicit homage. It is his peculiar merit as political thinker to have been refreshingly explicit in his many references to this first principle of his political science. It was his peculiar merit as political actor to have exploited this principle to build up the Union. . . .

Hamilton's opinions about society had the same style as his opinions about men: dispersed and yet consistent, intuitive and yet thoughtful, offhand and yet highly serviceable. His thinking was always oriented toward society rather than individuals, toward the public welfare rather than the private pursuit of happiness. The community as something more than the men who made it up was an inarticulate major premise of his political creed, and we may acclaim him as one of the first and most conspicuous *social* thinkers on the American scene. If he was not a full-blooded collectivist in his analysis of society, he was most certainly a man who had the higher purposes and claims of the community in full view. He had, moreover, a feeling for the community as an aggregate of men who had a "common national sentiment" and a "uniformity of principles and habits." A "heterogeneous compound" was not his idea of a healthy society. While variety was essential to a healthy social order, it needed a consensus on which to focus.

Like most men with a bias toward society and away from the individual, Hamilton seems to have thought of the community, perhaps more wishfully than analytically, as a working equilibrium of groups, interests, classes, even estates, each of which drew strength and support from all the others. . . . If Hamilton, like the men with whom he contested, seemed more solicitous about the place of some "parts" than of others in the "perfect harmony of all," he, unlike many of them, had an apparently guileless belief in the existence, real or potential, of "proportion" and "balance" among all groups and interests in society. For him the beauty of "the design of civil society" was that "the united strength of the several members might give stability and security to the whole body, and each respective member." It was, moreover, "in a civil society . . . the duty of each particular branch to promote, not only the good of the whole community, but the good of every other particular branch."

He was not, alas, precise about the terms he used to describe the component parts of the community. His favorite seems to have been "class," and the temptation to catalogue him as a "class thinker" is very strong until one notices that he used it as a label for all manner of social and economic divisions within the community: social strata, yes, but also levels of wealth, occupations, economic interests, sections, "factions," and even groups different from one another in tastes, opinions, manners, or morals. If society was, or was supposed to be, a "perfect harmony of all parts," the parts were many, various, and overlapping, especially under conditions of liberty.

One wishes that Hamilton had been a little more candid, or simply concerned, about the social strata of the young Republic. It may be noted that he acknowledged, without regret, the existence of social classes, and assumed, also without regret, that they would go on forever; that he, like most men of his generation (and of every American generation before and since), made economic achievement and possession the chief criterion of status; that he thought of society as a whole series of layers, yet could not resist the urge to reduce all these layers to two, "the *few* and the *many*," the "rich and wellborn" and "the mass of the people"; and that he betrayed, so far as one can tell, not the slightest interest in the middle class. He might have agreed with Adams, for whom this was a major theme, that the middle class was "that great and excellent portion of society upon whom so much of the liberty and prosperity of nations so greatly depends." He might have been persuaded by his mentor Hume to acknowledge that the "middling rank of men . . . are the best and firmest basis of public liberty." But he never did, and one is left with the feeling that he was essentially a prisoner, and a willing one at that, of the ancient habit of dividing all men simply into the few and the many. . . .

The notable marks of . . . society . . . were order, stability, and prosperity, and, at the same time, progress, adventure, and a solid measure of glory. He wanted his society to be good, but he also wanted it to be great, and he was not sure that it could ever be the one without being the other. In this as in all his hopes for America he wanted the best of both worlds, by which I mean the best features of both the traditional, organic, structured, prescriptive society and the progressive, open, fluid, self-directing society. He had great respect for custom and usage, and condemned "the spirit of innovation" and "the rage for change," yet he was better prepared psychologically than any other man of his time to hazard the fortunes of the Republic in political and social experiment. He put "substantial and permanent order in the affairs of a country" at the top of his list of social goods, yet he seemed to think that such order would be strengthened rather than sapped by the spirit of enterprise. . . .

If he was less committed than Jefferson to the idea of natural or social equality, he was more committed to the ideal of racial equality. One learns with surprise in an excursion through Hamilton's writings that this child of the West Indies (in many ways a harsher mentor in racial matters than Virginia) was singularly free of cruel or careless notions about the "natural" inferiority of the Negro. In a letter dated March 14, 1779, to John Jay, who was then President of the Continental Congress, he supported the quixotic proposal of his friend John Laurens to raise several battalions of Negroes in his native South Carolina. "I have not the least doubt, that the negroes will make very excellent soldiers," he wrote, "for their natural faculties are probably as good as ours." As to their supposed lack of talent and sensibility, "the contempt we have been taught to entertain for the blacks, makes us fancy many things that are founded neither in reason nor experience." One of these things, it is clear from other public and private musings on the plight of the Negro, was the alleged conformity of the institution of slavery to the dictates of social expediency or natural justice. While Hamilton was too much a man of his age and social milieu and too zealous an advocate of Union to push for emancipation through political action, he was moved deeply "by the dictates of humanity and of true policy" to hope for steady improvement in the fortunes of "this unfortunate class of men." The laws of slavery were "the laws of degraded humanity"; the surrender of escaped Negroes to slavery was as "*odious* and *immoral* a thing as can be conceived." . . .

13
On John Adams

John Ryerson

Though the following essay by John Ryerson does not analyze or dissect John Adams' social thought, it is the best I have found to describe the problem or the enigma of John Adams as a thinker. A man whose self-doubt permeates his private writings, which in Adams' case are his most revealing writings, only with difficulty instills a sense of confidence in later generations who read him. Most writers on Adams clearly see the deep strain of Puritan ethic and the exciting current of Enlightenment skepticism (not its confidence in human perfectibility). But though these characteristics are basic to his thinking, there is still the goal, the ethical purpose, which Adams pursues but somehow fails to grasp completely, or so it seems to him. Perhaps the elusive quality of what Adams sought was determined by the paradoxes in his thought. He was a revolutionary, yet he prized social order; he erased the historical past of the American colonies, yet he set upon finding a convincing constitutional history for the new American states; he was a moralist who dismissed the heady idealism of the French *philosophes*, Turgot and Condorcet; he believed in the complexity of human nature, yet he longed for simple government; he championed freedom, yet he wanted a well-regulated society under the authority of talented, educated, and propertied men. As Ryerson and others remind us, these intellectual traits lived on in the Adams family of statesmen and intellectuals from Massachusetts. Almost the entire first century of American national life had impressed upon it the public influence of this remarkable family. If "the New England character" can be found in the American mind, it is the Adams family that helped considerably to put it there.

For further reading: Bernard Bailyn, "Butterfield's Adams: Notes for a Sketch," *William and Mary Quarterly*, 17 (April 1962), 238-256; *Zoltan Haraszti, *John Adams and the Prophets of Progress* (1952); Clinton Rossiter, "The Legacy of John Adams," *Yale Review,* 46 (1957), 528-550; Stephen G. Kurtz, "The Political Science of John Adams, a Guide to His Statecraft," *William and Mary Quarterly,* 25 (October 1968), 605-613; *John R. Howe, Jr., *The Changing Political Thought of*

American Quarterly, 6 (Fall 1954), 253-258. Reprinted by permission of the author and the *American Quarterly*. Footnotes have been omitted.

John Adams (1966); *Adrienne Koch, *Power, Morals, and the Founding Fathers: Essays in the Interpretation of the American Enlightenment* (1961), chap. 5; Samuel Flagg Bemis, *John Quincy Adams and the Union* (1956).

The life of John Adams is not easy to understand because of its conservatism and its rebellious nature, and because John Adams was always trying to explain himself. The definitive biography (yet to be written) of John Adams must therefore be an unravelling of the nature of his conservatism and his rebellion, and an analysis of the validity of his own record. John Adams was an honest man, but he was excessively articulate, and the letters, diaries, records, and accounts in his own hand were written not merely to record their own present but also to anticipate posterity. They must be read with that in mind. Convinced (and perhaps determined) that he would never get satisfaction from his contemporaries, he made sure that posterity would know what the record was.

John Adams was known as a leader because of his public actions, not because of his diary and letters. He talked and argued and wrote and led. His own records may be revelations of the introspective life, but they lead us away from the truth of the public personality. These sources are complaining or vain, or irritable, or melodramatic, or self-justifying; these sources must be read with skepticism just because they are so complete, and because they are rationalizations.

John Adams was a much greater man than he could ever admit to himself. He was aggressive enough to enjoy a good fight, but when writing about his struggles he often felt guilty. Jefferson commented on the suspicious and jealous nature of Adams' opinion of others, but he was perhaps even more suspicious of himself than he was of others. What a difference, for example, there is between his bold essay "On the Canon and Feudal Law" or his "Instructions from the Town of Braintree" and his derogatory comments about them. He looked for signs of failure. In the letters of his old age to Jefferson, one gets the sense that he was happy, that he recognized he had not failed, and that he admitted how much he enjoyed the Yankee battle of life. He finally ceased being melodramatic.

The Adams sources are tempting—and they are melodramatic sources. But melodramatic emotion is at least an exaggeration, and probably a distortion for some unconscious reason of a much simpler emotion, distorted and exaggerated in order to overpower the reality of common sense or common feeling. Adams wrote his records to convince himself and his friends of his role, and to convince all concerned of the reality of the emotion he thought he ought to feel.

There were few simple and unselfconscious reactions for John Adams. Like an introspective man before a mirror, he is hard to catch in an unguarded moment before he becomes conscious of his own expression. Few diaries, autobiographies, or letters can provide us with spontantous insight, especially the diaries or biographies or letters of so true a New Englander as Adams. But from the marginal and offhand comments Adams made on his reading, Zoltan Haraszti has made a book that reveals John Adams more immediately, though not more completely, than the poses he struck before the mirror of his diary.

To construct a man from his marginal comments is an awkward biographical method. What makes it possible in Adams' case is that his marginal comments express his intellectual experiences in a concentrated form: his authors forced him (or he made them force him) to consider his fundamental principles. In the dialogue that took place between Adams and author the pace was often too fast for Adams to maintain the egocentric tone of the diary and the letters. The "prophets of progress" pushed him so hard he could sometimes answer only in desperate anger or, more significantly for the biographer's purpose, only by revealing *the desperation of his conservatism and the conflicted nature of his thought*.

Conservatism has never been easy to describe. John Adams' conservative political philosophy was not established on a simple intellectual position of upper-class power and resistance to change. In order to find a foundation for his conservatism, he had to meet his own skepticism and his own revolutionary impulse first. His own knowledge, his own convictions, his own experience, his own insight into human behavior prompted him to write at one moment of "benevolence, the sense of beauty, of grace in motion, of elegance, of figure, the wonderful effects of the face, attractions, sympathies of various kinds even before language or love would draw individuals together"; and at another moment to write cynically about the idealism of Turgot and Condorcet.

We must remember that he was only partly a lawyer seeking to perfect social regulation. He was also a revolutionary, forced into a constructive role. He struggled with Sam Adams in 1775 to make the Boston protest to Governor Hutchinson a practical protest rather than the doctrine of natural rights desired by Sam Adams, but one year later in the Continental Congress he was ready and willing to use the natural rights argument. His revolutionary activity set up its own need for depth of argument, but he could not completely accept the standard hopes of the eighteenth-century vision. The philosophers of social progress, he thought, were all alike. "Not one of them takes human nature as it is for his foundation. Equality is one of those equivocal words which the philosophy of the eighteenth century has made fraudulent." An angry, jealous, bitter, old man, he was unable fully to accept his own need for a conception of patriotism or religion or benevolence.

He sought order and he was a revolutionary. One sees in his response to these European writers his own reaction to his achievement. One understands how important it is to search out in the experience of John Adams the forces that made him a rebel and at the same time such an insistently orderly man. We can rely on Adams himself to describe the symptoms of his response but we cannot rely on him to describe the causes. His mind was not that simple. He had a deep desire to establish a well-regulated, authoritative society that would satisfy his search for a kind of potent benevolence, but he could only rely on his own efforts. And he was unable to believe that his efforts were satisfactory. The conflict thus created always forced him to explain himself. Like his son, he was never able to make himself understood.

He rebelled.

It is hard today to uncover the intensity of that rebellion, for his life has become compacted with the Federalist position, charges of monarchism, jealousy, and conservatism. He sensed the truth, we can suppose, when he gave that aggressively foreshortened toast on the day of his death and the fiftieth anniversary of the Declaration of Independence, "Independence Forever!"

It is an advantage for us that his rebellion did not come easily, and that its difficulty raised questions in his mind. As a youth he always wrote with something of the cynicism of an old man: the puritanic complaints of idleness, the self-abuse for throwing away his future on the movement for independence—one keeps finding in him an expectation of misery or failure, and at the same time an insistence upon the monumental nature of his work, a demand for recognition which he felt he could expect only from posterity. He was as dissatisfied with himself as with others.

No office ever brought him what he needed. He was insatiable, ambivalent about his revolutionary impulse and his sense of his own achievement. It was his ambivalence—coming out in the old scrapper so hard to satisfy, the defender of the British soldiers after the Boston Massacre, the President whose policy included a naval war with France and a peace mission, and who temporarily withdrew from his post by living in Quincy in the middle of his administration—which probably succeeded in making others as well as himself distrust his leadership. And it was his ambivalence which made him need a past while he was making revolutionary demands on the present. His histories of the Italian republics and Swiss cantons were to be incorporated into his life work as a means of satisfying a consuming historical and philosophical appetite and appeasing the revolutionary demands. Since he was going to destroy the past, he needed one too. The existence of God marked the boundary of his skepticism. All other absolutes became doubtful—but did not cease to be necessary.

He was fat, short, moody and garrulous.

He thought he could establish a theory of government on a theory of human nature. His theory of human nature was, in turn, established on his acceptance of the aggressive impulses in men in general and in himself in particular. Charles Beard has called to our attention the significance of Madison's economic doctrine in Number 10 of the Federalist Papers. Adams believed the same kind of control was needed but gave it a psychological twist. For John Adams, who had to make enemies in order to externalize the conflict that went on within him, property was not only a cause of feelings of aggression, property also provided a means of checking destructive aggression. "As the respect for property wears away, [man's] ferocity will return." Respect for property became a method of control, since property created the necessity of self-protection against destructive aggression.

His acceptance of personal and social aggression was an essential element in his theory of government. Human societies, he believed, were complex because human nature was complex. Absolute values could not be established which violated human nature; ideals had to be kept in line with the reality of evil; and the attempt to create a "simple" government was delusionary. "It is silly to be eternally harping upon simplicity in a form of government. The simplest of all possible governments is a despotism in one. Simplicity is not the summum bonum."

Men must search their hearts, and confess the emulation that is there: and provide checks to it. The gentlemen must be compelled to agree. They never will from reason and free will. Nothing short of an independent power above them able to check their majorities ever can keep them within valid bounds. It is the interest and the policy of the people for their own safety always to erect and maintain such a power over the gentlemen: and such another under them. Power must be opposed to power, force to force, strength to strength, interest to interest, as well as reason to reason, eloquence to eloquence, and passion to passion.

He and his son were isolated men and they paid for their isolation. He demanded of others the intensity of effort that he demanded of himself, he had strong feelings and sought regularity, and both he and his son tried to work out their conflicts through public service. Their public service was great but never was able to give them peace. In the mirror of introspection his image was never free of the burden of explanation. The guilt which John Bunyan had loaded upon Christian, fleeing from the City of Destruction with his fingers in his ears, turned up in Adams, who himself seemed to live out the words of Bunyan's Worldly Wiseman:

Why in yonder Village, (the Village is named Morality) there dwells a Gentleman, whose name is Legality, a very judicious man (and a man of good name) that hath such skill to help men off with burdens such as thine are from their shoulders: yea, to my knowledge he hath done a great deal of good this way: Aye, and besides, he hath skill to cure those that are somewhat crazed in their wits with their burdens.

John Adams was forced by his own needs to invent a system of government as carefully engineered, to put it in the words of his great grandson, as an electric dynamo and probably as fateful. This inventor had a vested interest in his machine: when it failed to work he could only task himself. Legislating, gardening, administering the national affairs, writing ceaselessly to friends and to himself, reading and commenting on books read—none of these compulsive activities could satisfy the demands he made of his own effort. The regularity he desired for the nation might be found in the rule of property or in an intellectual authority, but in neither case were the results fully satisfactory. He needed more. He had committed himself. His effort and his needed independence, committed to the American cause, gave him a political orientation which could be denied only if he denied his own identity. He could in no case relax the anxious grip he held on the revolution he had helped to start: he had invented a system and the system had to work. In his isolation and conflict between authority and rebellion, in his need to silence his own questions, he set up a standard of perfection which seldom permitted him to relax.

The journals and letters of John Adams and John Quincy Adams have not yet been fully understood. The lawyer's mind, the New England mind, the presidential mind, obscured and intensified by the Adams' mind and the relationship of father and son—all these provide us with a fascinating study. To understand both men one must understand the conflict they experienced between public life and private life, the conflict between an aggressive attitude toward the world and a withdrawal from it; the burden of responsibility and guilt which both carried, searching for a City of Morality and a man named Legality to free them of their burden; and finally the standard of perfection which they needed and which was so characteristically expressed by John Quincy Adams near the end of his life.

There has perhaps not been another individual of the human race of whose daily existence from early childhood to fourscore years has been noted down with his own hand so minutely as mine. . . . If my intellectual powers had been such as have been sometimes committed by the Creator of man to single individuals of the species, my diary would have been, next to the Holy Scriptures, the most precious and valuable book ever written by human hands, and I should have been one of the greatest benefactors of my country and of mankind. . . . But the conceptive power of mind was not conferred upon me by my Maker, and I have not improved the scanty portion of His gifts as I might and ought to have done.

Here is an expression of failure and simultaneously an expression of faith; here is a dream of perfection. Our responsibility is to understand John Adams by refusing to let him blind us to the conflicts in his life, by refusing to let him explain away his failures or idealize his successes, and by learning to understand that difficult experience of independence which he helped to make possible.

14
Thomas Jefferson Survives

Julian P. Boyd

Basic to the Jeffersonian intellectual position were a belief in the simplicity or "economy" of nature, a biological view of man, the empirical method in scientific inquiry, an emphasis upon present experience, a prudential approach to life, a deistic religious faith of humane morality, the conviction that man is endowed with a moral sense, and the political creed of republicanism. These and many other aspects of the Jeffersonian mind have been examined and clarified by intellectual historians. But nothing is so central to Jefferson's own thinking and to its legacy in the American mind as his argument and appeal for freedom of thought. This is the pinion that engages the entire larger cogwheel of his ideas. In no sense an empty or idle assertion was his famous declaration to Benjamin Rush in 1800: "I have sworn upon the altar of god, eternal hostility against every form of tyranny over the mind of man."

No better example of an idea being used as a weapon for American democracy could be included in this book than this essay by Julian P. Boyd, editor of *The Papers of Thomas Jefferson*. It speaks to the ever renewing and necessary quality of the Jeffersonian idea of freedom. It was written during the "McCarthy era" of witch hunting anticommunism in the early 1950s, when some writers, journalists, academic men, and even some men in high public office felt the repressive force of mass fear and hysteria directed against them.

There is another important Jeffersonian legacy that should be mentioned here simply because it is so closely interwoven with intellectual history, with the pursuits of all learned men, and with the thinking of almost all statesmen in the early republic. It is the Jeffersonian emphasis upon education to achieve an informed citizenry. Indeed, Jefferson's republicanism is as much defined by the idea of state-sponsored formal education to the highest level possible for those young men who merit it (girls and blacks were beyond his purview) as it is characterized by his idea that an agrarian people are informally educated to a natural state of true virtue by their closeness to the land.

American Scholar, 20 (Spring 1951), 163-173. Reprinted by permission of the author and the publishers.

For further reading: *Merrill D. Peterson, *The Jeffersonian Image in the American Mind* (1960); Dumas Malone, *Thomas Jefferson as a Political Leader* (1963); Henry Steele Commager, *Majority Rule and Minority Rights* (1943); *Adrienne Koch, *The Philosophy of Thomas Jefferson* (1943); *Daniel Boorstin, *The Lost World of Thomas Jefferson* (1948); *Leonard W. Levy, *Jefferson and Civil Liberties: The Darker Side* (1963).

James Parton's description of Jefferson as "a young man of thirty-two who could calculate an eclipse, survey an estate, tie an artery, plan an edifice, try a cause, break a horse, dance a minuet, and play the violin" is, for all its incongruity, only a partial analysis of his enormous versatility. To catalogue the areas of his explorations is to list most of the principal categories of knowledge: law, government, history, mathematics, architecture, medicine, agriculture, languages and literature, education, music, philosophy, religion, and almost every branch of the natural sciences from astronomy through meteorology to zoology. This exploration of science and culture, much of which Jefferson enriched and all of which he gathered within the orbit of his lofty purpose, is apt to be misunderstood in a day when the vast accumulation of knowledge has made universal inquiry impossible and specialization inevitable. Yet his insatiable thirst for knowledge was neither dilettantism nor pedantry. Its most salient characteristic was its purposefulness.

"Jefferson aspired beyond the ambition of a nationality," wrote Henry Adams, "and embraced in his view the whole future of man." Nevertheless this grand object could be achieved only through proof that government by consent as inaugurated in the American republic was practicable, that the ancient philosophical concept was able to survive its test before the eyes of the world. Jefferson wrote to John Dickinson a few days after his inauguration as president:

A just and solid republican government maintained here will be a standing monument and example for the aim and imitation of the people of other countries; and I join with you in the hope and belief that they will see from our example that a free government is of all others the most energetic; that the enquiry which has been excited among the mass of mankind by our revolution and its consequences, will ameliorate the condition of man over a great portion of the globe. What a satisfaction have we in the contemplation of the benevolent effects of our efforts, compared with those of the leaders on the other side, who have discountenanced all advances in science as dangerous innovations, have endeavored to render philosophy and republicanism terms of reproach, to persuade us that man cannot be governed but by the rod, &c. I shall have the happiness of living and dying in the contrary hope.

What for us is a proof was for him still an untried hope. Its realization depended upon the character of the citizens of the Republic. Hope and satisfaction alike would disappear if the standing monument fell. Its strength and virtue lay in its quality as an example to be emulated. Its force among the nations of the earth would, therefore, be a moral force, and its empire would not be one held together by armies, fleets or commerce, but bound by the strong ties of an idea holding sway through the ever-increasing Empire of Liberty. This being so, every citizen faced a responsibility to sustain the example and keep it from failing.

None realized this more clearly or met the responsibility more heroically than Jefferson. The urgency that permeated all of his versatile explorations of the fields of knowledge, the unremitting effort to improve himself and his countrymen, betrayed, perhaps, a fear that the great experiment might fail; that the mass of the people here might not be, as he knew they were not in some parts of the world, ready for the trial. If he exhibited a missionary zeal in what he called the "holy republican gospel," it was no doubt because he felt it necessary to set an example for his fellow citizens as they in turn were obligated to set it before the world. This idea, that the successful establishment of a republic governed by the consent of the people would "ameliorate the condition of man over a great portion of the globe," was one to which, for all his versatile and ramifying inquiry, Jefferson gave a singleminded devotion.

If this was the central core of his purpose, there were other beliefs and propositions that necessarily and logically followed. The citizens of a republic, to meet their exacting responsibilities, would need to know their rights and duties. Therefore, the establishment of a system of universal public education was necessary—not a system leveling all to a drab and uniform mediocrity, but a system so organized as to bring forth the best minds and elevate them to that position in which their talents would be best employed for the general welfare. If self-government was to succeed, the voice of the people must determine their affairs. Therefore, all barriers to free inquiry must be removed, freedom of access to information protected, freedom of speech and of assembly safeguarded. Since ecclesiastical systems had historically marched hand in hand with governments of varying kinds, had often asserted a power transcending that of the state, and had frequently opposed the spread of science and learning, the individual right of conscience must be protected by separating church and state. Since science and the progress of society daily brought about changes in the economic, social and spiritual status of mankind, it was necessary to establish fundamental constitutions which could not be altered by any power other than the people—though these should never be regarded as sacred and unalterable, but adjustable to inevitably changing conditions.

These necessary consequences of Jefferson's central purpose were not, of course, his beliefs alone. Their lineage was already ancient when he appeared on the scene. Yet, although he and his compatriots merely inherited the legacy of the sixteenth century at one of those pivotal moments of history when concept and opportunity are joined, Jefferson was the preeminent spokesman for the idea that became, under his felicitous pen, both the fundamental act of union and an exalted expression of the national purpose.

In the face of the capital fact that the nation which began such a great experiment under such high ideals has become the oldest, the largest, and by all standards the wealthiest and most powerful republic on earth, it seems needless thus to restate the principles which moved its founders and its chief spokesman. Are we not already sufficiently aware of our deep-rooted beliefs and principles: have we not glorified the Declaration of Independence, sanctified the Bill of Rights, proclaimed our allegiance to their principles in coast-to-coast broadcasts, speeches, loyalty parades, prizes, Freedom Trains, pledges, and many other ways—so much so that our ears and eyes are benumbed by the very din? Surely. But when we escape at last the noise and the public spectacles and the fervid orators, we are assailed by skepticism. And we conclude that there are at least two compelling reasons for reexamining and restating the Jeffersonian philosophy.

First, the voices that echo his words are often discordant, contradictory voices, lacking conviction and creating the uneasy suspicion that the true purpose is not so much to understand and apply his principles as to clothe hidden motives and attitudes with a semblance of justification through the employment of his name and his words. The voices do not ring true. Second, though actuality and ideal seldom if ever coincide, there is such a wide discrepancy between what the voices proclaim and what the proclaimers perform as to raise grave suspicions about their understanding of Jeffersonian ideals, or their intent, or both. The voices echo the word, but the action does not so much embody a constructive attitude toward mankind as special pleading for a group of men or for a restricted and unstated group of special interests. The principles are emblazoned on the billboards, in the subways, in children's comics, in the housewife's opiate taken in the form of true-to-life drama synthesized in the radio booths, repeated endlessly and (we suspect) on the cynical conviction that anything reiterated enough will at last be believed. But the principles, in large part, are not the touchstones of action and policy. The voices and the actions do not square.

Let us listen first to the contradictory voices that today re-echo the words of Thomas Jefferson. On the far Left, which of course becomes at full circle the far Right, we find Jefferson's stalwart championship of individual freedom voiced by those who, when in power, destroy all liberty which the individual may claim as of natural right. Their particular darling among historical American figures is, of course, Thomas Paine, but Jefferson's words are soothing and useful to them on occasion. Jefferson, who preferred chaos to government if government could be had only at the price of individual liberty, is quoted, but the one the quoters have in mind is Robespierre, progenitor of the modern totalitarian, who would sacrifice all personal liberty for the sake of order in society. Far off to the Right are those who, calling themselves Jeffersonians, embrace the doctrines of States' Rights not, as Jefferson did, for the purpose of advancing and strengthening the Empire of Liberty, but for the purpose of buttressing the status quo. Nearer the center, but still on the Right, are those who find solace not only in Jefferson's defense of States' Rights, but also in his assertion that the best government is that which governs least. They use—or more particularly in the past fifteen years they have used—Jefferson's words, but their allegiance really goes back to Hamilton and Marshall. They speak, for the most part, from honest conviction; they regard themselves as the true protectors of society and its institutions; they believe fervently in what they consider the American concept of government. But in actuality they cannot accept Jefferson's fundamental promise: that the people may be trusted to govern themselves. Near the Center and extending slightly to the Left are Fair Deals and New Deals, claiming not only legitimate descent from Jefferson but also an authority to wear his mantle and to employ his precepts. Here there is a measure of justification. Certainly, insofar as general policy and attitudes are concerned, there is some identity of statement and intent. But all too often there is a wide and, at this moment, an apparently increasing discrepancy between preachment and practice. The voices *ought* to ring true, but they rarely do.

Somewhere in this wide spectrum of opinion and belief somebody is bound to be wrong. Jefferson might on occasion have agreed with any of these groups on a given proposition, but on the fundamental principles of government and the inalienable rights of the individual he could only have agreed with those who have confidence in the people and who support individual rights as against any arbitrary and irresponsible power existing anywhere.

The thoughtful citizen may well ask himself which of the self-styled spokesmen for the Jeffersonian point of view is entitled to the claim. Which merely employs his words to fit a preconceived purpose? Which endeavors honestly to understand Jefferson's meaning, to discover what in his philosophy is living and valid today, and to strive toward the application of those principles that are not obsolete? The question is not an idle one. In many respects it is the gravest question that a citizen can ask himself today. For if, as I believe, Woodrow Wilson was correct in saying that the immortality of Jefferson lay not in any of his achievements but in his attitude toward mankind; and if, as I also believe, though many thoughtful men do not, his philosophy of government and of the individual's rights and responsibilities have not been rendered obsolete, though the natural law upon which these were based no longer seems worthy of historical or philosophical support, then it is a matter of grave concern to the American people and to the world that the conflicting echoes of his voice should be judged. For we are in serious danger of having, if we are honest, to give a new answer to Crèvecoeur's famous question, "Who is this new man, this American?" In his day the answer would have been Jefferson's: He is a man self-confident and self-reliant; he believes himself capable of governing himself; he is weak in physical resources and national power, but his inner convictions are indomitable and will prevail. Today, we should have to say: He is a citizen of the most powerful nation on earth, but he is frightened—or at least his leaders in government, in the press, in the church, and even in the universities tell him that he *ought* to be frightened—by the specter of communism. And fright has caused him to do violence to the things which he once prized most dearly.

As Tocqueville said with prophetic insight more than a century ago, "No form or combination or social policy has yet been devised to make an energetic people of a community of pusillanimous and enfeebled citizens." The weakness we have to fear is not one of material resources, but of the moral fiber of our nationhood and its principles. I do not mean to imply that the Jeffersonian precepts, however applicable they may have been to the society in which he lived, should be respected today merely because he entertained them or because they were once applicable to our national welfare. "The earth belongs in usufruct to the living; and . . . the dead have neither powers nor rights over it," he once declared, and his entire career reflects a magnet-like steadiness of aim in supporting this revolutionary and radical proposition. He not only recognized the absolute necessity of change if his dream of substituting reason and justice for authority and superstition were ever to be realized, but his ceaseless, versatile activity throughout life was, for all its diverse ramifications, a single, purposeful, dedicated effort to bring change about (though not "for light and transient causes") by peaceful means if possible, by revolution if necessary.

Though a revolutionary in deed and in thought, and one who calmly accepted the inevitability of turbulence and conflict in a republic, he was, in a true sense, the greatest of conservatives. For that which he sought to conserve was, by comparison with the objects of all other forms of conservatism, such as to make them seem almost trivial and irrelevant. All other forms of conservatism sought, in the end, to protect custom or property or established order; he sought to conserve the rights of men, over which neither the customs of society nor the property of individuals nor the order of established institutions nor any other earthly power should take precedence, since all found their ultimate justification in man who had formed society and created these things for the better protection of his rights. On all other matters his moral philosophy was relativistic; on *this* he was inflexible. "Nothing, then," he declared, "is unchangeable but the inherent and inalienable rights of man." Each generation should face its new problems in its own way, unfettered by the dead hand of the past. But none could justly or with impunity violate the basic assumption on which the state rested.

We may at once, then, dismiss the clamors of the extreme Right and the extreme Left, however much they may quote Jefferson in justification of their purposes. For by no stretch of reason or of the imagination could his lofty purpose be made commensurate with the kind of authoritarianism exhibited in these quarters. Indeed, we may dismiss all of those groups who appeal to the name of Jefferson either for the purpose of maintaining the status quo or for the purpose of returning to the past, so long as these purposes do not aim at the preservation of the "inherent and inalienable rights of man." They may quote Jefferson's words about the folly of directing agriculture from Washington; about the danger of a national debt and of high taxes; about the perfection of that government which governs least. There are many bold and quotable words on these subjects which, superficially, seem to lend the weight of Jefferson's authority to such a position. The words are the same, but the discordant voices quoting them are as out of key with the world of today as the pony express would be. Clearly, the government that governs least would in this twentieth century of corporate power be the worst possible form of government. I feel sure that Jefferson could detect the corporate abuse of the right to life, liberty and the pursuit of happiness, and would oppose it quite as readily as he did similar abuses by government in the eighteenth century.

James Bryce, half a century ago, observed that in Jefferson's day the restraining hand of authority was laid upon the individual by government, and that Jefferson and his contemporaries made the mistake of considering "the pernicious channels in which selfish propensities had been flowing for those propensities themselves, which were sure to find new channels when the old had been destroyed." Yet Bryce himself erred in thinking, with many today, that Jefferson feared only the power of government; that he set form above substance, channel above propensity. As for his attitude toward the abuses of power outside government, we need only recall his impassioned indictment of ecclesiastical authority, and of the power of manufacturing and commercial interests. As for government, it was what he called the "desolating pestilence" of power and its corrupting and abusive quality that he attacked, not its form. Proof of this is to be found in the Declaration of Independence itself: one of the self-evident truths there proclaimed was that "whenever *any form* of government becomes destructive of" the inalienable rights of man, the people could "institute new government, laying its foundations on such principles, and organizing its powers *in such form*, as to them shall seem most likely to effect their safety and happiness.

The voices on the Left and the Right are apt, like most of us, to read these exalted words in the context of 1776 and in reference to the single aim of justifying independence as against the supposed tyranny of George III. But they are for us now, as they were for Jefferson throughout life, not words to be remembered from the past as applicable to an obsolete purpose, but rather as a perpetual, living affirmation of an unalterable right, accessible at any time, in our day or in the distant future, to a people who will "suffer, while evils are sufferable" but who will not endure the intolerable. They are, of course, dangerous and inflammable words, useful to the subversive as well as to the reactionary, but their danger is a calculated risk and not regarded as a danger at all by those who, like Jefferson, regard the people as the safest, though not always the wisest, repository of power. They are also words of warning. They warn those who stand at the head of government—as well as those who represent economic, ecclesiastical, military, racial or other groups of society and who endeavor to bend government to their wishes—that the limits of sufferable evils must not be transcended.

These limits are being approached. The warning flags have been run up, but they have been disregarded. In 1948, despite the fearsome predictions of those whose preoccupation it is to instill a sense of fear, the people gave an overwhelming demonstration of the fact that they are not and have no intention of following after the false gods of communism. On top of this came the result of the loyalty investigation in government. Of the more than two million persons employed by government and investigated, less than one one-hundredth of 1 percent were found to be suspected of disloyalty. In the face of these irrefutable demonstrations of the sense and loyalty of the people of this nation, men may still be accused of disloyalty, may be denied the right to be confronted by the accuser, and may thereby stand in jeopardy of loss of reputation or livelihood. The highest legal officer of the government still possesses the power to say what organizations may be regarded as subversive, and citizens belonging to them may be placed under suspicion, investigated secretly, and made the object of humiliation and calumny. Elected representatives may still, though servants of the people, assume to themselves the supreme arrogance of defining for the American people what constitutes good American behavior, compounding insult, injury and denial of the principles they profess. State after state has required oaths of loyalty to America—oaths the real object of which is the illusory hope of exposing loyalty to Russia. Textbooks are being banned , writers boycotted, libraries told what can be safely placed before readers, teachers investigated, not for the competence of their teaching, but for the danger of their ideas. As the supreme evidence of confused thinking, an honored liberal journal has been struck from the list of school libraries in our greatest city, not because what it published was asserted to be untrue or libelous, but because three articles were said to be offensive to a particular church. These things, and more, are done often in the name of Thomas Jefferson, though by no tenet in the entire canon of his faith can any suppression of access to information, any denial of freedom of opinion, or any compulsory affirmation of belief be justified.

Despite the doctrine of fear on which moral, political, economic and other issues are being resolved, a few courageous voices re-echo the faith that Jefferson expressed when we experienced a similar wave of hysteria in the years 1798-1800. They believe, with him, that government by the people is the most energetic, though not necessarily the most orderly form; that the people may be trusted when left free to decide; and that those who offer false and seditious counsels should be allowed to "stand as monuments of the freedom with which error of opinion can be tolerated where reason is left free to combat it."

If I know anything about Thomas Jefferson and his principles, I believe these voices to be authentic echoes of his voice. They are honest, courageous, influential voices. They will not be silenced by the demand for conformity or for articulate hatred. They will grow in eloquence and influence. But they will influence only the spirit of the nation; they cannot yet determine policy.

For our policy as a nation is determined in the contest for power. This global struggle has brought forth two immense dangers, each of which threatens a betrayal of the principles for which Jefferson spoke. Internally, we profess that tolerance that is a necessary and essential element of society under a republic, but at the same time we are doing our utmost to compel uniformity, to level dissent, to suppress unorthodox ideas, and to organize a hysterical and potentially tyrannical public sentiment around the false proposition that the thing we hate can be eliminated if only we are unanimous in our hatred. Externally, we are in danger of forgetting, in our effort to win the peaceful nations of the earth to our side, that the world at this particular juncture may be more critically in need of moral leadership than of vast supplies of machines, arms, material goods and extensions of dollar credits. Either course, long continued, could destroy forever the kind of free republic composed of free men that Jefferson envisaged.

The compulsory uniformity now demanded of men in public life is the very antithesis of what Jefferson contemplated. For, as was observed by a wise philosopher a century before Jefferson, where there is uniformity, there also is tyranny. The temptation to adopt a new kind of imperialism which the mere possession of power brings with it may prove in the long run to be the undoing of ourselves as well as those who seem to stand in our path. At any rate, in pursuing either course, let us not malign the name of Jefferson by attempting to identify his ideals with our actions. Let those who would compel uniformity at home, who would deny the right of dissent to some, who would control our thinking and channel it in one single direction, who would decide our national issues by reference to the acts of another nation rather than by the principles we affirm, who would use our vast strength to mold and direct the governments of other nations to our desires, attempting to impose an international conformity similar to that now threatening the life of individuals and their freedom of choice—let all these reflect upon Jefferson's final affirmation of the meaning of American independence and of the establishment of a new nation: "May it be to the world what I believe it will be (to some parts sooner, to others later, but finally to all) the signal of arousing men to burst the chains under which Monkish ignorance and superstition had persuaded them to bind themselves and to assume the blessings and security of self-government. The form which we have substituted restores the right to the unbounded exercise of reason and freedom of opinion. All eyes are opened or opening to the rights of man."

We have had proof enough, in our lifetime, that all eyes are *not* opened to the rights of man. We have had proof enough that the right to the "unbounded exercise of reason and freedom of opinion" has indeed been bounded, and has in many respects been suspended. But, dismaying though this is, the greatest of tragedies in this conflict would be for this nation, which first erected a monument to stand as an example of man's capacity to protect his rights by a government of his own ordering, to deny its own birthright. The evidence that we are in danger of doing so, at home and abroad, is all too obvious. The final irony is that, in committing violence upon our professed principles, we should endeavor to justify our shameful default by appealing to the name of the man who was the author of that statement of our national ideal whose words we parrot while our acts desecrate its spirit.

Part III
Ideas for a Constitutional Democracy

15
The Great Mr. Locke: America's Philosopher, 1783-1861

Merle Curti

Broad reflection upon the course of American thought from the early eighteenth century onward brings one inevitably to consider the uses of John Locke. His writings, as well as the abridgments and popularizations made of them, became a significant part of any serious collection of books in the colonies or later in the new republic. Locke's philosophy and psychology (which are almost indistinguishable) and his political thought worked their way to the center of the American Enlightenment. Lockean principles were embedded in the development of New England Unitarianism, and it was from these principles that the Transcendentalists revolted in the 1830s because of their distaste for the Lockean view of the nature of man. John Locke's influence continued in nineteenth-century American college curricula; it was modified, but still germane, in Scottish common-sense realism, which became the established academic philosophy. Lockean influences carried into the teaching practices of American schools, into constitutional history, and into the growth of experimental psychology. There is still much for historians to do with these themes. Until they do, this essay by Merle Curti will remain the standard charting of specific appeals to Locke by writers and public men.

For further reading: *Louis Hartz, *The Liberal Tradition in America* (1955); Marvin Meyers, "Louis Hartz, *The Liberal Tradition in America:* An Appraisal," Leonard Krieger, "A View from the Farther Shore," Harry V. Jaffa, "Conflicts within the Idea of the Liberal Tradition," and Louis Hartz, "Comment," all in *Comparative Studies in Society and History,* 5 (1962-1963), 261-284, 365-377; Wilson Smith, "William Paley's Theological Utilitarianism in America," *William and Mary Quarterly,* 11 (July 1954), 402-424; *Robert Green McCloskey, *American Conservatism in the Age of Enterprise, 1865-1910* (1951), chap. 1.

Although no one has seriously questioned the great influence of John Locke on American thought during the later part of the eighteenth century, students of

Reprinted by permission of the author and the Henry E. Huntington Library from *The Huntington Library Bulletin,* no. 11 (April 1937), pp. 107-144, 147-151. All footnotes but one have been omitted.

American intellectual history have assumed by and large that his ideas were for the most part replaced during the first half of the nineteenth century by those of other philosophers. The purpose of this paper is, first, to test this assumption and, second, to explain the findings.

The importance of the first problem becomes clear when the extent of Locke's influence on Americans of the late eighteenth century is taken into account. Political thought both before and during the American Revolution was profoundly affected by the *Two Treatises on Civil Government*. Otis, John and Samuel Adams, and other leading revolutionists quoted "the great Mr. Locke" reverently; Franklin, Hamilton, and Jefferson read and praised him. His natural-rights philosophy, including the doctrine that all government rests on the consent of the governed and may be overthrown by revolution if it persistently violates individual life, liberty, and property, was incorporated in the Declaration of Independence itself. The similarity between his social and economic doctrines and those of the framers of the Constitution has likewise been pointed out. However, Locke had nearly as great an impact on theology as on political and social thought. Furthermore, the influence of his treatise on education should not be overlooked. His justification of religious toleration, his rationalistic theology, and his conception of the plastic character of human nature were all dear to America's children of the Enlightenment. It is scarcely too much to say, even when the importance of other thinkers is taken into account, that Locke was America's philosopher during the Revolutionary period.

Yet it has been generally assumed that, when the nation found itself torn by "the second American Revolution" in 1861, Locke's name was not cherished as it had been three-quarters of a century earlier. Indeed, even a superficial inspection of the conventional literature of the fifties indicates that his authority no longer figured in any lively way in theological discussions and that his "mental philosophy" had long been under attack, and, if we follow leading students of American philosophy, had been largely replaced by the Scotch school of "common sense," French eclecticism, and German idealism. Locke's political ideas, according to authorities on the history of American political thought, no longer enjoyed their pre-eminence.

The belief that Locke's influence during these seventy-five years was a waning one is probably due to a failure to examine sufficient evidence. Historians of ideas in America have too largely based their conclusions on the study of formal treatises. But formal treatises do not tell the whole story. In fact, they sometimes give a quite false impression, for such writings are only a fraction of the records of intellectual history. For every person who laboriously wrote a systematic treatise, dozens touched the subject in a more or less casual fashion. Sometimes the fugitive essays of relatively obscure writers influenced the systematizers and formal authors quite as much as the works of better-known men. The influence of a thinker does not pass from one major writer to another without frequently being transformed, or dissipated, or compressed in the hands of a whole series of people who responded to the thinker and his ideas. It is reasonably certain, moreover, that in the America of the early nineteenth century ephemeral writings, widely scattered as they were in pamphlets, tracts, and essays, reached a much wider audience and are often more reliable evidence of the climate of opinion than the more familiar works to which historians of ideas have naturally turned. The student of the vitality and modification of ideas may well direct his attention, then, toward out-of-the-way sermons, academic addresses, Fourth of July orations, and casual guides and essays.* By examining such irregular channels for the expression of ideas, it may be possible to learn to what extent Locke's ideas survived in any vital way during the period between the American Revolution and the Civil War.

Whether, on the one hand, Locke's ideas largely gave way to those of competing philosophers, or, on the other, they survived in some form, there is need for explanation. To a considerable extent students of intellectual history have sought to account for the disappearance of ideas, by assuming that they were supplanted by concepts that were either more valid or that in some way better fitted the spirit of newer times. This, however, is too vague an explanation to be very satisfactory.

The doctrine that men seek ideas to justify their activities and to promote their interests, that they think as they live, is hardly startling. If this is true it should follow that the vitality of ideas depends at least in part upon the effectiveness with which they function, on their usefulness to the interests which they serve. Ideas might be expected, then, to flourish when they answer a need and to wane when that need is no longer urgent. Although it is now almost thirty years since John Dewey asserted that thinking can best be explained in terms of functional relationships to human problems and needs, students of intellectual history have for the most part been little influenced by this concept. Nor have they been much affected by the still older but related contention that ideas are always associated with particular interests, and that the latter, broadly defined, have a way, in the never ending conflict with antagonistic interests, of adopting, modifying, and even inventing ideas serviceable to themselves. Before attempting to appraise this hypothesis, let us test it by finding out what light it throws on the survival or the disappearance of Locke's ideas in the three-quarters of a century following the American Revolution. In short, one should be able to determine what interests or groups challenged Locke's ideas, and for what reasons; what groups defended his teachings, and why; and what happened as a result of this contest.

Locke's ideas are, of course, closely interrelated and not always consistent. They can nevertheless be grouped, for present purposes, into fairly well defined categories, such as education, religion and theology, mental philosophy, and political and economic theory.

We may begin by considering the fate of Locke's educational theories which were embodied in *Some Thoughts Concerning Education* (1693). Horace Mann regarded this treatise as superior to all Locke's other works, and it was therefore with the more regret that the father of the common-school revival in Massachusetts, writing in 1840, felt compelled to admit that the great book had been "almost wholly neglected and forgotten." A study of contemporary educational literature confirms Mann's observation. Locke's *Thoughts* had been reprinted in the United States but once in all this period, and an examination of the leading educational periodicals

*The Huntington Library is particularly rich in this type of fugitive material. I have examined there some five hundred academic addresses, Fourth of July orations, and election sermons.

I wish to express my indebtedness to Professor Marjorie Nicolson and to Dr. Fulmer Mood for their contributions to my thinking on the problem of materials in intellectual history. I am also grateful to members of the staff of the Huntington Library for valuable comments on this paper.

and reports reveals that they mentioned Locke only very occasionally in the period between 1800 and 1860. Even when he was cited it was chiefly to buttress some particular school program: for instance, the Boston School Committee in 1837 quoted his recommendation that music be taught in the schools, on the ground that he had defined recreation as "easing the weary part by change of business" and that music admirably served such a purpose. Not until 1859 did Henry Barnard's *American Journal of Education* devote an article to Locke's pedagogy, and this, characteristically, was merely a translation of a critique of his educational theories from the pen of Karl von Raumer, a German whose word carried much weight among American schoolmen.

This apparent neglect of Locke's *Thoughts Concerning Education* is all the more interesting in view of the educational awakening that took place between 1825 and 1860. To say that the educational essay was, unlike his other writings, unknown even to eighteenth-century Americans, is inaccurate, because there is considerable evidence pointing to the familiarity of not a few colonial Americans with the work. To American children of the Enlightenment there was, indeed, a strong appeal in many of the educational doctrines it laid down. Liberal spokesmen of the middle class, which attached great value to enterprise, had welcomed Locke's emphasis on the importance of a sound body and on wisdom in managing affairs. As active, practical people, they had also relished Locke's insistence on the training of the senses rather than the memory; as critics of many sanctions of the past they had likes his stressing of reason rather than authority. Benjamin Franklin and Joseph Priestley had quoted Locke and were influenced by his educational theories: Franklin's *Sketch of an English School* reflected the utilitarianism of Locke, while Priestley helped to popularize his criticism of indoctrination, a practice which Locke had said was little more than the inculcation of error and prejudice in the name of imposing "right principles" on immature minds.

If Locke's educational theories were favorably known to liberal representatives of America's important middle class in the late eighteenth century, the absence of direct reference to them in the great quantity of educational literature in the first half of the nineteenth century is the more noteworthy. It must be remembered that Locke favored private rather than public education—his treatise, in fact, had been written primarily for tutors in the families of well-to-do gentry and merchants. Hence the groups in nineteenth-century American which stood for mass education at public expense naturally found little in Locke to give them aid or prestige. But those who adhered to the older concept of family or tutorial instruction, who went on thinking of education as a private matter, could continue to derive sustenance from Locke. And they did. An examination, not of the formal treatises and reports of the great leaders in the public-school revival but of the casual, fugitive guides for parental and tutorial education for middle-class families, shows that the ideas of Locke remained influential. . . .

Locke's educational precepts, as well as his "mental philosophy," were spread broadcast in the widely read *Improvement of the Mind*, by Isaac Watts, the famous English noncomformist writer of hymns and moral guides. This work, known familiarly as "Watts on the Mind," was almost universally used in the private academies and seminaries that sprang up so rapidly in the early years of the republic. It would, indeed, be hard to overstate the influence of Watts's popularization of Locke among middle-class Americans who patronized these institutions of learning.

However, it was not only through these informal pedagogical guides in the domestic circles of the well-to-do, and popular texts in the private seminaries, that Locke's educational ideas survived. While, as we have seen, the champions of the public schools did not find Locke's emphasis on private education useful, indirectly they were subject to his influence, for in going to school to Rousseau, Fellenberg, and Pestalozzi they went to school to Locke. In their emphasis on health, learning through doing, and character training, these men were reflecting Locke's teachings. Above all, they shared his faith in the possibility of modifying human nature by changing the environment of youth. It was this faith which inspired American democrats with devotion to education as the best means of insuring the success of their republican experiment and of solving social ills. Rousseau, Pestalozzi, and the French materialists, and back of them Locke, were the intellectual fathers of the American faith in education as the road to Utopia.

If one asks why the fathers of the common-school revival during the 1820s and 1830s turned to Continental writers rather than to Locke himself, an explanation has already been suggested in part. For inspiration and guidance, the Horace Manns, the Henry Barnards, and their colleagues quite naturally looked to the Continent, and especially to Germany, where a state system of public schools for all children had been put on a firm footing. They also cast their eyes on Switzerland, where the schools of Fellenberg and Pestalozzi, which combined learning with the doing of practical tasks, seemed particularly congenial to Americans who saw the value of an immediately useful education for a new society engaged in building a physical civilization in the wilderness. Locke, who had favored the private education of children of the middle class and who believed that a minimum of instruction in the principles of religion and trade was sufficient for the rest, seemed to have little to offer to sponsors of a truly democratic and publicly supported school system. So they did not quote him, but contented themselves with borrowing from the Continental writers that portion of his educational theory which did fit their needs. In this manner the ideas of Locke, insofar as they served interests or filled needs, continued to live on different levels and in different ways. On the one hand, they persisted directly in the casual manuals for private education; on the other, indirectly through the adoption of Lockean precepts which, combined with precepts of Continental educators, met the demands of practical-minded leaders of the public-school revival.

Turning from the educational to the theological doctrines of Locke, one recalls, first of all, that he was indirectly among the fathers of both English and American deism. In various writings, notably in *The Reasonableness of Christianity* and in *An Essay for the Understanding of St. Paul's Epistles* as well as in his *Letters on Toleration*, Locke subjected the tenets of Christian theology to reason and maintained that natural knowledge was more certain than miracles and revelation. These writings, like the *Essay Concerning Human Understanding* (1690), tended to break down barriers between the world of matter and the world of spirit, between man and nature—in short, tended to make it less difficult for men to believe that they themselves "correspond with the general harmony of Nature." Although Locke maintained that reason and experience are confirmed by divine revelation, his whole approach paved the way for the later and more thoroughgoing deists. For his God was, after all, a constitutional God, who did not trespass too much on the daily concerns of his creatures. Moreover, the *Essay Concerning Human Understanding* likewise fed the springs of deism, inasmuch as its plea for reliance on sensory experience and reflection, rather than on innate ideas and the ''mysterious,'' tended to undermine the traditional sanctions of orthodoxy. Locke's position was, in many respects, anticipatory of that maintained a hundred years later by the early Unitarians.

Indeed, it is clear that Locke and his disciples, particularly Samuel Clarke, explicitly influenced American Unitarians from Charles Chauncy to Joseph Buckminster, Joseph Priestley, Charles Follen, William Ellery Channing, and Andrews Norton. Locke's religious writings, including his *Letters on Toleration,* were frequently cited in the discussions of liberal Trinitarian as well as Unitarian clergymen, in their efforts to defend their position against both orthodox criticism and ''atheistic'' attacks. . . . Locke's writings were regarded by conservative Unitarians as a first line of defense when the transcendentalists raised the flag of revolt. On the other hand, the left-wing deists who popularized the cult—men like the militant, fearless Elihu Palmer—drew heavily on Locke, as well as on Holbach, Hume, and Bolingbroke. Palmer wrote in his *Principles of Human Nature*:

> *It was not the discovery of physical truths alone that bore relation to the revelation of the human species; it was reserved for Locke, and other powerful minds, to unfold the eternal structure of the intellectual world–explain the operations of the human structure of the human understanding–explore the sources of thought, and unite sensation and intellect in the same subject, and in a manner cognizable by the human faculties. Locke has, perhaps, done more than Newton, to subvert the credit of* divine Revelation.

In the forties and fifties, however, the religious writings of Locke no longer played a notable role in theological discussions. There was a variety of reasons for their decline in favor. Popular deism, reaching its high-water mark at the turn of the century, had been identified by conservatives with the excesses of the French Revolution. Discredited, it provided the soil for a conventional religious reaction which expressed itself, in part, in the evangelical revivals that swept the country. In such a climate of opinion and feeling, the rationalism of Locke lost its influence, for advocates of evangelical religion found no comfort in its cold, reasoned, apologetic treatises. Circuit riders, camp meetings, and revivals answered the emotional needs of pioneers and ill-adjusted city people far better than any kind of rationalism. The new conservative religious attitude toward Locke was well expressed in an article in the *Encyclopedia Americana* of 1836. In attempting to analyze the human soul, ''as an anatomist proceeds in investigating a body, piece by piece,'' Locke had, according to this article, unintentionally supported materialism, for he had suggested that God could, by his omnipotence, make matter capable of thinking—a doctrine considered dangerous to orthodox belief by virtue of its identification of God and mind. And when at length Locke's psychology and philosophy came to be rejected by a growing number of intellectuals, it was natural for liberal defenders of the faith to turn to writers, like De Wette, Baur, and Schleiermacher, whose basic philosophical assumptions were more congenial. . . .

Locke's influence on American philosophy and psychology has been profound. His leading theories in these fields—theories which at the beginning of the eighteenth century had been considered so subversive that Calvinistic Yale warned its students against the *Essay Concerning Human Understanding*—gradually made their way in academic circles. Samuel Johnson, a tutor at Yale, broke the ground at least as early as 1719; and Jonathan Edwards, in his fifteenth year, read and was deeply influenced by the *Essay*. Even after Samuel Johnson became a disciple of Berkeley, he recommended Locke to his pupils at King's College. Certainly by 1800 Locke dominated philosophic studies in American colleges.

In 1829, however, President Marsh of the University of Vermont could write to Coleridge that, whereas Locke had formerly been taught in colleges, Stewart, Campbell, and Brown had replaced him. Although Locke was restored at Harvard in 1833 by Joel Giles and used at least until 1841, the statement of President Marsh was substantially true.

Yet this fact need not be interpreted to mean that Locke's influence thereby came to an end. In 1830 a generation of young men trained by his *Essay* was just beginning its active life. Moreover, many of the American texts on mental and moral philosophy which were widely used in colleges embodied ample portions of Locke's philosophical treatise. . . . It will be recalled, also, that the widely read "Watts on the Mind" was a popularization of Locke. In conceiving of mind as possessing functions, powers, or faculties of behaving, such as memory, observation, and reason, it provided the basis of "faculty psychology." Implicit in this system of psychology was the belief in the desirability of formal discipline through concrete experiences and particular mental disciplines. Less used texts in mental philosophy, which were for the most part eclectic, seldom failed to pay high tribute to Locke and to draw heavily from his *Essay*.

Thus it was that an entire generation of Americans knew Locke's mental philosophy better than that of any other writer. The *Essay Concerning Human Understanding* was considered indispensable. . . . Even after it was subjected to frontal attacks, new champions, such as Frederick Beasley, Alexander Everett, Andrews Norton, and Francis Bowen, rose up to defend it. That the demand for it continued is borne out by the chronological distribution of the twelve American editions between the Revolution and the Civil War. So much, in fact, was the *Essay* a household phrase that James Kirke Paulding could make one of his characters in a novel of 1832 declare that Locke's analysis of the human understanding was the only one which the human understanding could comprehend. If further evidence of the persistence of Locke's philosophy be needed, a goodly number of references to it in academic addresses and similar fugitive literature could be cited. It is, in truth, the frequency of the Lockean assumptions in this sort of material which provides the most convincing proof of the pervasiveness and tenacity of Locke's philosophy.

What was back of this vogue for "the great Mr. Locke" during the first three or four decades of the republic? During a period of democratic faith in the future, in an age in which it was necessary to take an optimistic view of the possibilities of the

American experiment, a plastic conception of human nature was highly desirable if not indispensable. So those who were eager to demonstrate the possibility of a successful democracy welcomed Locke's concept that man is largely a creature of his experience, of his environment in the larger sense. If liberal, humane, and democratic influences could be guaranteed through proper training and institutions, the highest potentialities of mankind might be realized; then a democracy might function satisfactorily. . . .

Closely paraphrasing the essential ideas in the *Essay Concerning Human Understanding*, Abraham Holmes, of New Bedford, declared in an oration of 1796 that all social happiness depends on proper early experience, and that for the first time in history America, having thrown off tyranny, had established equal rights and individual freedom—had, in short, provided the proper environment for realizing man's potentialities. Have a care for public worship, universities, libraries, literary societies, and similar conditioning institutions, Holmes admonished, and the injurious and shameful practices which have long been a disgrace to the very name of human nature will disappear. Another champion of democracy, Tunis Wortman, a New York lawyer and publicist, likewise denounced the view that man's vices are stamped on his original constitution. He attributed the evils hitherto so destructive to human happiness to the errors and abuses that had inhered in political arrangements—that is, in monarchical and aristocratic institutions. He cited Locke to prove that man was not born with innate ideas, but that nine out of ten parts of a man's traits are what they are, good or evil, useful or not, by virtue of experience and training. Wortman insisted that, once human nature was thought of as malleable, there was no need for despairing of the ability of men to govern themselves intelligently and for the public good. Moreover, these were not lone voices, as any thorough investigation of the out-of-the-way literature of the early republic proves.

Such a picture of human nature was indispensable to certain groups and interests in the first decades of the nineteenth century. The period was one of rapid migration from rural areas to mill towns and cities, with consequent social poverty, vice, and general degradation. In the Old World, republican institutions were generally regarded as utterly incapable of dealing with these new evils or even with the most traditional problems of government. It was a period when the eighteenth-century vision of the heavenly city, temporarily beclouded by the chaos and fear of the French Revolution, was nevertheless seizing the imaginations of tender-minded Americans, who became pioneer exponents of the gospel of social progress. Locke's conception of human nature, differing as it did from the Calvinistic idea of predestination, was good ammunition for the humanitarian and reform groups which began, in the second decade of the last century, to form associations to uproot war, outlaw intemperance, and abolish slavery, poverty, and every social ill. The underlying psychology of Frances Wright, Robert Owen, and the Utopian Socialists is essentially that of "the great Mr. Locke." Although reformers did not find Locke's philosophy and psychology adequate for all their purposes, its importance to crusading humanitarianism can scarcely be overemphasized.

These three or four decades after the American Revolution were also years when the individual was being rapidly released from traditional ties. The industrial revolution was disrupting the system of apprenticeship and undermining the family as an economic unit, and both were still further thrown out of joint by the lure of free lands in the West. As a result the individual was more and more coming to think of himself as a free agent. In a relatively limited cultural environment the necessity of self-education was likewise good gospel. Thus Locke's philosophy, emphasizing the doctrine of individualism, the idea that man, within limits, was a free agent, ministered to the needs and desires of a people in such a time and on such a stage. As Professor [Carl] Becker has observed, men in general are influenced by writings that clarify their own notions, that suggest ideas which they are prepared to accept. In other words, ideas thrive according to the importance of the function that they serve.

American society during the first half of the nineteenth century, however, was by no means homogeneous. The wide variety of interests and needs that were in conflict with each other cannot even be suggested here. But one major contest in our intellectual life demands emphasis. By the early thirties the Northeast was becoming so rapidly industrialized that, to many, America seemed to stand for canals and railways, wharves and factories. From this industrialization sensitive souls drew back in horror and dismay, for it seemed to them that the mechanical trend in American civilization, the preoccupation with "curious mechanical contrivances and adaptations of matter, which it discovered by means of its telescopes, microscopes, dissections and other mechanical aids," was destroying human and spiritual values. And was not all this mechanism in our industrial organization, in morals, and in politics, the inevitable and direct result of a sensationalist philosophy which denied the primary intuitions of the soul? Was not the solution for such misfortunes to be found, in part at least, in a repudiation of Locke and the empiricists and in drinking deeply of the spiritual nourishment of the Cambridge Platonists, Coleridge, and the German idealists?

Some of these protestants against mechanism in American life, moreover, were sensitive to the social injustices seemingly inherent in the new mechanical order—injustices patent enough, they felt, to anyone whose eyes were not blinded. The empirical and sensationist philosophy, by virtue of the plastic character with which it endowed human nature, was sometimes used to support democratic ideals. But by 1840 a fresh generation of New Englanders saw that it could be used against the doctrine that all men are created equal. As Jonathan Saxton, farmer and transcendentalist, put it:

Sensation, then, does not, and by its own terms cannot, see man but in his outward condition, and his personal and social rights are such only, as can be logically inferred from the circumstances in which he is placed. Whatever is, in relation to society, is right, simply because it is. . . . [Sensation] finds man everywhere divided into high and low in social position, and concludes that gradation of ranks is of divine appointment. . . . This philosophy looks calmly on, and bids these ignorant, starving, scourged, and bleeding millions take comfort, for their lot is ordained by destiny that though the earth spreads out provisions liberally for all her children, the arrangements of nature would be defeated, if all should partake of them. . . . As this philosophy begets skepticism and infidelity in religion, so it has no faith, and no promise for man in his social and political relations. [1841]

Unwilling to reject faith in equality, which seemed divine and transcendent, some radicals thus felt forced to repudiate the whole philosophy of empiricism and sensationism and to fall back on that of innate ideas. For if the idea of equality of men did not originate in experience, if indeed it was refuted by the facts of observation and historical investigation, then it must be an innate idea, an inborn truth, having its validity in an appeal to "the universal spiritual intuitions of Humanity." There can be no doubt, as a study of the *Dial*, and more particularly of a vast quantity of random literature, indicates, that this social dissatisfaction with the new industrial order and all its abuses and inequalities and material emphasis led many to reject Locke's philosophy, or upheld them in their rejection of it. . . .

Abolitionists likewise found the doctrine of innate ideas more congenial than the teachings of Locke. When confronted by the argument of empiricists that the slaves needed experience for the proper use of liberty, William Hosmer insisted that liberty was both an innate idea and an innate capacity in every human being. "Liberty being the birth-right of man, the natural and normal condition of his existence, all the preparation he needs for its enjoyment is born with him. He gets his fitness for liberty, as he gets his hands and his feet—not by education, but by inheritance. It is born with him, and constitutes a part of his being." In short, it appeared to social reformers that the work of regeneration might best go forward with an anti-Lockean psychology, for Locke's political tenets were still held in high regard.

The revolt—for such it was—did not, of course, begin all at once. Even during his college days (1794-98) William Ellery Channing had been "saved," as he later put it, from Locke's philosophy by the reading of Dr. Richard Price's *Dissertations:* "He gave me the doctrine of ideas, and during my life I have written the words Love, Right, etc., with a capital." Price also gave Channing a zeal for humanitarianism and social reform. It was in Channing's study, in fact, that the peace movement was launched, and he became an early critic of slavery and of unfettered property rights.

One of the first explicit signs of the revolt against Locke was Sampson Reed's "commencement part" at Harvard in 1821—an address which young Ralph Waldo Emerson, an undergraduate, heard with eagerness. "The science of the human soul," declared Reed, who was already on the way to becoming a Swedenborgian, "must change with its subject. Locke's mind will not always be the standard of metaphysics. Had we a description of it in its present state, it would make a very different book from 'Locke on the Human Understanding.' " The reaction against Locke was indeed in the air. Four years later James Freeman Clarke, entering Harvard, read Coleridge and his American interpreter, President James Marsh of the University of Vermont, and was thereby confirmed in his longing for a "higher philosophy" than that of Locke and Hartley, from whom he had taken his first philosophical lessons in his grandfather's library. To use Clarke's own words, "Something within me revolted at all such attempts to explain soul out of sense, deducing mind from matter, or tracing the origin of ideas to nerves, vibrations, and vibratiuncles." Coleridge at this point rescued him. Accepting the English poet's "distinction between the reason and the understanding judging by sense," he lived again in the realization that knowledge begins *with* experience although it does not come *from* experience. At the Harvard Divinity School, Clarke and other candidates for the Unitarian ministry came in contact, after 1830, with Henry Ware, the younger, who led his students to Coleridge, Goethe, the Platonists, and church mystics, thus delivering them from "the wooden philosophy" of John Locke, before which as undergraduates they had been made to bend the knee.

The same revolt may be found in Emerson prior to the writing of his classic essay on Nature and his Divinity School address (1837). On July 4, 1834, at the age of thirty-one, he wrote in his *Journal* that Locke had given him little—that he was much more indebted to persons of lesser names. Locke is as surely the "influx of decomposition as Bacon and the Platonists [are] of growth," he wrote much later. In his essay, *The Transcendentalist* (1842), he went even further in his repudiation of the sensationist philosophy of Locke and in his hearty acceptance of Kant's "imperative forms"—intuitions of the mind itself through which experience is acquired. . . .

It was not only, however, from the neo-Platonists, from Coleridge, and from Kantian idealists that the American critics of Locke derived inspiration and a substitute philosophy. The eclecticism of Victor Cousin and Jouffroy was introduced by H. G. Linberg, Orestes A. Brownson, George Ripley, and the Reverend Caleb Sprague Henry. In this group the most unflagging efforts came from Henry, a man of personal magnetism, vivacity, and literary enthusiasm. . . . In 1834 he translated Cousin's *Elements of Psychology*, a treatise destined to become celebrated in American philosophical circles by reason of its criticism of Locke's *Essay Concerning Human Understanding*. Henry was attracted to Cousin by virtue of what appeared to him to be the most thorough, clear, and convincing criticism of Locke that had ever been made. This refutation, he believed, would establish the very foundations of morality and religion against the subversive principles of Locke and his disciple, [William] Paley. Cousin's doctrine of spontaneous reason (according to which reason, when uncontrolled by the will or when left free to develop undirected by the voluntary faculty, always apprehended things as they are) exerted considerable influence on the transcendentalists.

The appearance of the first edition of Henry's translation of Cousin's *Elements of Psychology*—there were four editions in all—stirred up much opposition, especially in Princeton circles, where Locke had not yet been replaced by the Scottish school. An article in the *Princeton Review*, early in 1839, attacked Henry and Cousin as "infidel expounders" of Locke who "sneered" at the great master for not having discovered a hypocritical way of making Christianity easily palatable to the critically minded. Cousin was represented as a mainstay of fatalism, as hostile to divine revelation in the Scriptures, as a pantheist, and even as an atheist who denied the personality of God and the essential difference between right and wrong.

In his preface to the third edition (1841), Henry replied to his Princeton critics by charging them with having displayed superficial and insufficient knowledge both of Cousin and of the German idealists with whom they confused the French philosopher. In fact Cousin, insisted Henry, made freedom of the will a fundamental part of his system, essential to any conception of moral obligation. He taught the absolute difference between right and wrong, the eternal and immutable nature of moral distinctions, and had explicitly denied the charge of pantheism.

The battle was on. Locke was attacked right and left. Dissatisfied with his compromising position on the problem of thoroughgoing materialism, disciples of that school in America (Dr. Thomas Cooper and Dr. Joseph Buchanan, for example) had long before refused to follow Locke when he implied that the physiological explanation of mentality was inadequate. Moreover, men who formerly entertained the highest regard for him, had, for one reason or another, transferred their allegiance to the Scotch common-sense school. . . . There were also men who, convinced that the philosophy of Locke "bordered hard upon the inner temple of sensualism," and believing that it was but a gradual descent from sensualism to materialism and thence to deism and rank atheism, found in Cousin an antidote against Locke and the French atheists.

The revolt against Locke aroused defense. Conservatives in religion and social outlook were alarmed at the spread of the intuitional philosophy. Bad enough was its association, in their eyes, with reform agitations of social questions and its menace to religious orthodoxy; but even worse was the possibility that it might beguile those who were guided by "enthusiasm" into endless strange cults unsettling to the authority of God, the past, and the present. . . .

The "back to Locke" movement was really inaugurated in 1819, when Alexander Everett published in the *North American Review* a long, closely argued paper, "The History of Intellectual Philosophy." This paradoxical and pragmatic critic undertook to explain the reaction among leading intellectuals against the *Essay Concerning Human Understanding*. To Everett it seemed clear that the main reason for the about-face was that conservative critics of the French Revolution and its aftermath had mistakenly denounced the essay as the real foundation of all the mischief which even more superficial commentators had attributed to Voltaire and Rousseau. . . .

After weighing the philosophies of Locke, the Scotch school, and Kant, Everett decided in favor of the great English empiricist who in rebelling against obscurantism and mysticism had done so much to inaugurate modern liberal thought. German idealism appeared to this man of the world as an unsubstantial dream, whose appeal arose from its supposed essential connection with the existence of God and the immortality of the soul. The present hysteria, Everett thought, was to be explained by reference to actions and reactions in the history of thought. The protest of the restless, disturbed intuitionalists against the materialism which they wrongly associated with Locke was merely a reversion to "the Platonic visions of the childhood of the race."

In a review of a new edition of Lord King's *Life of Locke*, Everett subsequently pointed out even more explicitly that the materialists or the philosophers of selfishness, in reality found no foothold in Locke for the degrading theories they cherished. At the same time, he held up for the highest esteem—without entire justification—the great philosopher's precision of ideas and correct use of language, "an indispensable instrument for correct thinking."

It was Francis Bowen, however, who, even more than Alexander Everett, admired Locke and his philosophical style, with its homely simplicity and its freedom from bizarre obscurantism and from dogmatism. What Bowen regarded as loyalty to American values and ideals led him, like Everett, to oppose the new fashion which abandoned plain English speech for "fantastic" German notions. Transcendentalism was, in his eyes, a kind of false, imported mixture of sublimated Fichtean atheism and the downright pantheism of Schelling. Moreover, in the transcendentalist reaction against Locke, the Harvard philosopher and historian detected the un-American tendency to divorce speculation from the everyday life of men. Bowen wrote for the *Knickerbocker* a popular paper, in the form of an imaginary discourse between Locke and Newton, which defended the former against the common misunderstanding which attributed to his denial of innate ideas the denial also of the certainty of ideas themselves.

An even more vigorous champion of "the great Mr. Locke" was the Reverend Frederick Beasley, who, like Bowen, resented the new tendency to borrow ideas from Europe and who regarded Locke as America's own philosopher. According to one of Beasley's friends, he could scarcely have shown greater warmth and zeal in Locke's defense had he been among his intimate and living associates. Indeed, Beasley went so far as to declare that Locke "never has been and never can be overthrown." Although he befriended him in his teachings and in his daily discussions, it was in *A Search for Truth in the Science of the Human Mind* (1822) that he mustered all his forces for the cause. Casting strictures on the Scotch school and on the French eclectics, Beasley exonerated his master from "the false and absurd charge of representative perception through mediate images." . . .

. . . Thomas C. Upham, of Bowdoin College, replied to Locke's critics by insisting that he had by no means supposed sensation to be the only source of knowledge. This rejoinder was needed, for transcendentalists had overlooked Locke's emphasis on reflection and his implication that there was also something like intuitive reason. What Upham chiefly valued in Locke, however, was his synthesis: Aristotle had seen the connection of the intellect with the material world, and had postulated the external origin of knowledge; Plato had directed attention chiefly to the internal origin of thought; and Locke combined these two great views. . . .

. . . It is, of course, impossible to determine finally the depth and persistence of the idealistic and eclectic attacks on Locke. There is evidence that they succeeded only in bringing about an increasing qualification and enrichment of the basic Lockean philosophy. No doubt American dependence on English thought was also lessened. But throughout later American thought, it appears certain that Locke's influence continued to be important, and that it did not die with the new emphasis on biology and the theory of organic evolution.

Subsequent developments in American philosophical and psychological thought reveal the tenacity of the ideas of the noted empiricist. In his widely read *Outlines of Cosmic Philosophy* (1874), John Fiske maintained that the doctrine of evolution harmonized Locke's great view that all knowledge was due to experience, with the Leibnitz-Kantian view that the mind even at birth possesses definite tendencies. In other ways, too, the Lockean empirical tradition was expressed in what have been regarded as characteristically American ideas. William James, according to his most authoritative biographer, belongs unquestionably to the British empirical school founded by Locke. More than once James referred to "the good Locke" and his "dear old book," and rejoiced in his devotion to experimentalism, his common sense, and his hatred of obscure, misty ideas. Furthermore, as Professor Perry points out, the chapter on "conception" in James's *Principles of Psychology* is quite definitely founded on Locke—with his view of the *priority* and *preeminence* of particulars, James heartily agreed. Even James's own more original thinking, as distinguished from his inheritance from Locke, was characterized by a functional relationship between ideas and reality—a position not so alien to Locke as to his critics, by reason of the fact that Locke had more or less recognized practical motives in the acquisition of knowledge.

Other American philosophers, too, in spite of non-Lockean influences on their thought, were not unaffected by the great empiricist so long regarded as America's particular master. In discussing the significance of Locke, John Dewey shows his own kinship with him. The philosophic empiricism initiated by Locke, Dewey writes, was designed to remove the burden which "blind custom, imposed authority and accidental association" had loaded on science and social obligation; and the best way to liberate man from this burden was "through a natural history of the origin and growth in the mind of ideas connected with objectionable beliefs and customs." Even the idealist Josiah Royce spoke well of Locke, while a contemporary philosopher, Frederick J. E. Woodbridge, pays great deference to him for having taught us that "we must go to our senses, not to our souls, if we are ever to enter into the realm of the mind." Moreover, the persistence, in contemporary thought, of the impact of Locke was not confined to philosophy. Notwithstanding the biological emphasis in modern psychology, the influence of Locke is still a factor to be reckoned with.

Thus, in spite of the defects in his system of knowledge, in spite of all the attacks levied on him, there was something in the empirical, middle-of-the-road, common-sense position taken by Locke which persisted in the main streams of American philosophy. May it not be that the explanation is partly to be found in the consideration that such a philosophy could best perform the work America needed done? Could it not break down the cleavage between speculation and everyday life, and safeguard our inherited, liberal, seventeenth-century English tradition from the "fantastic," imported, French and German notions, supposedly so alien to our Anglo-American civilization?

In the fields of political and economic theory, in the first seventy-five years of our national experience, the ideas of Locke were of peculiar importance—an importance not to be obscured by the varying interpretations given them. Locke's *Treatises of Civil Government*, published the same year (1690) as the famous *Essay Concerning Human Understanding*, was of course even more influential during the years of revolution than the philosophical and religious treatises. There is abundant evidence that his political theories did not die after the Revolution had become history. There was much work for them to do. True, the *Treatises of Civil Government* was seldom cited in the Constitutional Convention of 1787; but the cardinal doctrine that the people in themselves constitute a power superior to the government, that government may be dissolved without affecting civil society, had great weight in the minds of the men assembled in 1787 at Philadelphia to frame a new constitution, and was also a powerful factor in the fundamental assumptions of those who made and revised state constitutions.

Statesmen continued, during the early republic, to defer to Locke's *Treatises*. Jefferson, who had declared that "Locke's little book on Government is perfect as far as it goes," insisted that it be required reading for law students at the University of Virginia, where in general there were to be no requirements. Madison agreed, thinking that Locke was admirably suited to impress young minds with the right of nations to establish their own governments and to inspire a love of free ones. John Quincy Adams, when the question of the separation of powers was uppermost in the discussions of Congress, went straight to Locke rather than to Montesquieu, for he regarded the English thinker as the true originator of the theory. Charles Sumner and many less learned statesmen quoted Locke in their public speeches during the slavery controversy; and he was remembered during every contest between human and property rights and interests. Moreover, Locke's doctrine of the right of revolution figured largely in popular thought as reflected in hundreds of election sermons, academic addresses, and Fourth of July orations.

Part of the secret of much of Locke's influence on public thought lies in the very inconsistency of his political theories. In the *Essay Concerning Human Understanding* he had repudiated the theory of innate ideas; yet in his *Treatises of Civil Government* he assumed as innate ideas both the state of nature and the law of reason—conceptions which he could not have arrived at empirically. This incongruity, it will be recalled, was partly responsible for the repudiation of his empiricism by social radicals who, in a conflict between the "innate truths" of equality and the practical lessons of inequality, had no hesitancy in choosing the former. Forced thus to repudiate Locke's psychology and philosophy and aware that their leading defenders were social conservatives, radicals also discovered that Locke's political doctrines, once regarded as bold and even revolutionary, could be used as a bulwark for the *status quo* as well as for challenging it. Likewise, exponents of laissez-faire and of the sanctity of private property found comfort in Locke's individualism—in his natural rights of life, liberty, and property. Hence it was that divergent interests appealed to contradictory doctrines and implications in Locke's political thought.

It will be remembered that Locke not only refuted the doctrine of absolute monarchy, but also justified the right of revolution when a government willfully and over a considerable period of time violated the contract with civil society. He did not, however, indicate precisely how the people were to repossess themselves of the government, or just how it was to be determined that the contract had been broken. These questions, he implied, must be left to common sense, to the practical judgment of the majority. There could be no objective test. But clearly Locke denied the right of minorities to make a revolution, although revolutions (at least in their initial stage) are frequently, if indeed not always, minority movements. He was equally outspoken against "seditious factions." Thus hedged about and restricted, the right of revolution was stated and justified.

Still other aspects of Locke's thought appealed to American liberals and radicals in the first half-century of the republic. He stoutly adhered to the law of nature and reason, by which he meant "the law of good will, mutual assistance, and preservation," or, in other words, the sacred rights of life, liberty, and property. Under primitive conditions this law of nature or reason had, with some exceptions, governed men's relations. To avoid the confusion and awkwardness of exceptions, men had contracted with each other to form civil society and to delegate to government the single natural right of enforcing "the law of good will, mutual assistance, and preservation." Thus Locke's political philosophy was one of individualism. In the early days of the republic the principle of individualism best served the interests of radicals, for their fight was against the domination of favored classes and centralized government. Hence Locke's doctrine was in many respects as democratic in its implications as his theory of the plasticity of human nature, which, as we have seen, was beloved by antifederalists and social radicals. . . .

Critics of aristocratic tendencies in American life likewise appealed to "the great Mr. Locke." If his heritage of the consent of the governed was to be a thing of substance, then such antidemocratic groups as the Society of the Cincinnati must, it was urged, be restrained from promoting aristocracy and discord—behavior which would fatally wound civil liberty. During the debates in the Virginia Constitutional Convention in 1829, the liberals or reformers, who were contending for an enlarged suffrage and a redistribution of representation to weaken the Tidewater aristocracy, cited Locke and the doctrine of natural law in an effort to promote their cause. Locke taught that all government was based on consent, and an extension of political democracy in Virginia was necessary, they held, if this principle was to be realized in fact.

In other contests for an extension of suffrage, appeals were made to the doctrine of natural rights, the right of revolution, and similar teachings of Locke. The literature of the Dorr Rebellion, which came to a head in Rhode Island in 1842, is a case in point. As early as 1833 the labor leader, Seth Luther, told a Providence audience that every page in history was stained with blood shed in obtaining acknowledgment of the right of self-government, or in acquiring the exercise of it, or in defending it from encroachment. "In all cases, or nearly all, the rights of man have been wrested from the grasp of power, *vie et armis*, by force and arms. The people have been compelled to take by force that which has been withheld from them by force, to wit: the right to govern themselves, by laws made by themselves." In ringing words which appealed to the class consciousness of Rhode Island's disenfranchised thousands, Luther declared that the existing state government by depriving men of their natural rights, was violating the great tradition of English liberty and completely repudiating the doctrine of the consent of the governed—a doctrine hallowed by the Declaration of Independence. . . .

The same appeals to natural rights, and even to the right of revolution, emerged in the arguments of the more militant abolitionists. No sooner was the Revolution over than many men opposed to slavery held that the existence of that institution was a violation of all the rights for which the war had been fought. Dr. George Buchanan, in a Fourth of July oration in Baltimore in 1791, declared that slavery was a cruel, oppressive, and wanton abuse of the rights of man, that the fires of liberty might well be kindled among the slaves, and that they might rally under the standard of freedom and bring devastation and ruin on the country. "Alas," lamented Samuel Miller in speaking of slavery in a sermon delivered before the Tammany Society on July 4, 1793, "that we should so soon forget the principles, upon which our wonderful revolution was founded!" This note was struck again and again. Slavery, asserted the Reverend P. S. Cleland in a Fourth of July sermon at Greenwood, Indiana, in 1841, was diametrically opposed to the self-evident principles of the Declaration of Independence.

If slavery is right, the axioms set forth in that declaration as our apology to the world, for resisting unto blood, the oppressions of Great Britain, are glaringly false; the American Revolution was but a successful rebellion; and our fathers should be regarded as a band of rebels, engaged in unlawful resistance against the lawful tyranny of George III and his parliament. If the principles of the Declaration were fully adopted, we should no longer be guilty of contradicting our principles by our practice.

Other Fourth of July orators reproduced in detail the contract theory of the origin of government and the natural-rights philosophy, in a more or less orthodox Lockean fashion. Sometimes Locke and other revolutionary leaders or theorists of seventeenth-century England were specifically mentioned, but in any case their ideas were expressed with illuminating reiteration.

In the tension occasioned by slavery, particularly at the time of the fugitive slave law, some of the speakers even went to the length of advocating the right of revolution as perhaps the only means by which the free North could uproot the South's peculiar institution. "If the exigency is imminent, the perversion total, and other redress impossible, we must admit the desperate and fearful remedy of Revolution," declared the Reverend Samuel C. Bartlett at Manchester, New Hampshire, in 1853. "I need not argue the case that is so powerfully put in the immortal Declaration of Independence." But this was only one among dozens of such statements. Perhaps the most typical, but by no means the most thoroughgoing, of these expressions of the right of revolution is to be found in a leaflet, bearing the title "Revolution the only Remedy for Slavery," issued by the American Anti-Slavery Society. For the most drastic statements one must turn to the literature of the "higher law" doctrine and to radical abolitionists' justification of John Brown's attack on Harper's Ferry. The sermons of Gilbert Haven, a prominent Methodist leader, and the speeches and writings of such people as Wendell Phillips and Mrs. Child contain unequivocal assertions of the right of revolution. The transcendentalist, Theodore Parker, found Locke's theory of the right of evolution as useful to his scheme of values as he found his empirical psychology unserviceable. And, after the Civil War, abolitionists, in their advocacy of equal rights for the Negro, appealed to Locke more than once.

If, however, the slavery controversy resulted, on the one hand, in an appeal by the abolitionists to the natural-rights philosophy of Locke, on the other it stimulated exponents of slavery to redefine natural rights in such a way as to make slavery justifiable, or it led to a complete repudiation of the natural-rights philosophy itself. J. K. Paulding, novelist, satirist, and naval official, endeavored to reconcile slavery with natural-rights theories. President Dew, of William and Mary College, and Albert Bledsoe, a mathematical philosopher at the University of Virginia, undertook the same task. Discarding the traditional theory of individual natural rights, Bledsoe elaborated an idea of natural law which was based on public good and which definitely restricted individual liberty. The greatest number of proslavery apologists, however, rejected the theory of natural rights. They insisted that any observation of the facts of nature was an obvious refutation of the doctrine, for which they substituted the historical or organic conceptions of social development. Thus, interest led Southern intellectuals to try their hand at refuting the natural-rights philosophy of Locke which, when put to work by radical abolitionists, threatened the institution of slavery.

In their onslaught the apologists for slavery were aided by conservative Northerners who for one reason or another had no liking for the natural-rights philosophy. No doubt many responded to new currents of thought, particularly the theories of Burke, the utilitarianism of Bentham, and the ideas of the German historical school, whose leader, Savigny, exerted considerable influence on American intellectuals. But, at the same time, it is also true that these men were usually conservative by temperament and fearful lest extreme democratic tendencies should jeopardize the established rule of the wise, the good, and the well-to-do. Without completely renouncing all of Locke's political philosophy, John Quincy Adams in 1842 subjected the doctrine of the social compact to severe criticism. Appealing to historical facts, Adams demonstrated that the constitution of Massachusetts had been framed and adopted, not by all the citizens, but by only a certain portion, and that therefore the commonwealth could in no sense be thought of as democratic. . . .

In the years following the conclusion of peace with England in 1783, the Revolution was interpreted in the majority of Fourth of July orations in such a way as to temper the abstract right of revolution itself. Economic depression reminded everyone of the sacrifices which the Revolution had cost, and at least until 1786 times remained hard. It was therefore natural for ministers and orators to insist that the men of '76 had appealed to the sword only after every other recourse had been tried, and that the right of revolution had been resorted to most reluctantly. Since society was torn by factions, it was also desirable for orators and ministers to insist that the Revolution had been carried out by an overwhelming majority—Locke had made that a condition of a justifiable revolution. Little or nothing is to be found in the Fourth of July orations regarding the Tory opposition. And, save for avowed radicals (who were much less frequently called on to make addresses that found their way into print), little is said of the social changes and democratic upheaval which were unmistakably a part of the Revolution. Following Locke, the typical Fourth of July orator insisted that civil society had been in no way affected by the long years of the struggle. Such an attitude would obviously tend to counteract antifederalist restlessness and the rumblings of agrarian revolts in Massachusetts and Pennsylvania. . . .

. . . As reform got under way in the first decades of the nineteenth century, revolution was pushed more and more into the background. "A prudent man," the Reverend Joseph McKean pointed out in his election sermon before the governor of Massachusetts in 1800, "will not set fire to his house, and thereby endanger the lives of his family, because some parts are not so perfectly convenient, or some of its proportions not so agreeable to the eye, as they might be made in a new edifice." This refrain became a familiar one, and no doubt tended to help substitute the doctrine of gradualism for that of revolution. Although we meet with this argument in the literature of all reform movements, it was, as might be expected, especially evident in that of the peace movement.

Two circumstances help to explain the growing reliance on reform as a substitute for revolution. In the first place, as a result of faith in reason and enlightenment, sponsors of public schools spread the word that mass education, by raising the general level of intelligence, would remedy social abuses which might otherwise result in revolution. In the second place, it was generally believed that the existence of free lands provided a safety valve for discontent. Even though this belief may not have been well grounded, it must nevertheless have tended to make people think less in terms of revolution and more in terms of education and gradual reform as possible means of social amelioration. Occasionally, fear was expressed that, once free lands were exhausted, proletarian discontent might lead to a reign of terror. This fear was particularly strong in the minds of Southerners who were horrified at Fourierism and other radical social and economic doctrines, and who looked with dismay on the establishment in Paris of national workshops during the revolutionary days of 1848.

At the same time that these forces were diminishing the once generally cherished idea of the right of revolution, a still more powerful force was at work with similar effect, for, as an examination of Fourth of July orations clearly indicates, the tradition of the Revolution gave way before the spirit of nationalism and patriotism. Our revolution was regarded solely as the instrument by which our nationalism had come into existence. Once the historic mission of revolution had been fulfilled, once we were a nation, there could no longer be any use for revolution. It might even jeopardize the dearly bought nationalism which had not yet been consolidated.

In 1861, when the Southern states determined to embark on their separate path as a new nation, they chiefly justified their action by the doctrine of the right of secession, rather than by that of revolution. The idea of revolution was now in such bad odor that relatively few appealed to "the great Mr. Locke," whose theory of revolution had once done such good service. Some Northerners sought, on the one hand, to identify secession with revolution and to condemn it as such, but, on the other, denied that it was at all analogous to what happened in 1776.

Thus it was that, after the Revolution, various growing interests, particularly when challenged by competing ones, led to the qualification of Locke's idea of the right of revolution. In spite of the radicalism of much of Locke's political thought in the seventeenth and eighteenth centuries, it is plain that he himself would in general have approved of the qualifications of the natural-rights philosophy and of the doctrine of the right of revolution, which had been made in order functionally to serve dominant interests in the existing pattern of political and social arrangements. For in considerable part the sanctity of property rights was to Locke the chief reason and justification for the substitution of civil society and government for the original state of nature. It was likewise the sanctity of property rights which in his mind largely warranted men in making a revolution against a government jeopardizing them. Therefore he would have discountenanced attempts to apply his theory of the right of revolution to lend validity to movements to abridge or annihilate property rights.

Locke's belief that the preservation of property was the chief end of government had even more important social implications. In declaring that whatsoever a person "hath mixed his labor with and joined it to something that is his own" was a sacred right, to be protected by government, Locke laid the foundations of the concept of economic laissez-faire as well as of the theory that property, being a crystallization of personal achievement, is never to be lightly dissociated from private ownership. Although Locke himself defined property broadly and probably did not intend to give it the general and sweeping sanctity with which it was subsequently endowed, his doctrine became the gospel of liberty and property, in close association. For this development the march of events, which he could not have foreseen, must be chiefly blamed.

It is hardly defensible to attach too much weight to Locke's justification of property rights as he understood them, nor to assume that without his ideas on this subject events in nineteenth-century America would have shaped themselves in any fundamentally different way. Yet is is pertinent to note that Locke's theories of property influenced the thoughts and actions of the framers of the Constitution and the advocates of the stake-in-society theory of economics during the Jacksonian period. In other words, advocates of property rights found work for Locke's ideas. When Chancellor Kent was particularly concerned over the dangers to property which he feared the movement for an extension of suffrage involved, he declared, "Give me the writings of Addison and Locke." It is only necessary to examine the writings of such Federalists as Fisher Ames and such Whigs as Daniel Webster to note the similarity between their conceptions of property rights, individualism, and laissez-faire, and the teachings of Locke. In the debates of the state constitutional conventions which convened to discuss the enlargement of the suffrage, one finds clearly stated the Lockean-Federalist principle that "the great and chief end therefore of men's uniting into commonwealths, and putting themselves under governments, is the preservation of their property." Locke was quoted in those conventions, to the effect that men possessed of property must have power over those who were not.

In a pioneer society, with an abundance of free lands, the individualistic interpretations of the functions of government were not without their progressive, liberal connotations; but in an industrial, stratified society, the case was quite different, for there Locke's highly individualistic, laissez-faire conception of government and his regard for property rights could only check the development of social legislation and sanctify the accumulation of corporate wealth. Walton H. Hamilton has pointed out that Mr. Justice Sutherland, in condemning as unconstitutional an act of Congress regulating the conditions of labor of women in the District of Columbia, revealed a train of thought similar to that of Locke; even an occasional turn of expression was reminiscent of the seventeenth-century thinker. Without laboring the point, or attempting to establish any personal influence of Locke, it is clear, as Professor Hamilton has suggested, that here we have a continuing stream of thought. This is only one of the indications that Locke's influence remained vital long after the period with which this paper has been chiefly concerned.

The "great Mr. Locke" in a real sense remained America's philosopher, in spite of all the competition of new ideas. And he remained America's philosopher because many of his concepts were useful to interests in the tasks at hand. Above all, it is plain that many of his ideas admirably suited the needs of the more dominant American interests. His philosophy was practical and yet general; it appeared to be liberal, without endangering the individualistic conception of social relations and property rights. Moreover, his essential philosophy had the merit of emphasizing specific facts rather than general presuppositions. In varying degrees this emphasis served both conservatives and reformers. Clearly, Locke's thought—religious, educational, metaphysical, and political—survived to the degree that there was work for it to do; and those aspects of his philosophy which were functional to the needs of ascendant interests were destined to have the longest history.

16
The Background of the Unitarian Opposition to Transcendentalism

Clarence H. Faust

Throughout the first four decades of the nineteenth century eastern Massachusetts was rocked by theological dissension as, first, Unitarians gradually broke with Calvinists and then Transcendentalists broke with Unitarians. At the heart of theological debates in these years was the conflict between reason and revelation as a final authority in religious matters. It was much the same conflict that in academic moral philosophy pitted a prudential ethics (or theological utilitarianism), based upon the older Lockean sensationist psychology, against "common sense" moral judgments founded upon a renewed belief in man's innate moral faculty. This general conflict also played itself out across the broad stage of Western thought. It dramatized the challenge of the nineteenth century to the eighteenth, or (though it was known by different names at different times and places) the defiance of the Enlightenment by romanticisms. In America, the semantic significance of this conflict to the average educated person was that, generally speaking, the old Enlightenment meaning of "reason" as the empirical use of experience faded away. By the 1830s it became known as "understanding." And rational "understanding" was subordinated to the newer romantic idea of "reason" as intuited feeling arising from every man's internal moral sense. George Bancroft expressed the new meaning best in layman's terms when he said: "Reason exists within every breast. I mean not that faculty which deduces from the experience of the senses, but that higher faculty, which from the infinite treasures of its own consciousness, originates truth, and assents to it by the force of intuitive evidence."

Skillfully summing up the pamphlet literature of the Great Unitarian Controversy, which kind of literature was always profuse in any quarrel among learned men in those days, Clarence Faust here examines the rupture between Unitarians and orthodox Congregationalists and, next, the sources of Transcendentalist disenchantment with Unitarianism. Although Faust emphasizes nineteenth-century developments, the reader may be reminded that the start of liberal Unitarian thought in New England, like Enlightenment thought generally,

Reprinted by permission of the author and The University of Chicago Press from *Modern Philology*, 35 (1938), 297-324. Footnotes have been omitted.

may be traced to the mid-eighteenth century and to memorable latitudinarian clergymen like Jonathan Mayhew.

During this period, when Ralph Waldo Emerson and Theodore Parker emerge as brilliant spokesmen for what can only loosely be called a "transcendentalist" point of view, intellectual paradoxes were at work which etched themselves as continuing problems into varying levels of the American mind and character. Free scholarly inquiry in Biblical matters (generally the Unitarian position) came to be at loggerheads with free speculation in philosophical matters (generally the Transcendentalist position). The respectable people who thronged Unitarian churches in Boston became complacent and even acquiescent in the authority of Unitarian doctrine (liberal though it was) while they disavowed the younger men who were exercising the very "right of private judgment" that Unitarians long had cherished. Although the younger Transcendentalists were themselves connected by sentiment and education, if not by family, to "the best people," the Whigs of Massachusetts, their views of man in the mass and of nature were surely closer to the romantic American democratic (though not necessarily to the Jacksonian party) temper of the 1830s and 1840s. Finally, the intellectual Enlightenment waned after the 1820s in the very areas that first had best sustained it on these shores—in New England, where liberal Unitarianism hardened, and in Virginia, where the Jeffersonian temper was lost through stiffening resistance to free discussion and inquiry into the problems of a slave-holding society.

For further reading: *Conrad Wright, *The Beginnings of Unitarianism in America* (1955); Herbert W. Schneider, "The Intellectual Background of William Ellery Channing," *Church History*, 7 (March 1938), 3-23; Octavius B. Frothingham, *Boston Unitarianism, 1820-1850* (1890); *William R. Hutchinson, *The Transcendentalist Ministers* (1959); Sydney E. Ahlstrom, "The Scottish Philosophy and American Theology," *Church History*, 24 (September 1955), 257-272; Joseph J. Kwiat, "Thoreau's Philosophical Apprenticeship," *New England Quarterly*, 17 (1945), 51-69.

In the opening years of the nineteenth century, New England Calvinists—theological heirs, as they were fond of pointing out, of the founders of New England—were disquieted by indications, such as the appointment of Henry Ware to the Hollis chair of divinity at Harvard College, that the heresies of Socinus were making inroads upon American Congregationalism. The publication in 1815 of Thomas Belsham's *American Unitarianism,* which contained the announcement on no less authority than that of a Boston publisher, William Wells, that "most of our Boston Clergy and respectable laymen (of whom we have many enlightened theologians) are Unitarian," seemed to confirm their direct forebodings and roused them to battle. The controversy, thus precipitated, racked New England Congregationalism for three decades.

In 1827 there was added to the host of books, pamphlets, and articles which had appeared in the course of this controversy an anonymous review of a sermon entitled "Unitarian Christianity most favorable to piety," which had been delivered by William Ellery Channing at the dedication of the Second Unitarian Church of New York City in the preceding year. The reviewer, a staunch Calvinist, prefaced his criticisms of Channing's discourse by an illuminating survey of the conflict. In his view, it had moved through two phases and had entered a third. In the first of these, he wrote,

> *The weapons of attack and defense . . . were chiefly derived from* Biblical literature. *Erroneous readings, mistranslations, and wrong interpretations, were the charges perpetually preferred against the doctrines of the Orthodox, and the scriptural arguments by which they were maintained.*

In the second, "the trial of Orthodoxy was," he said, "transferred to another tribunal, that of philosophy. Its doctrines were declared to be irrational and absurd, wholly inconsistent with the perfections of God, and the freedom and accountability of man." Finally, the opposing creeds were "brought to another test, that of *tendency*," the "main question" being "which of the two systems, the Unitarian or the Orthodox, is of superior tendency to form an elevated religious character." The author thereupon presented a list of Unitarian publications in which the claim that the Unitarian doctrines were more likely than Calvinistic beliefs to promote piety and virtue had been strongly urged: Jared Sparks's *An inquiry into the comparative moral tendency of Trinitarian and Unitarian doctrines* (originally published in the *Unitarian Miscellany* in 1822); Channing's sermon at the ordination of his colleague Ezra Gannett (1824); a discourse by the Boston Unitarian, John Palfrey, in 1824; and a half-dozen articles and reviews in the *Christian Examiner, Christian Register*, and *Christian Inquirer*.

He might easily have expanded this catalogue by including such publications as Henry Ware's *The faith once delivered to the saints* (1825), in which the author contended that the claims of Unitarianism were supported by its being "peculiarly favorable" to virtue; Channing's "Unitarian Christianity" (1819), in which that acknowledged leader and spokesman of the "liberal" party declared that Calvinism "tends strongly to pervert the moral faculty"; and his "Objections to Unitarian Christianity considered" (1819), a large part of which was a reply to the charges that Unitarianism was not conducive to religious zeal and that it was " 'a half-way house to infidelity.' " The reviewer might, indeed, have observed that the most notable defense of Calvinism on philosophic grounds, the *Letters to Unitarians* published in 1820 by Leonard Woods, professor of Christian theology at Andover, was concluded by an elaborate discussion of the comparative tendencies of the two systems to "promote particular parts of Christian virtue and duty"; and that the most thoroughgoing defense of Calvinism on biblical grounds, the *Letters to Dr. Channing on the doctrine of the trinity*, published a year earlier by Woods's colleague, Moses Stuart, was climaxed with a stern warning that Unitarian principles of biblical interpretation were likely to induce infidelity.

The Calvinistic charge thus early formulated by Stuart that Unitarianism encouraged infidelity, that is, a rejection of the final authority of the Scriptures, was a particularly important aspect of the debate over the "tendencies" of the two opposing creeds; for, in the course of the controversy over this question, Unitarians assumed a position which they found peculiarly embarrassing when, late in the thirties of the century, Transcendentalism emerged in their midst. During the twenty years before Emerson delivered his divinity-school address at Harvard in 1838, they had been harassed by predictions, shrewdly particularized and vigorously supported, that their system of belief would carry them inevitably to the position with respect to the Christian Scriptures announced in that lecture and proclaimed by Theodore Parker in the years immediately after it. They had in defense committed themselves to principles that made it well nigh impossible for them to dissociate themselves from the new heresy. A survey of this aspect of the controversy will, I believe, contribute to our understanding of the Unitarian opposition to Transcendentalism and to its leading exponents—will, perhaps, make it easier to understand why Emerson was stigmatized as the purveyor of "the latest form of infidelity," and for many years denied further hearing at Harvard; why Parker was denounced as a "deist," "unbeliever," "atheist," and was invited to withdraw from the Boston Unitarian Association.

I

The Calvinistic opponents of Unitarianism, or, as they preferred to be called, "the Orthodox," had not been content simply to reiterate the warning that Unitarianism was "a half-way house to infidelity." They had supported this charge, which since the days of Tom Paine had been in New England a particularly grave one, by arguments based upon the nature of Unitarian belief, had strengthened it by comparisons with the course of similar movements abroad, and had rendered it ominous by arousing distrust for the character of the Unitarian leaders.

They asserted, for one thing, that Unitarianism was a merely negative system. "It is evident," wrote Samuel Miller, professor of theology at Princeton, in 1823, "that Unitarianism, according to the statement of one of its most zealous friends in the *United States*, consists 'rather in NOT BELIEVING.' " The zealous friend referred to by Miller was the Boston publisher William Wells, and the phrase quoted had been taken from a letter to the English Unitarian, Thomas Belsham, which had been published in the latter's *American Unitarianism*. A reviewer for the Calvinistic *Panoplist*, Jedidiah Morse, had put his finger on Wells's statement and had suggested its implications with respect to the religious influence of Harvard, which had long been regarded with sharp suspicion by Calvinists. It is clear, he wrote, that at Harvard college

> *the religion, which consists in* not *believing, is taught by a well concerted and uniformly executed plan of negatives. All systems but Unitarianism are openly, or secretly, impugned or ridiculed, while the "*not *believing" religion is dexterously substituted in their place.*

By 1834 Channing's colleague at the Federal Street Church in Boston, Ezra Gannett, was complaining, in a sermon called "Christian Unitarianism not a negative system," that this charge had been "reiterated in one form or another from north to south."

Not infrequently Calvinists represented Unitarianism as merely a stage in the decline from orthodoxy to general skepticism. Having renounced one creed, said Lyman Beecher in "The faith once delivered to the saints" (1823), Unitarians relinquish one doctrine after another until they have no clear convictions left. . . . The point was sometimes framed in more prophetic terms: Unitarianism, it was said, being by nature opposed to belief, and having abandoned one theological position after another, would eventually lapse into open infidelity. "The fire of unbelief has been the ruling spirit in your system," wrote George Cheever, for instance, in an article addressed to Unitarians through the columns of that militantly Calvinistic journal *The Spirit of the Pilgrims* in 1833. . . . Cheever devoted a section of his article to a consideration of the doctrines which Unitarians had already abandoned: the doctrines of human depravity, of the atonement, of the existence of Satan, of eternal punishment, and so forth. "Nor can you hope," he pressed on to say, "to keep the actual nature and tendencies of your system much longer concealed. They will not be repressed. Your system is displaying itself, and you need not expect to restrain its freaks and sallies of infidelity." In particular he expressed alarm over the rapid progress of "liberal Christianity" toward a rejection of revelation:

At present we must bend our efforts to the preserving of the Scriptures themselves from the grasp and sweep of your reckless infidelity. Were we to let you go on, we should very soon have no Bible whatever to appeal to.

In more ways than one you have shown your jealousy and dislike of the sacred volume. The publications that have emanated from the presses and institutions of your system, both in this country and in Europe, contain either an effective rejection of revelation or principles that lead to it.

What the Unitarian principles were which would lead to a rejection of revelation the author of this statement did not say; he contented himself with quoting passages from Unitarian writings which contained what he regarded as demonstrations of a tendency to infidelity or as covert embracings of it. Other Calvinists had, however, explored the subject in some detail. Moses Stuart, for instance, undertook in 1819 an analysis of Channing's statement of the Unitarian principles of exegesis. He agreed with Channing, he said, that the meaning of the Bible was "to be sought in the same manner as that of other books," that grammatical analysis of the biblical texts was the only justifiable method of interpretation. . . . Having stated this basic agreement with his opponent, Stuart took exception to Channing's position with respect to the relationship of reason and revelation. Channing had said

The Bible treats of subjects on which we receive ideas from other sources besides itself; such subjects as the nature, passions, relations, and duties of man; and it expects us to restrain and modify its language by the known truths which observation and experience furnish on these topics.

This principle Stuart felt obliged to reject, on the ground that it involved the ascription of final authority to reason rather than to revelation. He argued that once the claims of the Bible as a divine revelation had been allowed, as Channing professed to allow them, the only proper question was: What did the Bible teach? That question had to be answered, he said, by a careful, grammatical interpretation of the text. Once the meaning of the text had been ascertained, reason had performed its function. It had no authority to modify propositions thus derived from revelation so as to bring them into accord with conclusions arrived at independently. . . .

Quoting Channing's statement that Unitarians "do not hesitate to modify, and restrain, and turn from their most obvious sense" certain difficult passages of Scripture in which human beings are called gods, because the sense of these passages "is opposed to the known properties of the beings to whom they relate," Stuart wrote: "I must *hesitate* however to adopt this principle, without examining its nature and tendency." His investigation of its tendency led him to predict that those who applied it would end in infidelity:

> *I am well satisfied, that the course of reasoning in which you have embarked, [and the principles by which you explain away the divinity of the Saviour,] must eventually lead most men who approve of them to the conclusion, that the Bible is not of divine origin, and does not oblige us to belief or obedience. I do not aver, that they will certainly lead* you *[Channing] there. The remains of your former education and belief may still serve to guard you against the bolder conclusions of some of your brethren, who have not been placed under instruction such as you enjoyed in early life. You have more serious views of the importance of religion, than many, perhaps than most, of those who speculate with you.* Consistency, *too, will afford strong inducement not to give up the divine authority of the Scriptures. Yet many of your younger brethren have no inconsistency to fear, by adopting such views. . . . Feeling the inconsistency (as I am certain some of them will and do feel it), of violating the fundamental rules of interpretation, in order to make the apostles speak, as in their apprehension they ought to speak; and unable to reconcile what the apostles say with their own views; they will throw off the restraints which the old ideas of inspiration and infallibility of the Scriptures impose upon them, and receive them simply on the ground, on which they place any other writings of a moral and religious nature.*

Some Calvinists were confident that they could chart exactly the course which this subordination of revelation to reason would lead Unitarians to take. It was the road which German rationalism had traveled before their eyes. Again and again they pointed out that American Unitarians were treading in the steps of German heretics. It is true, wrote Samuel Miller of Princeton, in 1823, that the Germans, less restrained by public opinion, have gone a little farther; but Unitarians "will probably soon overtake them." Moses Stuart, watching the new movement from Andover, was very sure that they would "at last, go full length with the most liberal of them all." Reasoning as they did, he asserted they "must necessarily . . . come to the same conclusions with Eichhorn, and Paulus, and Henke, and Eckermann, and Herder, and other distinguished men of the new German school." I shall be ready to confess my apprehensions are quite erroneous," he wrote, "if the lapse of a few years more does not produce the undisguised avowal of the German divinity, in all its latitude." In 1829 Stuart's colleague at Andover, Leonard Woods, in his *Lectures on the Inspiration of the Scriptures* likewise pointed in warning to the decline of prominent German theologians into infidelity. Commenting on this section of the book, a Unitarian reviewer referred impatiently to those "who have rung all the changes of argument, warning, and sarcasm'' upon the parallels between Unitarianism and German rationalism ''till we should think it could scarcely yield another note.'' ''Is the learning of Germany, with its hasty, though monstrous growth, to deter all the world from inquiry?'' he asked.

Irritating these comparisons and prophecies must have been to Unitarians in the years before the appearance of Transcendentalism. They were made even more galling by an accusation which often accompanied them, namely, that Unitarians habitually and as a matter of policy concealed their subversive opinions.

This charge had gained its impetus from the circumstances under which the Unitarian controversy proper had begun in America. The provocative power of Belhsam's *American Unitarianism*, which had been the signal for that controversy, lay largely in a half-dozen letters from American to English Unitarians reproduced in it, reporting the gratifying progress of the movement in this country. Calvinists had professed to be shocked by the disclosure in these letters of the fashion in which Unitarianism had ''silently and covertly extended itself.'' The author of a widely read review of the work for the Orthodox *Panoplist* seems, indeed, to have represented the general feeling of his party when he wrote that the book had done good service to true Christianity by exposing the Unitarian program of stealthy penetration. The ''work of error,'' he wrote, ''was carried on for the most part in secret.'' Unitarians ''have not dared to be open. They have clandestinely crept into orthodox churches, by forebearing to contradict their faith, and then have gradually moulded them, by their negative preaching, to the shape which they would wish.'' This review was the starting point for a pamphlet skirmish, and the charge of ''concealment'' thus brought into prominence reappeared often in Orthodox journals and books. Linked with the assertion that Unitarianism induced infidelity, it made a formidable controversial weapon. . . .

II

It is not to be imagined, of course, that Unitarians endured in silence the reiteration of these charges that they had adopted a system of negations which must inevitably bring them, as it had the German rationalists, to open infidelity, and that they had deliberately fixed upon a policy of concealment which would lead unsuspecting folk into following them.

In countering these accusations, they insisted, for one thing, that instead of leading to infidelity, Unitarianism was a safeguard against it—a better safeguard, indeed, than Orthodoxy. Channing in 1819 laid down the main points in this line of defense. He admitted that one who had given up the doctrines peculiar to Calvinism might be expected to go on relinquishing one portion of his faith after another until he reached infidelity. Having found one part of his creed untenable, he would be inclined to distrust the whole of it. For this tendency Unitarians could not, however, be held responsible. The odium of it must be borne by their opponents, who had preached ''false and absurd doctrines.'' ''None are so likely to believe too little as those who have begun with believing too much; and hence we charge upon Trinitarianism whatever tendency may exist in those who forsake it, to sink gradually into infidelity.'' Unitarianism, on the other hand, fortified faith, because, having cast off the corruptions which through the centuries had fastened themselves upon Christianity, it did not, like the current Orthodoxy, bewilder and disgust thoughtful, morally sensitive souls. . . . Unless Christianity freed itself of these perversions, Channing pressed on to say, intelligent men would soon abandon it. Only a more "rational and amiable" system could save them. He was certain, then, that "Unitarianism does not lead to infidelity. On the contrary, its excellence is that it fortifies faith."

Unitarians often proclaimed this conviction in the years that followed Channing's sermon, and often repeated the arguments which he had employed to support it. They insisted that the time had come when "with men of intelligence and reflection the only question likely to arise" was whether they should have a "more rational religion or none"; and they published widely their certainty that the principles they had embraced, far from inducing infidelity, were the one sure protection against it. Their position was stated succinctly by the *Unitarian Miscellany* in 1823:

Unitarianism has been stigmatized as the half way road to infidelity. Let it be seen, in coming time, whether it is not rather the only barrier against a wild, unprofitable enthusiasm on the one hand, and a deadening unbelief on the other.

Calvinists had argued that the "new theology" tended to undermine faith in revelation because it was a negative system; Unitarians insisted, by way of objection to this conclusion, that their creed was favorable to faith because it was rational. But they went further: they attacked the premise of the argument, denying repeatedly that Unitarianism was merely negative. Thus, in 1834 Ezra Gannett preached a sermon, later published for distribution as a Unitarian tract with the title *Christian Unitarianism not a negative system*. According to Gannett, those who asserted that "liberal Christianity" consisted in not believing did so on the ground that it rejected certain Calvinistic doctrines. With equal reason Calvinism might be said to consist in not believing, he contended, since the disciples of Calvin rejected certain "peculiar dogmas of still larger divisions of the Christian Church." How, he inquired, could they reply to the Roman Catholic who declared that the discarding of the doctrines of transubstantiation and of purgatory made their system a negative one? In short, Gannett argued that the Calvinistic slur upon Unitarianism as a system of negations bound to end in infidelity, reduced itself upon examination simply to a narrow insistence that one must swallow the whole of Calvinism.

Against such arbitrary marking of the boundary between faith and unbelief Unitarians stoutly protested. They objected to the assumption that the denial of certain tenets of Calvinism, which they regarded as corruptions of Christianity, involved a complete abandonment of faith. . . . Unitarians accordingly protested against the refusal of orthodox Congregationalists to recognize as Christians those who could not accept the Genevan system. The *Unitarian Miscellany* of 1821 addressed Calvinists as follows:

You have defined Christianity in your own way; you have made its essence to consist in doctrines of your own choosing, and then declared, that whoever does not receive your definition, and believe the doctrines you have selected, is "no Christian."

In 1815 Channing censured this practice sharply in a sermon entitled "The system of exclusion and denunciation in religion considered." And in 1832 the American Unitarian Association published as a tract James Walker's *On the exclusive system*, in which Calvinists were denounced for denying "Christian fellowship, the Christian name, and all Christian privileges to such as differ from them beyond a certain mark; which they assume the right to fix for themselves and alter at pleasure." The principle here implied, it may be suggested at this point, was to cause Unitarians no little worry when, later on, they grappled with the problem of how to treat Emerson and Parker.

Unitarians prided themselves on being free from the fault of exclusiveness. At the annual meeting in 1830 of the Society for Promoting Theological Education at Harvard College, for instance, F. W. P. Greenwood, in an address often quoted, made a great point of the liberality of the Cambridge Divinity School. Unitarianism, he said, was not committed to "a timid creed-bound theology." It had, to be sure, its own peculiar doctrinal position; "but above the doctrinal opinions there is seated the high spirit of freedom." Again, "*Exclusiveness is its utter aversion*." Greenwood was plainly in harmony with the traditions of his party; indeed, Unitarians often assumed the title "Liberal Christians."

They prided themselves, furthermore, on recognizing the claims of unhampered inquiry in religious matters, particularly in biblical studies. "Free inquiry is a fundamental principle with Unitarians," wrote a reviewer for the *Unitarian Miscellany* in 1822. While urging the necessity of freedom in the study and interpretation of the Bible, they declared repeatedly, however, their confidence in its supernatural authority. At this point they met squarely the Calvinistic criticism that their system tended to produce infidelity. "Whatever doctrines seem to us to be clearly taught in the Scriptures," said Channing in 1819, "we receive without reserve or exception." His associates and followers were fond of asserting their allegiance to this Protestant principle. A writer for the *Christian Examiner*, discussing the "Misapprehensions of Unitarianism" in 1830, thought it not too much to say that Unitarians "recognize the divine authority of the Scriptures as completely as do our most Orthodox brethren." Not infrequently Unitarians declared themselves ready to support this assertion by submitting the doctrinal differences between themselves and Calvinists to the test of the Bible. The American editor of James Yates's *Vindication of Unitarianism* wrote in 1816 that his fellow believers

> *would esteem themselves but too happy, if the determination of the question, whether there is* one *Supreme Object of worship, or* three *Supreme Objects of worship, should be left to the clear and simple language of the Bible, explained by* any *consistent laws of interpretation.*

Indeed, Unitarians commonly remarked that if they could discover Calvinism in the Bible they would accept it. Wrote William Peabody in 1823:

> *We bring every doctrine and every duty to the test of Scripture; the reason of our rejecting certain doctrines, is, that we cannot find them taught in the Bible; if we did, we should embrace and avow them, as readily as we now disown and cast them away. No man can point to any sentiments which we have rejected because they are*

opposed to our reason merely; if we reject them, it is because we think they are not taught of God.

Since they were ready to submit their creed to the test of the Bible, Unitarians professed to be surprised at being accused of having an inadequate faith in revelation and of nurturing infidelity. The infidel rejects revelation, said a reviewer for the *Christian Examiner* in 1830, but the Unitarian confesses the "divine supernatural, miraculous origin of that system of interpositions and instructions, that is recorded in the Bible." And he added dramatically: "Was anything ever heard of, in all the annals of theological extravagance, more monstrous, than to charge men, who devoutly and gratefully profess to receive the Bible in this supernatural character, with being Infidels?"

III

By 1835 the chief points in the Orthodox attack on Unitarianism had often been stated and elaborated; they had, too, often been answered. There the matter apparently rested for a few years; and it might, in the fashion of such controversies, have gradually subsided had it not been for Ralph Waldo Emerson and Theodore Parker. In the decade beginning in 1838, these two young men embarrassed the leaders of the Unitarian movement, with which they had been identified, by assuming positions that seemed to Calvinists to justify their predictions concerning the tendency of the liberal theology toward infidelity.

In the summer of 1838, Emerson, addressing the graduating class of the Harvard Divinity School, urged candidates for Unitarian pulpits to forswear dependence upon the "Hebrew and Greek Scriptures." He frowned upon the "assumption that the age of inspiration is past, that the Bible is closed." He complained that "men have come to speak of revelation as somewhat long ago given and done, as if God were dead." Each of you, he assured his hearers, is "a newborn bard of the Holy Ghost."

Here was infidelity—an open rejection of the final and supernatural authority of the Bible. Unitarians, themselves, were among the first to point it out. Among the attacks on Emerson's address was one generally ascribed to Andrews Norton, professor of theology at Harvard. It contained the assertion that it was sufficient to say of Emerson that he "professes to reject all belief in Christianity as a revelation." For a later, more carefully considered statement of objections to the doctrine of Emerson's address, he chose the title "The latest form of infidelity."

Not all of Emerson's hearers, however, agreed with Norton. The young minister of the Unitarian congregation at West Roxbury, Theodore Parker, was delighted and stirred. "This week," he determined after listening to the address, "I shall write the long-meditated sermons on the state of the Church and the duties of these times."

The sermons which Parker, under the inspiration of Emerson's words, resolved to preach seem not to have disturbed his parishioners, countryfolk apparently unfamiliar with the nice aspects of the controversy. It was otherwise, however, when he spoke his mind in Boston before fellow Unitarian ministers. In May of 1841 he delivered the ordination sermon of Charles Shackford at the Hawes Place

Church in that city on the subject "The permanent and transient in Christianity." Less lofty than Emerson's address, his attack on the supernatural authority of the Bible was much more pointed and particular. Among the transitory elements in current Christianity, he placed the "doctrine respecting the origin and authority of the Old Testament." "It has been assumed at the outset, with no shadow of evidence," he said, "that those writers held a miraculous communication with God, such as he granted to no other man. What was originally a presumption of bigoted Jews became an article of faith, which Christians were burned for not believing." Surely, he continued, the belief that the Old Testament was miraculously inspired and infallibly true could not long endure. It was, in fact, already crumbling. Nor was the case for the infallibility of the New Testament any sounder. "Men have been bid to close their eyes at the obvious differences between Luke and John, the serious disagreements between Paul and Peter; to believe, on the smallest evidence, accounts which shock the moral sense and revolt the reason." Against this reverence for the Bible Parker protested. "An idolatrous regard for the imperfect scripture of God's word is the apple of Atalanta," he declared, "which defeats theologians running for the hand of divine truth." He dared to hope that it was passing away.

Such assertions did not, of course, remain unchallenged; Boston ministers refused to open their pulpits to this infidel. But a group of Boston laymen, interested in hearing him further, persuaded him to deliver a series of lectures in the city during the winter of 1841-42. In these discourses he elaborated his views of revelation, coming to the conclusion that

laying aside all prejudices, if we look into the Bible in a general way, as into other books, we find facts which force the conclusion upon us, that the Bible is a human work as much as the Principia of Newton or Descartes, or the Vedas and Koran.

When Calvinists read these pronouncements and those of Emerson, they felt justified in announcing that their predictions concerning the eventual decline of Unitarianism into infidelity had been fulfilled. They pointed to Transcendentalism as the end of the road along which "liberal Christianity," despite their warnings, had been traveling. From the strongholds of Orthodoxy at Princeton, New Haven, and Andover came such announcements. The *Biblical Repertory and Princeton Review* noted Emerson's attitude toward revelation, and minced no words in characterizing him as an infidel:

There is not a single truth or sentiment in this whole Address that is borrowed from the Scriptures. And why should there be? Mr. Emerson, and all men, are as truly inspired as the penmen of the sacred volume. Indeed he expressly warns the candidates for the ministry, whom he was addressing, to look only into their own souls for the truth. He has himself succeeded thus in discovering many truths that are not to be found in the Bible. . . . In a word, Mr. Emerson is an infidel and an atheist.

A review of the first series of Emerson's *Essays* two years later contained a blistering analysis of his "pantheism" and of his "characteristic profanation of scripture." This, said the reviewer, is what Unitarianism has come to. He found it a shocking, but not a surprising, development—one that had, in fact, been foreseen:

And this it is, which, if we are rightly informed, is to take the place of Unitarian Rationalism. The change is certainly great, but not surprising. Step by step the Unitarian theology has come down from the true position as to the inspiration of the scriptures, and thus having abandoned the only sure footing, those who are foremost in the descent have found themselves among the ooze and quicksands of atheistic philosophy.

In New Haven the *New Englander* likewise announced that the Transcendental infidelity was a logical outgrowth of Unitarianism. In the first of two articles on Theodore Parker in 1844, Parker's opinions were described as "the infidelity of the age"; and in the second the question was raised: "What is the process by which he was led to these results?" The author, Noah Porter, recently elected professor of metaphysics and moral philosophy at Yale College, felt sure that it was Parker's Unitarian training. He knew that Mr. Norton placed the blame for Parker's defection upon German metaphysics, but he was prepared to reject this defense.

Where learned Mr. Parker his philosophical system? Where did he discover that man himself might be so inspired, that his God could give him no added inspiration? . . . Mr. Norton will start up with his accustomed promptness, and reply: "Not from me–not from me. I have always taught as I do now, that man could not know God, or a future state, or his own moral nature, except as truths concerning these points are attested and confirmed by miracles. . . . But it is all German metaphysics, the adoption of the last importation from the dominion of tobacco smoke, and the taking up of the last extravagance that has come from the addled head of some German professor, that has done the mischief." Thus much might Prof. Norton say. But we are not quite certain that this is a complete and satisfactory account of the matter. We have some of us heard of Dr. Channing, and have known of his influence in shaping the principles and in forming the spirit of the liberal school. . . . We all know the relation in which he was accustomed to place man in respect to the Scriptures, and the office which he made the Bible fulfill to his wants. These views of Channing have pervaded, if indeed they have not constituted, the atmosphere of liberal Christianity. They have been as the unseen and impalpable particles which are diffused through the fluid, as the elements of future crystals. There was only wanting the fragment of some German system to serve as a nucleus, and behold they are gathered and shoot out from it at once, and we have them polished and hardened in all the beauty and symmetry of a perfect philosophic system.

After making a detailed analysis of "the principles and modes of thinking peculiar to liberal Christians," Porter concluded that Parker "is a consistent and logical thinker, and has carried them to no unnatural conclusions." A year later, writing about Parker's difficulties with the Boston Unitarian Association, he argued that Parker's strongest claim to recognition as a Unitarian in good standing was "that his opinions are the legitimate and logical consequence of the liberal theology."

At Andover, where every move among Boston Unitarians was keenly scrutinized, the doctrines of Emerson and Parker provoked a similar response. In 1846 Moses Stuart republished his letters to Channing of 1819, in which he had predicted the decline of Unitarianism into infidelity. He now added a long "postscript," pointing, not without pride, to the fulfilment of his prophecy. "A false prophet I was not, as it seems from the present state of *facts*," he wrote, "when I penned those remarks in my letters, twenty-six years ago." The opinions of Parker, he asserted, had derived lineally from those of older Unitarians, and must, if Unitarians remain consistent, eventually be shared by all of them. In the meantime, he was willing to credit Parker with superior consistency, frankness, and courage:

The fruits, in our own country, of beginnings like those in Germany during the years 1770-1800, are now plain and evident to all attentive observers. Had Dr. Channing lived until the present time, it is difficult to say what position he would have taken. But we know what position many of his friends and followers have taken. . . . But above all, the Rev. Theodore Parker, in his book Of Religion, *and other publications, has fully and openly taken the ultimate ground to which the principles in question naturally and even necessarily lead, in the mind of the bold and consistent men. . . . In my view, he has greatly the advantage, in respect to consistency and frankness and courage, over those Unitarians who are at variance with him, and who still cherish principles that must, at least if* logic *has any part to act, inevitably end in bringing them to the same views as those of Mr. Parker.*

In the face of these and similar reproaches, many Unitarians felt it necessary to cut the ties that bound Transcendentalists to them. Those who took this view, however, encountered a serious hindrance—their repeated declamations against the "exclusive system." With what grace, they were asked, can you, who have long inveighed against such a system, now exclude men like Parker and Emerson from your fellowship? This objection was first raised during the furor that followed Emerson's Divinity School address. At that time the *Christian Examiner* had proposed that hereafter the faculty of the Divinity School exercise a power of veto over student choices of lecturers. The proposal was vigorously denounced by James Freeman Clarke in the *Western Messenger*. He quoted at length from Greenwood's eulogy of the liberality of the Cambridge school and recalled how as a student there he had been warned against exclusiveness in religion and had been urged to independent pursuit of truth. Referring to the suggestion for faculty control of invitations to lecturers, he said: "This is indeed a 'New View.' " "At this late date," he asked, "is a new system to be introduced? Is that school really to become a college of propagandists? Is censorship to be established there?" Sadly he predicted the decline of the institution if this "novel policy" of "*religious exclusiveness*" should be adopted. A year later there appeared in the same journal a review of Norton's "The latest form of infidelity," in which Emerson's critic was reminded that in denying the Christian title to Transcendentalists he was employing the very tactics which he had formerly condemned. Much the same tone was adopted by George Ripley, who in his reply to Norton's pamphlet observed that the author's "Application of the exclusive principle is the more remarkable when we consider the vehemence with which he had opposed it in reference to his opinions."

Objections of the same character arose when Unitarians proposed expelling Parker from the Boston Association. The problem presented to "Liberal Christians" by the infidelity of Parker was far more acute than that raised by Emerson's doctrines, for, while Emerson had voluntarily stepped out of a Unitarian pulpit, Parker chose to remain in it. To the suggestion from the Boston Unitarian Association that, since he "hurt their usefulness, compromised their position," he ought to offer his resignation to the Association, he replied: "So long as the world standeth, I will not withdraw voluntarily while I consider rights of conscience at issue." When in January of 1843 the Boston Association debated in his presence his eviction from the society on the ground of his disbelief in the biblical miracles, he reminded them that no statement of belief had been required of him when he entered the society, and that Unitarians, unlike other sects had never set up creedal shibboleths—"had no symbolical books." When, a year later, he had been barred from "the great and Thursday lecture," Parker complained in a letter to the members of the Association that he was being made to suffer by their violation of their own principle that no man should be excluded from Christian fellowship on the basis of his theology. "Now, gentlemen," he said, "it seems to me that some of you are pursuing the same course you once complained of." One of the members of the Association to which this letter was addressed, Joseph Henry Allen, said, in reporting the difference between Parker and the Association: "Old memories of protest against 'the exclusive system' made a return to it impossible."

Thorny was the dilemma that was thus presented to Unitarians. To continue association with Parker was to lend color to the old charge of the Orthodox that Unitarianism was a halfway house to infidelity. To expel him was to abandon a principle that they had long fought for and earnestly cherished. Their predicament was shrewdly analyzed by Joseph Thompson in the *New Englander* for October of 1846. Thompson was reviewing George Putnam's sermon at the ordination of David Fosdick as minister of the Hollis Street Church in Boston. He found in the addresses delivered on that occasion evidence of "the difficulties that encompass the Unitarian body," in which "there is a great and portentous commotion." He discovered, too, the admission that Unitarianism "is a system of mere negations," and waxed facetious over Putnam's difficulty in framing a satisfactory definition of the movement, asking finally: "Is a Unitarian one who rejects miracles and the inspiration of the Scriptures? This appears to be the latest style of this indefinite character." This led him to an anlysis of the infidelity of Theodore Parker, and to the dilemma that Parker's views had forced upon Unitarians:

It is impossible to disown Mr. Parker without sacrificing their own consistency; it is impossible to retain him in their fellowship without giving up all pretence of being a Christian denomination. Yet one of the other of these things they must do. They must bring to light that unwritten creed; give it shape and expression; make it definite and stringent; make a new sect of orthodox Unitarians;–or they must evade all responsibility for such doctrines or their advocates, by disorganizing themselves completely; otherwise this new Rationalism must be regarded as the legitimate offspring, or the familiar associate of Unitarianism.

Unitarians were not at one concerning the solution of this uncomfortable problem. A few favored expelling Parker. Others suggested dissolving their Association to escape the odium of his attachment to it. The majority took a less strenuous, if less logical, course. Parker was not expelled, but he was vigorously denounced. He was allowed to remain in the Association, but he was shunned by most of its members. The *Christian Examiner* was at pains to make perfectly clear the general disapproval of him in Unitarian circles, and most of his colleagues refused to participate in the customary pulpit exchanges with him. His own account of his troubles, while bitter, seems amply justified:

At length, on the 19th of May, 1841, at the ordination of Mr. Shackford, a thoughtful and promising young man, at South Boston, I preached a "Discourse of the Transient and Permanent in Christianity" . . . a great outcry was raised against the sermon and its author. . . . I printed the sermon, but no bookseller in Boston would put his name to the title-page–Unitarian ministers had been busy with their advice. . . . Most of my clerical friends fell off; some would not speak to me in the street, and refused to take me by the hand; in their public meetings they left the sofas or benches when I sat down, and withdrew from me as Jews from contact with a leper. In a few months most of my former ministerial coadjutors forsook me, and there were only six who would allow me to enter their pulpits. . . . The controlling men of the denomination determined, "This young man must be silenced!" The Unitarian periodicals were shut against me and my friends–the public must not read what I wrote. Attempts were secretly made to alienate my little congregation, and expel me from my obscure station at West Roxbury.

Such intense antagonism and detestation Parker was to encounter from many Unitarians throughout his life. In 1857, for instance, the faculty of the Cambridge Divinity School canceled the invitation extended to him by the senior class to be its graduation lecturer; and at a meeting of Cambridge alumni two years later, when he was seriously ill, a resolution of sympathy for him was voted down.

The feeling which underlay actions of this sort is revealed in the *Reminiscences* of Samuel Lathrop, minister of the Brattle Street Unitarian congregation in Boston during the perturbation over Parker's beliefs. He is discussing the effects of Parker's discourse. "The transient and permanent in Christianity":

This outbreak, if I may call it so, of Mr. Parker disintegrated the clergy and the whole body of Unitarians, and dealt a blow from which Unitarianism has not, and probably as a religious denomination never will recover. The trouble caused ten years before by Mr. Emerson, when he preached against the Lord's supper and proposed to discontinue its administration, was slight and limited, because he resigned his charge and left the ministry; and, like an honest man, did not wish to make or hold the religious body to which he belonged and in which he had been educated responsible for his opinions. Mr. Parker insisted on retaining in all the ways that he could his connection with the Unitarians, and maintained that his views, opinions, and doctrines were not imported–not the result of his study of German theologians and philosophers,–but the logical result of the New England Unitarian theology. This made his influence damaging to Unitarianism, excited afresh the prejudice of the orthodox against it, and obtained for him sympathy and a large following, both of clergy and laity, among Unitarians themselves.

The resentment exhibited toward Emerson, who had left the Unitarian ministry before announcing his heresies, was, as is suggested by Lathrop's account, less harsh. Even so, Emerson observed that the Cambridge address had "given plentiful offense," and, writing in his journal concerning what he described to Carlyle as "the storm in our wash bowl," modestly reminded himself that "a few sour faces,—a few biting paragraphs,—is but a cheap expiation for all these shortcomings of mine." The *Christian Examiner* announced with respect to the doctrines of Emerson's address that "so far as they are intelligible, [they] are utterly distasteful to the instructors of the School, and to Unitarian ministers generally, by whom they are esteemed to be neither good divinity nor good sense." Andrews Norton of the Divinity School attacked them as "the latest form of infidelity," and was generally believed to be the author of an article in the Boston *Daily Advertiser* (August 27, 1838) in which the point was made that the officers of the Divinity School were in no wise responsible for Emerson's subversive discourse. His colleague, Henry Ware, published a sermon which the *Christian Examiner* hoped would "tend to disabuse the minds of many respecting the true character and tendency of a set of newly broached fancies, which, deceived by the high sounding pretensions of their proclaimers, they may have thought were about to quicken and reform the world." The sharpest words were written, perhaps, by Professor Felton, who found Emerson's discourse "full of extravagance and over-weening self-confidence, ancient errors disguised in misty rhetoric, and theories which would overturn society and resolve the world into chaos." Unitarians, said the *Western Messenger* in 1838, "have already fully vindicated themselves from the charge of agreeing with him [Emerson] in opinion. He has certainly been very soundly rated by them, in some instances we think with too much harshness and dogmatism."

Between the beliefs of the older group of Unitarians, to which men like Felton, Norton, and Ware belonged, and those of the new Transcendental school which sprang up among them, a wide chasm opened up. The opposition thus naturally engendered accounts in large part, of course, for the Unitarian dislike of Transcendentalism, even when full allowance is made for the amicable way in which men with differing theological views had cooperated in furthering the liberal movement. Its intensity, I am suggesting, can be fully understood only by considering the perplexing problems arising both from the character of the earlier Calvinistic attack upon Unitarianism and from the nature of the defense Unitarians had chosen to make. Squirming on the horns of a dilemma, many of them very naturally exhibited a bitter resentment toward those who, they felt, had forced them into their uncomfortable position.

17
Theodore Parker: Apostasy within Liberalism

Perry Miller

An intellectual history of democracy must deal largely with the ideas of freedom and equality. In the United States the story of freedom becomes mainly, though not exclusively, the history of liberalism. The origins of modern secular freedom are found in Enlightenment thought and in the Jeffersonian temper. Another root of American liberalism reaches back into the dissenting aspects of religious history, particularly to the time of the Great Awakening and again into the great Unitarian Controversy of the early nineteenth century. The memorable quality of the following essay lies in Perry Miller's ability to take the case of Theodore Parker, noble though it was in the cause of conscience and freedom of belief, and to probe its ambiguities, its meaning for intellectual criticism in our day, and to expose some strengths and weaknesses of American liberal thought then and now.

For further reading: *Henry Steele Commager, *Theodore Parker* (1936); Octavius B. Frothingham, *Transcendentalism in New England* (1876); John E. Dirks, *The Critical Theology of Theodore Parker* (1948); *Daniel Aaron, *Men of Good Hope* (1951), chaps. 1-2; John L. Thomas, "Romantic Reform in America, 1815-1865," *American Quarterly*, 17 (Winter 1965), 656-681; *George M. Fredrickson, *The Inner Civil War: Northern Intellectuals and the Crisis of the Union* (1965); *Martin Green, *The Problem of Boston* (1966).

I am not the first to detect in recent scholarship dealing with the transcendental period of New England a tendency toward vindicating, or at least toward putting in a good word for, the hitherto regularly berated opponents of Emerson and Theodore Parker. Because in the 1830s and 1840s and well into the 1850s the phalanx of those most outspoken in resistance were the Unitarian clergy, the custom has been for chroniclers of the literary and theological radicalism to heap derision upon the men who occupied established pulpits in the neighborhood of Boston and who

Harvard Theological Review, 54 (October 1961), 275-296. Reprinted by kind permission of the *Harvard Theological Review*.

spoke for the substantial portions of the community. In this indictment it is *de rigeur* to relate that after Parker's South Boston sermon of May 19, 1841, entitled *The Transient and Permanent in Christianity*, only eight of the local ministers would any longer exchange pulpits with him. Furthermore, after the publication in January 1842 of *A Discourse of Matters Pertaining to Religion*, the Boston Association directly challenged Parker to withdraw of his own accord. In the annals of American Protestant "liberality" these actions have long figured, axiomatically, as "persecution." Only within the last decade have voices been hesitantly raised to suggest that possibly something may be said on behalf of the alleged persecutors. Could it be that Unitarian Boston was not quite so bigoted as it has been represented?

Anyone brought up in the prevailing tradition, established by Parker's biographers in the later half of the century—by John Weiss, O. B. Frothingham, John White Chadwick—would assume as a matter of course that in the contests of the 1830s and '40s Emerson was the purest of white and Andrews Norton as black as the pit, that Parker was a gleaming Galahad while the Boston Association, with its eight memorable exceptions, was a nest of vipers. Interestingly enough, gestures toward a revision of this account have come from younger scholars. Possibly this phenomenon is a symptom of that swing toward "conformity" which elders with treasured memories of their own youthful deviations are prone to deplore. If to many fresh eyes Emerson and Parker are beginning to seem too fantastically obstreperous, as they did when judged by the organizational standards of a Samuel K. Lothrop or an Andrew Peabody, then we may no longer hold the comfortable persuasion that the Unitarianism of that time, which proclaimed itself "liberal," was entirely hypocritical.

What a revolution in our historiography is adumbrated, let alone enacted, by the very raising of this consideration! As early as 1848 James Russell Lowell posed, in *A Fable for Critics*, what had already become the ultraliberal query which no Unitarian might evade: how could the liberal Christianity conceivably accuse *anybody* of heresy, let alone a man of Parker's manifest sincerity? It should, of course, dissociate itself from professed atheists and deists, but how could there, within the community which owed allegiance to William Ellery Channing, be anything short of deism which deserved to be treated as apostasy? These "Socinians," as Lowell mischievously called them, said they believed something, though he confessed himself baffled as to just what it might be:

> I think I may call
> Their belief a believing nothing at all,
> Or something of that sort; I know they all went
> For a general union of total dissent:
> He went a step farther; without cough or hem,
> He frankly avowed he believed not in them;
> And, before he could be jumbled up or prevented,
> From their orthodox kind of dissent he dissented.

So the refrain continued even into 1926, with Vernon Parrington's *Main Currents*: Parker spoke out the truth which he had gathered at immense pains, said Parrington, and so was decried as a demagogue and agitator by "ministers and lawyers and merchants and politicians, men in high position, distinguished leaders of Boston society." Parker offended, according to Parrington, the Boston code of good breeding; he "pronounced judgment on Bostonians respected in the Back Bay, mighty in State Street." In 1936 the latest of Parker's biographers, Henry Commager, concluded with the familiar recitation that Parker had the courage as a young man, unknown and friendless, "to meet those black looks, those biting remarks, at the Berry Street Conferences." Parker had the great fortitude to endure the social ostracism, the odium. "Perhaps," mused Commager, "it would have been better if he had not fought back so hard; but he was a fighter, he couldn't help that." From Lowell to Commager, the scoundrels of the piece are the guardians of propriety, and these not the orthodox, not the Calvinists or the Methodists, but the liberal clergy, who, according to the sanctified narrative, turned upon him in a petulant rage which has exposed for all time, even until today, the hollowness of their pretensions to liberality. Instead of proving to be men of authentic probity, they showed themselves close hypocrites. Behind the courteous mask are disclosed the leprous features of what Parker thunderously denounced as "Hunkerism."

By the perfervid eloquence with which Parker presents himself as the martyr—in his public utterances, in his letters and journals—he contrives that any account of him must inescapably exhibit a saint crucified on Boston Common. His appeal overcomes the charges of his critics and even the frequent admissions of his followers that he obviously relished the role, that he embraced and exaggerated the contumely of his brethren. What free spirit among us can help being stirred into adherence by such a passage as this—announced to his "congregation" of three thousand, all refugees from conventional churches, in the Music Hall on November 14, 1852?

With such views, you see in what esteem I must be held by society, church, and state. I cannot be otherwise than hated. This is the necessity of my position–that I must be hated.

"Call me Ishmael," commenced the author of the most gigantic of American nonconformities, a romance entitled *Moby Dick*, published a year before Parker's "Some Account of My Ministry." For our century, which prides itself on having rediscovered Melville, on having for the first time divined the spiritual drive within Melville's diabolism, Parker becomes, even more dramatically than Frothingham or Chadwick could imagine, an archangel of dissent. For us, striving to breathe an atmosphere already filled with the filings of steel and perhaps soon to be permeated with particles of hydrogen, salvation is sought through vicarious identification with the figure of the rebel, the outsider, the angry young man—the more so while we are supinely submitting to the televised Hunkerism of the singing commercial. Hence Parker still looms for us, along with John Brown and Henry Thoreau, as one of the majestic nay-sayers in pre-Civil War America. So, if there are now murmurs against the canonization which liberals long ago bestowed upon him, we are indeed upon the threshold of a new crisis—if we have not already stumbled into it—similar to the agonizing one in which he was a principal actor—and victim.

Undoubtedly we today have to ask whether his habit of sentimentalizing his ostracism was not a form of self-pity. In his own time his friends would grant that he did a bit luxuriate in martyrdom, but they could then rally round what they held were his revolutionary teachings, and so maintain the standard attitude of militant defiance. For us, almost all his once earth-shaking pronouncements are commonplaces, have become in fact platitudes. Hence most of us are left sadly unmoved—where his friends were moved to tears of rage—by the disclosure of this passage from his journal on the eve of his forty-second birthday:

Poor dear father, poor dear mother! You little knew how many a man would curse the son you painfully brought into life, and painfully and religiously brought up. Well, I will bless you–true father and most holy mother were you to me: the earliest thing you taught me was duty–*duty to God, duty to man; that life is not a pleasure, not a pain, but a* duty.

Though we can hardly doubt the sincerity of this passage we are almost bound, I am sure, to detect in it an embarrassing mawkishness, a somewhat affected posturing before the mirror. And even many of the utterances to which his admirers have vibrated for a century may well appear to us slightly tinged with the sour envy of the plebian for the patrician.

I will go eastward and westward, and northward and southward, and make the land ring; *and if this New England theology, that cramps the intellect and palsies the soul of us, does not come to the ground, then it shall be because it has more truth in it than I have ever found.*

The reiterations of biographers and other celebrants—the facility with which they fall into the same incantations of denunciation for the respectable—eventually excite a suspicion among us that Parker seduces us into allegiance precisely because the targets of his most telling abuse are Boston and Harvard College. Satirizing the rigidities and sterilities of these communities has for many years become a sure-fire way of making a hit in Dubuque. They are always good for a laugh, as, to mention only two out of many recent examples, the commercial successes of John Marquand's *The Late George Apley* and Cleveland Amory's *The Proper Bostonians* demonstrate. The characters in such works who are shown in a comic light are almost always Unitarians—or if not, then former Unitarians who have sought a still more placid peace of mind by becoming Episcopalians. They are stereotypes cut from the same cardboard Santayana used for *The Last Puritan*. Therefore persons who are not Bostonians are happy to applaud when they find Parker writing in 1845: "I went to the meeting of the Unitarian Association; a stupid meeting it was, too. The brethren looked on me as the *Beni Elohim* looked on Satan, as he came last of all. However, they shook hands all the more tenderly, because the heart was not in it, and then turned the cold shoulder." However, this sort of thing is so infectious that Bostonians themselves join in the fun and discover a perverse pride in relishing all ridicule of themselves. The Harvard Divinity School has so hugged to its bosom the jibes Parker levied against it that I should perform a work of supererogation were I now to repeat the old chestnuts. Once Parker was safely dead and could no longer make a nuisance of himself, the most proper of Bostonians would graciously accept as the highest of compliments Parker's remark to his fellow agitator, Charles Sumner (whom the same classes also execrated in his life but whom they honored after his death by erecting his statue in Harvard Square), "Boston is a queer little city, the public is a desperate tyrant there, and it is seldom that one dares disobey the commands of public opinion."

Furthermore, as an encouragement to revisionist thinking, it manifestly is fair to admit that any fraternity has a constitutional right to refuse to accept persons it dislikes. The Unitarian clergy were an exclusive club of cultivated gentlemen—as the term was then understood in the Back Bay—and Parker was definitely not a gentleman, either in theology or in manners. Ezra Stiles Gannett, an honorable representative of the Sanhedrin, addressed himself frankly to the issue in 1845, insisting that Parker should not be persecuted or calumniated and that in this republic no power to restrain him by force could exist. Even so, Gannett judiciously argued, the association could legitimately decide that Parker "should not be encouraged nor assisted in diffusing his opinions by those who differ from him in regard to their correctness." We today are not entitled to excoriate honest men who believed Parker to be downright pernicious and who barred their pulpits against his demand to poison the minds of their congregations. One can even argue—though this is a delicate matter—that every justification existed for their returning the Public Lecture to the First Church, and so suppressing it, rather than letting Parker use it as a sounding board for his propaganda when his turn should come to occupy it. Finally, it did seem clear as day to these clergymen, as Gannett's son explained in the biography of his father, that they had always contended for the propriety of their claim to the title of Christians. Their demand against the Calvinist orthodoxy for intellectual liberty had never meant that they would follow "free inquiry" to the extreme of proclaiming Christianity a "natural" religion.

Grant all this—still, when modern Unitarianism and the Harvard Divinity School recall with humorous affection the insults Parker lavished upon them, or else argue that after all Parker received the treatment he invited, they betray an uneasy conscience. Whenever New England liberalism is reminded of the dramatic confrontation of Parker and the fraternity on January 23, 1843—while it may defend the privilege of Chandler Robbins to demand that Parker leave the association, while it may plead that Dr. N. L. Frothingham had every warrant for stating, "The difference between Trinitarians and Unitarians is a difference in Christianity; the difference between Mr. Parker and the Association is a difference between no Christianity and Christianity"—despite these supposed conclusive assurances, the modern liberal heaves repeatedly a sigh of relief, of positive thanksgiving, that the association never quite brought itself officially to expel Parker. Had it done so, the blot on its escutcheon would have remained indelible, nor could the Harvard Divinity School assemble to honor Parker's insurgence other than by getting down on its collective knees and crying "peccavi."

Happily for posterity, then, the Boston Association did not actually command Parker to leave the room, though it came too close for comfort to what would have been an unforgivable brutality. Fortunately, the honor of the denomination can attest that Cyrus Bartol defended Parker's sincerity, as did also Gannett and Chandler Robbins; whereupon Parker broke down into convulsions of weeping and rushed out of the room, though not out of the fellowship. In the hall, after adjournment, Dr. Frothingham took him warmly by the hand and requested Parker to visit him—whereupon our burly Theodore again burst into tears.

All this near tragedy, which to us borders on comedy, enables us to tell the story over and over again, always warming ourselves with a glow of complacency. It was indeed a near thing, but somehow the inherent decency of New England (which we inherit) did triumph. Parker was never excommunicated. To the extent that he was ostracized or even reviled, we solace ourselves by saying he asked for it. Yet, even after all these stratagems, the conscience of Christian liberality is still not laid to rest, any more than is the conscience of Harvard University for having done the abject penance for its rejection of Ralph Waldo Emerson's "Divinity School Address" of naming its hall of philosophy after him. In both cases the stubborn fact remains: liberalism gave birth to two brilliant apostates, both legitimate offspring of its loins, and when brought to the test, it behaved shabbily. Suppose they both had ventured into realms which their colleagues thought infidel: is this the way gentlemen settle frank differences of opinion? Is it after all possible that no matter how the liberals trumpet their confidence in human dignity they are exposed to a contagion of fear more insidious than any conservative has ever to worry about?

However, there is a crucial difference between the two histories. Emerson evaded the problem by shoving it aside, or rather by leaving it behind him: he walked out of the Unitarian communion, so that it could lick the wound of his departure, preserve its self-respect, and eventually accord him pious veneration. Parker insisted upon *not* resigning, even when the majority wanted him to depart, upon daring the fellowship to throw him out. Hence he was in his lifetime, as is the memory of him afterwards, a canker within the liberal sensitivity. He still points an accusing finger at all of us, telling us that we have neither the courage to support him nor the energy to cut his throat.

Actually, the dispute between Parker and the society of his time, both ecclesiastical and social, was a real one, a bitter one. It cannot be smoothed over by now cherishing his sarcasms as delightful bits of self-deprecation or by solemnly calling for a reconsideration of the justice of the objections to him. The fact is incontestable: that liberal world of Unitarian Boston *was* narrow-minded, intellectually sterile, smug, afraid of the logical consequences of its own mild ventures into iconoclasm, and quite prepared to resort to hysterical repressions when its brittle foundations were threatened. Parker, along with Garrison and Charles Sumner, showed a magnificent moral bravery when facing mobs mobilized in defense of the Mexican War and slavery. Nevertheless, we can find reasons for respecting even the bigotry of the populace; their passions were genuine, and the division between them and the abolitionists is clear-cut. But Parker as the ultraliberal minister within the pale of a church which had proclaimed itself the repository of liberality poses a different problem, which is not to be resolved by holding him up as the champion of freedom. Even though his theological theses have become, to us, commonplaces, the fundamental interrogation he phrased is very much with us. It has been endlessly rephrased, but I may here put it thus: at what point do the tolerant find themselves obliged to become intolerant? And then, as they become aware that they have reached the end of their patience, what do they, to their dismay, learn for the first time about themselves?

There can be no doubt, the Boston of that era could be exquisitely cruel in enforcing its canons of behavior. The gentle Channing, revered by all Bostonians, orthodox or Unitarian, wrote to a friend in Louisville that among its many virtues Boston did not abound in a tolerant spirit, that the yoke of opinion crushed individuality of judgment and action:

No city in the world is governed so little by a police, and so much by mutual inspections and what is called public sentiment. We stand more in awe of one another than most people. Opinion is less individual or runs more into masses, and often rules with a rod of iron.

Even more poignantly, and with the insight of a genius, Channing added—remember, this is Channing, not Parker!—that should a minister in Boston trust himself to his heart, should he "speak without book, and consequently break some law of speech, or be hurried into some daring hyperbole, he should find little mercy."

Channing wrote this—in a letter! I think it fair to say that he never quite reached such candor in his sermons. But Theodore Parker, commencing his mission to the world-at-large, disguised as the minister of a "twenty-eighth Congregational Church" which bore no resemblance to the Congregational polities descended from the founders (among which were still the Unitarian churches), made explicit from the beginning that the conflict between him and the Hunkerish society was not something which could be evaporated into a genteel difference about clerical decorum. Because he spoke openly, as Channing had prophesied someone might, with daring hyperbole, Parker vindicated Channing's prophecy that he who committed this infraction of taste would promptly discover how little mercy liberals were disposed to allow to libertarians who appeared to them libertines.

By reminding ourselves of these factors in the situation, we should, I am sure, come to a fresh realization, however painful it be, that the battle between Parker and his neighbors was fought in earnest. He arraigned the citizens in language of so little courtesy that they had to respond with, at the least, resentment. What otherwise could "the lawyer, doctor, minister, the men of science and letters" do when told that they had "become the cherubim and seraphim and the three archangels who stood before the golden throne of the merchant, and continually cried, 'Holy, holy, holy is the Almighty Dollar' "? Nor, when we recollect how sensitive were the emotions of the old Puritan stock in regard to the recent tides of immigration, should we be astonished that their thin lips were compressed into a white line of rage as Parker snarled at them thus:

Talk about the Catholics voting as the bishop tells! reproach the Catholics for it! You and I do the same thing. There are a great many bishops who have never had a cross on their bosom, nor a mitre on their head, who appeal not to the authority of the Pope at Rome, but to the Almighty Dollar, a pope much nearer home. Boston has been controlled by a few capitalists, lawyers and other managers, who told the editors what to say and the preachers what to think.

This was war. Parker meant business. And he took repeated care to let his colleagues know that he intended them: "Even the Unitarian churches have caught the malaria, and are worse than those who deceived them''—which implied that they were very bad indeed. It was ''*Duty*'' he said that his parents had given him as a rule—beyond even the love that suffused his being and the sense of humor with which he was largely supplied—and it was duty he would perform, though it cost him acute pain and exhausted him by the age of fifty. Parker could weep—and he wept astonishingly often and on the slightest provocation—but the psychology of those tears was entirely compatible with a remorseless readiness to massacre his opponents. ''If it gave me pleasure to say hard things,'' he wrote, ''I would shut up for ever.'' We have to tell ourselves that when Parker spoke in this vein, he believed what he said, because he could continue, ''But the TRUTH, which cost me bitter tears to say, I must speak, though it cost other tears hotter than fire.'' Because he copiously shed his own tears, and yielded himself up as a living sacrifice to the impersonalized conscience of New England, he was not disturbed by the havoc he worked in other people's consciences.

Our endeavor to capture even a faint sense of how strenuous was the fight is muffled by our indifference to the very issue which in the Boston of 1848 seemed to be the central hope of its Christian survival, that of the literal, factual historicity of the miracles as reported in the four gospels. It is idle to ask why we are no longer disturbed if somebody, professing the deepest piety, decides anew that it is of no importance whether or not Christ transformed the water into wine at eleven A.M. on the third of August, A.D. 32. We have no answer as to why we are not alarmed. So we are the more prepared to give Parker the credit for having taken the right side in an unnecessary controversy, to salute his courage, and to pass on, happily forgetting both him and the entire episode. We have not leisure, or the patience, or the skill, to comprehend what was working in the mind and heart of a then recent graduate of the Harvard Divinity School who would muster the audacity to contradict his most formidable instructor, the magisterial Andrews Norton, by saying that, while he believed Jesus, ''like other religious teachers,'' worked miracles, ''I see not how a miracle proves a doctrine.'' What indeed *has* happened to us? While we sagely approve this devastation of Parker's, we ourselves are not prepared to make of it a slogan against the miracles. It is worth an hour of our time to summon up the shade of Theodore Parker, if only to let him squarely put the question to us.

For clearly it is not enough to answer that we have exhausted the subject or that it has exhausted us, that we consider it wearisome and no longer worth disputing. That is an easy way out, which enables us to leave our churches on a Sunday morning and go placidly home to an unperturbed dinner. It precludes our having to participate in the ferocity with which Parker propounded, and with which his enemies condemned, the jolting thesis of the South Boston sermon:

> *If Jesus had taught at Athens, and not at Jerusalem; if he had wrought no miracles, and none but the human nature had ever been ascribed to him; if the Old Testament had forever perished at his birth–Christianity would still have been the word of God; it would have lost none of its truths.*

Either this passage is arrant nonsense or else it reveals that something more incendiary is at work than an academic discourse about the authenticity of the miracles. If the first, then we have gathered today for a ceremonial exhumation, after which we shall seal the coffin for at least another century. If the second, then we are obliged to probe further into hidden chambers and ask what actually was at stake when Parker offended his colleagues over the miracles.

All accounts attest the staggering range of his reading. He was literate in at least twenty languages, he collected an immense library, and he pored over the interminable literature of early nineteenth-century German examinations of the Biblical texts—a jungle which was and which still is impenetrable for most students of theology. Yet in his own publications, and even more in his preaching, he made strikingly little use of this fund of learning. Indeed, the one and only monument to his titanic labors in his library is his version of the treatise on the Old Testament by Wilhelm Martin Leberecht De Wette. Born in 1780 in a town near Weimar, De Wette had known Schiller and Goethe, received his inspiration immediately from Herder. Exiled from Prussia by royal decree in 1819, he was for three decades the entrenched and powerful theologian at Basel, whence he fought against the rationalists on his left and the evangelical pietists on his right. Americans understood little of the European situation, and were instinctively hostile to everything German. They had no awareness of De Wette's position, but they had heard vaguely that he was dangerous to every form of Christianity. Parker entitled his rendition, *A Critical and Historical Introduction to the Canonical Scriptures of the Old Testament*. He completed the first draft in 1837, worked it over and over, added copious notes and comments, and finally put the huge manuscript through the press in July 1843. Apparently it had no effect upon religious thought in America, except to advertise Parker's adherence to Germanism and to insinuate by his use of "Canonical" in the title that he was attempting to shatter the coherence of the Old Testament.

In addition to the translation and the footnotes, Parker also spoke briefly but effectively for himself. If we seek the true grounds for his intransigence, we shall find it in this book rather than in his more diffuse and scandalous declarations about the miracles. Or rather, the latter statements were consequences of what he had learned from his study of De Wette: they were the corollary of his scholarship, though he was sufficiently a child of the New England tradition to know instinctively that in the pulpit the use of art is to conceal art. Verbal though he was—indeed much too profuse—and garrulous as were his publications, he never allowed himself the time to explain precisely wherein his technique consisted in a use of history to destroy historicity. Hence it may be said that he was something of an enigma to his contemporaries, and was even a puzzle to himself. In which case, we must expound more exactly than he ever quite could do, or cared to do, why he is worth remembering a hundred years after he expired in Florence.

We have to attest that despite his omnivorous reading in the Biblical scholars he himself showed little or no originality in the technical areas. That which Emerson said of the whole transcendental group applies even to him: their scholarship exhibited the typically American superficiality. But the square-toed son of a Lexington farmer, and the forthright grandson of the commander of militia on the Lexington Common, could make out, from his service with De Wette, that the education purveyed by the Harvard Divinity School evaded what De Wette termed "negative criticism." The school was always saying—the more nervously because the orthodox accused it of merely negating—that such and such was true. Wherefore it had come, through no other compulsion than its own neurasthenia, to insisting that a man could not be accounted a Christian who disbelieved in the historicity of the miracles, though he might bask in the rays of salvation while serenely rejecting the Trinity. Parker hardly needed De Wette or any Continental scholar to point out the obvious discrepancy, though his Germanic importations supplied him with the authority to denounce it: the bias, not to say the shameless predilection, of his Unitarian elders in favor of the miracles and against the Trinity put blinders on their eyes. They could not freely employ any critical method. If they could not, then wherein were they actually more emancipated than the Calvinists? As Parker strove over and over again to make his point to the association, he was not worried whether they did or did not believe in miracles. What galled him was that they should dogmatize in advance as to the factualness of the performances, and then abhor as an Ishmael any who insisted, as Parker kept insisting, upon the preliminary need for an open-minded examination of the credentials. His apostasy within liberalism centers upon his elevation of this word "criticism," which came to be the term that his Unitarian opponents most detested. This was the more disturbing because they were persuaded that they had practiced all the critical rigor the civilized world any longer required.

Parker strove to demonstrate to the glib American student wherein real erudition consisted by giving translations as well as the originals of Latin, Greek and Hebrew quotations. To pile Pelion upon Ossa, or perhaps we should say in order to add insult to injury, he added out of his own reading masses of corroborative materials from patristic and modern commentators. The result was that he produced a De Wette which was nothing like what the *Einleitung* dared to be in its native language. Parker's rendition is a chronicle of how variously the Old Testament has been read by successive ages of Christendom, of how frequently the sense of one century has contradicted that of another. Thus he endeavored to teach the present generation to distrust its own dogmatics. He was, he tells us, tempted to entitle the book an "Introduction on the Basis of De Wette" rather than a "Translation," but he decided the latter more "modest." Yet by publishing this quandary, Parker effectively violated his own modesty, and we may well conclude that in this case arrogance was the better part of valor. Still, he made his critics aware that the two volumes were something more than a literal rephrasing, that they were specifically directed at the vitals of liberality. "I can only hope," he concluded, "the work will direct critical inquiries to a faithful examination of the Bible and that correct views of its origin and contents may at length prevail." This was an oblique way of announcing that so far only incorrect views were in circulation, at the Harvard Divinity School as well as at Andover. Parker's humble profession of hoping to be instrumental "in spreading the light of truth on this subject" could appear to his peers only as a conceited claim that he had a monopoly on that illumination.

He managed to highlight De Wette's basic statement of the method, of its scientific character, as being (the italics are Parker's) *historico-critical*. That is to say, as De Wette contended and as Parker gleefully translated, the Bible is to be considered a wholly historical phenomenon, completely subject to the professional rules of historical inquiry. Consequently, any consideration of it "in a religious view" comes into the range of De Wette's analysis only insofar as the dogma of inspiration and revelation is connected with the origin of the tests. It follows, De

Wette put into the crucial sentence, "This dogma itself, therefore, is likewise to be treated historically." What Parker manufactured out of his "translation" thereupon appears in a paragraph of his own composition, which is not so much an addition as a blunt interpolation, which he distinguished from the original by printing it in brackets, and thereby loudly calling attention to it.

"Most of the English and American theologians," he wrote with deceptive calmness, insist that the books of the Bible, especially those of the Old Testament, be considered from a religious point of view, "declaring [again, the italics are Parker's] *dogmatic theology* is the touchstone, wherewith we are to decide be tween the true and false, the genuine and the spurious." Hence they refuse to examine—or are incapable of examining—the Bible as a historical production. They force themselves to treat it as the highest standard of human faith and life.

Parker does not go out of his way to note that this condemnation applies as well to Andrews Norton's ponderous and stillborn volumes on the *Evidences of Christianity* as to the Calvinistic commentaries of Moses Stuart. But in 1843 everybody in eastern Massachusetts—and at Yale and Princeton—would know whom he attacked. When either of them, Unitarian or orthodox, approached the books of the Bible as a peculiar phenomenon, not to be judged by the same canons of criticism which apply to all other human writings—say, to the plays of Shakespeare—Parker roundly declared that their supposedly different methods remained in effect a single and erroneously stupid way of exposition—that which "strikes a death-blow to all criticism, and commits the Bible to a blind and indiscriminating belief."

The essence of Parker's thinking is here succinctly stated. We may say that throughout the last two hectic decades he did nothing but ring changes upon it, or merely repeat it. Some may then object that if this is all the shooting was about, then the provocation was trivial, that the whole commotion had better be forgotten rather than celebrated a century after Parker's self-imposed immolation.

I suspect that the issue is not dead. It is not only still with us, but in the era of Niebuhr and Tillich and Barth it has actually become, if anything, more pressing than it was in the 1840s. At any rate, of this we may be assured, that Parker, guided by De Wette and his readings in German romantic literature, faced up to the problem of criticism as no one else in his America did—as Emerson certainly never did and as in fact, strange though the conjunction at first sight appears, only Edgar Allan Poe came near to doing. Yet on second thought the conjunction is not too far-fetched. In the sense in which I use this phrase, "the problem of criticism," and as Parker was trying to spell it out both in the De Wette Introduction and the *Discourse*, it pertains equally to the fields of literary evaluation and Biblical scholarship.

In the *Discourse*, amid what was as usual his too gushing volubility, Parker managed (as occasionally he could) to frame several compact sentences which his opponents never understood and the full implications of which, in all areas of the mind, Parker himself may not have appreciated. For Parker was thinking only of the parochial issue of the miracles when he said that because of a literal belief in the narrative of the Bible, "A deference is paid to it wholly independent of its intrinsic merit." He had in mind mostly, maybe only, the then excitingly new discovery by the Romantic Age that history treated imaginatively need not be fettered by the history of historians when he declared that the mythology of the Bible should be surgically separated from its factual record, so that the critic could "take the Bible for what it is worth." This did not mean that he would reverence the factual and discard the mythological; on the contrary, knowledge of the distinction would make the latter meaningful for the first time in the life of Christianity. So he was speaking only as a Unitarian when he wrote that if we are required to "believe" the whole of the Bible, absurdities and all—if we stupidly make one part authoritative in the single sense by which we treat another as regulatory—"then we make the Bible our master, who puts Common Sense and Reason to silence, and drives Conscience and the religious Element out of the Church."

But suppose, if this be not too extravagant an interjection, we now substitute in Parker's sentences Hamlet for the Bible, and the cult of Shakespeare for the Unitarian Church. What have we, in either form, but a statement of the ever tormenting question of an individual's relation toward that to which he subjects himself—to that which is over and above him, more powerful than he can ever be, which he deeply loves but also in startling moments of awareness fears—against which he must preserve his own particular being? Parker's effort was to save the human spirit from becoming embalmed in Bibliolatry, just as a major effort of modern criticism has been to rescue living intelligence from Shakespeareolatry. The same obstacles persist: in Parker's day, his opponents did not know their souls had already atrophied amid their gracious conventions, as in our day academic instructors in Shakespeare courses are unaware their lungs have ceased to function. In that sense, Parker's campaign, at the Melodeon and at the Music Hall, was a contest for life against death, in which he used a timeless sense of historical fluctuations as his supreme weapon against the deadly illusion of historical finality.

Yet this is not to conclude—not by any means—that upon our reexamination we should join with Parrington and Commager in elevating Parker once more as the paladin of freedom against repressive Boston. Some of his critics were intelligent enough not to denounce him solely because he divorced belief in Christ from belief in the miracles. A few were astute enough—let this be chalked up to their credit—to note that he was himself guilty of the very crime he charged against them. He delighted, for instance, in disclosing how he, and he alone, had found in the Pentateuch "marks of a distinct plan and design on the part of the compiler." He deciphered the cunning plot, this subtle scheme, as though he were a cryptographer breaking a code—as though he were Edgar Poe constructing and then unraveling a detective story—and so could describe the tremendous fabrication as "artificial." Then, speaking as a modern man of letters, he announced that this was no disparagement of the compiler any more than a similar criticism would be of the legendary compiler known as Homer. Both had constructed a national epic. What Parker would blame was the ridiculous fancy among Christians of thrusting the authorship of the Biblical romance onto the Deity.

Yet Parker was unwilling to note—even though he assured his people that he and they entertained many opinions which future criticism would prove erroneous—that this sort of "historical" method, especially when it exposed some secret design behind an obfuscation of Scripture, was as fully prepared to impose its scheme of interpretation upon the Bible as were Unitarians to impose upon it their fable of the miracles. Parker was ready, in the end of all, to translate the untranslatable into the dreary prose of De Wette, just as any Calvinist had formerly been eager to translate the gospels into the five points of the Synod of Dort. Therefore it is not to be wondered at that there should arise in modern theology, as in modern literary discussion, a tribe of recalcitrants who consign all of Parker's and De Wette's annotations, along with those of Strauss or Baur or Moulton, to the realm of irrelevant footnotes—who proclaim anew the inner coherence of the Bible, just as cognate spirits in the other sorts of criticism summon us to contemplate the "essential" tragedy of Hamlet apart from all historical consideration of Elizabethan manners, diction, or of the belief in the objective reality of ghosts. In a sense, Parker's opponents, standing firm on a principle of interpretation which they would not yield to the formless relativity of historical anthropology, clinging fanatically to the sterile doctrine of the miracles, could rationally insist that they were the ones who came to the Bible for what it was worth, the ones who respected its intrinsic merit; whereas Parker, pretending to separate wheat from chaff, merely extracted verses which suited his preconception, and then called the rest chaff. The Unitarians were saying, as Norton's *Evidences* boldly contended, that the divine relevation could not be made less divine by any amount of explication of the historical circumstances, by any account of tribal customs, or by any demonstrations of how books were compiled or texts interlaced. Employ the *historico-critical* method as rigorously as you will, this generation of Unitarians in effect (though seldom as pungently as they should have) declared, the Bible remains the Bible. And the Bible, though it does not mention the Trinity and so should not bear the burden of this monstrosity, emphatically does tell of the miracles, exactly as Hamlet does contain a ghost. Parker, in their view, was deceiving not only to multitudes who flocked to the Music Hall instead of to decently constituted churches, but also himself. The glad tidings he gave out were not those of release, after all, but of an enslavement to a priori transcendentalism.

Meanwhile, out of his study of the Old Testament under De Wette's tuition, Parker acquired a deep respect for the prophets, even while he was learning an even deeper contempt for the priests. As he taught himself and his people to discard the notion that the prophets had ever pretended to be forecasters of events, he saw with what seemed to him absolute clarity that they had been men who grasped the nature of their social emergencies, who realized wherein lay the sinful complacency of the prosperous. As soon as he conceived the "truth" of the Old Testament in these terms he understood why priests who offered their congregations an explanation of the Bible which purported to be definitive for all time to come would by that very token not be disturbed by slavery, by the flourishing of prostitution in Boston, or by the cheats and hypocrisies of ordinary business conduct. They could not be prophets, for their theology rendered them insensitive to the crises of their time. We may suppose that merely by temperament Parker would have flung himself into all such "causes" as abolition and women's rights, but his doctrine of the prophet as opposed to the priest certainly supplied him with a formal justification. Only a prophet could denounce the rituals of the priests in the name of a Jehovah who was the eternal rule of virtue. The paradox with which the prophets could live but which terrified the sanctimonious priests consisted in the recognition that this standard or righteousness was to be apprehended only through familiarity with the historical, and so with the temporal and fleeting, manifestations of it. History thus elevated its own methodology into a destructive force, which over and over again became the purgation of false religion. Yet destruction was not an end in itself: it was the necessary prologue, age after age, to what Parker, in his most ecstatic moments, hailed as "absolute religion."

It is a distorted image of Parker that the ancient and honorable of Massachusetts held of him during his life, which they cherished after his death, that of the religious demagogue, the brash seeker for publicity by sensationally taking up every disreputable movement for "reform" then being agitated among New England's peculiarly active lunatic fringe. This judgment casts discredit upon the judges, not upon Parker, for it is blind to the majestic nobility of the man. It is, however, an equally distorted portrait that has been created by such libertarians as Parrington, by the epigoni of transcendentalism in the various "free religion" movements by cantankerous village noncomformists—that of the ever stalwart fighter for freedom in an age and against a society that had surrendered to cowardice. This view is blind to the neurotic compulsions which drove him to his maniacal ransacking of the world's scholarship without enabling him to use it beyond his edition of De Wette, to his pitifully limited aesthetic sense, to the facile nature of his few basic ideas, his intuitive and utterly dogmatic trust in his conception of God and immortality, and the repetitious banality of most of his published works.

Yet both these conceptions become useless once we penetrate to a more important context, because both of them are formulated on superficial levels of conventional categorization which bear only a distant relation to a deeper level wherein the true significance of Theodore Parker resides. On this other plane there is no such fundamental conflict between an oversimplified liberalism and a grotesque conservatism. On this level, both parties were, and in the American Protestant community still are, entangled within the same net of confusion. If we take the term "theological liberalism" to mean roughly the syndrome of propositions Parker put forth—historical criticism of the Bible, rejection of formalized creeds and most especially of the Westminster, assertion of the rights of intuition over speculation and of the heart over the head, along with an elevation of reason over authority, a boundless optimism as to human perfectibility along with a sacred obligation to fight eternally against social evils—then we may conclude that Parker dramatized the hitherto concealed terror within the assurance of progress. An advancing liberalism, he demonstrated, even though this was not his intention, is bound, the more it forges ahead, the more to slacken its attack on the enemy at its front and to turn back, in order to dismantle the great bastions it had formerly erected on what had been frontier outposts, beyond which it has passed. In practice, then, it can never entertain the prospect of ultimate or final victory, or any resting place. It can enjoy no surcease from insecurity and anxiety. Where the orthodox conservative must murder the Lamb of God, where Oedipus must murder his father, in order to enter their inheritance, the liberal has no time for either diversion. He is too busy killing himself. Or, more precisely, in slaying the previous incarnation of himself, as we in this present ceremony are dismembering Theodore Parker. The history of liberal religion is one of perpetual suicide.

Amid these tensions Parker strove to maintain his tremulous balance; amid these he suffered, until at last they did destroy him. What he demands of us is not so much love or even sympathy—though these are rewarding exercises of the spirit when extended to him—but more than these, a full and just comprehension of his and of our own predicament.

18 Emerson's Tragic Sense

Stephen E. Whicher

By going to some of Emerson's famous essays the reader can best receive that electric and startling charge of original ideas which first aroused Emerson's Concord friends, then the Boston community of letters and reformers, then all New England, and finally all the North. The background of Emerson's change from a Unitarian minister to a Transcendentalist philosopher is portrayed in *Essay 16;* the problem of Transcendentalism as a "liberal" stance is revealed in *Essay 17*. In this essay Stephen Whicher (1915-1961) exposes a side of Emerson seldom examined. It is a side that, in Whicher's view, reflects some of the pressing issues in twentieth-century "realism," particularly those concerned with the individual's sense of his own incapacity, his intellectual integrity, and his spiritual freedom.

For further reading: *Milton Konvitz and Stephen Whicher (eds.), *Emerson: A Collection of Critical Essays* (1962); *F. O. Matthiessen, *American Renaissance* (1941); Merrell R. Davis, "Emerson's 'Reason' and the Scottish Philosophers," *New England Quarterly*, 17 (June 1944), 209-228; *R. W. B. Lewis, *The American Adam: Innocence, Tragedy, and Tradition in the Nineteenth Century* (1955).

There is something enigmatic about most American authors. Poe, Hawthorne, Melville, Thoreau, Whitman, Mark Twain, Emily Dickinson, Henry Adams, Henry James, Frost, Faulkner—each has his secret space, his halls of Thermes, his figure in the carpet, which is felt most strongly in his best work and yet eludes definition. Sometimes it is quite opposed to what its possessor thinks he is or wants to be: for example, Hawthorne, envying Trollope his sunshine and his sales, whose best story was "positively hell-fired"; or Whitman, affirmer of life, whose poetry is never more powerful than when it treats of death; Poe, who liked to think himself icily logical and who wrote best from a haunted fantasy; Mark Twain, professional joker and amateur pessimist; or Frost, tough and humorous individualist, whose best

American Scholar, 22 (Summer 1953), 285-293. Reprinted by kind permission of Elizabeth Whicher and the publishers.

poems are often his saddest. Generally this is linked with an obscure fear or grief, even despair: American literature, closely read, can seem one of the least hopeful of literatures.

To all this, Emerson, representative American author that he is, is no exception. The more we know him, the less we know him. He can be summed up in a formula only by those who know their own minds better than his. We hear his grand, assuring words, but where is the man who speaks them? We know the part he played so well; we feel his powerful charm: we do not know the player. He is, finally, impenetrable, for all his forty-odd volumes.

Yet no man can write so much and so honestly and not reveal himself in some measure. We can see enough to sense in him an unusually large gap, even a contradiction, between his teachings and his experience. He taught self-reliance and felt self-distrust, worshiped reality and knew illusion, proclaimed freedom and submitted to fate. No one has expected more of man; few have found him less competent. There is an Emersonian tragedy and an Emersonian sense of tragedy, and we begin to know him when we feel their presence underlying his impressive confidence.

Of course I must stress the word "Emersonian" here. As Mark Van Doren has remarked, "Emerson had no theory of tragedy," unless to deny its existence is a theory. His oblivion can be prodigious.

The soul will not know either deformity or pain. If, in the hours of clear reason, we should speak the severest truth, we should say that we had never made a sacrifice. In these hours the mind seems so great, that nothing can be taken from us that seems much. All loss, all pain, is particular; the universe remains to the heart unhurt. Neither vexations nor calamities abate our trust. No man ever stated his griefs as lightly as he might.

As he explained in his lecture on "The Tragic," the man who is grounded in the divine life will transcend suffering in a flight to a region "whereunto these passionate clouds of sorrow cannot rise."

Such transcendence of suffering is one of the great historic answers to tragedy and commands respect. To be valid, however, it must "cost not less than everything." Emerson seems to pay no such price. When, in the same lecture on "The Tragic," he tells the "tender American girl," horrified at reading of the transatlantic slave trade, that these crucifixions were not horrid to the obtuse and barbarous blacks who underwent them, "but only a little worse than the old sufferings," we wonder if he paid anything at all for his peace. The only coin in which we can discharge our debt to suffering is attention to it, but Emerson seems to evade this obligation.

Yet this chilling idealism is not simple insensitivity. Emerson is teaching his tested secret of insulation from calamity: Live in the Soul. His famous assertion in *Experience* of the unreality of his devastating grief for his son is an impressive illustration of the necessity he was under to protect, at whatever human cost, his hard-won security. Yeats has said somewhere that we begin to live when we have conceived life as tragedy. The opposite was true of Emerson. Only as he refused to conceive life as tragedy could he find the courage to live.

By denying man's fate, however, Emerson did not escape it. His urgent need to deny it shows that his confidence was more precarious than he would admit. Who has not felt the insistence, the over-insistence, in such radical claims to freedom and power as *Self-Reliance*?

> *Trust thyself: every heart vibrates to that iron string. Accept the place the divine providence has found for you, the society of your contemporaries, the connection of events. Great men have always done so, and confided themselves childlike to the genius of their age, betraying their perception that the absolutely trustworthy was seated at their heart, working through their hands, predominating in all their being. And we are now men, and must accept in the highest mind the same transcendent destiny; and not minors and invalids in a protected corner, not cowards fleeing before a revolution, but guides, redeemers, and benefactors, obeying the Almighty effort, and advancing on Chaos and the Dark.*

What speaks here is self-*dis*trust, a distrust so pervasive that it must find an "absolutely trustworthy" seated at the heart before it can trust at all. Self-reliance, in the oft cited phrase, is God-reliance, and therefore not self-reliance. Contrast the accent of a genuine individualist like Ibsen: "The strongest man in the world is he who stands most alone." Or recall a truly self-reliant American: "It was about this time I conceiv'd the bold and arduous project of arriving at moral perfection. I wish'd to live without committing any fault at any time; I would conquer all that either natural inclination, custom, or company might lead me into. As I knew, or thought I knew, what was right and wrong, I did not see why I might not always do the one and avoid the other. . . . For this purpose I therefore contrived the following method." The free and easy assurance of Franklin is just what is missing in Emerson.

Certainly the first thirty years or so showed no great self-trust. A tubercular, like many in his family (two brothers died of the disease), he was engaged throughout his twenties in a serious battle of life and death in which he was not at all sure of winning. With his poor health went a disheartening self-criticism. He imagined he was incurably idle and self-indulgent, without force or wordly competence, constrained in the company of others, unresponsive in his affections. Though his early journals often show a manly courage and good sense, the dominant mood is a sense of impotence. He lacks all power to realize his larger ambitions and feels himself drifting, sometimes in humiliation, sometimes in wry amusement, before the inexorable flowing of time. He was the servant more than the master of his fate, he found in 1824; and later, in the depths of his illness, it seemed to him that he shaped his fortunes not at all. In all his life, he wrote, he obeyed a strong necessity.

The electrifying release of power brought to him by the amazing discovery, the start of his proper career, that God was within his own soul is understandable only against this early—indeed, this lifelong submission to a strong necessity. His subjection bred a longing for self-direction, all the stronger for his underlying sense of its impossibility. The force of his transcendental faith, and its almost willful extravagance, sprang from his need to throw off, against all probability and common sense, his annihilating dependence. He welcomed the paradoxical doctrine that "God dwells in thee" with uncritical delight, as the solution to all the doubts that oppressed him, and rushed in a Saturnalia of faith to spell out its revolutionary consequences for the solitary soul:

. . . The world is nothing, the man is all; . . . in yourself slumbers the whole of Reason; it is for you to know all, it is for you to dare all. . . . The height, the deity of man is, to be self-sustained, to need no gift, no foreign force. . . . All that you call the world is the shadow of that substance which you are, the perpetual creation of the powers of thought, of those that are dependent and of those that are independent of your will. . . . You think me the child of my circumstances: I make my circumstance. . . .

. . . Every rational creature has all nature for his dowry and estate. It is his, if he will. He may divest himself of it; he may creep into a corner, and abdicate his kingdom, as most men do, but he is entitled to the world by his constitution.

Yet this proclamation of the kingdom of man was always what he soon came to call it, a romance. He retained a common-sense awareness (and so retains our respect) that experience did not support it. Not merely were all manipular attempts to realize his kingdom premature and futile. The Power within, from which all capacity stemmed, was itself wayward. The individual relying on it was a mere pipe for a divine energy that came and went as it willed. With this hidden life within him, man was no longer hopeless, but he was still helpless. "I would gladly," Emerson wrote at the age of forty-one, "allow the most to the will of man, but I have set my heart on honesty in this chapter, and I can see nothing at last, in success or failure, than more or less of vital force supplied from the Eternal."

When Emerson wrote *The American Scholar*, seven years earlier, his imagination had kindled to a blaze at the thought of the divine power latent in the soul. Give way to it, let it act, and the conversion of the world will follow. As this millennial enthusiasm inevitably waned, the old helplessness it had contradicted emerged unaltered from the flames. The result was a head-on clash of belief and fact. His vision of man as he might be only intensified the plight of man as he was. Something resembling the Fall of Man, which he had so ringingly denied, reappears in his pages.

It is not sin now that troubles him, but "the incompetency of power." One may accuse Providence of a certain parsimony.

It has shown the heaven and earth to every child, and filled him with a desire for the whole; a desire raging, infinite; a hunger, as of space to be filled with planets; a cry of famine, as of devils for souls. Then for the satisfaction,–to each man is administered a single drop, a bead of dew of vital power, per day,*–a cup as large as space, and one drop of the water of life in it. Each man woke in the morning with an appetite that could eat the solar system like a cake; a spirit for action and passion without bounds; he could lay his hand on the morning star; he could try conclusions with gravitation or chemistry; but, on the first motion to prove his strength,–hands, feet, senses, gave way, and would not serve him. He was an emperor deserted by his states, and left to whistle by himself, or thrust into a mob of emperors, all whistling: and still the sirens sang, "The attractions are proportioned to the destinies." In every house, in the heart of each maiden and of each boy, in the soul* *of the soaring saint, this chasm is found–between the largest promise of ideal power and the shabby experience.*

This chasm is the Emersonian tragedy, a tragedy of incapacity. Man's reach must exceed his grasp, of course; that is not tragic, Emerson's chasm cuts deeper: between a vision that claims all power now, and an experience that finds none. Emerson's thought of the self was split between a total Yes and a total No, which could not coexist, could not be reconciled, and yet were both true. "Alas for this infirm faith, this will not strenuous, this vast ebb of a vast flow! I am God in nature; I am a weed by the wall."

There is an Emersonian skepticism as well as an Emersonian faith. Of the seven "lords of life" he distinguishes in his key essay, *Experience*, five are principles of weakness. A man is slave to his moods and his temperament, swept like a bubble down the stream of time, blinded and drugged with illusion, the captive of his senses—in a word, the creature of a strong necessity. To be sure, the God is a native of the bleak rocks of his isolation, and can at any moment surprise and cheer him with new glimpses of reality. But for all this miraculous consolation, he has no will or force of his own; self-reliant is precisely what he can never be. *The American Scholar's* assurance of the unsearched might of man is a feat of faith in view of the actual humiliating human predicament, "with powers so vast and unweariable ranged on one side, and this little, conceited, vulnerable popinjay that a man is, bobbing up and down into every danger, on the other."

It goes without saying that one can easily overstate the case for a tragic sense in Emerson. *Experience*, for instance, is not a tragic-sounding essay. Perhaps "sense of limitation" would be more accurate; I have deliberately chosen a controversial term, in order to stress a side of Emerson often overlooked. For all his loss of millennial hope, Emerson in fact came to allow much to the will of man, as any reader of *The Conduct of Life* can see. Nor do I mean to suggest that he did not find the secret of a serene and affirmative life. The evidence is overwhelming that he did. My point is that his serenity was a not unconscious *answer* to his experience of life, rather than an inference from it (even when presented as such). It was an act of faith, forced on him by what he once called "the ghastly reality of things." Only as we sense this tension of faith and experience in him can we catch the quality of his affirmation. He *had* to ascribe more reality to his brief moments of "religious sentiment" than to the rest of life, or he could not live.

The way he did so altered sensibly, as his first excess of faith in man diminished. A gentle resignation came to settle over his thought of human nature, an elegiac recognition that life perpetually promises us a glory we can never realize. As it did so, the center of his faith traveled imperceptibly from man to the order that included him. In moments of faith, as he explained even in the midst of his essay on *Self-Reliance*, "The soul raised over passion beholds identity and eternal causation, perceives the self-existence of Truth and Right, and calms itself with knowing that all things go well." Such dogmatic optimism, always a part of his faith, became more and more its sole content as his first dream of a kingdom of Man dwindled into reasonableness.

Emerson the optimist said some shallow and callous things, as he did in his lecture on "The Tragic." To restore our sympathy with his humanity, we must glimpse the prisoner that now and then looked out of the eyes above the smile. Within, he was sovereign, a guide, redeemer, and benefactor; without, he was a lecturing and publishing old gentleman. Each time his inner promise of ideal power came up against the narrow limits of his experience, the response could only be the same—a renewed surrender to the Power that planned it that way. He did not surrender to necessity because he found it good, so much as he found it good because he surrendered. Recurrently the Good he recognizes is more conspicuous for power than for goodness, a "deaf, unimplorable, immense fate," to which all man-made distinctions of good and ill are an impertinence. In some of his poems, particularly, those that have eyes to see may watch him swept into entranced submission to "the over-god" by the compulsion of his personal problems. This is how he meets the impossible challenge of social action, in the "Ode" to Channing. So the teasing evanescence of his moments of insight into reality is submerged in "The World-Soul." He bows to the same power for a bleak consolation in his "Threnody" for his son:

> Silent rushes the swift Lord
> Through ruined systems still restored,
> Broadsowing, bleak and void to bless,
> Plants with worlds the wilderness;
> Waters with tears of ancient sorrow
> Apples of Eden ripe to-morrow.
> House and tenant go to ground,
> Lost in God, in Godhead found.

In such poems we feel the hunger for strength that sent him first to his grand doctrine of Self-Reliance, and then swung him to its polar opposite, a worship of the Beautiful Necessity.

Like all puritans, Emerson was an extremist: he had to have entire assurance, or he had none at all. Though we have a tradition of mature tragedy in our literature, American authors have typically made the same demand. Either they have risen to his transcendental trust, like Thoreau and Whitman; or they have accepted shoddy substitutes, like Norris or Sandburg or Steinbeck; or they have dropped into blackness, like Henry Adams or Jefferson. Emerson himself teetered on the edge of this drop, as did Thoreau and Whitman too, sustained by little more than their own power of belief. Since then the impulse to believe has become progressively feebler and the drop quicker and harder, until now, John Aldridge tells us, our honest writers *start* in the pit. If we are ever to have a great literature again, one would conclude, it will not be until we can break decisively with the whole extremist Emersonian pattern and find some means to face this world without either transcendence or despair.

19
Constitutional Democracy: A Nineteenth-Century Faith

Ralph Henry Gabriel

Introducing some of the central themes that later appeared in his well-received book, *The Course of American Democratic Thought*, Ralph Gabriel works briefly in this essay with the ideas of nineteenth-century American nationalism. The "faith" of which Gabriel writes might be called "ideology" by a modern social scientist. To Karl Mannheim, who gave us its modern definition in his *Ideology and Utopia* (1929), the study of ideology means that "opinions, statements, propositions, and systems of ideas are not taken at their face value but are interpreted in the light of the life-situation of the one who expresses them." Surely Gabriel's central themes—the belief in a "higher law" operating in a moral order, or "cosmic constitutionalism," as he calls it, and the implicit doctrines of the free individual and a sense of mission—were once the function of American national existence. As operating assumptions they became a national ideology. Time would eventually modify, alter, or erode these assumptions, but in their heyday they were generally beyond the power of critical intelligence to change them. Nor were they the sole articles of a nineteenth-century American faith. Other widely shared opinions, attitudes, and systems of ideas flowing beneath the surface of popular American thought, such as expectations of change and newness, or the Puritan ethic described in Essay 7, enter into a consideration of American ideology or, as some choose to call it, the American character.

For further reading: *John William Ward, *Andrew Jackson: Symbol for an Age* (1955); *Marvin Meyers, *The Jacksonian Persuasion* (1957); *Henry Nash Smith, *Virgin Land: The American West as Symbol and Myth* (1950); *Irving Bartlett, *The American Mind in the Mid-Nineteenth Century* (1967); Perry Miller, *The Life of the Mind in America: From the Revolution to the Civil War* (1965); *Alexis de Tocqueville, *Democracy in America*, ed. Phillips Bradley (1945); David M. Potter, "The Quest for the National Character," in *John Higham (ed.), *The Reconstruction of American History* (1962), pp. 197-220; *David M. Potter, *People of Plenty: Economic Abundance and the American Character* (1954); *Henry

Reprinted by permission of Columbia University Press from Conyers Read (ed.), *The Constitution Reconsidered* (1938), pp. 247-258. Footnotes have been omitted.

Steele Commager, *The American Mind: An Interpretation of American Thought and Character since the 1890s* (1950).

The group of anxious men who assembled at Philadelphia in 1787 to frame a constitution for the new United States had almost universally that confidence in human reason which stemmed from Newton's scientific achievements of the century before, and back of that from the triumphs of the classical philosophers. Americans were interested in the individual man. Democracy is the appropriate political expression of the atomistic social emphasis, yet many of the framers had a healthy skepticism of democracy. To some it suggested the triumph of mediocrity, and to others the substitution of the rule of passion for that of reason. But the United States was committed to the principle of democracy by the logic of the Revolution, and, as a consequence, the framers established their government in frank Lockean style upon the consent of the governed. In the framing of their great document they were both rationalists and empiricists. When they were done, they rightly looked upon themselves as initiating a great experiment in popular government.

Fifty years passed. When Americans of the new generation met to celebrate the fiftieth anniversary of their constitution, they remarked that the experimental period had passed. The demonstration of the efficacy of popular sovereignty had been made. Under it the United States had become an important nation. The fears of the fathers concerning democracy had not been justified by later events, and with Andrew Jackson the common man, now skilled in the political art, had come to power.

Americans of the middle period lived in a climate of opinion different from that of the Founding Fathers. Eighteenth-century Deism, charged with causing the excesses of the French Revolution, had long since been driven underground. Tom Paine, returning as an old man to America, had found the doors of respectability closed and had gone to a lonely death. Evangelical Protestantism was covering the nation like a rising tide and reached its apogee in the middle decade of the nineteenth century. The popular symbol of social stability for this generation was not, as in our day, the Constitution of the United States or the Supreme Court, but was rather the village church, whose spire pointed significantly heavenward. "Civilization," remarked Emerson, "depends on morality." And it was the almost universal belief of his generation that morality rests upon religion. But Emerson was disgusted with the anthropomorphism of the conventional Christianity of his day and was dissatisfied with the pale negations of Unitarianism. He announced his transcendentalism in a little book entitled *Nature*, published in 1836, the year before the fiftieth anniversary of the Constitution. Four years later, an inconspicuous citizen, named George Sidney Camp, wrote a small volume which he called *Democracy*, and which Harper and Brothers thought expressed so well the mood of the age that they published it in their Family Library and later brought out a second edition. "Faith," said Camp, "is as necessary to the republican as to the Christian, and the fundamental characteristic of both." We are born believing," added Emerson. "A man bears beliefs as a tree bears apples." Faith is the clue to the understanding of the democracy of the middle period.

Among these Americans the word "democracy" took on two different but interrelated connotations; it had both a realistic and a romantic meaning. Realistic democracy was a behavior pattern which included caucuses and logrolling, the struggle for office among individuals, and the sparring for advantage among sections or pressure groups. Romantic democracy was a cluster of ideas which made up a national faith and which, though unrecognized as such, had the power of a state religion. Some of these ideas were as old as classical Greece and others were as new as the American nation. But, though most of the ideas were old and were borrowed, the configuration of the cluster was unique.

A secular national religion, such as the communism of Lenin's Russia or the national socialism of contemporary Germany, must meet certain basic psychological needs of the people who profess it. Among a disunited people it must emphasize the group and its solidarity. To a depressed people or to one suffering from a sense of inferiority it must give that illusion of superiority which springs from the doctrine that the nation has a great mission to perform in the world. To an anxious people, fearful of the future, a national religion must give a sense of security. In the America of the middle period, unity was a primary problem. Those transportation facilities which bind a nation together could not keep pace with the rapid westward advance of the frontier. Climatic differences had created a social problem which threatened the United States with division along sectional lines. The United States faced the menace of separatism. A lesser mid-nineteenth-century American need was for some defense against a sense of inferiority to Europe. This became acute in the middle period because in that age Americans were sensing their intellectual and their national power at a time when foreign travelers, some of them of the prominence of Dickens, were coming in increasing numbers and were returning to the Old World to write frequently unjust and almost universally offensive books. In such a scene Ralph Waldo Emerson threw off the robes of a Unitarian clergyman. He announced in 1836 the cosmic philosophy upon which his transcendentalism was founded. He proclaimed in 1837 in his famous Phi Beta Kappa address at Harvard College the American declaration of intellectual independence. "We have listened too long to the courtly muses of Europe," he said to the young scholars before him. "We will walk on our own feet; we will work with our own hands; we will speak our own minds." From that day Emerson became the Isaiah of that democratic faith which was at that very moment taking form spontaneously among the American people.

The foundation of this democratic faith was a frank supernaturalism derived from Christianity. The twentieth-century student is often astonished at the extent to which supernaturalism permeated American thought of the nineteenth century. The basic postulate of the democratic faith affirmed that God, the creator of man, has also created a moral law for his government and has endowed him with a conscience with which to apprehend it. Underneath and supporting human society, as the basis rock supports the hills, is a moral order which is the abiding place of the eternal principles of truth and righteousness. The reiteration of this doctrine of the moral order runs through mid-nineteenth-century social and political thought like the rhythm of the drums through the forest scene of O'Neill's *Emperor Jones*. "There are principles of abstract justice which the creator of all things has impressed on the mind of his creature man," said John Marshall in 1823 in an opinion from the bench, "and which are admitted to regulate, in a great degree, the rights of civilized nations." "In ascending to the great principles upon which all society rests," added Justice Joseph Story in 1828, "it must be admitted that there are some which are of eternal obligation, and arise from our common dependence upon our Creator. Among these are the duty to do justice, to love mercy, and to walk humbly before God." "There is a higher law," proclaimed William Ellery Channing long before Seward's famous speech in the Senate, "even Virtue, Rectitude, the Voice of Conscience, the Will of God." "The moral law," said Emerson in 1836, "lies at the center of nature and radiates to the circumference."

To trace the origin or the history of this doctrine of a higher or fundamental law is not our present task, for to do so would be to examine one of the more important strands of thought in Western civilization. Suffice it to say that in the United States in the middle years of the nineteenth century the existence of a moral order which was not the creation of man but which served as the final guide for his behavior was almost universally assumed among thinking persons. For Christians the moral law was the will of God; for the small company of articulate free thinkers it was the natural law of eighteenth-century Deism. Mr. Justice Story in his *Commentaries on the Constitution* succeeded in phrasing the doctrine in terms which would be acceptable both to those who still found their guide in reason and to those who looked for direction to the Scriptures. "The rights of conscience," said he, "are given by God, and cannot be encroached upon by human authority, without criminal disobedience of the precepts of natural, as well as of revealed, religion." Before the moral law all men stood on a footing of equality; from it they derived equal rights. Among the latter was the right to the private ownership of property.

The universal acceptance of the doctrine of the moral order suggests that it had uses in the culture of the time. American skies were darkened during the middle period by a storm which gathered momentum and increased in intensity with the passing years. The controversy over human slavery put the realistic democracy of American political institutions to the test of the hurricane. Anger mounted on either side, and, long before the final break occurred, passion threatened to replace reason in the councils of the nation. Garrison in the North and Yancey in the South early advocated breaking the ties which bound the sections together. Americans turned to the Constitution as the fundamental law of the land for those common agreements between the contending parties without which debate is impossible. But this instrument appeared to fail them. Instead of resolving the dispute, the Constitution became the very center of controversy as the sections divided on the question of its origin and of its nature. Webster for the North affirmed that the document drawn up at Philadelphia was the supreme law for a nation; Calhoun for the South replied that it was no more than a compact among sovereign states. The positions were at opposite poles and were irreconcilable; yet faith in constitutionalism was not shaken. Even after the final break the Confederacy did not abandon constitutionalism. The event suggests that the American faith in constitutional democracy did not have its ultimate origin in the constitution which established it. Emerson in 1854 sought to explain the paradox. "Whenever a man," said he, "has come to this state of mind, that there is no church for him but his believing prayer, no Constitution but his dealing well and justly with his neighbor; no liberty but his invincible will to do right, then certain aids and allies will promptly appear; for the constitution of the Universe is on his side.'' The doctrine of the moral order was, in effect, a doctrine of cosmic constitutionalism. The body of natural and of moral law was the fixed and unchangeable constitution of the world. The fundamental law of the Republic was thought to be but a man-made imitation of a divine archetype. When it failed to provide those common agreements necessary to rational debate, recourse must be had to those unwritten and eternal principles which, in the universal belief of Americans, made society possible. Emerson, in appealing to the ''constitution of the Universe,'' was discussing the Fugitive Slave Law to which he was opposed. Southern proponents of the peculiar institution, despairing of the Federal Constituion, were at the same time founding their defense of slavery upon the same moral law. ''Negroes are not free,'' said George Fitzhugh, ''because God and nature, and the general good, and their own good, intended them for slaves.'' The doctrine of the moral order was here providing those agreements which by functioning as the foundation of logical discussion made it possible for the democratic process to continue. Because Americans believed that fixed laws and eternal principles underlay society, they believed in written constitutions. But these, after all, were experiments, as the delegates at Philadelphia had suggested. If constitutions should fail, as the Federal Constitution failed in 1861, they should be reconstructed, as the Confederates tried to do, in accordance with unfolding human experience and with new light on the nature of the moral order.

The arguments of Emerson and of Fitzhugh sound strange in our post-Versailles world in which the prestige of Christianity has declined and naturalistic philosophies have captured the social disciplines. The absolutism of the nineteenth century which expressed itself in the theory of the moral law is out of fashion in our America. Faith in the eternal character of right and wrong is in retreat before the advance of the pragmatic ethics of expediency. But the retreat has not yet ended and, while it continues, modern Americans are confused. The bitter fruit of their confusion is a sense of intellectual and of social insecurity. Our age is witnessing many attempts of individuals and of groups to escape from the malaise of insecurity, but nothing in America is more pathetic or, perhaps, more menacing than the efforts of those who would set up the Constitution as a fetish and worship it in the spirit of the tribe which prays to idols of its own making. There was no Constitution-worship before Sumter fell. The Webster-Calhoun debate prevented it and the doctrine of the moral order made it unnecessary. That article of faith gave to mid-nineteenth-century Americans that mental peace and that sense of security which comes to the man who feels that he has planted his feet upon the eternal rock.

The second doctrine of the democratic faith of the middle period was that of the free individual. It contained a theory of liberty and of the relation of the individual to the state which he ultimately governed. The doctrine was derived from that of the moral order. The path which led from the one to the other was a philosophy of progress. This philosophy affirmed that the advance of civilization is measured by the progress of men in apprehending and in translating into individual and social action the eternal principles which comprise the moral law. The advance of civilization, in other words, is the progress of virtue. ''Nothing can be plainer,'' remarked William C. Jarvis, counselor at law, in 1820, ''than that the barbarian in the desert requires the restraint of a more powerful arm than the individuals whose passions and propensities are under the eternal restraint of moral and religious sentiments.''

"Civilization," added Frederick Grimke quaintly some thirty-six years later, "is that state in which the higher part of our nature is made to predominate over the lower." Out of this concept that the civilized man is the virtuous man and this hopeful philosophy that mankind is on the march toward a better world came the nineteenth-century theory of liberty. As men become more nearly perfect in obedience to the fundamental moral law, as they develop what Irving Babbitt used to call the "inner check," they need less the external control of man-made laws. "Hence," insisted Emerson, following Jefferson, "the less government the better. . . . The antidote to the abuse of formal government is the growth of influence of private character, the growth of the Individual. . . . To educate the wise man the State exists, and with the appearance of the wise man the State expires."

Henry Thoreau, Emerson's Concord friend, carried this reasoning to its logical conclusion. The man who has achieved moral maturity, he thought, should reject imperfect laws made by stupid majorities and should accept the higher law which is disclosed by his conscience as the sole guide and regulator of his life. In particular, he should practice civil disobedience when the state embarks upon an immoral policy. The fiery Thoreau emphasized his point by going to jail rather than pay a Massachusetts poll tax which he assumed would be spent to further iniquitous policies. That such extremism was rare in nineteenth-century America, however, was illustrated by Emerson's anxious visit to his friend behind the bars. "Henry," asked the great transcendentalist, "why are you here?" "Waldo," replied the jailbird, "why are you not here?" Emerson, the hardheaded Yankee farmer, thought such extremism in the nineteenth century would defeat its own ends. "We think our civilization is near its meridian," Emerson remarked, "but we are only yet at the cock-crowing and the morning star. In our barbarous society the influence of character is in its infancy." But before Emerson, as before Thoreau, shone the ideal of liberty as the ultimate goal, of liberty not as a means to an end but as an end in itself. "Liberty," said Emerson, "is an accurate index, in men and nations, of general progress." He was the greatest of the preachers of the democratic faith. He traveled from end to end of America preaching his gospel of self-reliant individualism. He moved the young men of the middle period as no other figure of the age. He opened doors for them which enabled them to escape from the stuffy confines of evangelical Protestantism into a glorious out-of-doors. He filled the disciples of the democratic faith with the hope of a better and freer world in the creation of which they would have a share.

It has commonly been said that the exaltation of the individual and the apotheosis of liberty of the mid-nineteenth century was the natural result of certain economic and social factors. A relatively small population was scattered over a vast area. Capitalistic enterprise had not developed beyond the stage in which its most important figure was the individual entrepreneur. Inevitably in such a social scene the focus of attention must be upon the individual. The conquest of a wilderness in the West and the attempt to establish a new industrialism in the East put a premium upon individual initiative and hence on individual liberty. Important as were these factors, there was another of equal, if not greater, significance for the doctrine of liberty. Down to the very eve of the fall of Sumter, Americans of the middle period enjoyed a sense of security rarely to be duplicated in modern history. Not only were there no dangerous potential enemies beyond the national frontiers holding the threat of invasion over the citizens of the Republic, but Americans marched in triumph into the capital of Mexico and dictated the terms of a profitable peace. An ocean guarded the eastern cities against attack from Europe. The opportunities of the frontier, moreover, offered to every able-bodied man the possibility of personal economic security. The doctrine of the moral law gave to the men of the middle period a sense of stability and of security in a world of change. The American philosophy of liberty had its seventeenth- and eighteenth-century origins in protests against established orders. It was then primarily a means to an end. In the middle of the nineteenth century, when it reached its maturity with the belief that liberty is an end in itself, it rested squarely upon a universal sense of security. When the traditional foundations of a culture crumble, as we are seeing them do today, and in the Western world crazed by nationalism, when government by law gives way to government by irresponsible force, the preoccupation with liberty as an end in itself is replaced by a new search for security, mental, social, economic, and even physical. In the middle period, however, when Americans felt safe, they could afford to enjoy their doctrine of the free individual.

The third doctrine of the democratic faith was that of the mission of America. It was a mid-nineteenth-century version of those myths of unique origin and of unique destiny so common in tribal tradition. Liberty, according to a widely accepted version of American mythology, had been established by deity in an empty western continent so that, freed from the burden of European tradition, it might flourish and become an inspiration to the world.

O God, beneath thy guiding hand
Our exiled fathers crossed the sea . . .

sang Leonard Bacon in 1833. George Bancroft, historian, saw the hand of the Omnipotent in the founding of the Republic. As late as 1866 Samuel Kirkland Lothrop, addressing a great Boston meeting upon the anniversary of the Declaration of Independence, proclaimed again the supernaturalistic interpretation of the origin of American democracy. "God in the hour of its utmost need," he declared, "gave . . . liberty an opportunity to plant itself on this new continent and strike its roots so deep that no despotic power could tear them up." The doctrine of mission was merely an extension of that origin. "Standing where we now do," prophesied A. A. Bennet, addressing his neighbors of the New York frontier on the national anniversary of 1827, "we may look forward to the period when the spark kindled in America shall spread and spread, till the whole earth be illumined by its light." "Already," added Justice Story in 1828, "has the age caught the spirit of our institutions." Whitman distilled a folk belief into deathless verse.

Sail, sail thy best ship of Democracy
of Value is thy freight . . .
Thou holdst not the venture of thyself alone, nor of the Western
continent alone . . .
With thee time voyages in trust, the antecedent nations sink or swim
with thee,
Theirs, theirs as much as thine, the destination port triumphant. [1872]

What was the significance of this doctrine of origin and of destiny? It provided the formula which expressed that sense of superiority that an in-group normally feels with respect to out-groups. It was the American way of saying: We are the Greeks; the rest of the world is made up of barbarians. As an expression of the American tribal ethnocentrism it assisted in that subtle osmosis by which a federation of particular states was transformed into a united nation. But it did more even than strengthen and glorify the nation. It provided for American democracy, with its emphasis upon diversity, a philosophy of unity. And this doctrine of the destiny of America held up before the humble democrat, whose drab world rarely extended beyond the main street of his village, a romantic vision in which he could see his inconspicuous efforts after righteousness invested with a world significance.

If Emerson was the prophet and Whitman the poet of the democratic faith, Herman Melville, ex-whaler, was its savage critic. Putting his thought for the most part into allegory but permitting himself at times direct, barbed thrusts, he assailed every doctrine of the ruling creed of his age. How do you know, he asked the Christians in effect, that God has created a moral order? God is past finding out. To the most urgent questions of men God answers nothing. If religion offers no security, thought Melville, neither does science, for science is but a lightship whose rays illuminate a circle in the darkness. It is man's incomprehensible fate that his days are set in mystery and that the essence of his life is hazard. Melville thought that the fundamental delusion in his age was that absolutism which held both religion and science in an iron grip and which was the foundation of the democratic faith. Out of this absolutism came the doctrine of the moral law, the belief in progress, and the gospel of liberty as an end in itself. Phantasms all, thought Melville. Melville rejected eternals. Each age, he taught, is new. Each age has its good and its evil and to the end of time neither will conquer the other. He assailed in particular the belief in progress. "There are many who erewhile believed that the age of pikes and javelins was passed," he said in *Mardi* in 1849, "that after a heady and blustering youth . . . [the world] was at last settling down into a serene old age; and that the Indian summer, first discovered in your land [of America], sovereign kings! was the hazy vapour emitted from its tranquil pipe. But it has not so proved. The world's peaces are but truces. Long absent, at last the red comets have returned. And return they must, though their periods be ages. And should [the world] endure till mountain melt into mountain, and all the isles form one tableland; yet would it but expand the old battle-plain." Turning to the doctrine of the mission of America to spread democracy throughout the world, Melville declared that the fate of the American Republic must be the same as that of its Roman predecessor. Democracy, thought the author of *Moby Dick*, is but a moment in history, not the end toward which all history runs. Yet Melville was not a pessimist, his critics to the contrary notwithstanding. Evil, he insisted, is both unconquerable and unconquering. A man can and must save his soul by fighting the evils of his day as Ahab on the deck of the "Pequod" pursued Moby Dick, well knowing that, though the chase must end in the defeat of the captain, yet it would not be a triumph for the white whale. If a man would be an individualist, taught Melville, if he would be free, let him stop running with the Christians to the Everlasting Arms, let him cease deluding himself with Emerson that the constitution of the universe is on his side. Melville in the middle years of the nineteenth century pitched overboard every one of the philosophies of individualism which dominated his age. Then the intellectuals of an era which proclaimed the ideal of liberty as an end in itself cast him out. His generation condemned Melville to nearly a score of years of living death as an outdoor clerk at the New York Customs House. He was defeated but he did not surrender. In *Billy Budd*, completed three months before his death in 1891, he challenged brilliantly and for the last time the democratic faith of America. Melville's was a troubled spirit which in coming to earth opened the door upon the wrong century.

20
The Reactionary Enlightenment

Louis Hartz

"The mind of the Old South" is an easy but deceptive phrase. It appears to mean a group of coherent regional attitudes, whereas few really existed. Virginia Tidewater planters did not always think alike with Piedmont Jeffersonians on social and political issues. South Carolina lowland people had their differences of opinion with up-country farmers. Planters of the raw, rich black belt in Mississippi formed different social ideas from the piney-woods settlers of Alabama or Georgia. The frontier nabobs and later the landed squirearchy around Lexington, Kentucky, or Nashville, Tennessee, saw things differently from the mountain people in the eastern parts of their states. The "plain people" of the South did not share all the same values with cotton kings. Above all, black people in their slavery held ideas about themselves, their culture, their religion, and the natural world which, though hard to document, historians are only now beginning to analyze. Yet "the mind of the South" is a phrase that sticks in American intellectual history like "the New England conscience." The mind of the South would still be a compelling issue for students of American thought even if they never had been aided by W. J. Cash's illuminating study of it.

Where the historical concept of a Southern mind may help in understanding today's problems it is valid, for the problems of the South were often the nation's. Racism that was magnified though not prevalent there alone has plagued the whole nation. Pride and inflated claims of regional differences amounting to "romantic nationalism," though exaggerated in the South to an explosive degree, had their counterparts in Northern self-righteous equalitarianism that was meant only for white people, in the literary smugness of writers and intellectuals in and around Boston or New York, and in the brassy expansionist psychology of the American West. But speaking with more saliency or relevance to modern America than any of the presumably "Southern" intellectual traits are the experiences of evil and tragedy in the Southern heritage. These experiences comprise, in C. Vann Woodward's phrase, "the burden of Southern history." They stand in contrast to the sense of innocence and social felicity, to the experiences of abundance and success of the North.

Louis Hartz's book, *The Liberal Tradition in America*, equates historic American liberalism with a "Lockean ethos" (the rights of private property and self-government). Challenging Vernon Parrington's older view of American thought as largely a contest of liberal and radical ideas against conservative ones, Hartz takes his theme from Alexis de Tocqueville and sees Americans as born free and lacking genuine radicalism simply because they never experienced feudalism. In his chapter on Southern thinkers, from which this selection is taken, Hartz describes leaders of the ante bellum South as being the first to take a truly objective look at the nation's Lockean liberalism. They chose to "invert" Locke and to emphasize property rights rather than natural rights. But still they themselves were held within the bounds of Lockean thought and, however penetrating at times their ideas were, they never quite escaped into the conservatism they sought.

For further reading: Paul F. Boller, Jr., "Calhoun on Liberty," *South Atlantic Quarterly*, 56 (1967), 395-408; *Richard N. Current, *John C. Calhoun* (1963); Ralph H. Gabriel, *The Course of American Democratic Thought* (2d ed., 1956), chap. 9; *William W. Freehling, *Prelude to Civil War: The Nullification Controversy in South Carolina, 1816-1836* (1966); *William R. Taylor, *Cavalier and Yankee* (1961); *C. Vann Woodward, *The Burden of Southern History* (rev. ed., 1968); *W. J. Cash, *The Mind of the South* (1941); *Winthrop D. Jordan, *White over Black: American Attitudes toward the Negro, 1550-1812* (1968); *Allen Weinstein and Frank Otto Gatell (eds.), *American Negro Slavery: A Modern Reader* (1968).

1. Conservatism in a Liberal Society

"We begin a great conservative reaction," Virginia's George Fitzhugh proclaimed in 1863 on the eve of the battle of Gettysburg. "We attempt to roll back the Reformation in its political phases." The first American revolution, Fitzhugh argued, had been a mere "reform." But the "revolution of 1861," which raised the banner of Tories everywhere and resurrected even the dream of Filmer, was a social upheaval that would ultimately shake the world.

Here, surely, was a strange note to be coming out of America in the midst of its liberal tradition. What had happened? Had America suddenly produced, out of nowhere, a movement of reactionary feudalism? Was it beginning to experience, seventy-five years late and in an inverted way, a French Revolution that it had managed to escape before? Was its social thought, nourished for years in the easy atmosphere of liberal agreement, suddenly beginning to explode with all of the old historic tensions of Europe? If these things were true, the distinctive meaning of American history would have been canceled out at a single stroke. Tocqueville's statement that the Americans had been "born free" would have become a fond illusion, the silent unity of Hamilton and Jefferson would have led nowhere, and the "promise of American life," to borrow the words that Croly used in another connection, would have become one of the falsest promises of modern times. By

1863, when Fitzhugh raised the Tory standard in the South, the battle over the "political phases" of the Reformation had ended even in Europe. The Holy Alliance had been dead for a generation.

Certainly we cannot deny that the American Southerners, when they began to break with their Jeffersonian past around 1830, duplicated in every essential aspect the argument of Europe's feudal reaction. We do not find here the mere parroting of a few of Burke's phrases. We find a most fantastic array of theoretical schemes, some of them to be sure as Aristotelian as they are Burkian, some of them passionately Hebraic in their emphasis on the Bible, but all of them dominated in the end by the basic concepts of the Western reaction. There are a group of ardent traditionalists who cherish the "conservative principle": the novelist N. Beverly Tucker, Governor Hammond of South Carolina, Albert Bledsoe. There are a group of "feudal socialists" who lash out at Northern capitalism in the spirit of Disraeli and Carlyle: Fitshugh, Chancellor Harper, George Sawyer, Edmund Ruffin. There are even a group of "sociologists" determined after the fashion of Bonald and Comte to turn the law of nature upside down and prove that Locke is "metaphysical": Fitzhugh again, Professor George Frederick Holmes of the University of Virginia, and that Mississippi prodigy who published his system at the age of twenty-five, Henry Hughes. Nor is Holmes the only academic figure in the reactionary renaissance. College professors rush to the Tory standard from all sides, Dew of William and Mary giving it a Hegelian touch, Smith of Randolph-Macon showering it with an indiscriminate idealism, J. B. De Bow of Louisiana buttressing it with a solid array of statistics. We have here, indeed, one of the great and creative episodes in the history of American thought.

And yet it would be a mistake, even on the basis of this lush evidence, to jump to conclusions about the collapse of the American liberal tradition. When we penetrate beneath the feudal and reactionary surface of Southern thought, we do not find feudalism: we find slavery. The distinction is not unimportant. For it leads us to see at a glance that this massive revival of Burke, Comte, Disraeli, and Hegel below the Mason-Dixon line was in large measure a simple fraud, and that instead of symbolizing the appearance of something new in American life, it symbolized the impending disappearance of something very old. Fraud, alas, was the inevitable fate of Southern social thought. If the trouble with Southern slave society had merely been that it did not fit the American liberal formula, as historians have often noted, its ideologists might not have had so hard a time. But the real trouble with it was that it did not fit any formula, any basic categories of Western social theory. And so when the Garrisons of the North arose to drive the Southerners out of their own Jeffersonian world, they were released from the anguish of one contradiction only to embrace the anguish of another even worse. They exchanged a fraudulent liberalism for an even more fradulent feudalism: they stopped being imperfect Lockes and became grossly imperfect Maistres. This is the meaning of Fitzhugh's "great conservative reaction," and once we understand it, its appearance changes enormously.

The Civil War, in other words, if it seems on the surface like a French Revolution in reverse, is really nothing of the kind. The fact that it seems like one in reverse, that fact that the "reaction" of the South is also a "revolution," ought to suggest this to us at once. For a feudalism that has once been liberal can never be really feudal, and its impact on the history of a nation is bound to be unique. A false Maistre, a Maistre who only a few years ago was a Jeffersonian democrat, confronts a set of problems entirely his own. He slaughters himself with the traditionalist logic he tries to use, he cannot terrify the men he seeks to terrify, and once he is defeated in war, he is not only likely to be forgotten but he is likely to forget himself. We can call America's great internal struggle whatever we like, a revolution, a rebellion, or a war, but if we identify the South with the feudalism it sought to imitate, we miss the significance of its social incongruity, of the ties it had to the liberalism it sought to defy, and above all of the swift disappearance of its Gothic dream. For the remarkable thing about the "great conservative reaction" of 1863, instead of being the way it scarred American political thought, was in fact the smallness of the impact it had upon it. Even our historians have pretty much forgotten the Disraelis and the Bonalds of the ante-bellum South.

There is a book to be written in the psychiatric vein, or at the very least a heart-rending romance, about the Southern search for a cultural code before the Civil War. In the time of Jefferson the agony of the South had been complex. Not only had John Taylor been embarrassed by slavery because of liberalism, but he had been embarrassed by liberalism because even then he had nourished a Disraelian streak. Now, in the age of Fitzhugh, when both of these problems would seem to have been solved, Taylor discovered that he could not be a real Disraeli even if given a chance to be one. He was a plantation capitalist, and in the Southwest, for all of its stratified social life, he was a very new, very raw, very fierce plantation capitalist. And so the sweat that had to go into making the South medieval was even greater than the sweat that had gone into making it modern. Henry Hughes had to twist slavery into a kind of feudal "warranteeism" when it was obviously nothing of the sort. George Frederick Holmes had to link it up historically with European serfdom when there was a gulf between the two. A thousand Southern gentlemen had to call themselves "The Chivalry" when a Northerner like Frederick Olmstead would only call them "Cotton Snobs." It is easy to understand, perhaps, why some Southerners occasionally gave up the idea of becoming imperfect feudal lords and tried the experiment of becoming imperfect ancient Greeks or imperfect Hebrew patriarchs. These roles, which just about exhausted the repertoire that Western culture offered, confused Holmes's historical pattern by shifting it back to ancient times, but the first of them had the merit at any rate of seeming to retain half of the Lockian world in which the Southerners had been accustomed to move. Parrington, seizing upon the idea of "Greek democracy," has actually identified Southern thought with it.

There were good reasons, however, apart from the stratified nature of Southern white society, why the Greek idea did not become the master image of Southern political thought. Locke's scheme had been fashioned not in response to Pericles but in response to Filmer, and when the Southerners were forced to assail it, they found themselves willy-nilly drifting in Filmer's direction. There is a categorical logic to political arguments that Mannheim has brillantly discussed. Since Garrison was using the doctrine of consent, Calhoun naturally replied with the doctrine of "Divine ordination." Since Garrison was using the concept of reason, Fitzhugh instinctively countered with the concept of human "prejudice." Since Garrison was using the idea of equality, Harper's course was clear: there was an "endless diversity in the condition of men.'' Actually what we have here is a most remarkable twist coming out of America's odd relationship to modern political thought. A nation built in the liberal image and yet without the feudalism that liberalism destroyed, once it challenged the liberal formula, it began to reproduce the philosophy of a feudal world it had never seen. This is why, even when the Southerners do not read the European conservatives, they write uncannily as if they did. Fitzhugh, who read the English conservatives but apparently not the French, resembles the French most. A ruthless and iconoclastic reasoner, he pursued the attack on Jefferson all the way back to a belief in absolute monarchy and a hatred of the Reformation.

But at this point a question arises, which brings us to the first of the various punishments that the American liberal world imposed on the feudal dreamers of the South. How can a man be an iconoclastic ''conservative''? How can Maistre breathe the spirit of Voltaire? Surely if any movement in American thought resembles the French Enlightenment in its sheer passion to shock, to tear down ancient idols, to stick pins in the national complacency, it is this sudden Burkian outburst in the South. And yet the argument of Burke is straight traditionalism. Shouldn't the Southerners, by their own reasoning, be clinging to Jefferson rather than trying to destroy him? Shouldn't they in fact be denouncing themselves?

There is no exaggerating the philosophic pain the Southerners endured as a result of this contradiction. Not to be quite genuine supporting the doctrine of Locke was one thing; not to be genuine supporting the doctrine of Disraeli was another, but to have the second doctrine constantly reaffirming one's ancient allegiance to the first was as keen a torture as the devilish brain of history could devise. How under such circumstances could John Taylor ever forget his democratic past? How could he ever hide his liberal origins? Long before, in the seventeenth century, America had laid this trap for the Southern thinkers. By being ''born free,'' by establishing liberalism without destroying feudalism, it had transformed the rationalist doctrine of Locke into the traditionalist reality of Burke, so that anyone who dared to use conservatism in order to refute liberalism would discover instead that he had merely refuted himself. I have said that the Southerners, simply by the logic of assailing Jefferson, were led to discover Bonald. But one thing has to be added to this: when they discovered him, they were no longer in America but in Europe. And when in triumph they tried to bring him back to America, he ceased to be Bonald and suddenly became Tom Paine. Surely Fitzhugh's attack on the Reformation, had he ever seriously extended it beyond its ''political phases,'' would have caused a turmoil in his own Protestant South.

Under such conditions it is not surprising that Southern thought should try to stick as much as possible to the European experience. After all, in a land where liberalism had destroyed nothing, unless it was the society of the Indians, which the Southerners were hardly trying to restore, it was very hard to denounce it in good conservative terms as being explosive, ''metaphysical,'' and utopian. In order to use the arguments of Burke or Comte, one had deliberately to twist American liberalism into the millennial molds of Europe. One had to make the same mistake about it consciously that Condorcet, observing the American Revolution from Europe, had made about it accidentally. This was very distasteful. An American knew that Jefferson was really not Robespierre, that the idea of compact had been used by the soberest men in American history since the sailing of the *Mayflower*. The Southerners could scarcely wait until they could blend their discussion of Jefferson into a discussion of the French Revolution, though of course they always hid their eagerness behind straight faces. "The prophets of Utopia," Holmes soberly said, were to be found "on both sides of the Atlantic." In the case of "feudal socialism" the situation was even worse, for if American liberalism had not been revolutionary, it had fulfilled itself to a remarkable degree in individual proprietorship. The Southern disciples of Carlyle and Disraeli were relieved of an awful burden when they managed to move from the miseries of the Northern worker to those of the English proletariat.

Locke, in other words, was too real, too empirical, too historical in America to attack: and the consequences of this are obvious. The God of the reactionaries was Himself on Locke's side, and the Southerners, when they assailed "metaphysicians," were committing a vigorous suicide. E. N. Elliott cherished the sociological relativism of Montesquieu, but the relative unfolding of America's culture had alas been liberal. Fitzhugh spoke of Burkian "prejudices," but the prejudices of America were alas the prejudices of liberty and equality. Indeed the "prejudice" argument was even more self-annihilating than the argument of cultural relativism. One might argue, insofar as slavery itself was concerned, that it was a historic institution, despite its sudden expansion after 1830, and that Montesquieu's lesson for the American Negroes was therefore different from his lesson for the American whites. But on the plane of "prejudice," the problem was not so simple: in its Jeffersonian youth the South itself had considered slavery bad. How then could Burke be used to assail Locke when even below the Mason-Dixon line Burke actually equalled Locke?

Few political theorists, save possibly in a nightmare dream, have ever found themselves in a predicament quite as bad as this. What it meant, of course, was that meaningful thought was practically impossible. The more consistently a man advanced the antiliberal arguments of Burke, the farther away he got from the traditionalist substance they were designed to protect. The more he cherished the traditionalist substance, the farther away he got from the antiliberal arguments. The only question was on which horn of the dilemma he wanted to impale himself. Most Southerners, unlike Fitzhugh whose logical passion usually led him to embrace only one of the horns, actually embraced both. Nor is this at all difficult to understand. It is not easy to work out a reactionary scheme of thought in twenty or thirty years, especially when it is far removed from reality. The Burkian power of America's liberal tradition manifested itself most clearly in the inability of the Southerners ever to get completely away from it. Down to the very end, to the Civil War, their theory was shot through and through with the Lockian principles they destroyed. In their glorification of "prejudice," they could not alas overcome the prejudices they had inherited.

Almost everywhere one turns one finds pathetic evidence of this. Calhoun repudiates the contractual rationalism of Locke, and yet when he assails the national tariff he advances a theory of minority rights and constitutional "compact" which carries it forward remarkably. Hammond poses as a defender of a feudal order, and yet he cannot help trying to preserve Jefferson insofar as the whites are concerned by building up a theory of race. Even Fitzhugh breaks down on one or two occasions. Denouncing Northern industrialism in the mood of the "English Tory Party," lamenting the emancipation of the serfs in Europe, he manages to smuggle into his theory a program for industrializing the South that would have delighted Henry Clay. W. J. Cash, in his remarkable portrait of the Southern mind, tells the story of one of the new Cotton Gentlemen who could not help telling his guests how much the furniture in his mansion cost. This is exactly the pathos of Southern "feudal" thought: the old liberal and the old bourgeois preoccupations keep sticking out all over it, betraying it, contradicting it. Even if the South had never been thoroughly liberal and never thoroughly bourgeois, it had been liberal and bourgeois enough to vindicate the insight of Burke by being unable to embrace him completely.

A confusion as subtle as this, a scheme of thought pitched to begin with on a half-fantastic plane and then destroying itself even there, is not designed to win political controversies. The next punishment that America imposed on the Voltairian Maistres of the South follows logically enough. They were not taken seriously by the North.

We must remember that all of the agony of the South was good fortune for the North. If the South was neither decently revolutionary nor decently conservative, the North was decently both. It had instigated the whole argument with its Garrisonian abolitionism, and hence was quite "jacobinical," but since it used the ancient arguments of the Declaration of Independence, and forced the Southerners to think up new arguments to refute them, it was quite traditionalistic as well. Having issued a violent attack, it could proceed to preserve ancient principles from the attack of others. This was the ironic replica in reverse of the whole Southern dilemma. Of course Garrison was forced to reject the Constitution, which recognized slavery, and in this sense could not play the part of a sober traditionalist. As a matter of fact he once exclaimed: "Thank God the Past is not the Present." But to the extent that it recognized slavery the Constitution had itself been a historic anomaly, contradicting the larger liberal tradition in which it had been created. To reject it on this score was to purge, not to repudiate, America's political past.

Thus if Burke equaled Locke in America, the North had the moral force of both, and so why should it bother to reply to a set of philosophic actors who had the moral force of neither? Inherently, inevitably, the grandiose feudal discoveries of the South slid off the Northern mind with scarcely a trace of impact. Instead of reconstructing the Declaration of Independence in terms of the reactionary attack, as Mill for example reconstructed Bentham or Constant reconstructed Rousseau, the North simply affirmed its principles with a new and wilder fury. Instead of bothering to look at the great Gothic cathedrals that were suddenly arising in the South, the North simply stuck to the ancient liberal ground where they should have been built in the first place. Hence, ironically, the greatest moral crusade in American history produced practically no original political thought. Garrison is not a creator of political ideas; neither is Phillips. Even Channing is not. Conservatism is always unreflective, and since these men, by the weird, upside-down logic that governed the slavery argument, are revolutionary conservatives, they unite with their very passion a strange and uncritical complacency. They will argue about the Bible, they will even say a few words in defense of the condition of the Northern worker, but insofar as the South's great "feudalist," "positivist," "corporatist" challenge to liberalism is concerned, it rarely occurs to them even to answer it. "Argument is demanded," Garrison once remarked, "—to prove what?"

This experience of being ignored, which every polemicist knows is the handwriting on the wall, produced a strange mixture of fury, gloom, and forced gaiety in the Southern literature. Chancellor Harper of South Carolina angrily assailed the North because it engaged in "denunciation disdaining argument," and then quietly, morosely, as if to himself, he said: "We can have no hearing before the civilized world." Fitzhugh, however, who pretended to believe in just the reverse idea, that the South was leading a worldwide revival of the principles of feudalism, would never let his anguish show. When the North paid no attention to his massive sociological proof that "free society" was a failure, he behaved happily as if he had won the argument: "The North is silent, and thus tacitly admits the charge." Fitzhugh was not naive: he knew that silence can be a sign of intellectual security as well as of intellectual bankruptcy. But what else could he say? If the liberal formula was hopelessly entrenched in the mind of the nation, even in the mind of the South, he had nothing to gain by pointing that fact out.

As a world revolutionary, then, Fitzhugh was in an odd position: his message was ignored by half of the country in which he lived. He was a Calvin not taken seriously by half of Geneva, a Lenin not taken seriously by half of Russia. This was a harsh fate, but it was hardly more than he had a right to expect. Even in 1776 America had not issued an apocalyptic clarion call to the liberals of the world, largely because the "cannon and feudal law" was not present here to inspire the inverted Christianity, the crusading secular visions of Rousseau and Condorcet. Was it reasonable to assume that America, nearly a hundred years later, would take a man seriously who issued such a call in defense of that law itself? The anguished fantasy of the Reactionary Enlightenment, its incredible contradictions, and its failure to impress anyone, all come out most vividly in the claim that it is going to sweep the world.

2. The Constitution: Calhoun and Fitzhugh

When we examine more closely the inner tensions of Southern thought, the inability of the Southerners to emancipate themselves from the liberal ideas they were in the process of destroying, we find a record of turmoil as vivid as one might expect. It is not easy to live at the same time in the dark world of Sir Walter Scott and the brightly lit world of John Locke. The contrasts are blinding, confusing, and in the end they drive a thinker mad. Calhoun, it seems to me, is our clearest proof of this.

One makes such a remark about Calhoun with some trepidation, for he is the philosophic darling of students of American political thought, the man who is almost invariably advanced when a thinker of European stature is asked for in the American tradition. And yet, despite the outward literary appearance of "rigor" and "consistency" in Calhoun's work, one is bound to affirm that the man is a profoundly disintegrated political theorist. What is "rigorous" about grounding the state in force and Providence after the fashion of Maistre and then creating a set of constitutional gadgets that would have staggered even Sieyés? What is "consistent" about destroying Locke's state of nature and then evolving a theory of minority rights that actually brings one back there for good? There are more impressive thinkers to whom the American historian can point. Fitzhugh, as I have suggested, must be ranked as one of these, for if on the surface he seems like a cracker-barrel commentator, at bottom he has a touch of the Hobbesian lucidity of mind. He, more than anyone else, sensed the awful way Calhoun betrayed the Reactionary Enlightenment when he based the sectional defense of the South on the ancient liberalism it tried to destroy. He fought continuously to substitute the concept of "organic nationality" for the concept of state "sovereignty," and there was the keenest logic to this substitution. By extracting a traditionalist type of Southern nationalism from the conservative theory of slavery itself, he was able to give up all of the compacts and all of the checks on which Calhoun relied.

We have to concede, however, that without this approach there was really no alternative to riding the two horses Calhoun tried to ride. For the theory of the reaction grounds itself on the divinity of existing coercions, and while this may serve a purpose for the defense of Negro slavery, it hardly serves a purpose for the liberation of the South from regional "slavery" to the North. The second type of slavery, if we take the Southerners at their word, was just as existent as the first, and if Calhoun's God ordained the one, how could he have failed to ordain the other? The irony of the Burkian position, even in Europe, was that it became articulate at precisely the moment it became untenable, at the moment when God had introduced a new reality to challenge his old one, which meant that when Burke denounced the French Revolution he had to become something of a rationalist himself. Under these circumstances, lacking Fitzhugh's faith in the South's romantic nationalism, it is not hard to see why Calhoun in his battle against the North kept applying the ethos of the Kentucky-Virginia Resolutions. After all, an inconsistency is better than a logical surrender.

But let us make no mistake about the fact of inconsistency: it is not merely striking, it is doubly and triply striking. Had Calhoun merely maintained an ordinary faith in the mechanics of the American Constitution at the same moment that he grounded government in force and tradition, this would have been one thing. But his faith is not an ordinary one. There is a weird quality about Calhoun: he has a wild passion for the conclusions his premises nullify, as if a pang of guilt made him redouble his affection for the things that he destroyed. The idea of state "sovereignty" shatters a meaningful American union, and yet he insists with the most anguished repetition that this alone can serve as a national "preservative." The idea of a fixed Southern minority and a fixed Northern majority amounts to civil war, and yet the scheme of the "concurrent majority" he builds upon it he describes in terms of compromise that are nothing short of idyllic. The best example of this mounting love in the midst of murder is the one that I have mentioned: the attempt to ground both of these mechanical schemes on the organic naturalism that his social defense of slavery inspired.

For surely the idea that the Constitution is a "compact" among "sovereign" states, that states may therefore nullify federal legislation, and that the proof of this is to be found in a diligent study of ratification procedures in 1787, is about as far away as you can get from the spirit of "Divine ordination." This not only makes the American system of government a rationalistic instrument of extreme delicacy but it pins its origin to a decisive moment in historical time, just as Condorcet, misunderstanding American constitutionalism, pinned it in the eighteenth century. If the Southerners usually had to distort American liberalism in order to denounce it as "metaphysical," they would not, ironically enough, have had to distort Calhoun's version of its constitutional embodiment in order to denounce it in that way. That version met all of the "metaphysical" standards. It left nothing to tradition, nothing to force, and nothing to God. Nor is it the only thing we have to consider. There is also Calhoun's theory of the "concurrent majority," which supplemented state nullification with the nullification of individual "interests." When we pile the one on top of the other, we have a scheme of man-made political instruments which the French Enlightenment in its palmiest days never dared to develop.

It is here, in his passionate defense of the minority interest, that Calhoun goes back to Locke's state of nature after having destroyed it in a blaze of organic glory. For there are of course minorities within minorities—as Unionists like Hugh Swinton Legare did not fail to remind Calhoun in South Carolina in 1832—and since Calhoun offers no reason why these should not be given a policy veto too, the idea of the "concurrent majority" quickly unravels itself into separate individuals executing the law of nature for themselves. When Locke accepted majority rule, in other words, he accepted more force in politics than Calhoun, the great theorist of force and slavery, was ready to accept. When Locke accepted majority rule, he was more pessimistic than Calhoun, the great pessimist, would permit himself to be. What could be worse for the logic of the Southern position? Here are grim traditionalists denouncing Northern liberalism as a code of "anarchy," and Calhoun supplies them with a political theory that even Daniel Webster can denounce as a theory to "anarchy." Here are ardent corporatists denying that a natural harmony of interests can ever exist—and Calhoun advances a logic of harmony that one would have to go to Godwin to duplicate.

Since Calhoun's mechanical suggestions were a failure, it is interesting that his new-found organic philosophy did not suggest the nature of their failure to him. One might say, as has often been said, that Calhoun was here merely extending the checking-and-balancing ethos of the Founding Fathers. If this is true, then his wild rationalism has a curious logic to it. Adams and Morris, instead of grounding their hope for America on a liberal unity that could support even their clumsy scheme of checks and balances, grounded it on the capacity of those checks and balances to contain and control frightful social conflicts that did not exist. In the only time in American history when such conflicts did appear, what was more reasonable than for a disciple of theirs to multiply passionately all of the checks and balances that were about to be exploded? But in his role as an antagonist of American liberalism, why didn't Calhoun see the futility of this reasoning? Why didn't his organic sense for the importance of social solidarity make him realize that however much you compounded "interest" checks with other checks none of them would work if the social fabric was actually torn apart? There was at least this relevance of traditionalism to the liberal cement of American life: that by concentrating on the solidarity that comes from "prejudice" it might have exposed the liberal prejudices that had held the country together to the view of "realistic" thinkers who had managed not to see them. Some Southern organicists actually caught this point, but Calhoun himself did not: the lesson of Adams ran too deep for a sudden correction by Burke.

And yet it would be unfair, after all of this has been said, not to notice that Calhoun was aware of the basic contradiction he faced. In his famous *Disquisition* he drew a distinction between "government" and "constitution." Governments were rooted in force and inspired by God, even as Negro slavery was, but constitutions were a different thing entirely. They controlled government, and being the product of a later age, when "invention" replaced "superstition," they could be used to abolish the South's regional enslavement to the North. Here was a straightforward effort to deal with the problem of Maistre and Sieyès. But it reminds us alas, for all of its ingenuity, of a man carefully placing a match on top of a stick of dynamite. For clearly if "consitution" and "government" ever come together at any point, if it is ever established that the one has any of the characteristics of the other, an explosion is bound to occur which wipes the Southern position off the face of the philosophic earth. Not only does the South become validly enslaved to the North, but the whole structure of "compact" and "concurrent majority" is swept away in a fierce tide of irrationalism. What difference then does it make whether a genuinely "American people" did or did not exist in 1787? God could have created one in the interval. What difference does it make whether minorities are coerced? Coercion is a law of life. What difference does it make whether the Southern "interest" is consulted? Interests can never work together freely and harmoniously anyway. This was a great deal to stake on a tenuous distinction between "constitution" and "government." And to say that the distinction was tenuous is putting the matter mildly. There are some who would argue that the control of government is actually the highest form of the governmental task.

Fitzhugh, then, was rightly terrified at the doctrines of the "Calhoun school." His theory of blood and solid nationalism, of "organic nationality," avoided all of the inner turmoil and the brink-of-destruction gyrations that the Calhounian position involved. Romantic, grounded in the claim of slave culture itself, it could never be assailed by the conservative theory that slavery produced. Nor should we assume that Fitzhugh was here a voice crying in the wilderness. Many Southerners, as the sense of their separateness was forced upon them and as the appeal of Scott and Disraeli grew, became attached to the principle of traditionalist nationalism with a genuine and ardent feeling. Of course, few of them became attached to it so much that they were ready to give up constitutional apologetics entirely, which meant that their original dualism of Burke and Locke was simply duplicated again on the plane of nationalism. But under the circumstances what is striking is not how little romantic nationalism there was in the political thought of the South but how little there was of it in the political thought of the "nationalistic" North. Daniel Webster remained as legalistic as Marshall, despite the fact that had he adopted some form of romantic nationalism (it would, of course, have to be a Rousseauan or a Mazzinian type in his case); he would have been able to explode against Calhoun much of the dynamite that he was playing with. There was much romanticism in the North, but with the exception of a few men like Barlow and Emerson, it spent itself in a Thoreauan individualism or a Garrisonian cosmopolitanism. Garrison denounced constitutional lawyers as fervently as Fitzhugh did, but he put on the masthead of the *Liberator*, "Our country is the world."

Thus, oddly, the South, the "sectionalist" South, became the real originator of romantic nationalism in American political theory. But one thing has to be said about that nationalism: it radicalized the whole Southern position. For it is hard to control the claim of nationalism, and especially the claim of Scott's nationalism, with its love of chivalry, its faith in force, its ethos of blood and soil. Implicitly the solution that Fitzhugh offered called for independence and beat the drums of war. And here the "Calhoun school," at least until 1860, might have offered a reply: it did not want independence and it did not want war. If it clung to Enlightenment contractualism because it wanted to defend the South against the North, it clung to it also because it wanted them both to live together. Its inconsistency pointed in two directions. This is the larger secret of Calhoun's intellectual madness: he appears at a moment when the South's fear of the North and its love of the Union hold each other in perfect balance, so that starting with explosive premises like sovereignty and conflict and force he drives himself somehow to avert the explosion with conclusions like nullification and the "concurrent majority." He was caught in the classic agony of the brink-of-war philosopher.

But the main point I want to emphasize is the coexistence in the Southern mind of its new Burkian traditionalism and its old Jeffersonian rationalism. Calhoun exemplifies it perfectly, a man whose thought is cut in two by the tug of the liberal past and the pull of the reactionary present. He slays Jefferson only to embrace him with a passion in the end, he destroys the Founding Fathers only to carry their work forward. Under such circumstances why should Garrison bother to reply to the elaborate Providential organicism of the South? The South was doing a good enough job of replying to it itself. The point illustrates again the basic dilemma the Southerners faced: their liberalism was so traditional that even they could not get away from it: Garrison the "jacobin" had the power of their own historic irrationalism on his side, and they, the historic irrationalists, could not even be decent "jacobins." They were, in a sense, outside of time and space, carrying on a reactionary conversation with themselves in a kind of Alice-in-Wonderland world where nothing was what it seemed to be, where nothing was what it ought to be, where liberalism was oddly conservatized and conservatism oddly liberalized. Or, if one prefers Stevenson to Carroll, they were a set of Dr. Jekylls constantly becoming Mr. Hydes—their own worst enemies and their own executioners.

Part IV
Ideas in a Darwinian Age

21 The Religion of Geology

Conrad Wright

For many years American historians stressed the "warfare" between scientific inquiry and religious faith. They were taking up the theme first exploited by John William Draper and Andrew Dickson White in the last quarter of the nineteenth century. That theme has been somewhat muted in recent decades. We now tend to see eighteenth- and nineteenth-century scientific methods and knowledge as independent intellectual currents within a broad stream of Western thought that often flowed from religious sources. This newer view does not so much gloss over the trauma American Protestant theology experienced when Darwinian thought emerged after 1859 as it seeks to describe pre-Darwinian science as intellectually respectable within the American experience and even as anticipating later findings in the natural sciences. By no means is the story of nineteenth-century science one of inevitable progress. There were dead ends, and partisanship was stultifying. From Benjamin Franklin to Josiah Willard Gibbs a century after him, America produced no major figure in theoretical or "pure" science, with the possible exception of Joseph Henry. America was inventive, not speculative. But the newer view recognizes scientific professionalism as coming to the fore in the Jacksonian era, supported by the appearance of scientific societies and journals. Conrad Wright's article in 1941 was one of the first to employ this revised portrait of scientific men in the 1840s who firmly used the Baconian or inductive method of inquiry to uncover the processes of nature in a still divinely ordered Newtonian cosmos. Yet these men were doing more than bringing up to date the natural theology of William Paley from the 1780s: by their classifying and cataloguing they were pushing forward the empirical understanding of geological history. Few branches of science then known were so fortunate. These academic men of western Massachusetts were making excursions into natural history from their orthodox religious base while at the same time Transcendentalists in eastern Massachusetts, most of whom could not be granted a hearing in any college, were exploring philosophical idealism from their discontent with orthodox religion.

The New England Quarterly, 14 (June 1941), 335-349, 353-358. Reprinted by permission of the author and *The New England Quarterly*. Footnotes and section 4 of the original essay have been omitted.

For further reading: I. Bernard Cohen, "Science in America: the Nineteenth Century," in Arthur M. Schlesinger, Jr., and Morton White (eds.), *Paths of American Thought* (1963), chap. 9; George R. Daniels, *American Science in the Age of Jackson* (1968); *Dirk J. Struik, *Yankee Science in the Making* (1962); *Charles C. Gillispie, *Genesis and Geology* (1951); John C. Greene, *The Deach of Adam: Evolution and Its Impact on Western Thought* (1959); *Nathan Reingold (ed.), *Science in Nineteenth-Century America: A Documentary History* (1964).

I

In the beginning, God created the heaven and the earth. And the earth was without form and void; and darkness was upon the face of the deep: And the spirit of God moved upon the face of the waters." With these words, the author of Genesis began his story of Creation, his attempt to unveil the awful mystery of the beginning of all things. His account, as part of the sacred writings of the Jews, was accepted by all Christendom as the infallible revelation of God. In the beginning, God created the heaven and the earth; on the sixth day, he created man in his own image; on the seventh day, God ended his work which he had made, and he rested on the seventh day from all his work which he had made. By computing the generations of Adam, the student could readily discover that the date of Creation was about four thousand years before the Christian era. These were the presuppositions of men's thinking, the framework within which all theories of Cosmogony were set.

During the nineteenth century, the Mosaic account of Creation was driven first from the minds of scientists, then from the minds of other educated men. But even though this change came within two or three generations, the evidence supporting the new theories had long been accumulating. That fossils represent organic remains, that they have been laid down under water in sequence, that they reveal a long period of sedimentation, that the surface of the earth has been undergoing constant change, and that earth processes are still in progress: each one of these views had to struggle for acceptance against the mass of inherited belief. The battles began in the sixteenth century, and continued through the eighteenth, until the whole structure of the new theory was unified by James Hutton (1726-1797).

Hutton's contribution was the doctrine of "uniformitarianism." No previous thinker had realized so clearly as he that the earth processes we can observe today are sufficient to explain the present surface of the globe. To other men, the peaceful landscape seemed stable and unchanging; he recognized that it was subject to constant erosion, and that the material removed was the source of the sediments in the sea. It followed that enormous lengths of time must have been necessary to build the beds of rock we encounter. Since erosion, long continued, should ere now have worn all the land away, there must be some counteracting force rebuilding the land masses. Hutton found this in vulcanism, declaring that molten matter pushed up from below served to maintain the continents. This opinion won for his followers the nickname "Plutonists."

Hutton's influence was not direct, because his first statement of the theory was printed obscurely, in 1785, while his later version was most tedious reading. The statement of the uniformitarian position which finally established it was Charles

Lyell's *Principles of Geology,* in three volumes (1830-1833). Lyell buttressed the Huttonian position with the results of recent developments in stratigraphy. The implications of Hutton's theory now struck the popular mind with full force; and for three decades, the conflict between the geologists' account and the Mosaic story of Creation raged furiously, both in England and America.

In New England, the attempt to reconcile the two was made most conspicuously by three geologists: Benjamin Silliman, Edward Hitchcock, and James Dwight Dana. The result was not only a reinterpretation of the Bible in the light of scientific knowledge, but also the use of geology to reveal the nature and attributes of the Creator. This body of thought was known as the "Religion of Geology."

II

Before 1802, when Benjamin Silliman was appointed to a professorship of chemistry and natural science at Yale, interest in geology in this country had been very sporadic. President Dwight, seeking in vain for someone competent to fill a proposed chair of natural science, was forced to appoint a bright young man and give him a chance to learn something about the subject before requiring him to teach. Silliman's only qualification was an alert mind. But Dwight's confidence was not misplaced. Silliman served as the channel through which European scientific progress reached this country, he trained the most prominent of the American geologists before the Civil War, he provided a scientific journal, and by his lecturing he spread a knowledge of geology and chemistry among the general public.

The most solid part of his geological training was received at Edinburgh, the city of Hutton and his followers, in the winter of 1805-1806. Silliman arrived in the midst of a furious controversy between the Plutonists and the disciples of the German mineraliogist, Abraham Gottlob Werner, who were known as "Neptunists" because of their belief that the earliest rocks had been formed by chemical deposition from a once universal ocean. Later formations, they conceded, involved mechanical deposition. In contrast with the Plutonists, their concept was one of stages in which different earth processes were at work.

Silliman became familiar with the arguments of both schools, though at first he was inclined to favor the Wernerians. Indeed, down to 1820 or 1825, American geologists generally were more or less Wernerian. This fact is important, because the Neptunist theory does not clash conspicuously with the Mosaic story of the Creation. After 1820, the Wernerian system rapidly lost ground; and in 1822 William Maclure wrote in the *American Journal of Science* that the German scientist's views were "fast going out of fashion." It would seem to be no accident that the first attempts in America to reconcile geology and the Bible should have coincided with the passing of the Wernerian geology. As Hutton's uniformitarian views gained wider acceptance, the need for such a reconciliation became increasingly acute.

In order to understand the attempted compromise of science and religion in the minds of American scientists, it is fully as important to know their religious background and training as their geological ideas. The three most prominent American geologists were all members of the orthodox wing of New England Congregationalism. More than that, they were all men of devout faith, believing sincerely in the prevailing Calvinism and in the plenary inspiration of the Scriptures.

Religious influences were important in Silliman's childhood. His father was "a decidedly religious man"; his mother taught the children prayers and hymns and required them to read the Bible regularly. The Westminster Catechism was the standard of their faith. In his college years, Silliman continued to be interested in religion. In his diary for 1795-1796 there are passages of introspection and self-appraisal, summaries of sermons, and mentions of the reading of Paley and of attendance at prayers. He wrote to his brother in April, 1797, "I am well convinced of the importance of an early and thorough examination of the evidence of the Christian religion, and intend that it shall be one of the first objects of my attention." When the revival of 1802 passed over Yale, it swept Silliman into the fold; and he joined the college church, to the great joy of many of his friends. None of his later scientific work could rob him of the deep piety which led him to this step.

It is not remarkable that the approach to the study of science of such a man was not based on mere utility or idle curiosity. Silliman was always conscious that what he was doing was investigating the laws by which the Creator works, and that part of his task was to glorify that Creator. In delivering his introductory lecture to his classes, he made no apology for speaking first of religion: "It is at the head of all sciences; it is the only revealed one, and it is necessary, to give a proper use and direction to all the others." Geology is of particular value; for in the study of the earth we find "decisive proofs of the power, wisdom and design of its author." This belief that "we honor the Divine Author by tracing the operation of his laws" recurs again and again in Silliman's writings. In 1836, he lectured at the Lowell Institute on chemistry. "The moral and religious bearing of the lectures was decided in illustration of the wisdom, power, and benevolence manifested equally in the mechanical and chemical constitution of our world." He lectured there again in 1841 and had the satisfaction "to contribute not only to the mental illumination of the people, but to the increase of their reverence for God."

It may be that Silliman's early acceptance of Werner's views softened the impact of geology on his inherited religious beliefs. Superficially, at least, the Mosaic account of Creation had much in common with Werner's description: both began with a watery abyss from which land emerged. In 1820, however, he was writing to his pupil, Edward Hitchcock, that he had become "still more convinced of the truth of the new views." A few years later, Professor Moses Stuart of Andover wrote to him about the problem, and he replied at length. Stuart was far from convinced, for he answered by letter, and in 1836 published an article stating his position. This correspondence led Silliman to prepare the first of four discussions of the conflict, as part of an "Outline of the Course of Geological Lectures Given in Yale College." This was printed in 1829 as the appendix to the first American edition of Bakewell's *Introduction to Geology*. Two of the other essays were supplements to successive editions; the fourth took the form of "Remarks Introductory to the First American Edition of Dr. Mantell's Wonders of Geology." These are not entirely different essays, for some material is reprinted verbatim from one to the next.

Silliman's ideas did not change essentially from year to year, and so it is possible to construct a synthesis of his position. He pointed out that the Bible is a code of moral instruction, rather than a system of science; hence it is not surprising that natural phenomena are described as they appear, rather than in scientific terms. Yet both declare that the world had a beginning, thereby proving the existence of a Creator. The order of events by which land appeared and was peopled with creatures in the sea and on land, culminating in man, is identical in the Mosaic account and in the fossil record. The difference lies in the amount of time required for the events before the creation of man. The solution is to conceive each "day" in the Mosaic account as a geologic period of indefinite length. Others had already made this suggestion; and Silliman was indebted for it to Cuvier and to Professor Jameson, under whom he had studied at Edinburgh.

Silliman rebutted other theories. One, which supposed that "the present earth was formed from the ruins and fragments of an earlier world, rearranged and set in order during the six days," was dismissed on the ground that it did not allow time for the deposition of fossil-bearing strata. Another theory declared that an indefinite period intervened "between the first creation 'in the beginning,' and the commencement of the first day." Silliman did not believe that an ordinary day was long enough for the emergence of mountains and the creation of many varieties of living beings, now entombed in the rocks. Finally, he denied the common view that the strata and surface deposits were laid down during Noah's flood. Yet there was ample geologic evidence that that deluge actually occurred; the nature of surface deposits was consistent with the account we have of it, and illustrated and confirmed the Bible story. In this connection, he recommended Buckland's *Reliquiae Diluvianae*. Believing that geology is an aid to faith rather than its enemy, he urged that theologians study science in order to become familiar with the evidence on which its conclusions are based.

One American geologist dissented very strongly from Silliman's doctrines. He was Thomas Cooper, an Englishman by birth, a friend of Jefferson, and President of South Carolina College. "Old Coot" had to use Silliman's edition of Bakewell in his classes, to his great annoyance; but was accustomed to try to counteract the influence of Silliman's appendix on his students. In 1833 he wrote a pamphlet, *On the Connection between Geology and the Pentateuch; in a Letter to Professor Silliman from Thomas Cooper, M.D.* This tract spoke of Silliman in none too cordial tones:

It is well for Professor Silliman, that his useful services to science have placed his reputation on a more stable foundation, than his absolute unconditional surrender of his common sense to clerical orthodoxy.

In his personal correspondence with Silliman, Cooper was equally outspoken. Finally he wrote a letter which, according to Silliman, "reviled the Scriptures, especially of the Old Testament, pronouncing them in all respects an unsupported and, in some respects, a most detestable book." To this letter, Silliman made no reply, and the correspondence came to an end.

Cooper's views were not typical of Americans at that time. They reveal the influence of a somewhat different religious background from that of New England Calvinism. Cooper was a close friend of Joseph Priestley, the English Unitarian. Priestley's materialism found little sympathy in New England, from either the orthodox or the liberal branch of the Congregational Church. Silliman's experience in Boston in 1835 and 1836 was that his views were received with favor by both Orthodox and Unitarian clergymen. Both, he declared, "thank me warmly for the manner in which they say that delicate points are treated."

III

Silliman's pupil, Edward Hitchcock, was even more concerned that science should be regarded as the handmaid of theology. He, too, belonged to the orthodox wing of Congregationalism. In his youth, he had been attracted by the specious charms of Unitarianism, but a serious illness led him to inquire on what foundation he was "building for eternity," and brought him back to the Orthodox fold. From 1819 to 1821 he studied at Yale, both reading theology and working in Silliman's laboratory. For four years he was minister of the church in Conway, Massachusetts; then, in 1825, he was appointed Professor of Natural History and Chemistry at Amherst, where he taught for most of the rest of his life. For nine years, from 1845 to 1854, he was President of the college; but at the same time he retained a professorship of natural theology and geology.

Amherst itself was a religious influence of no mean proportions. It was more orthodox and less secular-minded even than Yale. It had its own church, whose carefully worded creed began with a statement of belief in the infallibility of Scripture. Religious meetings were frequent, and revivals swept through the college with considerable regularity. Hardly a class graduated without having been touched in one of its four years by the Spirit of God. These revivals were approved and fostered by the college authorities, who became very skillful in directing their course. Some of the most effective religious meetings were held in President Hitchcock's own home; for he was accustomed to set aside a half-hour every Monday evening for prayer and conference with the students.

Hitchcock's appointment as President of Amherst made it necessary for him to give up the project of writing a full work on natural theology. He had long meditated on the subject, and regarded such books as *The Religion of Geology* as "insulated fragments" of a larger whole. This unwritten book he would have considered a greater monument than all his scientific research. His whole teaching career, indeed, had as its purpose not to explain scientific facts but to illustrate by those facts "the principles of natural theology." He made no claim to give his students more instruction in the natural sciences "than is necessary to understand their religious bearing. But this is their most important use, as it is of all knowledge."

The problems of Genesis and geology first began to concern Hitchcock as early as 1823, when he preached a sermon before the Pittsfield Medical Institution supporting the "new views." But though his theological opinions occasionally found incidental expression in the reports of his geological field work, it was not until 1835 that he began to write extensively on the subject. Three articles in the *Biblical Repository and Quarterly Observer* expressed his views on geology as proving the existence of God and revealing divine benevolence; and reviewed the various interpretations of the six days of Genesis. These essays caused a minor controversy. They were attacked by Professor Moses Stuart of Andover, in an article in the January 1836 number of the magazine. Certain positions the two men held in common. Both believed in the plenary inspiration of the Bible; both believed that the discoveries of geology should not clash with it. But Stuart was a literalist. It was clear to him that Moses knew nothing about the latest developments of science in the nineteenth century, and so knowledge of those developments can be of no use in the interpretation of Genesis. In the Bible, scientific matters are treated in the popular way; phenomena are described as they appear, not as the scientist views them. Stuart, the conservative literalist, was closer to the truth than the advanced thinkers of the time when he said, "If they please let it be a question, whether Moses has taught wrongly or rightly; but it never can be a question with philologists whether modern science is to be the final judge of what an ancient writing means." Stuart then turned to a philological examination of the first chapter of Genesis which combated Hitchcock's solution of the problem of the six days, and ended with a few tentative comments on purely geological matters.

Silliman had had correspondence with Stuart on earlier occasions, and had not formed a very favorable impression of his habits of mind. Now, with great eagerness, he wrote to Hitchcock to tell of new support the two had won for their side. His colleague, Professor Kingsley, had written an article showing that Stuart had applied his literal interpretation only when dealing with geological matters; when touching on astronomical questions such as the nature of the firmament, he had reinterpreted the words of Moses in just the fashion that the geologists insisted was necessary. Silliman asked Hitchcock for permission to publish this reply; and it appeared in the April 1836 number of the *American Journal of Science*. Hitchcock defended his own position in an article in the April 1836 number of the *Biblical Repository*. Then, the flurry of excitement over, he returned to his task of expounding the harmony of science and religion. Between January 1837 and January 1838 he published three articles on the Flood.

These essays were only preparation for his most important book, *The Religion of Geology*. It first appeared in 1851, being reprinted with an additional lecture in 1859. It combined treatments of the reconciliation of Genesis and geology with a discussion of the contribution of geology to natural theology. Hitchcock regarded scientific truth as a description of the laws of nature; or, in other words, of the way in which the Divine Mind operates. By studying scientific laws, therefore, we can learn something of the nature of God. "The principles of science are a transcript of the Divine Character." Such a study is what is meant by "natural theology." Both scientist and theologian seek to illustrate the character of God, one by investigating nature, the other by interpreting revelation. Hitchcock, like Silliman, defended with equal vigor the truth of geology and the plenary inspiration of the Scriptures. But since the Bible describes natural phenomena as they appear, rather than with scientific precision, he maintained that it is no more presumptuous to use scientific knowledge of geology to clarify the phrases of the Bible than it is to use Copernican astronomy for that purpose.

A careful philological examination convinced Hitchcock that the language of the Bible does not exclude the possibility that a long period intervened between the first creation "in the beginning" and the six demiurgic days. In that period, the processes of sedimentation were at work, and many species of plants and animals, whose remains are now found as fossils, were created by God, lived their allotted span of ages, and then passed away. The Mosaic account pays no attention to these creations, because they are irrelevant to the main moral purpose of the Bible. The six days were the latest period of new creation of species, during which the world was fitted up for man and its other present occupants. Silliman's view that the days represent indefinite periods seemed to Hitchcock unsound. The order of the creation in Genesis does not correspond with the order of fossils in the rocks as closely as Silliman thought.

One problem concerned Hitchcock to which Silliman had paid no attention. This was how death had entered the world. Genesis declares that it was because of Adam's sin; geology reveals long ages when plants flourished and died before the creation of Adam. But God knew that man would sin, and so he created a world in which death would exist. "Death . . . entered into the original plan of the world in the divine mind, and was endured by the animals and plants that lived anterior to man." By anticipation, the sin of Adam was the cause of death for all prior creation.

Next, Hitchcock turned to the problems of the Flood. He knew that God had sent a punitive deluge over the earth, for the Bible declared it. His observations informed him that great floods had occurred. The question at issue was whether the deposits on the surface of the earth had been laid down during the Biblical Deluge. Various geological considerations led him to the conclusion that no traces of the Flood can be identified today. But this involved no conflict between geology and revelation, for in the time that has elapsed, all traces might have been obliterated.

To show that there is no conflict between geology and the Bible was only the negative side of the religion of geology. Of equal concern to Hitchcock was the way in which geology contributes to natural theology. Most important, it proves the existence of God. Atheism rests on two assumptions: that matter itself is eternal, and that the laws by which it acts are sufficient explanation for the creation of all that is in the world. The evidence of geology, fairly considered, reveals "direct and repeated acts of creative power." Perhaps no more than the other scientists can the geologist prove that the earth was created out of nothing. But he can show that it was once a molten globe, on which life could not exist. Life, then, had a beginning, and requires a Creator for its explanation. The geologic record, Hitchcock asserted, is even more explicit. It reveals that again and again the earth has been peopled by creatures which have been completely erased from its surface, to be replaced by new species. Any suggestion that later races have developed from the earlier is tantamount to atheism; for it makes unnecessary the constant presence of divine benevolence and power in the universe. To such theories, geology gives no support.

The final evidence is the recent commencement of the human race. "And who will doubt that his creation demanded an infinite Deity?" Hitchcock did not, nor did he doubt that his creation was the end for which the whole system of nature was established. Geology furnishes numerous ways in which the earth has been prepared for his comfort and well-being. There is the soil, subject to weathering and disintegration, that vegetation might grow in it for man's use. The broken and upturned condition of the strata of the earth has made it possible for man to discover various mineral products. A conclusive argument is based on the distribution of water throughout the globe. "We should expect . . . that this element . . . must be very unequally distributed, and fail entirely in many places; and yet we find it in almost every spot where man erects his habitation."

The divine benevolence is most strongly impressed on our minds when we realize the unity of the divine plan. The laws of nature are seen to have been the same as far back as the geologic record runs. Present and past are tied together in one "great system of infinite wisdom and benevolence." In the same way that astronomy has increased our concept of the vastness of the divine plan by showing us almost unbelievably large distances in space, geology has increased it by revealing long periods of time. Throughout untold ages, God has been improving the universe, preparing it for the occupation of man, setting the stage for the great drama of man's fall and redemption. Thus scientific study heightens our sense of the power and majesty of God. . . .

IV

Of the religious background and experience of James Dwight Dana we have less detailed information than about Silliman and Hitchcock. Perhaps this is because of the discreetness of his biographer, who contented himself with a summary statement of his attitude—perpetually shown in his daily walk and conversation—the transcendent purpose of his soul is the service of his Master." Both of his parents, however, "were of strong religious convictions, based upon the moderate Calvinistic doctrines of the Congregational Church, to which they belonged." Dana was, of course, of a younger generation than Silliman and Hitchcock. He was born in 1813, and studied at Yale under Silliman. Perhaps the fires of the faith burned a little less fiercely in him than in his elders, yet he was in no sense a purely secular-minded scientist.

His first contribution to the literature of controversy was occasioned by a book entitled *The Six Days of Creation*. This was the work of Tayler Lewis, Professor of Greek at Union College. Although Lewis's most enduring claim to remembrance is based on his Greek scholarship, "the chief interest of his life . . . was the study of religion, and his main purpose was to show that revelation and scientific knowledge are not merely consistent but interdependent." Lewis was one of those who reached the conclusion that the "days" of creation represent long periods; but his train of reasoning and his incidental remarks on science caused great offence to Dana. Lewis, like Moses Stuart, was a literalist, believing that the meaning of the words of the Bible is a problem for philologists, without the aid of men of science. But the Bible is as infallible in its description of physical truth as in its moral teaching; the important distinction is that it does not use scientific language. The phrase "the sun rises" uses phenomenal language, not scientific; and in those terms it is everlastingly true. It is more correct, even, than scientific language, which tries to describe events in terms of their causes; for since causes can never be traced to the ultimate cause, the language of scientists is always shifting and unstable.

Dana had been told that Lewis supported the Silliman interpretation of the six days, and so he took up the book predisposed in its favor. He found in it "much truth, well expressed and argued," but also "much arrogance and error." It was accompanied by "sneers at geology and all science, which betokened a mind unfit for research." Dana was first of all concerned, then, to vindicate science and the work of scientists. The conclusions of science are no less true because they do not explain the ultimate causes of phenomena. Science proceeds by careful induction, which is a far cry from prescientific explanations of causes, reached by allowing the imagination to run free.

Dana's criticisms were presented in an essay in the *Bibliotheca Sacra* for January 1856; they were reprinted as a pamphlet, copies of which he sent to numerous scientific colleagues. Many favorable replies came back. Louis Agassiz thanked him heartily for it and for his "powerful vindication of science versus conceited theology." G. P. Bond, the astronomer, declared that he was "much gratified with its decisive statement of facts"; to him, the evidence Dana had brought forth was convincing. Benjamin Pierce regarded it as "the happiest possible reply to the attacks upon the religion of science," and went on to say, "It is fortunate for us that you have taken up this subject with your firmness, fidelity, and composure."

Dana had charged Lewis with teaching a development theory comparable to that of *Vestiges of Creation.* This charge rankled, and Lewis made haste to disavow such a doctrine. But Dana returned to the attack, and repeated the charge of infidelity in three more articles in the *Bibliotheca Sacra.* By attempting to discredit science, he said, Professor Lewis has done a disservice to the cause of the Bible. If people come to think that the two are hostile, they are likely to abandon the Bible. Dana regarded them as two revelations of God, in harmony with one another; but a sense of the independent standing of science pervades his work in a way that is not to be found in that of his predecessors. These articles, begun as an answer to Tayler Lewis, before long were transformed into a vindication of the scientific method and a defense of its conclusions. A wide gap separates them from *The Religion of Geology;* they usher in a new world. No longer is science a mere adjunct of religion, useful mainly for the added light it throws on revelation. The aura of religion still enshrouds it; it is still thought of as revealing to mankind the mind of God; but scientific truth becomes interesting for its own sake.

There was a second way, Dana felt, in which Lewis's work tended to infidelity; this was the use of the distinction between scientific and phenomenal language. Science admits that there is much that it does not know about the ultimate causes of phenomena; but it does not follow that what it knows about the immediate causes is false. The tendency of study is to clear away errors in our understanding of causes, not to lead us into deeper and deeper mistakes. If it were otherwise, man "would be forced, in just indignation, to write FALSE over the whole face of nature, and to replace the word GOD with that of DEMON."

V

How widely accepted was the religion of geology among those who shared the intellectual heritage of New England? No significant voice was raised against it from the purely scientific or naturalistic point of view. From the purely Biblical point of view, Moses Stuart and Tayler Lewis were important dissenters. What set them apart was not so much the precise conclusions they reached as their distrust of the findings of science. It seems probable that they were very much in the minority among religious thinkers. The warm response from the audience to which Silliman spoke, the favorable reception given to *The Religion of Geology*, and the fact that most of the controversial articles supported the harmony of Genesis and geology: these evidences seem conclusive.

Moreover, the Orthodox and the Unitarians in New England differed little in their acceptance of these views. Silliman was pleased to find the two groups united in his favor, when he lectured at the Lowell Institute. The Unitarians were considerably less concerned about the problem; but apart from that, the only difference that is clearly important is their recognition of the importance of Biblical criticism.

Presumably the minds of the ordinary people, who were neither scientists nor theologians, moved less rapidly. ,Yet it is safe to say that this body of ideas represents the same kind of thinking that the common man was doing. While Silliman, Hitchcock, and Dana were scientists, they shared the prevailing religious beliefs. And so the conflict which went on in society at large was perfectly mirrored within the minds of the geologists themselves. No doubt that conflict appeared sooner in their minds; perhaps a study of them minimizes unduly the extreme conservative position of those who had no real contact with geological knowledge; doubtless their thinking was more carefully reasoned out and elaborated. Yet their pathway was the same one trod by the ordinary mind, the same intellectual dilemmas confronted them, and the same compromise emerged from the harsh conflict of discordant intellectual concepts.

Silliman began to concern himself with the harmony of Genesis and geology about 1820. For the next forty years, after Huttonian geology superseded the Wernerian, no important new assumptions emerged. Geological facts were accumulated, and the glacial theory was introduced; the study of paleontology brought additional information; and the interpretation of the Bible in the light of science was elaborated and reworked many times, and improved by countless hands. The emphasis perhaps shifted slightly; in Dana science became the equal of revelation instead of being an adjunct to it. All in all, however, the foundations laid in the 1820s for this structure of ideas remained solid until 1859.

For many people, it continued to be an impressive structure. Silliman and Hitchcock never abandoned their early positions. Others carried on the controversy. But 1859 was the year of *The Origin of Species*. The battle front broadened as a new period in the debate began. The validity of the doctrine of evolution, and the question whether Darwinism was compatible with design and hence with the existence of God were surface aspects of the debate. More important was a new assumption which gradually emerged from the welter of conflict and which brought about the collapse of the beautiful structure Hitchcock had labored so hard to erect. It was Darwin who deprived men of the comfortable belief that man was specially created by God, and that the world was arranged for his habitation. It was Darwin who finally removed man from the center of the universe, and thereby crumbled the religion of geology to dust.

22
Darwinism and American Culture

Stow Persons

Few brief essays have so perceptively assessed the wide range of Charles Darwin's impact on major aspects of American thought as this one by Stow Persons, long a professor at the University of Iowa. The essay, moreover, distinguishes among the various American lines of Darwinian speculation that too easily can be seen as one. There is the Darwinian theory of evolution, which synthesized ideas that had been around for a long time. There is the Darwinian hypothesis of natural selection, which has been revised in the development of modern genetics. There is "Social Darwinism" (which is more properly called Spencerian or Malthusian evolutionism), the loose concept that transfers Darwinian themes from nature to culture. There is pragmatism and later instrumentalism, which replace the Social Darwinists' absolute idea of the environment with the view of environment as ever changing and directed by man's intelligence. There is the Darwinian view of history, which makes it a part of the social sciences and "a policy science." The continuing note in all of this, the Darwinian norm for all intellectual matters, is change. Darwinian man exists in a natural world of chance and uncertainty; no longer is he at the center of the cosmos.

For some thinkers at the end of the nineteenth century, like William Graham Sumner, Oliver Wendell Holmes, Jr., or Henry Adams, this picture of man's insignificance in nature put an end to cherished American beliefs in inevitable short-term progress. Other thinkers, whose most profound guide was Lester Frank Ward, fitted the Darwinian theme of long-term change to the purposes of social reform. They emphasized modern man's intellectual capacity for controlling his environment; they stressed adaptability, mutability, and cooperation in and among living groups. Ward saw the "struggle" for existence occurring between species rather than among individuals of one species. By freely interpreting Darwin's *Origin of Species* (1859) as bearing upon human social evolution when its sole concern was biological evolution—Darwin did not deal with social matters until his *Descent of Man* (1871), and then only broadly—pragmatic liberals kept alive the

Reprinted by kind permission of the author and The American Studies Association of Texas from Mody C. Boatright (ed.), *The Impact of Darwinian Thought on American Life and Culture* (University of Texas, 1959), pp. 1-10.

idea of progress in America. They helped nurture many of the early economic and social welfare measures of the twentieth century.

For further reading: Stow Persons (ed.), *Evolutionary Thought in America* (1950); Bert J. Loewenberg, "Darwinism Comes to America," *Mississippi Valley Historical Review,* 27 (1941), 339-369; *Paul F. Boller, Jr., *American Thought in Transition: The Impact of Evolutionary Naturalism, 1865-1900* (1969); *Edward Lurie, *Louis Agassiz: A Life in Science* (abridged ed., 1966); *A. Hunter Dupree, *Asa Gray* (1959); John C. Greene, *Darwin and the Modern World View* (1961); James Allen Rogers, "Darwinism and Social Darwinism," *Journal of the History of Ideas,* 33 (April-June, 1972), 265-280.

One might be able to defend the proposition that the Bible and certain of the works of Aristotle have had a more profound influence upon the history of American intellectual life than has *The Origin of Species*. But if we were to narrow the field to books written during the span of American history itself, and capable therefore of generating that kind of impact that arises out of the timely consideration of current issues, and of the novelty of their methods and solutions, then I doubt that any other book could successfully dispute the claim of Darwin's masterpiece to the distinction of being the most influential book of the past three centuries. Locke's *Treatise on Civil Government* might be thought to be a worthy competitor; but here one would have real difficulty in separating Locke's influence from that of the other seventeenth- and eighteenth-century writers who wrote in a similar idiom.

Nevertheless, in attempting to characterize the role of Darwinism in American culture I shall try to view *The Origin of Species* not as a first cause from which a train of consequences subsequently proceeded, but as a single episode in a chronological sequence of ideas proceeding by "descent with modification" from the middle of the eighteenth century to our own times. This, I take it, would be the approved Darwinian manner of looking at the matter; and, incidentally, I thus acknowledge my own obligations.

In America as in Europe Darwin's work represented the synthesizing of the data and concepts of natural history as that term was used in the late eighteenth and early nineteenth centuries. Natural history was one of two principal subdivisions of physical science (natural philosophy being the other), and it included everything from the biological and geological sciences to anthropology and linguistics. Darwin's place in natural history was comparable to that of Newton in natural philosophy two centuries earlier. For more than half a century before *The Origin of Species* was published the problems of variation, adaptation, heredity and environment had received considerable attention from field naturalists and closet scholars on both sides of the Atlantic. Some of these precursors even glimpsed the analogy between artificial and natural selection, without, however, realizing its possibilities as Darwin was to do.

But if in these respects Darwin's work represented the culmination of a tradition, in another it was a new departure. For more than a century there had been an intense interest in human and animal origins. The discovery and exploration of the New World had posed problems of the variation and distribution of species that had challenged the imaginations and resourcefulness of several generations of observers. The great strength of the religious tradition was apparent in the well nigh universal assumption that the findings of natural history were consistent with the outlines of history contained in the Biblical narratives. I have been greatly impressed by the extent to which the issues and hypotheses in natural history during the eighteenth century were framed in a perspective shaped by the Mosaic legends. Today we are obliged to make a considerable imaginative effort to recapture the climate of opinion in which the Pentateuch carried such weighty authority.

The Scriptural account of origins proved to be more accommodating to scientific investigations than one might have expected. Students of natural history had long been divided over the question of the unitary or multiple origin of the human species. Religious sanction was available to either party. Unitary creationists appealed to Adam and Eve; while those who were impressed with racial and varietal differences and with the subtle adaptations of life forms to their local environments adhered to the theory of multiple creation, and sought Biblical or extra-Biblical confirmation in the "Preadamites." Problems of geographical distribution of species and genera, and of variation under differing environmental conditions could be dealt with in terms consistent with the Biblical account of the confusion of tongues, the dispersion of tribes, and the wanderings of peoples. If the emergence and subsidence of continents and of land bridges as hypothesized by students of natural history seemed incredible to those who preferred their world as they found it, let them relieve their skepticism by recalling the Noachian flood and the parting of the waters of the Red Sea. Long after Darwin's time, the six days of creation, understood metaphorically to represent successive formative epochs, were still being hopefully stretched to embrace the rapidly accumulating evidence of geological and paleontological processes. The fact that should hold our attention, I think, is not the stubborn and pathetic rear guard resistance of twentieth-century fundamentalists, but the calm assurance of learned and cultivated Christians a century earlier that whatever science might discover could be reconciled with revealed truth. Far from acting as a straitjacket, the Biblical narratives were of positive assistance to science by providing a congenial soil in which the synthesizing concepts of natural history could take root.

One result of this confluence of ideas was an intimate association between natural history and natural theology. The fusion of these two traditions was best illustrated in Robert Chambers's *Vestiges of the Natural History of Creation* (1844). As A. O. Lovejoy pointed out some years ago, Chambers anticipated Darwin by effectively marshaling the various categories of data in support of the evolutionary hypothesis. The wide attention that Chambers's book received, in America as well as in Europe, undoubtedly paved the way for *The Origin of Species*. But the two books differed in at least one important respect. Chambers's work purported to be a history of creation. Its author was of course aware that the Bible also furnished a history of creation and that the two accounts must confirm or conflict with each other. Chambers professed to hope that although at first glance they might appear to conflict, they would eventually be found to be mutually compatible. His analysis of evolutionary transformations revealed a marked teleological emphasis. To him, evolution meant development. He referred repeatedly to the law or laws of organic development. By this he meant nothing but the sequential appearance of ever more complex forms of life culminating in *homo sapiens*. The pattern of history itself displayed a comprehensive design that was synonymous with the law of development of organic forms. Here was natural theology with a vengeance.

In this respect it would be difficult to overstate the difference between Darwin and his predecessor. *The Origin of Species* was concerned not with ultimate origins or destinations but with transformations in process. Darwin spoke not of "development," with all of the overtones implied by that term, but of "descent." Leaving aside for the moment the question whether natural selection was compatible with design in nature, it will suffice here simply to say that Darwin was apparently under no compulsion to reconcile his findings with cosmic purposes. In short, the problem that Darwin set for himself was much more narrowly defined, and all of the massive data he assembled were brought to bear on a single subject, namely, the mutability of species. Scientifically, this represented a great advance. The weight of evidence on this point was overwhelming, and except for a handful of men in Darwin's own generation the intellectual world promptly capitulated to evolution.

The immediate reaction of readers to *The Origin of Species* revealed a confusion of issues that long clouded discussions of organic evolution. Darwin not only showed that transmutation occurred; he also proposed natural selection as the principal causal factor. Although specialists employed the term "Darwinism" to indicate natural selection, the reading public did not always understand this usage, and much confusion resulted, some people rejecting evolution because they found natural selection objectionable.

With the passage of time, however, it became apparent that Darwin had been more successful in persuading the world of the fact of evolution than in establishing the method of its occurrence. Many biologists who accepted evolution rejected or questioned the efficacy of natural selection. Darwin had based natural selection upon the universal somatic variations among organisms. It was the struggle for existence among these dissimilar organisms that presumably resulted in the survival of the fittest. Darwin of course knew nothing of the principles of Mendelian genetics. He was incapable of distinguishing between genotype and phenotype, although he vaguely glimpsed such a possibility. No sooner had it been propounded than natural selection was subjected to searching theoretical scrutiny and experimental tests. The results were inconclusive. Scientific opinion was divided, and it remained so for nearly half a century. In the United States the influential Neo-Lamarckian school of Cope, Hyatt, and Packard that flourished briefly in the nineties was evidence of the continuing dissatisfaction with natural selection.

In order to understand the cultural history of Darwinism it is important, I believe, to make this distinction between evolution as such, which came to stay with *The Origin of Species,* and natural selection in its Darwinian form, which remained controversial until well into the twentieth century. The solution of the unsolved problems of natural selection came after 1900, with the new science of genetics. If I understand correctly such contemporary evolutionists as Dobzhansky, Huxley, and Simpson, their concept of natural selection is distinctly different from Darwin's. The genetic mutation is the principal evolutionary factor; while the universal somatic differences among organisms are not in themselves of great significance. Most important, perhaps, for cultural history is the fact that the "struggle for existence'' as an overt process is regarded as relatively insignificant. Simpson has defined natural selection concisely as differential reproduction; i.e., those organisms that reproduce more abundantly are *ipso facto* participating more effectively in the changing stream of genetic transmission. As Veblen had observed long ago, it is more important from an evolutionary point of view to produce food and children than to emerge victorious from combat.

The history of Darwinism will serve as a background for a brief consideration of its first cultural reflection in Social Darwinism. This is probably the most familiar chapter in the whole history of Darwinism, and there is little that I need to say about it. Social Darwinism was the attempt to modernize and refurbish the social ethic of competitive individualism by appealing to the authority of Darwin's version of natural selection. It emphasized the right, not to say the duty, of the individual to participate in the economic struggle for existence. It promised a higher standard of living for all as the social advantage to accrue from the unregulated economic struggle of the market place.

There was a certain appropriateness in this appeal from society to science. Darwin had acknowledged that the precise formulation of natural selection had occurred to him during a casual reading of Malthus's *Essay on Population*. Malthus had correlated human population statistics with environmental factors in a naturalistic manner, and his correlations had subsequently been incorporated in the foundations of nineteenth-century laissez faire economic theory. Darwin was now in a position to repay his debt by bringing the prestige of science to the support of a social theory and policy.

If what I have said about the scientific fate of Darwin's version of natural selection is correct, then it is apparent that social Darwinism lost its presumed scientific validity in the twentieth century. No doubt it would enhance the symmetry of this analysis if it could be shown that Social Darwinism was undermined by the demise of Darwinian natural selection. But this cannot be demonstrated. As social analysis, Social Darwinism was superficial, and it soon lost the support of the few intellectuals who had sponsored it. With the rapid growth of large-scale enterprise a steadily increasing number of individuals found that their social roles entailed bureaucratic competition rather than entrepreneurial competition, a situation to which the tenets of Social Darwinism had little relevance. In the political and economic struggles of the turn of the century even the business class found the Social Darwinian doctrine more a liability than an asset. The principles of welfare capitalism proved to be far more suitable to the American situation.

A more sophisticated attempt to apply evolutionary ideas to social theory was made by Thorstein Veblen. Whereas the Social Darwinists had dealt with individuals as competing units, Veblen concentrated upon institutionalized behavior in a social evolutionary continuum. He borrowed from Morgan and the Comtean positivists the idea of the emergence of civilized culture from savagery and barbarism. He propounded a technological interpretation of social progress which he seems to have complacently regarded as a salutary innovation, but which in fact had been current in various forms for at least a generation.

It was as a social evolutionist, paradoxically enough, that Veblen was least impressive. What was most impressive was his transfer of Darwinian concepts from nature to culture. He did not attempt to reduce culture to nature as the Social

Darwinians had done. He took society as he found it, and attempted to analyze its structure and dynamics in Darwinian terms. Because human behavior was almost entirely institutionalized behavior it was the social institution that was seen to be subject to selection. The fate of racial groups rather than of individuals was found to be the significant outcome of the adaptive process. Technological innovation was the potentially fruitful variation. Although none of these explicitly Darwinian propositions of Veblen's can be said to have achieved a permanent place in modern sociological analysis, they did furnish significant aid as models for the objectification of social situations that is the central feature of modern sociology.

In the meanwhile, a more radical and potentially far-reaching use of Darwinian concepts had been suggested by Charles Sanders Peirce. Philip Wiener tells us that in Peirce's hands the concepts of universal random variation and selection suggested a statistical approach to aggregates of phenomena, whether in the natural or the social sciences. Probabilities calculated from statistical data replaced the causal determinism of the older logic. Chance now became the basis of a new scientific logic. The individual particle or person was thus left partially undetermined as to the laws of its behavior. Culturally, this was an important means of avoiding naturalistic determinism in all its forms. But many years were to pass before Peirce's work received attention. Although he is customarily hailed as a founder of pragmatism, I must confess that I am incapable of detecting any traces of this aspect of his thinking in the more familiar writings of James and Dewey.

In any event, the work of the pragmatists occupies a central place in the history of the evolutionary influence. As seen from a cultural perspective their function was to free the individual from the restraints imposed upon him by the Social Darwinists. James and Dewey in turn, and in a thoroughly Darwinian manner, addressed themselves to the problem of the relationship of the individual to his environment. They pointed out that the Social Darwinists had clung to an absolutist conception of environment, where the environment posed selective standards against which organic and human characteristics and behavior were to be measured. As opposed to this environmental determinism Dewey insisted that, when properly understood, significant variation was found to result in the release of a new environment. In his opinion, the evolution of environments remained the relatively neglected aspect of natural selection theory. But if the environment was undergoing constant modification it was not available as a norm for the evaluation of adaptive modifications. Change was the only constant. Man must establish his own norms and guide change intelligently toward useful objects. Professor Edward S. Corwin has pointed out that when Darwinism was translated into social terms it became pragmatic reformism; and the state became the obvious agency by which to implement reform.

Just as social theory under the impact of Darwinism passed through Social Darwinism to pragmatic reformism, so historical thought moved from the earlier positivistic conception of the savagery-barbarism-civilization sequence to the modern sophisticated relativism of Carl Becker and Charles A. Beard. Dewey put the new point of view succinctly: "Intelligent understanding of past history is to some extent a lever for moving the present into a certain kind of future."

This, it seems to me, is an authentic expression of the Darwinian view of history. The present is a fulcrum from which we use the past as a lever to move the future where we want it. This is an eminently practical view of history, measuring the value of that discipline in terms of its relevance to present problems. It attaches history to the social sciences, and makes it a policy science. It declares an obvious preference for recent history as opposed to the more remote past. All evolutionists have a characteristic sense of reality as an ongoing process, and thus a similar consciousness of the relationship between past, present, and future. But the Darwinian brand of evolution had the effect of destroying an authoritative past independent of its present uses. In the cultural implications of their theories this was the great difference between Darwin and Chambers.

If we should ask how American culture today differs from that of a century ago, I think we might agree that in one respect we have lost any sense of an authoritative past. We accept change as a normal condition. The past and the future radiate out from the present as measured by a series of changes, and both are increasingly obscure as they recede from the present. The temporal solipsism of historical relativism is a problem with which our more reflective modern historians have all struggled. It is a problem peculiar to the modern mentality, and I believe that Darwinian evolution is largely responsible for it, by imprisoning the modern consciousness in its own present.

Finally, I would like to direct your attention to the way in which the Darwinian influence has severed the traditional relationship between nature and culture. When we consider the American civilization of a century ago we cannot fail to note how intimately religion was involved in the total range of cultural and intellectual activities. It would have been hard then to find an informed and influential opinion or conviction about life or the nature of the universe that was not compatible with religious teachings or had not been scrutinized with a view to integration with religious convictions.

This cultural involvement of religion was especially impressive with respect to science. We cannot dismiss the massive evidence of the compatibility of science and religion as indicating a mere marriage of convenience. Science and religion marched hand in hand because they shared common presuppositions. These presuppositions constituted a natural religion, the conviction that the universe was a divine creation displaying the evidences of design in its physical features. In studying the creation man was thinking God's thoughts after Him. Natural religion was found not only in orthodox religious thought, in Deism, and in transcendental naturalism, but also in psychology, geology, economics, and historical thought. Leading scientists like Silliman, Dana, Agassiz, and Gray were among its most eloquent exponents. Natural religion was the bond that united nature and culture.

Evolution as such could be absorbed into natural religion. God could if He chose create in time. Enormous energy was expended by the theologians of the later nineteenth century to accomplish the reconciliation. But they generally avoided the difficult question, which was whether natural selection could be reconciled with rational design in nature. The leaders of thought in Darwin's own generation had divided on this issue. Asa Gray and James McCosh thought a reconciliation feasible; Charles Hodge and Darwin himself thought it impossible.

We must all have noticed how frequently in the past men have survived the crises of history not by solving the issues at stake but by circumventing them. It was the judgment of John Dewey, expressed on the semi-centennial of *The Origin of*

Species, that Darwinism had had the effect of outmoding the old issue of creative design versus chance. Thanks to the influence of Darwinism, said Dewey, "philosophy foreswears inquiry after absolute origins and absolute finalities in order to explore specific values and the specific conditions that generate them." Whatever you may think of Dewey's presumption to speak for modern philosophy you will have to grant, I think, that modern American culture as a whole has foresworn an interest in origins and finalities.

The effect of this circumvention upon religion has been considerable. There is no longer any widespread interest in natural religion as a cultural mediator. This in turn means that formal religion is on the cultural periphery because the major intellectual activities are carried on in terms that cannot be cast in traditional religious forms, or at least they are not. The result is a pallid and negative religion, one that can complain of our shortcomings but cannot participate in our activities. We have our Jeremiahs but not our Aquinases.

In the retrospect of a hundred years it may seem futile to attempt to isolate the changes stemming from a purely intellectual source from all of the institutional and industrial changes that bulk so large in our understanding of the immediate past. But perhaps we can risk the following generalization about the evolutionary influence in American culture. A theory of process proclaiming the sovereignty of the present had the effect of undermining traditional intellectual authorities. These authorities had entrenched themselves—as authorities always do—in institutions, which consequently felt the Darwinian impact. Some of them, notably the churches, were weakened in their intellectual influence; others, such as the colleges, were transformed. In the place of the relatively unified and quasi-official intellectual culture of mid-nineteenth-century America emerged the bewildering variety of autonomous and mutually contradictory authorities with which we are familiar. The Darwinian theory by its very nature facilitated this transformation. It emphasized variety, change, the image of the world as a "blooming, buzzing confusion." Darwinism did its work well. It is difficult to conceive of anything like a return to the old state of affairs.

23
The Influence of Darwinism on Philosophy

John Dewey

John Dewey (1859-1952) delivered this lecture at Columbia University in 1909 during an observance of the fiftieth anniversary of *The Origin of Species*. It has become a classic expression of the subject, written by a philosopher caught up in the technique of inquiry whose birth he describes. The Darwinian revolution in ideas meant an emphasis upon change, both as biological fact and as intellectual method. This emphasis became Dewey's unique style. Coming early from Hegelian idealism, he made the "instrumentalist" concepts of change, process, and experience the keynotes of his long career. His leadership in the revolt against formalism in philosophy and social thought, together with his advocacy of "reconstruction" in philosophy, are fundamental lessons for students of twentieth-century American ideas. Although his philosophy stressed flux and newness in human affairs as in all nature, there was still much of the traditional in him (which Charles Frankel tells us in Essay 32). Dewey's critics are now beginning to suspect that he did not so much "solve" some of the old problems as "get over" them—a trait that both he and George Santayana thought typically American (see Essay 27). Nevertheless, Dewey in his lifetime put forward some of the precepts for intellectual inquiry that still have validity even in areas that are finding nineteenth-century rules of empirical evidence not wholly satisfying. Up to date is his assertion that, in their asking, some questions make assumptions that render the questions meaningless. And his vision of the aim of science endures: "Science is compelled to aim at realities lying behind and beyond the processes of nature, and to carry on its search for these realities by means of rational forms transcending ordinary modes of perception and inference."

For further reading: *Gertrude Himmelfarb, *Darwin and the Darwinian Revolution* (1962); *Richard Hofstadter, *Social Darwinism in American Thought* (rev. ed., 1955); *Charles C. Gillispie, *The Edge of Objectivity: An Essay in the History of Scientific Ideas* (1960); Herbert W. Schneider, "The Influence of Darwin and Spencer on American Philosophical Theology," *Journal of the History of Ideas*, 6 (January 1945), 3-18; *Arthur M. Schlesinger, Sr., *A Critical Period in American Religion, 1875-1900* (1932).

I

That the publication of the *Origin of Species* marked an epoch in the development of the natural sciences is well known to the layman. That the combination of the very words origin and species embodied an intellectual revolt and introduced a new intellectual temper is easily overlooked by the expert. The conceptions that had reigned in the philosophy of nature and knowledge for two thousand years, the conceptions that had become the familiar furniture of the mind, rested on the assumption of the superiority of the fixed and final; they rested upon treating change and origin as signs of defect and unreality. In laying hands upon the sacred ark of absolute permanency, in treating the forms that had been regarded as types of fixity and perfection as originating and passing away, the *Origin of Species* introduced a mode of thinking that in the end was bound to transform the logic of knowledge, and hence the treatment of morals, politics, and religion.

No wonder, then, that the publication of Darwin's book, a half century ago, precipitated a crisis. The true nature of the controversy is easily concealed from us, however, by the theological clamor that attended it. The vivid and popular features of the anti-Darwinian row tended to leave the impression that the issue was between science on the one side and theology on the other. Such was not the case—the issue lay primarily within science itself, as Darwin himself early recognized. The theological outcry he discounted from the start, hardly noticing it save as it bore upon the "feelings of his female relatives." But for two decades before final publication he contemplated the possibility of being put down by his scientific peers as a fool or as crazy; and he set, as the measure of his success, the degree in which he should affect three men of science: Lyell in geology, Hooker in botany, and Huxley in zoology.

Religious considerations lent fervor to the controversy, but they did not provoke it. Intellectually, religious emotions are not creative but conservative. They attach themselves readily to the current view of the world and consecrate it. They steep and dye intellectual fabrics in the seething vat of emotions; they do not form their warp and woof. There is not, I think, an instance of any large idea about the world being independently generated by religion. Although the ideas that rose up like armed men against Darwinism owed their intensity to religious associations, their origin and meaning are to be sought in science and philosophy, not in religion.

II

Few words in our language foreshorten intellectual history as much as does the word species. The Greeks, in iniating the intellectual life of Europe, were impressed by characteristic traits of the life of plants and animals; so impressed indeed that they made these traits the key to defining nature and to explaining mind and society. And truly, life is so wonderful that a seemingly successful reading of its mystery might well lead men to believe that the key to the secrets of heaven and earth was in their hands. The Greek rendering of this mystery, the Greek formulation of the aim and standard of knowledge, was in the course of time embodied in the word species, and it controlled philosophy for two thousand years. To understand the intellectual face-about expressed in the phrase *Origin of Species*, we must, then, understand the long dominant idea against which it is a protest.

Consider how men were impressed by the facts of life. Their eyes fell upon certain things slight in bulk, and frail in structure. To every appearance, these perceived things were inert and passive. Suddenly, under certain circumstances, these things—henceforth known as seeds or eggs or germs—begin to change, to change rapidly in size, form, and qualities. Rapid and extensive changes occur, however, in many things—as when wood is touched by fire. But the changes in the living thing are orderly; they are cumulative; they tend constantly in one direction; they do not, like other changes, destroy or consume, or pass fruitless into wandering flux; they realize and fulfill. Each successive stage, no matter how unlike its predecessor, preserves its net effect and also prepares the way for a fuller activity on the part of its successor. In living beings, changes do not happen as they seem to happen elsewhere, any which way; the earlier changes are regulated in view of later results. This progressive organization does not cease till there is achieved a true final term, a τελὸς, a completed, perfected end. This final form exercises in turn a plenitude of functions, not the least noteworthy of which is production of germs like those from which it took its own origin, germs capable of the same cycle of self-fulfilling activity.

But the whole miraculous tale is not yet told. The same drama is enacted to the same destiny in countless myriads of individuals so sundered in time, so severed in space, that they have no opportunity for mutual consultation and no means of interaction. As an old writer quaintly said, "things of the same kind go through the same formalities "—celebrate, as it were, the same ceremonial rites.

This formal activity which operates throughout a series of changes and holds them to a single course; which subordinates their aimless flux to its own perfect manifestation; which, leaping the boundaries of space and time, keeps individuals distant in space and remote in time to a uniform type of structure and function: this principle seemed to give insight into the very nature of reality itself. To it Aristotle gave the name ἐῖδος. This term the scholastics translated as *species*.

The force of this term was deepened by its application to everything in the universe that observes order in flux and manifests constancy through change. From the casual drift of daily weather, through the uneven recurrence of seasons and unequal return of seed time and harvest, up to the majestic sweep of the heavens—the image of eternity in time—and from this to the unchanging pure and contemplative intelligence beyond nature lies one unbroken fulfillment of ends. Nature as a whole is a progressive realization of purpose strictly comparable to the realization of purpose in any single plant or animal.

The conception of ἐῖδος, species, a fixed form and final cause, was the central principle of knowledge as well as of nature. Upon it rested the logic of science. Change as change is mere flux and lapse; it insults intelligence. Genuinely to know is to grasp a permanent end that realizes itself through changes, holding them thereby within the metes and bounds of fixed truth. Completely to know is to relate all special forms to their one single end and good: pure contemplative intelligence. Since, however, the scene of nature which directly confronts us is in change, nature as directly and practically experienced does not satisfy the conditoins of knowledge. Human experience is in flux, and hence the instrumentalities of sense-perception and of inference based upon observation are condemned in advance. Science is compelled to aim at realities lying behind and beyond the processes of nature, and to carry on its search for these realities by means of rational forms transcending ordinary modes of perception and inference.

There are, indeed, but two alternative courses. We must either find the appropriate objects and organs of knowledge in the mutual interactions of changing things; or else, to escape the infection of change, we *must* seek them in some transcendent and supernal region. The human mind, deliberately as it were, exhausted the logic of the changeless, the final, and the transcendent, before it essayed adventure on the pathless wastes of generation and transformation. We dispose all too easily of the efforts of the schoolmen to interpret nature and mind in terms of real essences, hidden forms, and occult faculties, forgetful of the seriousness and dignity of ideas that lay behind. We dispose of them by laughing at the famous gentleman who accounted for the fact that opium put people to sleep on the ground it had a dormitive faculty. But the doctrine, held in our day, that knowledge of the plant that yields the poppy consists in referring the peculiarities of an individual to a type, to a universal form, a doctrine so firmly established that any other method of knowing was conceived to be unphilosophical and unscientific, is a survival of precisely the same logic. This identity of conception in the scholastic and anti-Darwinian theory may well suggest greater sympathy for what has become unfamiliar as well as greater humility regarding the further unfamiliarities that history has in store.

Darwin was not, of course, the first to question the classic philosophy of nature and of knowledge. The beginnings of the revolution are in the physical science of the sixteenth and seventeeth centuries. When Galileo said: "It is my opinion that the earth is very noble and admirable by reason of so many and so different alterations and generations which are incessantly made therein," he expressed the changed temper that was coming over the world; the transfer of interest from the permanent to the changing. When Descartes said: "The nature of physical things is much more easily conceived when they are beheld coming gradually into existence, than when they are only considered as produced at once in a finished and perfect state," the modern world became self-conscious of the logic that was henceforth to control it, the logic of which Darwin's *Origin of Species* is the latest scientific achievement. Without the methods of Copernicus, Kepler, Galileo, and their successors in astronomy, physics, and chemistry, Darwin would have been helpless in the organic sciences. But prior to Darwin the impact of the new scientific method upon life, mind, and politics had been arrested, because between these ideal or moral interests and the inorganic world intervened the kingdom of plants and animals. The gates of the garden of life were barred to the new ideas; and only through this garden was there access to mind and politics. The influence of Darwin upon philosophy resides in his having conquered the phenomena of life for the principle of transition, and thereby freed the new logic for application to mind and morals and life. When he said of species what Galileo had said of the earth, *e pur se muove*, he emancipated, once for all, genetic and experimental ideas as an organon of asking questions and looking for explanations.

III

The exact bearings upon philosophy of the new logical outlook are, of course, as yet, uncertain and inchoate. We live in the twilight of intellectual transition. One must add the rashness of the prophet to the stubbornness of the partisan to venture a systematic exposition of the influence upon philosophy of the Darwinian method. At best, we can but inquire as to its general bearing—the effect upon mental temper and complexion, upon that body of half-conscious, half-instinctive intellectual aversions and preferences which determine, after all, our more deliberate intellectual enterprises. In this vague inquiry there happens to exist as a kind of touchstone a problem of long historic currency that has also been much discussed in Darwinian literature. I refer to the old problem of design *versus* chance, mind *versus* matter, as the causal explanation, first or final, of things.

As we have already seen, the classic notion of species carried with it the idea of purpose. In all living forms, a specific type is present directing the earlier stages of growth to the realization of its own perfection. Since this purposive regulative principle is not visible to the senses, it follows that it must be an ideal or rational force. Since, however, the perfect form is gradually approximated through the sensible changes, it also follows that in and through a sensible realm a rational ideal force is working out its own ultimate manifestation. These inferences were extended to nature: (*a*) She does nothing in vain; but all for an ulterior purpose. (*b*) Within natural sensible events there is therefore contained a spiritual causal force, which as spiritual escapes perception, but is apprehended by an enlightened reason. (*c*) The manifestation of this principle brings about a subordination of matter and sense to its own realization, and this ultimate fulfillment is the goal of nature and of man. The design argument thus operated in two directions. Purposefulness accounted for the intelligibility of nature and the possibility of science, while the absolute or cosmic character of this purposefulness gave sanction and worth to the moral and religious endeavors of man. Science was underpinned and morals authorized by one and the same principle, and their mutual agreement was eternally guaranteed.

This philosophy remained, in spite of sceptical and polemic outbursts, the official and regnant philosophy of Europe for over two thousand years. The expulsion of fixed first and final causes from astronomy, physics, and chemistry had indeed given the doctrine something of a shock. But, on the other hand, increased acquaintance with the details of plant and animal life operated as a counterbalance and perhaps even strengthened the argument from design. The marvelous adaptations of organisms to their environment, of organs to the organism, of unlike parts of a complex organ—like the eye—to the organ itself; the foreshadowing by lower forms of the higher; the preparation in earlier stages of growth for organs that only later had their functioning—these things were increasingly recognized with the progress of botany, zoology, paleontology, and embryology. Together, they added such prestige to the design argument that by the late eighteenth century it was, as approved by the sciences of organic life, the central point of theistic and idealistic philosophy.

The Darwinian principle of natural selection cut straight under this philosophy. If all organic adaptations are due simply to constant variation and the elimination of those variations which are harmful in the struggle for existence that is brought about by excessive reproduction, there is no call for a prior intelligent causal force to plan and preordain them. Hostile critics charged Darwin with materialism and with making chance the cause of the universe.

Some naturalists, like Asa Gray, favored the Darwinian principle and attempted to reconcile it with design. Gray held to what may be called design on the installment plan. If we conceive the "stream of variations" to be itself intended, we may suppose that each successive variation was designed from the first to be selected. In that case, variation, struggle, and selection simply define the mechanism of "secondary causes" through which the "first cause" acts; and the doctrine of design is none the worse off because we know more of its *modus operandi*.

Darwin could not accept this mediating proposal. He admits or rather he asserts that it is "impossible to conceive this immense and wonderful universe including man with his capacity of looking far backwards and far into futurity as the result of blind chance or necessity." But nevertheless he holds that since variations are in useless as well as useful directions, and since the latter are sifted out simply by the stress of the conditions of struggle for existence, the design argument as applied to living beings is unjustifiable; and its lack of support there deprives it of scientific value as applied to nature in general. If the variations of the pigeon, which under artificial selection give the pouter pigeon, are not preordained for the sake of the breeder, by what logic do we argue that variations resulting in natural species are pre-designed?

IV

So much for some of the more obvious facts of the discussion of design *versus* chance, as causal principles of nature and of life as a whole. We brought up this discussion, you recall, as a crucial instance. What does our touchstone indicate as to the bearing of Darwinian ideas upon philosophy? In the first place, the new logic outlaws, flanks, dismisses—what you will—one type of problems and substitutes for it another type. Philosophy forswears inquiry after absolute origins and absolute finalities in order to explore specific values and the specific conditions that generate them.

Darwin concluded that the impossibility of assigning the world to chance as a whole and to design in its parts indicated the insolubility of the question. Two radically different reasons, however, may be given as to why a problem is insoluble. One reason is that the problem is too high for intelligence; the other is that the question in its very asking makes assumptions that render the question meaningless. The latter alternative is unerringly pointed to in the celebrated case of design *versus* chance. Once admit that the sole verifiable or fruitful object of knowledge is the particular set of changes that generate the object of study together with the consequences that then flow from it, and no intelligible question can be asked about what, by assumption, lies outside. To assert—as is often asserted—that specific values of particular truths, social bonds and forms of beauty, if they can be shown to be generated by concretely knowable conditions, are meaningless and in vain; to assert that they are justified only when they and their particular causes and effects have all at once been gathered up into some inclusive first cause and some exhaustive final goal, is intellectual activism. Such argumentation is reversion to the logic that explained the extinction of fire by water through the formal essence of aqueousness and the quenching of thirst by water through the final cause of aqueousness. Whether used in the case of the special event or that of life as a whole, such logic only abstracts some aspect of the existing course of events in order to reduplicate it as a petrified eternal principle by which to explain the very changes of which it is the formalization.

When Henry Sidgwick casually remarked in a letter that as he grew older his interest in what or who made the world was altered into interest in what kind of a world it is anyway, his voicing of a common experience of our own day illustrates also the nature of that intellectual transformation effected by the Darwinian logic. Interest shifts from the wholesale essence back of special changes to the question of how special changes serve and defeat concrete purposes; shifts from an intelligence that shaped things once for all to the particular intelligences which things are even now shaping; shifts from an ultimate goal of good to the direct increments of justice and happiness that intelligent administration of existent conditions may beget and that present carelessness or stupidity will destroy or forego.

In the second place, the classic type of logic inevitably set philosophy upon proving that life *must* have certain qualities and values—no matter how experience presents the matter—because of some remote cause and eventual goal. The duty of wholesale justification inevitably accompanies all thinking that makes the meaning of special occurrences depend upon something that once and for all lies behind them. The habit of derogating from present meanings and uses prevents our looking the facts of experience in the face; it prevents serious acknowledgment of the evils they present and serious concern with the goods they promise but do not as yet fulfill. It turns thought to the business of finding a wholesale transcendent remedy for the one and guarantee for the other. One is reminded of the way many moralists and theologians greeted Herbert Spencer's recognition of an unknowable energy from which welled up the phenomenal physical processes without and the conscious operations within. Merely because Spencer labeled his unknowable energy "God," this faded piece of metaphysical goods was greeted as an important and grateful concession to the reality of the spiritual realm. Were it not for the deep hold of the habit of seeking justification for ideal values in the remote and transcendent, surely this reference of them to an unknowable absolute would be despised in comparison with the demonstrations of experience that knowable energies are daily generating about us precious values.

The displacing of this wholesale type of philosophy will doubtless not arrive by sheer logical disproof, but rather by growing recognition of its futility. Were it a thousand times true that opium produces sleep because of its dormitive energy, yet the inducing of sleep in the tired, and the recovery to waking life of the poisoned, would not be thereby one least step forwarded. And were it a thousand times dialectically demonstrated that life as a whole is regulated by a transcendent principle to a final inclusive goal, nonetheless truth and error, health and disease, good and evil, hope and fear in the concrete, would remain just what and where they now are. To improve our education, to ameliorate our manners, to advance our politics, we must have recourse to specific conditions of generation.

Finally, the new logic introduces responsibility into the intellectual life. To idealize and rationalize the universe at large is after all a confession of inability to master the courses of things that specifically concern us. As long as mankind suffered from this impotency, it naturally shifted a burden of responsibility that it could not carry over to the more competent shoulders of the transcendent cause. But if insight into specific conditions of value and into specific consequences of ideas is possible, philosophy must in time become a method of locating and interpreting the more serious of the conflicts that occur in life, and a method of projecting ways for dealing with them: a method of moral and political diagnosis and prognosis.

The claim to formulate *a priori* the legislative constitution of the universe is by its nature a claim that may lead to elaborate dialectic developments. But it is also one that removes these very conclusions from subjection to experimental test, for, by definition, these results make no differences in the detailed course of events. But a philosophy that humbles its pretensions to the work of projecting hypotheses for the education and conduct of mind, individual and social, is thereby subjected to test by the way in which the ideas it propounds work out in practice. In having modesty forced upon it, philosophy also acquires responsibility.

Doubtless I seem to have violated the implied promise of my earlier remarks and to have turned both prophet and partisan. But in anticipating the direction of the transformations in philosophy to be wrought by the Darwinian genetic and experimental logic, I do not profess to speak for any save those who yeild themselves consciously or unconsciously to this logic. No one can fairly deny that at present there are two effects of the Darwinian mode of thinking. On the one hand, there are many sincere and vital efforts to revise our traditional philosophic conceptions in accordance with its demands. On the other hand, there is as definitely a recrudescence of absolutistic philosophies; an assertion of a type of philosophic knowing distinct from that of the sciences, one which opens to us another kind of reality from that to which the sciences give access; an appeal through experience to something that essentially goes beyond experience. This reaction affects popular creeds and religious movements as well as technical philosophies. The very conquest of the biological sciences by the new ideas has led many to proclaim an explicit and rigid separation of philosophy from science.

Old ideas give way slowly; for they are more than abstract logical forms and categories. They are habits, predispositions, deeply ingrained attitudes of aversion and preference. Moreover, the conviction persists—though history shows it to be a hallucination—that all the questions that the human mind has asked are questions that can be answered in terms of the alternatives that the questions themselves present. But in fact intellectual progress usually occurs through sheer abandonment of questions together with both of the alternatives they assume—an abandonment that results from their decreasing vitality and a change of urgent interest. We do not solve them: we get over them. Old questions are solved by disappearing, evaporating, while new questions corresponding to the changed attitude of endeavor and preference take their place. Doubtless the greatest dissolvent in contemporary thought of old questions, the greatest precipitant of new methods, new intentions, new problems, is the one effected by the scientific revolution that found its climax in the *Origin of the Species*.

24
Evolution in American Philosophy

Max H. Fisch

Dominant currents of American thought have all had some relationship to the broader history of Western ideas. The persistence of an Atlantic community of ideas since the seventeenth century dispels any claim that America has ever lived in intellectual isolation. The dissemination of Darwinian ideas after 1859 in America well illustrates the close collaboration of that day between British and American learned and academic men. Insofar as a prime mover or publicist is always necessary for popularizing a body of ideas, Edward L. Youmans (1821-1887) served that purpose for Darwinism in the United States with his *Popular Science Monthly*, founded in 1872. This era had much in common with the intellectual history of the later eighteenth century. While that period saw the powers of observation, sensation, and reflection turned to verifying the Lockean meaning of mind which abandoned the Cartesian dualism of mind and body, this later period witnessed the "naturalization" of mind—the attempt to locate man's reason in evolutionary time. Because of this thrust, evolutionary biology after Darwin meant more of an abrupt break with past American philosophy and theology than did the findings of geologists before 1859 (see Essay 21). The spurt given to social philosophy by the newer view of man's mind was dramatic. With their faith that the struggle of human evolution meant essentially man's constant efforts to apply intelligence to holding at bay the conflicting forces of his own nature and of the nature around him, the new social sciences were born out of the old moral philosophy. American academic life was rejuvenated. It experienced what Charles A. Barker has called "the second American Enlightenment." Suffusing and supporting it all were the spirit and writings of the American pragmatists whom Max Fisch discusses here. These gentlemen of the Metaphysical Club in Cambridge, Massachusetts—Chauncey Wright, Charles Sanders Peirce, William James, Oliver Wendell Holmes, Jr., and Nicholas St, John Green—had all been schooled in mid-nineteenth-century philosophical thought—in Scottish common-sense realism and in British utilitarianism, though perhaps less in German idealism. None came from botany or zoology, the two fields most revolutionized by Darwin's findings; yet each man was

Philosophical Review, 56 (1947), 357-373. Reprinted by kind permission of the author and the editors of *The Philosophical Review*. Footnotes have been omitted.

partial to empirical inquiry and, especially in the case of Wright and Peirce, to mathematical logic. Their commitment to an experiential basis for knowledge made the early pragmatists warmly receptive first to the work of Herbert Spencer and then to the writings of Charles Darwin, whose critical yet persuasive supporters they became.

For further reading: Bert J. Loewenberg, "The Reaction of American Scientists to Darwinism," *American Historical Review*, 38 (1933), 687-701; *Philip P. Wiener, *Evolution and the Founders of Pragmatism* (1949); *Ralph Barton Perry, *The Thought and Character of William James* (abridged ed., 1948) *W. B. Gallie, *Peirce and Pragmatism* (1952); E. H. Madden, *Chauncey Wright and the Foundations of Pragmatism* (1963).

In the middle period of the century of American thought with which [this essay] is concerned, there was one idea which so far overshadowed all others that we may fairly confine our attention to it. That idea was evolution. Like the ideas of earlier periods, it was imported, and imported chiefly from Britain. But the cultural lag, the interval between publication there and assimilation here, was rapidly lessening. Indeed, except for a slow start due to the Civil War, the idea of evolution spread as rapidly here as abroad. Moreover, American thinkers were from the start acknowledged though junior partners in shaping, criticizing, and confirming the idea in its biological and other applications, and they have led the way in working out the logic of evolutionary theory and the theory of evolutionary logic.

Both in preparing the *Origin of Species* and for defending it after its appearance, Darwin leaned heavily on his American friend Asa Gray, much as he did on Joseph Hooker in England. Other American biologists, geologists, and paleontologists, before and after 1859, discovered and adduced some of the most telling evidences of evolution. To cite but one instance, when Huxley came to America in 1876 to deliver the inaugural lecture at Johns Hopkins, he spent a week with O. C. Marsh in New Haven studying his collection of fossil horses, which for the first time established the direct line of descent of a living animal, and his collection of fossil toothed birds, which completed the series of transitional forms between birds and reptiles. Huxley recast his New York lectures on evolution to take account of these evidences and said he knew of "no collection from any one region and series of strata comparable, for extent, or for the care with which the remains have been got together, or for their scientifc importance." Darwin wrote to Marsh in 1880 that his work on these fossils "afforded the best support to the theory of evolution" that had come forward in the twenty years since the *Origin*.

A convenient symbol for the way in which, with respect to evolution, Britain and America formed from the start a single intellectual community may be found in the following fact. The famous Wilberforce-Huxley debate at the Oxford meeting of the British Association in 1860, just a few months after the appearance of the *Origin*, took place in the course of discussion of a paper by John W. Draper, the New York physiologist, "On the Intellectual Development of Europe Considered with Reference to the Views of Mr. Darwin and Others That the Progression of Organisms is Determined by Law."

No good cause should be without an eminent and vigorous adversary, who prevents it from being ignored. Such an adversary was Louis Agassiz. Many of the American scientists who declared for evolution in the first generation had been his pupils and were converted to it by his arguments against it. To some of them it seemed that he had laid the "whole foundation of evolution, solid and broad," and then "refused to build any scientific structure on it." So it seemed to laymen also. John Fiske, for instance, says that "the immediate cause which drove me to the development theory was the mental reaction experienced in reading Agassiz's arguments against that theory in his Essay on Classification, in 1859, shortly before Darwin's book was published." And Fiske became the most influential American proponent of evolution as an idea of general and even cosmic application.

The age of evolution, however, was also the great age of American enterprise, and the most distinctly American service to the cause was to provide it with an entrepreneur. The New York firm of Appleton had been cautiously edging into the hitherto unprofitable field of scientific book publishing, at the instigation of Edward L. Youmans. As a rival publisher, Henry Holt, later put it, "Youmans became the scientific adviser of the house, and brought to it so many of the important books on the great questions of that epoch, as to place the house first on those subjects, and the rest nowhere." It was on Youman's initiative that the first volume of Buckle's *History of Civilization* was reprinted by Appleton's in 1858, and that they got out an American edition of Darwin's *Origin* within two months of its publication in England. When Ticknor & Fields of Boston, who had previously published Herbert Spencer's *Social Statics*, declined his *Education* in 1860, Youmans secured it for Appleton's by writing to Spencer: "I thought . . . that if our house had the management of the work I might possibly in various small ways contribute to urge it forward; for we have found on this side that the straight and narrow way that leads right up to the heaven of success is traversable by but one motor—namely, *push*." Three years later, Youmans wrote to Spencer: "I am an ultra and thoroughgoing American. I believe there is great work to be done here for civilization. What we want are ideas—large, organizing ideas—and I believe there is no other man whose thoughts are so valuable for our needs as yours are."

John Fiske describes the pushing Youmans did as follows:

> *As soon as [books] were ready for the market he wrote reviews of them, and by no means in the usual perfunctory way. His reviews and notice were turned out by the score, and scattered about in the magazines and newspapers where they would do the most good. Not content with this, he made numerous pithy and representative extracts for the reading columns of various daily and weekly papers. Whenever he found another writer who could be pressed into the service, he would give him Spencer's books, kindle him with a spark from his own blazing enthusiasm, and set him to writing for the press. The effects of this work were multifarious and far-reaching, and–year in and year out–it was never for a moment allowed to flag. The most indefatigable vender of wares was never more ruthlessly persistent in advertising for lucre's sake than Edward Youmans in preaching in a spirit of the purest disinterestedness the gospel of evolution.*

When Appleton's sent Youmans to visit Spencer and other British scientists in

1862, he learned that only five hundred copies of Spencer's *Psychology* had been printed, and that three hundred remained unsold; that five hundred of his *Education* had been printed, and only two hundred were sold; that the *Social Statics* had been more popular, but that eleven years had not sufficed to exhaust the seven hundred and fifty copies printed. By the time Youmans' Spencer boom subsided, Appleton's alone had sold five hundred thousand copies of his twenty-five works. Of the *First Principles* alone, 162,000 copies were sold in less than thirty years.

One of the best essays on the derivations of American thought, but an essay not yet as widely known as it should be, is Merle Curti's "The Great Mr. Locke: America's Philosopher, 1783-1861." The period with which we are concerned deserves a similar essay: "Herbert Spencer: America's Philosopher, 1861-1916." The difference is that whereas Locke had long been dead before his American vogue began, Spencer was adopted, subsidized, and promoted by America during his lifetime, and owed the completion and success of his *Synthetic Philosophy* in large part to that fact. His thus becoming American intellectual property did not, however, increase his honor in his own country. Justice Holmes could write to Sir Frederick Pollock in 1895: "H[erbert] Spencer you English never quite do justice to. . . . He is dull. He writes an ugly uncharming style, his ideals are those of a lower middle class British Philistine. And yet after all abatements I doubt if any writer of English except Darwin has done so much to affect our whole way of thinking about the universe."

As a promotional medium for the scientific books brought out under his editorship, Youmans founded the *Popular Science Monthly* in 1872 and continued as editor until his death in 1887. The early numbers carried installments of Spencer's *Study of Sociology*, written at Youmans' suggestion to prepare the public for the *Descriptive Sociology* which appeared in later years. Within a year and a half the *Monthly* reached a circulation of twelve thousand. Students of American philosophy remember with amusement but with a strange lack of curiosity that Peirce's "Illustrations of the Logic of Science" were published in it as a series of six articles. Even as unacademic a philosopher as James spoke with a certain condescension of "those hardheaded readers who subscribe to the *Popular Science Monthly* and *Nature*, and whose sole philosopher Mr. Spencer is"; but the fact is that the *Monthly* was then the chief medium of periodical publication for so much of American philosophy as was in touch with science.

Not content with reprinting here the works of overseas scientists, Youmans conceived and launched in 1873 the International Scientific Series of books published simultaneously on both sides of the Atlantic. Within Youmans' lifetime the Series ran to fifty-seven volumes, and eventually to nearly a hundred. The first was Tyndall's *Forms of Water*, the second Bagehot's *Physics and Politics*, the classic of social Darwinism. Among other early volumes were Bain's *Mind and Body*, Spencer's *Study of Sociology*, Cooke's *The New Chemistry*, Stewart's *Conservation of Energy*, Whitney's *Life and Growth of Language*, Huxley's *The Crayfish*, Darwin's *Formation of Vegetable Mould*, Stallo's *Concepts and Theories of Modern Physics*, Romanes' *Animal Intelligence*, and Clifford's *Common Sense of the Exact Sciences*. The best seller was Draper's *History of the Conflict between Science and Religion*, which ran through fifty printings and was translated into nearly every language of commercial publication.

While Youmans was enthusiastic in propagating, both through the International Scientific Series and through the *Popular Science Monthly*, modern views in physics, chemistry, geology, and biology generally, everything was tributary to the philosophy of evolution. As Fiske puts it: "As presenting the supreme organizing idea of modern thought, his chief effort at all times lay in directing inquirers to Mr. Spencer's works, in explaining their doctrines, defending them from misquotation and misunderstanding—in being, in short, the American apostle of evolution, fervid, instant in season and out of season, making opportunities where he did not find them."

A symbol for the relationship between the intellectual and the industrial entrepreneur in the age of enterprise may be found in the fact that when Spencer was about to board ship for home after his visit to America in 1882, he seized the hands of Edward Youmans and Andrew Carnegie and cried to the reporters; "Here are my two best American friends."

A complete sketch of the fortunes of the idea of evolution in America would include the early opposition from the side of religion, the ironic work of religious-minded biologists like Gray, the reconciliations of evolution and religion, the theologies of evolution which sought to make religious capital of it, the American forms of social Darwinism, the cosmic philosophies of Fiske and Abbot, the rise of the distinctively American science of sociology, the attempts of idealists like Howison to fix the limits of evolution and of others like Royce to digest evolution and entropy together in the Absolute, the genetic social philosophies of Baldwin, Mead, and others, and the emergence of those forms of evolutionary naturalism that are still current among us. . . .

The crux of the theory of biological evolution was of course man, and the difficulty was not so much that of finding the links between the human organism and those of lower animals, as it was that of finding the links between animal instinct and human reason. Darwin made a beginning in those chapters of his *Descent of Man* devoted to comparison of the mental powers of man with those of lower animals, and to the development of the intellectual and moral faculties during primeval and civilized times. The naturalization of the human mind there begun was continued by the pragmatists. The story goes back to a time which Charles Peirce remembered, as follows, nearly half a century later:

I was away surveying in the wilds of Louisiana when Darwin's great work appeared, and though I learned by letters of the immense sensation it had created, I did not return until early in the following summer when I found [*Chauncey*] *Wright all enthusiasm for Darwin, whose doctrines appeared to him as a sort of supplement to those of Mill. I remember well that I then made a remark to him which, although he did not assent to it, evidently impressed him enough to perplex him. The remark was that these ideas of development had more vitality by far than any of his other favorite conceptions and that though they might at that moment be in his mind like a little vine clinging to the tree of Associationalism, yet after a time that vine would inevitably kill the tree He asked me why I said that and I replied that the reason was that Mill's doctrine was nothing but a metaphysical point of view to which Darwin's, which was nourished by positive observation, must be deadly.*

Peirce saw in the idea of evolution a welcome antidote to the prevailing nominalism and associationalism, but what Wright valued most in Mill was neither of the latter but the principle of utility, and he projected a synthesis of utilitarianism and Darwinism. Leslie Stephen in his classic work on the English Utilitarians has called attention to the paradox of their indifference to history combined with their appeal to experience. They and the British empiricists generally seemed always to be in need of, and yet always to reject by anticipation, some theory of evolution. Their difficulty was that theories of evolution appeared to them to involve something mystical and transcendental. "This," says Stephen, "may help to explain the great influence of the Darwinian theories. They marked the point at which a doctrine of evolution could be allied with an appeal to experience." So it seemed to Wright.

Though he was a mathematician and a computer for the Nautical Almanac, Wright had had some training in biology under Asa Gray and had published essays on the origin and uses of the arrangements of leaves in plants and on the architecture of honeycombs. Gray had sent some of these essays to Darwin in 1859, but the mathematics had been too much for him.

Over a period of some months after his first reading of the *Origin of Species*, Wright composed a review essay which Gray forwarded to Darwin in 1861 and Darwin turned over to Huxley for publication in the *Natural History Review*; but apparently it was thought too philosophical and was never published.

At that time Herbert Spencer's *First Principles* was coming out in parts. William James, who was scarcely twenty, later wrote: "I . . . was carried away with enthusiasm by the intellectual perspectives which it seemed to open. When a maturer companion, Mr. Charles S. Peirce, attacked it in my presence, I felt spiritually wounded, as by the defacement of a sacred image or picture, though I could not verbally defend it against his criticisms."

Peirce and Wright, though intellectually far apart in some respects, were agreed that there was no way of being a good Darwinian and a Spencerian at the same time, and they had no qualms about renouncing Spencer and adhering to Darwin. James soon came around to their view and used Spencer as his chief whipping boy for thirty years.

In 1865 Wright published in the *North American Review* an article on "The Philosophy of Herbert Spencer," in which, in the course of criticizing Spencer, he indicated the philosophy of science in terms of which the pragmatists were to resolve Darwin's problem.

Ideas are developed by the sagacity of the expert, rather than by the systematic procedures of the philosopher. But when and however ideas are developed science cares nothing, for it is only by subsequent tests of sensible experience that ideas are admitted into the pandects of science. . . . Science asks no questions about the ontological pedigree or a priori *character of a theory, but is content to judge it by its performance. . . . The principles of modern natural philosophy, both mathematical and physical. . . are rather the eyes with which nature is seen, than the elements and constituents of the objects discovered. . . . Nothing justifies the development of abstract principles in science but their utility in enlarging our concrete knowledge of nature. The ideas on which mathematical Mechanics and the Calculus are founded, the morphological ideas of Natural History, and the theories of Chemistry are such working ideas,–finders, not merely summaries of truth.*

By 1870 the pragmatic case was much further developed. In an article on the "Limits of Natural Selection," Wright gave it as his opinion that consciousness, language, and thought were so far from being beyond the province of natural selection, as Alfred Wallace supposed, that they afforded one of the most promising fields for its future investigations. In a long and revealing footnote applying the principle of natural selection to the development of the individual mind by its own experiences, he argued that "our knowledges and rational beliefs result, *truly and literally*, from the survival of the fittest among our original and spontaneous beliefs." He suggested that the chief prejudice against this conclusion would be removed if we adopted Bain's definition of belief. Now it will be remembered that the Metaphysical Club, of which Wright, Peirce, James, and Holmes were members, was meeting at this time. Peirce says that Nicholas Green, a lawyer among them, often urged the importance of applying Bain's definition of belief as that upon which a man is prepared to act. From this definition, Peirce adds, pragmatism is scarce more than a corollary. I shall therefore quote enough of Wright's note to show that one application of Bain's definition was to the solution of the problem our pragmatists had inherited from Darwin.

Human beliefs, like human desires, are naturally illimitable. The generalizing instinct is native to the mind. It is not the result of habitual experiences, as is commonly supposed, but acts as well on single *experiences, which are capable of producing, when unchecked, the most unbounded beliefs and expectations of the future. The only checks to such unconditional natural beliefs are* other *and equally unconditional and natural beliefs, or the contradictions and limiting conditions of experience. Here, then, is a close analogy, at least, to those fundamental facts of the organic world on which the law of Natural Selection is based; the facts, namely, of the "rapid increase of organisms," limited only by "the conditions of existence," and by competition in that "struggle for existence" which results in the "survival of the fittest." As the tendency to an unlimited increase in existing organisms is held in check only by those conditions of their existence which are chiefly comprised in the like tendencies of other organisms to unlimited increase, and is thus maintained (so long as external conditions remain unchanged) in an unvarying balance of life; and as this balance adjusts itself to slowly changing external conditions, so, in the history of the individual mind, beliefs which spring spontaneously from simple and single experiences, and from a naturally unlimited tendency to generalization, are held mutually in check, and in their harmony represent the properly balanced experiences and knowledges of the mind, and by adaptive changes are kept in accordance with changing external conditions, or with the varying total results in the memory of special experiences. This mutual limitation of belief by belief, in which consists so large a part of their proper* evidence, *is so prominent a feature in the beliefs of the rational mind, that philosophers had failed to discover their true nature, as elementary facts, until this was pointed out by the greatest of living psychologists, Professor Alexander Bain. The mutual tests and checks of belief have, indeed, always appeared to a great majority of philosophers as their only proper evidence; and beliefs themselves have appeared as purely intellectual phases of the mind. But Bain has defined them, in respect to their ultimate natures, as phases of the will; or as the tendencies we have to* act *on mere experience, or to* act *on our simplest, most limited experiences. They are tendencies, however, which become so involved in intellectual developments, and in their mutual limitations, that their ultimate results in rational beliefs have very naturally appeared to most philosophers as purely intellectual facts; and their real genesis in experience has been generally discredited, with the exception of what are designated specially as "empirical beliefs."* [1870]

About the same time another application of Bain's definition was being made by Holmes. He was developing a conception of law in terms of expectancies or predictions and the readiness to act upon them. In the *American Law Review* for July, 1872, he criticized Austin's view that command was the essence of law, that custom only became law by the tacit consent of the sovereign manifested by its adoption by the courts, and that before its adoption it was only a motive for decision. What more, Holmes asked, was the decision itself in relation to any future decision?

What more indeed is a statute; and in what other sense law, than that we believe that the motive which we think that it offers to the judges will prevail, and will induce them to decide a certain case in a certain way, and so shape our conduct on that anticipation? A precedent may not be followed; a statute may be emptied of its contents by construction, or may be repealed without a saving clause after we have acted on it; but we expect the reverse, and if our expectations come true, we say that we have been subject to law in the matter in hand.

Holmes does not expressly connect his prediction theory of law with evolution, but it seems likely that he had it in mind, for he published a criticism of Spencer in the following year.

It has always seemed to us a singular anomaly [he said] *that believers in the theory of evolution and in the natural development of institutions by successive adaptations to the environment, should be found laying down a theory of government intended to establish its limits once for all by a logical deduction from axioms. . . . Mr. Spencer is forever putting cases to show that the reaction of legislation is equal to its action. By changing the law, he argues, you do not get rid of any burden, but only change the mode of bearing it; and if the change does not make it easier to bear for society, considered as a whole, legislation is inexpedient. This tacit assumption of the solidarity of the interests of society is very common, but seems to us to be false. . . . In the last resort a man rightly prefers his own interest to that of his neighbors. . . . The more powerful interests must be more or less reflected in legislation; which, like every other device of man or beast, must tend in the long run to aid the survival of the fittest.*

We return now to Chauncey Wright. In July, 1871, he published an essay "in defence and illustration of the theory of Natural Selection" against the criticisms of

St. George Mivart. He sent advance proof sheets of this essay to Darwin. "My special purpose," he said, "has been to contribute to the theory by *placing* it in its proper relations to philosophical inquiries in general." Darwin was so pleased with this essay that, with Wright's permission, he had it reprinted at his own expense in London, along with an appendix supplied by Wright, and distributed it to the leading naturalists of the British Isles and to some abroad.

Mivart replied to Wright, and Wright met his new criticisms in an essay published in July, 1872, of which again he sent proof sheets to Darwin, who replied:

Nothing can be clearer than the way in which you discuss the permanence or fixity of species. . . . As your mind is so clear, and as you consider so carefully the meaning of words, I wish you would take some incidental occasion to consider when a thing may properly be said to be effected by the will of man. I have been led to the wish by reading an article by your Professor Whitney. . . . He argues, because each step of change in language is made by the will of man, the whole language so changes: but I do not think that this is so, as man has no intention or wish to change the language. It is a parallel case with what I have called "unconscious selection," which depends on men consciously preserving the best individuals, and thus unconsciously altering the breed.

Shortly thereafter Wright made a trip to England and the Continent. Late in August he wrote Darwin a long letter from London, indicating the line he would take, and referring to his criticism of Wallace two years before. A few days later he visited overnight with Darwin at Down, where the problem was further discussed and a plan laid which Wright reported to a friend as follows:

I am some time to write an essay on matters covering the ground of certain common interests and studies, and in review of his "Descent of Man," and other related works, for which the learned title is adopted of Psychozöology,–as a substitute for "Animal Psychology," "Instinct," and the like titles,–in order to give the requisite subordination (from our point of view) of consciousness in men and animals, to their development and general relations to nature.

Wright died with the intended book unwritten, or at least unpublished, but a preliminary sketch of a part of it was written that winter and appeared in the following spring under the title "The Evolution of Self-Consciousness." In the latter part of this long essay Wright applied the principles of spontaneous variation and natural selection to the origin and development of language and worked out a solution to Darwin's problem. "So far as human intentions have had anything to do with changes in the traditions of language," he argued, "they have . . . been exerted in resisting them." In the course of the argument Wright drew a parallel between the development of language and that of law.

The judge cannot rightfully change the laws that govern his judgments; and the just judge does not consciously do so. Nevertheless, legal usages change from age to age. Laws, in their practical effects, are ameliorated by courts as well as by legislatures. No new principles are consciously introduced; but interpretations of old ones (and combinations, under more precise and qualified statements) are made, which disregard old decisions, seemingly by new and better definitions of that which in its nature is unalterable, but really, in their practical effects, by alterations, at least in the proximate grounds of decision; so that nothing is really unalterable in law, except the intention to do justice under universally applicable principles of decision, and the instinctive judgments of so-called natural law. [1873]

This was to be one of the themes of Holmes's great lectures on "The Common Law," published seven years later. . . .

In November, 1872, shortly after Wright's return from his visit to Darwin, the Metaphysical Club met to hear Peirce read a paper expounding some of the views which he later said he "had been urging all along under the name of pragmatism." He began by saying that "each chief step in science has been a lesson in logic" and that "the Darwinian controversy is, in large part, a question of logic," as some of Wright's papers had shown it to be. "Mr. Darwin," he said, "proposed to apply the statistical method to biology. . . . While unable to say what the operation of variation and natural selection in every individual case will be, [he] demonstrates that in the long run they will adapt animals to their circumstances." Peirce proceeded to outline the lesson in logic of this new step in science. The now familiar argument runs as follows:

The irritation of doubt is the only immediate motive for the struggle to attain belief. . . . Hence, the sole object of inquiry is the settlement of opinion. . . . The problem becomes how to fix belief, not in the individual merely, but in the community. . . . The method must be such that the ultimate conclusion of every man shall be the same. Such is the method of science. . . . The essence of belief is the establishment of habit, and different beliefs are distinguished by the different modes of action to which they give rise. . . . There is no distinction of meaning so fine as to consist in anything but a possible difference of practice. . . . Our idea of anything is *our idea of its sensible effects. . . .* [*The way to make our ideas clear is to*] *consider what effects, which might conceivably have practical bearings, we conceive the object of our conception to have. Then, our conception of these effects is the whole of our conception of the object. . . .* [*If we apply this prescription to the ideas of truth and reality, we get this result:*] *The opinion which is fated to be ultimately agreed to by all who investigate, is what we mean by the truth, and the object represented in this opinion is the real.* [1877, 1878]

This paper was later published as two articles in the *Popular Science Monthly* and followed by four others on "The Doctrine of Chances," "The Probability of Induction," "The Order of Nature," and "Deduction, Induction, and Hypothesis"; all six under the general title, "Illustrations of the Logic of Science." It will be noted that Peirce's version of Darwinian logic, like Wright's, turns on Bain's definition of belief. . . .

James was trained in medicine. He had known Darwin's writings from his student days. In 1868 he had reviewed Darwin's *Variation of Animals and Plants under Domestication* for both the *Atlantic Monthly* and the *North American Review*, remarking, among other things, that there was no law explaining the origin of variations. In the year 1872-1873, and during the five years from 1874 to 1880, he gave a course in Harvard College on "Comparative Anatomy and Physiology." In the first half-year he tended to use comparative anatomy as affording proofs and illustrations of evolution, and in the second half-year to use physiology as an approach to psychology.

In 1878 James published his first original philosophical article, "Remarks on Spencer's Definition of Mind as Correspondence," or "adjustment of inner to outer relations." He argued that in the working out of his theory Spencer made mind "pure product" and ignored the role of emotion, volition, and action.

I, for my part, cannot escape the consideration, forced upon me at every turn, that the knower is not simply a mirror floating with no foot-hold anywhere, and passively reflecting an order that he comes upon and finds simply existing. The knower is an actor, and co-efficient of the truth on one side, whilst on the other he registers the truth which he helps to create. Mental interests, hypotheses, postulates, so far as they are bases for human action–action which to a great extent transforms the world–help to make *the truth which they declare. In other words, there belongs to mind, from its birth upward, a spontaneity, a vote. It is in the game, and not a mere looker-on. . . .*

In this and later attacks on Spencer, James identified himself with Darwin. The identification is most complete in the lecture on "Great Men and Their Environment," delivered before the Harvard Natural History Society and published in 1880. He began with this sentence: "A remarkable parallel, which I think has never been noticed, obtains between the facts of social evolution on the one hand, and of zoological evolution as expounded by Mr. Darwin on the other." James's memory was at fault, for it had been often noticed by Wright. He went on to say, as Wright had, that the great merit of Darwin was to discriminate clearly between the causes which originally produced variations and the causes that preserved them after they were produced. James applied this distinction, as Wright had, to mental evolution.

*. . . The new conceptions, emotions, and active tendencies which evolve are originally produced in the shape of random images, fancies, accidental out-births of spontaneous variation in the functional activity of the excessively instable human brain, which the outer environment simply confirms or refutes, adopts or rejects, preserves or destroys,–*selects, *in short, just as it selects morphological and social variations due to molecular accidents of an analogous sort. . . .* [*Even the conceiving of a law*] *is a spontaneous variation in the strictest sense of the term. It flashes out of one brain, and no other, because the instability of that brain is such as to tip and upset itself in just that particular direction. But the important thing to notice is that the good flashes and the bad flashes, the triumphant hypotheses and the absurd conceits, are on an exact equality in respect of their origin.*

From this lecture it is an easy step to James's *Principles of Psychology* published a decade later, and particularly to the last chapter, on "Necessary Truths and the Effects of Experience," in which he applied the Darwinian notions of variation and selection to the a priori factors in human knowledge.

What was really novel in James's lecture of 1880 was the further use of Darwin's distinction to defend against Spencer the great-man theory of history.

> *The causes of production of great men lie in a sphere wholly inaccessible to the social philosopher. He must simply accept geniuses as data, just as Darwin accepts his spontaneous variations. For him, as for Darwin, the only problem is, these data being given, How does the environment affect them, and how do they affect the environment? Now, I affirm that the relation of the visible environment to the great man is in the main exactly what it is the "variation" in the Darwinian philosophy: It chiefly adopts or rejects, preserves or destroys, in short* selects *him. And whenever it adopts and preserves the great man, it becomes modified by his influence in an entirely original and peculiar way.*

Such a man, I imagine James would say, is John Dewey. Though born in the year the *Origin of Species* appeared, he came to Darwin by way of Hegel and did not reach him until nearly the end of the century. Since that time, however, he has worked in the legitimate line of descent from Darwin, and the whole development whose early steps I have traced may be said to have reached a kind of culmination in 1938 in his *Logic: The Theory of Inquiry*. It rests on the principle of the continuum of inquiry and on the theory that "all logical forms (with their characteristic properties) arise within the operation of inquiry and are concerned with control of inquiry so that it may yield warranted assertions." Dewey reminds us that the movement away from Aristotelian logic is closely connected with "the reversed attitude of science toward change."

> Completion *of the cycle of scientific reversal may be conveniently dated from the appearance of Darwin's* Origin of Species. *The very title of the book expresses a revolution in science, for the conception of biological species had been a conspicuous manifestation of the assumption of complete immutability. This conception had been banished before Darwin from every scientific subject save botany and zoology. But the latter had remained the bulwark of the old logic in scientific subject-matter.*

Consciously following Peirce, Dewey expounds the new logic which claims to have learned the lesson of the reversal the early pragmatists helped to complete.

25 The Moralist Rigorism of W. G. Sumner

Robert B. Notestein

Textbook discussions of William Graham Sumner tend to have a kind of tunnel vision into this curmudgeon from the Yale faculty. He usually is described, but not analyzed, as the leading spokesman for conservative Social Darwinism in the Gilded Age. Accurate though the label may be, it does justice neither to the complexity of Sumner's thought nor to the many lines of speculation touched by it. Robert Notestein clearly outlines here Sumner's intellectual breadth as economic thinker and "father" of American sociology.

It may help the reader to consider that Sumner's "timeless moral code" was not basically the same code of Christian ethics to which he had subscribed as an Episcopalian clergyman before entering his Yale professorship. Rather it was Herbert Spencer's code of hedonistic ethics developed by evolving human society. Here is the point at which most Protestant churchmen of Sumner's day rejected Spencerian evolutionism. If man is the product of animal evolution, they argued, how then account for his God-given intuited ideas of good which make him superior to lower forms? Although theological utilitarianism (the pleasure-pain principle seen as divinely instilled in man to guide him to right choices) had been fashionable for Lockean and Paleyan moralists since the eighteenth century, Herbert Spencer's hedonist ethics meant untenable relativism to mid-nineteenth-century American theologians. But not so to Sumner. Why this did not, however, put him in the same camp with the pragmatists who shaped their ideas in good measure from the later British utilitarians is made clear in the illuminating quotations from Chauncey Wright in Essay 24. Sumner's idea of expediency, found in his men of basic natural drives, is not the same as the pragmatic test of truth conducted by reasoning men. For the early pragmatists, "natural beliefs" were the result of a Darwinian natural selection from among man's illimitable individual experiences; they were not merely the result of the limited Spencerian and Sumnerian logic of habit.

For further reading: Ralph H. Gabriel, *The Course of American Democratic Thought* (2d ed., 1956), chap. 18; *Richard Hofstadter, *Social Darwinism in*

Journal of the History of Ideas, 16 (June 1955), 389-400. Reprinted by permission of the author and the *Journal of the History of Ideas*. Footnotes have been omitted.

American Thought (rev. ed., 1955); *Robert G. McCloskey, *American Conservatism in the Age of Enterprise, 1865-1910* (1951); John William Ward, "The Ideal of Individualism and the Reality of Organization," in his *Red, White, and Blue: Men, Books, and Ideas in American Culture* (1969), pp. 227-266.

William Graham Sumner, Professor of Political and Social Science at Yale from 1872 to 1910, has left behind many images. To some sociologists he is variously conceived, as one of the "fathers" of their discipline, as the author of the most influential single volume in the social sciences, *Folkways,* as the first teacher of sociology in the United States in terms of both time and ability.

To Albert Galloway Keller, Professor of the Science of Society at Yale from 1900 to 1942, and Sumner's most devoted student, Sumner was conceived of as a social scientist of the stature of Herbert Spencer and Vilfredo Pareto, and as an incomparable guide to those "correct" moral choices which the citizen could ignore only at his own and his nation's peril. Keller's devotion to the memory of Sumner led him to devote many years of his own academic life to editing and preparing for publication the enormous mass of ethnographic material gathered by Sumner. When he retired from teaching, Keller organized the William Graham Sumner Club. This group became a "cult," using Sumner's works as a club to belabor the Democratic administration and their policies during the 1940s.

To John Chamberlain, a student of A. G. Keller and the editor of *The Freeman,* Sumner was a farsighted spokesman for and a progenitor of a contemporary conservative ideology. Chamberlain has been at work for several years on a biography of Sumner which will, it is hoped by Professor Keller, establish Sumner in his rightful place as the Darwin of the social sciences.

At the opposite end of the ideological spectrum is the image of a Sumner who was "the prime minister in the empire of plutocratic education," who was "the St. Paul of the Gospel of Wealth," and who preached in both the classroom and in the pages of the periodical publications of the last quarter of the nineteenth century a "stark, drastic Social Darwinian philosophy unrelieved by any humanitarian sentiments."

These diverse images are partially due to the differing social and personal backgrounds of the observers, which have structured their perceptions. They are also due to the fact that Sumner, to a degree unique among American intellectuals, was motivated not so much by the goal of acquiring and disseminating disinterested knowledge, but rather by the goal of demonstrating to his audiences the timeless validity of a moral code. This motive was in turn evoked by the profound changes in American life during the last third of the nineteenth century, which repeatedly outraged his conception of individual and national virtue.

Sumner's transitions from clergyman to economist to sociologist, his prolific writing, the profound attraction he had for generations of Yale students, the devotion of Professor A. G. Keller, the barbed shafts hurled at him by men as diverse as Upton Sinclair, Lester F. Ward, and William McKinley, the almost total neglect of his work by contemporary social scientists, were and are due to his moralist rigorism.

Sumner, as Robert Green McCloskey has aptly said, was a man "whose moral predispositions were soundly conservative, yet who disclaimed all moral predispositions, one who rightfully wore the mantle of the scholar, yet shared the simple materialism of his less-schooled contemporaries, one who would fight for what he believed like a religious zealot, yet not surrender to the sentimentalism religion sometimes begets."

His influence on American political and social thought stems from the vigor, the incisiveness and the dogmatism of his work.

II

The categories which lie behind Sumner's conceptual apparatus were the common property of many men and women in the last half of the nineteenth century. These categories were the structure of the intellectual climate of opinion from the Civil War until the turn of the century, or roughly from the demise of transcendentalism to the rise of pragmatism. Hence an analysis of the categories used by Sumner does not give insight into the unique quality of his work.

Such insight can however be gained from the consistency of his use of those concepts he believed were applicable to the intellectual problems which evoked his writings. Through the analysis of Sumner's concepts and the use to which he put them, the content of his moralist rigorism will be inferred.

A. Human Nature

He regarded human nature as fixed and constant. "One psychical power to be assumed is the ability to distinguish pleasure and pain." Why is pleasure attached to some types of action, and pain to others? The answer of Sumner: "Pleasurable acts are those which bring adaptation to life conditions, painful acts do not." He is saying that pleasurable acts are those which enhance survival chances. His hedonism is a deduction from the postulates of Darwinism.

Even if this type of psychological hedonism would explain individual actions, it would not explain human interaction. How does he deal with this problem? "Men do not associate with one another because of an innate quality of sociability implanted in his germ plasm." Rather, "association has at length and with great difficulty become a characteristic habit of mankind because of its high survival value in the evolution of civilization." Why does association have a high survival value? "Association has high survival value because it is to the individual's interest in the face of the rigors of nature."

Men everywhere possess these motives, hunger, sex passion, vanity and fear (of ghosts and spirits). These motives come into play when men live together under the same life conditions. Under each of these motives there are interests. "Life consists in satisfying interest, for life in a society is a career and an effort expended on both the material and the social environment."

The "felicific calculus" of pleasure-pain is hitched to adjustment to life conditions producing an almost complete social conservatism. All the individual can do in the face of these inexorable conditions is to practice renunciation and self-denial.

B. Life Conditions

Life conditions become the foundation on which the pursuit of individual interest produces societies. Man solves his problems of existence not in terms of "creation'' but rather in terms of adjustment to the folkways and mores. Mores and institutions in turn conform to the external conditions of life. Of these external conditions, the economic is the most fundamental.

This facet of Sumner's thought has received little attention, having been overshadowed by his theory of the folkways and mores, but it is far more fundamental than ''culture'' in determining man's way of life. Sumner's interpretation of economic determinism differs crucially from that of Marx. The contribution of Marx to this topic lies in his dialectical construction of ''productive forces,'' ''production relations,'' and ''property relations.'' Antagonistic polar opposites produce social structures with developmental laws leading from Asiatic to ancient to modern bourgeois societies. Sumner's construction of economic determinism is merely a summation of factors, as when he puts Mediterranean slavery, medieval life and modern society together with the monogamic family. He continually moves outside history to arrange the stream of evolution.

Before specifying what ''economic'' meant to Sumner, it is desirable to elaborate the proposition by specific examples.

In regard to marriage he said, ''It is the variation in life conditions, chiefly economic, which have made and slowly modify the marriage-institutions, producing the innumerable varieties which are encountered along the course of its evolution.''

The state is also based on property relations. Property arose through force and the process of consolidating property relations was also the beginning of state relations. Sumner accepted the class theory of the state as elaborated by Gumplowitz.

What then is the state? It is an instrument for class domination, power in the hands of the most powerful class in the society. ''Chiefs, kings, priests, warriors, statesmen, and other functionaries have put their own interests in the place of group interests, and have used the authority they possessed to force the societal organization to work and fight for their interests.''

Sumner was not always consistent in his conception of the state. There is implicit, particularly in his more polemic essays, the conception of the state as a beneficent mediator of the claims of the various classes of society. He could not accept the logical conclusion of the class theory of the state, and continually exhorted his students and readers to allow the state to perform its sole ''legitimate'' function, to guarantee to each and every man the fruits of his own labor. He feared that the state would be ''perverted'' to favor a ''new privileged class of the many and the poor,'' or would be captured by the big bourgeoisie and ''perverted'' into a plutocracy. This fear increased until in 1909 the future presaged for him a period of class conflict and misery.

Ideals also had their basis in economic factors. ''Notions of right and wrong and conceptions of rights are a product of economic relations which have been adopted because expedient and successful, philosophical and religious dogmas are a result of reflections on experience furnished by the operation of existing systems of societal economy.'' Humanitarianism, democracy, the doctrine of natural rights were the product of economic surplus in relation to a scarcity of men and were therefore [hostile] to Sumner transitory ideas. The impermanence of the ideals was a product not only of changing life conditions, but also of Sumner's dislike of democracy, hatred for revolutionary natural law philosophy and acceptance of conservative natural law philosophy.

What did Sumner mean by "the economic" in his deterministic approach? Three concepts are involved

a. Monopoly.—"One of the prime characters worked out in the struggle for existence and bequeathed as an instinct to all animals is that which leads them to make a monopoly of the means of self-provision . . . to complain of property as a monopoly is like complaining of the force of gravitation." Private property was to Sumner a datum of nature. But the ability to accumulate property was dependent on the land-man ratio

b. Land-man ratio.—Men ultimately draw their living from the soil, and the quality of their existence, their method of obtaining it, and their mutual relations in the process are all determined by the proportion of population to the available land. When men were few and soil was abundant, the struggle for existence was mild; when population presses on the supply of land, the struggle for existence becomes hard. Sumner believed that the man-land ratio could be mitigated by what was for him the prime condition for the development of society, capital

c. Capital.—"Capital is energy stored up against the struggle for self maintenance." This energy is embodied in tools and machines which subjugate natural forces and make them the servant of man. How is capital to be accumulated? Capital accumulation "is the result of human foresight, rendered possible by consistent renunciation of the present in favor of the future." Here has entered into these deterministic forces an indeterminant element. The importance of this factor in understanding Sumner's values cannot be overestimated, as will subsequently be shown.

The economic basis of social life, in Sumner's emphasis, receives its importance not because it is a hypothesis to be tested but rather because it is an ontological fact. It is more "real" than art, music, law, religion, etc. Retrospectively, first man works to accumulate capital before he can indulge in "dythyrambic rhetoric." Prospectively, the important task is to promote capital accumulation, to enhance industrial efficiency, not to develop aesthetic and intellectual potentialities.

With this emphasis on the economic order goes an image of the "ideal man." In a revealing interview, a magazine writer asked Sumner, in the last years of his life, whom he regarded as the "great men" on the American scene during his lifetime. Sumner quickly answered, Thomas Edison, Andrew Carnegie, and John D. Rockefeller. His ideal is "homo faber," man in pursuit of "real tasks," which implies a depreciation of and suspicion toward the expressive aspects of human conduct.

C. Social Darwinism

Men, as they struggle with nature to adjust to the "land," enter into competitive relationships with one another. To succeed in this struggle capital is indispensable, and so private property became for Sumner a feature of society organized in accord with the natural conditions of the struggle for existence.

Inequalities in wealth derived from varying degrees of aptitude for the struggle for existence. The "weak" were then the poor, the idle, the extravagant, the ignorant. The "strong" were the industrious, the frugal, the talented, the wealthy. For Sumner the pursuit of self-interest was identical with the pursuit of society's best interest. This assumption was possible only because the "fittest" survived.

Property became for Sumner an inalienable right. Yet during his lifetime the alienation of the worker from the means of production proceeded at an extremely rapid rate. What he does in considering those so alienated is to forget his social determinism and to introduce epithets such as "delinquent," "improvident," "those who lack merit," etc. He heaps scorn on those who suffer from capitalism after he had introjected social conditions into the individual.

How can one reconcile his equation of strength with virtue, thrift, foresight, and merit with his statements that "the historical or selected classes are those which, in history, have controlled the activities and policies of generation"? "Merit and societal value, according to the standards of their time, have entered into their status only slightly and incidentally."

Like Marx, Sumner saw the end result of the class struggle as the division of society into the plutocrats and the masses with the destruction of the middle classes. This was the logical conclusion. His hero was "The Forgotten Man," the hard-working, self-sufficient, small-propertied, middle-class individual, who does not complain. This was the logical conclusion of his version of social Darwinism, but he could never accept this conclusion.

D. Folkways and Mores

1. Reification of the mores and conservative natural law —As Sumner's work progressed the mores became an entity. As Vincent has said, Sumner fell victim to "a fallacy against which he gives frequent warning, viz., the danger of being deceived by words and phrases to which an almost magic power is attributed. . . . The mores seem to be almost objective and independent things, determining right and wrong, creating status, and having aims."

He is engaging in reification and putting the mores on a plane of causal equality with what echoes throughout his economic and political essays, the doctrine of conservative natural law.

Not only is there this equivalence in causal efficacy, but he conceived of folkways and mores as the fulfillment of natural laws inherent in the universe. What Sumner is saying is that reason is too weak to transcend the present and penetrate into the future, although reason is strong enough to comprehend the whole past of human history through evolutionary constructions. Why cannot reason be projected forward? Because he had no hope for the future, only fear, therefore he has no interest in mastering the future. All he can propose is "adjustment." This philosophy of conservative natural law which posits "eternal" human motives, "eternal" laws of society is discouraging to any hope of men to master the "irrational" features of society

2. Moral relativism.—Sumner's greatest contribution to the social sciences was his emphasis on the relativity, between cultures, of cultural values. But in attempting to elaborate this position, he very clearly demonstrates the difficulty that any observer has in getting outside his own culture. This difficulty enables one to isolate the fundamental value premise of Sumner. Considering his equation of the causal

efficacy of the mores with natural law, it would not follow that mores are relative to time and place.

What is right and what is wrong? Right is what is permitted by the mores, wrong is what is condemned by the mores. The problem of freedom (Jesus: "It is written but I say unto you"), and spontaneity (George H. Mead's ineffable "I"), is divorced from any a priorism and relegated to the complex of the mores. Reason, as formerly embodied in the rational utopian element of sixteenth-century puritanism and as secularized in the liberal progressivism of Adam Smith, is surrendered. Ethical universalism is surrendered. Morality and reason are divorced. Reason can only contemplate, describe slowly changing mores.

Sumner's statement that right is what is permitted, wrong is what is condemned by the mores, is a tautology. But he could not stop here, he wanted some more objective criteria. One answer he gave was that the mores were "adjustments" to the struggle for existence. "The adjustment of men to their surroundings is the controlling thought of this book. . . . The essence of evolution is the adjustment of life to life conditions." So whatever mores have survived selection have been "expedient" to their time. They are "expedient" because they lead to "societal welfare." Moral conduct is conduct useful to the society. But men in making the inference from utility have "been liable to the most pernicious errors. . . . Men have turned their backs on welfare and reality, in order to pursue beauty, glory, poetry and dithyrambic rhetoric." These "false values" enter at the second stage of the act-thought-act sequence and give rise to error concerning what is actually the conduct best calculated to serve societal welfare.

But since right and wrong have no meaning apart from the mores, why the epithet "pernicious, false values"? There must be some value by which Sumner is evaluating the mores. The value is "societal welfare." But the phrase must be given some content. Obviously beauty, glory, poetry, and dithyrambic rhetoric lack such value, for they are pernicious errors. When the mores are wrong it is because "energy is expended on acts which are contrary to welfare." But still, what is "societal welfare"? "What is true is that there are periods of social advance and periods of social decline, that is advance or decline in economic power, material prosperity, and group strength for war."

So "societal welfare" is measured in terms of material or economic power. Good is whatever contributes to material and economic power, bad is what diminishes such power. Moral questions are determined by expediency, and expediency is determined by economic power. It is this material ethic which enables him to judge social policy and individual behavior. This value premise of Sumner's is most clearly implied in his economic and political essays, where he emphasizes again and again the necessity for the accumulation of capital if a society is to advance. When this value is linked with Social Darwinism the result is the belief that the most capable will be those who gain the greatest material advantage. "The men who are competent to organize great enterprises and to handle great amounts of capital must be found by natural selection, not by political election. . . . The aggregation of large amounts of capital in few hands is the first condition of the fulfillment of the most important tasks of civilization which now confront us."

He says that these "leaders" must be found by "natural selection," and he obviously believed that most of them were so found. But Sumner was not unique. Most Americans also believed that these men did not inherit their power but rather achieved their status. This "myth" goes roughly as follows: "A poor immigrant boy arrived on the shores of a new nation which abounded in endless opportunity. As the boy was the son of a workingman, he had little or no formal education and was forced by circumstances to seek employment at a tender age. His first job was a lowly one, but in short order he rose to prominence, usually as a result of cleverness, diligence, or luck. In this manner, the top-level businessman was but a generation removed from poverty and anonymity." William Miller has, however, clearly indicated that "selection" was more often ascription on the basis of certain social characteristics found in the middle and upper classes.

The successful businessmen were then, for Sumner by his logic, the élite of the nation. But he did not approve completely of the destination to which his material ethic had led him. His hero was not the millionaire but the hard-working, self-sufficient, middle-class "Forgotten Man." Success was never for him a motive which carried its own justification. His abhorrence of the plutocrat who succeeded by political means was due to his belief that the Goulds and Fisks of his era seldom exemplified the virtues of industry, frugality and self-reliance.

E. Contraditions and Resolution

Several contradictions in Sumner's thought have been pointed out.

1. He never settled on the role of the state in society. In his earlier and more polemic work, the state was the mediator performing its "legitimate function of guaranteeing to each and every man the fruits of his labor." In his sociological writings the state is the servant of the class which controls it. He combats the increasing power of the government with the weapons of the classic laissez-faire liberal, and at the same time he wants the state to be powerful enough to enforce standards guaranteeing that everyone gets his just due from his labor.

2. Capital accumulation was to Sumner the foundation of civilization. Therefore anything that diminishes the possibility of capital accumulation in the hands of the "fittest" was harmful to the society. Did this mean that capital accumulation contained its own justification? For Sumner it did not.

3. Sumner's Social Darwinism clearly implies an economic élite, and his derivation of "morals" from societal self-maintenance implies the economic determination of morality. This would then mean that the economic élite is also the moral élite. But this conclusion Sumner would not completely accept.

Behind these contradictions is found the fundamental value premise which pervaded his life work.

III

"Capital is the fruit of industry, temperance, prudence, frugality and the other industrial virtues. It comes to this: that the question how well off we can be depends at the last on the question how rational, virtuous, and enlightened we are . . . whatever deficiencies there are in our society which are important—or radical—that is to say, which surpass in magnitude the harm which comes from defects in the social machinery—are due to deficiencies in our moral development. We are as well off as we deserve to be."

Quotations such as the above recur throughout his writings. The good man for Sumner was temperate, chaste, frugal, industrious and devoted to duty. This type of virtue would find its own reward. Why? Because for Sumner the priest they were the external signs of inward grace, and for Sumner the social scientist they were the prerequisites for survival and success in a world governed by natural law. Richard Hofstadter has said that "like some latter-day Calvin, he came to preach the predestination of the economically elect through the survival of the fittest." This statement misses the mark. While it is, I believe, true that Sumner's basic value was the ethic of intra-world asceticism, the reasons why this value was held and the goals it would achieve differ fundamentally in Calvin and in Sumner.

The explanation of human personality as a "calculus" of pleasure-pain is phrased in terms of the universal life goal of adjustment to the inexorable laws of nature. This makes of life a continual process of renunciation and self-denial. But the historical Puritan renounced his world to remake it. Sumner has transposed this old impulse into righteous indignation against "abuses." He then feels called upon to agitate against these "abuses" of the laws of nature. These "calls" distract him from his proper vocation, which is science. But science is not the use of reason to remake the world, but rather the contemplation of a world governed by natural la. The "call" to agitation comes not from reason but from conscience. Hence reason and morality are divorced from one another.

But what is this conscience? It provides guidance for "adjustment." Such guidance must lead to the acquisition of the "virtues." You get the legitimation of these virtues, not by religious salvation, but rather in terms of the degree to which they bring success in this world. So the ethical legacy of Puritanism becomes an ideology according to which the "successful" are the moral superiors of the "unsuccessful."

As a consequence of this "ideology," Sumner endorses property as work-property. He feels outraged by those types of activity which transmit economic power on to political power, as was the case in the nineteenth-century American policy of tariff protection. He is indignant when activities depart from the political order and its institutions to intervene in the economic order as the regulation of economic activities in conformity with legal standards, such as the Sherman Anti-Trust Law.

This emphasis on the strict separation of economics and politics, which is the "utopian" element in the thinking of Sumner, stems from classical economics. But Sumner stood at quite a different phase of capitalist development. The last quarter of the nineteenth century in America saw not the demise of mercantile monopolies, of privileged trading companies, but rather the insecurity of small businessmen in the face of competition from large-scale corporate units, with their tremendous aggregation of capital and rationality of production. These changes explain his insecurity, his fear for the future and, of greatest importance, the contradictions to be found in his writings. What is the nature of his ambivalence?

He felt optimistic about the ability of industrialists to meet the economic challenge of the twentieth century. He takes his stand with these "big entrepreneurs," and he conceives of them in terms of work-property acquired through the "virtues." The logic of "natural selection" supported by illustrations from ethnography makes it unnecessary to question who they are and how they actually acquired their power.

On the other hand he fears and fights "plutocracy." This phenomenon is not for him the normal result of competition in the market, and hence a purely economic fact of life, but rather it is a moral issue. There are then "good" and "bad" businessmen.

He can then attack plutocracy by the epithets of jobbery, protectionism, imperialism, and also praise Rockefeller and Carnegie as good and great men. He can praise the end and criticize the means.

He can eulogise the "Forgotten Man," the small shopkeeper, the indebted farmer, who demanded political protection against the policies of the railroads, and he can defend the policies of the creditors, the banks and the corporations.

He does not fight against big capital for small property, but differentiates between "plutocracy," which is immoral and exploitative political capital based on "jobbery," and big capital as demanded for the tasks the nation faced, and beneficial because based upon achievement and leadership.

Sumner was a confused spokesman of the small-propertied middle class in its struggle against the rise of big monopolies, which he would nevertheless defend when it came to political interference with their policies.

But history had passed him by. So one of his students, who graduated from Yale in 1910, and hence knew a different America than did Sumner, has said: "This mind, immense and clumsy, with traces of the moralist, moved in his last years to regions uncomfortable for the mainly literary. . . . The book [*Folkways*] is a ghost. . . . Sumner himself seemed a little ghostly in his last years, a bulky stern figure moving in heavy robes of an academic procession or listening in the rear of a huge lecture hall while Richard Lull [Professor of Paleontology at Yale] chivalrously deplored the extinction of the sabre toothed tiger and the amiable little eohippus. . . . Indeed the old man seemed most at home in dim, high places of that museum where man is but one form of many that live and have lived, where beasts stuffed and strung on wires are ranged to show another age what once stirred and drew its breath in freedom."

26

The Limits of Social Science: Henry Adams' Quest for Order

Henry S. Kariel

Historians of ideas, no less than writers on American government, politics, or foreign affairs, have been fascinated by a quiet little resident of Washington during the Gilded Age who was reserved in his social acquaintances yet saw everything that was changing his city, his country, and the Western world. They find in Henry Adams (1838-1918) a historian, biographer, and essayist who exposed and pursued the most perplexing themes about the changing condition of modern man. They see that Adams, like most men of playful and inquiring mind, defies easy labeling. The attempt to use him as a guide into one broad area of knowledge often leads profitably into another, as here Henry Kariel's use of Adams as a guide to the boundaries of social science advantageously brings us closer to the humanities, to fundamental questions on the limits of man's freedom.

Though without a systematic philosophy, Adams in his diversity comes close to being America's first philosopher of history. He wrote a monumental history of the early republic from the mental outlook and high-toned parochialism of a great regional family that had made the nation its business since the Revolution. At the same time he inhabited the world of letters and of historical reflection that used centuries of Western man as its natural elements. His breadth of view forced him to search constantly for meaning in the nineteenth-century American experience. The search took him beyond even the great definitions of national character, given us earlier by Tocqueville, to the forces of science, especially steam, then transforming the Atlantic world. A witness to what his brother, Brooks Adams, called "the degradation of the democratic dogma," Henry Adams sought to explain why in his century the power of moral integrity and of the person was giving way to general social forces whirling in a mechanistic universe, why man was being replaced by the machine, faith by force, the virgin by the dynamo.

His suggestions are perhaps viewed too easily as those of the ultimate pessimist, finally acquiescent to universal chaos. For, as William H. Jordy tells us, Adams was able to distinguish people as the source of character, not of power, which has its sources elsewhere. In this respect he was a great moral historian. By virtue of his

American Political Science Review, 50 (June 1955), 1074-1089, 1092. Reprinted by permission of the author and The American Political Science Association. Footnotes have been omitted.

unremitting probing into the meaning of human existence amid vast impersonal natural forces, Adams moreover gave the humanist's answer to total despair. This answer indicates a triumph of human spirit, not because that spirit wins out over nature, but precisely because it retains its human integrity. It is the answer of the literary artist whose total work can grant him esthetic fulfillment, which science, faith, or scholarship do not give him. In this essay the author calls such esthetic fulfillment, in Adams' case, "the integrating of ambiguities." Adams' life suggests what John Dewey some decades later tells us about art as experience. Despite all the peculiar perversity or lack of "fit" to his life as he himself saw it, the reading of Henry Adams' works may well be the beginning of wisdom for students of nineteenth-century America.

For further reading: *William H. Jordy, *Henry Adams: Scientific Historian* (1952); J. C. Levenson, "Henry Adams," in Marcus Cunliffe and Robin Winks (eds.), *Pastmasters: Some Essays on American Historians* (1969), pp. 39-73; *Richard Hofstadter, *The Progressive Historians: Turner, Beard, Parrington* (1969); *Henry Adams, *The Education of Henry Adams* (1918).

Contemporary social scientists generally regard Henry Adams as a brilliant but erratic figure in the history of American thought. Their image of him is that of a gifted but unreliable and unscientific writer. Yet it is striking how, upon a reexamination of his approach to his world, there emerges a cluster of attitudes and preoccupations which clearly anticipate much of what is significant in the work of these social scientists themselves. The reason why Adams is not, however, regarded as a forerunner of present-day students of society is that he never kept himself from pushing his theories to conclusions. If those who share his scientific ideals must ultimately reach his conclusions, the limits of their science might be exposed by a reconsideration of his personal battle, of his peculiar pains, trials, and failures.

Anticipating familiar tendencies, Adams made a case for irrationalism insofar as he pleaded for the conversion of theory into action; for conservatism insofar as he supported the reduction of discords by a manipulative science of means; and for elitism insofar as he permitted the practitioners of empirical science to settle the social conflicts left open to debate by the traditional methods of politics and philosophy. But Adams' formulation of this case was more than merely prescient. It was so consistent, elaborate, and thoroughgoing—and yet so free from the burden of technical jargon—that intentions and goals unclear or concealed in modern social science may be illuminated by a retracing of his search for genuine knowledge of society, by a retracing of his tenacious effort to cut through an infinite succession of wholly baffling events.

It is apparent from both Adams' "study of twentieth-century multiplicity," the subtitle he gave his *Education,* and his prodigious correspondence that the environment in which he had found himself never ceased to baffle him. From the moment when, as a young man, he was mystified by the behavior of English diplomats to the time he constructed his final survey of the meaning of history, Adams was to remain impressed by the inexplicability of politics and society, of nature and culture, of life and death. He saw unmanageable, incoherent forces frustrating, twisting, and deflecting all human plans. Nothing ever, it seemed, turned out as schemed. British statesmanship during the American Civil War was "a pointless puzzle." That Senator Sumner and Secretary Hoar should become the victims of the Grant Administration was a meaningless fact. After a study of Secretary Seward, it was impossible to conclude which part of him "was the mask and which was the features." The political machinery and the moral standards supporting "an eternity of Grants, or even of Garfields or of Conklings or of Jay Goulds" were, for Adams, inconceivable. The panic of 1893 was beyond understanding, the cultural output of Paris at the turn of the century a chaos, Paris and London "fantastic," Garibaldi an inscrutable sphinx, the ruins of Rome "bewildering." Confronted by the fact that his sister was painfully dying, he could not help but conclude the senselessness of it all. Nature itself, in the form of Mont Blanc, "looked to him what it was—a chaos of anarchic and purposeless forces."

Once more [Adams wrote Charles Milnes Gaskell in 1907] I find myself pitchforked across the ocean into this inconceivable kettle of absurd humanity, and the only change is that I feel each time more bewildered than before by the fact of my own continued existence, which seems now to connect back with nothing. This world has no relation whatever with my world, and I go on living in dreams.

The universe, in its very foundations, was incomprehensible, profoundly meaningless and absurd. Where it had been possible for John Adams and John Quincy Adams—as it seemed to their great-grandson and grandson—to see the world whole, where they had really known the relations between experienced events to be perfectly natural and rational, Henry Adams saw these relations as nothing but subjective acts of will. Such acts, to be sure, did connect disconnected events; but the connections were not in the nature of things. They were artificially created by man, established not by reason but by convention or force. To anyone who would honestly look after extricating himself from personal prejudice and social habit, nothing but an infinite number of discrete, opaque facts existed. Behind them was the great void.

However Adams' nineteenth-century contemporaries tied up disparate particulars, whatever resolutions commended themselves to them, he was alienated from their law. "Outlawry," he affirmed, was his peculiar birthright. The existing formulas failed to account for the sequence of events, for the Grants, Garfields, Conklings, and Goulds. With such a sequence, Adams could not come to terms. He was unable to find the unifying terms either in or for his world. Life's tensions and tests, contingencies and mysteries, could not be subordinated to any significant end or purpose.

The alternatives for Adams—for anyone seeking to bear up after denying validity to all points of orientation—were to impose order in practice or to conquer disorder in theory. In his search for education, for an underlying natural law, in his attempt to effect a systematic reduction of variables to some operationally valid framework, Adams might have tried to add his will and his power to existing pressures. He might have acted and imposed order in practice. Yet to a large extent, either he closed the active road himself or the America of his day, constituted as it was, closed it for him. He was not, at any rate, to be the politician. If his concern was ultimately to be with the political order, as indeed it was, he gave little immediate indication of it. If he forever struggled for balance in practice, as he modestly did when, at past fifty, he "solemnly and painfully learned to ride the bicycle," he effectively covered this up by concentrating on the problem of balance in theory.

Haphazardly yet inflexibly, he set out to perceive a scheme in things which were apparently wholly devoid of scheme, to find reasons for behavior which seemed wholly random and irrational. His encyclopedic, tortuous quest was not only far less playful and idle than Adams managed to make it appear—it actually was desperately serious after the suicide of his wife, an event so irrational that it never did fit the plan of the *Education*—it was also far from superficial. Taking him into virtually all the disciplines of learning, including geology and paleontology, the search was to be lifelong. Adams tried everything but the laboratory experiment. Though always carefully rationed out, the energy and passion with which he proceeded would make it appear reasonable to speak of him as being driven. But his style and bearing alone indicate that after every interpretation of Adams as nothing but the frustrated actor, something remains. Adams and not some autonomous drive obviously did the directing. His constant awareness of what he was about makes it evident that he was thoroughly in control. And this fact alone should make it necessary to refrain from psychoanalysis or socio-analysis, to treat his ideas respectfully in and for themselves, to move economically within the circle of his beliefs.

I

What Adams consistently reached for, it should be clear, was "some great generalization which would finish one's clamor to be educated," some constitutive order basic to change, underlying history. He was plainly dismayed by the conception of history as the manifestation of individual actions to be artistically arranged by the historian. And unwilling to conceive of history as nothing but the capricious and indeterminate behavior of men, he hoped to grasp it as the interplay and the interaction of forces, forces which man himself might somehow discern and learn to master. This meant approaching history as something other than one thing happening after another *at random*. It meant finding a *necessary* sequence, necessary relations between events. To find such a plot, or such law, required that Adams disentangle himself from the play that was history. He had to gain, however fleetingly, a moment of insight, a point for perspective. He had to free himself from contingencies and the laws conventionally assumed to govern them, looking upon events from the outside, from some undetermined, freely posited vantage point. Assuming the characteristics of the free-floating intelligentsia made familiar by the sociology of knowledge, Adams expressly recognized the philosopher's need to place himself above history "as though he were a small God immortal and possibly omniscient."

From such an all-determining vantage point, he resolved to lay out a framework exposing history's fixed pattern, coinciding with it. He was to write, that he "had even published a dozen volumes of American history for no other purpose than to satisfy himself whether, by the severest process of stating, with the least possible comment, such facts as seemed sure, in such order as seemed rigorously consequent, he could fix . . . a necessary sequence of human movement.'' One result of this depersonalization, of the elimination of the subjective and the arbitrary, was the austerity and dryness of his nine-volume *History of the United States during the Administrations of Jefferson and Madison* (1889-91). There he wanted to let the facts, or the documents, speak for themselves, permitting them to reveal their natural order, their objective condition. And indeed he kept his comments repressed, checked himself from embellishing the record, made history as pure and positive as seemed possible.

Yet he fully knew that he could not succeed. Unquestionably, if the short span of history he had covered could be identified with certainty, if it could be positively known, the key to all that followed and preceded would be bared. But the attempt to achieve this by means of traditional historical scholarship was obviously senseless. Adams therefore pushed through to another realm of knowledge for a possible answer to the riddle of man's existence and history—its conception, its end, its very point. ''Satisfied that the sequence of men led to nothing and that the sequence of their society could lead no further, . . . he turned at last to the sequence of force. . . . '' To wrest an answer from the facts, he turned to the physical sciences, hoping that perhaps their unity ''would serve.'' He accepted, for analytical purposes, not only their specific discoveries—for which he has been soundly criticized—but, more crucially, their method and conventions of investigation.

Natural history, it seemed worth assuming, is governed by the same laws as human history. The physical universe and human society are systematically related. A substructure of forces refers to both; knowledge is basically one. There is a pattern in history just as there is in the stuff studied by the physical scientist. This pattern had to be discerned pure and simple, that is, without the subjective presuppositions which spoiled the social physics of Comte and his precursors. As Adams made clear in the undelivered presidential address he communicated to the American Historical Association in 1894, the challenge had been issued to the historian. It was now essential to go beyond mere analogies and to treat man as the physical scientist had been treating nature. The creation of a science of history, Adams wrote, was a most natural tendency of historical scholarship. Historians had to cooperate with the inevitable. ''Historians will not, and even if they would they can not, abandon the attempt. Science itself would admit its own failure if it admitted that man, the most important of all its subjects, could not be brought within its range.'' Historians, Adams wrote, were standing ''on the brink of a great generalization that would reduce all history under a law as clear as the laws which govern the material world.'' The hope for a ''self-evident, harmonious, and complete system'' emphatically existed. All that was needed was just one sudden inspiration, one corner turned. Sheer persistence and a lucky break—not genius—would pull it off. ''The law was certainly there, and as certainly was in places actually visible, to be touched and handled, as though it were a law of chemistry or physics.'' And if it should be discovered, ''if some new Darwin were to demonstrate the laws of historical evolution,'' historians, while necessarily coming into conflict with that part of the *status quo* for which there could unfortunately be no future, would attain power. Where at present they were deprived of direct access to centers of power or denied themselves the satisfaction of exercising it, they would finally reach its very core. They would be able to achieve control in the realm of practice. Reflective insight would become operative. Writing to Henry Osborn Taylor, Adams suggested in 1905 that "it will not need another century or half century to tip thought upside down. Law, in that case, would disappear as theory or *a priori* principle, and give place to force. Morality would become police." What has been the traditional philosophical quest for knowledge, the indispensable prerequisite for prudent action, would become a dispensable vocation. The body of knowledge concerning first principles being complete, the historical moment to cease philosophizing and to commence action would have arrived. Morality, *a priori* principles, would be justifiably enforced.

The method by which the "physicist-historian" might achieve control, the method which yielded Adams' own science of history, was (1) to disregard the view of history as an unbroken, undifferentiated continuum in time, as an even flow of "events," (2) to search for possible *natural,* self-evident breaks in the continuity of history, and (3) to examine the forces in the periods between the breaks. Each of these periods—or phases, as Adams called them—would constitute some sort of equilibrium, more or less stable, which would always be qualitatively modified by succeeding periods. The historian's concern would be with the intensity and potency of the forces composing the respective equilibriums. Having taken account of the intensity of force, assigning values to it, he could engage in comparative analysis and possibly make predictions.

In a generally guarded tone, Adams found it useful to posit the existence of four intelligible, discontinuous periods, and from these he projected a fifth. The first was instinctual; the second, characterized by religious fetishism (beginning some 90,000 years ago and ending in 1600); the third, mechanical (1600-1870); and the last, electrical (1870-1917). He had confidence only in the relative accuracy of the mechanical phase, one he therefore used as base. It was from this base that he consequently projected. Since he had to delimit *some* period, he had to risk the misleading impression created by the specificity of dates. Whatever the impression, however, he was always willing to take or to leave a decade, knowing that this would scarcely affect the ultimate outcome very much.

Projection became possible the moment he was struck by two things: the critical breaks between periods came ever closer together and, in every new period, human energy had increasingly dissipated. This led him to conclude (1) that the dates of equilibrium change are set by a law of acceleration, specifically the law of inverse squares, and (2) that social and intellectual energy is in an ever-accelerating state of disintegration and leveling out—not in fine gradations but in jumps. It was the law of inverse squares which led him to extrapolate, and talk about, an ethereal period. If the base period were really correct, the ethereal one, as he called it, would last from 1917 to 1921, the year in which man, unable to hold off the force of nature, would finally lose control. As the Virgin was the symbol for the age of religious fetishism, as the dynamo was the symbol for that of electricity, so radium symbolized this last phase of man. Its ethereal nature made discussion of it necessarily vague, though Adams was never inhibited about characterizing a present which implied a future:

The play of thought for thought's sake had mostly ceased. The throb of fifty or a hundred million steam horse-power, doubling every ten years, and already more despotic than all the horses that ever lived, and all the riders they ever carried, drowned rhyme and reason. No one was to blame, for all were equally servants of the power, and worked merely to increase it. . . .

Modern politics, is, at bottom, a struggle not of men but of forces. The men become every year more and more creatures of force, massed about central power-houses. The conflict is no longer between the men, but between the motors that drive the men, and the men tend to succumb to their own motive forces.

Power leaped from every atom, and enough of it to supply the stellar universe showed itself running to waste at every pore of matter. Man could not longer hold it off. Forces grasped his wrists and flung him about as though he had hold of a live wire or a runaway automobile. . . .

These things he wrote in the *Education*. But already three years before he had told his brother Brooks that it was his belief "that science is to wreck us, and that we are like monkeys monkeying with a loaded shell. . . . It is mathematically certain to me that another thirty years of energy-development at the rate of the last century, must reach an *impasse*."

The conclusions of the physical sciences of Adams' day proved to be all too easy to use for support and extension of his own insight. Adams welcomed Lord Kelvin's second law of thermodynamics less as scientific hypothesis than as final truth. Here was an authoritative, handy formulation stating the universality of entropy. The fact that man, like nature, would come to a dead end, both being subject to the same law, Adams was wholly ready to accept, solicitously noting that man, whose mass was strikingly less great than nature's, would meet annihilation first.

In responding to this formula uncritically, he surely betrayed his temper. Yet an inner check kept the betrayal from being complete. However dogmatic he could sound when making predictions, with whatever exactitude and certainty he might make his repeated announcements of impending catastrophe, he actually accepted no law of physics as conclusive. He never quit the great debate, never let up reviewing the literature of science. On the contrary, he doggedly continued his search for "a spool on which to wind the thread of history without breaking it," his search for some object which was more than mere plaything, hypothesis, or force among forces.

To the tired student, the idea that he must give it up seemed sheer senility. As long as he could whisper, he would go on as he had begun, bluntly refusing to meet his creator with the admission that the creation had taught him nothing except that the square of the hypotenuse of a right-angled triangle might for convenience be taken as equal to something else.

Knowing his own theory provided no answer—that his answers were not generated by his science—he kept raising his question of what might account for man's behavior, of what might give it meaning. And for Adams, there was to be no conclusive victory over the facts of history. While the extent of his discernment has been remarkable enough to all students of his work, the world did remain mysterious, irreducible to any set of symbols. Order might be the dream of man, but chaos persisted as the law of nature. The sequence of history, of society, of men, had led to nothing; the relation of cause and effect was artificial; the sequence of thought was unintelligible. There was to be no formula. Adams laid claim to no meaning. He offered no conclusion, either to philosopher or ruler.

. . . in the chaotic and unintelligible condition in which I found–and left–the field of knowledge which is called History, I became overpoweringly conscious that any further pretence on my part of acting as instructor would be something worse than humbug. . . . As History stands, it is a sort of Chinese Play, without end and without lesson.

History remained "a tangled skein that one may take up at any point, and break when one has unravelled enough. . . . " The historian, it turned out, was purely arbitrary. What end or purpose might be discerned in history, the historian had supplied it. History, beyond all appearance, had no goal or purpose. All Adams could see, at the end, was endless flux and change—no necessary development.

Ultimate reality was to him nothing but motion, nothing but force and its intensity. Consequently no perceived particulars could be related to anything but one another—a conclusion which even physical science was compelled to reach. If motion is all, if everything is relative, there can be no durable truth—and Adams knew it—"when he came to ask himself what he truly thought, he felt he had no Faith. . . . " For a while, he said, he believed in the truth of Darwinism. But he was certain "that whenever the next new hobby should be brought out, he should surely drop off from Darwinism like a monkey from a perch. . . . " He knew "that the idea of one Form, Law, Order, or Sequence had no more value for him than the idea of none; that what he valued most was Motion, and what attracted his mind was Change." And he added that he "was the first in an infinite series to discover and admit to himself that he really did not care whether truth was, or was not, true." In the absence of truth, there could be no success, for there would be nothing to measure it by. In the absence of any point of orientation, there could only be the aimless pursuit—"the pursuit of ignorance in silence" which had "led the weary pilgrim into such mountains of ignorance that he could no longer see any path whatever, and could not even understand a signpost." There was, indeed, no ground for support, no point from which to survey self or world. One might search for a reliable order, but Adams had foreknowledge of the necessary defeat.

II

To support Henry Adams' intellectual position, truly to embrace it, is to block all alternatives, to absolute, intensely personal despair. To believe, without compromise, without qualification, (1) that, in the final analysis, everything about man, about society, about history, about the universe itself, everything which man himself has not fabricated, is totally mysterious, (2) that, again in the final analysis, there is no point to anything, that nothing has intrinsic significance, that nothing is coherent except that which man himself has forced to cohere, (3) that man is but a force—a self-generating, self-activating, self-replenishing one—in a universe of forces, that all is ultimately force, and (4) that no particular event, no discrete thing, is autonomous but, when truly understood, related to some substructure of forces—to value and act on this combination of propositions is to permit the human enterprise to become literally unbearable.

The despair of this position has always invited attempts to bear up by removing the conflict between the self and the environment, to gain direct, immediate knowledge of the nature of things, to dispense with the ambiguities of all forms of mediation—basically those of language. It is revealing to note to what extent Adams himself edged toward the various forms assumed by man's desperate effort to reach spiritual truth directly, to bridge the gap between the self and the universe. Thus he significantly played with self-annihilation, making overtures to both total quietism and unreserved activism.

Those who have covered Adams' trail, his friends, critics, and biographers, have unearthed no record whatever of suicidal thoughts he might have entertained. But his abiding "hunger for annihilation," his conscientious effort to deny himself, has been fully evident. "I have deliberately and systematically effaced myself," he wrote Brooks in 1895, "even in my own history." He managed to keep himself concealed again and again—publishing anonymously, resisting every portrait photographer, unwilling "to talk or write or appear," refusing to address the American Historical Association, turning away from the honorary degree Harvard offered to bestow upon him, contriving to objectify himself by keeping the first person singular out of the account of his life.

His same inability to come to terms with himself, his same inability to see the self as essentially and ultimately meaningful, found expression in an approval of a straightforward activism which makes it perfectly explicable that Adams conceived of mindless selfishness as "the only spring of success," and confessed, "I like best Bergson's frank surrender to the superiority of Instinct over Intellect. You know how I have preached that principle, and how I have studied the facts of it. In fact I wrote once a whole volume . . . in order to recall how Education may be shown to consist in following the intuitions of instinct." It was in one of the most impressive passages of this volume that Adams paid his respect to the education of his grandfather. On one summer morning, he recalled, the old President had done with unreasoning, silent display of authority what, of necessity, *had* to be done—taken the rebellious Henry to school, and "without a word." This inclination, an admittedly permanent one, to appreciate that silent strength and mastery which needs no apologetic other than its massive effectiveness, which justifies itself by virtue of its sheer potency, is a natural enough conclusion from Adams' premises. Assuming that none of the particular things within human experience can have meaning, he might nonetheless have conceived of the undifferentiated whole as meaningful. But to accept as meaningful only the universe in its awful entirety is to deprive oneself of any ground for making distinctions and discriminations, for caring about parts and articulations. Knowledge of such a universe must remain inexpressible, beyond symbolization, language, discourse. It is not surprising, therefore, that if reflection on the universe as well as on history is not enough to teach man anything-

—permitting him only to make what he will or to enjoy his nonsensical tautologies—all he can do, if act he must, is to act without reflection, without thought. While thoughtful action may still seem possible in the absence of a meaningful cosmos, it must lack a basis beyond the subjectivity of individuals, becoming altogether optional. Dependent on utility and efficiency, thought must appear either as a variety of action, as mere instrument for domination, or else as wasteful check on action and expansiveness. . . .

. . . When reason is useless, when thought merely travels "round and round," when certain knowledge is ever contradicted, one is driven to the "study of . . . ignorance in silence," revering St. Francis' way of repudiating "the thread spun by the human spider" as "the most satisfactory—or sufficient—ever offered." When all relations between facts are hypothetical, nothing can be affirmed with certainty: "The student had nothing to say. For him, all opinion founded on fact must be error, because the facts can never be complete, and their relations must be always infinite." Realizing "he could teach his students nothing"—that is, nothing truly educating them—"the greatest good he could do them was to hold his tongue." There being no final science of history, it became necessary to stress, as Adams did, that "silence next to good temper was the mark of sense." "The situation seems to call for no opinion," he wrote in "The Tendency of History," "unless we have some scientific theory to offer. . . ." Either a finished theory—or nothing.

III

. . . His self-depreciation was never quite complete. His quietism was as constantly restrained as his activism. His pursuit of ignorance in silence was after all what he had reluctantly called it: his "final *profession*." He had always fully responded to the example provided by Henry James in a letter he addressed to Adams in 1914:

> Of course *we are lone survivors, of course the past that was our lives is at the bottom of an abyss–if the abyss* has *any bottom; of course, too, there's no use talking unless one particularly* wants *to. But . . . one* can, *strange to say, still want to–or at least can behave as if one did. Behold me therefore so behaving–and apparently capable of continuing to do so. I still find my consciousness interesting–under* cultivation *of the interest. Cultivate it* with *me, dear Henry. . . . You see I still, in presence of life (or of what you deny to be such,) have reactions–as many as possible–and the book I sent you is a proof of them. It's, I suppose, because I am that queer monster, the artist, an obstinate finality, an inexhaustible sensibility. Hence the reactions–appearances, memories, many things, go on playing upon it with consequences that I note. . . .*

Undeniably, Adams did act on the suggestion that, although the world is black, although all is pointless, one can yet want to go on, keep talking, cultivate interests, react, and take note. While he was certain that there were no certainties, that therefore all was absurd, he not only kept on looking, for he was an insatiable traveler, but also kept on professing, articulating, writing. He never ceased taking part in the perennial human debate and thus never completed his alienation from society, hanging on as its diffident participant while ever departing from it.

This unresolved tension between engagement and disengagement persisted. To maintain it, Adams invariably avoided giving his convictions secular power. He consequently communicated no sense of commitment to any dogma, remaining exasperatingly fuzzy and inconclusive to every generation of readers of the *Education*. He notably failed to *argue* any position to its terminus, aware that in an America enjoying its gilded age no opponents could be enlisted in systematic debate. There was, he lamented, no audience: "No one cares." In an America pervaded, as Louis Hartz has shown, by an irritatingly effective, all-corrosive liberalism, Adams was unable to come to the point and challenge the national creed head-on. It was his very indirectness, supported by the doctrine that there were no certainties, that kept him from feeling free either to create his own truth or, by a shock of recognition, to intuit some specific truth immanent in history. Thus he rejected the Nietzschean view that the artist-historian should impose on his material and simply fabricate his myth no less than the Hegelian one that History is permeated by Spirit moving in a determinable way. He never arbitrarily filled the nothing he encountered: he patented no Dialectic, identified no True Leader, held no brief for Reason manifest, designated no Elite, Party, or Race. That he institutionalized no insight, translated no transcendental truth into secular reality, imposed no law of science, is worth emphasizing for it distinguishes his effort from historicism such as that of Marx and Engels. Whatever law there seemed to be, whatever science appeared to be true, for Adams it required infinite qualification. Thus he found it easy to call his "Rule of Phase" his last plaything, "not meant to be taken too seriously"; he noted he was a Darwinian "for fun"; he regarded his "Letter to American Teachers of History" as a "fable," as a "form of humor." And by holding that the relation between facts must be always infinite, he put every relation between facts, every correlation, in doubt—making all statements equivocal, leaving all histories ambiguous, inverting every formulation until it affirmed its opposite, and then denying that too. His assertion that "no one means all he says, and yet very few say all they mean, for words are slippery and thought is viscous" can well stand as his final disclaimer.

To see Adams employ this process of integrating ambiguities is to see the artist at work. The artist can provide a dimension for understanding politics and society whenever he disciplines his implacable urge to negate the world, whenever he harnesses the impulse which makes him shatter, as André Malraux has argued, the forms he has inherited. In qualifying and requalifying whatever did find expression, whatever did become manifest, Adams expressed himself ironically, elliptically, artistically. It is as artist that he used symbols pointing at both the obvious and the concealed. By plausibly relating the concealed to the obvious, he denied what is affirmed, cancelled what is credited. He thus helped make the unbelievable believable, the impertinent pertinent, the unconventional conventional. To carry this off, the artist must be playful. He must be entertainingly, dramatically serious in order to lead man into the dark caverns of experience—caverns he lights up, illuminating what without the light touch would be unbearable. And yet he will keep men from embracing and fighting for the very truth he has revealed, committed as he is to mock that too. At his finest, which is also at his most anti-social, he cannot help but reveal that whatever implausibility his exploration has made plausible it too is streaked and freakish, not to be taken in earnest, something already too comfortable to justify human discomfort, too domestic to merit sacrifice.

The result of the artist's elliptical method—if it is successful—is to provide a fuller view of any specific situation, to broaden perceptions, enhance imaginative sympathies, heighten and refine consciousness. . . . Keeping contradictions in suspense, the artist projects possibilities which it is unconventional to consider. Taking stock for individuals too absorbed in their immediate environment, too captivated by present urgencies, the artist will expose their usual business and politics as incomplete ventures, as meager preoccupations, as flat and stale and unpromising. Developing new analogies and utopias, he may detect riches men fail to appreciate. And pointing to the concrete sources of vitality and impotence which tend to escape extremists—activists too much in touch and quietists too much out of touch—he may not only emancipate men from the dictates of the past but also provide a basis for mediation and reconciliation. Sensitive to continuities he may chasten those who are merely expansive and fitful. He may make it possible for men to reorder and stabilize their existence, in the words of Herbert J. Muller, "by systematically complicating all issues, stressing the defects and the excesses of all values, insisting on tension, imbalance, uncertainty, and contradiction . . . by ironically qualifying the great triumphs and reverently qualifying the great failures. . . ."

To do this is to deprive any particular era or generation of its balance and success. By proclaiming himself to be a failure—by so labelling all of his impressive achievements—Adams outwitted expectations and implied that no one had really encountered success, that his contemporaries were far from triumphant, that it was rash to consider the time of his lifespan as one of equilibrium and fulfillment for American politics and statesmanship. In placing in a wider context the manners and formulas of an America which had yet to come of age, he perceived characteristics to which his compatriots were blind. He saw complexities where others saw simplicities, challenging the prevailing definition of practicality and efficiency, the formula of progress, the belief in inevitable victory, the faith in the necessary destiny of American democracy.

By creating the complicating perspectives which placed American experience in a new light, by establishing new relationships, Adams redeemed a scientific failure which was unmitigated and genuine. For he offered a statement—given actuality in the very way he shaped his life—which is at once elegant and humanistic. Seemingly denying everything, he still affirmed good form—including a deep responsibility to the integrity of the philosophical and scholarly quest. In implying that if men must waste their resources and fail it is imperative that they do so with dignity, he reveals his values—values which the assumptions of his science had to discredit. His immense "failure"—and now the word must be put in quotes—is significant: for he was successfully sustained not by his scientific conclusions but by his artistic commitment. Indeed, he fought heroically: recognizing the necessity of defeat he remained intellectually upright, unhumiliated by nature. Yet it is obvious that the way Adams redeemed his failure as scientist could not lead him to the only education, the only success, he valued—success in formulating a model for comprehending society, in making society the subject of the law.

IV

Whether the task is to affect historical events or to gain understanding of them, Adams offered two methods, one by explicit statement, the other by the way he himself proceeded. Events may be dealt with either by the physicist-historian or else by the artist, either by those who master the forces of society or those for whom every view, every conclusion, is too provincial, too specific, too narrow. Characteristically, Adams jeopardized the validity of both methods. Thus he had held not only that scientific, positive history led to nothing but also that art, as a critical, negativist enterprise, had its limits no less: "The mania for handling all the sides of every question, looking into every window, and opening every door, was, as Bluebeard judiciously pointed out to his wives, fatal to their practical usefulness in society." Yet Adams never followed up his doubt. He never openly stated that neither of his alternative approaches makes it possible to deal with the events of this world in a reasonable manner, that is, by persuading men in terms of a rationally held and defended standard, one which is on the one hand admittedly less final than a Law of History but on the other immune to the irresponsible relativism implicit in the artistic method, a standard exposed to the impact of debate but beyond the endless mockery of irony. Only by acknowledging the relevance of such standards, of such political theory, is it possible (1) to conceive of "an eternity of Grants, or even of Garfields or Conklins or Jay Goulds" and, more importantly, (2) to deal with them by political, non-violent means. In the face of every imperfect, chaotic array of politicians, in the face of the innumerable gradations of human error, Adams counseled either control of conflicting social forces in terms of a determinate, absolute law or else suspension of all articulation. Thus it was easy for him to write, for example, that he saw "no hope for the government [the McKinley Administration] short of sweeping it out of existence." Man had to impose forcefully upon politics or else decline to take it seriously. . . .

. . . He could scarcely have been pleased by the prospect of a control of social forces so total that men would find themselves living in a realm in which spontaneity and necessity were indistinguishable. If, however, he entertained doubts about all prospects, he must have doubted the inevitability of the potential triumph of social science. Yet the only basis for such doubt is the belief in the possibility of appealing to an incommensurable human quality, the faith in the continuing possibility of using language to educate and enlighten men, the expectation that they will tend to act rightly once they are made aware of what they do, once they are led to see the tension between the real and the ideal, once the artist has raised the implications of their actions to a level of consciousness which makes them feel uncomfortable and rebellious. Adams' resignation was never so complete as to cause him to repudiate this faith or shirk the work it demands. For he had emphatically seen it as his duty "to fit young men, in universities or elsewhere, to be men of the world, equipped for any emergency. . . ." If despite all his digressions he ultimately clarified the failure of positivist science and negativist art to provide a sufficient grounding for dependable knowledge of man and society, he may have equipped the student better than he had reason to hope.

Part V
Ideas in the Progressive Era

27
The Genteel Tradition in American Philosophy

George Santayana

Complete philosophical systems or even full histories of philosophical thought do not abound in America. One of the few largescale histories is *The Life of Reason* (1905-6), written by George Santayana (1863-1952) toward the end of his forty years' residence in Boston and Harvard University. This was a kind of prelude to the construction of his own philosophical system, which appeared as *The Realms of Being* (1927-40) after he turned to England and Europe for the last forty years of his life. Within the context of American thought, one can hold that there is some irony in Santayana's accomplishments. His mind was "un-American" in the sense that it rejected emotion and intuition as these had earlier been used here in academic Scottish common-sense philosophy. His premises were naturalistic and materialist; they lay outside the American traditions of Calvinism or Transcendentalism. His own esthetic philosophy led systematically through the disciplined life of reason from human desires to ideal concepts of truth, goodness, and beauty. Yet he was quite the native son in his understanding of what makes Americans tick. His portraits of the American mind, brilliantly set forth in precise and elegant language in this essay and in his *Character and Opinion in the United States* (1920), rank with the insights left us by Tocqueville, Lord Bryce, and D. W. Brogan.

Or it can also be held that Santayana's philosophy is permeated with his American experience. Herbert W. Schneider contends that there is much of "the ultimate Puritan" in the austerity of Santayana's later works, and so much naturalistic metaphysics that they "necessarily betray" their natural origin in America. Morton White brings the question of Santayana's American identity to focus upon a contrast between Emerson and Santayana. For White, Emerson is "the sage of American idealism who had a poetic fancy and a gift for observation and epigram," while Santayana is "the similarly endowed sage of American materialism" All agree that the American experience of this Spanish-born philosopher is an indispensable consideration for the student of ideas. Along with William James, whose philosophy he admired because it broke the genteel

Reprinted by permission of J. M. Dent & Sons, Ltd., from George Santayana, *The Winds of Doctrine* (1913). This essay is an address delivered before the Philosophical Union of the University of California, August 25, 1911.

tradition, and with Josiah Royce, whose idealism he disputed, Santayana was a master craftsman in the Golden Age of Harvard philosophy.

For further reading: *George Santayana, *Character and Opinion in the United States* (1920); John Dewey, "The Development of American Pragmatism," *Studies in the History of Ideas*, 2 (1925), 353-377, reprinted in *David Van Tassell (ed.), *American Thought in the Twentieth Century* (1967), pp. 9-28; *Morton White, *Science and Sentiment in America* (1972), chap. 10; *Henry F. May, *The End of American Innocence* (1959), pp. 9-19.

LADIES AND GENTLEMEN,—The privilege of addressing you to-day is very welcome to me, not merely for the honour of it, which is great, nor for the pleasure of travel, which are many, when it is California that one is visiting for the first time, but also because theire is something I have long wanted to say which this occasion seems particularly favourable for saying. America is still a young country, and this part of it is especially so; and it would have been nothing extraordinary if, in this young country, material preoccupations had altogether absorbed people's minds, and they had been too much engrossed in living to reflect upon life, or to have any philosophy. The opposite, however, is the case. Not only have you already found time to philosophise in California, as your society proves, but the eastern colonists from the very beginning were a sophisticated race. As much as in clearing the land and fighting the Indians they were occupied, as they expressed it, in wrestling with the Lord. The country was new, but the race was tried, chastened, and full of solemn memories. It was an old wine in new bottles; and America did not have to wait for its present universities, with their departments of academic philosophy, in order to possess a living philosophy—to have a distinct vision of the universe and definite convictions about human destiny.

Now this situation is a singular and remarkable one, and has many consequences, not all of which are equally fortunate. America is a young country with an old mentality: it has enjoyed the advantages of a child carefully brought up and thoroughly indoctrinated; it has been a wise child. But a wise child, an old head on young shoulders, always has a comic and an unpromising side. The wisdom is a little thin and verbal, not aware of its full meaning and grounds; and physical and emotional growth may be stunted by it, or even deranged. Or when the child is too vigorous for that, he will develop a fresh mentality of his own, out of his observations and actual instincts; and this fresh mentality will interfere with the traditional mentality, and tend to reduce it to something perfunctory, conventional, and perhaps secretly despised. A philosophy is not genuine unless it inspires and expresses the life of those who cherish it. I do not think the hereditary philosophy of America has done much to atrophy the natural activities of the inhabitants; the wise child has not missed the joys of youth or of manhood; but what has happened is that the hereditary philosophy has grown stale, and that the academic philosophy afterwards developed has caught the stale odour from it. America is not simply, as I said a moment ago, a young country with an old mentality: it is a country with two mentalities, one a survival of the beliefs and standards of the fathers, the other an expression of the instincts, practice, and discoveries of the younger generations. In all the higher things of the mind—in religion, in literature, in the moral emotions—it is the hereditary spirit that still prevails, so much so that Mr. Bernard Shaw finds that America is a hundred years behind the times. The truth is that one-half of the American mind, that not occupied intensely in practical affairs, has remained, I will not say high-and-dry, but slightly becalmed; it has floated gently in the back-water, while, alongside, in invention and industry and social organization, the other half of the mind was leaping down a sort of Niagara Rapids. This division may be found symbolised in American architecture: a neat reproduction of the colonial mansion—with some modern comforts introduced surreptitiously—stands beside the sky-scraper. The American Will inhabits the sky-scraper; The American Intellect inhabits the colonial mansion. The one is the sphere of the American man; the other, at least predominantly, of the American woman. The one is all aggressive enterprise; the other is all genteel tradition.

Now, with your permission, I should like to analyse more fully how this interesting situation has arisen, how it is qualified, and whither it tends. And in the first place we should remember what, precisely, that philosophy was which the first settlers brought with them into the country. In strictness there was more than one; but we may confine our attention to what I will call Calvinism, since it is on this that the current academic philosophy has been grafted. I do not mean exactly the Calvinism of Calvin, or even of Jonathan Edwards; for in their systems there was much that was not pure philosophy, but rather faith in the externals and history of revelation. Jewish and Christian revelation was interpreted by these men, however, in the spirit of a particular philosophy, which might have arisen under any sky, and been associated with any other religion as well as with Protestant Christianity. In fact, the philosophical principle of Calvinism appears also in the Koran, in Spinoza, and in Cardinal Newman; and persons with no very distinctive Christian belief, like Carlyle or like Professor Royce, may be nevertheless, philosophically, perfect Calvinists. Calvinism, taken in this sense, is an expression of the agonised conscience. It is a view of the world which an agonised conscience readily embraces, if it takes itself seriously, as, being agonised, of course it must. Calvinism, essentially, asserts three things: that sin exists, that sin is punished, and that it is beautiful that sin should exist to be punished. The heart of the Calvinist is therefore divided between tragic concern at his own miserable condition, and tragic exultation about the universe at large. He oscillates between a profound abasement and a paradoxical elation of the spirit. To be a Calvinist philosophically is to feel a fierce pleasure in the existence of misery, especially of one's own, in that this misery seems to manifest the fact that the Absolute is irresponsible or infinite or holy. Human nature, it feels, is totally depraved: to have the instincts and motives that we necessarily have is a great scandal, and we must suffer for it; but that scandal is requisite, since otherwise the serious importance of being as we ought to be would not have been vindicated.

To those of us who have not an agonised conscience this system may seem fantastic and even unintelligible; yet it is logically and intently thought out from its emotional premises. It can take permanent possession of a deep mind here and there, and under certain conditions it can become epidemic. Imagine, for instance, a small nation with an intense vitality, but on the verge of ruin, ecstatic and distressful, having a strict and minute code of laws, that paints life in sharp and violent chiaroscuro, all pure righteousness and black abominations, and exaggerating the consequences of both perhaps to infinity. Such a people were the Jews after the exile, and again the early Protestants. If such a people is philosophical at all, it will not improbably be Calvinistic. Even in the early American communities many of these conditions were fulfilled. The nation was small and isolated; it lived under pressure and constant trial; it was acquainted with but a small range of goods and evils. Vigilance over conduct and an absolute demand for personal integrity were not merely traditional things, but things that practical sages, like Franklin and Washington, recommended to their countrymen, because they were virtues that justified themselves visibly by their fruits. But soon these happy results themselves helped to relax the pressure of external circumstances, and indirectly the pressure of the agonised conscience within. The nation became numerous; it ceased to be either ecstatic or distressful; the high social morality which on the whole it preserved took another colour; people remained honest and helpful out of good sense and good will rather than out of scrupulous adherence to any fixed principles. They retained their instinct for order, and often created order with surprising quickness; but the sanctity of law, to be obeyed for its own sake, began to escape them; it seemed too unpractical a notion, and not quite serious. In fact, the second and native-born American mentality began to take shape. The sense of sin totally evaporated. Nature, in the words of Emerson, was all beauty and commodity; and while operating on it laboriously, and drawing quick returns, the American began to drink in inspiration from it aesthetically. At the same time, in so broad a continent, he had elbow-room. His neighbours helped more than they hindered him; he wished their number to increase. Good will became the great American virtue; and a passion arose for counting heads, and square miles, and cubic feet, and minutes saved—as if there had been anything to save them for. How strange to the American now that saying of Jonathan Edwards, that men are naturally God's enemies! Yet that is an axiom to any intelligent Calvinist, though the words he uses may be different. If you told the modern American that he is totally depraved, he would think you were joking, as he himself usually is. He is convinced that he always has been, and always will be, victorious and blameless.

Calvinism thus lost its basis in American life. Some emotional natures, indeed, reverted in their religious revivals or private searchings of heart to the sources of the tradition; for any of the radical points of view in philosophy may cease to be prevalent, but none can cease to be possible. Other natures, more sensitive to the moral and literary influences of the world, preferred to abandon parts of their philosophy, hoping thus to reduce the distance which should separate the remainder from real life.

Meantime, if anybody arose with a special sensibility or a technical genius, he was in great straits; not being fed sufficiently by the world, he was driven in upon his own resources. The three American writers whose personal endowment was perhaps the finest—Poe, Hawthorne, and Emerson—had all a certain starved and abstract quality. They coult not retail the genteel tradition; they were too keen, too perceptive, and too independent for that. But life offered them little digestible material, nor were they naturally voracious. They were fastidious, and under the circumstances they were starved. Emerson, to be sure, fed on books. There was a great catholicity in his reading; and he showed a fine tact in his comments, and in his way of appropriating what he read. But he read transcendentally, not historically, to learn what he himself felt, not what others might have felt before him. And to feed on books, for a philosopher or a poet, is still to starve. Books can help him to acquire form, or to avoid pitfalls; they cannot supply him with substance, if he is to have any. Therefore the genius of Poe and Hawthorne, and even of Emerson, was employed on a sort of inner play, or digestion of vacancy. It was a refined labour, but it was in danger of being morbid, or tinkling, or self-indulgent. It was a play of intra-mental rhymes. Their mind was like an old music-box, full of tender echoes and quaint fancies. These fancies expressed their personal genius sincerely, as dreams may; but they were arbitrary fancies in comparison with what a real observer would have said in the premises. Their manner, in a word, was subjective. In their own persons they escaped the mediocrity of the genteel tradition, but they supplied nothing to supplant it in other minds.

The churches, likewise, although they modified their spirit, had no philosophy to offer save a new emphasis on parts of what Calvinism contained. The theology of Calvin, we must remember, had much in it besides philosophical Calvinism. A Christian tenderness, and a hope of grace for the individual, came to mitigate its sardonic optimism; and it was these evangelical elements that the Calvinistic churches now emphasised, seldom and with blushes referring to hell-fire or infant damnation. Yet philosophic Calvinism, with a theory of life that would perfectly justify hell-fire and infant damnation if they happened to exist, still dominates the traditional metaphysics. It is an ingredient, and the decisive ingredient, in what calls itself idealism. But in order to see just what part Calvinism plays in current idealism, it will be necessary to distinguish the other chief element in that complex system, namely, transcendentalism.

Transcendentalism is the philosophy which the romantic era produced in Germany, and independently, I believe, in America also. Transcendentalism proper, like romanticism, is not any particular set of dogmas about what things exist; it is not a system of the universe regarded as a fact, or as a collection of facts. It is a method, a point of view, from which any world, no matter what it might contain, could be approached by a self-conscious observer. Transcendentalism is systematic subjectivism. It studies the perspectives of knowledge as they radiate from the self; it is a plan of those avenues of inference by which our ideas of things must be reached, if they are to afford any systematic or distant vistas. In other words, transcendentalism is the critical logic of science. Knowledge, it says, has a station, as in a watchtower; it is always seated here and now, in the self of the moment. The past and the future, things inferred and things conceived, lie around it, painted as upon a panorama. They cannot be lighted up save by some centrifugal ray of attention and present interest, by some active operation of the mind.

This is hardly the occasion for developing or explaining this delicate insight; suffice it to say, lest you should think later that I disparage transcendentalism, that as a method I regard it as correct and, when once suggested, unforgettable. I regard it as the chief contribution made in modern times to speculation. But it is a method only, an attitude we may always assume if we like and that will always be legitimate. It is no answer, and involves no particular answer, to the question: What exists; in what order is what exists produced; what is to exist in the future? This question must be answered by observing the object, and tracing humbly the movement of the object. It cannot be answered at all by harping on the fact that this object, if discovered, must be discovered by somebody, and by somebody who has an interest in discovering it. Yet the Germans who first gained the full transcendental insight were romantic people; they were more or less frankly poets; they were colossal egotists, and wished to make not only their own knowledge but the whole universe centre about themselves. And full as they were of their romantic isolation and romantic liberty, it occurred to them to imagine that all reality might be a transcendental self and a romantic dreamer like themselves; nay, that it might be just their own transcendental self and their own romantic dreams extended indefinitely. Transcendental logic, the method of discovery for the mind, was to become also the method of evolution in nature and history. Transcendental method, so abused, produced transcendental myth. A conscientious critique of knowledge was turned into a sham system of nature. We must therefore distinguish sharply the transcendental grammar of the intellect, which is significant and potentially correct, from the various transcendental systems of the universe, which are chimeras.

In both its parts, however, transcendentalism had much to recommend it to American philosophers, for the transcendental method appealed to the individualistic and revolutionary temper of their youth, while transcendental myths enabled them to find a new status for their inherited theology, and to give what parts of it they cared to preserve some semblance of philosophical backing. This last was the use to which the transcendental method was put by Kant himself, who first brought it into vogue, before the terrible weapon had got out of hand, and become the instrument of pure romanticism. Kant came, he himself said, to remove knowledge in order to make room for faith, which in his case meant faith in Calvinism. In other words, he applied the transcendental method to matters of fact, reducing them thereby to human ideas, in order to give to the Calvinistic postulates of conscience a metaphysical validity. For Kant had a genteel tradition of his own, which he wished to remove to a place of safety, feeling that the empirical world had become too hot for it; and this place of safety was the region of transcendental myth.

I need hardly say how perfectly this expedient suited the needs of philosophers in America, and it is no accident if the influence of Kant soon became dominant here. To embrace this philosophy was regarded as a sign of profound metaphysical insight, although the most mediocre minds found no difficulty in embracing it. In truth it was a sign of having been brought up in the genteel tradition, of feeling it weak, and of wishing to save it.

But the transcendental method, in its way, was also sympathetic to the American mind. It embodied, in a radical form, the spirit of Protestantism as distinguished from its inherited doctrines; it was autonomous, undismayed, calmly revolutionary; it felt that Will was deeper than Intellect; it focussed everything here and now, and asked all things to show their credentials at the bar of the young self, and to prove their value for this latest born moment. These things are truly American; they would be characteristic of any young society with a keen and discursive intelligence, and they are strikingly exemplified in the thought and in the person of Emerson. They constitute what he called self-trust. Self-trust, like other transcendental attitudes, may be expressed in metaphysical fables. The romantic spirit may imagine itself to be an absolute force, evoking and moulding the plastic world to express its varying moods. But for a pioneer who is actually a world-builder this metaphysical illusion has a partial warrant in historical fact; far more warrant than it could boast of in the fixed and articulated society of Europe, among the moonstruck rebels and sulking poets of the romantic era. Emerson was a shrewd Yankee, by instinct on the winning side; he was a cheery, child-like soul, impervious to the evidence of evil, as of everything that it did not suit his transcendental individuality to appreciate or to notice. More, perhaps, than anybody that has ever lived, he practised the transcendental method in all its purity. He had no system. He opened his eyes on the world every morning with a fresh sincerity, marking how things seemed to him then, or what they suggested to his spontaneous fancy. This fancy, for being spontaneous, was not always novel; it was guided by the habits and training of his mind, which were those of a preacher. Yet he never insisted on his notions so as to turn them into settled dogmas; he felt in his bones that they were myths. Sometimes, indeed, the bad example of other transcendentalists, less true than he to their method, or the pressing questions of unintelligent people, or the instinct we all have to think our ideas final, led him to the very verge of system-making; but he stopped short. Had he made a system out of his notion of compensation, or the over-soul, or spiritual laws, the result would have been as thin and forced as it is in other transcendental systems. But he coveted truth; and he returned to experience, to history, to poetry, to the natural science of his day, for new starting-points and hints toward fresh transcendental musings.

To covet truth is a very distinguished passion. Every philosopher says he is pursuing the truth, but this is seldom the case. As Mr. Bertrand Russell has observed, one reason why philosophers often fail to reach the truth is that often they do not desire to reach it. Those who are genuinely concerned in discovering what happens to be true are rather the men of science, the naturalists, the historians; and ordinarily they discover it, according to their lights. The truths they find are never complete, and are not always important; but they are integral parts of the truth, facts and circumstances that help to fill in the picture, and that no later interpretation can invalidate or afford to contradict. But professional philosophers are usually only apologists: that is, they are absorbed in defending some vested illusion or some eloquent idea. Like lawyers or detectives, they study the case for which they are retained, to see how much evidence or semblance of evidence they can gather for the defence, and how much prejudice they can raise against the witnesses for the prosecution; for they know they are defending prisoners suspected by the world, and perhaps by their own good sense, of falsification. They do not covet truth, but victory and the dispelling of their own doubts. What they defend is some system, that is, some view about the totality of things, of which men are actually ignorant. No system would have ever been framed if people had been simply interested in knowing what is true, whatever it may be. What produces systems is the interest in maintaining against all comers that some favourite or inherited idea of ours is sufficient and right. A system may contain an account of many things which, in detail, are true enough; but as a system, covering infinite possibilities that neither our experience nor our logic can prejudge, it must be a work of imagination and a piece of human soliloquy. It may be expressive of human experience, it may be poetical; but how should any one who really coveted truth suppose that it was true?

Emerson had no system; and his coveting truth had another exceptional consequence: he was detached, unworldly, contemplative. When he came out of the conventicle or the reform meeting, or out of the rapturous close atmosphere of the lecture-room, he heard Nature whispering to him: "Why so hot, little sir?" No doubt the spirit or energy of the world is what is acting in us, as the sea is what rises in every little wave; but it passes through us, and cry out as we may, it will move on. Our privilege is to have perceived it as it moves. Our dignity is not in what we do, but in what we understand. The whole world is doing things. We are turning in that vortex; yet within us is silent observation, the speculative eye before which all passes, which bridges the distances and compares the combatants. On this side of his genius Emerson broke away from all conditions of age or country and represented nothing except intelligence itself.

There was another element in Emerson, curiously combined with transcendentalism, namely, his love and respect for Nature. Nature, for the transcendentalist, is precious because it is his own work, a mirror in which he looks at himself and says (like a poet relishing his own verses), "What a genius I am! Who would have thought there was such stuff in me?" And the philosophical egotist finds in his doctrine a ready explanation of whatever beauty and commodity nature actually has. No wonder, he says to himself, that nature is sympathetic, since I made it. And such a view, one-sided and even fatuous as it may be, undoubtedly sharpens the vision of a poet and a moralist to all that is inspiriting and symbolic in the natural world. Emerson was particularly ingenious and clear-sighted in feeling the spiritual uses of fellowship with the elements. This is something in which all Teutonic poetry is rich and which forms, I think, the most genuine and spontaneous part of modern taste, and especially of American taste. Just as some people are naturally enthralled and refreshed by music, so others are by landscape. Music and landscape make up the spiritual resources of those who cannot or dare not express their unfulfilled ideals in words. Serious poetry, profound religion (Calvinism, for instance), are the joys of an unhappiness that confesses itself; but when a genteel tradition forbids people to confess that they are unhappy, serious poetry and profound religion are closed to them by that; and since human life, in its depths, cannot then express itself openly, imagination is driven for comfort into abstract arts, where human circumstances are lost sight of, and human problems dissolve in a purer medium. The pressure of care is thus relieved, without its quietus being found in intelligence. To understand oneself is the classic form of consolation; to elude oneself is the romantic. In the presence of music or landscape human experience eludes itself; and thus romanticism is the bond between transcendental and naturalistic sentiment. The winds and clouds come to minister to the solitary ego.

Have there been, we may ask, any successful efforts to escape from the genteel tradition, and to express something worth expressing behind its back? This might well not have occurred as yet; but America is so precocious, it has been trained by the genteel tradition to be so wise for its years, that some indications of a truly native philosophy and poetry are already to be found. I might mention the humorists, of whom you here in California have had your share. The humorists, however, only half escape the genteel tradition; their humour would lose its savour if they had wholly escaped it. They point to what contradicts it in the facts; but not in order to abandon the genteel tradition, for they have nothing solid to put in its place. When they point out how ill many facts fit into it, they do not clearly conceive that this militates against the standard, but think it a funny perversity in the facts. Of course, did they earnestly respect the genteel tradition, such an incongruity would seem to them sad, rather than ludicrous. Perhaps the prevalence of humour in America, in and out of season, may be taken as one more evidence that the genteel tradition is present pervasively, but everywhere weak. Similarly in Italy, during the Renaissance, the Catholic tradition could not be banished from the intellect, since there was nothing articulate to take its place; yet its hold on the heart was singularly relaxed. The consequence was that humorists could regale themselves with the foibles of monks and of cardinals, with the credulity of fools, and the bogus miracles of the saints; not intending to deny the theory of the church, but caring for it so little at heart that they could find it infinitely amusing that it should be contradicted in men's lives and that no harm should come of it. So when Mark Twain says, "I was born of poor but dishonest parents," the humour depends on the parody of the genteel Anglo-Saxon convention that it is disreputable to be poor; but to hint at the hollowness of it would not be amusing if it did not remain at bottom one's habitual conviction.

The one American writer who has left the genteel tradition entirely behind is perhaps Walt Whitman. For this reason educated Americans find him rather an unpalatable person, who they sincerely protest ought not to be taken for a representative of their culture; and he certainly should not, because their culture is so genteel and traditional. But the foreigner may sometimes think otherwise, since he is looking for what may have arisen in America to express, not the polite and conventional American mind, but the spirit and the inarticulate principles that animate the community, on which its own genteel mentality seems to sit rather lightly. When the foreigner opens the pages of Walt Whitman, he thinks that he has come at last upon something representative and original. In Walt Whitman democracy is carried into psychology and morals. The various sights, moods, and emotions are given each one vote; they are declared to be all free and equal, and the innumerable commonplace moments of life are suffered to speak like the others. Those moments formerly reputed great are not excluded, but they are made to march in the ranks with their companions—plain foot-soldiers and servants of the hour. Nor does the refusal to discriminate stop there; we must carry our principle further down, to the animals, to inanimate nature, to the cosmos as a whole. Whitman became a pantheist; but his pantheism, unlike that of the Stoics and of Spinoza, was unintellectual, lazy, and self-indulgent; for he simply felt jovially that everything real was good enough, and that he was good enough himself. In him Bohemia rebelled against the genteel tradition; but the reconstruction that alone can justify revolution did not ensue. His attitude, in principle, was utterly disintegrating; his poetic genius fell back to the lowest level, perhaps, to which it is possible for poetic genius to fall. He reduced his imagination to a passive sensorium for the registering of impressions. No element of construction remained in it, and therefore no element of penetration. But his scope was wide; and his lazy, desultory apprehension was poetical. His work, for the very reason that it is so rudimentary, contains a beginning, or rather many beginnings, that might possibly grow into a noble moral imagination, a worthy filling for the human mind. An American in the nineteenth century who completely disregarded the genteel tradition could hardly have done more.

But there is another distinguished man, lately lost to this country, who has given some rude shocks to this tradition and who, as much as Whitman, may be regarded as representing the genuine, the long silent American mind—I mean William James. He and his brother Henry were as tightly swaddled in the genteel tradition as any infant geniuses could be, for they were born before 1850, and in a Swedenborgian household. Yet they burst those bands almost entirely. The ways in which the two brothers freed themselves, however, are interestingly different. Mr. Henry James has done it by adopting the point of view of the outer world, and by turning the genteel American tradition, as he turns everything else, into a subject-matter for analysis. For him it is a curious habit of mind, intimately comprehended, to be compared with other habits of mind, also well known to him. Thus he has overcome the genteel tradition in the classic way, by understanding it. With William James too this infusion of worldly insight and European sympathies was a potent influence, especially in his earlier days; but the chief source of his liberty was another. It was his personal spontaneity, similar to that of Emerson, and his personal vitality, similar to that of nobody else. Convictions and ideas came to him, so to speak, from the subsoil. He had a prophetic sympathy with the dawning sentiments of the age, with the moods of the dumb majority. His scattered words caught fire in many parts of the world. His way of thinking and feeling represented the true America, and represented in a measure the whole ultra-modern, radical world. Thus he eluded the genteel tradition in the romantic way, by continuing it into its opposite. The romantic mind, glorified in Hegel's dialectic (which is not dialectic at all, but a sort of tragi-comic history of experience), is always rendering its thoughts unrecognisable through the infusion of new insights, and through the insensible transformation of the moral feeling that accompanies them, till at last it has completely reversed its old judgments under cover of expanding them. Thus the genteel tradition was led a merry dance when it fell again into the hands of a genuine and vigorous romanticist like William James. He restored their revolutionary force to its neutralised elements, by picking them out afresh, and emphasising them separately, according to his personal predilections.

For one thing, William James kept his mind and heart wide open to all that might seem, to polite minds, odd, personal, or visionary in religion and philosophy. He gave a sincerely respectful hearing to sentimentalists, mystics, spiritualists, wizards, cranks, quacks, and impostors—for it is hard to draw the line, and James was not willing to draw it prematurely. He thought, with his usual modesty, that any of these might have something to teach him. The lame, the halt, the blind, and those speaking with tongues could come to him with the certainty of finding sympathy; and if they were not healed, at least they were comforted, that a famous professor should take them so seriously; and they began to feel that after all to have only one leg, or one hand, or one eye, or to have three, might be in itself no less beauteous than to have just two, like the stolid majority. Thus William James became the friend and helper of those groping, nervous, half-educated, spiritually disinherited, passionately hungry individuals of which America is full. He became, at the same time, their spokesman and representative before the learned world; and he made it a chief part of his vocation to recast what the learned world has to offer, so that as far as possible it might serve the needs and interests of these people.

Yet the normal practical masculine American, too, had a friend in William James.

There is a feeling abroad now, to which biology and Darwinism lend some colour, that theory is simply an instrument for practice, and intelligence merely a help toward material survival. Bears, it is said, have fur and claws, but poor naked man is condemned to be intelligent, or he will perish. This feeling William James embodied in that theory of thought and of truth which he called pragmatism. Intelligence, he thought, is no miraculous, idle faculty, by which we mirror passively any or everything that happens to be true, reduplicating the real world to no purpose. Intelligence has its roots and its issue in the context of events; it is one kind of practical adjustment, an experimental act, a form of vital tension. It does not essentially serve to picture other parts of reality, but to connect them. This view was not worked out by William James in its psychological and historical details; unfortunately he developed it chiefly in controversy against its opposite, which he called intellectualism, and which he hated with all the hatred of which his kind heart was capable. Intellectualism, as he conceived it, was pure pedantry; it impoverished and verbalised everything, and tied up nature in red tape. Ideas and rules that may have been occasionally useful it put in the place of the full-blooded irrational movement of life which had called them into being; and these abstractions, so soon obsolete, it strove to fix and to worship for ever. Thus all creeds and theories and all formal precepts sink in the estimation of the pragmatist to a local and temporary grammar of action; a grammar that must be changed slowly by time, and may be changed quickly by genius. To know things as a whole, or as they are eternally, if there is anything eternal in them, is not only beyond our powers, but would prove worthless, and perhaps even fatal to our lives. Ideas are not mirrors, they are weapons; their function is to prepare us to meet events, as future experience may unroll them. Those ideas that disappoint us are false ideas; those to which events are true are true themselves.

This may seem a very utilitarian view of the mind; and I confess I think it a partial one, since the logical force of beliefs and ideas, their truth or falsehood as assertions, has been overlooked altogether, or confused with the vital force of the material processes which these ideas express. It is an external view only, which marks the place and conditions of the mind in nature, but neglects its specific essence; as if a jewel were defined as a round hole in a ring. Nevertheless, the more materialistic the pragmatist's theory of the mind is, the more vitalistic his theory of nature will have to become. If the intellect is a device produced in organic bodies to expedite their processes, these organic bodies must have interests and a chosen direction in their life; otherwise their life could not be expedited, nor could anything be useful to it. In other words—and this is a third point at which the philosophy of William James has played havoc with the genteel tradition, while ostensibly defending it—nature must be conceived anthropomorphically and in psychological terms. Its purposes are not to be static harmonies, self-unfolding destinies, the logic of spirit, the spirit of logic, or any other formal method and abstract law; its purposes are to be concrete endeavours, finite efforts of souls living in an environment which they transform and by which they, too, are affected. A spirit, the divine spirit as much as the human, as this new animism conceives it, is a romantic adventurer. Its future is undetermined. Its scope, its duration, and the quality of its life are all contingent. This spirit grows; it buds and sends forth feelers, sounding the depths around for such other centres of force or life as may exist there. It has a vital momentum, but no predetermined goal. It uses its past as a stepping-stone, or rather as a diving-board, but has an absolutely fresh will at each moment to plunge this way or that into the unknown. The universe is an experiment; it is unfinished. It has no ultimate or total nature, because it has no end. It embodies no formula or statable law; any formula is at best a poor abstraction, describing what, in some region and for some time, may be the most striking characteristic of existence; the law is a description *a posteriori* of the habit things have chosen to acquire, and which they may possibly throw off altogether. What a day may bring forth is uncertain; uncertain even to God. Omniscience is impossible; time is real; what had been omniscience hitherto might discover something more to-day. "There shall be news," William James was fond of saying with rapture, quoting from the unpublished poem of an obscure friend, "there shall be news in heaven!" There is almost certainly, he thought, a God now; there may be several gods, who might exist together, or one after the other. We might, by our conspiring sympathies, help to make a new one. Much in us is doubtless immortal; we survive death for some time in a recognisable form; but what our career and transformations may be in the sequel we cannot tell, although we may help to determine them by our daily choices. Observation must be continual if our ideas are to remain true. Eternal vigilance is the price of knowledge; perpetual hazard, perpetual experiment keep quick the edge of life.

This is, so far as I know, a new philosophical vista; it is a conception never before presented, although implied, perhaps, in various quarters, as in Norse and even Greek mythology. It is a vision radically empirical and radically romantic; and as William James himself used to say, the visions and not the arguments of a philosopher are the interesting and influential things about him. William James, rather too generously, attributed this vision to M. Bergson, and regarded him in consequence as a philosopher of the first rank, whose thought was to be one of the turning-points in history. M. Bergson had killed intellectualism. It was his book on creative evolution, said James, with humorous emphasis, that had come at last to "*écraser l'infâme*." We may suspect, notwithstanding, that intellectualism, infamous and crushed, will survive the blow; and if the author of the Book of Ecclesiastes were now alive, and heard that there shall be news in heaven, he would doubtless say that there may possibly be news there, but that under the sun there is nothing new—not even radical empiricism or radical romanticism, which from the beginning of the world has been the philosophy of those who as yet had had little experience; for to the blinking little child it is not merely something in the world that is new daily, but everything is new all day.

I am not concerned with the rights and wrongs of that controversy; my point is only that William James, in this genial evolutionary view of the world, has given a rude shock to the genteel tradition. What! The world a gradual improvisation? Creation unpremeditated! God a sort of young poet or struggling artist? William James is an advocate of theism; pragmatism adds one to the evidences of religion; that is excellent. But is not the cool abstract piety of the genteel getting more than it asks for? This empirical naturalistic God is too crude and positive a force; he will work miracles, he will answer prayers, he may inhabit distinct places, and have distinct conditions under which alone he can operate; he is a neighbouring being, whom we can act upon, and rely upon for specific aids, as upon a personal friend, or a physician, or an insurance company. How disconcerting! Is not this new theology a little like superstition? And yet how interesting, how exciting, if it should happen to be true! I am far from wishing to suggest that such a view seems to me more probable than conventional idealism or than Christian orthodoxy. All three are in the region of dramatic system-making and myth to which probabilities are irrelevant. If one man says the moon is sister to the sun, and another that she is his daughter, the question is not which notion is more probable, but whether either of them is at all expressive. The so-called evidences are devised afterwards, when faith and imagination have prejudged the issue. The force of William James's new theology, or romantic cosmology, lies only in this: that it has broken the spell of the genteel tradition, and enticed faith in a new direction, which on second thoughts may prove no less alluring than the old. The important fact is not that the new fancy might possibly be true—who shall know that?—but that it has entered the heart of a leading American to conceive and to cherish it. The genteel tradition cannot be dislodged by these insurrections; there are circles to which it is still congenial, and where it will be preserved. But it has been challenged and (what is perhaps more insidious) it has been discovered. No one need be browbeaten any longer into accepting it. No one need be afraid, for instance, that his fate is sealed because some young prig may call him a dualist; the pint would call the quart a dualist, if you tried to pour the quart into him. We need not be afraid of being less profound, for being direct and sincere. The intellectual world may be traversed in many directions; the whole has not been surveyed; there is a great career in it open to talent. That is a sort of knell, that tolls the passing of the genteel tradition. Something else is now in the field; something else can appeal to the imagination, and be a thousand times more idealistic than academic idealism, which is often simply a way of white-washing and adoring things as they are. The illegitimate monopoly which the genteel tradition had established over what ought to be assumed and what ought to be hoped for has been broken down by the first-born of the family, by the genius of the race. Henceforth there can hardly be the same peace and the same pleasure in hugging the old proprieties. Hegel will be to the next generation what Sir William Hamilton was to the last. Nothing will have been disproved, but everthing will have been abandoned. An honest man has spoken, and the cant of the genteel tradition has become harder for young lips to repeat.

With this I have finished such a sketch as I am here able to offer you of the genteel tradition in American philosophy. The subject is complex, and calls for many an excursus and qualifying footnote; yet I think the main outlines are clear enough. The chief fountains of this tradition were Calvinism and transcendentalism. Both were living fountains; but to keep them alive they required, one an agonised conscience, and the other a radical subjective criticism of knowledge. When these rare metaphysical preoccupations disappeared—and the American atmosphere is not favourable to either of them—the two systems ceased to be inwardly understood; they subsisted as sacred mysteries only; and the combination of the two in some transcendental system of the universe (a contradiction in principle) was doubly artificial. Besides, it could hardly be held with a single mind. Natural science, history, the beliefs implied in labour and invention, could not be disregarded altogether; so that the transcendental philosopher was condemned to a double allegiance, and to not letting his left hand know the bluff that his right hand was making. Nevertheless, the difficulty in bringing practical inarticulate convictions to expression is very great, and the genteel tradition has subsisted in the academic mind for want of anything equally academic to take its place.

The academic mind, however, has had its flanks turned. On the one side came the revolt of the Bohemian temperament, with its poetry of crude naturalism; on the other side came an impassioned empiricism, welcoming popular religious witnesses to the unseen, reducing science to an instrument of success in action, and declaring the universe to be wild and young, and not to be harnessed by the logic of any school.

This revolution, I should think, might well find an echo among you, who live in a thriving society, and in the presence of a virgin and prodigious world. When you transform nature to your uses, when you experiment with her forces, and reduce them to industrial agents, you cannot feel that nature was made by you or for you, for then these adjustments would have been pre-established. Much less can you feel it when she destroys your labour of years in a momentary spasm. You must feel, rather, that you are an offshoot of her life; one brave little force among her immense forces. When you escape, as you love to do, to your forests and your sierras, I am sure again that you do not feel you made them, or that they were made for you. They have grown, as you have grown, only more massively and more slowly. In their non-human beauty and peace they stir the sub-human depths and the superhuman possibilities of your own spirit. It is no transcendental logic that they teach; and they give no sign of any deliberate morality seated in the world. It is rather the vanity and superficiality of all logic, the needlessness of argument, the relativity of morals, the strength of time, the fertility of matter, the variety, the unspeakable variety, of possible life. Everything is measurable and conditioned, indefinitely repeated, yet, in repetition, twisted somewhat from its old form. Everywhere is beauty and nowhere permanence, everywhere an incipient harmony, nowhere an intention, nor a responsibility, nor a plan. It is the irresistible suasion of this daily spectacle, it is the daily discipline of contact with things, so different from the verbal discipline of the schools, that will, I trust, inspire the philosophy of your children. A Californian whom I had recently the pleasure of meeting observed that, if the philosophers had lived among your mountains their systems would have been different from what they are. Certainly, I should say, very different from what those systems are which the European genteel tradition has handed down since Socrates; for these systems are egotistical; directly or indirectly they are anthropocentric, and inspired by the conceited notion that man, or human reason, or the human distinction between good and evil, is the centre and pivot of the universe. That is what the mountains and the woods should make you at last ashamed to assert. From what, indeed, does the society of nature liberate you, that you find it so sweet? It is hardly (is it?) that you wish to forget your past, or your friends, or that you have any secret contempt for your present ambitions. You respect these, you respect them perhaps too much; you are not suffered by the genteel tradition to criticise or to reform them at all radically. No; it is the yoke of this genteel tradition itself that these primeval solitudes lift from your shoulders. They suspend your forced sense of your own importance not merely as individuals, but even as men. They allow you, in one happy moment, at once to play and to worship, to take yourselves simply, humbly, for what you are, and to salute the wild, indifferent, noncensorious infinity of nature. You are admonished that what you can do avails little materially, and in the end nothing. At the same time, through wonder and pleasure, you are taught speculation. You learn what you are really fitted to do, and where lie your natural dignity and joy, namely, in representing many things, without being them, and in letting your imagination, through sympathy, celebrate and echo their life. Because the peculiarity of man is that his machinery for reaction on external things has involved an imaginative transcript of these things, which is preserved and suspended in his fancy; and the interest and beauty of this inward landscape, rather than any fortunes that may await his body in the outer world, constitute his proper happiness. By their mind, its scope, quality, and temper, we estimate men, for by the mind only do we exist as men, and are more than so many storage-batteries for material energy. Let us therefore be frankly human. Let us be content to live in the mind.

28
Veblen and Progress: The American Climate of Opinion

David W. Noble

More broadly conceived than its title indicates, this essay treats the thought of Richard T. Ely (1854-1943), Simon Nelson Patten (1852-1922), and Thorstein Veblen (1857-1929). David Noble, for many years an intellectual historian at the University of Minnesota, examines these three economic thinkers in their relation to the changing idea of progress among social scientists. (See also essay 35.) He separates the ideas of Ely and Patten from those of Veblen in a way that other writers have tended to overlook. Just as the evolutionary and historically relativist theories of Ely and Patten passed beyond those of the classical defenders of laissez-faire capitalism, so Veblen's thought went even further. In place of a theory of progress, Veblen posited his science of causation. True science is "causal," which meant to him "impersonal" and "cumulative." Noble, moreover, briefly explains why these American social theorists were not Marxists—a theme unfortunately missing from too many social histories of this era. Having singled out their differences over the development of human societies, the author finds these three men have a fundamental though perhaps "unconscious" similarity. They were subject to "the paradox of Progressive thought." For them, progress meant "a return to human primitive qualities, set free by industrialism." They and many other new social scientists in the last quarter of the nineteenth century found no conflict between the primitive norms of primary human groups and increasingly complex social organizations. Moralists as most of them were—even Veblen, in spite of himself—they sought to return to "the altruistic ethics of the natural man." A later generation would claim that their vision of human nature became confused by their belief in an ancient ideal state of man held simultaneously with a desire for change and social reform.

For further reading: *Morton White, *Social Thought in America: The Revolt against Formalism* (1949); David Riesman, *Thorstein Veblen, a Critical Interpretation* (1953); *Walter P. Metzger, *Academic Freedom in the Age of the University* (1955); Samuel Haber, *Efficiency and Uplift: Scientific Management in*

Ethics, 65 (July 1955), 271-286. Reprinted by permission of the author and The University of Chicago Press. Footnotes have been omitted.

the Progressive Era, 1890-1920 (1964); *Henry May, *The End of American Innocence: A Study of the First Years of Our Own Time, 1912-1917* (1959).

The recent book of David Riesman, which has interpreted Thorstein Veblen in the light of the scholarship of the last two decades, has placed Veblen in a well-defined perspective as an individual reacting to the various social currents of his times. But while Riesman has suggested in a succinct manner the basis of many of Veblen's theoretical contradictions in the nineteenth-century intellectual background, he has not chosen to emphasize, in the short space allotted him in the book, this particular aspect of Veblen's writings. The essay of Abram L. Harris, which recently appeared in *Ethics,* again stressed several of the important contradictions of Veblen's theories which were based on nineteenth-century viewpoints, but neither did he try to connect Veblen, in detail, with the intellectual history of the late nineteenth and early twentieth century.

These two publications and those of the last quarter century have brought to the attention of students of American thought the fact that Veblen was not the completely original thinker, the far-reaching innovator, claimed by his earlier commentators. This essay is put forward to supplement these writings in suggesting the manner in which Veblen's contradictions, his deep commitment to older ways of thinking, fitted the climate of opinion of his generation.

It is somewhat fitting that this concept of a climate of opinion, which is used as a tool of historical analysis, is applied to Veblen—for Veblen believed that man is a creature of habit, that his ideas reflect these habits, that man, in his psychological make-up and his ideas, is a product of group habits that have hardened into traditions and institutions. Veblen might very well have agreed, therefore, with Carl Becker that men are, to a great extent, prisoners of certain fundamental ideas of their age; that these ideas are so much a part of them that they are held without self-conscious appraisal. Yet no man ever acted with the certainty of Thorstein Veblen that he had freed himself from all hidden preconceptions which could bind him to an ideal world not based on the brute facts of existence. He, Veblen, was the prophet of a new age; its ideas might be called a climate of opinion, but they differed radically from all other ages. Matter-of-fact knowledge was the beginning and end of this new world. Only things that could be measured or weighed or counted were to hold the attention of man. All questions of ultimate reality were banished, along with all ideals. This was to be the world of scientific objectivity.

In *The Heavenly City of the Eighteenth-Century Philosophers,* Becker described other men who insisted that they were interested only in facts, that abstract reason was the whole of their climate of opinion. But Becker went on to say that their claim of disillusioned indifference was a facade to hide "their eager didactic impulse to set things right," that "they were out for the cold facts" but only "to spoil the game of the mystery mongers." And he went on to describe how the *Philosophes* gradually discarded abstract reason, which could not provide the absolute values for the coming Heavenly City on earth, for a historical method which could give them such values based on the revelation of an enduring human nature. After vigorously and vociferously discarding with Locke the concept of innate ideas, they brought them back surreptitiously as the permanent and universal essentials of human nature. "Is it possible," writes Becker, "that they were engaged in that nefarious medieval enterprise of reconciling the facts of human experience with the truths already, in some fashion, revealed to them?" It is just at this theoretical point that recent students have emphasized the contradictions in Veblen's theory; for Veblen insisted that there was no such thing as human nature in general when he attacked the classical economists, and yet the core of his anthropology, which he held to be so important for the social sciences, was his belief in "a generically human type of spiritual endowment, prevalent as a general average of human nature throughout" and that "these native proclivities alone make anything worthwhile, and out of their working emerge not only the purpose and efficiency of life, but its substantial pleasures and pains as well."

Becker, in his essay on the eighteenth century, suggested the pragmatic unity of believing, at once, that man is the product of his environment and, at the same time, has universal qualities. On one hand, the reformers of that century had to demonstrate that man was capable of regeneration, that he was not bound by original sin, that a better environment would provide a better man. Having destroyed to their satisfaction the conservative defense of the status quo, based on the insistence of innately evil qualities of man, they must, as moral men, substitute a code of values for those which they had destroyed. And so they proclaimed that man, in civilization, had been led astray from the essential goodness of the universal natural order; if he could strip off the errors of his artificial institutional life, if he could conform to the pattern of nature, then all would be well.

Traditionally, scholars have come to believe that this belief in the virtue of the primitive man, related to a world of natural law, gave way in the nineteenth century to the forces of historicism, evolutionism, and relativism. The record, as revealed by historical investigations, is clear that scholars in post-Civil War America had made the break from this pattern of thinking. Veblen's own discipline of economics is one example. By the 1870's, young Americans, eager for knowledge, were making pilgrimages to Germany to study new currents in economic thought. Not content with the conservative statics of English neoclassicism, they desired to get in touch with the German emphasis on history, an emphasis which insisted that man's economic life changed through time, and economic principles, therefore must also change.

I

One such young American was Richard T. Ely, who abandoned philosophy for economics while in Germany and who studied with Karl Knies at Heidelberg—Knies whom Ely classed with Wilhelm Roscher and Bruno Hildebrand as a father of German historical economic thought. It was Ely who pronounced that the ideas which most influenced his generation were those of evolution and relativity. It was Ely who issued a challenge to the older American economists in 1884 in his *The Past and Present of Political Economy*. These older Americans, he wrote, based their ideas on the English school, which was outdated because it was idealistic in that its principles were ready-made in the mind and deductive because it took these premises and evolved an economic system around them without recourse to the external world. Outdated, he continued, because we of the new generation realize that economics must be a science, and science is not based on idealistic and deductive philosophy; it is realistic and inductive, and that is why we have based our thinking on German precedent which accepts the outer world as a source of principles and studies it empirically, inductively. The unscientific basis of all previous economic thinking in this country must, therefore, necessarily call into question its major tenets: that universal self-interest is the basic cause of all economic phenomena; that all men love ease and are averse to exertion; that there is no friction in economic life; that "the beneficent powers of nature . . . arrange things so that the best good of all is attained by the unrestrained action of self-interest."

This whole system has been given the dignity of natural law; its postulates are called the reflection of universal attributes of man and nature. Now, with the knowledge drawn from the German economists, Ely declared, we can scientifically affirm that there are no natural economic laws, that there is only the growth and development of new concepts of economics which differ with the particular context of the time and place in which they find expression, that "in every stage of its progress, the theory of political economy is the generalization of truths recognized up to a certain point of time, and this theory cannot be declared complete, either as respects its form or substance."

While Ely was proud of the scientific aspects of his theory, he was also frankly a moralist, a Christian moralist. He openly wanted to reform not only economics but all of America, and he saw in the American Economic Association, which he helped to found, a means to both ends. Classical economics had failed as abstract theory when it postulated "that there is an entire harmony of interests between the different classes of society" because this "is at complete variance with the teaching of modern science." But more important for him was the failure of self-interest to further a Christian moral life, and he ended this book on the note that the German economists were also moralists, that they conceived of the nature of society as organic so that it must find its basic principle in co-operation and love. The German school, he wrote, "denotes a return to the grand principle of common sense and Christian precept," the Golden Rule. Ely was not a man divided between his Christian moralism and his science; in his mind, he was a Christian when he was a scientist and a scientist when he was a Christian. Consciously, he looked on his theoretical tools of historicism, evolution, and relativism as means to establish a better Christian world. The question of undermining laissez-faire economics was not merely a question of abstract science; it was necessary for the reform of America. Laissez-faire economics, as it found expression and prestige in the philosophy of Herbert Spencer, was blocking Americans from taking action to end the crisis in which they found themselves.

Ely, when he returned from Germany, in the 1880's, had been impressed by the social chaos that marked the new industrial America. Industrialism, he felt, was the cause of this crisis which was appearing in every part of the world where new methods of production had come into being. It was to be explained by the fact that the new machine processes had broken up the old patterns of life; men who had lived in tight-knit groups up to this time were suddenly caught up in great population shifts; men were now no longer social animals but individual atoms trying to work out their own selfish destinies because there were no longer community values and ideals. Out of this period of confusion developed laissez-faire thinking, a negative philosophy designed to protect the necessarily self-sufficient individual. It was in the context of this particular historical situation that Herbert Spencer's thought was to be explained; more than a century after this period had begun, he was still stressing that liberty was negative and political. This was the great weakness of Spencer—he represented a period of history which had been left behind.

The nature of man, Ely postulated, was the product of his environiment, and his thinking reflected the behavior patterns of that environment. Spencer's thought was relevant to a period of past history but not to the present because industrialism continued to alter the human environment and to demand new values and new ideas. It was now bringing new patterns of community life out of the initial chaos it had caused. Man was being molded into co-operative habits by a new urban, industrial environment, which was constructing a social solidarity beyond that known before. The crisis resolved into a conflict between the new habits of organization and thought which had been felt by those classes most under the discipline of industrialism, the workers, and the older institutions of laissez-faire capitalism in which the behavior and thought patterns of the past had hardened. This, then, was the conflict between socialism, through which the workers were groping for means of expressing their new needs and desires, and capitalism.

Ely expressed the seriousness of this crisis; it was his belief that it might possibly not be resolved peacefully. But his greatest emphasis was optimistic; there was no need of class warfare, a successful resolution was in sight. It was in sight because more and more people were feeling the discipline of industrialism; they were living a life of social solidarity; they were prepared to scrap the old, outdated institutions under which they had lived. Indeed, the transition would come easily, almost spontaneously, because the discipline of industrialism was not so much coercive as it was liberating.

According to Ely's theology, man was not innately evil but good, he was not selfish but loving; according to his anthropology, primitive man had not lived an isolated life, short, nasty, and brutish; rather, the first men were social animals who lived a co-operative, loving life in small groups. Man's history had not been a pleasant one because there had been no way for these socially healthy groups to communicate and thus understand one another. Now Ely could assure his generation that the ethics of industrialism were the right ones because they were those of the Christian and natural man. Industrialism was making possible the organization of men into one world-wide, tight-knit community whose standards and values would be those of Christianity and the socially healthy primitive men. In the fashion of the *Philosophes,* Ely had blamed the vices, the injurious theories of his time, to the ephemeral environment of shifting social institutions. All that was bad in man's nature had been caused by forces which could be overcome. Ely, searching history for the universal man, had found him in the perfection of primitivism and Christianity. He had used the theories of abstract reason or science to defeat his enemies, but he had forsaken these concepts when it was time to advance his own set of values and standards. Evolution had brought man full cycle to a complete expression of his initial attributes.

II

Among the group of young economic rebels who joined with Ely in creating the American Economic Association was an awkward farm boy from Illinois, Simon N. Patten. Like Ely, he had completed his emancipation from the Calvinism of his family and the secular orthodoxies of post-Civil War America by the study of economics in Germany; like Ely, Patten returned to an America that he saw desperately in need of salvation. Unlike Ely, however, Patten did not expend most of his energies in popular causes. It was not enough to attack the Manchester economics with the ideas of the German professors and then ask the American people to accept these academic abstractions as the guiding principles for the future reconstruction of their life. The authority of his German teachers, for Patten, was that only of ground-breakers. These men were pioneers; they had undermined the English theories; they had suggested the paths for a new economic philosophy; it was up to men such as Patten to work out the details of this philosophy.

In his first book *The Premises of Political Economy*, however, Patten was still the bright young student using the critical weapons of his German mentors to undermine the American version of English neoclassical economics. The keystone of this older school, its main line of defense, was the insistence that its major premises were based on natural laws. Candidly, Patten confessed that he was going to attack this philosophy in order to clear the ground for a solution of the problems of industrial America, and so he wrote, "If the doctrines of Ricardo are not universally true, a civilization is possible in which each individual, by complying with the surrounding external conditions, can obtain all that reward which nature offers. . . ." And, of course, for Patten, the student of the German theories of historical relativism, there were no universal laws of economics. Systematically, he went on to show that the limiting and pessimistic doctrines of Ricardo and Malthus were based on a static conception of human nature which was demonstrably untrue, not only in terms of historical relativism, but also of the Darwinism that the exponents of laissez-faire were attempting to use to defend their position. ". . . What is natural changes with the intelligence and moral character of the laborers and with changes in political and social institutions." This was the true message of Darwin, that the characteristics of animals, including man, change with each new environment.

Against the conservative claim that man was a creature of universal traits, Patten had aggressively asserted that man was a plastic being molded by the conditions under which he lived. To fully illustrate this contention, Patten wrote *The Development of English Thought,* a study, he said, in the economic interpretation of history. In it, he worked out a psychology to fit the facts of the changing nature of man and his environment. There were, he wrote, two fundamental aspects of the psychology of the individual: his sensory and his motor apparatus. The human being is able to adjust to his environment because his ingoing nervous currents bring him knowledge of the external world. This is the function of the sensory side of man. Because of his senses, he is able to create conscious ideas of what the environment is like. Essentially passive, the senses necessarily influence greatly what the active motor responses of man will be to the environment. As the individual grows in knowledge, in sense experience, his ideas are interrelated and associated, growing into complex patterns. This results in the ability of one sense fact to call forth a complex picture of the surrounding conditions and allows man to react quickly and almost instinctively to a complex problem. Man, for Patten, was not completely passive. He was capable of motor responses to signals brought by the senses, responses that tried not only to adjust the organism to the environment but also tried to control, to a degree, the environment so that it would become more favorable.

When man lives under a set of conditions for a long period, as he did in savagery, a certain set of motor responses become habitual with him; they become part of his heredity, difficult to change or to eliminate. The stage is set, therefore, for a disharmony between human psychology and the environment—because the environment changes more quickly than do these motor reactions. History becomes a series of conflicts between new environments and old motor reactions, conflicts that are compromised by the secondary habits created by the temporary environments and the institutions which rest on these habits. In this way, Patten could write without animus about Ricardo and Malthus and the institutions of laissez-faire capitalism. They represented the reactions of men to a certain set of economic conditions; if these conditions had not been rationalized by Malthus and Ricardo, they would have, by necessity, found other rationalizers, because in this period of history such institutions were inevitable. And like Ely, Patten pronounced the passing of the stage of laissez-faire capitalism. Mankind had entered a new economic environment; he must develop fresh habits, ideas, and institutions that would fit it.

Ely had frankly believed in the necessity of progress; it was part of his version of a coming Christian "Kingdom of God on Earth." He had stressed the necessity of the wilful activity of man to make the culmination of progress possible, but generally when he thought in terms of science, he postulated the economic scientist's task as the revelation of the predetermined laws of economic development which would lead to an economic utopia based on primitive and Christian virtues. Patten reacted against the unsophisticated elements in the thought of Ely. He would not defend a literal Christian position, nor would he admit that evolution was a predetermined scheme of progress, let alone a progress that would culminate in a return to primitive conditions. Indeed, in *The Premises of Political Economy* he had written, "The original man was a slave to his appetites and passions, and enjoyed only those pleasures which are of a physical nature." Ely had written about the importance of variation in the evolutionary process and the increasing plasticity of human nature, but he had not developed these ideas or tried to reconcile them with his presuppositions about Christianity and the natural man. But Patten, the self-conscious philospher, was going to develop these ideas to reinforce the notion of the independence of man from any universal characteristics, ideas that found expression in Patten's next major book *Heredity and Social Progress,* the central theme of which was the increasing plasticity of human nature and its continual transformation with the addition of new traits. Taking his notion that motor responses actually work to reform objective conditions around man, Patten now insisted that when such an improvement was made, the successful organism enjoyed such a surplus of energy that new aspects of the organism could be developed, changing its character.

Working to by-pass the universals of the American conservative position of the late nineteenth century, Patten seems to have arrived at an appreciation of the meaning of evolution in terms of novelty and change which far exceeded that of Ely; he also seems much more impressed by the necessary correlation of a philosophy of science with such a concept of evolution. Patten, however, was not just an abstract economist or philosopher; he was a reformer. While he did not perhaps believe in Ely's Christian "Kingdom of God on Earth," he did want a better America. He had used the new intellectual theories of evolution and historical relativity to undermine the conservative position. Now he must replace that position with a better set of values. What philosophy would be the source of these values?

The answer to this question can be found in the ambiguities of his book *Heredity and Social Progress*. There, with increasing frequency, "new" and "changed" characteristics are associated with "natural" characteristics. If man's nature is changing, what can Patten mean by natural? Once he had written with disapproval of original man, but now he came to associate the semi-permanent motor responses of primitive man with social virtues. Primitive man was unselfish, co-operative, peaceful, everything that men of the capitalist era were not. But the selfish, competitive, warlike character of the capitalistic man was the habit pattern of only a brief epoch in history. Western man had entered a new economic environment, an economy of pleasure or plenty as against the economies of pain and scarcity that had marked all previous epochs except that of primitive man. And, continued Patten, man's natural character is made active by surplus energy, by the surplus energy coming from the new economy; it is brought to light after having been held dormant throughout the ages by the deficit economy which allowed the individual to be determined by acquired characteristics from the immediate environment, such characteristics as selfishness or combativeness.

This was the promise Patten held out to an America which, like himself, was caught up in the enthusiasm of the progressive movement. In the tones of warning used by Ely, he could tell the people, "Confusion and defeat stare us in the face politically, morally and economically, if the disappearance of old customs, traditions and modes of thought is not followed by the rise of new concepts, ideas and institutions." But, in the midst of cultural crisis, he could not help but tell Americans that if they acted, they must be saved; they could not help but tell Americans that if they acted, they must be saved; they could not help but be saved because the conditions of the new industrial society were automatically bringing in the new concepts, ideas, and institutions, which were based on the social virtues of the primitive man. This was the message of Patten's next book *The New Basis of Civilization*. The discipline of industrialism was forming new habits and ideas which conformed to the social inheritance of mankind brought down through racial heredity from savagery.

At that time, man had lived in cohesive family groups with a moral code of altruism; somehow, with the growth of population, this altruism had been replaced by selfishness. Perhaps it was that with increasing size, society inevitably became more complex, and it lost its simple and healthy homogeneity. Men ceased to be brothers, and some became tribute givers, others tribute takers. On the solid substratum of workers were added the artificial and parasitic military and priestly classes. These classes developed what has been known as culture and, through generation after generation, culture has passed down through the leisured classes. The development of the badges of class superiority, however, affirmed Patten, actually spelled the spiritual poverty of the aristocrats; they had not added anything to their spiritual endowment but had been alienated from it. Fortunately for the future of mankind, he continued, the number of these aristocrats who were the creatures of artificial traditions and institutions has been small. The bulk of mankind, the tribute givers, have remained in the primitive stage. "There have flowed then, side by side, two streams of life, one bearing the working poor, who perpetuate themselves through the qualities generated by the stress and mutual dependence of the primitive world, and the other bearing the aristocracies, who dominate by means of the laws and traditions giving them control of the social surplus." Paradoxically, perhaps, Patten believed that the vast extension of the complexity of civilization through the large scale industrial units and closely packed cities of the new economic order would restore the solidarity of primitivism. Confidently, he proclaimed that the new "economic life will make them [men] more social by reviving the impulses of the primitive world," and "the growth and influence of cities are renewing and intensifying in all classes the motives to cooperation."

In his last major book of social theory, *The Social Basis of Religion,* Patten attempted a synthesis of his conflicting ideas of historical and evolutionary relativism with primitivism and rationalism. He was, he informed his readers, a pragmatist because the meaning of evolution for philosophy was that the human mind was not a mechanism with certain innate characteristics but was active and flexible, changing with the environment around it. Thus the conservative position that human traits were fixed and a radical reconstruction of society was therefore impossible was obviously untenable, based as it was on pre-Darwinian ways of thinking. Then Patten began to do strange things with his pragmatism. The conservatives, such as Spencer, he wrote, reflected a definite stage in the development of human thought, namely, the second. Agreeing with Auguste Comte that man's thought necessarily passed through three historical stages, Patten merged Comte's metaphysical and positive stages together as the second and proclaimed pragmatism the third and final epoch. In the future, men would not be able to think in terms of fixed qualities; they must think in terms of process, of genetic change. They must perceive that it is possible for society to be altered from the principles of laissez-faire economics to something better.

Patten further made it clear that this could be done because mankind was not under the control of physical law. The history of the human race was the history of its traditions which had been impressed on it at the beginning of civilization in the Near East. These traditions, as against the peacefulness and co-operativeness of primitive man, were those of selfishness and conflict because of the poor climatic conditions at that time. Now man would escape from these traditions because the new environment of surplus and prosperity allowed the flowering out of hereditary altruistic nature. When dealing with the conservatives, the human mind, for Patten, was the changing product of external conditions. When he talked of reform, the human mind suddenly became a thing of fixed characteristics. And given the absolute standards for the good society found in human nature, the task of economic science would be to survey the sweep of history to find the one set of conditions which would provide the best possible environment for man, the environment which would obliterate all the harmful acquired character traits that civilization had produced and which would foster the full expression of the natural man. Pragmatism had been left far behind. Needless to say, modern industrialism was in the process of providing many of the necessary conditions for such a utopia. Like Ely, Patten rejected the necessity of a Marxian type class struggle to destroy the old order, which must inevitably disappear under the new discipline of industrial life. Patten also found that one important tradition of modern civilization had not been in conflict with man's primitive nature: this was Christianity which, in its insistence on peace and unselfishness and brotherly love, had helped to sustain the original nature of man. Patten looked to Christianity, therefore, to help man through this transition from a society of competing classes and individuals to the better world of classless solidarity and perfect harmony.

III

In a recent study of the influence of the idea of evolution on American academic economics, it has been said that Simon Patten was second only to Thorstein Veblen in his insistence on the importance of evolution for economic theory. In one way, the line of connection between Ely and Patten and Veblen might be interpreted as one of increasing sophistication as Americans became more cognizant of the implications of evolution for philosophy. Ely believed that evolution was to be equated with progress; Patten believed that evolution made progress possible if not inevitable; Veblen rejected both theories and insisted that evolution merely provided man with a tool to know his society objectively, that it did not provide the power to know the future or to control the future. Indeed, Veblen, the man of science, the man without values, would abandon Ely and Patten to the past as pre-Darwinian thinkers as they, in turn, had abandoned the defenders of laissez-faire capitalism to the limbo of outdated philosophy.

In the modern climate of opinion, for Veblen, there was no more room for men of science as reformers than there was for men of science as defenders of the status quo. This climate of opinion, he insisted, the scientific climate of opinion, postulates the fact of consecutive change; it is interested in process; it is a sharp break from the past, part of an intellectual revolution that may be conveniently dated with the popularization of Darwin's theories. Before this time scientists were interested in taxonomy; they thought in terms of definition and classification; they searched for the first cause and the consummation of whatever they studied. The heart of their science was the discovery of "the body of natural law, governing phenomena under the rule of causation." Now the post-Darwinian scientists were no longer interested in first causes, final consummations, or natural laws. They were concerned only in a description of "what has taken place and what is taking place."

With this definition of what the science of the post-Darwinian epoch is, it is clear, continued Veblen, why the discipline of economics is not an evolutionary science. The new science is realistic; it emphasizes facts, but so did the economists of the nineteenth century. The new science demands a theory of process that will give meaning to disjointed and scattered facts, but again recent economists have emphasized processes in economic life. Wherein is the obvious sign, then, that economics is not yet an evolutionary science? This sign, said Veblen, "is a difference of spiritual attitude . . . it is a difference in the basis of valuation of the facts for the scientific purpose, or in the interest from which the facts are appreciated." The modern scientist is concerned only with the mechanics of cause and effect, the "colorless impersonal sequence" in its cumulative character. But the classical economists place their study of process, of cause and effect, within the power of natural law. "To meet the high classical requirement, a sequence—and a developmental process especially—must be apprehended in terms of a consistent propensity tending to some spiritually legitimate end."

The keystone of the classical belief in the essentially static nature of economics has been its theory of human psychology. Criticized in the light of modern psychology, which tells us that man is an active, changing being whose activity is an important part of the economic process, the classic position sees man as a creature of fixed qualities, always calculating the pleasure and pain to be gained from his economic endeavors. For this school, man "has neither antecedent nor consequent. He is an isolated, definitive human datum, in stable equilibrium except for the buffets of the impinging forces that displace him in one direction or another." To be a science, economics must accept the individual as active and changing. It must place him in the stream of history and search out the historical forces that have made him what he is. And "in all this flux there is no definitively adequate method of life and no definitive or absolutely worthy end of action, so far as concerns the science which sets out to formulate a theory of the process of economic life. . . . An evolutionary economics must be the theory of a process of cultural growth as determined by the economic interest, a theory of a cumulative sequence of economic institutions stated in terms of the process itself."

With this theoretical position, with these theoretical weapons of historicism, evolution, and relativism, Veblen set out to march up and down the nineteenth century to show how every economist, whether he was conservative or liberal, shared in the antiquated thinking of natural rights. There was John Bates Clark who wanted to save American capitalism from increasing monopoly and bring it back to its "normal" state of free competition, and whose law of "natural" distribution placed him squarely at the historical level of the physiocrats or Adam Smith. There was Karl Marx whose propaganda was based on "natural rights ideals, but his theory of the working out of these ideals in the course of history rests on the Hegelian metaphysics of development, and his method of speculation and construction of theory is given by the Hegelian dialectic." Because of this dependence on pre-Darwinian patterns of thought, all of Marx's major economic points, the class struggle, the increasing distress of the proletariat, his theory of labor value, were untenable. None of the economists of the past had accepted the fact that evolution "is a scheme of blindly cumulative causation, in which there is no trend, no final term, no consummation," and their economic theories must, therefore, fall.

But what of the future? Would Veblen become the first modern economist as he had become the first thoroughgoing critic of past economics? Would he describe American conditions with complete objectivity, without praise or censure, as was fitting in a world without values? At this point, one is reminded of the description of Hume in Becker's *Heavenly City* who, in his *Dialogues Concerning Natural Religion,* came to the conclusion that reason could not establish the existence or the goodness of God and, for that matter, the foundation for any system of values; who then locked the manuscript in his desk and turned to the study of history where one could establish a system of values based on the permanent characteristics of man, because, in Hume's own words, "mankind are so much the same, in all times and places, that history informs us of nothing new or strange in this particular. Its chief use is only to discover the constant and universal principles of human nature."

Veblen had not locked his manuscript away; he had asserted and reasserted that reason, the scientific method of the post-Darwinian epoch, could not establish values. He had even denied the ability of history to perform such deeds because man changed constantly throughout history. But when Veblen began to write his descriptions of the American social and economic scene, when he began to discuss subjects other than the theory of science, his philosophy of history and of human psychology shifted radically. Ely and Patten, too, had used evolution and historical relativism to undermine the theories of their opponents, but they had based their positive values on a set of absolute principles, the principles of the natural man who stood above history, who was more than a complex of shifting habits and desires. They were careful to replace what they destroyed. And so it was with Veblen, who denied his role as reformer, but who presented for the edification of his liberal readers, who delighted in his destruction of conservative absolutes, a set of values in the tradition of his fellow reformers, Ely and Patten, the altruistic ethics of the natural man.

Even in his scientific essays, the central role the idea of the natural man played in his thinking comes to attention. In his important essay "The Place of Science in Modern Civilization," while he is discussing the fact that modern civilization is now under the influence of science and is "peculiarly matter-of-fact," Veblen asks the question, "How far is the scientific quest of matter-of-fact knowledge consonant with the inherited intellectual aptitudes and propensities of the normal man?" And he answers it by writing, "it may seem a curious paradox that the latest and most perfect flowering of the western civilisation is more nearly akin to the spiritual life of the serfs and villeins than it is to that of the grange or the abbey"; this means, in the context of the essay, that modern science coincides very closely with the qualities of the normal man who, in the era of savagery, was motivated by the instinct of idle curiosity which is also the foundation for modern science and that the savage traits have been carried largely uncorrupted in the lower classes through history, although they were overpowered superficially in the next stage of history, the barbaric, by the characteristics of the aristocrats, the barbaric aristocrats who dwelt in grange and abbey. It means that Veblen believed modern conditions were making possible the revival of the savage spiritual life.

These were the very terms used by Patten when he divided men into aristocrats who were creatures of history, creatures of cumulative habit, and the lower classes who retained the qualities of their original savage state, who were submerged but not obliterated by history and who were not re-emerging to stamp the new epoch with their permanent and good characteristics. This theme of contrasting a lost Garden of Eden with the evils of the present and forecasting the return of this primitive purity under the discipline of industrial conditions, this "outmoded" philosophy which was used so enthusiastically by Ely and Patten, became the biting edge of Veblen's criticism of his America and his solution to its problems.

Veblen's description of the economic manners of the American upper class in *The Theory of the Leisure Class* would have lost much of its satire if Veblen had been true to his statement that he was not making value judgments. The whole theory of history and anthropology of the book, however, is designed to give the reader standards by which to criticize the foibles of America's upper class. Here was no presentation of facts within an evolutionary process without a beginning, without meaing, and without a culmination. History has a beginning in the state of savagery, and man had gained a permanent nature during that period, a nature of goodness, of altruism, of peacefulness which somehow had been suppressed in the next stage of history, that of barbarism, in which some men had drifted away from their real nature under the sway of competition and invidious comparison and conspicuous consumption and conspicuous waste. Veblen then gave the reader the impression that history had moved beyond barbarism to civilization (was it the last, the final historical era?), and the characteristics of the leisure class were survivals of barbarism in the modern age and, therefore, objects of ridicule. And Veblen could also assure his reader that these were bound to pass because they were not part of a permanent human psychology but were the product of history, of the cumulative growth habits: "The habits derived from the predatory and quasi-peaceable culture are relatively ephemeral variants of certain underlying propensities and mental characteristics of the race."

In his next book *The Theory of Business Enterprise,* Veblen criticized modern business in terms of the wastefulness characteristic of the leisure class, but he did so now, not in terms of his theory of historical stages and his anthropology of primitive purity, but on the basis of the other important aspect of his philosophy, the discipline of the machine process. There is a conflict between the scope and methods of modern industry which are formed by the machine process and the management of that industry by businessmen whose outlook was formed in an earlier historical period, who are not geared to the discipline of the machine that calls for efficiency of production but who think in terms of profits, profits that may disrupt the running of the whole industrial system. Veblen saw a contest for power going on between the businessmen of the barbarian past, whose habits of thinking were entrenched in the institutions of private property, and the rest of the community, which was coming under the discipline of the machine, which had lost the habits of thought of barbarism, and which now gave no allegiance, therefore, to the institution of private property. "Broadly, the machine discipline acts to disintegrate the institutional heritage of all degrees of antiquity and authenticity. . . . It hereby cuts away that ground of law and order on which business enterprise is founded." For Veblen, there was no possibility of business successfully resisting the machine because, in the last analysis, business was based on control of the machine.

The Instinct of Workmanship draws together the two themes of these earlier books and shows their relationship. It was the machine process that had made possible the extreme objectivity of post-Darwinian science because "the discipline of the machine process enforces a standardization of conduct and of knowledge in terms of quantitative precision, and inculcates a habit of apprehending and explaining facts in terms of material cause and effect. It involves a valuation of facts, things, relations, and even personal capacity, in terms of force. Its metaphysics is materialism and its point of view is that of causal sequence.'' This had the effect that ''the mechanically trained classes, trained to matter-of-fact habits of thought, show a notable lack of spontaneity in the construction of new myths or conventions as well as in the reconstruction of the old.''

Did this then mean that civilization was to be without values? Not at all. Modern man had no need for new values, for new conventions; he had them built in, ready-made, from his savage inheritance. Stripped of all that was false and pernicious, man could, at last, go back to the native proclivities that ''alone make anything worthwhile.'' These are the instinct of workmanship that leads men to high social and material productivity and pride in their jobs; the instinct of parental bent which is broader than a family feeling and leads men to a broad humanitarianism and concern for the welfare of the whole community; and idle curiosity which is the basis of all progressive knowledge.

As these instincts are expressed through habit and as habits become conventionalized in institutions, a complex pattern of life emerged in which the instincts contaminated each other and led to the regressive stage of barbarism where men came under the habits of predation and self-aggrandizement. This weakness in man is unavoidable. ''It appears, then, that so long as the parental solicitude and the sense of workmanship do not lead men to take thought and correct the otherwise unguarded drift of things, the growth of institutions . . . will commonly run at cross purposes with serviceability and the sense of workmanship.''

As modern capitalism has developed, Veblen saw the progressive freeing of the instinct of workmanship from the bonds of barbarian habits; the machine process has made possible the flowering of the instinct of idle curiosity; and the destruction of class divisions and distinctions in the industrial order would further the community spirit of the parental bent. Perhaps the discipline of the new machine civilization would prevent the contamination of these instincts and keep man living according to his normal propensities. By obliterating the habits of barbarism, perhaps the machine had helped man escape from history, from the curse of unending cumulations of habits without values and meaning.

Indeed Veblen, as he was about to enter his openly reformist years of World War I and after, began to sound even more suspiciously like the Christian philosopher Ely and the quasi-Christian thinker Patten. Both had agreed that the historical traditions of man, with the exception of Christianity, had worked at cross purposes to his primitive nature. Both had seen in Christianity a spiritual tradition that had kept alive the ideals of primitive goodness; and both had looked to Christianity as a source of cultural stability that would ease the transition of society from its competitive basis to the era of co-operation. Veblen, writing in 1910, followed the pattern of thinking of Ely and Patten almost to the letter. Western civilization, he wrote, is based at the moment on two major traditions, that of competitive business and that of Christianity. It was important, Veblen believed, to discover if they ''further and fortify one another? Do they work together without mutual help or hindrance? Or do they mutually inhibit and defeat each other?'' These questions were important to Veblen because he had a still more basic question in mind: Could Western civilization survive if one or the other of these traditions disappeared?

The answers to all of the questions could only be found through the establishment of their historical background. Christianity, Veblen explained, was based on two principles: humility and brotherly love. It appeared as a force in Western civilization during the collapse of the Roman Empire for two reasons which explain the two principles which were its foundation. In the first instance, that of humility, the discipline of daily life for most of the people was the experience of defeat and the necessity of submission. This was the cultural source of humility in the habits of the day. Brotherly love, however, came not from habit but rather from its destruction. During the period of disaster, "the pride of caste and all the principles of differential dignity and honor fell away, and left mankind naked and unashamed and free to follow the promptings of hereditary savage human nature which make for fellowship and Christian charity." This, to Veblen, explained the lasting power of Christianity through the ages; it was based on a permanent human nature which "springs eternal" when the pressure of conventionality is removed.

As against the bedrock on which Christianity was grounded, Veblen stated that the competitive principle of business went back no farther than the eighteenth century and reflected the cultural values of this limited historical period. Anchored only on ephemeral habits of mind and the institutions which rested on those habits, the competitive principle was disappearing from a world in which the machine process was inculcating new habits of thought.

Veblen was not in a position to answer his questions concerning the relations of Christianity and the competitive system. They did not further each other, they did not help each other, nor did they mutually defeat each other. One was dying and one was growing stronger. One represented a phase in Western civilization and one represented the essence of it. Western civilization would survive, therefore, the disappearance of the competitive principle. And the machine process with its impetus to the savage instincts of workmanship, idle curiosity, and parental bent would further the development of the Christian tradition. Expressing as much enthusiasm as was possible in his scientific and objective prose, Veblen wrote:

There is little in the current situation to keep the natural right of pecuniary discretion in touch with the impulsive bias of brotherly love, and there is in the spiritual discipline of the situation much that makes for an effective discrepancy between the two. Except for a possible reversion to a cultural situation strongly characterized by ideals of emulation and status, the ancient racial bias embodied in the Christian principle of brotherhood should logically continue to gain ground at the expense of the pecuniary morals of competitive business.

Veblen's faith in inexorable progress is much less apparent than that of Ely and Patten; but it is also inescapably evident that he shared their paradoxical concept of progress defined as a return to primitive human qualities, set free by industrialism, a concept shared by other thinkers of their generation. His deep allegiance to an intellectual pattern, predating the new theories of evolution stemming from the influence of Darwin, ironically, is both a justification and condemnation of Veblen as a social theorist. Few, if any, of his contemporaries did more to suggest the manner in which man is enmeshed in the historical process, incapable of any sudden escape from the conditioning influences of the past. In his insistence on the social nature of man and the slow, cumulative growth of social patterns, Veblen has always provided his interpreters with the insight that it was impossible for his generation to cut suddenly its commitments to the past and to follow fully and completely whatever novel implications were to be found in Darwinian evolutionary theory. And yet no one wanted to believe in this possiblity more passionately than Veblen, no one worked more adroitly to give it theoretical sanction. Indeed, he blended ardor and technique so compellingly that, for a generation, his interpreters could not help but accept Veblen in his self-appointed role as the ahistorical, self-contained, unique thinker, a role which openly contradicted so much of his social theory.

29
Toward Racism: The History of an Idea

John Higham

Racial prejudice in the American past has been studied with increasing intensity by historians. Focusing upon the institution of black slavery and thereby underscoring racism as the idea of white superiority, David B. Davis and Winthrop D. Jordan have produced memorable studies. Examinations of white racist attitudes toward American Indians and Mexican Americans are still comparatively limited. This chapter from John Higham's book, *Strangers in the Land,* deals with yet another kind of racism. It is the ethnic prejudice of white Anglo-Saxon Americans directed toward other white Americans from different ethnic backgrounds. Since this variety of racism was partly promulgated out of Darwinian or Spencerian hypotheses, which some of the preceding essays explore, it is important to point out that applications of evolution theory to the question of "race" have been greatly modified by the development of modern genetics. For a time, Mendelian genetics generally replaced the Darwinian theory of natural selection in formulating evolutionary ideas. But by 1937, with the appearance of Theodosius Dobzhansky's *Genetics and the Origin of Species,* evolution theory and genetics theory were integrated. Present discussions of "race" owe much to the "gene pool" concept as it is used in the field of population genetics. Here evolution appears to be the result of change in the proportional distribution of genes in a normally unchanging pool. Work along this line, together with the findings of scientific anthropologists and biochemists, has transformed thinking about "race" in intellectual history.

Yet applications of scientific findings to theories of human *social* development are tentative and often metaphorical. The biological discussion of "race" is not the same as a historical account of racism. We may remember that for biologists and anthropologists "race" has only two large meanings. For one, it is a category of classification, an attempt to give names to the wide and wild variety of living organisms so that they can be grouped for a scientific understanding of them. Secondly, "race" is a biological phenomenon. This means that the visible

Reprinted by permission of Rutgers University Press from John Higham, *Strangers in the Land* (1955), pp. 131-158. Footnotes have been omitted.

differences among men in different parts of the world are partly genetic. Whereas there are differences between any two people, even between brothers or sisters (except identical twins), "race" differences are genetic differences between Mendelian populations. Races do differ in the same traits in which individuals differ. But confusing and dangerous "typological thinking," as Dobzhansky calls it, arises when a specifically named racial group is assumed to be composed of individuals who are similar or even alike. Biology has been tending to abandon typological misconceptions. When the same effort has been applied to social theories about "race" based upon evolution, the issue has not been simple.

Some social thinkers insist that the human species has no "races," that if an individual has any "racial" identity at all, it exists in his participation in an intrabreeding group; it has nothing to do with his genetic or physical characteristics. For those of this persuasion, neutral terms such as "ethnic group" or "human variety" now seem preferable to the word "race." Other social thinkers, in accord with Dobzhansky's view, hold that once we get over typological misjudgments which assume that an individual is a manifestation of a racial type, and once we realize that human diversity is a biological fact which is not to be confused with social inequality, then we can accept racial differences as *relative*, not as absolute biological differences. Races differ in the frequency of some genes more often than they differ in the absence of one gene. This relativity in the gene-pool picture of mankind means that there can be no strict rules of thumb about racial differences. Thus the old Darwinian idea of evolution is now widely interpreted through the findings of modern geneticists. Natural selection is seen through the concept of differential reproduction, that is, the integration of organisms with their environment determined by the frequency or larger number of offspring they produce. The "struggle for existence," if the term still has meaning, is usually a peaceful and unconscious process for the individual. Putting the biological hypothesis as a metaphor for human society can suggest that violence and war may retard the adaptation of the human species to the total environment. So the racial, ethical, and political determinism of Darwinian and Spencerian struggle is being abandoned. (See essay 37.)

Even more significant in the social implications of recent biology is the waning of the old idea of the "social organism." Biologists find that each separate organism must sustain itself; the whole species is not sentient. Social evolution occurs through the strengthening or the fulfillment of each individual, not through its subjection to an imagined "social organism" or to one dominant individual. In a special sense this challenges the idea of "rugged" individualism in social philosophy so that *individuality* becomes a more telling concept.

For further reading: *John Higham, *Strangers in the Land: Patterns of American Nativism, 1860-1925* (1955)' *Thomas F. Gossett, *Race: The History of an Idea* (1963); *Oscar Handlin, *Race and Nationality in American Life* (1957); *Barbara M. Solomon, *Ancestors and Immigrants* (1956); *Allen Weinstein and Frank Otto Gatell (eds.), *The Segregation Era, 1863-1954: A Modern Reader* (1970); *David B. Davis, *The Problem of Slavery in Western Culture* (1966); *Winthrop D. Jordan, *White over Black: American Attitudes toward the Negro, 1550-1812* (1968).

Hardly any aspect of American xenophobia over its course from the eighteenth to the twentieth century is more striking than the monotony of its ideological refrain. Year after year, decade after decade, the same charges and complaints have sounded in endless reiteration. Variously combined, formulated, and documented, adapted to different and changing adversaries, rising and falling in intensity and acceptance, nearly all of the key ideas persisted without basic modification.

But in one major respect the pattern of nativist thought changed fundamentally. Gradually and progressively it veered toward racism. Absent from the strictures of the eighteenth century nationalist, notions of racial superiority and exclusiveness appeared in the mid-nineteenth, but they were to undergo a long process of revision and expansion before emerging in the early twentieth century as the most important nativist ideology. Several generations of intellectuals took part in transforming the vague and somewhat benign racial concepts of romantic nationalism into doctrines that were precise, malicious, and plausibly applicable to European immigration. The task was far from simple; at every point the race-thinkers confronted the liberal and cosmopolitan barriers of Christianity and American democracy. Ironically and significantly, it was not until the beginning of the present century, when public opinion recovered much of its accustomed confidence, that racial nativism reached intellectual maturity.

Of course racial nativism forms only a segment, though a critical and illuminating segment, of the larger evolution of race consciousness in modern times. The greater part of the complex phenomenon which is now fashionably called "race prejudice" lies beyond the scope of this book; its history is tangled and still largely unwritten. What concerns us is the intersection of racial attitudes with nationalistic ones—in other words, the extension to European nationalities of that sense of absolute difference which already divided white Americans from people of other colors. When sentiments analogous to those already discharged against Negroes, Indians, and Orientals spilled over into anti-European channels, a force of tremendous intensity entered the stream of American nativism.

The whole story of modern racial ferment, nativist and otherwise, has two levels, one involving popular emotions, the other concerning more or less systematic ideas. Most of the emotions flow from a reservoir of habitual suspicion and distrust accumulated over the span of American history toward human groups stamped by obvious differences of color. The ideas, on the other hand, depend on the speculations of intellectuals on the nature of races. The distinction is partly artificial, for the spirit of white supremacy—or what may be labeled race-feeling—has interlocked with race-thinking at many points. Indeed, their convergence has given the problem of race its modern significance. But at least the distinction has the merit of reminding us that race-feelings and explicit concepts about races have not always accompanied one another. The Anglo-Saxon idea in its early form did not entail the biological taboos of race-feeling. Nor did the pattern of white supremacy, in all likelihood, depend at the outset on formal race-thinking. Traditional religious beliefs, often hardly articulated at all, served the pragmatic purposes of the English colonists who enslaved Negroes and who scourged Indians as Satanic agents "having little of Humanitie but shape." However, the evolution of white supremacy into a comprehensive philosophy of life, grounding human values in the innate constitution of nature, required a major theoretical effort. It was the task of the race-thinkers to organize specific antipathies toward dark-hued peoples into a generalized, ideological structure.

To the development of racial nativism, the thinkers have made a special contribution. Sharp physical differences between native Americans and European Immigrants were not readily apparent; to a large extent they had to be manufactured. A rather elaborate, well-entrenched set of racial ideas was essential before the newcomers from Europe could seem a fundamentally different order of men. Accordingly, a number of race-conscious intellectuals blazed the way for ordinary nativists. . . .

From Romanticism to Naturalism

Two general types of race-thinking, derived from very different origins, circulated throughout the nineteenth century. One came from political and literary sources and assumed, under the impact of the romantic movement, a nationalistic form. Its characteristic manifestation in England and America was the Anglo-Saxon tradition. Largely exempt through most of the century from the passions of either the nativist or the white supremacist, this politico-literary concept of race lacked a clearly defined physiological basis. Its vague identification of culture with ancestry served mainly to emphasize the antiquity, the uniqueness, and the permanence of a nationality. It suggested the inner vitality of one's own culture, rather than the menace of another race. Whereas some of the early racial nationalists attributed America's greatness (and above all its capacity for self-government) to its Anglo-Saxon derivation, others thought America was creating a new mixed race; and, such was the temper of the age, many accepted both ideas at the same time. But whether exclusive or cosmopolitan in tendency, these romantics almost always discussed race as an ill-defined blessing; hardly ever as a sharply etched problem. During the age of confidence, as Anglo-Saxonism spread among an eastern social elite well removed from the fierce race conflicts of other regions, it retained a complacent, self-congratulatory air.

Meanwhile a second kind of race-thinking was developing from the inquiries of naturalists. Stimulated by the discovery of new worlds overseas, men with a scientific bent began in the seventeenth and eighteenth centuries to study human types systematically in order to catalogue and explain them. While Anglo-Saxonists consulted history and literature to identify national races, the naturalists concentrated on the great "primary" groupings of *Homo sapiens* and used physiological characteristics such as skin color, stature, head shape, and so on, to distinguish them one from the other. Quite commonly this school associated physical with cultural differences and displayed, in doing so, a feeling of white superiority over the colored races. On the whole, however, the leading scientific thinkers did not regard race differences as permanent, pure, and unalterable. A minority insisted that races were immutable, separately created species; but the influence of this polygenist argument suffered from its obvious violation of the Christian doctrine of the unity of mankind. For the most part, early anthropologists stressed the molding force of environmental conditions in differentiating the human family.

In the course of the nineteenth and early twentieth centuries, the separation between the two streams of race-thinking gradually and partially broke down.

Racial science increasingly intermingled with racial nationalism. Under the pressure of a growing national consciousness, a number of European naturalists began to subdivide the European white man into biological types, often using linguistic similarity as evidence of hereditary connection. For their part, the nationalists slowly absorbed biological assumptions about the nature of race, until every national trait seemed wholly dependent on hereditary transmission. This interchange forms the intellectual background for the conversion of the vague Anglo-Saxon tradition into a sharp-cutting nativist weapon and, ultimately, into a completely racist philosophy.

Behind the fusion—and confusion—of natural history with national history, of "scientific" with social ideas, lay a massive trend in the intellectual history of the late nineteenth and twentieth centuries. Hopes and fears alike received scientific credentials; and men looked on the human universe in increasingly naturalistic terms. In religion, literature, philosophy, and social theory ancient dualisms dissolved. Human affairs and values were seen more and more as products of vast, impersonal processes operating throughout nature. The Darwinian theory represented a decisive step in this direction; in the eyes of many, it subsumed mankind wholly under the grim physical laws of the animal kingdom.

While the whole naturalistic trend encouraged race-thinking and lent a sharper flesh-and-blood significance to it, Darwinism added a special edge. By picturing all species as both the products and the victims of a desperate, competitive struggle for survival, Darwinism suggested a warning: the daily peril of destruction confronts every species. Thus the evolutionary theory, when fully adopted by race-thinkers, not only impelled them to anchor their national claims to a biological basis; it also provoked anxiety by denying assurance that the basis would endure. Although most Anglo-Saxonists still identified their race with an indwelling spiritual principle, now they had also to envision the bearers of that principle as combatants in the great biological battle raging throughout nature.

On the other hand, it is not true that Darwinian (and Spencerian) ideas led directly to an outburst of racial nativism or to an overriding hereditarian determinism. The whole scientific revolution of the nineteenth century merely prepared the way and opened the possibility for those developments. Actually, the evolutionary hypothesis left major obstacles to a rigidly racial creed.

First of all, the general climate of opinion in the early Darwinian era inhibited the pessimistic implications of the new naturalism. What stood out in the first instance, as the great social lesson of the theory of natural selection, was not the ravages of the struggle for survival but rather the idea of "the survival of the fittest." To a generation of intellectuals steeped in confidence, the laws of evolution seemed to guarantee that the "fittest" races would most certainly triumph over inferior competitors. And in their eagerness to convert social values into biological facts, Darwinian optimists unblinkingly read "the fittest" to mean "the best." They felt confirmed in their supremacy over the immigrants, who in turn seemed the winnowed best of Europe. Darwinism, therefore, easily ministered to Anglo-Saxon pride, but in the age of confidence it could hardly arouse Anglo-Saxon anxiety.

Secondly, Darwinism gave the race-thinkers little concrete help in an essential prerequisite of racism—belief in the preponderance of heredity over environment. Certainly the biological vogue of the late nineteenth century stimulated speculation along these lines, but the evolutionary theory by no means disqualified a fundamentally environmentalist outlook. Darwin's species struggled and evolved within particular natural settings; they survived through adaptation to those settings. This aspect of the theory ultimately impressed itself so forcefully on American social scientists that toward the end of the century one of them acclaimed the doctrine of evolution for actually discouraging racial as opposed to environmental interpretations. And while liberal environmentalists drew comfort from the new scientific gospel, it left the race-thinkers with no definite knowledge of how hereditary forces function or persist. Darwinism explained only the survival, not the appearance, of biological variations from pre-existing types. The origins of and relationships among races remained obscure.

Obviously both of these difficulties would have to be overcome if the Anglo-Saxon nationalism of the 1870's was to evolve into a fully effective instrument for race-feelings. Even to begin the transition the race-thinkers would have to cast loose from Darwinian optimism, discarding the happy thought that the fittest, in the sense of the best, always win out. That done, they would still lack a strict racial determinism. To divorce race entirely from environment and to put biological purity at the center of social policy, American nationalists would need further cues from the developing natural sciences.

Patricians on the Defensive

Americans were slow to take that second and more drastic step. Although sweeping theories and pretentious sciences or pseudo-sciences of race developed in continental Europe in the late nineteenth century, American intellectuals of that period knew practically nothing of them. Nor did American scientists make any contributions to race-thinking similar to those of Broca, Ammon, or Lapouge. In the United States psychologists dealt with individuals rather than groups, sociologists with institutions rather than peoples. Anthropologists immersed themselves in narrowly empirical studies of primitive folk, chiefly the Indians. The movement toward racism was an up-hill fight in democratic America.

But a number of Anglo-Saxon nationalists in the eighties and nineties did begin to break away from evolutionary optimism. At first, instead of trying to qualify or rebut the principle of the survival of the fittest, the race-thinkers simply turned from complacent contemplation of America's Anglo-Saxon past to an anxious look at its future. This swing to a defensive outlook marks the initial phase of racial nativism. It required no fresh intellectual stimulus; it was precipitated by the general crisis in American society.

The same internal crisis that reactivated the older nativist traditions crystallized the new one. Until unrest and class cleavage upset the reign of confidence in the 1880's, the assimilationist concept of a mixed nationality had tempered and offset pride in Anglo-Saxon superiority. But when the Anglo-Saxon enthusiasts felt their society and their own status deeply threatened, they put aside their boasts about the assimilative powers of their race. They read the signs of the times as symptoms of its peril. Contrary to an impression widespread among historians, the new racial xenophobia did not originate as a way of discriminating between old and new immigrations. It arose from disturbances, within American society, which preceded awareness of a general ethnic change in the incoming stream. At the outset, Anglo-Saxon nativism vaguely indicted the whole foreign influx. Only later did the attack narrow specifically to the new immigration.

The current social scene presented a troubling contrast to the image of America that Anglo-Saxon intellectuals cherished. The tradition of racial nationalism had always proclaimed orderly self-government as the chief glory of the Anglo-Saxons—an inherited capacity so unique that the future of human freedom surely rested in their hands. But now the disorders of the mid-eighties cast doubt on the survival of a free society. The more anxious of the Anglo-Saxon apostles knew that the fault must lie with all the other races swarming to America. Did they not, one and all, lack the Anglo-Saxon's self-control, almost by definition? So, behind the popular image of unruly foreigners, a few caught sight of unruly races; and Anglo-Saxon nativism emerged as a corollary to anti-radical nativism—as a way of explaining why incendiary immigrants threatened the stability of the republic.

The explanation came out clear-cut in the convulsion that followed the Haymarket Affair. A writer in a business magazine stated the racial lesson of the riot in the baldest terms: anarchy is "a blood disease" from which the English have never suffered. "I am no race worshipper," he insisted, "but . . . if the master race of this continent is subordinated to or overrun with the communistic and revolutionary races, it will be in grave danger of social disaster." During the same fateful summer a leading Congregational theologian equated race and unrest in words so sharp that he withheld them from publication for a year and a half. The Reverend Theodore T. Munger, an exponent of evolutionary theology, had long admired the Anglo-Saxons, the most highly developed, the most individualistic, and indeed the most Christian of races. As he surveyed the strife of 1886, he saw "anarchism, lawlessness . . . labor strikes, and a general violation of personal rights such as the Anglo-Saxon race has not witnessed since Magna Charta . . . This horrible tyranny is wholly of foreign origin." Fundamentally, however, the problem was not just foreign. It was "physiological": how to restrict immigration "so that the physical stock shall not degenerate, and how to keep the strong, fine strain ascendant."

Compared to the common and simple attack on radical *foreigners,* the attack on radical *races* was at first a minor theme. Indeed, it did not immediately displace the older kind of race-thinking. During the eighties many Anglo-Saxonists still clung to the traditional pride and confidence in America's powers of assimilation. Josiah Strong, for example, was still celebrating the absorptive capacities of the Anglo-Saxons after he had begun to attack the immigrants as socially disruptive. And in 1890 James K. Hosmer's glowing constitutional history of the Anglo-Saxon race still conceded that racial mingling invigorated it, although Hosmer was equally certain that immigration was diluting the Anglo-Saxons' blood and subverting their social order.

During the 1890's, as the social crisis deepened, racial nativism became more defined and widespread. If one may judge, however, from Congressional debates, newspapers, and the more popular periodicals, Anglo-Saxonism still played a relatively small part in public opinion. The rising flood of popular xenophobia drew much more upon conventional anti-foreign ideas.

On the whole, the Anglo-Saxon tradition in its new nativistic form still found its support within the patrician circles where it had persisted throughout the age of confidence. Now, as then, the race-thinkers were men who rejoiced in their colonial ancestry, who looked to England for standards of deportment and taste, who held the great academic posts or belonged to the best clubs or adorned the higher Protestant clergy. Some, like Frank Parsons or Albert Shaw, were active reformers, especially in the municipal field. But, in general, racial nativists worshipped tradition in a deeply conservative spirit, and in the tumult of the nineties it seemed to them that everything fixed and sacred was threatened with dissolution. Among them were Episcopalian Bishop A. Cleveland Coxe, who added the final "e" to his family name in order to re-establish its antique spelling; Woodrow Wilson, then a historian with aristocratic sympathies, a disciple of Burke and Bagehot who believed heartily in evolution because it moved so slowly; John W. Burgess, who brought from German seminars a love for "the race-proud Teutons" rather than the Anglo-Saxons and whose political science proved that racial amalgamation endangered private enterprise; and of course Henry Cabot Lodge, who mourned for the days when society venerated the old families, their traditions, and their ancestors. No one expressed the state of mind in this group better than the Presbyterian clergyman in New York who thought nature's great principle of inequality endangered by a "specious humanity," liberty-loving Anglo-Saxons beset by socialistic foreigners, and the intelligent people in the clutches of the unintelligent.

A substantial number of these patrician nativists belonged to the cultivated intelligentsia of New England, the region where the Anglo-Saxon idea was most firmly entrenched. There the proportion of foreign-born in the total population was rising more sharply than in any other part of the country. There too the declining vitality of the native culture contributed to a defensive attitude. Brahmin intellectuals such as Lodge, Henry Adams, and Barrett Wendell knew that the historic culture of New England had entered its "Indian Summer," and the knowledge gave them added cause to see their race and region beleaguered by the alien. In other places also a pessimistic spirit was creeping into intellectual life as the century wanted. What the German writer Max Nordau was calling "vague qualms of a Dusk of the Nations" darkened various minds receptive to social anxieties or to the grimmer implications of Darwinian naturalism. But New Englanders particularly succumbed to the melancholy, *fin de siècle* mood and gave it a racial form. Thus at Harvard, Barrett Wendell, whose English accent matched his Anglophile interpretation of American literature, was settling into the conviction that his own kind had had its day, that other races had wrenched the country from its grasp for once and all.

Many if not most of these men in the early nineties remained oblivious of the new immigration, assuming that the immigrants as a whole lacked the Anglo-Saxon's ancestral qualities. However, the avant-garde of racial nationalists was discovering during those years the shift in the immigrant stream. The discovery was important, because it lent a new sharpness and relevance to race-thinking. By making the simple (and in fact traditional) assumption that northern European nationalities shared much of the Anglo-Saxon's inherited traits, a racial nativist could now understand why immigration had just now become a problem. Also, the cultural remoteness of southern and eastern European "races" suggested to him that the foreign danger involved much more than an inherited incapacity for self-government: the new immigration was racially impervious to the whole of American civilization! Thus Anglo-Saxon nativism, in coming to focus on specific ethnic types, passed beyond its first, subordinate role as a corollary to anti-radical nativism. It found its own *raison d'être,* and in doing so served to divide the new immigrants from their predecessors in an absolute and fundamental way. Racial nativism became at once more plausible, a more significant factor in the history of immigration restriction, and a more precisely formulated ideology.

Three prominent intellectuals of the day illustrate this evolution in the Anglo-Saxon idea. Each of them embarked on anti-foreign agitation in the loose terms provoked by the internal events of the eighties, and each of them ended by fixing on the new immigration as constitutionally incapable of assimilation.

Nathaniel S. Shaler, the Kentucky-born geologist who presided over the Lawrence Scientific School at Harvard, was in some ways a reluctant and unlikely nativist. One of the most benign of individuals, Shaler felt a real sympathy for disadvantaged groups; and his professional training impressed upon him the large influence of the physical environment in creating human differences. But his early southern background had given Shaler an indelible race consciousness. He easily shared the belief of his Brahmin colleagues that American democracy rested on an English racial heritage. At first he stated the racial argument against immigration in class terms, contending that the immigrants threatened social stability because, as peasants, they lacked the Americans' inborn instinct for freedom. In 1894, however, he shifted to a more specific and sweeping attack on the new immigration. Instead of indicting the immigrants as a whole, he now drew a sharp racial contrast between northwestern and southeastern Europeans, maintaining that the new "non-Aryan" peoples were wholly different from earlier immigrants and innately impossible to Americanize.

Henry Cabot Lodge arrived by a similar route at the same conclusion but carried it much further. What was perhaps his earliest public attack on immigration reflected simply a nationalist reaction to the crisis within American society. At that time, in 1888, he actually repudiated the injection of racial considerations into political issues. His own Anglo-Saxonism still conformed to the traditional eulogistic pattern. Events, however, soon turned his attention to invidious racial comparisons. In 1891 Lodge published a statistical analysis, which cost him much time and effort, concerning "the distribution of ability" in the American population. By classifying the entries in a biographical encyclopedia, he tried to show "the enormous predominance" of an English racial strain over every other in contributing to the development of the United States. Although the figures in this study suggested the inferiority of every non-English group in America, thereafter Lodge concentrated his fire on the new immigration, arguing that it presented a supreme danger transcending political or economic considerations: it threatened "a great and perilous change in the very fabric of our race."

To support this view, Lodge went far beyond his American contemporaries in the direction of a racial philosophy of history. During a summer in France in 1895, he happened upon a new book by Gustave Le Bon, *The Psychology of Peoples.* Le Bon was a poetic social psychologist, an enemy of democracy, and a man who lived in dread of an imminent socialist revolution. His book treated nationalities as races and races as the substrata of history. Only through crossbreeding, according to Le Bon, could a race die or miss its destiny. He saw little hope for continental Europe but thought that the English, alone among European races, had kept their purity and stability. Lodge took these ideas back to the United States and repeated them almost verbatim on the floor of the Senate in 1896 in leading the fight for the literacy test. Without restriction of the new immigration, he warned, America's fixed, inherited national character would be lost in the only way possible—by being "bred out."

Lodge was exceptional both in his direct contact with European race-thinking and in the degree to which he embraced an ideal of racial purity. It was not so easy for others to ignore the influence of environment or to understand how a supposedly backward, inferior type could overwhelm the puissant Anglo-Saxons.

A third member of the Yankee upper crust moved more cautiously into racial nativism but exerted in the long run a more telling intellectual influence. Francis A. Walker, president of the Massachusetts Institute of Technology and one of the outstanding economists of his day, was virtually the only American who made an original contribution to nativist thought in the late nineteenth century. Unlike Lodge, Shaler or the rest, Walker faced up to the key Darwinian issue of the survival of the fittest.

When he awoke to the menace of the foreign-born during the great labor upheaval of the mid-eighties, it was not race but rather the European's characteristic "insolence and savagery" that gave Walker visions of "great cities threatened with darkness, riot, and pillage." He continued to think of labor unrest as the most important aspect of the foreign peril and, in fact, never indulged in comprehensive racial theorizing. But as early as 1890 he trembled at a new influx of totally unassimilable races, representing "the very lowest stage of degradation." That these were laggards in the struggle for existence Walker had no doubt. Lest anyone should still defend the old Darwinian notion of migration as a selective process bringing America the most energetic and enterprising of Europeans, Walker neatly turned the tables, declaring that natural selection was now working in reverse. Due to the cheapness and ease of steamship transportation, the fittest now stay at home; the unfit migrate. The new immigrants, he declared in phrases that rang down through the restriction debates of the next three decades, "are beaten men from beaten races; representing the worst failures in the struggle for existence. . . . They have none of the ideas and aptitudes which . . . belong to those who are descended from the tribes that met under the oak trees of old Germany to make laws and choose chieftains."

But still there was the hard question: How and why can such unfit groups endanger the survival of America's strong native stock? Walker held the clue long before it occurred to him to ask the question. As superintendent of the United States census of 1870, he had noticed that the rate of population growth in America was declining. At the time and for many years afterward he interpreted the decline very sensibly as a result of urbanization and industrialization. Then, when the events of the eighties and early nineties turned his attention to racial significance of immigration, the old problem of population growth appeared in a new light. Might not the dwindling birth rate be a prudential response by the old American stock to a Darwinian struggle with immigrants capable of underbidding and outbreeding them? With an ingenious show of statistics, Walker argued in 1891 that the reproductive decline was occurring largely among the native population and that immigration rather than domestic conditions was responsible for it. In order to compete with cheap foreign labor, he said, Americans preferred to reduce the size of their families rather than lower their standard of living. Thus the foreign-born were actually replacing the native stock, not reinforcing it; in the very act of maintaining social and economic superiority, native Americans were undergoing biological defeat. In view of the new influx from southern and eastern Europe, Walker was sure that this long process of replacement would now enter an increasingly ominous stage.

From a racial point of view, the argument had the disadvantage of resting on social and economic determinants and therefore failing to make any real distinction between immigrant types. Nevertheless, it did effectively counter Darwinian optimism while defining the foreign danger in plainly biological terms. Like Lodge's bluster about crossbreeding, Walker's birth-rate hypothesis suggested that unobstructed natural selection might insure the survival of the worst people rather than the best. The recasting of the Anglo-Saxon tradition into the mold of a gloomy, scientific naturalism was under way.

Optimistic Crosscurrents

Before this naturalistic trend made further headway, in fact before nativists paid much attention to Walker's theory, events temporarily twisted race-thinking in a very different direction. The fears and forebodings that were pushing Anglo-Saxonism toward sharper, more dogmatic formulations suddenly lifted at the end of the century; a new era bright with hope and flushed with well-being relieved the need to define enemies and explain failures. At a time when every xenophobia subsided, racial nationalism softened, relaxed, and resumed once more its historic air of triumphant confidence. Yet, oddly, it flourished as never before.

Actually, two currents of racial nationalism had developed among American intellectuals during the 1890's. One was defensive, pointed at the foreigner within; the other was aggressive, calling for expansion overseas. Both issued, in large measure, from the same internal frustrations; both reflected the same groundswell of national feeling. But one warned the Anglo-Saxon of a danger of submergence, while the other assured him of a conquering destiny. By 1898 the danger and doom were all but forgotten, and the conquest was made. An easy and successful adventure in imperialism gave racial nationalism both an unprecedented vogue and a cheerful tone. In a torrent of popular jubilation over the Anglo-Saxon's invincibility, the need to understand his predicament scientifically dissolved in a romantic glow.

Imperialists happily intent on absorbing Filipinos and Puerto Ricans felt little doubt of the Anglo-Saxons' powers of assimilation. Instead of Lodge's dread of racial mixture and his insistence on the fixity of the Anglo-Saxon folk, the country now heard once more the earlier theory of John Fiske: that Anglo-Saxons possess a unique capacity to merge with other peoples while retaining their own dominant traits. Franklin H. Giddings, the first professor of sociology at Columbia University, dressed up in scientific language the old notion that immigration was recapitulating in the United States the same blend of European strains from which the English had originally emerged. His proof that the United States was still English moved the editor of the *Ladies' Home Journal* to congratulate the home of the oppressed for its success in assimilation. Others admitted that America's racial composition was changing but insisted that its Anglo-Saxon (or Teutonic) ideals were imposed on all comers. Albert Shaw, once one of the leading racial nativists, explained his shift away from a restrictionist position by asserting that America's power to assimilate had increased. Another imperialist felt so strong a sense of national homogeneity that he gave a new definition to the term Anglo-Saxon. All who stand together under the stars and stripes and fight for what it represents, he declared, have a right to that proud designation.

Of course, there was another, less uplifting side to this frame of mind. The prime object of the imperialist ideology, after all, was to justify imposing colonial status on backward peoples. Every Anglo-Saxonist knew that the United States was taking up "the white man's burden" in extending American control over the dark-skinned natives of the Philippines, Hawaii, and Puerto Rico. Under these circumstances the Anglo-Saxon idea easily associated itself with emotions of white supremacy. In other words, while welcoming the immigrant population into the Anglo-Saxon fold, imperialists were also linking their ideal of nationality to a consciousness of color. Although a romantic idealism temporarily blurred the ideological sharpness of racial nationalism, at a deeper and more permanent level the Anglo-Saxon would henceforth symbolize the white man par excellence.

The imperialist excitement itself lasted only a short while, leaving the Anglo-Saxon tradition freighted with race-feelings and exposed again to a defensive, nativistic reaction. Overseas adventures lost their savor as soon as they engendered difficult moral problems and serious international entanglements. As early as 1901 the bloodshed necessary to impose United States rule on the "new-caught, sullen peoples" of the Philippines was deflating enthusiasm for expansion. And by 1905, when Japan emerged as a new world power menacing American interests in the Far East, American opinion was nervously repudiating the conquering, global destiny of a few years before. Confronted by the "Yellow Peril," the Anglo-Saxon abandoned his rampant stance and resumed a somewhat defensive posture.

There were various indications in the early years of the twentieth century that race-thinking was entering a fretful, post-imperialist phase. One very direct reflection of the change of mood came in a book published in 1905 by a United States Army surgeon on his return from a tour of duty in the Philippines. In *The Effects of Tropical Light on White Men*, Major Charles E. Woodruff passed a depressing verdict on the racial results of imperialism. The blond, blue-eyed race, he argued, is born to command and to conquer; but in expanding southward from its foggy, overcast homelands in northern Europe it always succumbs to intense sunlight, which only the brunette races can withstand. And as Woodruff glanced apprehensively at the complexion of the immigrants pouring into the United States at the time, he added a significant afterthought. Perhaps the blond Teutons cannot expect to survive even under the climatic conditions prevailing throughout most of the United States. Woodruff displayed all of the color feelings aroused by imperialism and none of its buoyant idealism. Much the same can be said of the gloomy tracts that California's leading race-thinker, Homer Lea, wrote in the next few years on the decline of American militancy and the spread of the Yellow Peril.

Among other racial nationalists the reaction from imperial euphoria brought back the vague fears of the nineties about the Anglo-Saxons' stamina. They spoke of the old stock becoming decadent and being elbowed aside, of the Anglo-Saxon race as doomed, of the native Americans suffering from all manner of moral, physical, and psychic deterioration, due in large measure to immigration. Since nativism was at a low ebb in early years of the century, the complaints usually sounded a mournful note rather than a belligerent or defiant one. Professor George E. Woodberry, one of the old-guard literary critics, even tried to find some comfort in the dismal spectacle. Lecturing on "race power" in literature in 1903, he suggested that the dissolution of the English race would fulfill a historic, sacrificial principle by which each great race succumbs in order to bequeath its heritage to a broader humanity.

A less spiritually satisfying but more scientific explanation of the Anglo-Saxon's flagging energies could be found in Francis A. Walker's theory that immigration discouraged reproduction among the older stock. The theory was more and more widely discussed, with hardly anyone equipped statistically to challenge it. Instead of critical scrutiny, Walker's sober argument now got a popular currency as it was inflated into the more grandiose concept of "race suicide." This happened in a curiously roundabout fashion. In 1901 Edward A. Ross used Walker's ideas in an address before the American Academy of Political and Social Science to explain how unchecked Asiatic immigration might lead to the extinction of the American people. When a higher race quietly eliminates itself rather than endure the competition of a lower one, said Ross, it is committing suicide. At the time, Ross was too confident of America's powers of assimilation to write about European immigration in these terms. Before "race suicide" did become directly pertinent to the problem which Walker himself had had in mind, Theodore Roosevelt simplified it into an argument against birth control. For all of his booming optimism, Roosevelt could not entirely repress lurking doubts over the future. His nativist tendencies being in check, he discharged his anxieties through vague, thundering appeals to mothers to arrest the suicide of "the race" by having more children.

The President's campaign for fecundity popularized the notion of race suicide. During the period from 1905 through 1909 the general magazines published over thirty-five articles dealing directly with the topic. Once it became a minor national phobia, the original, nativistic implications of the idea speedily reasserted themselves. In reply to a Rooseveltian tirade, *Harper's Weekly* remarked caustically in 1905 that exhortation would have little effect on the native birth rate as long as unlimited European immigration continued to reduce it. Soon books were being written to warn that race suicide would "toll the passing of this great Anglo-Teuton people" and the surrender of the nation "to the Latin and the Hun." In the end, the whole discussion probably caused more race-thinking than reproduction. At least it brought to a wider audience the racial pessimism previously confined to a limited group of upper-class intellectuals.

It would be wrong to suppose, however, that any despairing note sounded very loudly or struck very deeply during the first decade of the twentieth century. Pessimistic anxieties crept about the fringes of American thought; at the heart of it was a supreme confidence. As the ebullience of imperialism ebbed away, much of the slack in American spirits was taken up by another enthusiasm. Progressivism inherited and sustained a good deal of the verve and exuberance which imperialism had generated. Many of the empire-builders of 1900 became apostles of social reform in the following years, their crusading élan shifting from expansion abroad to improvement at home. As long as progressivism kept that psychological tone, as long as it radiated a sense of promise and victory, it limited the impact of imperialism's other heritage of race-thinking.

Furthermore, the premises of progressive thought, as well as its optimistic spirit, blunted the force of Anglo-Saxon nativism. By renewing faith in democracy, progressivism tended to challenge belief in racial inequalities. By concentrating on environmental reconstruction, it implicitly disputed all racial determinisms. At a time when politicians, public, and intelligentsia, alike, quickened with a vision of intelligence recasting environment, the Anglo-Saxon tradition faced powerful opposing currents. If nativistic intellectuals were to capitalize on the race consciousness left in the wake of imperialism, they would have to breast the mainstream of progressive thought.

Thus the race-thinkers of the early twentieth century belonged in considerable degree to the same social minority that had sustained the Anglo-Saxon tradition during the late nineteenth. Conservative patricians were less likely than most Americans to share the prevailing optimism and environmentalism. To men like Lodge and the founders of the Immigration Restriction League, like Major Woodruff and Professor Woodberry, the crusading spirit of progressivism brought little solace. Surely reform was not restoring the more stable social order of the past, and those who above all valued family and tradition often relapsed into a gloomy view of their racial future once the appeal of imperialism faded. A number of patrician intellectuals, it is true, were caught up in the wave of social reform and surrendered some of their ethnic worries in the process. Theodore Roosevelt, for example, who had applauded Lodge's racial tirade in 1896 and rushed off to France an order for Le Bon's books, by 1904 was calling into question the whole tendency to use racial criteria in judging nationalities. But others of Roosevelt's background felt increasingly their own social displacement in a democratic age and hugged ever more tightly—in Henry James' words—"the honor that sits astride of the consecrated English tradition."

In short, when imperialism subsided, the Anglo-Saxon tradition moved again in the nativist direction it had taken during the early and mid-nineties. Yet the subsequent compulsions of empire-building and progressive reform decisively affected its course—one in a positive, the other in a negative, way. Imperialism left a heritage of race-feelings that enriched the emotional appeal of Anglo-Saxon nativism; progressivism challenged its intellectual basis. The democratic, environmentalist outlook adopted by most of the leading social scientists and historians of the Progressive era weakened the intellectual respectability of the confused, ill-defined concepts of race prevalent in the nineteenth century. To vindicate its intellectual pretensions and rationalize its emotional tone, the Anglo-Saxon tradition more than ever needed restatement in the form of a scientific law. And this was exactly what happened.

Enter the Natural Scientists

In the 1890's nativist intellectuals had barely begun to think of European races as a biological threat or to associate national survival with racial purity. Even Walker's birth-rate theory offered no logical reason to suppose that the country would suffer from the replacement of old stock by new. Perhaps the most serious intellectual handicap of American race-thinkers before the twentieth century was the lack of a general scientific principle from which to argue the prepotency of heredity in human affairs. But at the turn of the century, when social science and history came increasingly under the sway of environmental assumptions, biologists advanced dramatic claims for heredity and even helped to translate them into a political and social creed.

The new science of heredity came out of Europe about 1900 and formed the first substantial contribution of European thought to American nativism after the time of Darwin. The study of inheritance suddenly leaped into prominence and assumed a meaningful pattern from the discovery of the long-unnoticed work of Gregor Mendel and its convergence with August Weismann's theory of germinal continuity. Together, these hypotheses demonstrated the transmission from generation to generation of characteristics that obeyed their own fixed laws without regard to the external life of the organism.

Amid the excitement caused in English scientific circles by these continental discoveries, Sir Francis Galton launched the eugenics movement. Galton, who was England's leading Darwinian scientist, had long been producing statistical studies on the inheritance of all sorts of human abilities and deficiencies. But it was only in the favorable climate of the early twentieth century that he started active propaganda for uplifting humanity by breeding from the best and restricting the offspring of the worst. To Galton, eugenics was both a science and a kind of secular religion. It certified that the betterment of society depends largely on improvement of the "inborn qualities" of "the human breed," and Galton preached this message with evangelical fervor. Thus he provided biologists and physicians, excited over the new genetic theories, with a way of converting their scientific interests into a program of social salvation—a program based wholly on manipulation of the supposedly omnipotent forces of heredity.

In the latter part of the 1900's the eugenics movement got under way in the United States, where it struck several responsive chords. Its emphasis on unalterable human inequalities confirmed the patricians' sense of superiority; its warnings over the multiplication of the unfit and the sterility of the best people synchronized with the discussion of race suicide. Yet the eugenicists' dedication to a positive program of "race improvement" through education and state action gave the movement an air of reform, enabling it to flourish in the backwash of progressivism while still ministering to conservative sensibilities. By 1910, therefore, eugenicists were catching the public ear. From then through 1914, according to one tabulation, the general magazines carried more articles on eugenics than on the three questions of slums, tenements, and living standards, combined.

The leading eugenicist in America was Charles B. Davenport, a zoologist of tremendous ambition and drive who established the country's first research center in genetics at Cold Spring Harbor, Long Island. Davenport's father, a descendant of one of the Puritan founders of New England, was a genealogist who traced his ancestry back to 1086, and Davenport himself often mourned "that the best of that grand old New England stock is dying out through failure to reproduce." His early experiments at Cold Spring Harbor were devoted to testing the Mendelian principles in animal breeding; by 1907 he was beginning to apply them to the study of human heredity. In 1910 he persuaded Mrs. E. H. Harriman to finance a Eugenics Record Office adjacent to his laboratory with the aim of compiling an index of the American population and advising individuals and local societies on eugenical problems. Over a course of years she poured more than half a million dollars into the agency, while Davenport—already one of America's leading biologists—gave the rest of his life to studying the inheritance of human traits and spreading the gospel of eugenics. An indefatigable organizer, Davenport was also one of the leaders of the American Breeders' Association, where the eugenics agitation first centered. Established in 1903 by practical plant and animal breeders who wanted to keep in touch with the new theoretical advances, the association enlarged its field in 1907 to embrace eugenics.

The racial and nativistic implications of eugenics soon became apparent. From the eugenicists' point of view, the immigration question was at heart a biological one, and to them admitting "degenerate breeding stock" seemed one of the worst sins the nation could commit against itself. It was axiomatic to these naïve Mendelians that environment could never modify an immigrant's germ plasm and that only a rigid selection of the best immigrant stock could improve rather than pollute endless generations to come. Since their hereditarian convictions made virtually every symptom of social disorganization look like an inherited trait, the recent immigration could not fail to alarm them. Under the influence of eugenic thinking, the burgeoning mental hygiene movement picked up the cry. Disturbed at the number of hereditary mental defectives supposedly pouring into the country, the psychiatrists who organized the National Committee for Mental Hygiene succeeded in adding to the immigration bill of 1914 an odd provision excluding cases of "constitutional psychopathic inferiority." By that time many critics of immigration were echoing the pleas in scientific periodicals for a "rational" policy "based upon a noble culture of racial purity."

None were quicker or more influential in relating eugenics to racial nativism than the haughty Bostonians who ran the Immigration Restriction League. Prescott F. Hall had always had a hypochondriac's fascination with medicine and biology, and his associate, Robert DeCourcy Ward, was a professional scientist. They had shied away from racial arguments in the nineties, but in the less favorable atmosphere of the new century their propaganda very much needed a fresh impulse. As early as 1906 the league leaders pointed to the new genetic principles in emphasizing the opportunity that immigration regulation offered to control America's future racial development. Two years later they learned of the eugenics sentiment developing in the American Breeders' Association. They descended upon it, and soon they were dominating its immigration activities. The association organized a permanent committee on immigration, of which Hall became chairman and Ward secretary. Ward proceeded to read papers on immigration legislation before meetings of eugenicists, and for a time the two considered changing the name of their own organization to the "Eugenic Immigration League." Meanwhile they seized every occasion to publicize the dogma that science decrees restrictions on the new immigration for the conservation of the "American race."

Obviously the eugenics movement had crucial importance for race-thinking at a time when racial presuppositions were seriously threatened in the intellectual world. But basically the importance of eugenics was transitional and preparatory. It vindicated the hereditarian assumptions of the Anglo-Saxon tradition; it protected and indeed encouraged loose talk about race in reputable circles; and in putting race-thinking on scientific rather than romantic premises it went well beyond the vague Darwinian analogies of the nineteenth century. On the other hand, eugenics failed utterly to supply a racial typology. In their scientific capacity, the eugenicists—like their master Galton—studied individual traits and reached conclusions on individual differences. When they generalized the defects of individual immigrants into those of whole ethnic groups, their science deserted them and their phrases became darkly equivocal. Indeed, the more logical and consistent eugenicists maintained that America could improve its "race" by selecting immigrants on the ground of their individual family histories regardless of their national origins.

In the end the race-thinkers had to look to anthropology to round out a naturalistic nativism. Anthropology alone could classify the peoples of Europe into hereditary types that would distinguish the new immigration from older Americans; it alone might arrange these races in a hierarchy of merit and thereby prove the irremediable inferiority of the newcomers; and anthropology would have to collaborate with genetics to show wherein a mixture of races physically weakens the stronger.

American anthropology remained cautiously circumspect on these points. The influence of the foreign-born progressive, Franz Boas, was already great; in 1911 he published the classic indictment of race-thinking, *The Mind of Primitive Man*. In the absence of interest on the part of American anthropologists, a perfected racism depended on amateur handling of imported ideas. In a climate of opinion conditioned by the vogues of race suicide and eugenics, however, it is not surprising that scientifically minded nativists found the categories and concepts they needed without assistance from American anthropologists.

Again the inspiration came from Europe. There, chiefly in France and Germany, during the latter half of the nineteenth century anthropologists furnished the scientific credentials and speculative thinkers the general ideas out of which a philosophy of race took shape. The first of the thoroughgoing racists, Count J. A. de Gobineau, reached a limited audience of proslavery thinkers in America on the eve of the Civil War and then was forgotten. His successors were even less effective. Once in a while an immigrant writer tried to translate some of this literature into terms that might appeal to an American public, but the stuff simply was not read. Not until the beginning of the twentieth century did the invidious anthropological theories which had been accumulating in Europe for over thirty years reach a significant American audience. And when they did, they were delivered in a characteristically American package.

William Z. Ripley was a brilliant young economist who had the kind of mind that refuses to stay put. In the mid-nineties, before he was thirty years old, Ripley was teaching economics at the Massachusetts Institute of Technology, while simultaneously developing a unique course of lectures at Columbia University on the role of geography in human affairs. In its conception this course reflected Ripley's conviction of the basic importance of environmental conditions in molding the life of man; but he quickly came up against the problem of race. The question led him to the controversies among continental scholars on the anthropological traits of European peoples, and he chose the locale of Europe as a crucial test of the interplay of race and environment. In *The Races of Europe*, a big, scholarly volume appearing in 1899, he anatomized the populations of the continent, pointing temperately but persistently to ways in which physiological traits seemed to reflect geographical and social conditions.

This was cold comfort to nativists, but the book had another significance apart from the author's well-hedged thesis. Ripley organized into an impressive synthesis a tripartite classification of white men which European ethnologists had recently developed. For the first time, American readers learned that Europe was not a land of "Aryans" or Goths subdivided into vaguely national races such as the Anglo-Saxon, but rather the seat of three races discernible by physical measurements: a northern race of tall, blond longheads which Ripley called Teutonic; a central race of stocky roundheads which he called Alpine; and a southern race of slender, dark longheads which he called Mediterranean. Here was a powerful weapon for nativists bent on distinguishing absolutely between old and new immigrations, but to make it serviceable Ripley's data would have to be untangled from his environmentalist assumptions.

It is ironical that Ripley himself did some of the untangling. For all of his scholarly caution he could not entirely suppress an attachment to the Teutonic race that reflected very mildly the rampant Teutonism of many of the authorities on which he relied. In the early twentieth century the new genetic hypotheses and a growing alarm over the new immigration turned his attention from environmental to inherited influences. He began to talk about race suicide and to wonder about the hereditary consequences of the mixture of European races occurring in America.

Before abandoning anthropology completely to concentrate in economics, Ripley delivered in 1908 a widely publicized address in which he suggested an answer to the old problem of how the crossing of superior and inferior races can drag down the former. His roving eye had come upon the experiments that some of the Mendelian geneticists were making on plant and animal hybrids. Hugo De Vries and others were demonstrating how hybridization sometimes caused a reassertion of latent characters inherited from a remote ancestor. The concept of reversion was an old one, discussed by Darwin himself, but the rise of genetics brought it into new prominence. Ripley fastened on the idea and raised the question whether the racial intermixture under way in America might produce a reversion to a primitive type. In contrast to the theory of race suicide, this doctrine—torn from the context of genetics and applied to the typology of European races—provided a thoroughly biological explanation of the foreign peril. Presumably race suicide might be arrested by legislation and by education raising the immigrant's standard of living; but reversion seemed remorseless. All of the pieces from which a sweeping statement of racial nativism might be constructed were now on hand.

The man who put the pieces together was Madison Grant, intellectually the most important nativist in recent American history. All of the trends in race-thinking converged upon him. A Park Avenue bachelor, he was the most lordly of patricians. His family had adorned the social life of Manhattan since colonial times, and he was both an expert genealogist and a charter member of the Society of Colonial Wars.

Always he resisted doggedly any intrusion of the hoi polloi. On his deathbed he was still battling to keep the public from bringing cameras into the zoo over which he had long presided.

In addition to a razor-sharp set of patrician values, Grant also had an extensive acquaintance with the natural sciences and a thoroughly naturalistic temper of mind. Beginning as a wealthy sportsman and hunter, he was the founder and later the chairman of the New York Zoological Society, where he associated intimately with leading biologists and eugenicists. In the early years of the twentieth century he published a series of monographs on North American animals—the moose, the caribou, the Rocky Mountain goat. He picked up a smattering of Mendelian concepts and, unlike his eugenicist friends, read a good deal of physical anthropology too. Ripley's work furnished his main facts about European man, but he also went behind Ripley to many of the more extreme European ethnologists. Thus Grant was well supplied with scientific information yet free from a scientist's scruple in interpreting it.

By 1910 Grant's racial concepts were clearly formed and thoroughly articulated with a passionate hatred of the new immigration. He showed little concern over relations between whites and Negroes or Orientals. His deadliest animus focused on the Jews, whom he saw all about him in New York. More broadly, what upset him was the general mixture of European races under way in America; for this process was irretrievably destroying racial purity, the foundation of every national and cultural value.

Grant's philippic appeared finally in 1916. It bore the somber title, *The Passing of the Great Race*, summing up the aristocratic pessimism that had troubled nativist intellectuals since the 1890's. Everywhere Grant saw the ruling race of the western world on the wane yet heedless of its fate because of a "fatuous belief" in the power of environment to alter heredity. In the United States he observed the deterioration going on along two parallel lines: race suicide and reversion. As a result of Mendelian laws, Grant pontificated, we know that different races do not really blend. The mixing of two races "gives us a race reverting to the more ancient, generalized and lower type." Thus "the cross between any of the three European races and a Jew is a Jew." In short, a crude interpretation of Mendelian genetics provided the rationale for championing racial purity.

After arguing the issue of race versus physical environment, Grant assumed a racial determination of culture. Much of the book rested on this assumption, for the volume consisted essentially of a loose-knit sketch of the racial history of Europe. The Alpines have always been a race of peasants. The Mediterraneans have at least shown artistic and intellectual proclivities. But the blond conquerors of the North constitute "the white man par excellence." Following the French scientist Joseph Deniker, Grant designated this great race Nordic. To it belongs the political and military genius of the world, the daring and pride that make explorers, fighters, rulers, organizers, and aristocrats. In the early days, the American population was purely Nordic, but now the swarms of Alpine, Mediterranean, and Jewish hybrids threaten to extinguish the old stock unless it reasserts its class and racial pride by shutting them out.

So the book turned ultimately into a defense of both class and racial consciousness, the former being dependent on the latter. The argument broadened from nativism to an appeal for aristocracy as a necessary correlative in maintaining racial purity. Democracy, Grant maintained, violates the scientific facts of heredity; and he was obviously proud to attribute feudalism to the Nordics. Furthermore, Grant assaulted Christianity for its humanitarian bias in favor of the weak and its consequent tendency to break down racial pride. Even national consciousness ranked second to race consciousness in Grant's scale of values.

This boldness and sweep gave *The Passing of the Great Race* particular significance. Its reception and its impact on public opinion belong to a later stage in the history of American nativism, but its appearance before America's entry into the First World War indicates that the old Anglo-Saxon tradition had finally emerged in at least one mind as a systematic, comprehensive world view. Race-thinking was basically at odds with the values of democracy and Christianity, but earlier nativists had always tried either to ignore the conflict or to mediate between racial pride and the humanistic assumptions of America's major traditions. Grant, relying on what he thought was scientific truth, made race the supreme value and repudiated all others inconsistent with it.

This, at last, was racism.

30
The Rebellion of the Intellectuals, 1912-1917

Henry F. May

In his book, *The End of American Innocence, A Study of the First Years of Our Own Time, 1912-1917* (1959), Professor Henry May of the University of California (Berkeley) brought the years immediately preceding America's entry into World War I into fresh and clear focus for students of intellectual history. Because of his work, we now read this time as a forecast of much that was the intellectual temper of the 1920s. May's interpretation, moreover, pointed up the break with the genteel tradition and with Victorian attitudes that occurred just before the First World War. This essay is May's précis, or at least preliminary excursion into the argument of his book.

For further reading: *David W. Noble, *The Progressive Mind, 1890-1917* (1970); *Charles B. Forcey, *Crossroads of Liberalism: Croly, Weyl, Lippmann and the Progressive Era, 1900-1925* (1961); Heinz Eulau, "Man against Himself: Walter Lippmann's Years of Doubt," *American Quarterly*, Laurence R. Veysey, "The Academic Mind of Woodrow Wilson," *Mississippi Valley Historical Review*, 49 (March 1963), 613-634.

As the nineteen-twenties move from memory into history, a standard picture of the decade emerges from reminiscence and research into the textbooks. This picture is a puzzling one. The decade is still, as it was in the thirties, the last island of normalcy and isolation between wars and crises. Yet it is also, clearly, a period of major cultural revolution. Both the "revolt of the highbrows" and the "rebellion of youth," first sketched by F. L. Allen, are a standard part of our semiofficial self-picture. In response to current historical fashions and perhaps also to their own changing worries about their country, historians are giving more attention to the revolutionary aspect of this conservative decade.

Having dealt with other revolutions, historians should be able to appreciate both

American Quarterly, 8 (Summer 1956), 114-126. Reprinted by permission of the author and the University of Pennsylvania. Footnotes have been omitted.

the importance and complexity of this one. For instance, they should be able to avoid taking to task the rebellious intellectuals of the twenties in the manner of some critics of the forties. The spokesmen of a revolution are not, after all, its sole cause, and a healthy regime is seldom overthrown. Yet anybody, today, must recognize that revolutions are expensive. They may release, as this one certainly did, a burst of creative vigor; but they inevitably leave behind division, hatred, and shock. In the twenties, for instance, beliefs and customs that still commanded the deepest loyalties of one part of the population became to another group a dead and repressive Genteel Tradition, to be ceremonially flouted whenever possible. Suspicions dating from this cultural cleavage still poison the air. The historian must hope that analysis of the revolution and its causes can eventually help a little to clear away some of the resentment.

Starting backward, as historians must, we arrive immediately at the First World War, and there many have stopped. It is obvious that America's first major venture into world tragedy, with its rapid cycle of national exaltation, exhaustion, and revulsion played a very large part in the emotional life of the postwar rebels. By contrast with 1918 or 1919 or even 1925, hundreds of autobiographies paint the prewar period as a time of unity, moderation, progress, and sheltered childhood.

Yet we all know that postwar reminiscence, whether of the old plantation or the old literary culture, is a dubious guide for history. Those who have looked even briefly at the social and literary criticism of the prewar years know that the period 1912-1917 was itself, for some, a time of doubt and fragmentation, of upheaval in ideas, of the disintegration of tradition—in other words it was a pre-revolutionary or early revolutionary period. Nearly every phenomenon of the twenties from Freudianism to expatriation or the abandonment of politics was present before the war, on a smaller scale and with certain differences. If we can recapture any of the meaning or content of this prewar ferment, we may be able to understand better in what sense the revolution of the twenties was and was not postwar. In this way we may even get a few suggestions as to the perenially baffling problem of the relation between ideas and events.

In an essay published in 1913 George Santayana made an attempt to catch and pin down on paper "The Intellectual Temper of the Age." To do this for one's own time is one of the hardest tasks a writer can undertake, yet for anybody who has been for a while immersed in the records of that period it is astonishing how well this brilliant essay seems to order and illuminate the times. To Santayana it seemed that "the civilisation characteristic of Christendom has not disappeared, yet another civilisation has begun to take its place." In the resulting age of confusion and transition, men were giving up the search for lasting values and firm intellectual conclusions. Instead of these, they were placing a premium on sheer vitality, on movement, change, and emotion. According to Santayana, who sometimes enjoyed but did not admire this taste, the result was that in thought and art, his generation was "in full career toward disintegration."

Whether or not Santayana's cool disapproval of the tendencies of his day, the vitalist spirit he describes stares out from the sources. One recognizes on all sides its gaiety, its irresponsibility, its love of change, and also its contempt for reason. And it does not take much knowledge of American intellectual history to know that this spirit meant trouble. For a century and a half the dominant ideas in the national faith had been a confidence in secure moral values and a belief in progress. These two commitments had often been in conflict and formed at best a somewhat unstable compound. Now both at once were brought under devastating attack.

If one starts, as Santayana does, with philosophy, the tendencies he describes emerge very clearly. The young intellectuals of America were still most widely influenced by pragmatism, by What Morton G. White has called the revolt against formalism. Experience and movement were reality; potentiality more important than actuality. Dewey's program for intelligence remaking both the world and itself probably attracted the largest number of conscious disciples, some of them, like Randolph Bourne, soon to break away in a more emotionally satisfying direction. But it may well be that the influence of James, with his catholic and dangerous acceptance of the irrational, personal, and mysterious went deeper in a generation nourished on idealism. Emerson, universally read though misunderstood and underrated, and Whitman, the sole American patron of some of the rebels, as well as the German idealists casually studied in college courses, must have prepared them for a philosophy of intuition. Whatever the reason, it was the destructive elements in pragmatism that were the most influential. The avant-garde of 1912-17, the aggressive young innovators, were perfectly willing to see all of life as an experiment. But their purpose in experimenting was rather to express themselves and experience emotion than to solve problems in a disciplined manner.

Those who were sensitive to Atlantic breezes felt most keenly the swelling winds of antirationalism, which had been gathering force for a long time. Nietzsche, for long known vaguely by the American public as an Anti-christ, was becoming a major prophet. The most vigorous, though not the most accurate, of his American interpreters was H. L. Mencken, who in a widely read and widely praised book published first in 1908 and again in 1913 used the German prophet to belabor religion, women, and, most roughly of all, democracy in his already familiar manner. But the most fashionable of Europeans was the still living and lecturing Henri Bergson, who pushed the current tendency to an extreme, contending that reality, being in constant flux and change, is only distorted by efforts to think about it and must be apprehended through intuition. His was not the only, but it was probably the dominant direction in which philosophy was moving in 1913, and there is plenty of evidence that he was extraordinarily attractive to up-to-date American intellectuals. Irving Babbitt, already an alarmed defender of traditional values, saw the rise of Bergsonism as the culmination of a long, deplorable irrationalist trend, and found it in 1912 "allied with all that is violent and extreme in contemporary life from syndicalism to 'futurist' painting."

Psychology, as well as philosophy, was dealing heavy blows to dominant assumptions and beliefs. From the time of Freud's famous trip to Clark University in 1908, the Viennese theories cropped up in popular magazines and political treatises as well as learned journals. Whether or not, as his supporters claim, Freud is to be regarded as himself a brave and determined champion of reason, the first impact of his doctrines in the United States seemed to confirm and deepen the hedonism, emotionalism, and egocentricity that were beginning to spread so widely. On the other hand, Behaviorism, a movement launched in its most dogmatic form by John B. Watson in 1912, had to wait for its vogue until after the war. Its extreme practicalism, its rejection not only of reason but of consciousness, its suspicion of emotion, did not fit the tastes of the prewar rebels.

It does not need demonstrating that restless and vigorous innovation in the graphic arts got its American start before the war. Two major tendencies already dazzled the intellectuals and startled the public. One was apparently native, the harsh and sometimes violent Ash Can realism of Sloan, Bellows and the *Masses* cartoons. The other was imported from Paris, and consisted of a kaleidoscopic series of schools of experiment in form and technique. Commenting on "Current Impressionism," a term already well out of date but helpful as a catch-all, Louis Weinberg extended his observations from and beyond contemporary art:

Impressionism as a technique is a means of recording the transitory nature of phenomena and the fluidity of motion. As a principle it is based on a philosophy of change. . . .

But this is not alone a description of the art of our times. It is the very essence of our lives.

Wherever the impressionist or vitalist tendency arose, it was expressed most frequently and characteristically not in painting or philosophy, but in politics and literature. These are the forms in which most American cultural change has been recorded, and it is to them that we must turn for a slightly closer look at prewar tendencies. Santayana's brilliant summary suggests that in politics alone the current drift toward fragmentation and chaos may have reversed itself in the constructive and integrating (though to Santayana most uncongenial) movement towards collectivism. In this one opinion, regarding an area which concerned him little, I think Santayana missed the current drift and underrated the force of his own generalization. It is true that progressivism, optimistic, gradual, and in some forms mildly collectivist, was the officially dominant ideology; and that socialism was a swelling movement on the left that seemed to many sober Americans to possess the future. Yet both these political tendencies were in the early teens already under devastating attack, and from much the same irrationalist quarter.

Progressivism in all its varieties took for granted one or both of the two fundamental assumptions which had so far underlain the whole American political tradition. One of these was that we possess secure criteria by which we can judge our political achievement, the other that human beings are able consciously to remold their environment. Now both of these basic assumptions were being seriously shaken by new doctrines that had penetrated the house of progressivism itself.

Recent studies have shown that moral standards of a highly traditional sort motivated a great many of the prewar progressives. Truth and falsehood, good and evil, stand out in nearly all the speeches of Theodore Roosevelt and Wilson and good men threw out bad in most American cities. These venerable distinctions were the first to go; the younger progressive intellectuals, nourished on Dewey and H. G. Wells, were quite willing to throw out moral categories and rely on the shaping intelligence. On a popular level Lincoln Steffens spread the picture of the good boss and the honest crook. James Harvey Robinson, speaking for the main organ of the pragmatic progressives, lumped together as obsolete the ideals of "sound doctrine, consistency, fidelity to conscience, eternal verities, immutable human nature, and the imprescriptable rights of man."

With these went the state and law, the traditional locus and method of American reform. Many of the ablest political theorists of various schools, led by the brilliant Harold Laski, were redefining the state almost out of existence. To some it was a congeries of associations, to others the tool of a class, to still others the expression of the wish of those at present in authority. Its acts were no more final and deserved no greater obedience than those of other human groups, and it was less likely than many to be rationally motivated. Similarly, law, to the followers of the French positivist Leon Duguit or the American Roscoe Pound was no longer either the embodiment of a principle nor the command of a sovereign, but the complex resultant of social forces, prevailing opinion, and judicial will.

There remained the conscious intelligence, remolding the goals of action together with its methods. This was a moving conception, and a sufficient loyalty for many in this generation. Yet this too was seriously menaced by ideas that were attractive to the youngest generation of progressives. From the new and flourishing disciplines of sociology, anthropology and social psychology came an increasingly fashionable emphasis on custom and group emotion. It was sometimes hard to see what function this newest tendency left for intelligence and purpose.

Walter Lippmann's two prewar studies, *A Preface to Politics* (1913) and *Drift and Mastery* (1914) bring together the pragmatist attack on tradition and the implicit Freudian attack on pragmatism. Appealing for a radically instrumental state, he denounces the "routineers" who rely on political machinery, law, and conventional morality. His fellow progressives seem to draw most of his fire for their naïve adherence to literal numerical democracy and narrow utilitarian goals. What is needed in politics is passion and creative emotion, still of course somehow constructively channeled and used by the far-seeing for purposes which will transcend woman suffrage or the eight-hour day.

. . . the goal of action is in its final analysis aesthetic and not moral–a quality of feeling instead of conformity to rule.

This formulation seems to me far closer to the view of postwar literary intellectuals than to that of the progressive standard-bearers. And the sources are explicit. Lippmann's friend Graham Wallas, the British author of *Human Nature in Politics* had opened the eyes of his Harvard seminar to political psychology. Steffens had helped to guide Lippmann and so, in a negative direction, had his brief experience with municipal socialism in Schenectady. But beyond these immediate guides one finds recurring references to James, Nietzsche and Bergson and frequent, specific acknowledgment of the work of Freud.

All these new insights enriched the social sciences, and for many they doubtless furnished in practice new sources of power and freedom. Traditional progressivism, with its facile assumptions and sometimes shallow purposes needed—and for that matter still needs—rethinking. Yet much had been accomplished under the auspices of ideas that were beginning to seem stale and boring. And the new beliefs that buzzed and swarmed through the immediate postwar years were not easy to introduce into the progressive hive. To combine Lippmann or Laski with Wilson was, and soon proved to be, as difficult as to match Bergson and Nietzsche with Lyman Abbott.

It is tempting to wonder whether the actual practical difficulties of progressivism from about 1914 to 1917 were not related in part to confusion of purposes and motives. It is true at least that the Wilsonian impetus began to bog down in these years. Already one finds in the up-to-the minute *New Republic* troubled editorials that ask the common postwar question: what has happened to the progressives?

On the far left much the same process was taking place, whether one labels it fertilization or disintegration or both. Not the Marxian dialectic, but the Bergsonian and mystical syndicalism of Sorel or the anarchism of Max Stirner or Emma Goldman seemed most exciting to the younger radical intellectuals. Not the earnest socialism of Milwaukee or Schenectady, with its respectability and its reliance on the discredited machinery of the state, but the romantic activism of the I.W.W. captured the emotions of the sympathizers. One of America's waves of labor violence, running through the Northwest, Colorado, West Virginia and other centers of direct action, reflecting the primitive brutality of employers' methods in the same areas, aroused the generous emotions and seemed to some to make political action irrelevant. The climax came in 1912 at Lawrence and in 1913 at Paterson, when the I.W.W. penetrated the East and the writers and artists went to its aid, when Bill Haywood was a Greenwich Village social lion and John Reed staged an immense pageant in Madison Square Garden with the letters I.W.W. flaming from the roof in red electric signs ten feet high. Even Lippmann, viewing radicalism from the outside, approved the I.W.W. rather than the Socialist Party as less formalist and more in possession of the kind of emotional force that needed only to be constructively channeled.

Naturally, when Max Eastman, a young man of impeccable ministerial stock, joined the Socialist Party, he chose the left wing rather than the gradualists. Under Eastman's editorship the *Masses,* focus of so much later radical nostalgia, became perhaps even more clearly than the sober *New Republic* the organ of youth. Publishing the magnificent and not always political cartoons of Sloan and Bellows, an occasional Picasso drawing, stories by Sherwood Anderson, and reporting by Reed, it fought for the new literature and the new sexual morality as well as the social revolution. The *Masses* was rich in humor and human emotion—qualities often enough lacking on the far left—and practically negligible in social program. Smashing idols was, in these years as after the war, a flourishing business, while Socialism as a political movement was already losing momentum in 1914-16.

More spectacularly than anywhere else, the new spirit of 1910 or 1912 to 1917 was reflected in a literary renaissance. The story of this sudden creative outburst has often been told, and only two points need making for our present purpose. One of these is that literary departures in the prewar years were closely related to contemporary movements in other fields of thought, the other that prewar writing contains in embryo nearly all the developments of the twenties.

Here too the stimulus came in large part from abroad. Young Americans, brought up on Matthew Arnold and Thackeray, were following before he gave it the advice of Yeats at the *Poetry* dinner in 1912 to forget London and look to Paris for all that was excellent. In Kroch's bookstore in Chicago, in the translations issued by a series of daring new publishers, in the eager if undiscriminating reviews by the young critics, this generation of rebels was nourished on a whole series of movements extending over the last generation in Europe. All the writers that had for so long been belaboring the European bourgeoisie—French symbolists and decadents and naturalists, Scandinavian pessimists and social critics, Russian apostles of mysticism and emotion; even from England D. H. Lawrence as well as Shaw, suddenly began to penetrate the American barrier. What this series of reagents produced was a series of explosions, and what exploded was more than the genteel tradition in literature, more than conventional moral categories. With the conventions of literary form and language went the underlying assumptions about thought and communication. Randolph Bourne perhaps described this grand explosion better than he realized in June, 1917:

What becomes more and more apparent to the readers of Dostoevsky, however, is his superb modern healthiness. He is healthy because he has no sense of any dividing line between the normal and the abnormal, or even between the sane and the insane.

When Harriet Monroe, full of civic feeling as well as poetic zeal, founded *Poetry* in 1912 she seemed to tap immediately a rich underground gusher of poetic impulse. Soon the flood of experiment became too thick and varied even for *Poetry* to contain and overflowed into *Others* and the *Little Review*. As in the visual arts, a rapid series of schools succeeded each other, but perhaps the literary movement most characteristic of the period, and most obviously related to its philosophic tendencies was that of the Imagists, with its manifestoes in favor of complete freedom, concentration on the fleeting and immediate image for its own sake, and refusal to assign an image any "external" meaning or reference. Already before the war the revolution in the use of language was under way toward its ultimate destinations; Joyce was being published in the London *Egoist* and Gertrude Stein, settled in Paris, had developed her opinions and her characteristic style.

It would be misleading to divide this literary outpouring into precise categories, yet one can find suggestions of two emergent ways of thinking and feeling among writers. One group demanded freedom from European forms, confidence in emotion and spontaneity, and in general preached democratic optimism in the Whitman tradition. The other, more disciplined but also more deeply rebellious against American culture, called for concentration, rejection of irrelevant moral and political purposes, and the development of conscious intellectual atistocracy.

Obviously the former, democratic and optimist group is more distant than the other from postwar directions. This is the tendency one associates particularly with the sudden and brief Chicago Renaissance, with Sandburg and Lindsay and Miss Monroe, though it is found also in other areas, for instance in the organized and vigorous character of what Francis Hackett labeled and dated forever as Miss Amy Lowell's "Votes for Poetry movement." Yet even the most exuberant of the Chicago poets were, like contemporary political radicals, destroying for the sake of redemption, like Sandburg's personified city "Shovelling, wrecking, planning, building, breaking, rebuilding."

And even in Chicago pessimistic and sceptical tendencies were also, and had long been, at work. Dreiser's not exactly rosy picture of American city life was finally finding its audience; and the small town, from E. A. Robinson's New England Tilbury town to Masters' Middlewestern Spoon River, was preparing the way for Winesburg and Gopher Prairie. In the bosom of *Poetry* magazine, at the official heart of the Chicago movement, Ezra Pound, the magazine's foreign editor, was chafing at its cover slogan, the statement of Whitman that "to have great poets there must be great audiences too." Pound preferred Dante's pronouncement that the wisest in the city is "He whom the fools hate worst" and denied that poets have any need for the rabble.

It is true that the great artist has always a great audience, even in his lifetime; but it is not the vulgo *but the spirits of irony and of destiny and of humor, sitting with him.*

In that sentence lies the germ of a dozen ponderous manifestoes of the postwar Young Intellectuals. Pound stayed on *Poetry* long enough to persuade Miss Monroe to publish Eliot's "Prufrock" in 1915 and then found a refuge from uplift and Whitmanism in the *Little Review*.

In the Eastern centers of the new literary movement the mixture of optimism and nihilism, of reform and rejection was somewhat different. Harvard, which was incubating an extraordinary number of important writers, seemed to produce a strange and special mixture of ideas. The dominant note in its teaching of literature was aestheticism, worship of Europe, and contempt for the native production. Irving Babbitt's vigorous attack on democratic sentimentality was already a major influence. Yet Walter Lippmann, for one, managed to combine presidency of the Harvard Socialist Club with assisting Professor Santayana. A certain survival of Emersonian and Puritan responsibility seems to have been a part of the prevalent passionate concern for literature. America might be vulgar and materialistic and nearly hopeless; if so one's duty was to search the harder for seeds of literary springtime, and literary revival would bring social regeneration as well. Like so many writers after the war, Van Wyck Brooks went to Europe to look for these seeds. He found in London in 1913-14 Ezra Pound, T. S. Eliot, John Gould Fletcher, Conrad Aiken, Elinor Wylie, Robert Frost and Walter Lippmann. Across the channel he could already have run into an equally significant group of fellow-countrymen. It was in London that Brooks began to struggle seriously with the typical problem of the expatriate of the next decade: the love of European tradition and the nostalgic turning toward American vitality. He solved this problem by writing, in London in 1914, the book that most influenced the writers of the next decade, an attack on the Genteel Tradition and an appeal for a literary renaissance that seemed then, as its title implies, to mark an arrival and not just a beginning: *America's Coming-of-Age*.

From here we can see, even more clearly than Santayana could in 1913, the unrest, the disintegration of old standards, the search for vitality and movement that already was under way at that time. We know, too, that what was then unrest later became cultural revolution and angry intellectual civil war. This brings us to the compelling question, what started it all? Why did this search for novelty, this gay destruction of traditional standards, occur at just this moment in the midst of an apparently placid and contented period?

This is hardly a question that can be answered with certainty. All that we know for sure is that a movement so general and noticeable in the prewar years was not started by the war. Perhaps the most obvious forces at work in early twentieth-century civilization were technological change and urban growth, but these had been at work reshaping American culture for several generations and do not afford a direct and simple explanation for the sudden restlessness of 1912-17. Moreover, an increase of mechanistic materialism rather than a new vitalism would seem a more easily understandable product of machine civilization. It may be that the prewar rebellion was in part a protest against such a long-run tendency; in 1915 the *Nation* suggested that the rising "Bergsonian school . . . owes not a little of its popularity to its expression of revolt from the dreary materialistic determinism of the closing years of the last century."

One is tempted to wonder whether the new physics was at work already disintegrating the comparatively simple universe of nineteenth-century science. It seems, however, that although the Einstein revolution was being discussed before the war by American scientists and reported in the serious periodical press, it did not directly affect as yet the literary and political intellectuals to any great extent, and it was not, as it became after the war, a newspaper sensation.

In part the American intellectual rebellion may be considered merely a belated phase of an European antirationalist tendency. Yet it remains puzzling that Nietzsche and Dostoevsky and Baudelaire waited for their most telling American impact until they competed with Freud and Joyce. Part of the violence of the American literary and intellectual battles of the next decade arises from the fact that influences that had gradually permeated European thought presented themselves to many Americans all at once and in their extreme forms.

The time and special character of the prewar rebellion were, I believe, determined in part by the very surface placidity of the Progressive Era. Traditional American beliefs in moral certainty and inevitable progress had for some time been subjected to inner strain and external attack, yet in the prewar decade, for the last time, the official custodians of culture were able to maintain and defend a common front. Yet these almost hereditary leaders—Roosevelt and Royce and Howells in their several spheres—were growing weaker. A new generation, full of confidence and provided with leisure and libraries, was fairly literally looking for trouble. What attracts us about the standard culture of America in the early years of the century is its confident consensus, its lack of passion and violence. Passion and violence were exactly the demand of the young intellectuals of 1913 and 1914, of Lippmann and Brooks and Bourne and Pound. This was what they wanted, and this was what they got.

The war, then, was not the cause of the cultural revolution of the twenties. It played, however, the immense part that the Civil War played in the economic and political revolution of the mid-nineteenth century, speeding, widening and altering in kind a movement already under way.

The experiences of 1917-19 darkened and soured the mood of the rebels. Even at its most iconoclastic and even in those spokesmen who adopted the most pessimistic doctrines, the prewar renaissance was always exuberant. Pound, amid his fierce negations, still found it possible to make his famous and somewhat rash prophecy that the coming American Risorgimento would "make the Italian Renaissance look like a tempest in a teapot!" The rejection of easy rationalism, the spurning of dull politics were to make America better and brighter. In the war and its aftermath however the rebellious generation learned something of the price of destruction and experienced personally both tragedy and (in 1919) failure. Many who had been rebellious optimists became despairing nihilists and those who had already been preaching the futility of conscious effort preached it with different emotional corollaries.

The other effect of the war was that the disintegration of traditional ideas spread far more widely among the population. Most of the prewar rebellion was confined to a small and isolated, though articulate and potentially influential, group of intellectuals. As yet the overwhelming bulk of the people took for granted the truth of the old political and moral slogans. As long as this was so rebels could be ignored or patronized; they did not have to be feared and fought. Without the political events of 1917-19 traditional beliefs might perhaps have been slowly adapted to new realities instead of, for the moment, either smashed or blindly defended. And without the currents of doubt and disintegration already abroad, these political events themselves might have lacked their willing and ready Cassandras.

In 1913 *Sons and Lovers, A Preface to Politics,* and *Winds of Doctrine* were published, but *Pollyanna* and *Laddie* were the best-sellers. In 1925 the best-seller list itself had to find place for *An American Tragedy.*

Part VI
Ideas for the Twentieth Century

31
The Freudian Revolution Analyzed

Alfred Kazin

Intellectual history has profited greatly from the contributions of literary critics such as Alfred Kazin, Lionel Trilling, and Edmund Wilson. Tracing humanistic themes, they tend to view the field in its largest dimensions. In this instance Alfred Kazin displays brevity, appreciation in the best critical sense, and fresh insight into the range and limits of Sigmund Freud's influence upon the mind of modern educated Americans. When so much has been written about Freud's work, Kazin's essay is a major accomplishment in brief compass; it stands well with Trilling's brief essays on Freud (cited below).

Kazin, in passing, discerns what has escaped most writers who inquire into the success of Freudian psychoanalysis in the United States. Though acknowledging it, he does not linger with the old theme of Americans liberated from Victorian prudery after World War I. Instead he emphasizes the attraction that Freud's rational search for the subconscious sources of personal happiness had for Americans dedicated to older Lockean or even Aristotelian ideals of happiness. The search for "individual self-realization," Kazin reminds us, is a fairly recent development in Western culture, and Americans have long believed themselves to be in the vanguard of that search. In this respect, then, the Freudian pessimism about human nature, its skepticism about the elevation of biological man in the natural world, and its tough materialism, although outside the main streams of Jeffersonian and religious idealism in America, do come to terms with a modern quest for happiness. Of course, it is by now almost a first lesson in American thought that, like Jefferson, Darwin, and Dewey, Freud (1856-1939) had his name given without his consent or knowledge to a body of dogma that went beyond what he knew or intended.

Just as in the 1880s a small group of physicians and psychologists around Boston anticipated Freudian analysis by emphasizing environment, sexuality, childhood experiences, and family in the makeup of personality, so also an even larger number of disciples and revisionists, for good or ill, have expanded Freud's work since the master first came to the United States for a brief lecture visit in 1909 (see Essay 30). The early work of Alfred Adler and Carl Gustav Jung in Europe, of Harry Stack

Sullivan, Karen Horney, and Erich Fromm in the United States and, more recently, the social philosophy of Herbert Marcuse and the political thought of members of the Frankfurt school who fled from Hitler to America, and, most striking for its revision of the classic Freudian portrait of personality development, the work of Erik H. Erikson—all have carried forward Freud's ingenious inquiries into the forces motivating the individual and society.

For further reading: Lionel Trilling, "Freud and Literature," in his **The Liberal Imagination: Essays on Literature and Society* (1950), pp. 44-64; Lionel Trilling, "Freud within and beyond Culture," in his **Beyond Culture: Essays on Literature and Learning* (1965), pp. 89-118; F. H. Matthews, "The Americanization of Sigmund Freud: Adaptations of Psychoanalysis before 1917," *Journal of American Studies,* 1 (April 1967), 39-62; *Philip Rieff, *Freud: The Mind of the Moralist* (1959); *J. A. C. Brown, *Freud and the Post-Freudians* (1961); Nathan G. Hale, Jr., *Freud and the Americans: The Beginnings of Psychoanalysis in the United States, 1876-1917* (1971).

It is hard to believe that Sigmund Freud was born over a century ago. Although Freud has long been a household name (and, in fact, dominates many a household one could mention), his theories still seem too "advanced," they touch too bluntly on the most intimate side of human relations, for us to picture Freud himself coming out of a world that in all other respects now seems so quaint.

Although Freud has influenced even people who have never heard of him, not all his theories have been accepted even by his most orthodox followers, while a great many of his essential ideas are rejected even by many psychoanalysts. In one sense Freud himself is still battling for recognition, for because of the tabooed nature of the materials in which he worked and the unusually speculative quality of his mind, Freud still seems to many people more an irritant than a classic.

On the other hand, Freud's influence, which started from the growing skepticism about civilization and morality after the First World War, is now beyond description. Freudianism gave sanction to the increasing exasperation with public standards as opposed to private feelings; it upheld the truths of human nature as against the hypocrisies and cruelties of conventional morality; it stressed the enormous role that sex plays in man's imaginative life, in his relations to his parents, in the symbolism of language.

It is impossible to think of the greatest names in modern literature and art—Thomas Mann, James Joyce, Franz Kafka, T. S. Eliot, Ernest Hemingway, William Faulkner, Pablo Picasso, Paul Klee—without realizing our debt to Freud's exploration of dreams, myths, symbols and the imaginative profundity of man's inner life. Even those who believe that original sin is a safer guide to the nature of man than any other can find support in Freud's gloomy doubts about man's capacity for progress. For quite other reasons, Freud has found followers even among Catholic psychiatrists, who believe that Freud offers a believable explanation of neurosis and a possible cure, and so leaves the sufferer cured to practice his faith in a rational way.

Many pschologists who disagree with Freud's own materialism have gratefully adopted many of Freud's diagnoses, and although he himself was chary about the psychoanalytical technique in serious mental illness, more and more psychiatrists now follow his technique, or some adaptation of it. For no other system of thought in modern times, except the great religions, has been adopted by so many people as a systematic interpretation of individual behavior. Consequently, to those who have no other belief, Freudianism sometimes serves as a philosophy of life.

Freud, a tough old humanist with a profoundly skeptical mind, would have been shocked or amused by the degree to which everything is sometimes explained by "Freudian" doctrines. He offered us not something that applies dogmatically to all occasions, but something useful, a principle of inquiry into those unconscious forces that are constantly pulling people apart, both in themselves and from each other.

Freud's extraordinary achievement was to show us, in scientific terms, the primacy of natural desire, the secret wishes we proclaim in our dreams, the mixture of love and shame and jealousy in our relations to our parents, the child as father to the man, the deeply buried instincts that make us natural beings and that go back to the forgotten struggles of the human race. Until Freud, novelists and dramatists had never dared to think that science would back up their belief that personal passion is a stronger force in people's lives than socially accepted morality. Thanks to Freud, these insights now form a widely shared body of knowledge.

In short, Freud had the ability, such as is given to very few individuals, to introduce a wholly new factor into human knowledge; to impress it upon people's minds as something for which there was evidence. He revealed a part of reality that many people before him had guessed at, but which no one before him was able to describe as systematically and convincingly as he did. In the same way that one associates the discovery of certain fundamentals with Copernicus, Newton, Darwin, Einstein, so one identifies many of one's deepest motivations with Freud. His name is no longer the name of a man; like "Darwin," it is now synonymous with a part of nature.

This is the very greatest kind of influence that a man can have. It means that people use his name to signify something in the world of nature which, they believe, actually exists. A man's name has become identical with a phenomenon in nature, with a cause in nature, with a "reality" that we accept—even when we don't want to accept it. Every hour of every day now, and especially in America, there are people who cannot forget a name, or make a slip of the tongue, or feel depressed; who cannot begin a love affair, or end a marriage, without wondering what the "Freudian" reason may be.

No one can count the number of people who now think of any crisis as a personal failure, and who turn to a psychoanalyst or to psychoanalytical literature for an explanation of their suffering where once they would have turned to a minister or to the Bible for consolation. Freudian terms are now part of our thought. There are innumerable people who will never admit that they believe a word of his writings, who nevertheless, "unconsciously," as they would say, have learned to look for "motivations," to detect "compensations," to withold a purely moralistic judgment in favor of individual understanding, to prize sexual satisfaction as a key to individual happiness, and to characterize people by the depth and urgency of their passions rather than by the nobility of their professions.

For much of this "Freudian" revolution, Freud himself is not responsible. And in evaluating the general effect of Freud's doctrines on the modern scene, especially in America, it is important to distinguish between the hard, biological, fundamentally classical thought of Freud, who was a determinist, a pessimist, and a genius, from the thousands of little cultural symptoms and "psychological" theories, the pretensions and self-indulgences, which are often found these days in the prosperous middle-class culture that has responded most enthusiastically to Freud.

There is, for example, the increasing tendency to think that all problems are "psychological," to ignore the real conflicts in society that underlie politics and to interpret politicians and candidates—especially those you don't like—in terms of "sexual" motives. There is the cunning use of "Freudian" terms in advertising, which has gone so far that nowadays there's a pretty clear suggestion that the girl comes with the car. There are all the psychologists who study "motivations," and sometimes invent them, so as to get you to buy two boxes of cereal where one would have done before.

There are the horrendous movies and slick plays which not only evade the writer's need to explain characters honestly, but, by attributing to everybody what one can only call the Freudian nightmare, having imposed upon a credulous public the belief that it may not be art but that it is "true"—that is, sex—and so must be taken seriously. And, since this is endless but had better stop somewhere, there are all the people who have confused their "urges" with art, have learned in all moral crises to blame their upbringing rather than themselves, and tend to worship the psychoanalyst as God.

The worst of the "Freudian revolution" is the increasing tendency to attribute all criticism of our society to personal "sickness." The rebel is looked on as neurotic rather than someone making a valid protest. Orthodox Freudians tend to support the status quo as a matter of course and to blame the individual for departing from it. Freud himself never made such a mistake, and no one would have been able to convince him that the Viennese world around him was "normal."

The identification of a military group, or a class, or a culture, with an absolute to which we must all be adjusted at any price is a dangerous trend. And the worst of it is that to many people psychoanalysts now signify "authority," so that people believe them on any and all subjects.

On the other hand, the greatest and most beautiful effect of Freudianism is the increasing awareness of childhood as the most important single influence on personal development. This profound cherishing of childhood has opened up wholly new relationships between husbands and wives, as well as between parents and children, and it represents—though often absurdly overanxious—a peculiar new tenderness in modern life. Similarly, though Freud's psychology is weakest on women, there can be no doubt that, again in America, the increasing acknowledgment of the importance of sexual satisfaction has given to women an increasing sense of their individual dignity and their specific needs.

But the greatest revolution of all, and one that really explains the overwhelming success of Freudianism in America, lies in the general insistence on individual fulfillment, satisfaction and happiness. Odd as it may seem to us, who take our striving toward these things for granted, the insistence on personal happiness represents the most revolutionary force in modern times. And it is precisely because our own tradition works toward individual self-realization, because private happiness does seem to us to be both an important ideal and a practical goal, that Freudianism has found so many recruits in this country. . . .

Freud's work appealed to the increasing regard for individual experience that is one of the great themes of modern literature and art. The sensitiveness to each individual as a significant register of the consciousness in general, the artistic interest in carrying human consciousness to its farthest limits—it was this essential side of modern art that Freud's researches encouraged and deepened. He brought, as it were, the authority of science to the inner promptings of art, and thus helped writers and artists to feel that their interest in myths, in symbols, in dreams was on the side of "reality," of science, itself, when it shows the fabulousness of the natural world.

Even if we regret, as we must, the fact that Freud's influence has been identified with a great many shallow and commercially slick ideas, the fact remains that if Freud's ideas appealed generally to the inwardness which is so important to modern writers and artists, it was because Freud thoroughly won his case against many aggressive but less intelligent opponents. . . .

Civilization as we know it, Freud said, had been built up on man's heroic sacrifice of instinct. Only, Freud issued the warning that more and more men would resent this sacrifice, would wonder if civilization was worth the price. And how profoundly right he was in this can be seen not only in the Nazi madness that drove him as an old man out of Vienna, that almost cost him his life, but in the increasing disdain for culture, in the secret lawlessness that has become, under the conformist surface, a sign of increasing personal irritation and rebelliousness in our society. More and more, the sexual freedom of our time seems to be a way of mentally getting even, of confused protest, and not the pagan enjoyment of instinct that writers like D. H. Lawrence upheld against Freud's gloomy forebodings.

For Freud the continuous sacrifice of "nature" that is demanded by "civilization" meant that it was only through rationality and conscious awareness that maturity could be achieved. Far from counseling license, his most famous formula became—"Where id was, ego shall be"—the id representing the unconscious, the ego our dominant and purposive sense of ourselves. However, consciousness meant for Freud an unyielding insistence on the importance of sexuality. And it was just on this issue that, even before the first World War, his movement broke apart.

Jung went astray, as Freud thought, because he was lulled by the "mystical" side of religion; Adler, through his insistence that not sex but power feelings were primary. Later, Harry Stack Sullivan and Erich Fromm tended to emphasize, as against sex, the importance of personal relatedness to others, and nowadays many psychoanalysts tend to value religion much more highly than Freud ever could. But the root of the dissidence was always Freud's forthright insistence on the importance of sexuality and his old-fashioned, mid-nineteenth century positivism. For Freud always emphasized the organic and the physical rather than the social and the "cultural."

In fact, it is now possible to say that it is precisely Freud's old-fashioned scientific rationalism, his need to think of man as a physical being rather than a "psychological" one, that explains the primacy of Freud's discoveries. Psychoanalysis, especially in America, has become more interested in making cures than in making discoveries, and it is significant that there has been very little original thought in the field since Freud.

Freudianism has become a big business, and a very smooth one. The modern Freudian analyst, who is over-busy and who rather complacently uses his theory to explain everything, stands in rather sad contrast to that extraordinary thinker, Sigmund Freud.

Perhaps it is because Freud was born a century ago that he had the old-fashioned belief that nothing—not even a lot of patients—is so important as carrying your ideas beyond the point at which everybody already agrees with you. Nowadays everybody is something of a Freudian, and to many Freudians, the truth is in their keeping, the system is complete. But what mattered most to Freud was relentlessly carrying on the revolution of human thought.

32
John Dewey's Legacy

Charles Frankel

Biographies of John Dewey (1859-1952) are beginning to appear. There is some irony here. For no matter how revealing a study of his life may be, as history it still cannot be, for the Deweyite, "definitive" in the book reviewer's sense of a final statement on the subject. Dewey's own system of inquiry defies any perception of biography or history as conclusive. Our perceptions of the past, for Dewey, are transient in nature, the result of our ever changing experiences. By the same token, however, biography and history may be quite valid or "true" for our intellectual growth when they fill some current aesthetic or moral need. For these reasons, brief critical studies of Dewey's life and work may prove to be more rewarding to successive American generations than full-scale biographies. Among brief essays on Dewey, this one by Charles Frankel is outstanding. Writing as a younger professor from Dewey's Department of Philosophy at Columbia University to celebrate the centennial of his birth, Frankel is sympathetic to Dewey's philosophical position, yet critical of his unclear writing, his "semantic mayhem." Frankel illuminates the instrumentalist theory of truth at the center of Dewey's thought. Although that theory was forged to meet the needs of twentieth-century urban democratic culture, Frankel believes it is, like Dewey the Vermonter, characteristically American in its fundamental moral concern for the individual in his environment. It originates in a naturalistic view of human intelligence and in Charles Sanders Peirce's early work on pragmatism (see essays 23 and 24). Although Dewey may be considered America's greatest *social* philosopher—and here he differs from his great predecessor in pragmatic method, William James, who emphasized the individual—Dewey's harmonious society, the truly democratic society, is one that exists with no controls but the constant exercise of intelligence by informed individuals. Every choice made by an individual in a world of constant choice-making is a moral choice. Thus Dewey's lifelong dedication to education, to informed intelligence, which is the lifeblood of democracy. Although Dewey's critics are quick to point out ambiguities and inconsistencies in his social and educational philosophy, some of which Frankel mentions here, Dewey appears

Reprinted by permission of the author and Harper & Row, Publishers, from Charles Frankel, *The Love of Anxiety and Other Essays.*

to have made a lasting contribution to the philosophy of science, to esthetics, and to the social theory of democracy.

For further reading: George H. Mead, "The Philosophies of Royce, James and Dewey in Their American Setting," *Ethics,* 40 (1930), 211-231; Stow Persons, *American Minds: A History of Ideas* (1958), chap. 23 *Gail Kennedy (ed.), *Pragmatism and American Culture* (1950); *Lawrence A. Cremin, *The Transformation of the School: Progressivism in American Education, 1876-1957* (1961); *Richard Hofstadter, *Anti-Intellectualism in American Life* (1963), chaps. 13-14.

Even during his lifetime John Dewey suffered the unfortunate fate that the gods seem to reserve for those who become too influential in philosophy. He disappeared as an individual and became a symbol. Plato, it will be remembered, fought in his letters to preserve the image of his poor singular self, and insisted that what he had taught could not be condensed into a doctrine. Even Karl Marx felt the need to remind his friends wistfully that, after all, he himself was not a Marxist. And it is difficult now to remember that John Dewey was a man, not an institution, a philosopher and not a social movement.

For more than two generations the mention of this unassuming man's name has been less an invitation to the discussion of his philosophy than a signal for the start of large debates about the ailments of the modern world. To be for Dewey has been to be for progress, reason and enlightenment. To be against him has been to be for God, the ancient values of our civilization and the triumph of spirit over matter. To himself Dewey must have seemed to be what any philosopher who is not self-deceived must seem to himself to be—an individual, working ultimately in solitude, plagued by doubts, impatient with his deficiencies, and taking a chance on such ideas as he might happen to have. But to his admirers Dewey was and is a representation of all that is most hopeful in American civilization. And to his detractors he was and remains a paradigm of some of the worst ills of our society.

Indeed, even those for whom Dewey's name is not a battle cry find it difficult to approach his work with detachment. For whatever Dewey's influence may really have been, his ideas are in the air and his name has echoes. He stood astride an era in American thought with which we are still busy making our peace. To read Dewey's works is to be forced to ask what we ourselves, facing our own problems, really think about progressive education, the welfare state, the moral implications of science, the meaning of liberalism, or almost any one of the other contemporary issues around which intellectual controversies rage. Even when we turn to aspects of the present scene with which Dewey cannot be associated—the vogue of Zen Buddhism or existentialist theology at one extreme, the influence of linguistic philosophy on the other—Dewey's image comes to mind, teasing us to decide whether we have fallen from grace or have finally begun to recover our senses. For Dewey stands there as a palpable presence, a possible alternative. To know where we stand toward Dewey's ideas is to find out, at least in part, where we stand with ourselves.

It may be good to be reminded, therefore, as the Dewey centennial celebrations have recently done, that he was born a hundred years ago. For he lived so long and vigorously, he remains so inextricably associated in the public mind with what is "new" and "progressive," and he is still so substantial a figure among us, that it is easy to forget that he grew up in a world very different from our own. Indeed, the problems that gave Dewey's thought the shape it retained throughout his life were different in fundamental ways from the problems we face.

Dewey was born before Lincoln was President. He was fifty-five years old when the long peace of the nineteenth century collapsed into permanent war, revolution and tension. When he was a graduate student at Johns Hopkins, the most speculative of philosophies, idealism, dominated the university scene, and not the most anti-speculative of philosophies, logical empiricism. The great idea that had to be absorbed into Western thinking was the theory of evolution. Socialism was a mere ideal, communism in Russia unthinkable, fascism unimagined. And Freud was unheard of, Kierkegaard forgotten, and the Orient a reality only to exotics.

In the law and social thinking Dewey was faced by the principles of Social Darwinism and the doctrine of "natural rights" applied to the behavior of impersonal corporations. In economics he saw unbridled competition on one side, and insecurity and indignity for masses of men on the other. In politics he had to worry about a state that did too little, not a state that did too much. In the schools there was political patronage, antiquarianism and a discipline so senseless that children might even be prohibited from turning their heads in class. And in American intellectual life generally Dewey had to wrestle, not so much with the slick vulgarity that troubles us today, but with prudishness, gentility, and conceptions of culture and the good life to which only a few in a democratic and industrial age could hope to aspire.

What does a man who grew up in such a world, and whose basic ideas were shaped as answers to such problems, have to say to us? The question is all the more pertinent because Dewey was so honestly and eagerly a creature of his time. And it becomes more insistent when we examine the curious equipment that Dewey brought to his philosophical tasks.

To begin with, he wrote badly—almost, indeed, as though it were a matter of principle. Most of his books were unorganized and repetitious, many of his arguments imprecise and incomplete. At times his sentences have vigor and bite. At other times we enter a sentence of Dewey's and find ourselves in a trackless thicket, from which we emerge at the other end scratched, shaken and relieved. In Dewey's hands even individual words play tricks on us, snarling when we expect them to purr, evaporating when we expect them to stand for something solid. Dewey did not invent his own system of notation, but he did not write in ordinary English either. With some help from his long apprenticeship in German idealism, he made ordinary English over into an artificial tongue.

To be sure, there was a purpose behind this semantic mayhem. Dewey had a sense of the nuances of terms and a shrewd Yankee judgment about their ambiguities. He saw, or thought he saw, that many words we habitually use—including words like "experience," "reality," "true" and "good," which are fundamental in building our conception of the world and our place in it—have quite the wrong meanings attached to them as a result of their historical careers. He wanted to squeeze the wrong meanings out of these words and attach new and better meanings to them. So he used the words not as they are ordinarily used, but as he thought they ought to be used, and he frequently gave old terms new depth and power in the process.

Unfortunately, however, he did not always remember that his readers needed to be warned about what he was doing. And he frequently replaced an old ambiguity simply with a new and more troublesome polyguity. Surely, for example, it is confusing to remark, as Dewey once did, that his book *Experience and Nature* might just as easily have been called *Culture and Nature,* and that the title would not have changed its meaning with this change in its terms. Whatever the reasons may have been, Dewey wrote tortuously, inexactly, carelessly.

Nor is it only Dewey's prose that we must take into account in considering his deficiencies. It must also be said, I think, that Dewey regularly ignored important ideas and issues that were clearly relevant to the themes he chose to discuss. He wrote about logic, but he was largely indifferent to symbolic logic and the revolutionary work of Bertrand Russell and Alfred North Whitehead. He devoted much of his time to questions about the growth of personality and the education of children. But even though he continued to pay attention to these questions after 1920, he did less than disagree with Freud: he virtually ignored his existence.

Perhaps most disconcerting of all, Dewey repeatedly claimed that his ideas were supported by the logic of science and pleaded continually for the use of scientific method in all fields. But the examples of scientific thinking that Dewey offered and analyzed were only rarely examples of scientific thought at its theoretical or system-building levels. They were much more often examples taken from practical life—a doctor diagnosing a disease, an engineer planning a bridge. Compared with Russell, Whitehead, Morris Cohen or even Josiah Royce—to mention only a few of his distinguished contemporaries in philosophy—Dewey's knowledge of the sciences, and particularly of mathematics and the physical sciences, was secondhand.

Dewey had, to be sure, an original and powerful insight into certain issues. He is clearly one of those most responsible for helping us to recognize the constructive and creative aspects of scientific thought and the difference that scientific habits of mind make in any culture that accepts them. But in the history of the interpretation of science there are men like Francis Bacon or Voltaire, who look at science from the outside, seize on some one of its features, and then go on to explain to the nonscientist the general difference that science can make in human attitudes or in standards of right reason. There are, on the other hand, men like Descartes or Immanuel Kant, who understand science from the inside, and who deal, so to speak, with some of its professional problems of logic and method as well as with its general relation to other styles of life and thought. Dewey falls somewhere between these two groups. He was neither so clear and dramatic, nor quite so superficial, as Bacon or Voltaire. But he did not have the precise grasp of details or the informed authority of Kant or of other philosophers in the American tradition, like Charles Peirce.

In fact, there is rather generally a curious remoteness about Dewey, a habit of talking around a subject without coming to close grips with it. He showed this trait even when he dealt with subjects about which he knew a good deal. Much of his philosophic writing, for example, consists of criticisms of the great historical traditions in philosophy. There are few historians of philosophy at work today, however, who would not regard the picture that Dewey drew of his philosophic ancestors as slanted and inaccurate. Again, although Dewey's central interest was in social affairs, one cannot find anywhere in his work a direct, systematic examination of major social philosophies—for example, competitive capitalism, socialism, anarchism, syndicalism, guild socialism—that were competing for men's allegiance in his day.

In short, although Dewey argued that philosophy must be a guide to the solution of concrete, practical problems, he repeatedly left his readers guessing what he himself thought about such issues. He was a man of rugged courage who was not afraid to take sides in public controversies. But in his writing he regularly stopped at just the point where we are anxious to see, if only in outline, the kind of practical, positive program he thought his ideas implied. He was a social reformer whose position toward socialism in America, even in the thirties, was unclear. He was a writer on morals who never discussed questions of sexual morality. He was an innovator in education whose views about progressive education are still a legitimate subject for debate. He was modest and had good sense, and this may explain why he was unwilling to pontificate in areas where no man, and least of all a philosopher, can be sure of himself. But it cannot explain the difficulty there is in determining where Dewey stood, simply as one man among other men, on many of the issues that he himself raised for discussion.

What, then, remains? Why did Dewey make the stir that he did? What did he leave that was important, and that we can choose to forget only at a great loss to ourselves?

The answer can be found, I think, only if we are prepared to look at Dewey from a point of view that is not habitual in philosophical circles today. He did not have some of the qualities that a professional philosopher ought to have. He was not an elegant thinker and not always a disciplined one. But he had a quality which can make the difference between a merely skillful philosopher and a first-rate original mind. In his own cheerful, unaggressive way he was a visionary.

It is not easy to think of this quiet, patient man in this way. He was easygoing, unimpassioned and temperate. He did not go in for flights of fancy or bursts of indignation, or indulge in the consolations of paradox and irony like those other visionaries of his generation, Shaw and Russell. He simply kept going, year after year, sticking to his guns, insistent, indefatigable, and always returning—the sure mark of a visionary—to the same basic theme.

And it was a distinctive theme, which the comparison with Shaw and Russell highlights. Shaw was fundamentally disturbed, as he once remarked, by stupidity; it was the direction of life by a consistent view of things that excited him. In Russell's work there are the twin visions of certainty in intellectual matters and justice in the arrangement of human affairs. But while Dewey did not like stupidity and injustice, what basically disturbed him was the decline of any human being's life into a state of passivity. It seemed to him to be the denial of the human birthright.

There is a sentence in Karl Marx's *Capital* which, with appropriate alterations, suggests what Dewey thought the basic human problem of his day was. Under capitalism, Marx wrote, the advance of technology and the accumulation of capital, far from helping the worker, "mutilate the laborer into a fragment of a man, degrade him to the level of appendage to a machine, destroy every remnant of charm in his work and turn it into hated toil. . . ." Dewey could not speak with the scorn and bitterness of a Hebrew prophet. Moreover, he thought too steadily in terms of the individual's day-to-day experience to believe that an abstract change in the law of property would be enough to change a man's relation to his work. He would have asked whether factories were still organized in an authoritarian manner or whether the economic revolution had been imposed without the consent of those affected. And he would have looked at other areas where human behavior is governed and human personality is shaped or misshaped—for example, at philosophies that suggest that the answer to men's problems can be found simply by consulting fixed principles, or at educational systems that make submissiveness the child's central experience in the classroom.

But Dewey would have agreed that it was the "mutilation" of the individual, the imposition upon him of an external, mechanical routine, which was the basic moral problem of industrial society. He would have thought, indeed, that it had been the moral problem of all major forms of social organization that had ever existed. And he would have felt an immediate sympathy, it may be suspected, with the direct language, the immediate and aesthetic language, that Marx employed in this passage. For the program of reconstruction in philosophy, morals and society which Dewey proposed can be understood only if we see that Dewey took the daily experience of individuals more seriously than he took anything else, and that he ultimately evaluated everything as an instrument for the enrichment of such experience.

This is the heart of Dewey's philosophy, I suggest, and the ultimate meaning that is to be attached to calling him a "pragmatist" or "instrumentalist." What Dewey wanted to see diffused throughout human life, and what he thought that democracy, science, and technology could diffuse, were qualities that we find best exemplified in the arts—spontaneity, self-discipline, the involvement of the personality, and the marriage of individuality and order, the delightful and the meaningful. His enemies were routine, drill, external dictation and the ready-made in ideas; and the targets he attacked were social arrangements, educational methods or philosophical systems that seemed to promote such qualities.

Oddly enough, this philosopher who wrote so badly, whose thinking seems so homely and prosaic, and who is remembered for his glorification of science, had essentially a poet's vision of the possibilities of human life. He wished to see men's environments so ordered that the life of art was possible for all. His ideal was a world in which individuals lived with a sense of active purpose, exerting their individual powers, putting their mark on their environments, sharing their experiences, and making their own contribution to the common enterprises of humanity. He did not seem to think that this was a utopian ideal—or perhaps he did not care if it was. For he was convinced that it could be more closely approximated in the modern world than it had ever been before, and it was the only ideal which could give our power and wealth some meaning beyond themselves.

"Democracy," Dewey once wrote, and he said the same thing in one way or another again and again, "is belief in the ability of human experience to generate the aims and methods by which further experience will grow in ordered richness." It is an odd definition, and a dark one. But it becomes clearer when we put it alongside a

remark he made in his book on aesthetics, *Art as Experience*. "Ultimately," Dewey wrote, "there are but two philosophies. One of them accepts life and experience in all its uncertainty, mystery, doubt and self-knowledge and turns that experience upon itself to deepen and intensify its own qualities—to imagination and art. This is the philosophy of Shakespeare and Keats."
Shakespeare and Keats."

It is a long way from the poetry of Shakespeare and Keats to a philosophy of democracy, but Dewey had a way of bringing distant things together. And the bridge by which he made such transitions was his theory of human experience—his conception of human life in its ideal form. He rejected any philosophy that seemed to cut human life or society to a pre-arranged form. He preferred philosophies that liberated men from leading strings and allowed them to take control of their own lives. And so he framed his moral philosophy, his educational theory and his conception of democracy not primarily in terms of abstract ideals or institutional arrangements, but in terms of the diffusion throughout a society of this distinctive sort of personal experience.

This is the vision that stands behind the freshness and power of John Dewey's insights. With this vision he turned logic, the history of philosophy, and even that most abstruse and apparently artificial of philosophical subjects—the theory of knowledge—into subjects with moral and cultural significance. He connected theory not only to practice but to a coherent image of what human life might be. And he made philosophy what it has always been when it has been most vigorous—a commentary on things outside itself and a challenge to men to make up their minds about the terms on which they were willing to conduct their business in this world. Underneath the difficulties of his language and the technicalities of his arguments Dewey's vision, it seems to me, is the source of the excitement and the sense of importance that his work communicated, and still communicates, to others.

Despite the looseness and occasional tedium of John Dewey's books, they have, then, an inner dynamism. There is a coherent theory of experience that propels them. This theory is best formulated in *Art as Experience,* the most revealing of Dewey's books, I think, and the one to which too little attention is paid. But it also controls Dewey's thinking in his books on education, morals, democracy and science. What was this theory? To what notions about human culture did it lead Dewey? How did it affect his philosophy of education and of science? These are the questions to which we must turn.

There are for Dewey two extremes between which our experience moves. At one extreme we live by habits, which include, of course, habits of mind and feeling as well as habits of motor behavior. Without habits our lives would be unendurable: every action that was not instinctive would call for a decision. And so long as we do not meet new situations in which our habits come a cropper, our lives move smoothly. But they also move without awareness on our part, without questions, without self-consciousness.

At the other extreme from the life of habit, there is the sudden break in our routine activity, the event so new and different that we are startled into noticing it. This is what it means, in Dewey's special language, to have a "sensation." It is not a mere feeling, like the feeling of being tickled or the seeing of a brown patch of color. It is to be aroused by the unusual, to have the kind of experience in which "sensational" journalism specializes. And just as an individual is passive when he is wholly a creature of habit, he is also passive when he is overcome by sensation. It is something that happens to him, that plays over him, and that he may enjoy because it releases him from routine and returns an edge to his consciousness. But he cannot do anything about it except notice it. The moment that he can fit it into his own normal pattern of life and work it ceases to be merely sensational. It becomes something he can use, grist for his intellectual mill. It stops being a "sensation" and becomes something he can make sense of.

But these extremes of routine and shock between which so much human experience oscillates suggest what it is to have "experience" in the ideal sense. We have "an experience" when our habits are interrupted, when novelty intrudes, and when we master this novelty by developing the ideas that allow us to fit it into a new pattern of successful action. We have experiences, in short, when we solve problems. And the point of successful problem-solving for Dewey is not simply that it allows us to return to the even, habitual tenor of our ways, but that it provides us with those moments in which we are most intensely conscious of our surroundings, most aware of our own purposes, and most cognizant of the relation between our surroundings and our purposes. To have an experience is to have a story to tell. It is to move in an orderly way from a blocked purpose through a series of exploratory actions to a conclusion in which our purpose is realized or at least intelligibly defeated. Experience, in this sense, is its own reward. It is a means to having other experiences, but it is also—although Dewey did not like the expression—an end in itself. And in terms of this view of experience, the problematic is more interesting than what is settled, and taking risks and acting deliberately on hypotheses is to be preferred to the illusions of safety and certainty.

Dewey, it is plain, was using the word "experience" in his own way. Moreover, his theory of experience was not quite what he made it seem. Until the end of his life Dewey retained the habits of a not quite reformed philosophical idealist. He did not believe that there is a clear distinction to be made between descriptions of the facts and judgments of value, and he presented his theory of experience as though he were giving an account of the growth of experience out of habit and sensation. He admitted that human experience in fact contained many moments that were merely passages to something else and had no intrinsic worth of their own, and that there were other moments that were just dead ends. But instead of deploring these facts on explicit moral or aesthetic grounds he preferred to suggest that they were somehow instances of experience nipped in the bud, cut off before it had come to full development.

But the notion of "development" always contains an implicit standard of what is normal or desirable. We want a ten-year-old boy to grow, for example, but at some point we should also like to see him stop growing. Dewey, I believe, would have helped his readers immeasurably, and would have avoided much unnecessary controversy, if he had presented his theory of experience for what it was. It was not a psychologist's account of the laws that govern human perception or motivation, or a sociologist's account of the relation of the individual's attitudes and behavior to his culture, class or social role. It leaned on such facts (or on guesses about such facts). But its purpose was not description for its own sake; its purpose was to describe a kind of experience that sometimes occurs and that Dewey thought ought to occur more frequently, and to show the conditions under which such experience may be blocked or realized. Facts are not irrelevant to it; but appeal to facts alone will not suffice to justify it. We also have to share Dewey's implicit ideals.

Once we adopt these ideals even provisionally, however, a new landscape opens before us. For Dewey employed his notion of ideal experience to develop a remarkably trenchant and comprehensive critique of Western philosophy and culture. The views of human experience that had prevailed in the past were not, to his mind, transcripts of unchanging truths about the human scene. They were reflections of specific social conditions, and of conditions that need no longer exist. Men had lived in a world which for the most part they could not control. So they had looked to pure reason to provide them with a refuge, and had used philosophy to paint a picture of another and better world—a "real" world behind phenomena—where everything was permanent and safe. Even more to the point, men had lived in a social world rigidly divided into separate classes. The great majority had done manual work; a tiny minority had enjoyed leisure and "culture." So the practical, the useful, the material, had been denigrated; the contemplative and useless had been the things to admire.

In short, such conditions had created, Dewey believed, the traditional philosophical "dualisms," the sharp divisions that philosophers had characteristically set between mind and matter, reason and the senses, values and facts. In Dewey's view intelligence, when properly understood, is the activity of a biological creature, caught in mid-passage by some block to his habits or interests, and seeking and finding new habits that will be effective in place of the routines that do not work. In such a view of intelligence there is no place for separating the work of thought and the work of the senses, the movements of the mind and the effective manipulation of the physical environment. All are phases of the same activity and all support one another. In such circumstances, mind and matter, reasoning and sensing, are effectively one, and philosophical dualisms that place them in separate categories merely reinforce attitudes and habits of behavior that prevent men from having experience in its ideal form.

Once more, of course, all this raises questions. But before we turn to these questions, it is important to see what we can easily fail to see. In a sense, Dewey's ideas suffer from their very sanity: we may not recognize how fresh and radical they were. For Dewey's conception of intelligence restored men to a view of themselves that the most powerful traditions in Western philosophy and religion had tended to obscure.

If Dewey was right, then the mind is not a mysterious ghost in the machine of the body. It is simply one type of physical disposition and activity. If Dewey was right, there is no world of eternal ideas, and no order of original, pure perceptions, to which our ideas must conform. Our ideas derive their meaning from the uses we give them in specific contexts of language and inquiry. And if Dewey was right, our thinking does not normally fall into neat, military divisions marked "thinking about facts" and "thinking about values." Accordingly, moral insight is not the special prerogative of the humanities or religion or metaphysics; and if men in these fields have opinions about either facts or values, these opinions must meet the same tests that beliefs in any other field must meet.

But questions remain. There are questions, for example, about the accuracy of

Dewey's account of the philosophical past, and questions, as well, about the lengths to which Dewey's fear of "dualisms" led him. To argue, for instance, that thinking about values is not independent of thinking about facts is one thing. But to say that a value judgment cannot be distinguished from a judgment about the facts is quite another. Yet this is what Dewey sometimes seems to suggest. But perhaps the greatest question raised by Dewey's theory of experience and culture, which is to say his notion of right experience and right culture, is the implicit value judgment that it involves. "Ideas are worthless," Dewey wrote, "except as they pass into actions which rearrange and reconstruct in some way, be it little or large, the world in which we live." Surely it can be agreed that a life devoted exclusively to the mental rehearsal of possibilities would be a thin and cold affair; and it can also be agreed that a society which does not use its ideas to guide its behavior will be blind or reckless in what it does. But the kind of play of the mind that is sheer play, that does not involve an irritable reaching after decisions and programs, seems to me to have a place in any calendar of the virtues that is circumspectly drawn.

No doubt Dewey did not mean to deny this value utterly. Passages certainly can be found in his books where he tries to make a place for it and emphasizes its importance in enriching experience and in bringing it the qualities of humor and compassion. But I do not think that even his stanchest defenders will say that he did not emphasize doing and acting even more, or that it was not characteristic of him to be impatient with thought for thought's sake. He spoke for men in a rising democracy, energetic, busy, committed. But a democratic culture will be richer if it can also find a place for the disengaged mind and for a kind of thinking that is not necessarily a prelude to action.

This element of distortion in Dewey's point of view seems to me to affect his views on both science and education. His most important contribution to the philosophy of science is undoubtedly his "instrumentalist" theory of ideas. Although he owed this theory in large part to Charles Peirce, he developed and applied it with an originality that was his own. Very briefly, this theory holds that an idea is an instrument by which we move from situations in which we do not know what to think or act to situations in which our perplexities are dispelled. Ideas are leading principles, rules which tell us what observations to make and what inferences to draw from our observations. The truth of an idea, therefore, is a matter of its effectiveness in leading to successful predictions and to actions in which our purposes are realized—in short, its effectiveness in dealing with the particular problem that it was created to solve.

The instrumentalist theory is an immensely liberating one. It explains the function of fundamental scientific ideas like the theory of the atom and tells us what we mean when we call such ideas true even though we cannot directly observe the objects whose structure they purportedly describe. And it can be used—Dewey, in fact, did use it with great success—to dispel a host of perennially disturbing problems. In moral philosophy, for example, it has traditionally been thought that we cannot rationally determine how we ought to behave unless we have some abstract definition of "good" and "right" with which to work. But Dewey argued that our moral dilemmas arise only in definite situations where individual or social interests are blocked. What we do in such circumstances is to work out some plan of action that will eliminate the specific conflict that is troubling us. And we test this plan, not by its agreement with some general definition of "the good," but by its feasibility and its consistency with other values we actually hold. Particularly when Dewey dealt with the logic of our practical judgments he exhibited, it seems to me, a shrewd, close grasp of the facts and a stubborn resistance to traditional intellectual follies—two qualities, it must be confessed, that are not entirely usual among philosophers.

But Dewey had the defect of this virtue. As one of his early essays, "The Logic of Practical Judgment," states explicitly, he believed that scientific thinking could be made to fit the model of practical judgment. At the very least, this is an overstatement. For while it is true that many fundamental scientific ideas have an instrumental function, it is a gross simplification (as Dewey himself sometimes recognized) to say that they are tools for manipulating the environment. Their acceptance in a scientific system depends equally on purely intellectual considerations such as economy, elegance and the possibility of connecting them with other systems. Moreover, Dewey's insistence that thinking always remakes and reforms the materials on which it works makes it difficult to find a place for the clearly primary objective of theoretical science—namely, to understand a world whose structure does not depend on what we think or do about it. Dewey repeatedly failed to distinguish between facts as they exist and those beliefs about the facts that have the warrant of science at some particular time. But unless this distinction is kept clearly and uncompromisingly in mind we cannot explain what Dewey himself thought the hallmark of scientific thinking—its openness to correction by further evidence.

Dewey's view of science, indeed, has something a little dated about it. It seems to be the view of a man whose fundamental ideas about science had been formed before the rise of modern physics, which, for all its practical and ominous usefulness, describes a world that transcends almost all our practical and habitual expectations. When Dewey argued that "scientific method" or "scientific habits of thought" should be diffused throughout society, what did he mean by these elusive phrases? The science that played the greatest role in Dewey's thinking was biology; and what he meant by "the scientific attitude," I would suggest, was primarily the evolutionary attitude—a recognition that nothing is exempt from change, that new circumstances require new ideas and institutions, and that we should measure the worth of these ideas and institutions not in terms of allegedly eternal truths, but in terms of their contribution to the control of the human environment and the satisfaction of human interests. He was right to have believed that if such an attitude could be generally diffused in a society, a remarkably liberating revolution would take place. And he would be equally right to say, as he surely would today, that some appreciation of the intellectual significance of contemporary science should be regarded as a necessity for all educated men in our society. But the view of science and scientific method which he held is not one which is likely to warn us about the extraordinary difficulty of this task.

And so we come, by a quite natural transition, to Dewey's philosophy of education. I must be brief, and I speak with the diffidence that befits any discussion either of Dewey or of education. Dewey's philosophy of education, as Sidney Hook has argued, rests on two pillars—first, a commitment to democracy and a belief that the habits developed in the classroom are as important to a student's effective participation in democracy as the facts and ideas he acquires; second, a belief that the content and methods of instruction should be governed by the best scientific knowledge available. To this certain other propositions may also be added. Teaching is effective only when the student's perspective is taken into account and only when his active interest and participation in the work of the classroom is aroused. Further, since we do not understand facts or ideas until we know how to use them, the student must be provided with facts and ideas in contexts in which he can put them to use and test them for himself.

Any teacher can report how easy it is to forget these principles in everyday practice, and yet they may seem too obvious to constitute a significant educational philosophy. But if they do seem obvious, this is a measure of Dewey's achievement. For they were not at all obvious when he first began to write on education. In 1892, for example, Joseph Rice made a survey of American schools in thirty-six cities. He told the story of a teacher in Chicago who, after asking a question, would say "Don't stop to think. Tell me what you know!" In New York, Rice asked a school principal whether students were allowed to turn their heads. The man replied, "Why should they look behind when the teacher is in front of them?" This is the sort of thing that Dewey was thinking about when he emphasized that teachers teach students and not only subjects, that a spirit of inquiry should animate the classroom, and that play too has its educational uses. It is grossly untrue to say that Dewey had insufficient respect for the intellectual goals of education. His philosophy was not an attempt to make the schools more frivolous. It was an attempt to return the schools to seriousness.

But Dewey, unhappily, did write vaguely. In the hands of eager disciples, his language, never an adequate instrument for the communication of ideas, has been converted into a jargon that hides them. Moreover, as Dewey himself pointed out late in life in his little book *Experience and Education,* his philosophy of education had merely been an attempt to emphasize neglected issues in education. But many of his admirers have taken a matter of emphasis for the whole story. Although I remain diffident, I cannot forebear saying that the results have frequently been bizarre.

I can mention only one issue, an issue raised by Dewey's emphasis on "the practical." It has led, I would suggest, to a mistaken conception of the kind of thing that needs to be done to involve a student actively in the learning process. Dewey was right to think that a student will master an idea only when he has had a chance to use it for himself. But it is wrong to conclude that the student can learn the use of important ideas by focusing primarily on homely problems within the round of his daily experience. If ideas have a direct bearing on such issues, that is all to the good. The alert teacher will exploit the opportunity. But we learn the distinctive function of an important idea when he see it at work, not simply reorganizing the world we have known, but leading to other worlds we might never have imagined otherwise. Accordingly, unless the student's attention to things outside his ordinary world is deliberately engaged, and unless his perceptions are liberated from domination by the familiar, the school will not have done its job.

Although Dewey would undoubtedly have agreed with this truism, I believe that he must bear some of the responsibility for the tendency of those who espouse his educational philosophy, to forget it. For there is a repeated error into which Dewey falls in his educational philosophy and in his philosophy in general. He wished passionately to show that the everyday practical experience of men could have an ideal dimension. But he slid from this idea to the quite different one that a man's—or a child's—experience must always have a practical dimension.

And yet these criticisms do not touch the heart of what John Dewey succeeded in doing. He thought that philosophy was an instrument by which a society criticizes itself, throwing off the ideas that block its development and finding the possibilities within itself that it might work to realize. He set himself to this task and performed it with a quiet, steady passion, magnanimously, imaginatively, without nostalgia for the past or regret for the comforting dogmas that had to be sacrificed. And he put his finger on the two main issues of his day—the steady growth in the importance of science and the struggle to extend democracy—and revealed their moral meaning, their possibilities for our day-to-day experience.

Dewey helped men to see that science meant something much more than an increase in their power to control their environment. He showed that science challenged inherited forms of authority and offered an alternative way by which men could stabilize their lives. And despite all his emphasis on practical manipulations and control, Dewey also showed that science represented a revolution in the human imagination, extending human horizons and making men aware of remote and unfamiliar things. So he brought science to the same test that he brought everything else—its impact on men's immediate experience; and he taught men to value science for what it could do to enhance the meanings they found in their everyday lives.

He transformed the theory of democracy in a similar way. "The one thing in the world of value," Emerson once wrote, "is the active soul." This was the central point of Dewey's theory of experience, and it is the source of his conception of democracy. Only in a society in which the lines between classes are fluid and in which men freely mingle and communicate with one another, Dewey believed, can active souls be generated everywhere. And so he saw that democracy could mean something much more than a political form. It could mean a change in the quality of a culture, an opportunity for men to experience more and to live more intensely.

Without vanity or pretentiousness, John Dewey made himself a spokesman for the best hopes of his generation. And to our generation he leaves the image of a man of unforced courage and honesty, living by choice in the mainstream of events, and yet rising above events to a coherent vision of what men might make of themselves. He helped us to see farther and to move more freely. It is to him as much as to anyone that we owe what belief we have that our own place in history can be an opportunity and not a fatality.

33 Holmes, Brandeis, and Frankfurter: Differences in Pragmatic Jurisprudence

Robert Goldecke

Although much that is creative and exciting in American intellectual life never passes into the case opinions of United States Supreme Court justices, informative intellectual history can be drawn from their judicial decisions. Historians of ideas have generally been inclined to pass over court opinions as grist for their mill for two reasons. For one, until this century high court opinions usually were on the side of established tradition; the law and the men who spoke for it were affirmative, not innovative. Secondly, legal and judicial opinions do not, in the main, conform to the wider-ranging style of narrative or analytical history. Conversely, written history rarely fits the requirements of a legal brief. But early in this century the arrival upon the supreme bench of men who discussed underlying ideas, who took official cognizance of social and economic theories, did much to change historians' attitudes toward judicial pronouncements. In a period of rapid change, the country was fortunate to have on its highest tribunal the three penetrating minds discussed here: Oliver Wendell Holmes, Jr. (1841-1935), Louis Dembitz Brandeis (1856-1941), and Felix Frankfurter (1882-1965). Throughout the 1930s, as again in the 1950s, '60s, and '70s, Americans became aware of the Supreme Court's meaning for their lives. Virtually every informed citizen came to know the terms "sociological jurisprudence" or "judicial restraint." But what even most scholars did not detect were the differences among the "pragmatists" in the federal court system.

Professor Goedecke analyzes these differences and centers his discussion in the concept of a higher unity above even the binding elements of a legal system, the tough-minded spirit of national community which Holmes cherished and which Brandeis and Frankfurter saw in different ways. The reader will want to consider, moreover, that although Holmes was present at the founding of pragmatism and was sympathetic to it as a method of inquiry (see Essay 24), his was basically a naturalistic rather than a pragmatic outlook upon life. He held a certain disdain for humanitarians and altruists; he was attracted to the view of man as predatory and always in battle. He saw no good reason to support the idea of a moral order in the

Ethics, 74 (January 1964), 83-96. Reprinted by permission of the author and The University of Chicago Press. Footnotes have been omitted.

universe, breaking here with a major tradition in Anglo-American law. For him, man is not cosmically important, and the highest loyalty man can give for his own survival is loyalty to his group.

For further reading: Irving Bernstein, "The Conservative Mr. Justice Holmes," *New England Quarterly*, 23 (December 1950), 435-452; Samuel J. Konefsky, *The Legacy of Holmes and Brandeis: A Study in the Influence of Ideas* (1956); *Eugene V. Rostow, "The Realist Tradition in American Law," in Arthur M. Schlesinger, Jr., and Morton White (eds.), *Paths of American Thought* (1963), chap. 11; Alpheus T. Mason, "The Supreme Court: Temple and Forum," *The Yale Review*, 48 (Summer 1959), 524-540, reprinted in *Leonard W. Levy (ed.), *American Constitutional Law: Historical Essays* (1966), pp. 225-241; *Wallace Mendelson (ed.), *The Supreme Court: Law and Discretion* (1967).

Mr. Justice Holmes was appointed to the Supreme Court by Theodore Roosevelt in 1902 and stayed for thirty years, always admired and respected, although frequently in the posture of dissent, until retirement in 1932. Soldier, scholar, aristocrat, and thinker, as well as judge, his judicial opinions were the first to carry the "revolt against formalism" to the Supreme Bench. Holmes attacked "mere words" and "logic" as the bases of the law and held that conceptions of the demands and needs of civilization were basic for law. Mr. Justice Brandeis was appointed by President Wilson in 1916 to the highest tribunal, amid a storm of protest from conservatives, and stayed on until 1939. An attorney and reforming publicist before his appointment to the Supreme Court, Brandeis had lectured and written on matters of policy which his opponents regarded as within the domain of private business, while Brandeis considered them within the domain of public consideration and action. His "Brandeis briefs" were another aspect of the attack on formalism and legalism in constitutional law. Rather than deducing conclusions from prior laws, Brandeis indicated social evils and possible legal remedies through vast compilations of statistics and expert opinions on the matter under consideration. Mr. Justice Frankfurter had been an assistant to Brandeis in the compilation of some such briefs, and as a professor of law at Harvard he had continued to insist on recognition of the policy-making role of the judiciary, as opposed to notions of "mechanical jurisprudence." Appointed by Franklin Roosevelt to the Supreme Court in 1939, he has now retired from that body, bringing to a close three generations of antiformalist thought, sixty years after Holmes first came to the Bench.

It is now obvious that there were differences among these three justices. Holmes was aloof from the immediate issues of politics and economics and not particularly sympathetic with notions of social reform. Brandeis was a fighter for reform, both before and after he was on the Supreme Court. Frankfurter during his last years on the Supreme Court became a "champion of self-restraint" and extremely wary of applying judicial vetoes on state laws and practices, whether these were in the realm of economics and taxation, or in the realm of religion and freedom of speech.

It is perhaps necessary to insist on the similarities of legal method held in common by the three justices. All three were agreed that extreme formalism and legalism were inappropriate to crucial constitutional problems in a changing world. The change in conditions and the change in the meaning of words meant that it was impossible to go back to the eighteenth-century document and expect that it would contain within it all the answers to modern problems without need for interpretation and practical judgment. All three were aware of the useful and yet treacherous ambiguity of words and phrases, and of the underlying social and economic purposes to which such terms as "liberty of contract" and "property" served as legal masks. All three were aware that interpretation of the words in laws and the Constitution was so flexible that the Court was in effect a policy-making body, and not simply a guardian of cold and fixed restrictions. All three saw that social life was filled with the conflict of interests and values, a conflict of various social forces, and they all saw the Court as having a role in solving the problems and disputes that arose because of such multiple interacting forces and values. All three were concerned about the obvious changes in the circumstances of the nation, from the end of the Civil War through the development of modern industrialism and urbanism in America. The slogan started by Holmes; "Think things, and not words!" was repeated faithfully by Brandeis and by Frankfurter: a logic of the facts, a logic of history, an empiricism concerned with the concrete process of events, was for all of them more real than the abstractions, general propositions, and deductive logic of the Old Law. All three justices were pragmatists in the sense that the words of the law are subordinate and instrumental to the realities, and that definition must be given to situations, not to words. All three saw the duty of the Court to remain "disinterested," rather than biased, scientific rather than opinionated, and practical rather than formal. In the words of Frankfurter, proper judicial interpretation

> *requires an evaluation based on disinterested inquiry, pursued in the spirit of science, on a balanced order of facts exactly and fairly stated, on the detached consideration of conflicting claims, and on a judgment not* ad hoc *and episodic but duly mindful of reconciling the needs both of continuity and change in a progressive society.*

Given such a similarity in method, how are the ultimate differences in jurisprudence to be explained? The answer can be given irrationally in terms of differences in social background and fundamental psychological attitudes among the three men; but such obviously true clichés do not yield much information about differences in jurisprudence. In terms of pragmatic jurisprudence, each judge had to find the dynamic area where any distinction between fact and value was false and unrealistic. Each of the three justices, Holmes, Brandeis, and Frankfurter, did find such an area. But each discovered area was different. Holmes discovered such an area in the comprehensive unity of society as a whole, within which legislative and economic battles could proceed without hurting the fundamental social unity. Brandeis discovered the area on the level of the wisely directed interaction of various groups in society. The co-operation of groups, rather than their senseless competition, was the area where facts and values would form the unity needed for pragmatic social theory. And finally, Justice Frankfurter followed a method of extreme empiricism, in which such unities as Holmes and Brandeis found were rejected as abstractions, and unity of value could be found only on the level of actual individual men and actions, and even there only rarely. The higher music that Justice Holmes intuited as the essence of constitutional law became a faint reedy pipe indeed on the level of tangled particulars in taxations, jurisdiction, and conflicting traditions that Justice Frankfurter saw as the area of empirical jurisprudence. To expand on this thesis, and to indicate with somewhat greater clearness the differences stated, the jurisprudence of each justice will be expounded briefly.

Holmes's writing on the history of the law, his insistence on experience rather than logic as the "life" of the law, and his willingness in later life to talk about battles and fighting as basic, led both friends and enemies to class him as an extreme pragmatist, who accepted change and brute power as the fundamental facts of life and the facts of life as the beginning of all jurisprudence. But this common view of Holmes is false to his continued insistence on a unity of thought and social life above the clashes of opinion. For Holmes, life could not be reduced to mere facts, although he sometimes longed for it to be so. In correspondence he lamented that he could not live life on the level of "splendid good dinners" and "fine rattling walks"; but metaphysical questions, which Holmes linked with constitutional questions, prevented satisfaction on this level. Holmes made a point of never reading newspapers. He would not go with Brandeis to visit factories when Court was in recess, despite his colleague's pleas. For Holmes life was much more ideas and incessant reading. But the reading disclosed a pluralism and conflict of ideas which pointed, Plato-fashion, to a cosmos beyond such clashes.

Holmes's view of legislation was that it was on the level of ideas, or rather in the realm where creativity, experimentation, ideas, and facts mingle in human action. This was a pluralistic realm, and not the province of constitutional jurisprudence. It was an area for "the making of social experiments." Therefore, in general, Holmes was not concerned about the facts upon which such legislation was based, nor was he concerned as to whether he agreed with the theories behind such laws. Such theories were various and relative; which ones were new and which ones were old and acceptable was largely a matter of "accident," and theories dominant at one time would go out of fashion at another. All theories, all economic views, all legislation, had limitations, and therefore no permanency or false absolutism should be expected or forced by the Court in these areas. Holmes's most constant complaint about the other members of the Court was that they based their opinions on economic and social theories.

Investigators looking at the economic theories of Justice Holmes, discovered in conversation and correspondence, have found his theories unsophisticated and conservative. He believed in the wage-fund theory of compensation to labor; he believed that differences in ownership of property made no difference, in comparison with "the stream of goods" and actual consumption; and he believed that combination in business enterprise was an unmitigated good thing. But these views rarely affected his judicial opinions, if ever, because he did not think his own views were relevant; his uncritical acceptance of oversimplifications in economics probably was due to the very insignificant place such a subject had in his scheme of jurisprudence. The realm of economics was for the makers and doers, not the thinkers and judges.

With the rejection of facts and theories as the locus of value and judicial principle, what is left? The student of Holmes is driven to the realization that what was most real for Holmes in constitutional legal judgment was the over-all unity of the whole process of the clash of opinions, theories, and interests. It was this over-all unity which the Supreme Court was to guard, allowing "free play in the joints" in the areas of industrial conflict and legislative experiment within such unity. Such a constitutional unity was discovered not verbally and logically, which would have reduced it to cold theory, but by "an intuition more subtle than logic could discover." This unit was not a unity on the level of facts, for the facts of life were struggle and a Darwinian conflict of interests; nor was this unity on the basis of theories, for there were many theories of economics and government, and the Constitution was designed to include them all, and in the course of time theories and faiths go down before other theories and faiths. But, for Holmes, beyond facts and the variety of faiths there was in America an over-all unity of the pluralistic social process, and this unity was maintained and protected by the Supreme Court.

Before Holmes was on the Court, he had been suggesting in speeches that there was an area above facts and ideas. In his famous essay, "The Path of the Law," Holmes started with law as factual and predictive. On the level of facts, the government is power, and the business of the lawyer is to predict successfully how that power will be exercised. However, Holmes did not stay on such a factual level. He recommended vast reading in economics, history, and jurisprudence to reach an appreciation of the values found in the science of the law. He indicated that readings in Roman law and German jurisprudence were as valuable as studies in the Common Law. The purpose of such reading, Holmes stated, is not practical at all, it is theoretical. Theory is ultimately more important than practice, and ideas are more powerful than guns and brute power. Holmes stated: "See how much more the world is governed today by Kant than by Bonaparte." But even Kant is not ultimate truth—simply one of the great thinkers—and Holmes mentioned Descartes as just as powerful. The pluralism on the level of philosophic systems points to a more unified level, beyond pragmatic success and beyond theory, where the intellect can connect law with the universe, "catch an echo of the infinite, a glimpse of its unfathomable process, a hint of the universal law."

In his first written opinion for the Supreme Court, *Otis* v. *Parker*, Holmes indicated that facts are not the province of the Court, but of the legislature: "Considerable latitude must be allowed . . . for possible peculiar conditions which this court can know but imperfectly, if at all." Similar latitude must be given to theories, opinions, and values, which are in the realm of the changing. What is left Holmes described as "relatively fundamental rules of right, as generally understood by all English-speaking communities." It should be noted that these fundamentals are above "ethical and economic theories" which do not have an over-all unifying tendency:

General propositions do not carry us far. While the courts must exercise a judgment of their own, it is by no means true that every law is void which may seem to the judges who pass upon it excessive, unsuited to its ostensible end, or based upon conceptions of morality with which they disagree. Latitude must be allowed for differences of view, as well as for conditions which this court can know but imperfectly, if at all. Otherwise a constitution, instead of embodying only relatively fundamental rules of right, as generally understood by all English-speaking communities, would become the partisan of a particular set of ethical or economic opinions, which by no means are held semper ubique et ab omnibus.

Thus a unity must be sought above ordinary ethics and economics, but not on the level of brute facts; rather on the level of tolerance and insight of a supervising judiciary. Holmes's famous dictum in his *Lochner* dissent, that "the Fourteenth Amendment does not enact Mr. Herbert Spencer's *Social Statics*," was meant to cut two ways: both against the brother justices who based their judicial opinions on their privately held theories of government and economics, and thus on opinion rather than truth; and against Herbert Spencer, whose "atomistic" views were a denial of Holmes's fundamental convictions about the need for sovereign law in civilization. A social unity is above all views, and because there are different views, such a unity is needed: "A constitution is not intended to embody a particular economic theory, whether of paternalism or of *laissez faire*. It is made for people of fundamentally differing views."—Holmes continued in his *Lochner* dissent to state the basis of constitutional law—intuition. Later pragmatic thinkers have attempted to overlook this aspect of Holmes's view of experience and to relate intuition to facts alone. But Holmes thought that the facts were the province of legislatures; the intuition is of the over-all unity: "General propositions do not decide concrete cases. The decision will depend on a judgment or intuition more subtle than any articulate major premise."

It is this subtle and silent contact with the transcendent unity of the action of society which Holmes found at the basis of jurisprudence and politics. Such a view informs all his writings, and gives them that peculiar quality, which, not fully understood, has been called "literary charm." Since articulate major premises cannot state these subtle intuitions, his *dicta* have a flavor of boyish irresponsibility, Olympian detachment, and, at the same time, usually suggest immediately fundamental problems of morality, statesmanship, and law.

Holmes was willing to accept not only differences, but also futilities, stupidities, and even poisons, on the lower and changing levels of commerce and legislation, if these actions and laws did not damage the going unity. He hated the notion that mere words would be used to "prevent the making of social experiments . . . in the insulated chambers afforded by the several states, even though the experiments may seem futile or even noxious to me." But Holmes was not above voiding legislation if it was going to disrupt the foundations of social unity; to guard against disintegration of that sort was the duty of the Court. Holmes saw the Sherman Antitrust Act as such a potentially disruptive law. In such a case (which did not actually arise), the law no longer represented merely another economic theory with which he was not in agreement; it would have been an unconstitutional usurpation of powers:

I am happy to know that only a minority of my brethren adopt an interpretation of the law which would make eternal the bellum omnium contra omnes *and disintegrate society so far as it could into individual atoms. If that were its intent I should regard calling such a law a regulation of commerce a mere pretense. It would be an attempt to reconstruct society. I am not concerned with the wisdom of such an attempt but I believe Congress was not entrusted by the Constitution with the power to make it.*

On matters of civil rights, Justice Holmes consistently maintained that the "sovereign" power was the sole and proper judge of its exercise, against whom the citizens had no rights. However, his view changed and broadened from an earlier, more strict denial of the rights of the ruled, to a later position in which Holmes insisted that the legislative and executive branches of the government, like the judiciary, should realize the diversity of opinions and developments in social theory as inevitable realities in the human situation, and therefore exercise tolerance (except in cases of immediate danger to the sovereignty). The earlier position was maintained most obviously in the Moyer case in which Moyer sued the governor of Colorado for putting him in jail for ten weeks without any sort of court action. Holmes's view was that the governor could have killed Moyer if he had seen fit to do so and that the jail term was, relatively speaking, lenient. . . . Holmes's later view does not admit less power to the rulers, but calls upon legislators to recognize the facts of change on the level of theory and opinion, action and reaction:

But when men have realized that time has upset many fighting faiths, they may come to believe even more than they believe the very foundations of their own conduct that the ultimate good desired is better reached by free trade in ideas.

In one of his more extreme *dicta*, Holmes suggested that the Supreme Court could preside over a change from democracy to dictatorship without complete disruption of society:

If in the long run the beliefs expressed in proletarian dictatorship are destined to be accepted by the dominant forces of the community, the only meaning of free speech is that they should be given their chance and have their way.

In sum, Holmes was quite prepared to admit conflict and change on the partial and lower levels of facts, economics, ethics, laws, and ideas, if the dynamic unity of society were maintained through judicial intuition. The pragmatism and moral relativism for which he is praised and blamed are subordinate in his thought and in his judicial opinions to an ongoing unity above the conflict of classes and theories.

No such unity above social interests was seen by Holmes's great friend and junior colleague, Mr. Justice Brandeis. Brandeis could not maintain an Olympian disinterest in the clash of labor with management and capital, because for Brandeis this was the significant reality, and unity must be worked and fought for on the level of past and present social conflict. The real problem for America was whether the laboring classes would be so degraded and devitalized by abuse and indifference that the economy would suffer and a democracy based on awareness of different views and interests would never be realized. Brandeis was not willing to leave facts and opinions to others. His method of thought, made famous before he became a justice, was to accumulate all the facts of a situation, and then to accumulate all the opinions relevant to the situation or similar ones all over the civilized world.

Brandeis then worked with these opinions to discover a common unity and direction, not subject to reasonable opposition. Such a unified and proper opinion would then be the basis for industrial agreement, legislative action, and judicial decision. Through a close scrutiny of facts and opinions, action could be taken which would replace the destructive Darwinism of competition and monopolies with a co-operative unity on a level which recognized the validity of different groups and different interests and values, but refused to see conflict as economic or as civilized. His method can be seen in three examples, characteristic of Brandeis' concern with evils on a social and economic level: life insurance for the working classes, regulation of hours of employment for women, and the nature and function of employment agencies. . . .

Such instances show how Brandeis believed in facing facts and opinions to advance the public welfare through governmental and judicial action. Brandeis discovered that ways could be found to overcome factual conflicts and conflicts of interest and value, but only through patient study of these facts and interests. Social interests could then be unified, and it was as much the duty of the Supreme Court to act on such developments as to do any other tasks. Karl Llewellyn has indicated the difference between Holmes and Brandeis on the proper role of Court and judge: "A Brandeis sustains a new industrial regulation because he sees and demonstrates its utility—a Holmes sustains it in magnificent disinterest." Brandeis found a unity on the level of economic action and legislative development which Holmes did not, and consequently Brandeis found a different area upon which to found the fundamental decisions of law. For Holmes, groups and interests were changing, variable, and thus unable to form a solid and unified foundation for constitutional decision. Brandeis found that groups and interests were the reality of social life, which must be recognized in politics and law. Groups and people were more real than individuals in social life:

This right of development on the part of the group is essential to the full enjoyment of rights by the individual. For the individual is dependent for his development (and his happiness) in large part on the group of which he forms a part.

Legal individualism is therefore deficient:

Enlightened countries grant to the individual equality before the law; but they fail still to recognize the equality of whole peoples or nationalities. We seek to protect as individuals those constituting a minority; but we fail to realize that protection cannot be complete unless group equality also is recognized.

What is true of the reality of groups in domestic life is also true of the reality of peoples and nations on the international level; these groups are the true individuals in the social process:

The movements of the last century have proved that whole peoples have individuality no less marked than that of a single person, that the individuality of a people is irrepressible, and that the misnamed internationalism which seeks the obliteration of nationalities or peoples is unattainable.

It is this recognition of the reality of groups and their interests that is fundamental in Brandeis' jurisprudence of constitutional law and action. He insisted that the interplay of group interests was a fact of public life and rejected other views as theoretical. For Holmes, who thought such a conception of the co-operation of social groups unrealistic, Brandeis always remained "one of those onward and upward fellers," while, as we shall see, for Frankfurter, such a conception of the reality of groups is unempirical: only individuals exist and even the Supreme Court is an abstraction. In emphasizing group realities Brandeis could overlook the brute problems of life on the individual level, for the sake of developments on the larger social scene. His ability in his chosen area is unsurpassed. In his patience in gathering facts, and in his ability to marshal opinions, he was a great arbiter and judge. But his unity is not the transcendent unity of the jurisprudence of Justice Holmes, and his individuality of groups is not the factual individuality of Justice Frankfurter.

Justice Frankfurter's restraint in stating his own views might make it seem difficult to discover what, for him, is the locus of value and activity in constitutional law. But the massive scholarship and brilliant legal technique which seem a screen for personal views in Frankfurter's opinions are part of a philosophy of extreme nominalism and individualism. For the jurisprudence of Justice Frankfurter, the immediate action and the immediate situation, together with historic antecedents and considered consequences, are the reality of the social process and the law. Consequently there are not obvious larger unities to which social policy and constitutional decision can be addressed. In the immediate workaday world of individual facts, it is not obvious that conflicting interests can be reconciled: if a state tax is constitutional, the state gets the tax money; otherwise the corporations keep it. If a guilty criminal can successfully claim violation of his constitutional rights, he goes free and society suffers; otherwise he goes to prison and suffers. Most legal conflicts on the individual level mean that someone will lose. In such situations it is the wisdom of the Court not to impose its will arbitrarily, but to keep within the restrictions imposed by precedent and tradition. Every case is a hard case, and judges have the painful duty of declaring judgment against one individual and set of values, and for another. Experience for Frankfurter gave no insight into the abstractions of groups or higher social unities; experience gave a grasp of the historical facts of precedent in the judicial process and conflict of men and interests as the difficult facts of social life.

Frankfurter cautioned against seeing the Supreme Court as a unity:

We speak of the Court as though it were an abstraction. To be sure, the Court is an institution, but individuals, with all their diversities of endowment, experience, and outlook, determine its actions. The history of the Supreme Court is not the history of an abstraction but the analysis of individuals acting as a Court who make decisions and lay down doctrines, and of other individuals, their successors, who refine, modify, and sometimes even overrule the decisions of their predecessors, reinterpreting and transmuting their doctrines.

. . . However, abstractions, such as the law, the Supreme Court, and general propositions are real insofar as they have an actual effect in practical life. "The raw material of modern government is business.'' The Supreme Court has influenced this business through legal devices:

It cannot be denied that the Supreme Court has enormously furthered corporate growth. By devising facilities for business . . . the decisions of the Court themselves have operated as economic factors.

And general propositions can be seen in their concrete effects on decisions:

I am not unmindful of Mr. Justice Holmes' caution that ''general propositions do not decide concrete cases.'' Whether they do or not often depends on the strength of the conviction with which such ''general propositions'' are held. A principle may be accepted ''in principle'' but the impact of an immediate situation may lead to a deviation from the principle. Or, while accepted ''in principle,'' a competing principle may seem more important. Thus, a decision may turn on whether one gives the Fourth Amendment a place second to none in the Bill of Rights, or considers it on the whole a kind of nuisance in the war against crime.

Thus general propositions are not completely unreal, but they are real only insofar as they affect concrete and immediate decisions.

This emphasis on particular actions and men, and their particular effects in the stream of history, which Justice Frankfurter called the ''empiric process,'' to be studied by the method of ''empiricism,'' leads to a view of the judicial process different from the view of Brandeis. Values on this level are in conflict, and no obvious harmony can be attained through judicial action. In cases of broad political conflict, reconciliation by the Court is impossible; and it would be better if the judiciary did not intervene at all:

History teaches that the independence of the judiciary is jeopardized when courts become embroiled in the passions of the day and assume primary responsibility in choosing between competing political, economic, and social pressures.

The Supreme Court, for Frankfurter, was not the institution to provide remedy for such social problems. At the opposite end of social disputes, the petty injustices of minor officials and policemen against citizens, remedies are also unavailing from the Court; for it cannot ''regulate the quotidian business of every traffic policeman, every registrar of elections, every city inspector or invesitgator, every clerk in every municipal licensing bureau in the country.'' This ''self-restraint,'' for which Frankfurter became famous, is an avoidance of imposing policy decisions on persons in conflict, where there is no obvious unity that can be attained by such a procedure. At times Frankfurter has expressed suspicion of the whole process of judicial review: if the people and their representatives cannot find their way to the solution of a conflict, it will do them no good to have the Court impose a solution, ''garbed in the abstractions of the law.''

Not infrequently Frankfurter argued for the side whose interests he was going to deny, indicating that right was not obviously and completely on one side in such controversies. For instance, in a case involving deportation of an alien, Frankfurter argued for the alien who had just claims but then decided against him because of other just claims:

Since he is a "person," an alien has the same rights as a citizen under the due process clause, and deportation . . . strikes one with a harsh sense of incongruity. . . . If due process bars Congress from enactments that shock the sense of fair play, is it not beyond the powers of Congress to deport an alien who was duped into joining the Communist Party?

In the abstract, "were we writing on a clean slate," such claims are valid; but in the concrete historical process things are messier. Frankfurter continued:

But the slate is not clean. . . . That the formulation of policies [respecting aliens] *is exclusively entrusted to Congress has become about as firmly embedded in the legislative and judicial tissue of our body politic as any aspect of our government.*

On the concrete empirical level, values do not interplay with the same resultant harmony that they may on the group level. . . . The Brandeis method of "letting the facts speak for themselves" did not give a "scientific" answer to the problem, for the evidence indicated that society was marching in different directions, or standing still.

The difficulties of deciding value conflicts legally led Frankfurter frequently to look to England as a place where the grass is greener. The unanimity of popular opinion there makes the problems of a free society easier of solution, and also they avoid the abstractions of "Bills of Rights:"

Neither court and counsel nor police and prosecution are ultimate reliances for the liberties of the people. These rest in ourselves. The liberties that are defined by our Bill of Rights are, on the whole, more living realities in the daily lives of the Englishmen without any formal constitution, because they are part of the national habit, they are in the marrow of the bones of the people.

The police are better in England:

In this country policy testimony is often rejected by juries precisely because of the widely entertained belief that illegal methods are used to secure testimony. Thus, dubious police methods defeat the very ends of justice by which such methods are justified. No such cloud rests on policy testimony in England.

The desire to remain close to the concrete facts of life with an empirical philosophy such as Frankfurter's means that if there must be ideals, they can be concrete ideals, such as the practices of another country.

Some of the confusion surrounding certain of Justice Frankfurter's dissenting opinions can be cleared up if proper regard is given to his insistence on empirical and particular facts, and empirically held and concrete values. His hesitancy with respect to protecting religious rights against demands to participate in salutes to the flag arose because he saw conflicting values in the situation, "the right to awaken in the child's mind considerations as to the significance of the flag contrary to those implanted by the parent,'' and because the concrete empirical values would have been affected otherwise by the abstract and imposed values of formal law: ''personal freedom is best maintained when it is ingrained in people's habits and not enforced against popular policy by the coercion of abjudicated law.'' His refusal to recognize constitutional rights to the reapportionment of voting districts within states was a refusal to substitute the abstract and imposed directions of the Court for the concrete and historical patterns of voting in the states involved. His willingness to allow state taxation of corporations involved in interstate commerce came from an empirical insistence that the property involved actually was within the confines of the state, while considerations involving higher costs of national commerce were relatively abstract.

Finally, Justice Frankfurter found within the flow of history an impersonal standard of ideals, which was not simply a product of emotional whim on the part of judges of the law. ''Canons of decency and fairness'' have developed, and, although each person has a slightly different opinion as to what they are, they are in fact objective and commonly accepted.

Judicial review inescapably imposes upon this Court an exercise of judgment upon proceedings in order to ascertain whether they offend those canons of decency and fairness which express the notions of justice of English-speaking peoples. These standards of justice are not authoritatively formulated anywhere. . . . The judicial judgment must move within the limits of accepted notions of justice and is not to be based upon the idiosyncrasies of a merely personal judgment. The fact that judges may differ among themselves, whether in a particular case a trial offends accepted notions of justice is not disproof that general rather than idiosyncratic standards are applied.

Therefore the jurisprudence of Justice Frankfurter is signalized by his insistence that an empirical method demands that the locus for the solution of judicial problems be found in the concrete individualities and value conflicts of immediate everyday life. Within his jurisprudence Justice Frankfurter was able to distinguish many things: general propositions; social issues; concrete, abstract, and ambiguous words; rights and interests; theories of government; private and public problems; men and actions—but in the empirical realm all these various factors were to be seen in terms of their practical and concrete effect. Justice Frankfurter has been a lifelong admirer of Justice Holmes, but in his repeated praises of Holmes, it is not the philosophy of the man that matters so much as that of a philosopher affected the actual constitutional law of the country in a particular way.

The method of solution of difficulties in pragmatic jurisprudence involves a judicious weighing of considerations on both sides of a dispute and reaching a fair and workable solution in terms of a formal law which is judged flexible in new circumstances, general considerations of social policy, and the particular circumstances of place and time actually involved in the dispute. All three justices, Holmes, Brandeis, and Frankfurter, followed such a pragmatic method self-consciously. They all attacked formalism, abstract notions of rights, and traditional or ''mechanical'' logic. But within this common method each found a different unity of fact and value. Holmes saw conflicts of value in economic and legislative processes but found a more comprehensive unity of the social process guarded by the Court, which allowed for tolerance of much conflict on partial and changing levels. Brandeis sought for a harmonious unity on the level of group interaction, in which various groups would be recognized and yet would not continue to conflict with other social groups. Frankfurter denied any higher unities above factual individualities, and saw the law as having limited duties of maintaining a stable and yet flexible tradition in a concrete historical process where the law cannot solve al problems, nor unite all interests.

Some significance must be given to each of the three general areas of final value indicated by Holmes, Brandeis, and Frankfurter, beyond the scope of constitutional law and jurisprudence. If, above the facts of power and death, a man can discover a Holmesian unity in life, the clashes and defects and stupidities become interesting, affording variety and change. Or, if a man can find in life an area of social adjustment, agreement, and unanimity, then his personal drives can unite with his social conscience in social action toward goals shared by all. Finally, it is hard to escape the brute empirical facts that in the concrete and individual flow of history opinions clash, rights go unrecognized, and taxes must be paid every year.

The three areas of finality are philosophically incompatible and psychologically diverse. Holmes's position demands a clash of ethical and economic systems, for the higher tolerance, while Brandeis insists that through proper arbitration such clashes can be avoided. Brandeis discovered a possibility of social progress that made Court "activism" a Good Thing, while Justice Frankfurter discovered that, in the painful task of denying interests, recourse to impartial tradition and judicial self-restraint constituted the highest wisdom. It would be impossible for any one man, at the same time, to see a wisdom above ethical differences, and complete agreement on the level of social ethics, and the factual conflicts and frustrations of life, all united and constituting the pragmatic values on which to base decisions. However, despite philosophy and psychology, Holmes and Brandeis were the greatest of friends, Frankfurter and Brandeis were co-workers in many causes for years, and Frankfurter's admiration for Holmes is unbounded. Life goes on while the theory of human values is stopped in perplexity.

34
The New Orthodoxy

Walter M. Horton

Neo-orthodoxy in twentieth-century American Protestant theology has meant a reappraisal of the Puritan outlook upon the nature of man. While not embracing Puritan literalism or fundamentalism about the Bible, nor subscribing to Puritan social views, neo-orthodox theologians have preached that man's powers are indeed limited, that he is ever subject to error or sinfulness, and that he is the victim of his own hubris and overreaching.

The chief spokesman and leader for this point of view since the 1920s has been Reinhold Niebuhr (1892-1971). Reared in a Midwestern German Lutheran parsonage, pastor of a Detroit church when industrial unionism was struggling for recognition, and then for thirty-two years on the Union Theological Seminary faculty in New York City, Niebuhr believed that Christian morality should be manifest in social and political action. For this reason he was a proponent of pragmatism in American public affairs. The complexities of modern life, he contended, afford people no simple, clear-cut choices that are "right." The answers to public questions can only be approximate, never neat or absolute. This attitude toward public policy Niebuhr called "modern Christian realism"; it is perhaps more descriptive of his work and writing than the adjective "neo-orthodox." If he saw men as sinful, it was their collective guilt which he recognized and warned against, not private immorality. This vision of modern man was first stated in *Moral Man and Immoral Society* (1933). Niebuhr was not one to emphasize Christian conversion, preferring to stress a Christian realism by which one can try to change the environment as best one can. He took issue with Protestant evangelists on his right, like Billy Graham, and with liberal Protestant clergymen like Norman Vincent Peale, who preached self-help through faith. Yet Niebuhr expressed his own tough-minded Christian faith. He taught that religious belief is "basically a trust that life, however difficult and strange, has ultimate meaning." The influence of his theology was already recognized in the 1930s, as Walter M. Horton indicates in this article which traces the European background of neo-orthodoxy in the thought of Karl Barth, Emil Brunner, and Søren Kierkegaard.

American Scholar, 7 (Winter 1938), 3-11. Footnotes have been omitted.

But Niebuhr came to have even more influence upon American leadership after the Second World War. Academic men, journalists, government workers, and statesmen in the highest councils of the nation were swayed by his view of man's limited capacities for good and his "realistic" appraisals of American domestic and foreign affairs. (See also Essay 5.)

For further reading: *Charles W. Kegley and Robert W. Bretall (eds.), *Reinhold Niebuhr: His Religious, Social and Political Thought* (1956); *Charles Frankel, *The Case for Modern Man* (1955); *Morton White, *Social Thought in America: The Revolt against Formalism* (1957 ed.), epilogue; Kenneth Cauthen, *The Impact of American Religious Liberalism* (1962); L. Harold DeWolf, *The Religious Revolt against Reason* (1949); *Daniel Day Williams, *What Present-Day Theologians Are Thinking* (1952); Martin Luther King, Jr., "Letter from the Birmingham Jail," in his **Why We Can't Wait* (1963), pp. 76-95.

To the average college-trained American, church-goer or not, "orthodoxy" means "fundamentalism." And since that memorable occasion when fundamentalism took its stand, Canute-like, with William Jennings Bryan at Dayton, Tennessee, defying the sea of science to advance another inch, our college man is very likely to be convinced that only a rustic ignoramus can be truly orthodox. (So, in the declining days of the Roman Empire, it was only the *pagani,* the ignorant countrymen, who clung to their faith in the old Olympian gods.) Imagine his bewilderment then when he hears that many of the younger preachers and theologians—some of whom had their university course at Princeton or Harvard and their theological course in schools as pronouncedly liberal as Chicago Divinity School or Union Seminary—are now beginning to go "orthodox"! Imagine his distress when he is told that Professor Reinhold Niebuhr, whose shrewd analyses of current social issues have won his respect, is now bearing "theologically to the right" and (some say) heading full steam for orthodoxy!

The news is correct in the main though somewhat misleading unless rightly interpreted. Active young minds in the churches and seminaries *are* beginning to show a marked conservative trend. A generation ago young preachers and theological students were likely to be in revolt against traditional Christian theology wherever it came into collision with modern scientific or philosophical ideas. Today they are still in revolt—the perpetual prerogative of youth—but they are in revolt against liberalism. The statement is not, of course, true without qualification. In many churches and seminaries, especially in the South, the conflict between fundamentalism and liberalism still goes on and youth is on the liberal side. But precisely where the victory of liberal Christianity has been most complete, in the Northern urban centers, the reaction against it is most pronounced and the trend toward orthodoxy most unmistakable.

This new conservative movement is essentially different from fundamentalism. Fundamentalism was pre-modernistic; the new orthodoxy is post-modernistic. Fundamentalism was a defensive movement, designed to protect the historic "deposit of faith" against the destructive inroads of its modern environment; the new orthodoxy is an aggressive pioneering movement, already adjusted to its modern environment but pushing on through the increasingly arid desert of modern existence with the help of ancient maps and ancient travelers' songs—the rediscovered legacy of an "Eternal People" whose "Eternal Road" has often taken them through that self-same wilderness.

The new orthodoxy has only recently appeared in America but it has flourished for fifteen years in Continental Europe. American delegates to the church unity conferences which met at Oxford and Edinburgh this summer became aware of its pervasive influence when they encountered opposition of "the Continentals" on every major issue. At first with amusement or indignation, then with some respect, they were repeatedly obliged to listen to a point of view in which the German and Scandinavian Lutherans, the French and Dutch Calvinists and the Eastern Orthodox seemed all substantially at one, but which was as remote from the "Anglo-Saxon" (British or American) position as Timbuktoo from Kalamazoo.

Sometimes this Continental point of view was described as "Barthian" by its American critics. This was undoubtedly a misnomer. Most of the Continentals would have refused—perhaps with some heat—to be called followers of Karl Barth; and he himself had he been present might have unchurched the great majority of them. Yet somehow the Continental delegation did look "Barthian" to the Americans and might properly be called Barthian in a relative sense as Canada is British to the Americans and American to the British. For Barth is the pioneer of the new orthodoxy and its most extreme representative. Few accept his teachings *in toto* but all Europe feels the pull of his influence. The easiest way to define any European theologian's position is to ask "Where does he stand in relation to Barth?"

Karl Barth is not (like Bishop Manning) a constitutional conservative. With quizzical eyes peering out from behind thick lenses and a leering, lopsided grin he looks more like a Bolshevik than like an ecclesiastic, and his appearance is not deceptive. Before the World War he was what used to be called an "advanced" thinker: A Christian Socialist, a sharp critic of the modern *bourgeois* church, and a theological liberal of the neo-Kantian variety, trained under Wilhelm Herrmann at Marburg. He is still a Socialist in politics and his suspicion of the decadence of the modern church has grown to prophetic certainty, but he does not identify the Socialist Utopia with the Kingdom of God and in theology he has pushed beyond liberalism, through radical skepticism, to a militant, revolutionary orthodoxy reminiscent of Luther and Calvin.

It was during the War, as minister of a little Reformed church in northwest Switzerland, that Barth passed through the radical crisis which made him orthodox. Trying to preach his liberal social gospel in wartime, while big guns over the horizon in Alsace punctuated his exhortations with ironical comments, he was thrown, he tells us, into a profound "embarrassment." Here were people pathetically expectant, longing to be assured of the reality of God in a world suddenly gone mad. Here was a Book the burden of whose every page was the reality of God. And here stood he, supposed to preach the Word of God to these people but unable to believe in his own sermons!

One thing he found he could no longer do with honest conviction—explain God by identifying him with any contemporary social movement or tendency or with anything temporal or human. Hegel might do that, Utopian Socialists might do that, but Kierkegaard and current events had conspired to remove the scales from Barth's eyes. Taught by the great Danish critic, whose works had such a vogue in the German-speaking world during the War, he learned to doubt whether the antitheses of human society were really leading on toward a glorious divine synthesis which would comprehend all tragic differences in some equable and rational "Both . . . and." Human life, as he observed it and as he found it magnificently analyzed in Dostoievsky's novels, seemed to be an insoluble paradox, a question without an answer. Both the Christian Church and the Socialist party seemed to be rushing to perdition rather than marching toward the Millennium. A God one could trust and reverence must be wholly above and beyond all this. There must be, as Kierkegaard said, an "infinite qualitative difference" between the temporal and the eternal.

Such pessimism as this was no doubt irreligious according to liberal Christian notions, but as Barth despairingly searched the Scriptures it struck him that a certain pessimism about human affairs was characteristic of their teachings, and when he turned to the Biblical commentaries of Luther and Calvin he was pleased to discover that these men of faith viewed the secular scene pretty much as he did. Perhaps after all it was not wrong to be "embarrassed" when one attempted to make God intelligible in terms of contemporary social movements; perhaps a God who could be discovered on the human plane would not be God; perhaps "embarrassment," inability to talk without involvement in verbal contradictions and rational paradoxes, was something one was *bound* to experience in the presence of the true and living God who is "wholly other" (*totaliter aliter*) than all our ideas of him. Perhaps theology itself is but "the description of this embarrassment." This was Barth's first great theological insight and it has remained fundamental for him.

The book which brought Barth to the attention of the world was his Commentary on the Epistle to the Romans, which has passed through many editions and radical revisions since it first appeared in 1918. It is a strange book, full of the most astonishing paradoxes—deliberately so, since Barth is convinced that wherever God impinges upon human life he reveals himself in some apparent contradiction; death that is life, despair that is hope, an insoluble enigma which is its own triumphant answer. It is not a conventionally pious book, for in the name of God Barth heaps his scorn upon religion and the church—above all upon that liberal Christianity which fails to see that "one can *not* speak of God simply by speaking of man in a loud voice." But for all this, it is a religiously stirring book, for Barth has now found in the Bible what he regards as the absolute Word of God, lifted high above all the perishable counsels of men. This does not mean that he has turned his back upon the critical, scientific study of the Bible or failed to recognize the human and fallible elements in the teachings of the prophets and apostles. He has no animus against the "high criticism"; but for him the real task of Biblical interpretation begins where the critic's task ends, where the interpreter stops to listen for the Word which the God who produced the Bible has to speak to our own time. Barth's *Romans,* coming after a generation of cool, objective Biblical scholarship, gave the theological world a sudden shock, for it dared to translate Paul's epistle to the Romans into a special-delivery letter from God to the 20th century.

This crisis in the life of Karl Barth is typical of the crisis through which multitudes of Europeans—some independently, some stimulated by his leadership—have been passing in the post-war era. They have turned back from liberal Christianity toward more classical sources of inspiration because they have become convinced that modern civilization, with all its indubitable achievements, is now in a blind alley from which we must back out before we can hope to go ahead again. They have abandoned the liberal Christian emphasis upon the indwelling ("immanence") of God in the world and in man because God no longer appears to them as the Patron of modern humanistic culture but as its Adversary and Judge. In this general attitude Barth is at one not only with "Barthians" who accept his theology but also with many of his Protestant critics and even with Roman Catholic and Eastern Orthodox thinkers. Whether we listen to Maritain the Catholic on *Freedom in the Modern World* or Berdyaev the Russian Orthodox on *The Fate of Man in the Modern World* or Barth's Protestant antagonist Schweitzer on *The Decay and Restoration of Civilization* we always get the same diagnosis: modern man, having attempted to make himself the center of the universe, has fallen victim to his own mechanical ingenuity and unless he can find a new center for his existence above and beyond himself, in God, his mechanized civilization is doomed to suffer the fate described in *The Decline of the West*. Unanimity vanishes, of course, when these thinkers pass from criticism to construction. All agree that a strategic retreat to some impregnable fortress of Christian faith is necessary but each builds his fortress at a different spot in accordance with the pattern of the Christian tradition to which he adheres. Maritain calls us back to St. Thomas, Berdyaev to the mystics and philosophers of the Eastern Church, Barth to the Protestant Reformers and their *sola Scriptùra, soli Deo gloria,* and Albert Schweitzer, less radically anti-modern, calls us back to the Christian humanitarianism of the Age of the Enlightenment.

Barth is less influential and representative on this constructive side of the new orthodoxy than on its critical side. His contempt for all that is merely human or temporal, his distrust of human reason as an avenue of approach to God, are so thoroughgoing that he is left without any intellectual cement wherewith to hold the jagged fragments of his faith together or to build a bridge between faith and knowledge. He has lately parted company with his most able disciple, Emil Brunner, because Brunner made room in his theology for a real though incomplete knowledge of God derived from direct observation of nature and human society; and others have left him for similar reasons.

Unless all signs fail, the future development of the new orthodoxy is going to follow Brunner's lead rather than Barth's. One cannot imagine the Catholic or Eastern Orthodox Churches giving up their rational *preambula fidei* whereby the acceptance of superhuman revelation becomes itself a reasonable act. Still less can one expect theologians trained in the Liberal Protestant tradition to turn their backs collectively upon philosophic reason as a guide to the knowledge of God. What one may expect and what seems to be occurring is a shift of base in philosophy—from idealistic optimism and "world-affirmation" to realistic pessimism and "world-denial." As the monks in medieval Europe withdrew to their monasteries, where they treasured and studied the records of Christian antiquity and prayed to a God who was above the battle that raged around their walls, so the modern church, in Europe, is beginning to interiorize her life, to live less on surrounding culture than on her own precious heritage, and to pin her faith to a transcendent God who will survive the coming doom of Western civilization.

What will America do about the new orthodoxy? So far she has done very little. Our relative peace and isolation make it hard to believe, on this side of the water, that European thinkers are really in earnest when they talk about the impending doom of civilization and the inability of man to avert it by his own efforts. Only quite recently, during the economic depression, did the American mind begin to lose something of its ingrained optimism and consider whether there might not be something really and basically wrong with the world. It was during this period that Reinhold Niebuhr rose to a position of commanding influence in the theological world. In him we probably have the best measuring-rod that could be devised to test the extent of our response to the new orthodoxy and the distance which divides it from yesterday's fundamentalism and modernism.

Like his friend Paul Tillich—who has now become his colleague at Union Seminary—Niebuhr has always lived "on the boundary" between rival currents of thought. A German-American, well-grounded in the conservative traditions of the Lutheran and Reformed churches but equally versed in the political philosophy of John Dewey and the intricacies of the American labor movement, he has for years been reading Continental theology and applying it to the American scene. This practice has long since led him to view his native America with a detached and somewhat ironical gaze. It has also led him to criticize the Continental point of view from the American angle. The result—to employ his favorite term—has been the development of a powerful "tension" in his mind, where Europe and America are perpetually tugging in opposite directions. So long as America continues to tug he will never go completely orthodox in the Barthian sense. So long as Europe continues to tug he will never cease to pull American theology toward a deeper appreciation of the truth in orthodoxy. In all his recent books, orthodoxy and liberalism are made to carry on a continuous process of mutual criticism which should be for the ultimate benefit of both. The verdict in this internal debate would run like this:

Liberal Christianity, especially in its American form, has been unrealistic and romantic in its estimate of the difficulties which beset mankind. It has believed it possible to realize the Kingdom of God on earth by collective moral effort, forgetting that society is largely made up of sinners and has a way of corrupting even the virtues of saints through collective self-deception. Orthodox Christianity, notably in its European form, has been so pessimistic about human nature, so transcendental in its view of God, that it has tended to make all moral distinctions vanish in a universal condemnation of sin-in-general, thus cutting the nerve of effort and rendering history meaningless. Actually we face a world where the Christian Gospel is "relevant" at every moment but never finally reaches its goal. "No absolute limit can be placed upon the degree to which human society may yet approximate the ideal. But it is certain that every achievement will remain in the realm of approximation."

This verdict of Niebuhr's is comparable at many points with the verdict which British theology—closer to the Continent than we are—has already reached in its discussion of the new orthodoxy. Led by Dean Inge and others, contemporary British theology has abandoned the Utopian expectation of reaching the Kingdom of Heaven on earth by cooperative human effort; it conceives of history as a perpetual struggle between a transcendent divine Will and a creative process dependent on that Will but capable of resisting it to the point of self-destruction. With British common sense, however, it insists upon the possibility of tracing the hand of God even in the history of his rebellious creatures and continues to hope for divine victories in this earthly sphere, victories of such a quality that man may learn from them to know the taste of eternity in the midst of time.

If such an attitude is remote from the modernism which floats blissfully down the stream of contemporary civilization, confident of the divinity, yea, the Christlikeness of its prevailing currents and the happiness of the condition toward which it is tending, it is equally remote from the fundamentalism which identifies the Word of God with an ancient Book. For Niebuhr (as indeed for Barth himself, with all his anti-modernism) the Word of God is something contemporaneous, or rather something eternal, which impinges upon our age through a human and fallible historic medium. Literal faith in the *ipsissima verba* of Scripture is a form of idolatry which God will punish as He will punish the idolatrous State-worship of our nationalistic contemporaries. But let the words of Scripture be taken as what Niebuhr calls "myths" and Barth calls "tokens"—symbolic expressions of truths too transcendent for human science to grasp, on which nevertheless our human fate depends —and they will lead us back to a fresh appreciation of Christian orthodoxy.

In its great ages orthodoxy has not stifled intelligence or shackled the present to an archaic past. It has been a living tradition, perpetually reborn through reapplication to the needs and problems of each new generation, perpetually confirmed by the disasters which ensue when humanity departs from it. In G. K. Chesterton's famous figure, orthodoxy careens down the pathway of the centuries like a charioteer, reeling but erect, spilling out heretics and extremists to the right and left but managing by the grace of God to maintain its balance.

35
The Belief in Progress in Twentieth-Century America

Clarke A. Chambers

The idea of progress has been an essential part of intellectual history since the Enlightenment, if not since the Renaissance or earlier. It can be argued that belief in progress, in the sense of an improved destiny for man on the new American continent, was present long before the American Enlightenment in the minds of colonial Americans. Even the Puritan city on a hill, though it was designed as a model of Christain living for the Old World to follow, was implicitly a statement of belief that men, by withdrawing to unspoiled wilderness, could point human society in a desirable direction. As a somewhat systematic theory of human advance and decline, the Enlightenment idea of progress was cyclical. Civilizations, as Jefferson and Adams saw them, follow the recurring life cycle of the seasons or of human beings. They gradually grow to a peak of power and influence, then they decline and fade away, only to be eventually reborn in favorable historical circumstances. A civilization can maintain its vigor, so John Adams argued, only so long as its moral integrity is unimpeached. With Benjamin Franklin Americans heard the first prominent voice for unilinear progress in America. Franklin's confidence in the ability of science and technology to improve the condition of mankind, like the aging Jefferson's faith in the capacity of the human mind for indefinite (though not infinite) improvement, became a characteristic nineteenth-century American attitude. What has happened to that attitude in twentieth-century America is traced here by Clarke Chambers of the University of Minnesota.

For further reading: *Charles Frankel, *The Case for Modern Man* (1956); Sidney Pollard, *The Idea of Progress: History and Society* (1968); *J. B. Bury, *The Idea of Progress* (1932); Alfred Cobban, *In Search of Humanity: The Role of the Enlightenment in Modern History* (1960); David W. Noble, "The Religion of Progress in America, 1890-1914," *Social Research*, 22 (Winter 1955), 417-440; W. Warren Wagar, *Good Tidings: The Belief in Progress from Darwin to Marcuse* (1972).

Journal of the History of Ideas, 19 (April 1958), 197-224. Reprinted by permission of the author and *Journal of the History of Ideas*. Footnotes have been omitted.

Celebrating the great American success story, Henry Luce, prophet of "The American Century," recently proclaimed: "The business of America is to progress; and Progress is the business of America. We are a nation forever on the march." Here summarized is a tenet of the American creed to which the American people, for generations, have committed themselves: the belief that America's mission was to lead the world in the unfolding of an ever finer tomorrow, that the direction of history, in America at least, was onward and upward. That the reaffirmation of this faith came in the midst of what others have known as an "Age of Anxiety" was remarkable; remarkable that is if one chooses not to recognize the tremendous force that the belief in progress has exerted throughout the whole sweep of the American past. That such a reaffirmation appears fatuous optimism to many other observers of the contemporary American scene may warrant still another survery of the idea of progress and an analysis of what that belief has meant for twentieth century America.

The belief, in the classic words of J. B. Bury, that "civilization has moved, is moving, and will move in a desirable direction," was, as so many scholars have pointed out, a product of the modern era of Western history. As a way of looking at the course of human events, it demanded the rejection of traditional authority, for to believe in progress was to insist that far better ways of life were still to be discovered, and that truth was in a continual process of revelation. It required, moreover, a scientific view of the universe as responsive to uniform, immutable laws, laws that men of intelligence and good will could discover and then use for the creation of ever better ways of life on earth. Upon these postulates, elaborated by seventeenth- and eighteenth-century scientists and philosophers, later champions of progress—Turgot, Condorcet, Comte, Marx—came to declare that through an understanding of the laws of society, men could establish direction over the course of history and could thus mold the future to fulfill their own needs and desires.

Most of these disciples of progress, however, were not yet prepared to assert that the forward advance of man was inevitable. Even such an optimistic partisan of progress as Condorcet insisted that the realization of such potential was contingent upon man's freedom to think and to act. Only if man were released from the burdens of ignorance, superstition, and tyranny, only if outmoded institutions were broken and abandoned, could the progress of the human spirit be assured.

In what the champions of progress considered as the wonderful century that stretched from Waterloo to Sararjevo, the belief in the contingent possibility of progress was transformed into a belief in the inevitability of progress. Here operative were not only the internal logic of the idea itself but also the historical conditions of the nineteenth century that permitted Western civilization to embark upon exuberant adventures in the full confidence that progress was "not an accident, but a necessity," and that it was "certain that man must become perfect." It was a century of peace, broken only by short, limited wars that seemed to prove that victorious nationalism was an indication of advancing civilization. It was a century marked by substantial economic expansion, in which it seemed that the machine, man's servant, would assure higher standards of living for all. It was a century during which the Western world advanced steadily toward the realization of all those humanitarian and equalitarian goals against which real progress could be measured.

In America, especially, conditions favored an absolute faith in and a nearly universal, popular acceptance of progress as the rule of life. The whole history of the American nation seemed to suggest an unbroken continuity of betterment. America came into existence after Western feudal institutions had lost their vigor; and those vestiges of the old Europe that were transplanted across the ocean failed to take root in the virgin soil of the new world. America, unlike Europe, never had to turn against its own past in order to progress, it had only to extend and perfect lines of development that were present from the beginning. The American continent, moreover, was blessed with natural resources awaiting exploitation. Material plenty, product of science and technology, meant rising spirals of prosperity and of national power. Here, in the triumph of industrial capitalism, was progress that could be measured, in miles of railroad built, in tons of steel forged, in billions of dollars accumulated. Machines—"engines of democracy"—became symbols of America's advance. And when America celebrated, in the depths of a great depression, a "Century of Progress," science and technology and the machine were the dominant symbols chosen to represent a nation's progress.

In a land and in an age in which individual opportunity was maximized, in which everyone could "get along" and nearly everyone could "get ahead" or, at the least, "keep up," popular faith in the reality of progress was understandably exuberant. The American mission to lead the world in the paths of progress seemed to be justified by the good works of nineteenth-century America. No wonder that Professor E. E. Channing, setting out to tell the American story, professed to see "in the annals of the past the story of living forces, always struggling onward and upward toward that which is better and higher in human conception." To Americans, all things were possible. Even those who saw the evils that had been insinuated into American society by the machine, the factory, and the city were confident that reform could right what was wrong.

America, and the Western world generally, did not require a theory of biological evolution to persuade them of the soaring flight of life; but the writings of Darwin, and of his followers, who argued the creed of social evolution by analogy from the biological world, gave a fillip to man's faith in progress in the latter decades of the nineteenth century. Life, it was taught, all life, had evolved from simple to complex forms; man, descended from lower orders of life, had ascended. "So far from degrading Humanity," wrote the American historian John Fiske, "the Darwinian theory shows us distinctly for the first time how the creation and the perfecting of Man is the goal toward which Nature's work has all the while been tending." Just as the species had evolved upward, just as man had learned to manipulate the universe through science for his own comfort and security, so had civilization evolved toward "spiritual ends" through the innate tendencies of the human heart toward altruism, brotherhood and peace. "The future is lighted for us with the radiant colours of hope," he rejoiced. "Strife and sorrow shall disappear. Peace and love shall reign supreme."

Clearly, however, men, although agreed upon the indisputable fact of progress, were not agreed upon the nature of the methods of social evolution. To some the logic of progress was teleological: man was drawn inevitably upward toward ultimate perfection. To others progress depended on the discovery of and obedience to the natural laws of the physical, social, and moral universe. To spokesmen for industrial capitalism, progress was to come through unfettered competition, through the free exploitation of resources both natural and human, and through the preservation of the sanctity of property. To still others, who in America rejoiced in the label of "progressivism," social advance depended upon the "application of intelligence to the construction of proper social devices," and the deliberate manipulation of society through the "instrumentality" of government, guided by a humane concern for the promotion of the general welfare.

Here were scholars, politicians, editors, men of the cloth, men of affairs, who came to dominate thought and action during the early years of the twentieth century. They believed in the sufficiency of democracy because they believed in man, in his capacity for rational behavior, in his "contriving and constructive intelligence." Rejecting the notion that progress would come with the release of man's competitive instincts, they posited instead a faith in man's natural instinct for cooperation and love. They believed, moreover, in the efficacy of man's will. Men were not passive instruments of either divine will or natural processes; they were, potentially at least, masters of their own fate if only they would take thought, apply the methods of science to man and society, and strive purposefully for reform. Through such methods, wrote the youthful Walter Lippmann just before the first World War, man could come to assert "mastery" over the "drift" of life. All men need do, he wrote, was deal deliberately with life, "devise its social organizations, alter its tools, formulate its method, educate and control it. In endless ways we put intention where custom has reigned. We break up routines, make decisions, choose our ends, select means." Thus, but always contingent upon man's will to use his social intelligence, was progress assured. Man, if he would, had history in his grasp.

The belief in progress, like other religions, was syncretic: it picked up all manner of attitudes through the generations, adding scraps and bits along the way and sloughing off others. Although their rhetoric often borrowed from Darwinism and pragmatism, progressives more often stood upon old-fashioned postulates. It became the goal of many reformers, moved by the Social Gospel, to transform "life on earth into the harmony of the heavens." To the eighteenth-century belief in man's rationality and goodness, and in the existence of an all—encompassing moral order, was added a nineteenth-century romantic belief in the soundness and benevolence of man's emotions, and a Transcendental faith in his infinite perfectibility.

One can see in the thought of William Allen White the way in which progressivism drew upon diverse concepts and incorporated them into one conglomerate system. Delivering a Phi Beta Kappa address at Columbia University in 1908, he traced "A Theory of Spiritual Progress." Science, he noted, was just beginning to push back the veil of mystery that obscured the truths of life; but science could vouchsafe, at least, that life had direction, and that "determinate and purposeful change" was the rule of modern society. If life were "outward bound, but to an unknown port," the more proximate goal, towards which civilization assuredly was advancing, was the enlargement of man's sensibilities and knowledge. Awareness of human suffering, kindness, concern for the welfare of one's brothers, these qualities were ever more coming to dominate over the baser passions of the human race. Through inventions, life was made easier for all men; through social justice, the fruits of technology were more equitably distributed; and as life moved forward, "in the way of the Lord," mercy and charity conquered over cruelty. In the modern era, biological and material evolution could advance into the spiritual realm. Looking about at the moral advances of the modern age, man could not but conclude that "Progress to some upward ideal of living among men is the surest fact of history."

White decried the fancy that men of wealth could lead the nation in the paths of true progress. Like the Hebrew prophets of old, he cried that the rich "get things and things oppress them. Things curse them. Things corrupt their children. . . . Things make men cowards and cheats, and bind them to unholy tasks." Rather, the nation was exalted by the leadership of the humble and the unselfish who alone could direct the people's course in the paths of righteousness. The unselfish would lead, and the nation would follow, because man's nature demanded progress: "The divine spark is in every soul. In a crisis the meanest man may become a hero. . . . This holy spirit is in every heart. . . . It is the fundamental claim men have upon one another as brothers. . . . Over and over the spark is planted in untold billions of hearts as the ages pass; and slowly as our sensibilities widen, our customs change. So comes progress, and the fire grows larger in our common lives."

Here in one great peroration were so many of the varied strands that had been woven into the fabric of the belief in progress during the nineteenth century; science and technology, Darwinism, romantic humanitarianism, Christian moralism, and Transcendental idealism. This vision of progress drew but slightly from the pragmatic rebellion of that era.

Progressives, then, were exuberantly confident of the future, and they invested their enthusiasms with the faith that men of good will would act with good will toward man. But other voices were heard in the land. The Irish bartender and philosopher, Mr. Dooley, wryly noted: "I sometimes wondher whether prog-gress is anny more thin a kind . . . of merry-go-round. We get up on a speckled wooden horse an' th' mechanical pianny plays a chune an' away we go, hollerin'. We think we're thravellin' like th' divvle, but th' man that doesn't care about merry-go-rounds knows that we will come back where we were. We get out dizzy an' sick an' lay on th' grass an' gasp: 'Where am I? Is this the meelinyum?' An' he says: 'No, 'tis Arrchey Road.' "

And then the war came, striking down the dreams of a secular millennium. In Europe, and even in America, men set out to inventory what remained. Disenchantment and disillusion set in; disillusion exactly because these same men had believed so firmly in eternal progress and in the regeneration of the human race. War, and its attendant evils, persuaded many that if knowledge were power, men would not necessarily manipulate power virtuously. Indeed, the very same advances in technology that had promised enlarged vistas for civilization could also become instruments of retrogression. A young journalist, writing in the postwar era, summed up his generation's disillusionment: "after the colossal follies of the twentieth century, what sensitive and thoughtful person can believe in the natural goodness of man?" In full flight from the "Age of Rousseau," he wrote, Americans had become critical "of the democratic ideal, of humanitarian gospels, or romantic enthusiasms of all kinds." The suspicion is, he despaired, "that man, far from being virtuous when undisciplined by a civilized culture, is selfish, irrational and unwittingly absurd."

Frederic C. Howe, an old-line progressive embittered by war and the collapse of the reform movement, confessed his own disenchantment. The attack upon civil liberties, product of wartime intolerance, had been led by members of Wilson's New Freedom administration. Liberal critics had been hounded into silence, and with the return of "normalcy" the crusade against the "orgy of commercialism" had collapsed. Wilson had betrayed international idealism, and a new mood of corruption and reaction prevailed. "Facts were of little value; morality did not guide man. In America, as in Europe, there was conquest, plunder." His earlier belief that an enlightened middle class, "aroused from indifference, from money-making, from party loyalty and coming out into the clear light of reason," had given way before the revival of economic self-seeking. "I now began to see that men were not concerned over the truth," he concluded. "It did not interest them when economic interests were at stake."

The first world war undoubtedly marked a great turning point in the belief in progress. It again accustomed man to violence, made him callous to humane values and to human suffering. A crude amoralism was fostered by what Harold Stearns, one of that generation that thought of itself as "lost," called the "cynicism and brutality and meaninglessness" of war. Progressives had thought, with Wilson, that war could be waged against the institution of war, only to discover in the post-1920 world it had been foolish to dream that men could "pluck liberal flowers from the wastelands of violence and unreason."

It was not war alone, however, that conjured up the spectre of degeneration and even catastrophe. The disenchantment ran deeper into the essentials of modern life. War, it appeared to many mourners, was but a symptom of the cancerous diseases that ate at the vitals of modern civilization. The mechanization and urbanization of society, so it was said, stunted man's creative urges, stultified his initiative, deprived him of his wholeness, and uprooted him. Not harmony and altruism, but cacophony and devisiveness were the rules of life. Cultural aridity, oppressive standardization, levelling mediocrity, the corruption of art and taste were the products of a technically progressive society. Lost in the infinite complexities and distractions of modern life were the sense of belonging and the sense of community, lost were all the moral sanctions and disciplines of personal restraint. The individual was engulfed by the increasing corporateness and collectivization that marked all areas of life. The machine, that "undreamed of reservoir of power," had been harnessed to the dollar, wrote John Dewey, rather than to the "liberation and enrichment of human life." Technical and industrial progress had led to the "supremacy of mechanism over organism, and organization over spontaneity." Lewis Mumford, decrying the impoverishment of the internal life, described the crisis in civilization: "External order: internal chaos. External progress: internal regression. External rationalism: internal irrationality."

Even more central to the attack upon the belief that civilization was bound to move forward was the charge that history had gotten out of control, that man had surrendered his capacity for the intelligent and deliberate ordering of life to forces quite beyond his control. Walter Lippmann, who had once celebrated man's capacity to assert mastery over life, now resigned himself to man's abdication of the exercise of significant decision. The people "are managed, if they are managed at all," he wrote, "at distant centers, from behind the scenes, by unnamed powers."

The private citizen, he concluded, "does not know for certain what is going on, or who is doing it, or where he is being carried. . . . He lives in a world in which he cannot see, does not understand, and is unable to direct."

Above all, men came to doubt that progress could be the law of life when the new sciences of psychology and society described human nature in terms of behaviorism and determinism. The portrait of man as essentially rational and innately good gave way to a sketch of man as a creature of passion and subconscious impulses over which he had little, if any, control, and of which he was, in all probability ignorant. On the other hand, it was fancied that man was totally dominated by his external environment. Man appeared now as a creature rather than a creator, victim rather than hero, a passive bit of nature rather than an active participant in the drama of destiny. If one accepted these new concepts of the nature of human nature, one was bound to question the validity of earlier theories of democracy which proposed that a citizenry was competent to decide and govern itself. Now it appeared that the citizen could gain neither the capacity to understand the issues of politics nor the competence to exert a sustained direction over program and policy. The American voter, pictured by a leading political behaviorist, was: "chock-full of passions and prejudices, easily affected by personalities and propaganda, swayed by the popular currents and winds, susceptible to clap-trap and humbug."

Edward Sapir, noted linguist and anthropologist, writing in the 1920's, pointed out that the apparent advances in civilization constituted spurious progress when measured against the criterion of a "harmonious, balanced, self-satisfactory" culture. Suggesting that much of modern civilization was "spiritually meaningless," marked by "a sense of frustration, of misdirected or unsympathetic effort," he noted that modern industry, beyond harnessing machines to man's use, harnessed man to the machine. In such a world the individual suffered from "spiritual disharmony," from a "fragmentary existence." "Part of the time we are dray horses; the rest of the time we are listless consumers of goods which have received no least impress of our personality." True culture, measured by the "spiritual primacy of the individual soul," he concluded, may decay while the technical apparatus of civilization continues to progress. So ran the indictments of the old-fashioned, simplistic belief in progress. How deeply the ordinary citizen was moved by the disaffection of the intellectuals, it is difficult to determine.

Then came the Great Depression and the eclipse of the popular belief that American capitalism guaranteed the material advance, at the very least, of society. Although the Great Depression shook the confidence of Americans in the seemingly irreversible upward trend of economic development, faith in the possibilities of progress was partially revived under the buoyant leadership of Franklin D. Roosevelt. Having assured the nation that it had nothing to fear but fear itself, Roosevelt proceeded to enact a program for relief, recovery, and reconstruction; and although the New Deal achieved only partial success toward these goals, a mood of confidence was restored—confidence, as the President said, that even in the "darkest moments" of crisis men could master their destiny, and "improve their material and spiritual status through the instrumentality of the democratic form of government." Particular problems were attacked by specific programs. Science and technology were mobilized through the agency of government for the well-being of the entire community. The participation of all individuals and groups, at every level of decision-making, guaranteed that planning would be democratic, vital, and effective.

Novel as the methods of reform occasionally were, the ultimate objectives for which the New Deal strove were shamelessly old-fashioned; and much of the political effectiveness of the New Deal arose out of Roosevelt's ability to give new content and life to the hallowed traditions of American liberalism. Again and again he returned to those principles that other generations had held as essential to a belief in progress: the capacity of man to uncover the natural harmony of society and through understanding to reach that neighborly accord which was the mark of a democratic society; the equal and original goodness of all men in the spiritual democracy of creation; the sufficiency of the individual and group will to win orderly advance toward the goals of full opportunity, security, social justice, and a life more abundant for all men. The final truth of these axioms made possible "infinite progress in the improvement of human life," so long as democracy prevailed. "Among men of good will," Roosevelt proclaimed, "science and democracy together offer an ever-richer life and ever-larger satisfaction to the individual. With this change in our moral climate and our rediscovered ability to improve our economic order, we have set our feet upon the road of enduring progress."

Elsewhere in the Western world, however, there was less cause for confidence. The rise of the coercive states in Italy, Germany, and Russia disturbed such optimism that had survived the first great war. Then came a second world war, more terrible than the first. Guernica, Buchenwald, Lidice, the Siberian camps could hardly serve as symbols of advance. The mushroom clouds over Hiroshima and Nagasaki suggested that science, far from guaranteeing progress, was morally ambivalent; and at least one observer, Norman Cousins, raised the query of modern man's obsolescence. The disintegration of the victorious coalition of the United Nations, the cold war with all its attendant anxieties, the race for weapons of massive destruction, Korea—all gave men cause to wonder about the direction that history was taking. In the United States, the experience of national frustration gave rise to suspicions of disloyalty and treason. Many wondered if America were not about to surrender its peculiar insulation from the stream of history.

Back in 1912, Frederick Lynch, soon to become executive secretary of the Carnegie-endowed Church Peace Union, had confidently asserted: "It looks as though this were going to be an age of treaties rather than an age of wars, the century of force." As late as 1923 Professor E. P. Cheyney, in his presidential address before the American Historical Association, was willing to proclaim the certainty of an historical "law of moral progress." But Joseph Wood Krutch, who had in 1929 suggested that "The Modern Temper" made untenable a belief in progress, had concluded by mid-century that "man's ingenuity has outrun his intelligence," and that "we are believers in catastrophe rather than evolution." Many others agreed. Arthur M. Schlesinger, Jr., liberal historian and adviser to liberal politicians, spoke of the "inadequacy of man to most of the problems which confront him," and concluded: "I think that if there is anything the twentieth century knows, it is that the more knowledge people have of more manipulations, the more that knowledge is used for evil purposes."

In such an atmosphere it was natural that American theological neo-orthodoxy, a revival led most notably by Reinhold Niebuhr, should stress again the emergence of human evil not out of imperfect institutions and a deficient environment, but rather out of man's inclinations to assert his radical freedom for selfish ends and out of the tendency of all power to corrupt even the highest and most worthy of ideals. Denying that progress was the necessary direction of history, neo-orthodoxy insisted that every advance in life was precarious, that every particular interest and position was partial and relative, that there were no final resolutions of man's problems on earth, and that a sentimental and uncritical devotion to the creed of progress was bound ultimately to lead to disillusion and despair for it rested upon false assumptions regarding the nature of man. If knowledge were power, knowledge was not necessarily virtue; in this regard Bacon had the better of Socrates. Here the confession of St. Paul was relevant: "The good that I would do, I do not; and the evil that I would not, that I do." The twentieth century should have taught men what other generations had known, wrote Niebuhr in 1940: "History does not move forward without catastrophe, happiness is not guaranteed by the multiplication of physical comforts, social harmony is not easily created by more intelligence, and human nature is not as good or as harmless as had been supposed."

The neo-orthodox movement proposed that to insist upon man's limitations, his capacity for error, the corruption of his will by pride and self-interest was not to deny his potentialities and his responsibilities to seek the reform of specific evils in society, even if there were no final assurance that a reformed environment would lead to a regneration of humanity. Man stood under the commandment of love and under the ultimate judgment of God. A more just society was possible, if progress itself were not inevitable.

How widely this critique of the belief in progress was felt cannot easily be judged. There is evidence, however, that many had taken it to heart. The mood was reflected, for example, by Adlai Stevenson in his "Call to Greatness." In this series of lectures, delivered at Harvard University in 1954, Stevenson warned against the ingrained American habit of seeking total solutions through panaceas. The world itself was tough, and the love of men for the good not as absolute as Americans had easily assumed. American traits of "impatience, arrogance, and our faith in quick solutions" were likely, in modern circumstances, to lead to irresponsibility of national action. "As long as this habit of mind persists—and it is fundamentally an un-Christian attitude, ignoring the pervasiveness of evil and loaded with arrogance and pride—we shall never be able to face our problems realistically. Our first job, it seems to be, is to school ourselves in cold-eyed humility; to recognize that our wisdom is imperfect, and that our capacities are limited." He urged upon his audience the "conscious acceptance of Christian humility" as a necessary temper for national greatness. Even the most "innocent" of nations, it would seem, was liable to the common tendency of the race toward the corruption of ideals by the cardinal sin of pride.

Many of the attacks that neo-orthodoxy made upon the "herctical" creed of progress were paralleled by the admonitions of those intellectuals who, in recent years, have been labelled as the "neo-conservatives." A motley lot, differing in doctrine from the flexible to the dogmatic, in tone from the relaxed to the strident, they shared a firm conviction of the invalidity and insufficiency of the belief in progress. American civilization had fallen short of greatness, they believed, because it had been too fervently committed to the romantic notion that man, being rational and good, could and would channel history along an ascending path of virtue. A civilization, they said, was a product of long and painful experience through time and liable to perversion at any juncture. Central to their argument at every point was the belief "that evil arises from the nature of man, not from a lack of more science, or more education, however laudable these things may be." It is no purpose of this essay to analyze the roots and consequences of this revival among intellectuals, but to note merely that it was consistent with the new conservative mood of the post-World War II era, and that it necessarily entailed an explicit rejection of the belief in the beneficence of change.

Whatever the influence of neo-orthodoxy and neo-conservatism upon popular attitudes, there is little doubt that the actual historical experience of this generation did little to support faith in progress. That there was confusion and turmoil, doubt, uncertainty and insecurity no sensitive person wished to deny. Political regimentation, social disorganization, intellectual bewilderment were all part of the new climate, if not its whole truth. "Technology, while adding daily to our physical ease, throws daily another loop of fine wire around our souls," wrote Adlai Stevenson. "It contributes largely to our mobility, which we must not confuse with freedom." The "massiveness" of modern life, he continued—"mass population, mass education, mass communications—yes, and mass manipulation"—threatened to undermine and corode the foundations of human dignity. We are more in danger of "becoming robots than slaves." There was a great deal to fear beyond fear itself, for always there was the chance that some untoward and unforeseen act would trigger the hydrogen bomb. As Vannevar Bush, scientist and educator, concluded at mid-century: "the first World War shook our optimism, the depression shook it further, and the second World War nearly destroyed it. Now, though we may still hope that our race will go forward in progress, we are confronted with facts that take all the former exuberance out of our hope, reducing it almost to a wish of despair." Professor Edward Arlington Ross, once a harbinger of progressive dreams, put it still more bluntly: "After the horrors of Nazi concentration camps, the butcheries of the Jews, the treatment of civilians in occupied Russia, the easy optimism of a half century ago will be left to born ninnies and youths in their early 'teens."

Yet we know that such doubts were not universally entertained; men who were neither born ninnies nor in their 'teens did continue in the traditional faith of progress. To them the modern era held forth promise that somehow civilization would survive and grow. The militant force of Fascism, Nazism, and Japanese imperialism had been overcome; and in a decade of uneasy armistice the world had not slipped over the precipice of nuclear war.Two total wars had been fought, they noted, without that sacrifice of democratic institutions, which many had feared. The principle that government must exercise responsibility for the general welfare of the community had been established without that consequent regimentation of which some had warned. The advance of the medical sciences contributed surcease from pain, healthier and longer life for millions, and partial relief from the pangs of mental derangement. Fantastic advances in modern technology had already raised the standards of living of millions so that they mignt lead decent and secure lives, while automation and atomic power promised even further progress within the foreseeable future. To many it seemed that if the ledger had not been balanced, no clear and simple conclusion of progress or retrogression was possible.

It was understandable, then, that Henry Luce could still rejoice that "Progress is the business of America." Acknowledging the possibility of another war, he proclaimed in what was admittedly a "brief overstatement," that "we have almost solved all the internal problems which have been the traditionally proper subjects for political agitation and debate." An "American Age of Plenty" was in the making; abundance, widely shared, promised release from drudgery, increased leisure, and the opportunity to advance beyond the satisfaction of material needs toward the realization of spiritual and moral values." Machine technology guaranteed that the "monstrous offenses" of plague, famines, mass hysteria, superstitions, fanaticisms" would be dispelled, gave assurance of a "decent life, a life of air and light and chosen food and education and recreation and length of years." Drawing upon the inspiration of Lecomte du Nouy's *Human Destiny*, Luce returned to that theme which had done so much to fortify man in his will to believe; that evolution could not have happened by chance; that it had been a response to God's will. Then, somewhere along the long line of evolution, God had breathed freedom of will into a species, and it became man. Man was then on his own, free to work with Providence for the mission of spiritual evolution.

In America, man had learned the methods of progress: "the gospel of work ('free enterprise') and the social gospel ('humanitarianism')," science, voluntary cooperation, and organization (by which Luce meant not only the modern "responsible" corporation but all the intricate organizations of state of society). "The habit and spirit of voluntary cooperation form the ideal base for Organization. Today, to a degree never before known, man is Organized Man. . . . We have brought to birth that cooperative society . . . which Kropotkin foresaw in his answer to Darwin." The individual could, if he would, be the mutation that impelled mankind forward; but, at the same time, progress was a transcendent force. "For if, as we believe, the Spirit is at work in the race of man, then the work of the Spirit is done not only in the atom of the individual but also through the generations of men and in traditions and in treasured wisdom and in the moral law slowly apprehended and in the beloved community and in the Church."

If evidence were required of the syncretic nature of the religion of progress, it is certainly supplied here. Many others, captivated by the amazing increases in technological efficiency, joined in the hymn to progress. David Sarnoff, President of the Radio Corporation of America, took up the refrain in the first of a series of articles by notable Americans published by *Fortune* magazine in celebration of its twenty-fifth anniversary, on the theme of what the next twenty-five years held in store. The marriage of human freedom and science had brought to America, "the classic land of technology . . . the largest freedom from destitution, ignorance, and disease, along with political rights and social improvements unique in history." Science was not, as some had claimed, "the natural enemy of the soul." Evil arose, not out of technology, but out of the failure of man to keep pace with accelerating changes in the economic sphere; but cultural lag could be overcome if man applied his intelligence to the resolution of social problems, just as man's mind had learned to control the physical universe. As long as American liberties, and particularly the freedom of the mind, were maintained and extended, 1980 promised to be an immeasurably richer age.

Writing in the same series, Robert Sherwood, endorsing President Eisenhower's admonition that "there is no longer any alternative to peace," warned that unless the world disarmed within the next twenty-five years it would, in all probability, commit suicide. This eventuality he refused to entertain. By 1980, he concluded, the "threat of a third world war will be a malodorous memory." Why? Because God had created man in His own image, and man's unique spirit had impelled him ever forward. "Thus believing, I find it inconceivable that man is about to destroy himself with the products of his own God-given genius."

Gilbert Burck elaborated upon the same themes. A belief in progress was itself the essential ingredient for the achievement of real progress. This faith America had practiced. The American "genius for innovating, adapting, simplifying, and improving," the American willingness to experiment, the American system of free enterprise had all propelled the nation forward. The American character, "individualistic and competitive yet cooperative," ingenious, confident, practical, and ambitious had placed the nation in "the vanguard of that progress" which all other peoples now wished to emulate. No need to cry that the machine had demeaned life; quite the contrary, "the machine provided the only way . . . of making life decent and even of ennobling it."

These sentiments, far from being peculiar in mid-twentieth century, probably constituted a main stream of American aspiration. The best was yet to come. To Morris Ernst the ushering in of a Utopia of abundance would be possible if only men believed that progress was attainable and acted confidently upon that faith. Science and technology would provide the environment in which potentialities of man for good would be released. He foresaw an age in which security and plenty would release all men from jealousy, envy, antagonism, and strife. New folkways of male-female comradeship would be evolved, children would be raised with neither complexes nor repressions, and the growth of premarital experience would make sexuality in marriage less inept. Abundance and leisure would permit Americans to transcend the present status of an "audience society" and enter a "fully participating culture." All this was possible, if men took heart, because man was inherently rational and good. "I abhor the dogma—man is inherently evil. I decry it. Man is potentially good and tender, limited only by prior environment. The new setting will invite and make possible the best—and the best is unbelievably heartening."

One can select similar evidence of continuing belief almost at random. Charles Merriam, distinguished political scientist, placed his faith in man's proven capacity to control the world and society for his own finer purposes. Referring to the anxiety created by the atomic bomb, he countered Norman Cousins' fears: "To say that modern man is obsolete is an interesting literary phrase, but the precise opposite is true. Modern man is coming of age. . . . The mind is king, not the atom. We trapped the atom; we have mastered some secrets of its latent forces, not by accident, but by deliberate design, by organization and ingenuity." Sidney B. Fay, American historian, while not as confident as John Fiske or E. E. Channing, or E. P. Cheyney before him, and while admitting that civilizations had displayed "oscillations of advance and retreat," concluded, in 1947: "Progress is not constant, automatic, and inevitable in accordance with cosmic laws, but it is possible and even probable as a result of man's conscious and purposeful efforts.'' Ashley Montagu, anthropologist and philosopher, held that society was ''infinitely perfectible,'' if only men realized the eternal truth that the way to social evolution was not through competition and strife, but through cooperation and love. All the evidence of modern biology and psychology indicated ''that human beings are born good—'good' in the sense that there is no evil or hostility in them.'' *''Human nature,''* he continued, ''is good. It is our present *human nurture* that is bad.'' The acceptance and practice of a new theory of learning that would place emphasis upon ''cooperation, on adaptive association, on love, on shared relationships,'' would hasten the day when all problems would be more capable of solution than ever before in the long history of humanity.

Even Adlai Stevenson who, in addressing non-political audiences, expressed his personal reservations about the adequacy of a belief in progress, was moved, on purely political occasions, to express more traditional and popular ideas. During the campaign of 1952, he exclaimed: ''I do say to you soberly and sincerely that on the evidence of science, of technology, and of our own common sense, the United States at mid-century stands on the threshold of abundance for all, so great as to exceed the happiest dreams of the pioneers who opened the vast Western country. Unless we allow ourselves to be held back by fear, we shall in God's good time realize the golden promise of our future.'' If the presidential aspirant spoke from the heart on this occasion, it is significant of the continued force of the idea of progress upon the liberal mind; if he spoke rather what he felt might be politically expedient, what the American voter wished to be assured of, his optimism was even more significant for an evaluation of the persistence of this belief.

The belief in progress has exhibited remarkable toughness in twentieth-century America. Despite the weight of historical evidence to the contrary, many Americans seemed determined still to believe in the necessary advance of society and culture. This faith traditionally rested upon certain axioms: the beneficence of Providence, the lawfulness of the world, the potential coherence and harmony of social organizations, the innate rationality and goodness of natural man, his capacity to compel the material world to serve his purpose through science and his ability to evolve ever-higher systems of law and government, morality and ethics through the exercise of social intelligence. But even in its most exuberant phase, the faith was a conditional one, contingent upon the preservation or creation of particular circumstances conducive to the realization of man's potentialities for infinite perfectibility. At various times different conditions were declared to be essential: machine technology, social mobility, free enterprise, the cooperation of men in voluntary associations, the willingness to experiment, the will to believe, and always, above all else, freedom of the mind.

The last two prerequisites were often linked together, for in the last analysis man's intelligence stood at nought unless he was determined to use his intelligence constuctively for human advance, while his will was rudderless without the guidance that the free mind could apply. To believe that progress was possible was to make that progress probable. Time and again, during the past decade of mounting crises, Americans were exhorted to believe.

From the academic world, where pessimism, such as it was, was perhaps the deepest, came the call "to recover confidence in social progress and in man's ability to adjust his difficulties through human intelligence." Clark Kerr, Provost of the Universtiy of California in Berkeley, taking note that the evidence of the recent past did not exactly support a view of historical progress called upon educational leaders not to be "intimidated by history." The University, he said, was dedicated to freedom of investigation and the discovery of truth in order that men may "control their destiny" and "consciously direct human progress." A spokesman for liberal elements of the business community put the same thought directly and bluntly: progress is not automatic, it depends upon "human intelligence." The same confidence in the efficacy of faith was uttered by Adlai Stevenson during the presidential campaign of 1952 when he proclaimed: "We can win the war against war because we must. Progress is what happens when inevitability yields to necessity. And it is an article of the democratic faith that progress is a basic law of life."

Willing would make it so. President Eisenhower, then of Columbia University, hammered home the same point in March, 1950: "we must not be discouraged by the inescapable slowness of world progress. However disappointing may be the lack of speed, every new evidence of advance brings immediate hope of a brighter tomorrow to millions; and peoples hopeful of their domestic future do not use war as a solution to their problems. Hope spurs humans everywhere to work harder, to endure more now that the future might be better; but despair is the climate of war and death. Even America, without American optimism, can accomplish nothing beyond the needs of each day.

The will to believe, then, was one of the necessary ingredients to make possible that progress for which men yearned. The other prerequisite was freedom of the mind. Upon this last condition, advocates of progress would admit of no dispute, although they rejected the practice in the Soviet Union where men tyrannized over the mind and spirit of man while still professing a belief in the progress of humanity. Freedom of inquiry was the one undeniable postulate that the liberal mind cherished. Progress might not be inevitable but it was not even possible unless the mind were free, for as David Sarnoff emphasized: "if freedom is lost, if the dignity of man is destroyed, advances on the material plane will not be 'progress' but a foundation of a new savagery."

Only in a pluralistic, open society were no limits set to the inquiring mind; only in a democratic society in which all men enjoyed continuous access to full and candid information was faith in the judgment and conscience and common sense of the people justified as a means to promote the progress of the nation, spiritually as materially. This faith constituted the hard irreducible core at the heart of the belief in progress. All else was relatively peripheral and friable. In the end, faith in the possibility of progress, or even in its probability, had swung full circle back to the original formulations of Francis Bacon.

It was significant, therefore, that in mid-twentieth century another pure scientist, J. Robert Oppenheimer, should explore the domain of "The Open Mind." Science had wrought a revolution in what men conceived to be the nature of their world and of themselves; technology had accelerated the pace of social change. Atomic scientists had discovered that adequate as the Newtonian concept of an ordered and determinate universe was for most of the common problems of "statistical mechanics," at the heart of the universe, in the infinitely minute world of the atom, lay causal anomalies, unpredictability. This view in itself was deeply disturbing to traditional systems of thought and action. "Short of rare times of great disaster, civilizations have not known such rapid alteration in the conditions of their life, such rapid flowering of many varied sciences, such rapid changes in the ideas we have about the world and one another. . . . the ways that we learned in childhood are only very meagrely adequate to the issues that we must meet in maturity." For those who participated in the creation of a new world view and a new world there was "terror as well as exaltation." In particular, the creation of a new instruments of "massive terror" out of the free search of devoted scientists for truth made men "anxiously aware that the power to change is not always necessarily good." The use of science for the alleviation of "hunger and poverty and exploitation" depended now upon the need to eliminate organized violence among nations.

Atomic physics could not be repealed; the methods of science could not be scrapped. "To assail the changes that have unmoored us from the past is futile, and in a deep sense, I think, it is wicked. We need to recognize the change and learn what resources we have." In a world of terrifying complexity one could strive only to render "partial order" out of "total chaos." That much was possible for the very methods of free inquiry had vastly extended man's freedom and had given to society the instruments with which the ancient problems of humanity might be solved. Science and democracy flourished or foundered together; without the freedom to inquire, science and man could not progress. Given such conditions, man's ways "point not merely to change, to decay, to alteration, but point with a hopeful note of improvement that our progress is inevitable."

It was fitting that Professor Oppenheimer should commend to one of his audiences a letter of Thomas Jefferson:

> *I am among those who think well of the human character generally. I consider man as formed for society, and endowed by nature with those dispositions which fit him for society. I believe also, with Condorcet, . . .that his mind is perfectible to a degree of which we cannot as yet form any conception. . . .*
>
> *. . . I join you therefore in branding as cowardly the idea that the human mind is incapable of further advances. This is precisely the doctrine which the present despots of the earth are inculcating; and applying especially to religion and politics; "that it is not probable that anything better will be discovered than what was known to our fathers." . . . But thank heaven the American mind is already too much opened, to listen to these impostures; and while the art of printing is left to us, science can never be retrograde; what is once acquired of real knowledge can never be lost. To preserve the freedom of the human mind then and freedom of the press, every spirit should be ready to devote itself to martyrdom; for as long as we may think as we will, and speak as we think, the condition of men will proceed in improvement. . . .*

The belief in progress had arisen during an age of faith in man's capacities for rational and effective action. Could it survive when many men could cling no longer to the Enlightenment's view of human nature? It had been elaborated at a time when science and machine technology appeared to promise material abundance and the increasing control of men over their environment. Could it survive when the acceleration of technological change threatened to engulf man and to alienate him from traditional systems of morality and value? It had grown in force during generations of relative peace and advancing democracy. Could it survive an era of war, social chaos and totalitarianism? The evidence would suggest that if widespread doubts were entertained throughout (Western civilization, most Americans were still inclined to act upon the faith that the future held forth the promise of ever better things to come.) America, at mid-century, was not yet prepared to reject as no longer relevant or viable the belief in progress, rooted as that faith was in the experience of generations. Continuity of thought and hope survived the discontinuities posed in an age of anxiety. ''Progress'' was still ''the business of America.'' The nation, ''forever on the march,'' was certain that it was advancing into a better land.

36
American Intellectuals and American Democracy

William G. Carleton

The place of the intellectual in American life is a topic that fascinates cultural historians, social thinkers, and men of letters generally. While it is surely a subject that affects their personal lives, it is also a problem concerned with the delicate if not precarious relationship between the life of ideas and a modern industrial democracy. The concept of the intellectual is itself rather new in Western culture; it comes mainly though not exclusively from the Marxist idea of an *intelligentsia* or intellectual class within a society. In American usage the concept has had a loose and inexact meaning, which is possibly to its advantage. The historian Richard Hofstadter, who wrote an outstanding work on anti-intellectualism in America, characterized an intellectual as a person who has both a pious and playful attitude toward ideas. The following piece by William G. Carleton is more descriptive of the defensive posture of the pragmatic liberal intellectual in the 1950s than analytical about the place of intellectuals in a democracy generally. Yet the complaints that Carleton registers about the departure of some intellectuals from the pragmatic liberalism which he cherishes give us a clear picture of the ideological tensions that arose in America after the Second World War. Some of these tensions remain today the center of intense speculation and vigorous debate.

For further reading: *Richard Hofstadter, *Anti-Intellectualism in American Life* (1963); John William Ward, "The Intellectual: Cleric or Critic," in his *Red, White, and Blue: Men, Books, and Ideas in American Culture* (1969), pp. 315-329; Merle Curti, *American Paradox: The Conflict of Thought and Action* (1956); Seymour Martin Lipset, "American Intellectuals: Their Politics and Status," Arthur Schlesinger, Jr., Karl W. Deutch, David Riesman, Talcott Parsons, and Daniel Bell, "Comments on 'American Intellectuals: Their Politics and Status,' " *Daedalus*, 88 (Summer 1959), 460-498; *C. Wright Mills, *White Collar* (1951), chap. 7; George B. deHuszar (ed.), *The Intellectuals: A Controversial Portrait* (1960); Morton and Lucia White, "The Intellectual versus the City," in Arthur M. Schlesinger, Jr., and Morton White (eds.), *Paths of American Thought* (1963),

The Antioch Review, 19 (Summer 1959), 185-204. Reprinted by permission of the author and *The Antioch Review*.

chap. 14; *Jacques Barzun, *The House of Intellect* (1959); *Daniel Bell, *The End of Ideology* (rev. ed., 1962); *Michael Paul Rogin, *The Intellectuals and McCarthy: The Radical Specter* (1967); David Felix, *Protest: Sacco-Vanzetti and the Intellectuals* (1956); *C. P. Snow, *The Two Cultures: And a Second Look, an Expanded Version of the Two Cultures and the Scientific Revolution* (1963); Lionel Trilling, "The Leavis-Snow Controversy," *Commentary* (June 1962), reprinted in his **Beyond Culture: Essays on Literature and Learning* (1965), pp. 147-177.

The work and values of American intellectuals of the 1920's and 1930's have been under critical fire since World War II. But what of the intellectuals of the 1940's and 1950's? Perhaps by now it is not unduly presumptuous to begin attempting to put the American intellectuals of mid-century in some kind of historical perspective.

First, a word about the intellectuals of the 1920's and 1930's. The present generation tends too much to regard American thinkers and creative artists of those years as "radical." True, many of them were excited by the constructive possibilities of the Russian Revolution and enormously interested in the Soviet Union as a laboratory for vast social experimentation. However, as Granville Hicks and others have repeatedly pointed out, very few of America's intellectuals of the 1930's were Communists. Even among those who went pretty far to the left, there were many who survived their earlier enthusiasm to make valuable contributions to democratic thinking in the 1940's and 1950's. Some of these—Edmund Wilson, Malcolm Cowley, Robert Gorham Davis, Hicks himself, and others—reveal an awareness of twentieth-century realities, born of their earlier probings and experiences, too often lacking in our younger contributors. Others, with the God-that-failed mentality, having become disillusioned with the authoritarian "truth" of the left, have been searching ever since for some brand of authoritarian "truth" on the right. These embittered futilitarians, often extroverts in their personalities, have been among the leading assailants of their own generation.

It is my own feeling that the intellectual temper prior to World War II was more in harmony with the dominant American tradition than is the intellectual temper today; and more, that in general the intellectuals of the earlier period were coming to grips more realistically with the central problems, domestic and international, of our time.

Much has been written about how we were "betrayed" by the intellectuals of the 1930's. But as we move deeper into the twentieth century, we may find that it was the intellectuals of the 1940's and the 1950's, and not those of the 1930's, who departed more widely from the American tradition—at the very time, too, when that tradition needed to be reinterpreted, and applied to the realities of today.

I

What is the dominant American tradition? It is optimistic, democratic, rational, experimental, and pragmatic. It maintains that men are not the slaves of social conditions and blind historical forces, that to a large extent men can rationally mold their own institutions, without an hereditary or a privileged elite to guide them, and within the value-framework of human dignity and individual freedom. Although this tradition is often rationalized in terms of Locke, the Enlightenment, and Rousseauean humanitarianism, it came out of the historical interplay of creative man and indigenous American conditions: vast land and resources and a relatively small population; the relative absence of feudal, manorial, communal village, guild, and internal mercantilistic practices and traditions; the lack of aristocracy, priesthood, status, and "orders" generally; frontier realities; and the obviously howling success of the American experience.

America's Declaration of Independence boldly proclaimed the equality of men, regardless of birth, status, race, or religion. It was a revolutionary document when proclaimed, and it is a revolutionary document today. The Constitution of 1787, "struck off by the mind of man," created a government structure so contrived as to guarantee liberty; it set an example of how man might literally "make" his own institutions. Even the Transcendentalists, in revolt against rationalism, were optimistic and practical idealists. Like the older American rationalists and the later American pragmatists, they were ready to make a future to order. "Why should we not also enjoy an original relation to the universe?" asked Emerson. As H. S. Commager has pointed out, the Transcendentalists, with all their faith in *a priori* truths, took a chance that the heart knew better than the head and labored heroically to make the good come true. Even the most lasting impression of Darwinism on the American mind was not the rationalizations of the Social Darwinians glorifying the plutocrats as the "survival of the fittest," but the assurance that there is constant change; and change, to most Americans, was something that could be directed to the good, be made "progressive." And at the turn of the century came William James's pragmatism, that marriage of American optimism and practicality with the bright promise of science. Pragmatism harmonized with American tradition and practice, for it emphasized the importance of experimentation, breaking with the past, rejecting custom and habit, trying new methods, creating a future on order.

American intellectuals of the 1920's and 1930's were in the dominant American tradition. John Dewey emphasized the plasticity of man's instincts, the malleability of human nature. Truth was not only what worked out for the individual but for society. Individuals sought, in common with their fellow men, for secular, immediate, and particular truth that had meaning for the community. Thorstein Veblen, fusing economics, sociology, and anthropology, and posing as an objective, if ironic, observer, sought through an analysis of the conflicts between business and industry, between technology and the price system, to realize the possibilities of the new technology. Charles A. Beard and Herbert Croly saw in the marriage of Hamiltonian centralization and Jeffersonian democracy solutions of contemporary industrial problems through democratric national planning. Vernon L. Parrington wrote passionately of the history of American thought as the history of an evolving revolutionary liberalism; the central theme was that of the battle between conservatism and liberalism, reaction and revolt, with liberalism and revolt triumphant; the American tradition emerged as the identification of Americanism with democracy. Roscoe Pound, Oliver Wendell Holmes, Jr., Louis Brandeis, and Benjamin Cardozo were in revolt against legal abstractionism and scholasticism, and were busy infusing the law with pragmatic values and social realism. Sinclair Lewis was writing of the ugliness of commercial civilization; Dos

Passos and Steinbeck and Farrell were portraying social injustices; but in all of these writers, even in the determinism of Dreiser and Darrow, there was the unspoken assumption that man could overcome ugliness and evil by changing his environment. Even Wolfe, at the close of his life, was groping toward a recognition of something larger than himself.

In contrast, the most vocal and conspicuous of the present generation of American intellectuals have surrendered to non-involvement or non-commitment, or retired into formalism, or become obsessed with techniques, or retreated into the individual psyche, or fled into the non-rational and the irrational diversity, or seriously distorted the American democratic tradition, or sought to substitute for evolving and fluid democratic values the fixed values of status and aristocracy. Exponents and exemplars of each of these points of view have all played down the wondrously rich diversity and flexibility of American life.

Now, of course, the older trends have not disappeared; the dominant points of view of the 1920's and 1930's still have creative exponents today; and vistas opened by earlier thinkers continue to be explored. In some areas, notably law and jurisprudence, pragmatism and social realism continue to make notable gains. Also, it must not be supposed that the new conservative points of view are entirely new; all of them had antecedents in the 1920's and 1930's and even earlier. Nor can it be denied that some of the work of America's uncommitted and conservative thinkers and creators of today is deepening insights, sharpening tools and techniques, penetrating psychic mysteries and complexities, intensifying aesthetic perceptions, and in some aspects of thought and life making Americans a more discriminating and sophisticated people.

What is novel in the current situation is the popularity of non-involvement and non-commitment and of conservative and aristocratic values. Conservatism is being proclaimed as the truly traditional attitude of Americans. Conservatism, it is said, has been our dominant tradition all the time; what is new, it is claimed, is our belated recognition of conservatism as our naitonal traditon.

Let us examine some of the values of the New Conservatism and kindred schools of thought popular today, inquire into the authenticity of their claim to be our national values, examine whether they square with today's social realities and the facts of contemporary society, and suggest some of the consequences likely to follow were we to accept them as our "traditional"and guiding values.

II

Many intellectuals of the post-war generation have fled from all values whatsoever. They have taken refuge in non-commitment and non-involvement and called it objectivity or sophistication or wisdom. The great vogue among textbook writers and publishers for anthologies and collaborative works which acquaint the student with "all points of view" is today a much-used way of escaping integration and commitment. Sampling opinion, taking polls, and compiling the results of interviews constitute another way of escaping commitment by merely tabulating statistically the relative opinions and values of others on comparatively surface or safe questions. More and more, authors of books and magazine articles merely report opinion, but do not express an opinion of their own. They indicate trends, but seldom pass judgment on them. And as for moral judgments—these are to be avoided as "hortatory" and "evangelistic." There is not even a commitment to eclecticism, to an avowed defense of a society in which the existence of plural and diverse values is taken as a positive good, the hallmark of a healthy, vital, free, and infintely fertile civilization. This would be a defensible postion, for it may be that the American society has in fact become such and eclectic society. But few contemporary intellectuals are committed to eclecticism as a positive value in itself.

Closely akin to the trend to non-commitment is the emphasis on form, technique, and methodology. One way of escaping commitment in subject matter is to concentrate on form. In all the intellectual disciplines today, even in the humanities and the social sciences, there is a growing concentration on forging methods and techniques that will make the discipline truly "scientific." Now, of course, nobody objects to sharpening the tools of investigation and research, but an excessive concern for methodology may also be a way of avoiding all substantive import. For instance, had Kinsey waited to "perfect" his methodology, or retreated into a minuscule area of investigation, or confined himself to a safe aspect of his subject, or been frightened by the moral and social implications of his researches, we would have been denied one of the few illuminating works of our time.

In literature, too, there has been an almost obsessive preoccupation with form, with style. If the 1920's and the 1930's represented a revolt from formalism, the present generation is chatacterized by a retutrn to formalism. T. S. Eliot and the New Critics began the trend to form; today, form has become the vogue and most of our influential writers have been molded by the canons of the New Criticism. Norman Podhoretz has commented on the high stylistic polish, the precociously sophisticated craftsmanship, of our rising young novelists, even when these have little to say.

In matters of substance, many of this generation have retreated from social considerations into the individual psyche. There is an enormous preoccupation with individual man's motivations, love life, sex drive, frustrations, complexes, and neuroses; and there is a neglect, even an ignoring, not only of social considerations and problems but even of the impact of society and environment on individual man himself. Podhoretz has also commented on the concentration of today's young novelists on the individual's psychological drama. To our rising novelists, the supreme fact is personality and the main business of life is love. There is an almost total lack of awareness of the social environment as a molder of character and as a maker of the traumatic situations themselves.

In even many of our mature novelists and playwrights, life has been reduced to the individual's viscera, his gonads, and an eternal contemplation of his navel. There is, of course, a certain insight and fascination in the plight of the neurotic hero enmeshed in his own complexes and in the interplay of his little circle of family, friends, loves, and hates. But is this the ultimate wisdom in art? On this question, Arthur Miller eloquently writes:

What moves us in art is becoming a narrower and narrower esthetic fragment of life. . . . The documentation of man's loneliness is not in itself and for itself ultimate wisdom. . . . Analytical psychology, when so intensely exploited as to reduce the world to the size of a man's abdomen and his fate equated with his neurosis, is a re-emergence of romanticism. It is inclined to deny all other forces until man is only a complex. It presupposes an autonomy in the human chartacter that, in a word, is false. A neurosis is not a fate but an effect.

Is all of this an escape? Miller suggests strongly that it is, that we actually are more aware than previous generations of the impact of the city, the nation, the world, and now of the universe on our individual lives; yet we persist in refusing to face the consequences of this in art—and in life.

The degree to which non-social and even anti-social attitudes have come to prevail in literature and humanities faculties of our colleges and universities today is perhaps realized only by those of us who teach in them. Recently, by way of illustration, it was argued in the humanities staff of one of our state universities that Steinbeck's *Grapes of Wrath,* which for many years had been required reading in a course in twentieth-century literature, should be dropped from the readings because it was "only a social tract and not literature." The book was dropped.

Historians and biographers, whether they have the training for it or not, increasingly use the psychoanalytic approach in writing the lives of famous leaders. This method is also used by Harold Lasswell and his followers to analyze the careers of prominent politicians. When this is the approach, the tendency is to emphasize personal motivations, often running back into childhood, and not the social consequences of the leader's mature activities. Since conservatives are less "troubled," are likely to come off as agitators, extroverts, and cranks, as victims of frustrations, complexes, and neuroses. This method, which minimizes the larger social setting of a leader's work and the social results of his work, tends to reduce all leadership, conservative and liberal alike, to the trivial and the commonplace, to rob it of its historical and social significance.

During the 1920's and 1930's, advances had been made in treating the leading philosophers and political and social thinkers in terms of the historical time and social milieu in which they did their thinking. Many intellectuals of this generation are in revolt from this. Exponents of the "great books" approach, the neo-Thomists, and, among others, David Easton in political theory argue that this method reduces thought to a mere sociology of knowledge. There is now a new emphasis on "pure thought," on theories separated from their historical and social context, on sheer logical analysis of the ideas themselves in an attempt to discover absolute truths. However, the emphasis does not seem to be on all the acknowledged ranking thinkers in the Western tradition. All too often greater emphasis seems to be placed on the equally important thinkers in the skeptic-nominalist-inductive-empirical-pragmatic tradition. Now, intellectuals engaged in this business are certainly not running from commitment. On the contrary, these are seeking, through a new exegesis and a new scholasticism, absolute commitment and eternal verity.

III

Many of today's intellectuals are putting a new emphasis on non-rational values. The rationalist values of the Enlightenment are more and more under attack. This is particularly true among the New Critics, the Southern Agrarian Romantics, and the increasingly influential Neo-Thomists. Arnold Toynbee, who has a greater vogue in the United States than anywhere else, speaks disparagingly of the Enlightenment as turning its back on the Christian virtues of faith, hope, and charity, and emphasizing the Mephistophelian maladies of disillusionment, apprehension, and cynicism. A political scientist, Eric Voegelin, is writing a gargantuan work, an attempt to build "order" in history and politics on Thomist thought. It seems that the apple of discord appeared with the Greek skeptics and Medieval Gnostics.

Now, of course, rationalism is not enough to explain history and life, but neither is non-rationalism. In order to be aware of the importance of the non-rational, one need not embrace non-rationalism completely; indeed, a rational respect for non-rational values may be the beginning of wisdom. Our society today, conscious of both, has a better chance of reconciling rational and non-rational values—of balancing the Apollonian and the Dionysian (to use Ruth Benedict's terms), the prudential and the passionate (to use Bertrand Russell's terms)—than any society which ever existed. But this new balance and this new wisdom will not be attained by denunciation or rejection of rational values.

Closely connected with the revolt from rationalism is the revolt from democracy and the bold affirmation of the values of an aristocratic society. The intellectual revolt from democracy had it origins in the 1920's with H. L. Mencken, the New Humanism of Irving Babbitt and Paul Elmer More, Southern Agrarian Romanticism, and the New Criticism. Ortega y Gasset's *The Revolt of the Masses*, which appeared in 1930, has had a tremendous, though often unacknowledged, impact on non-democratic and anti-democratic thinking in America. Today, Southern Agrarianism lives on in John Crowe Ransom, Allen Tate, and a number of younger votaries. The Neo-Thomism of Mortimer Adler has increasing influence. And the New Criticism of T. S. Eliot, Ezra Pound, and Kenneth Burke has become the dominant influence in literary criticism. "America," according to Burke, "is the purest concentration point of the vices and the vulgarities of the world." The New Criticism has been summarized by Robert Gorham Davis as a way of thinking in which "authority, hierarchy, catholicism, aristocracy, tradition, absolutes, dogmas, and truths become related terms of honor while liberalism, naturalism, scientism, individualism, equalitarianism, progress, protestantism, pragmatism, and personality become related terms of rejection and contempt.

In his *The Conservative Mind*, Russell Kirk finds in conservatism a unified movement and a consistent body of first principles from the time of Edmund Burke right down to the present. He sees these first principles as belief that a divine intent rules society; affection for the mystery of traditional life; conviction that society requires orders, classes, status, social gradations, and hierarchy; persuasion that property and freedom are inseparably connected; faith in prescription; recognition that change and reform are not identical. This, of course, is a far better description of traditional European conservatism than of American tradition or even of American business "conservatism."

Peter Viereck, in his *Conservatism Revisited*, finds in Metternich and in the Metternich system of 1815-1848 a sagacious attempt to conserve the traditional values of Western civilization and to bridle the forces of liberalism, nationalism, and democracy, which, according to Viereck, have led in the twentieth century to the mass man, fierce class and international wars, and totalitarian statism. A defense of the Metternich system is something novel in American historians, for up to this time every school of American history—Federalist, Whig, and Democratic—has seen in the Metternich system mostly obscurantist reaction. Many American specialists in international relations are searching in the Metternich system and the diplomacy of the reactionary Castlereagh for techniques and methods for coping with the revolutionary ferment of our time.

There is a disposition, too, to import from anthropology the "tenacity of the mores" as reason for resisting change. "Respect for the mores" played its part in the decision to retain the Mikado in Japan; it is being employed to sabotage new racial adjustments in the South. A century, it seems, is hardly long enough to allow Southern whites to adjust to the changes of the Civil War. Anthropology, of course, deals with the ways and techniques of change as well as with the resistances to change, but the emphasis of the conservative intellectuals who go to anthropology for rationales is on resistance to change.

America's New Conservatives describe the European past in too glowing terms; they romanticize it; they hearken back to a Golden Age which in fact never existed. They minimize the good of an industrial society. They do not give enough credit to the enormous gains made by industrialism over poverty, ignorance, disease, and personal brutality. They make conservatism both too comprehensive and too simple. They tend to appropriate for conservatism the whole humanistic tradition of the Western world, whereas, of course, that tradition has become a part, in somewhat varying ways, of Western reaction, conservatism, liberalism, radicalism, and socialism. Again, a consciousness of tradition, habit, and the organic continuities of social life are in themselves not so much a matter of conservatism as of the maturity and profundity of one's social understanding. The New Conservatives see in historic conservatism a consistency, a unity, and a continuity it never had in fact. If the need today is to weld aristocrats, businessmen, Catholics, and Protestants into a common front against Marxism, such was not the case in the past; indeed, such a combination represents a putting together of historic enemies. The contemporaries of Metternich did not consider him an impartial mediator between aristocrats and bourgeoisie; they knew him to be the friend of aristocracy and the enemy of the bourgeoisie. Very often these New Conservatives think of conservatism as being above the battle, as being the wise judge composing conflicting interests, snugly fitting moderate change into social and historical continuity. They too often forget that conservatives, like everybody else are motivated by their interests. Conservatives are likely to overestimate the virtues and underestimate the injustices of an existing order and of their own position. As William Lee Miller has pointed out, "relative justice" will usually not be found with the conservatives, however cultured or humane or "new," but with their opponents.

The New Conservatism is an attempt to substitute European conservative values for the American liberal tradition. It is as transparent a fraud as the Southern antebellum feudal dream of Fitzhugh, Harper, Ruffin, Holmes, Hughes, Dew, DeBow, Tucker, Bledsoe, and Hammond. (How many Americans, how many

Southerners, remember these names today?) Kirk and his cohorts are attempting to foist Burke's traditionalism on America, and as Louis Hartz has acutely pointed out, Americans, including Southerners, cannot become Burkian traditionalists without becoming Lockians, because the predominant tradition Americans have had is that of Locke.

IV

Some other thinkers are guilty not of falsifying the American tradition but of distorting it. Frederick Hayek, who has had an influence on contemporary American thought, erects free enterprise into a rigid system and decries all departures from it as "the road to serfdom." Walter Lippmann, in his *The Public Philosophy*, takes natural law concepts, which are capable of both a liberal and a conservative interpretation, and gives them a conservative Thomist slant. (Lippmann himself is an illustration of many of the older generation who have travelled spiritually from left to right. Lippmann has moved from democratic socialism to liberalism to conservatism—and to the urbane observer above the battle.) Louis Hartz, Clinton Rossiter, and Daniel J. Boorstin emphasize the private property drives of Americans to the point of distortion.

Americans have believed that they began in revolution and that by a continuous process of experience and free experiment have been in a continuous revolution, a "permanent revolution," ever since. Hartz gives American history a different twist. He contends that Americans have never had a revolution, that they were born free. Unlike the European, they escaped the feudal-manorial-guild society, the society of aristocracy, status, and fixed orders, and were literally born into the new society of the free market. The result was a property-owning, middle-class society which took Locke for its patron saint; and if Locke had never existed, this society would have had to invent him. Now, of course, there is much truth in this, but it overstates the ease with which the American society came to birth and maturity and it understates the difficulties of building and maintaining a free and democratic society in the face of constantly recurring tendencies in the human situation to privilege, complacency, stratification, and ossification. In spite of the relative absence of an inhibiting cake of custom from the past and in spite of the favorable conditions of the American environment, a free society did not just occur automatically. Even in America, inhibiting left-overs of the European past were considerable. To realize the possibilities of the new environment, to mold America's free society and adapt it to constantly changing conditions, required vision, imagination, and humanitarian impulse; it required the experimental and pragmatic spirit; it required struggle and the willingness to do battle; it required innovators and fighters and innovating and fighting movements.

Kirk claims that the American Revolution was "a conservative restoration." Viereck calls it a "conservative revolution" in the pattern of the Revolution of 1688. (This would indeed be a surprise to Macaulay, who described the American experiment as "all sail and no ballast.") But Hartz says it was no revolution at all. (How "hot-house" all this would have seemed to the expropriated and exiled Tories!) The American Revolution, with its Declaration of Independence and its sweeping away of Old World legal, political, economic, and social "vestiges," *was* a revolution, a revolution of considerable radical propensities.

Even though most of the subsequent political and social drives in American history represented "merely" a further breaking down of the status society, an extension of the free market, and a more widespread distribution of private property, they also showed a continuing humanitarian and innovating spirit. The great mass movements to abolish indentured servitude and imprisonment for debt, to enfranchise the propertyless, to emancipate women, to educate the masses at public expense, to abolish slavery, and to insure social justice in an industrial society are not to be set down as merely putting the finishing touches on a system pre-ordained by indigenous American conditions. The struggles between theocracy and Independencey, Old World tyranny and New World freedom, seaboard and frontier, federalism and republicanism, agrarianism and capitalism, slavery and freedom, industry and labor were hardly picayune. Even the party battles of Hamilton and Jefferson, Clay and Jackson, McKinley and Bryan were not the hollow shams a whole host of young historians and political scientists are now "demonstrating" them to have been. While the drive in America to private property, to "American Whiggery," and to Horatio Algerism, so emphasized by Hartz, is undeniable, so also have been the drives to the freedom of the mind, equality of opportunity, and relative social justice—as exemplified in varied ways by Roger Williams, Daniel Shays, Franklin, Paine, Jefferson, Benjamin Rush, Jackson, Dorothea Dix, Horace Mann, Emerson, Greeley, Theodore Parker, Ellery Channing, Wendell Phillips, Lincoln, Whitman, Peter Cooper, Henry George, Edward Bellamy, Peter Altgeld, Susan Anthony, Jane Addams, George Norris, John Dewey, and scores of others.

Hartz raises some basic questions about the very nature of the political process. Are the conflicts of politics, even in Europe, rendered meaningful only when they involve class and the dialectics and ideology of class? Cannot problem-solving and the clashes of group interests, as distinct from those of class, also be meaningful? Granted that American politics have involved little class and ideological conflict, have not the clashes of America's amazingly diverse group interests over the distribution of the benefits of the American economy been most significant? Was the New Deal any less significant because its approach was non-ideological, that of "mere" problem-solving? Cannot Americans make decisive contributions to the underdeveloped peoples today by a problem-solving rather than a dialectical-ideological approach?

The Hartz thesis, that America has had no feudal and aristocratic right, no Marxist left, but only a liberal center, does much to clarify the difficulty Americans are having in understanding the "isms" abroad. But in playing down the humanitarian and the experimental elements in American life, Hartz and other conservatives are making it more difficult to bridge the spiritual gap between Americans and the non-Communist social-democratic revolutionary forces abroad. We cannot bridge this gap by harping on America's "monolithic liberalism," but we may bridge it by emphasizing the innovating, pragmatic, and basically non-doctrinaire naure of Americans and American society.

V

Those Americans writing about the American economy in a large and significant way—and beginning with World War II these have dwindled in number—are guilty of one kind of distortion or another.

A. A. Berle, who with Gardiner Means in the 1930's wrote a most meaningful book about America's big corporations, has now become an apologist for the economic concentrates. In his *The Twentieth Century Capitalist Revolution*, he likens the big corporations to the feudatories of old and to the modern sovereign state. Indeed, Berle sees the modern corporation taking over some of the functions of the state. According to him, we need not fear this corporate power because the big corporations will check one another, and they will go a long way toward checking themselves because of the sense of benevolence and social responsibility they are developing, the self-restraints of natural law, and the infusing spirit of a kind of twentieth-century City of God. Berle's distortion is that of optimism.

C. Wright Mills, in his *The Power Elite*, sees big business and the political state as merged, and the United States as a monolithic oligarchy ruled by the corporate rich, the high political directorate, and the war lords. These orders of the American society have an interlocking membership and transfer among them takes place at the top. But what is the common goal of this elite? What common interest holds its parts together and gives it a common direction? Mills develops no concept of class which might hold this elite together, and he suggest no other bond of unity. What, then, prevents rifts and conflicts in the elite itself? The truth seems to be that the American society is more complex and diverse and has more vital conflicts and clashes on all levels than Mills will concede. America's elite is not as exclusive, concentrated, and unified as he makes out, and its decisions are not as free from the influence of Congress, political leaders, political parties, group associations and pressures, mass organizations, journalistic opinion, and public opinion generally as he contends. Mill's distortion is that of oversimplification and pessimism.

John K. Galbraith, until recently, strongly suggested that we may enjoy the economic benefits of oligopoly and at the same time escape the evils of concentrated power because of the operation of what he calls countervailing power, new restraints on economic power which have come into existence to take the place of the old competition. The new restraints appear not on the same side of the market but on the opposite side, not with competitors but with customers and suppliers. Galbraith admits that under the inflationary pressures of demand, countervailing power weakens and then dissoves. But even in the absence of inflationary pressures, countervailing power is not pervasive but sporadic, because while in our economy some customers and suppliers are large-scale and organized and able to exert countervailing power against original power, others are small-scale and unorganized and unable to exert countervailing power. Galbraith suggests that government step in and create countervailing power where bargainers are small-scale and unorganized. But government is not something isolated from society, above the battle, forever standing ready to act in a disinterested way to correct imbalances. Government itself is subject to pressures. Why doesn't government encourage the countervailing power of small business to oppose the original power of the concentrates? Because the concentrates have access to government, too;

they can put pressures on government; indeed, their pressures are likely to be more effective than those of small business. Galbraith's distortion is that of seeing too much symmetry and balance, of substituting countervailing power for the old "unseen hand" as a built-in regulator, as an automatic balancer.

However, one can scarcely classify Galbraith as a conservative. In his more recent *The Affluent Socety*, he has revealed some skepticism about his own concept of countervailing power, and he has emphasized the importance of the public sector, the area of government-produced goods and services, in our economy. . . .

VI

Perhaps the most pervasive distortion today is the belief that we live in a completely mass society and mass culture and that these are evil. Many intellectuals and aesthetes, and their numerous imitators, speak rather glibly of mass man, organization man, the crowd mind, group conformity, "togetherness," non-autonomous man, stereotyped man, the other-directed society, and the monolithic society. This conception may be selling our liberal society short. On the other hand, this may be symptomatic of a growing awareness of the importance of cultural freedom, in addition to political and economic freedom, a manifestation of a cultural revolution which is already far along the way. People were not so conscious of agrarianism's narrow limitations and its non-autonomy, but at least we are now increasingly conscious of the non-autonomy produced by industrialism.

The truth seems to be that while in some of its aspects our society is more integrated than the pre-industrial societies of the past, in some other aspects it is less integrated. In its economic and political areas it is more integrated, and there are threats to personal autonomy in these areas. However, we are increasingly conscious of them, and it is precisely in the political and economic areas that the American liberal tradition is strongest. This liberal tradition needs to be reinterpreted and then applied to the new realities. Certainly, rejecting the liberal tradition at this time would be a surrender to the forces of impersonality and not a challenge to them.

But in many of its other facets our society is less integrated. People in an industrial society have been freed from the old restraints of localism, from customary status and class, from the traditional primary groups of family, neighborhood, and parish. They are mobile. They can escape to the anonymity of the cities. There is a much wider range of choice in careers than there was in the past. And all people, no matter what they do, work less and less and have more and more time on their own. But do they escape the old fetters only to be absorbed in the crowd? There is escape into privacy and into sub-groups of one's own choosing as well as absorption into the crowd.

W. H. Auden, in his *The Dyer's Hand*, observes that advanced technological society, by putting at our immediate disposal the arts of all ages and cultures, has completely changed the meaning of the word "tradition." It no longer means a way handed down from one generation to the next. It means a consciousness of the whole of the past of all societies—with their infinite ways and values—*as present*.

In our society, all sorts of values—pre-industrial and industrial, rural and urban, non-scientific and scientific, non-rational and rational—compete and jostle within communities, neighborhoods, families, and even individuals. (In some individuals, this produces neuroses; in many others, it produces personal emancipation and cultural enrichment.) In their personal lives, Americans display a wide variety of recreational, aesthetic, religious, moral, and sex values—perhaps the widest variety in the history of human societies. The amazing variety of attitudes and practices in sex found by Kinsey would likely be found also in other aspects of personal living, if these were given similar scrutiny.

The mass media, which are often said to impair autonomy and creativity, are in fact Janus-faced. They widen the outlets for banality and mass vulgarity, but they also widen the outlets for good reading, good drama, good art, good music, knowledgeable interpretation of events, and live history-in-the-making. Actually, in consumption, there seems to be at the present time more discriminating connoisseurship in food, drink, clothing, dress, housing, sex, entertainment, travel, reading, music, and the arts than there was in the days before mass advertising and the other mass media. And in production, creativity, far from drying up, has never been so alive. Never before has it been so easy for so many people to have careers in research, scholarship, science, and the pure arts. Since 1901, American scientists have in each successive decade been receiving a larger and larger portion of the Nobel prize. Since the 1920's, Americans have had five winners of the Nobel prize for literature. We may deplore the current avoidance of social realism by our contemporary American writers, but we can only applaud their increasing sophistication and craftsmanship. And the practical arts grow and multiply. There has been an enormous expansion and proliferation of the service industries, of applied social science and psychology (like social and personnel work and psychiatry), of applied writing (like public relations, trade journalism, criticism), of applied art (like architecture, landscape gardening, commercial art, dress design).

A self-confessed middle-brow, Russell Lynes, comes closer than any intellectual to summing up the nature of our culture:

Ours is a "You-name-it-we-have-it" kind of culture. It is a vast market place of conflicting tastes, conflicting ambitions, and conflicting needs. In guaranteeing "the pursuit of happiness," we recognize that not every man's happiness is measured by the same yardstick. We may do our damnedest to convince him that our yardstick is better than his, but we do not beat him over the head with it. . . . Out of the crowd that the voyeurs *of culture call "the mass," many single voices are heard. So long as this is true, what we have is not a "mass culture," but neither is it an aristocratic culture. It is a highly competitive culture.*

Is not ours a society without a metaphysical base? Is not ours an amazingly diverse, pluralistic, and eclectic society held together by a kind of humanistic pragmatism? And is not ours the probable prototype for other advanced industrial societies of the future?

To discover the actual nature of our society, the individual must for the most part look to the realities about him and trust to his own observations of life. Our researchers are currently bogged in methodology, minutiae, timidity, and bureaucracy; and our humanistic and literary intellectuals, with a passion for monistic unity, symmetry, conceptualism, and abstraction (most of all the New Humanists, the Neo-Thomists, the New Critics, and the New Conservatives), are busy constructing some homogeneous pattern for our society and culture, a pattern which simply does not exist. In a recent issue of *Commentary*, Robert Gorham Davis has pointed out how during this century American literary critics, with thorough Judeo-Puritan-Brahmin bookishness, have given the whole American literary tradition a homogeneity which in fact it does not possess.

VII

It would be a cruel paradox if we Americans failed in the world contest of today because we had succeeded too early and too well in developing the industrial society of the future. Our very wealth, as a society and as individuals, is producing a spiritual and psychological gulf between us and the world's poor folks which under the very best of circumstances is going to be difficult to bridge. Most of the world is in revolutionary ferment. The anti-imperialist revolutions in Asia, the Middle East, and Africa are the most important political event of our time, and these revolutions are seeking not a rationale for the status quo but a justification for basic change. They may find that justification in Marxism. They may find it in the dynamic, democratic, libertarian, experimental, and pragmatic tradition, the dominant tradition of the American society. But they will never find it in the non-rational, non-democratic, anti-democratic, aristocratic, authoritarian, and ritualistic attitudes of America's New Conservatism. Politically, the attitudes of the New Conservatives make sense only if the United States is about to undertake to erect a Neo-Metternich system to underwrite a conservative and reactionary status quo in the world or to build an outright American empire. But if the United States is to win the anti-imperialist revolutions from the Marxists and put itself squarely at the head of all those forces determined to build a future democratic world, then the New Conservatism is working untold damage to American foreign politicy, even to American survival.

The New Conservatism distorts and even falsifies the American tradition. It does not square with the facts of our modern industrial society. It is playing into the hands of the Marxists. It is giving verity to the Marxist theory of history that a bourgeois society, when confronted with the Marxist challenge, must necessarily commit suicide by going reactionary. It is damaging America's appeal to the revolutionary, but democratic, forces abroad, and weakening the democratic attitudes in America necessary for a sustained and successful democratic appeal abroad.

On the other hand, America's optimistic, democratic, libertarian, rational, experimental, and pragmatic tradition is the dominant and authentic American tradition. Moreover, it is the only tradition ample and flexible enough to allow and give meaning to our culturally heterogeneous and eclectic society produced by advanced industrialism. And this authentic American tradition is the only one available to us Americans that will appeal to foreign peoples in revolutionary mood, justify their drives for basic change outside a Marxist framework, and give sense to the kind of societies their new industrialism will eventually evolve.

37 Scientific Concepts and Cultural Change

Harvey Brooks

Employing some of the style of argument used by earlier writers on the influence of Darwinian ideas (see Essays 22, 23, and 29 headnote), Harvey Brooks, Professor of Applied Physics at Harvard University, here explains how themes from the physical and biological sciences are today entering our general culture. The reader may well want to ask if the newer ''finite aims'' of scholarship, derived from the methods of scientific research, will in the long run prove advantageous to the humanistic quality of intellectual history itself.

For further reading: Everett Mendelsohn, ''Science in America: The Twentieth Century,'' in *Arthur M. Schlesinger, Jr., and Morton White (eds.), *Paths of American Thought* (1963), chap. 23; *James B. Conant, *Modern Science and Modern Man* (1952); *Werner Heisenberg, *Physics and Philosophy: The Revolution in Modern Science* (1958); Percy W. Bridgman, ''The New Vision of Science,'' in his *Reflections of a Physicist* (2d ed., 1955), pp. 167-189, reprinted in *David Van Tassel (ed.), *American Thought in the Twentieth Century* (1967), pp. 109-123; Percy W. Bridgman, ''P. W. Bridgman's 'The Logic of Modern Physics' after Thirty Years,'' *Daedalus*, 88 (Summer 1959), 518-526; *Thomas S. Kuhn, *The Structure of Scientific Revolutions* (1962); *Sir Charles Sherrington, *Man on His Nature* (1940); Robert Oppenheimer, ''Perspectives in Modern Physics,'' in Robert E. Marshak (ed.), *Perspectives in Modern Physics* (1967).

There are many difficulties of communication between the sub-groups within our culture—for example, between the natural sciences, social sciences, and humanities. But there are also ways in which they are becoming increasingly united, and most of this essay will be an effort to trace a few common themes and viewpoints derived from science which I see as increasingly pervading our culture as a whole.

Perhaps one of the most important is the common allegiance of scholarship to the

Daedalus, 94 (Winter 1965), 66-76, 79-82. Reprinted by permission of *Daedalus*, Journal of the American Academy of Arts and Sciences. Three footnotes have been omitted.

ideal of objective research, to the possibility of arriving by successive approximations at an objective description of reality. Whether it be concerned with the structure of a distant galaxy or the sources of the art of the nineteenth century poet, there exists a common respect for evidence and a willingness to follow evidence wherever it leads regardless of the preconceptions or desires of the scholar. This is, of course, only an ideal; but failure to conform to this ideal, if detected, damns a scholar whether he be a scientist or a humanist. In a sense the whole apparatus of academic scholarship is an attempt to bring scientific method into the pursuit of knowledge through progressive refinements in the uncovering and use of evidence.

A characteristic of scholarship, as of science, is that it prefers to tackle well-defined, finite problems that appear to be soluble with the methods and evidence available. This often means eschewing the more fundamental, the more "metaphysical" issues, in the belief that the cumulative result of solving many smaller and more manageable problems will ultimately throw more light on the larger issues than would a frontal attack. One of the paradoxes of modern science has been that the greater its success in a pragmatic sense, the more modest its aims have tended to become in an intellectual sense. The goals and claims of modern quantum theory are far more modest than those of Laplace, who believed that he could predict the entire course of the universe, in principle, given its initial conditions. The aim of science has changed from the "explanation" of reality to the "description" of reality—description with the greatest logical and aesthetic economy. The claims to universality of nineteenth century physics have been replaced by a greater awareness of what still remains to be discovered about the world, even "in principle." The day of global theories of the social structure or of individual psychology seems to have passed. Experience has taught us that real insight has often been achieved only after we were prepared to renounce our claim that our theories were universal. The whole trend of modern scholarship has been towards greater conservatism in deciding what can be legitimately inferred from given evidence; we are more hesitant to extrapolate beyond the immediate circumstances to which the evidence applies. We are quicker to recognize the possibility of unrevealed complexities or unidentified variables and parameters. Even in artistic criticism we tend to recognize greater diversity in the influences playing on an artist, greater ambiguity in his motives or artistic intentions. Art, scholarship, and science are united in looking further behind the face of common-sense reality, in finding subtleties and nuances. It is, of course, this search for subtlety which has made communication between disciplines more difficult, because to the casual observer each discipline appears to be working in an area beyond common sense.

The admission of finite aims in scholarship has been connected with an increasingly sophisticated view of the scope and limitations of evidence in all fields. But the emphasis on finite and limited aims in scholarly inquiry has also been paralleled by the extension of scientific and scholarly attitudes to practical affairs. One sees a close analogy between the preoccupation of science with manageable problems and the decline of ideology and growth of professional expertise in politics and business. One of the most striking developments of the post-war world has been the increasing irrelevance of political ideology, even in the Soviet Union, to actual political decisions. One sees the influence of the new mood in the increasing bureaucratization and professionalization of government and industry and in the growth of "scientific" approaches to management and administration. The day of the intuitive entrepreneur or the charismatic statesman, seems to be waning. In a recent volume of *Daedalus* on "A New Europe?" the recurring theme is the increasing relegation of questions which used to be matters of political debate to professional cadres of technicians and experts which function almost independently of the democratic political process. In most of the western world the first instinct of statesmanship is to turn intransigent problems over to "experts" or to "study groups." There appears to be an almost naive faith that if big problems can be broken down sufficiently and be dealt with by experts and technicians, the big problems will tend to disappear or at least lose much of their urgency. Although the continuing discourse of experts seems wasteful, "Parkinsonian," the fact remains that it has worked surprisingly well in government, just as it has in science and scholarship. The progress which is achieved, while slower, seems more solid, more irreversible, more capable of enlisting a wide consensus. Much of the history of social progress in the twentieth century can be described in terms of the transfer of wider and wider areas of public policy from politics to expertise. I do not believe it is too fanciful to draw a parallel between this and the scientific spirit of tackling soluble problems.

The trend towards the acceptance of expertise has been especially striking in Europe where both ideology and the apolitical professional bureaucracy have been stronger than in the United States. But even in this country there has been increasing public acceptance of expert analysis and guidance in such areas of government as fiscal policy and economic growth. In the realm of affairs, as in the realm of knowledge, the search for global solutions or global generalizations has been replaced by the search for manageable apolitical reformulations of problems. The general has been replaced by the specific. Concern with the theoretical goals and principles of action has been replaced by attempts at objectively predicting and analyzing the specific consequences of specific alternative actions or policies. Often the problems of political choice have become buried in debates among experts over highly technical alternatives.

It remains to be seen to what degree this new reign of the bureaucrat and the expert reflects the influence of science and scientific modes of thinking and to what degree it represents a temporary cyclic phenomenon resulting from unprecedented economic growth and the absence of major social crises. However, the modes of thought which are characteristic of science have penetrated much deeper into scholarship and practical affairs than the hand-wringing of some scientists would tend to suggest, and the general adoption of these modes of thought does not appear to have relegated genuine human values to the scrap heap to the degree which some of the humanists would have us believe. Indeed it has brought us closer to a realization of many of the human values which we regard as desirable.

On the other hand, it must be recognized, that some of this reliance on expertise has moved us in directions in which we would not have gone had we been more aware of the unspoken and unrecognized assumptions underlying some of our "technical" solutions. For example, economic growth and technology have come to be accepted as valuable in themselves. The assembly line has brought more and more goods to more and more people, but it has also introduced monotony into work and a sometimes depressing standardization into our products. The technology of production tends to accept as its goals values which technology alone is well adapted to achieving without balanced consideration of other, equally important goals. The very definition of gross national product connotes measurement of economic progress in purely quantitative terms without reference to changes in the quality of the social and physical environment or improvement and deterioration in the quality and variety of the products available. The inclination to tackle the soluble problems first often extrapolates to the view that the more intractable problems are less important.

In the preceding paragraphs I have argued that both scholarship and practical affairs have increasingly adopted the spirit and mode of thought of the natural sciences. An interesting question is to what extent the actual concepts and ideas of science have entered into other disciplines and into our culture generally. There are, of course, some very obvious ways in which this has occurred. Scarcely any other scientific theory, for example, has influenced literature and art so much as Freud's psychoanalytical theory. Though some of Freud's ideas might be said to contain dogmatic elements which are essentially non-scientific or even anti-scientific in spirit, nevertheless, psychoanalysis is based on largely empirical observation and professes to test itself against objective evidence. It is clearly a scientific theory which, though extensively elaborated and modified, is still basically valid in its description of the irrational and subconscious elements in human motivation and behavior. It has completely altered our view of human nature, and this changed viewpoint is reflected almost universally, though in varying degrees, in modern literature and art, as well as in the interpretation of history and political behavior. The orderly Lockean world embodied in the American Constitution, in which each man acts rationally in his own self-interest, can no longer be accepted in quite the undiluted way that the Founding Fathers believed in it. There is ample evidence of neurotic and irrational behavior on the part of whole communities and social systems, often in opposition to their own self-interest. Even organized religion has largely accepted and adapted many of the principles of psychoanalysis, while rejecting some of the world views which have been extrapolated from it.

A more problematic example is the parallel between the increasingly abstract and insubstantial picture of the physical universe which modern physics has given us and the popularity of abstract and non-representational forms of art and poetry. In each case the representation of reality is increasingly removed from the picture which is immediately presented to us by our senses. As the appreciation of modern physics requires more and more prior education, so the appreciation of modern art and music requires a more educated—some would say a more thoroughly conditioned—aesthetic taste. In physics the sharp distinction which used to be made between the object and its relations to other objects has been replaced by the idea that the object (or elementary particle) is nothing but the nexus of the various relations in which it participates. In physics, as in art and literature, form has tended to achieve a status higher than substance.

It is difficult to tell how much psychological reality there is to this parallel. It is not sufficient to reply that a physical picture is still a definite model which can be related by a series of clear and logical steps to the world which we see and that no such close correspondence exists between abstract art and the sensible world. For physical models depend to a larger degree on taste than is generally appreciated. While correspondence with the real world exists, this probably is not sufficient by itself to constitute a unique determinant of a model. Yet the successful model is one that has evolved through so many small steps that it would take a bold imagination indeed to construct another one which would fit the same accumulation of interconnected facts or observtions. What is regarded as acceptable evidence for a model of reality, even in physics, is strongly dependent on the scientific environment of the time. Evidence which favors theories already generally accepted is much less critically scrutinized than evidence that appears to run counter to them. One always makes every effort to fit new evidence to existing concepts before accepting radical modifications; if a theory is well established the contradictory evidence is usually questioned long before the theory, and usually rightly so. Established theories depend on many more bits of accumulated evidence than is often appreciated, even by the scientist himself. Once a principle becomes generally accepted the scientific community generally forgets much of the detailed evidence that led to it, and it takes a real jolt to lead people to reconsider the evidence. In fact, scientific theories are seldom fully displaced; rather they are fitted into the framework of a more comprehensive theory, as Newtonian mechanics was fitted into the formulations of relativity and quantum mechanics. This, in itself, suggests that there are many theories or models which will fit given facts.

All of this points to the fact that a scientific theory is the product of a long evolutionary process which is not strictly logical or even retraceable. The mode of presentation of science, especially to the non-scientist, usually suppresses or conceals the process by which the results were originally arrived at, just as the artist does not reveal the elements which went into his creation. Thus it seems possible that there is some common or universal element in the modern mentality which makes quantum theory acceptable to the physicist, abstract art to the artist, metaphysical poetry to the poet, atonal music to the musician, or abstract spaces to the mathematician. The attack on these aspects of modern culture by totalitarians of both the right and the left perhaps lends further credence to these common threads. It is interesting to observe that children with previously untrained tastes have little trouble in appreciating and enjoying modern art or music and that the younger generation of physicists has no trouble in absorbing the ideas of quantum mechanics quite intuitively with none of the sense of paradox which still troubles some of the older generation. It is probable that the main elements of taste, whether it be scientific or aesthetic, are formed quite early in our experience and are strongly conditioned by the cultural climate. Science, as one of the most dynamic of contemporary intellectual trends, is undoubtedly a strong factor in creating this cultural climate, but it would be rash to ascribe causal connections. It would be interesting to know whether some psychologist, by studying current tastes in art or poetry, could predict what *kinds* of theories were likely to be acceptable in elementary particle physics, or perhaps vice versa!

Another obvious but superficial way in which scientific ideas enter our culture is through some of the dominant "themes" of science. One such theme, for example, is evolution and natural selection, and the derived philosophical concept of progress. Today we take the idea of evolution so much for granted that we are inclined to forget that until the nineteenth century it was generally believed that the present state of society and man was the result of degeneration from some antecedent golden age or hypothetical ideal "state of nature." The Puritan Revolution in England and the French Revolution had ideologies which appealed to a hypothetical prehistoric past for their model of an ideal society. Only with Marx did revolution present itself as a forward movement into a more "advanced," previously non-existent state of human society.

In the nineteenth century the idea of evolution and particularly the concepts of natural selection, competition between species, and the "survival of the fittest" were seized upon as an explanantion of and justification for the contemporary laissez-faire capitalist society. State intervention in the competitive economic process was regarded as an almost immoral interference with the "balance of nature" in human society. In the United States and Britain the first science of sociology was built upon an interpretation of the ideas of natural selection. A whole generation of future American businessmen was educated in the ideas of men like Sumner. This sociology stressed the dangers of permitting organized society to tamper with the inexorable laws of social evolution.

In the early part of the twentieth century Darwin's ideas lost some of their original influence, but now, in the second half, they have regained much of their influence in biology and have tended to be reinforced by recent discoveries in biochemical genetics. However, it is interesting to note that a subtle change of emphasis has crept into the interpretation of natural selection. The modern evolutionary biologist tends to stress the concept of the "ecological niche" and the fact that natural selection, when looked at more carefully, leads to a kind of cooperation among species, a cooperation which results from finer and finer differentiation of function and of adaptation to the enviornment. Indeed, biologists stress the fact that natural selection generally leads not to the complete domination of one species, but rather to a finer and finer branching of species, a sort of division of labor which tends ultimately to minimize competition. Is it too much to suggest a parallel here between the changing scientific interpretations of biological evolution and changing attitudes towards cooperative action in human societies? Is there any connection between the modern view of ecology and the progressive division of labor and specialization of function which are characteristic of modern economic organization? Certainly the analogies with biological evolution have been extremely suggestive in the development of modern cultural anthropology.

Another theme which is involved here is that of dynamic equilibrium or balance, also fruitful in the study of chemical equilibrium. When dynamic equilibrium exists, a complex system can be apparently static from the macroscopic viewpoint even though rapid changes are taking place in its elementary components. All that is necessary is that the rates of changes in opposite directions balance. This is the kind of equilibrium that is envisioned as occurring in an ecological system or in a social or economic system. It would, perhaps, be wrong to suggest any causal or genetic relation between the growth of such ideas of chemical theory and their application to social or biological systems. The fact is, however, that the concepts arose at similar periods in scientific development and helped to establish a kind of climate of taste in scientific theories which undoubtedly facilitated intuitive transfer from one discipline to another. One finds the images and vocabulary of chemical equilibrium theory constantly recurring in descriptions of social and economic phenomena.

Two of the germinal ideas of twentieth-century physics have been "relativity" and "uncertainty." Philosophers generally recognize that both of these themes have had an important influence on their attitudes, but the physical scientist finds it more difficult to connect the philosophical view with its role in physics. At least the connection is not so self-evident as it is in the case of evolution or of psychoanalysis. Indeed, both relativity and uncertainty are words which have rather precise operational meanings in physics, but which have been given all sorts of wishful or anthropomorphic interpretations in philosophy. Indeed scientific popularizers have themselves been especially guilty of this type of questionable semantic extrapolation. The situation has been aggravated by the tendency of physicists to use words from everyday discourse to denote very subtle and precise technical concepts. The popularizer and the layman then use the technical and the everyday term interchangeably to draw conclusions bearing little relation to the original concept.

Let us consider relativity first. The basic idea of relativity is that all the laws of mechanics and electromagnetism are the same, independent of the state of uniform motion in which the observer happens to be moving. Relativity is "relative" in the sense that there is no "absolute" motion, no fixed reference point in the universe that has greater claim to validity than any other. On the other hand, the elimination of absolute motion is achieved only at the price of introducing an absolute velocity which is the same in all reference systems, namely, the velocity of light. Thus it may be legitimately questioned whether "relativity" or "absolutism" is the correct name for the theory. Nevertheless, the first terminology was the one that caught the popular and speculative imagination and provided the basis of a revolution in viewpoint which affected many areas of knowledge. Not long after relativity was absorbed into physics, the anthropologists were stressing the extraordinary diversity of human customs and ethical norms and were arguing that moral standards had to be viewed not in an absolute sense but relative to the particular culture in which they were found. The judgments of history became less moralistic; the actions of individuals tended to be viewed in the context of the ethical norms of their time. The realistic novel or drama in which human behavior was depicted without moral judgment became fashionable. Yet if these things have little to do with "relativity" in the sense that Einstein intended, the very fact that the word caught fire so easily suggests there does exist a kind of common taste in such matters and that this taste forms part of the intellectual climate of the time.

The other key idea of physics is "uncertainty," as embodied in the Heisenberg Uncertainty Principle. The philosophical interpretation of this principle has been the subject of interminable debate by both scientists and laymen. On one extreme, people have viewed the uncertainty principle as repealing the laws of causality and reintroducing "free will" into the physical as well as the mental universe. Most working physicists tend to take a somewhat more pedestrian view of the principle. They interpret it as being the result of an attempt to describe the state of the universe in terms of an inappropriate and outmoded concept, namely that of the point mass or "particle," a concept derived by analogy with macroscopic, i.e.

common sense, physics. Nevertheless, regardless of the exact interpretation, the uncertainty principle does imply that the idealized classical determinism of Laplace is impossible. The laws of quantum theory are deterministic or "causal" in the sense that the state of the universe at any time is determined by its "state" at some previous time. The lack of determinism in the Laplacian sense comes from the impossibility of specifying the "state" at any time in terms of any set of operations which will not themselves change its state and thus spoil the assumptions. What is wrong in the old determinism is the idea that the universe can be uniquely and unequivocally distinguished from the observing system, which is a part of it. In this sense the uncertainty principle can be seen as merely a further extension of the concept of relativity. Interpreted in this light, we find the same idea cropping up in many fields of knowledge. The social scientist is increasingly conscious that the measurements that he can make on any social system affect the future behavior of the system. A good example is public opinion polls, which, if made public, affect the attitude of the public on the very matters the polls are supposed to measure "objectively." Another example is educational tests, which not only measure human ability, but tend to change the cultural and educational norms which are accepted and sought. This aspect of the uncertainty principle in the social sciences is, in quantitative terms, a matter of some debate, but it is an important factor in social measurement, which has to be dealt with just as in physics. In many social situations the mere fact that the subjects know they are being observed or tested affects their behavior in ways which are difficult to discount in advance. Even in a subject like history a sort of analog of the uncertainty principle is found. It lies basically in the fact that the historian knows what happened afterwards and therefore can never really describe the "initial conditions" of his system in a way which is independent of his own perspective. In seeking to discern the underlying causes of events he inevitably tends to stress those factors which demonstrably influenced events in the way they actually came out, minimizing factors or tendencies which did not develop even though the relative strengths of the two tendencies may have been very evenly balanced at that time. The modern historian, of course, tends to be very aware of this uncertainty principle and to allow for it as much as possible. Again, while there is probably little intellectual connection between these various attitudes in the different disciplines, there is a general intellectual climate which stresses the interaction between the observer and the system being observed, whether it be in history, physics, or politics.

There are a number of themes in science having a somewhat more direct and traceable intellectual connection between different disciplines. Here I should like to mention three, namely, energy, feedback, and information. Each of these is a highly technical concept in physics or engineering; however, each also has broad and increasing ramifications in other disciplines. Of these, the oldest and most loosely used is probably energy. This concept is closely associated with that of "transformation." That is, the reason energy is a useful concept is that it has many different forms or manifestations which may be transformed into each other. In physics it is probably the most general and unifying concept we have. All physical entities or phenomena, including "matter" or "mass," are forms or manifestations of energy. Though it may be transformed, its quantity is "invariant," and this is what makes it important. The concept of energy has, of course, been important in biology almost as long as in physics. Living matter functions by transforming energy, and much of the early science of physiology was concerned with studying the transformations of energy in living systems. But the term "energy" has also found its way into many other fields of knowledge, where it is used often more metaphorically than with precise significance. Nevertheless, even in its metaphorical use it tends to partake of some of the characteristic properties of physical energy; namely, it is subject to transformation into different forms, and in the process of transformation the total energy is in some sense preserved. One speaks of psychic energies, historical energies, social energies. In these senses energy is not really measurable, nor is it directly related to physical energy. Nevertheless, like physical energy it can be released in the form of enormous physical, mental, or social activity; and, when it is, we tend to think of it as somehow "potential" in the pre-existing situation. The term "tension" denotes a state of high potential energy, like a coiled spring; and a high state of tension, whether social or psychological, is usually followed by a "release" or conversion into kinetic energy or activity of some variety. Thus the language of energy derived from physics has proved a very useful metaphor in dealing with all sorts of social and psychological phenomena. Here the intellectual connection is more clear than in the case of relativity or uncertainty, but it is more metaphorical than logical. . . .

It seems highly likely that the business cycle in the economy as a whole represents a form of feedback instability to which many individual elements of decision making contribute through their time lags. In fact all forms of social decision making tend to contain an inherent time lag arising from the fact that anticipations of the future are simply linear extrapolations of past trends. Thus one can even discern a similar tendency in history for political and social attitudes towards public issues to be those appropriate to the experience of the recent or distant past rather than to the actual situation which is faced. For example, the philosophies of laissez-faire economics were conditioned by the mercantile and pre-industrial era in which the principal problem was the inhibiting effects of state interference in the economy. Or, to take a more recent example, early post-war American economic policy was based on the fear of a major depression similar to what followed the first war, while much of present public thinking is based on the fear of inflation of the type which followed World War II. Such lags in social attitudes probably contribute to many of the cyclic phenomena which are often attributed to history. Of course, the examples given above are somewhat crude oversimplifications, but the basic idea is one which may have quantitative as well as suggestive or metaphorical value.

Another possible example is the cycle in moral attitudes. Attitudes towards moral values, because of the long time they take to diffuse throughout society, tend to lag behind the actual social conditions for which they were most appropriate. Thus, for example, Victorian attitudes towards sex arose partly as a reaction to the extreme laxity which existed in previous times, and conversely modern liberal attitudes towards sex are to some extent a response to the social and psychological effects of Victorian repression. Such attitudes tend to go in cycles because their inherent time lag produces unstable feedback in the social system. Such lags are especially important in the dynamic or "high gain" cultures characteristic of the West.

The problem of stability in feedback theory is relevant to situations in which the environment without considering feedback is more or less constant. When an unstable feedback situation exists, the system "hunts" about the stable situation of adjustment to the environment. The other important concept, however, is that of the response of the system to environmental changes imposed from without, or, in amplifier terminology, the faithfulness and speed with which the output follows the input. This introduces the idea of "optimization" in control systems. An optimized system is one which responds to its environment in the best way as defined by some quantitative criterion. Of course, the optimal configuration of the control system will be dependent on the properties of the environment to which it is expected to respond or adapt. We can imagine an environment which is subject to short-term and long-term changes and a feedback system which is optimized for the short-term changes occurring during a certain period. If the nature of the short-term changes also varies slowly in time, then the feedback system will not remain optimum. We could then imagine a feedback system whose properties change with time in such a way as to keep the response optimal as the short-term changes in the environment occur. The continuing optimization can itself be described as a form of information feedback. For example, we can imagine a man learning a game requiring great physical skill. When he has learned it, his muscular and nervous system may be thought of as a feedback system which has been optimized for that particular game. If he then engages in a new game, his muscles and nerves will have to be optimized all over again for the new game, and the process of learning is itself a form of information feedback. In this way we arrive at the concept of a whole hierarchy of feedback systems—of systems within systems, each operating on a different time scale and each higher system in the hierarchy constituting the learning process for the next lower system in the hierarchy. In the technical literature these hierarchies are referred to as adaptive control. Adaptive control systems appear to "learn" by experience and thus come one step closer to simulating the behavior of living systems. In fact we may imagine that biological and social systems are information feedback systems with many more super-imposed hierarchies than we are accustomed to dealing with in physical control systems.

The other key idea from engineering which has had an important impact on social and biological theory is that of information, and the closely associated concept of noise. The idea that information was a concept that could be defined in precise mathematical terms was recognized by Leo Szilard in 1929. Szilard was the first to point out the connection between the quantity of information we have about the physical world and the physical concept of the entropy of a system. However, Szilard's ideas lay fallow until twenty years later when they were rediscovered by Shannon and precisely formulated in their modern form—the form which has revolutionized modern communications. There is a very close relation between information and probability. In fact, the amount of information in an image or a message is closely connected with its deviations from a purely random pattern. The concept of information is basic to the quantitative study of language and has provided one of the cornerstones of a new science known as mathematical linguistics. It is also generally recognized that the transmission of genetic properties from generation to generation is essentially a communication of information. This has led to the idea of the "genetic code" which contains all the information necessary to reproduce the individual. So far the attention of biologists has mostly been focused on the elementary code, that is, on the relationship between the structure of the DNA molecule and the genetic information which it carries. The possibility of precise definition of the quanity of information in a system, however, opens up the possibility of considering evolution from the standpoint of a system of information transmission—a type of study which is still in its infancy. A remarkable consequence of information concepts is the realization that the information embodied in the biological constitution of the human race is essentially contained in the total quantity of DNA in the human germ cells—at most a few grams in the whole world. One suspects that it may be possible to apply information concepts similarly to the study of cultural evolution and to the transmission of culture from generation to generation.

One cannot talk about information without considering noise, which is the random background on which all information must ultimately be recognized. By its very nature noise is the absence of information. When an attempt is made to transmit a definite piece of information in the presence of noise, the noise destroys a definite amount of the information in the transmission process. No transmission system is completely faithful. Noise is, in the first instance, a physical concept; but, as in the case of information and feedback, the concept may be extended in a somewhat vague way to social and biological systems. For example, in evolutionary theory the "noise" is the random variations in the genetic constitution produced by cosmic radiation and other external influences on the genetic material. In the transmission of cultural information, the "information" communicated by a piece of literature or a work of art depends not only upon the intrinsic information content of the work but also on the experience and education of the recipient. Unless the artist and the recipient have had the same experience, the communication is always less than faithful.

In the foregoing I have tried to suggest how a number of important themes from the physical and biological sciences have found their way into our general culture, or have the potential for doing so. In the case of the concepts of feedback and information, the ideas appear to have an essentially quantitative and operational significance for social and cultural dynamics, although their application is still in its infancy. The most frequent case is that in which a scientific concept has served as a metaphor for the description of social and political behavior. This has occurred, for example, in the case of the concepts of relativity, uncertainty, and energy. In other cases, such as evolution and psychoanalysis, the concept has entered even more deeply into our cultural attitudes.

38
Human Nature in American Thought: Retreat from Reason in the Age of Science

Merle Curti

Retracing some major themes that have concerned American thinkers since the age of Darwin, Merle Curti here provides a useful summary of much that has been discussed in the preceding sixteen selections. Professor Curti delivered this essay as the second of two lectures at Columbia University in 1953.

For further reading: Citations in the headnotes for Essays 34, 35, and 37.

The century from 1860 to the present has marked a steady retreat from reason. This retreat has recently become headlong, so that at present we are living in a new age of faith. But at the beginning of the century, in 1860 let us say, reason was still enthroned in the United States. In the 1860's the traditional Christian approach was still dominant, and continued to be, for that matter, in the succeeding decades. Orthodox doctrine taught the reality of original sin, but it also taught men to believe in their ability to struggle against sin and in the possibility of redemption. In an expanding Christian circle the idea of the malleability of human nature, of its potentialities for good, was finding fresh emphasis; and in this circle the idea was coming to be held that sin is social rather than individual in character, and that the Christian effort must concentrate on reforming society. Christian ideas about human nature also squared with age-old proverbs: people accepted the maxim, "You can't change human nature", but they also quoted the conflicting proverb, "As the twig is bent, so the tree inclines."

On a more sophisticated level men still largely subscribed to the faculty psychology which Professor Thomas Upham of Bowdoin College had done so much to popularize. This assumed a duality of body and mind. The body was the seat of those base impulses which to the orthodox meant original sin. But the mind was made up of capacities classified under the faculties of understanding, feeling and will. Through the will man could rule his baser impulses and translate his innate moral ideas into action. Properly disciplined by early formal training, reason and

Political Science Quarterly, 68 (December 1953), 492-505, 507-508. Reprinted by permission of the author and *Political Science Quarterly*. Footnotes have been omitted.

will could enable individuals to eliminate traditional shortcomings in themselves and in society. Thus the academic scheme of human nature represented a synthesis of Christianity and the Enlightenment.

Such optimistic views of human nature were firmly entrenched in American thought of 1860 despite some dissident notes. These ideas had so long been dominant in the thinking of leading Americans that by that time they were commonplace even among the masses. They were reflected in dime novels, in the popular women's magazines, and in Fouth of July orations.

It is not strange that so dominant a philosophy of human nature was very little affected by a tremendous event in 1859, the publication of Darwin's *The Origin of Species*. This did provoke a lively response as the years passed, particularly in intellectual circles. But it did not at first cause even intellectuals to doubt *their* ability to get at *the* truth. Not for perhaps fifty years did this doubt even begin to be a serious one in their thinking—not indeed until William James and John Dewey spoke so plainly that they had to listen. No wonder that the retreat from reason was a very slow one.

Just as the traditional formulations about human nature continued after 1859 to enjoy wide credence, so did the social "sciences" associated with these formulations. Economics, political science, sociology and history continued to appeal to the older ideas about human nature for validity. Even as late as the turn of the twentieth century the academic social studies were for the most part formal, rational and highly schematic. Each one, as synthesized by eminent writers, postulated universal and unchanging laws—laws comparable to those governing the mind in faculty psychology or the physical universe in Newton's system. These laws, discovered by the use of reason, were all highly reasonable and abstract. And they were well cloaked with moral virtue.

It is possible to comment only briefly on these formal and rationalistic social disciplines. The classical and neoclassical economics assumed that the individual acts rationally, and that reason leads him to avoid pain and seek pleasure. It also assumed that the economy is governed by abstract and unchangeable laws of supply and demand. It further assumed that any complete economic equality as between individuals is out of the question—it does not for one thing square with the inequality of endowment of individuals. Neither, so the neoclassical economy held, does it square with universal economic laws. But on the other hand, if these laws are obeyed, then a reasonable equilibrium between desires and satisfactions can be counted on. The way is open to economic progress if not to economic utopia.

In the field of political thought we again find the assumption of a system governed by certain laws of nature. According to these laws, formulated in the seventeenth century and analogous to Newton's laws of gravitation, every individual possesses inalienable rights to life, liberty and property. Government exists to protect the individual in these rights. It cannot properly interfere with their natural operation by favoring the weak and improvident at the expense of the strong and capable. To do so would deny to the latter their natural rights to liberty and property. The national sovereign state can, however, use its police powers in war to protect the natural rights of its citizens when these are menaced by aggressors beyond the national boundaries. Such was the prevailing synthesis of political science familiar to our grandfathers in the 1870's and 1880's and in a sense, to our fathers on the threshold of our own century.

In the sphere of social relations, the sociology of three quarters of a century ago was coming to terms with the nineteenth-century doctrine of evolution in a greater degree than had the sister disciplines of economics and political science. But sociology was also formal and rationalistic—theoretical and schematic in its conception of absolute laws. These permitted the able and ambitious to climb the social ladder; but if one failed to take advantage of the ladder, or slipped in the effort, he must be content with his status. The social laws also included the acceptance by women of their limited role. So too the inferior races must accept their inferiority. But in each case there was room for improvement—within the proscriptions set by nature.

At the very time that the formal, moralistic and rational synthesis of the social studies was achieved, new and revolutionary developments had begun to challenge the dualistic faculty psychology with its emphasis on an innate rationality and morality in human nature. In America it was not a scientist but a poet who first proclaimed an entirely naturalistic and monistic view of man. Walt Whitman rejected all antitheses between body and soul and identified morality with obedience to nature's law of the organic unity of man. Such evil as the Good Grey Poet saw in "flippant people with hearts of rag and souls of chalk" he laid at the door of man's refusal to accept the unity of body and soul. But few took Whitman's startling and shocking message very seriously.

If at first a similar hostility greeted kindred ideas blown to our shores by the new scientific currents, in the long run these proved telling. In 1867 Edward Livingston Youmans called attention to the progress that had been made, chiefly abroad, in the scientific study of human nature. He pointed to the implications of the physiological discoveries of Sir Charles Bell and Dr. Marshall Hall; of the far-reaching theory of Sir Charles Darwin; and of the application by Helmholtz and others of the techniques of physics to the study of sensations. Other Americans discovered the pioneer work of Wundt in the laboratory study of mental activity. In later decades careful observations and controlled experiments, especially in relation to the behavior of animals and young children, showed the continutiy of animal and human behavior. All this was, of course, in line with the theory of organic evolution.

One highly significant result of the development of biology in the later half of the nineteenth century was the more specific content given to the hitherto loosely used term instinct. A German Darwinian, Preyer, elaborated a list of specific instincts which he applied to an analysis of child and adult behavior. In America William James listed some fifty instincts which his pupils Thorndike and Woodworth still further extended. The discoveries of the geneticists, Mendel, Weismann, Morgan and others, led to a sharpened and more precise analysis of instincts in purely biological terms. In time it became evident that many of the so-called instincts were in truth not inherited mechanisms but rather acquired patterns of behavior. But before this became fully evident many psychologists, including James and, especially, G. Stanley Hall, taught that inherited patterns of behavior provided the natural if not the inevitable foundation for the subordinate role of women and of the backward races, for war, and for competitive capitalism.

The darker view of human nature which in the earlier Age of Reason and Morality had found only such exceptional literary exponents as Hawthorne and Melville was now buttressed both by the new Darwinian emphases and by incoming literary currents from abroad. Half-whimsically, half-seriously, Mark Twain held man up to scorn for pretending to a morality denied the higher animals. The satirist went so far in *The Mysterious Stranger* as to dub man "such an unreasoning creature that he is not able to perceive that the Moral Sense degrades him to the bottom layer of animated beings and is a shameful possession." Dr. Oliver Wendell Holmes wrote his "medicated novels" in which he made a sweeping use of the mechanistic and unconscious factors in human behavior. His proto-Freudian essay, "Mechanism in Thought and Morals," discussed these on the scientific level.

Conservatives who opposed the program of feminists, pacifists and socialists declared, "You can't argue with an instinct." When Henry George asked Edward Livingston Youmans what could be done about the poitical corruption and the selfishness of the rich in promoting it, the disciple of Darwin and Spencer replied: "Nothing! It's all a matter of evolution. Perhaps in four or five thousand years evolution may have carried men beyond this state of things." The same conviction that selfishness, competition and struggle, based on an instinctive nature, governed social relations was reflected in the Middletown of the 1930's—"the strongest and best survive—that's the law of nature after all—always has been and always will be."

But you would be left with a very false impression if you supposed that the newer biological study of human nature did nothing more than to buttress faith in the inevitability of war, racial and sex inferiority, economic competition and the *status quo* generally. In undermining the older view of human nature as innately rational and moral, the new psychology did not close the doors entirely to the traditionally American faith in meliorism. In the functionalist phase which the new psychology in the United States assumed under the leadership of James, Mead and Dewey, mind was thought of as the capacity of the organism to adapt itself to situations, to solve problems. The traditional concept of motivation and learning was rejected for the more realistic one of the adaptation of the organism to changing situations through problem-solving.

In John Dewey especially the new views about human nature reenforced the optimistic faith in man's capacity to shape his future in ways that seemed desirable and good. It is worth nothing that Dewey developed his views in the first two decades of the twentieth century when the movement for social, political and economic reform was at high tide. At the very turn of the century he argued that all concepts of human nature are, as it were, politically determined. The theory that human nature does not and cannot change was, he insisted, a view functional to and prevalent in aristocracies. The democratic scheme of human nature emphasized thinking as problem-solving and living as a cooperative social enterprise in which experience was reconstructed on ever more satisfying levels, individual and social. In other words, far from conceding that the new psychology struck a blow at the old faith in man's capacity for progress and democracy, Dewey held that it actually opened new avenues to those objectives. His view of human nature was at its core essentially American in its emphasis on mind-in-use and on man's ability to make adjustments in a changing environment which he himself could direct. "True psychology", he declared, "is itself a conception of democracy."

In rejecting dualism, in questioning the sweeping scope so many psychologists gave to instincts and to imitation in learning, above all in repudiating the idea of mind as fixed structure, Dewey advanced a democratic and one may say an American conception of human nature. Some now think he was too optimistic, but one must nevertheless note that much empirical investigation in school, clinic, industry, and mass communication supports his thesis. And in the current programs for the study and improvement of human relations we have an impressive tribute to his theory of human nature.

Dewey represented not only a retreat from the earlier rationalistic conception of the autonomous individual. He also in a sense represented a qualification of the emphasis of the early scientific studies of human nature in terms of biology and physics. In supplementing this emphasis with a consideration of man in his social context Dewey supported the cultural anthropologists. Many of these shared his optimistic views about the potentialities of human nature. For cultural anthropologists questioned the assumption that all the traits common to Western civilization represented absolute laws governing all human behavior everywhere. On the contrary, careful scientific investigations of many primitive peoples seemed to indicate that competition and aggression, presumably universal traits, scarcely exist in certain cultures. Moreover, far from regarding women as mentally inferior, some peoples assumed that women are more highly endowed in intelligence and other desirable traits than men. And it was something of a shock to learn that just as we looked down on primitive peoples as innately inferior to us, so they regarded us as innately inferior to them. If we spurned the long-haired Kaffirs as little more than baboons, they regarded our almost bald pates and our inability to get along in their forests as proofs of innate inferiortiy.

The implications of all this gave a much larger sphere to culture than to biology in explaining complex characteristics of collective behavior; undermined the assumption that universal economic, political and social laws govern all peoples; and postulated a relativism in discussions of human nature. Also if culture is more important than biology in many hitherto unsuspected spheres, the way is open to an enlarged and reenforced faith in the possibility of uprooting man's exploitation of man, war and other customs assumed to rest on inborn characteristics.

These emerging ideas of human nature rested not only on the functional psychology and the pragmatic instrumentalist philosophy of James and Dewey and on cultural anthropology. They also drew support from and gave support to vigorous nonconformist and protest movements on the political, social and economic stage in the era of progressivism and the new freedom. Also related to the newer ideas about human nature and to protests against the *status quo* was a new approach to social, economic and political problems. The breakdown of the older, rationalistic, schematic conception of human nature inevitably weakened the various syntheses of the social studies that had drawn support from the traditional rationalistic conception of human nature.

Equally important was the fact that in the later decades of the nineteenth century and in the first decade of our own, the pressure of industrial and urban problems became so great that social scientists began to study these problems empirically. Field surveys, case histories, and, above all, quantitative or statistical techniques revolutionized the older rational social studies by imbuing them with both empiricism and faith. Economists now concerned themselves no longer with studying abstract economic principles or laws which they applied to imaginary problems, such as Robinson Crusoe's classical economic behavior on a lonely island. They turned rather to specific, fact-finding studies of price behavior, of depressions, and of actual economic institutions, such as corporations, labor unions, and cooperatives; for these were now seen to influence economic activity in ways that failed to correspond to the older ideas about economic law.

Skillful advertising technicians, appealing to sex, prestige and desire to conform, proved that demand could be vastly expanded. One advertisement pictured a hopeful, hard-working business man bent over his papers as he weighed a new investment versus a household demand. The caption read, "No use balancing your books if your wife can't balance a teacup." Experiments in paying higher wages for a bigger output upset older ideas about the iron law of wages. Friction between labor and management often yielded to insights gleaned from the new knowledge about human nature. This emphasis on the application to specific problems of the new insights reenforced the faith both in man's power to shape his economic future and in the democratic belief that the poorest need not always be with us.

And there were similar changes in political studies. Empirical investigations of concrete problems proved that it was possible greatly to improve administration and efficiency in a democracy. Other studies suggested that lawmaking is the result of various pressures of interested groups rather than of any use of abstract reasoning. Laws came to be increasingly regarded, not as timeless, unchanging absolutes, but as instruments for adjusting in varied ways to changing human needs. All this strengthened the belief that, however great the difficulties, men are not governed by absolute political and economic laws, but that economic and political phenomena are far more complex and relative, and therefore more malleable, than had been assumed.

These implications are even more striking when we turn to the rising empirical studies of crime, delinquency, and other social problems. The new theories of human nature suggested that aberrant behavior may be more largely the result of conditioning, of the impact of specific and unfortunate experiences and situations, than of faulty will power or deficient reasoning. In proving the direct relation between unfortunate environment and crime and delinquency, and in demonstrating the useful potentialities of counseling, social workers still further strengthened the belief that man need not helplessly submit to a fate he cannot control. New knowledge about the relation of inadequate nutrition or of deficient glandular activity or of harrowing childhood fears to mental illness revolutionized attitudes in this sphere. And the teachings of the cultural anthropologists and, in later years, of the social psychologists about the cultural as opposed to the biological bases for differences among men encouraged Negroes and their white champions in their fight against discrimination. Psychologists proved that women possess as a group quite as high intelligence as men and have potentially quite as varied interests, and such finding reenforced the democratic movement to enlarge the opportunities of women in every sphere—educational, political, economic and social. It came to be recognized that the Victorian authority Havelock Ellis quoted was wrong in regarding the suggestion that women possess sexual feelings as "a vile aspersion". The current Kinsey report speaks to this point!

The conception of human nature associated with the name of John Dewey has continued to be applied in many fields of human relations. But currents of thought in many ways quite opposite have gained increasing vogue. I have already called attention to the pessimistic overtones of the hereditarian emphasis on instincts—to the weight given to biology in the nature-nurture controversies. The early efforts to measure intelligence also seemed to run counter to the traditional view that all men possess rational faculties in a relatively high degree. But before commenting on the sweepingly antirationalistic and antidemocratic interpretations given to the testing movement I must recall to mind the gloomy overtones implicit in the teachings of Freud.

Freud's message had already been heralded, at least in part, by the pioneer work of the Boston psychiatrist, Dr. Morton Prince. This too-often neglected American emphasized the large rôle of the unconscious, of repression, and of conflict in mental aberrations. He welcomed Freud who visited the United States in 1908. Freud's teachings became increasingly familiar in the era after World War I. Without using the experimental techniques and the controlled observations of the objective psychologists, the Freudians developed a theory of human nature which, in emphasizing the importance of sex, contributed to a better understanding of motivation and behavior. This was particularly to the point in view of the traditional neglect of sex in the early faculty psychology and even in the great *Principles* of William James.

The newer views about the nonrational factors in behavior were abundantly illustrated in the First World War, an event which both in itself and in its aftermath did much to shake the older confidence in the inevitability of progress. In this country intellectuals were shocked to see evidences of sadism and cruelty on the battlefield and in the prison camp. The widespread sense of catastrophe, futility and defeat was expressed in a cartoon which pictured a baboon contemplating an endless sea of soldiers' graves and saying, "If this goes on we will have to start all over again!" On another level thoughtful men and women were horrified to see how readily a highly charged emotional war propaganda was stimulated and how quickly a frightening mass hysteria resulted. What lay in store in the 1950's was anticipated at the trial in 1917 of fifteen professors at the University of Nebraska for alleged pro-Germanism on the most flimsy testimony, and the senseless persecution of countless citizens whose German-sounding names suggested guilt by association. Even more shocking than all this was the way in which the war forced almost everyone to take the recital of wholesale slaughter without turning a hair. All these things illustrated grimly enough the newer revelations about the irrationality of the human make-up.

In the years that followed the First World War new evidences of irrationality weakened still further the older confidence in the ability of an essentially reasonable and moral human nature to shape a future of freedom, democracy and peace. Propaganda was organized on a huge scale and used not only by advertising men and pressure groups. Some political leaders who had formerly trusted "the people's will" now began to see that those in power could call on the skillful techniques of the public relations specialists and other experts to sway large masses of human beings. Grave doubts increased as to whether the people are rational and moral, whether the people are really always right. The psychological testing done during the war seemed to indicate so low a general intelligence that some jumped to the conclusion that the average person is simply too dumb to perform the functions of citizenship with any competence. Even when more critical psychologists demonstrated the inadequacy of the first tests and the errors in interpreting them, the idea of the average dumbness remained—and bolstered the doctrine of the elite as preached on the one hand by the eugenicists and on the other by the new humanists of the Irving Babbitt and Paul Elmer More persuasion. Many climbed on the bandwagon of Henry Mencken and echoed his gibe that democracy is, in view of the low IQ of the masses, only boobocracy. These ideas did not die even when psychologists pointed out that the IQ was only an arbitrary measure, needing still more careful analysis, and not even fixed in any individual.

The faltering record of the League of Nations did not do much to keep alive a confidence that man can uproot war. It did not add to the peace of mind of thinking people, either, when social scientists demonstrated the emptiness of mere verbal professions of peace, such as personal pledges never to fight—or even the Kellogg-Briand Pact. In the 1830's Professor Thomas C. Upham of Bowdoin College had argued that if only the peoples would insist that their rulers renounce war, peace would be at hand. Ironically, now in the 1930's they were insisting, but peace seemed farther away than ever.

In the 1930's the new revelations about the irrationality of men were even more shockingly illustrated. The inhuman atrocities committed by Fascists and Nazis against their fellow men weakened the belief that it is possible to control men's social behavior intelligently for truly social ends. Reports of purges in the Kremlin began to blast the earlier roseate predictions of well-known American authorities that in eliminating competition and insecurity the Soviet experiment was creating a happier version of human nature than Western man had known. I need hardly add that the experiences of the post-war world have confirmed the growing doubts—the tension and fears, the uncertainties and anxieties associated with the atom bomb and the cold war are all too much with us. One example, which will be easily recalled, is symptomatic of the waning faith in man's ability to shape his social destiny into moral and rational channels. I refer to the articles in *Colliers Magazine* for October 7, 1952. The story, told by our distinguished playright and biographer, Robert E. Sherwood, and a galaxy of well-known writers, describes the third world war—*the war we did not want but could not prevent*. This shocking profession of inability to direct our future as we want it to be was indeed not quite all-inclusive and absolute. For even the *Colliers* writers envisaged the reconstruction of a defeated Soviet Union in accordance with dominant American ideas about freedom and comfort—including a style show in the Kremlin to give Soviet women the fashions they have been unhappily pining for these thirty odd years! But if some faith survives in our ability to shape our future at least in part, the picture is indeed very different from that associated with the doctrine of human nature widely held in the Age of Reason and Morality and in the first phase of the intellectual revolution of the early twentieth century. . . .

. . . In the nineteenth century the great value attached to individual freedom—a value functional to so much elbow room and to such wide and varied opportunities—was complemented by the habit of forming and joining voluntary associations. Thus men and women escaped in at least some degree the loneliness that individualism often meant. We still have our voluntary associations. But, though the crowds are bigger than they were in the Age of Reason and Morality—if they are not lonelier—one must now think at least twice before running the risk of possible guilt by association! Man himself may not be obsolete, even in a world of incalculable and perhaps uncontrollable instruments of destruction. But in some quarters the feeling prevails that freedom and the will to use it for social reconstruction are more or less obsolete.

Finally, the reaction against the intellectual revolution of the later nineteenth century and the early twentieth may perhaps also be seen in the distrust in many circles of the scientific method itself as an instrument for guiding men out of chaos and darkness into peace and light. Perhaps it is another irony of American history that the scientific methods and techniques to which we owe so much can also be used to incite hysterical emotion and to make man's destruction of humanity more efficient. Thus in the amazing atomic age the retreat from reason has led many to abandon faith in science. No substitute, no new faith, has as yet been found which seems completely to fill the gap left by the retreat from reason. Neither neo-Thomism nor neo-orthodoxy has swept the country. May, perhaps, the future historian conclude that the dominant faith of our time is the religion of nationalism—the American way? This of course is not a new faith. It goes back to our colonial experience. It was nourished by the Enlightenment and by its romantic aftermath. It was consolidated and sharpened as the nineteenth century ran its course. Yet nationalism now seems to have fewer competing loyalties than ever before.

All this suggests that the exponents of the newer theories of human nature and of the empirical approach in the social sciences expected too much, too soon. Many feel that science has been a god, and a false one no longer to be trusted to establish goals and to determine values by which man is to live. Hence the tendency of many to seek for security in authoritarian philosophies or orthodox religious faith. Hence the tendency of others to turn their faces against the unresolved conflicts of our time and to find solace in the arts. Hence the tendency of still others to despair of man's faith in his ability to bring about that which ought to be, to give way rather to the dark and hopeless cult of irrationality, or to brood on the rediscovery and implications of the problem of evil. Hence the renewed faith in American nationalism, and renewed opposition in many quarters to internationalism.

Time, of course, may prove that the current reaction against both the surviving heritage of the Age of Reason and Morality and the intellectual revolution of the last part of the nineteenth century and the early years of our own is only temporary. Certainly the historian may properly suggest that this may be the case. If so, the historian of the future will attach less importance to the reaction than do many thoughtful men and women today. It is of course natural for those who came to maturity in a world of depression, war, and prospects of war to expect little—to expect *too* little, to reconcile themselves too easily to an acceptance of what is and what seems likely to be. It is also understandable that many of my generation whose hopes have been dimmed by mankind's crucifixion in the past quarter of a century should share the view so common apparently among younger people in this country and in so many others. But I for one am convinced that this is not the part either of realism or of wisdom. Or of sound historical perspective. For, should the world crisis persist, should fear and suspicion and hatred and reliance on force continue to be man's chief outlet, then we may be sure that we shall have to face crises that will shake the world—and events that may quite possibly destroy civilization.

Each of us, whether he knows it or not has some kind of a world view, vague and inarticulate, or clear and expressed. Each must take some stand in the current crisis. Not to take one is, in effect, to take one. . . .

39
The Spirit of American Philosophy

John E. Smith

This selection is part of the final chapter in a book by Professor John E. Smith of Yale University. His definition of a philosophic "spirit" in America, particularly the America of the last one hundred years, is a fitting conclusion to these readings and an invitation to consider whether the history of ideas will continue along the paths charted in the past as Americans enter the last quarter of the twentieth century.

For further reading: *George Santayana, *Character and Opinion in the United States* (1920); Ralph Barton Perry, *Characteristically American* (1949); Henry Steele Commager, "The Twentieth Century American," in his **The American Mind: An Interpretation of American Thought and Character since the 1880s* (1950), pp. 406-443; David M. Potter, "The Quest for the National Character," in *John Higham (ed.), *The Reconstruction of American History* (1962), pp. 197-220; *C. Wright Mills, *The Sociological Imagination* (1959).

The "golden period of American philosophy," as it has been called, the period of James, Royce, and Peirce, extends from just after the Civil War to the nineteen-thirties. It falls between what is generally known as the "classic background" of American thought—the age reaching back to Jonathan Edwards and Samuel Johnson of King's College—and the developments of the present. The golden period marks the coming of age of philosophical thinking in America and it embraces our best-known philosophical minds. They shaped and brought to clearest expression what we have called the "spirit of American philosophy." Can we now summarize that spirit as a prelude to asking about its presence on the current scene?

The answer to this question must begin with a word about the idea of "spirit" itself. By the spirit of a philosophical development is meant something which is at once more and less than a set of doctrines. A spirit is something more because it means, in addition to formulated beliefs, a style, a stance toward life in the world, and strong convictions about the importance of reflective thought. A spirit is something less than a body of consciously formulated doctrines because it stands deeply rooted in the life of a people as a kind of unwritten philosophy. In the figure used by Peirce, it would be in our muscles prior to finding its way into our learned tradition. Unfortunately, the annoying fact about styles and unwritten philosophies is that, while we may apprehend them in some not very clear way by living in the society animated by them, we are unable to communicate them to others unless we express them in the form of definite beliefs or doctrines. This we must do, but accompanied by the hope that what has been said about the peculiar character of a "spirit" will not be forgotten.

There are three dominant or focal beliefs through which our philosophic spirit can be articulated. First, the belief that thinking is primarily an *activity* in response to a concrete situation and that this activity is aimed at solving problems. Second, the belief that ideas and theories must have a "cutting edge" or must *make a difference* in the conduct of people who hold them and in the situations in which they live. Third, the belief that *the earth can be civilized* and obstacles to progress overcome by the application of knowledge. Taken together, these beliefs define a basically humanistic outlook—in the end, the spirit of philosophical thinking in America represents another outcropping of that ancient tradition established by the reflective genius of Socrates and Plato in which the Good is the dominant category. From this perspective all things derive their value from the contribution they make to the founding and securing of the good life.

These three beliefs are equally basic, although the philosophers whose views we have considered do not illustrate them in the same manner or to the same degree. When it is said that thought is an activity and a response to a situation, several distinct but related ideas are involved. For the pure rationalist fond of emphasizing the timeless character of conceptual meanings and of logical connections, it appears beside the point to describe thought in terms of the concrete setting in which it takes place. For the rationalist, to emphasize the fact that thinking is an activity, that it takes time, and that it is carried on by individual human beings, means no more than to call attention to a "psychological" aspect which really does not enter into the essential nature of thought. Not so for Peirce, James, Royce, and Dewey. Each in his own way started with the insight that thought—better, thinking—is an activity which is engaged in by human beings and that it emerges in human life under specific conditions. In other words, what Dewey called the *context* of thought, the historical setting and its problems, enters essentially into the meaning of reflective activity. Thinking is not something which happens in a world apart from or beyond the one in which all live; on the contrary, it is called forth by circumstances in our own world and it is responsive both to the demands imposed by the environment and to the interests of the individual thinker.

Of special importance is the reciprocal relation that exists between demand and response. The doctrine that reflective thinking is and must be oriented toward specific problems is the counterpart of the thesis that such thinking is called forth only upon occasions when there is some incongruity or lack of adjustment between the thinking individual and the concrete situation confronting him. The theory underlying this description expresses a teleological process not always acknowledged. It tells us that since reflective thinking arises only when the smooth operation of habit is interrupted by a problem, the whole function of such thinking must be to solve that problem. Thinking becomes a means to an end; its purpose is solving problems. This theory has been the occasion for sharp differences of opinion among the thinkers we have considered.

While each of them accepted the general thesis that thinking is directed by purposes and oriented toward the good, Peirce, Royce, and Whitehead differed sharply from James and Dewey on the issue of thought's autonomy. The first three argued for the universal character of thought and for its independence of *individual* plans and purposes. It is interesting to notice that, in contrast with James and Dewey they were all proponents of *formal* logic and their interest in this subject and in the related mathematical fields led them to reject any theory which puts thought wholly under the constraint of extra-rational factors or purely practical considerations.

The difference of outlook is by no means unimportant. James and Dewey, though divided in their views at several crucial points, were at one in rejecting the ancient rationalist ideal according to which reason has its own goal and canons of truth. Pragmatism meant in the end the subordination of rational thought to an immanent, human, and practical goal; for the pragmatists the criterion of reason stands outside of reason in the sense that it is found in the success or failure of thinking to reach a desired practical goal. While Royce was willing to speak of logic as the expression of rational purpose; while Peirce was ready to say that thought has the function of producing belief and shaping habit; and while Whitehead could speak of the practical reason which Ulysses shares with the foxes; *no one of them was willing to make the test of reason consist in wholly non-cognitive terms*. Instead each maintained the ancient ideal of rational truth. Royce spoke of the rational will to know the whole truth as known to the Absolute Self. Peirce envisaged a community of knowers seeking a truth independent of the interests of any one member. Whitehead laid down criteria for judging the validity of a speculative scheme which presuppose that reason can exercise a distinctively intellectual function. The doctrine, therefore, that thinking is an activity performed by man, that it is a means of answering questions and of resolving problems, is broader than pragmatism itself. The latter position is one form only of the general thesis. Characterized by the special claim that since reflective thinking arises only when the situation presents a challenge or a difficulty, it finds its final test in its ability to achieve a practical goal. Not all of our philosophers would accept that claim.

To understand the spirit of American philosophy it is necessary to take full account of the distinction just developed. While thinkers like Peirce, Royce, and Whitehead had their own interpretation of thought as an activity carried on by individual persons in an historical setting, they did not accept the pragmatist thesis that the practical context of thought sets all the conditions for judging the validity of the ideas and theories which result from rational activity. This does not mean that in rejecting pragmatism as a philosophical doctrine they wanted to return to an older rationlism in which the concrete setting of thought does not count. On the contrary, they believed that reason can intervene in human life, that it can establish connections with human purposes and goals without at the same time losing its autonomy. It is an error to ignore, as critics sometimes have, the fact that many American thinkers who have talked about the function of reason in human life or the intimate connection between logic and the human will have at the same time refused to accept a place in the ranks of the pragmatists.

The second feature of the philosophic spirit in America—the belief that ideas must have a "cutting edge," that they must make a difference in human life and conduct—has long been regarded as the essence of the American character. Two basic ideas are involved: one is that thinking should be focused not on the universal, general, and "timeless" problems, but rather on specific difficulties arising here and now; the second is that the power of ideas to shape the course of events depends directly on the extent to which they are acted upon and used to guide the conduct of men.

By specific problems are meant such questions as, how to improve *this* school system; how to resolve *this* conflict between labor and management; how to tame *this* river and turn it into a source of power. Such questions came to be regarded as the proper targets of thought because of the feeling that, since they have a "here and now" about them, their solutions can readily be used to transform a situation or guide our conduct. The contention has been that our total intellectual energy should be aimed at meeting these issues and that we have no time for dealing with problems of a generalized nature which have no clear focal point in time. Dewey expressed this point very well when he said that all our efforts should be aimed at eliminating the *evils* of human life, but that we have no time to speculate about the *problem of evil*. The complaint is that the latter is a metaphysical and religious question and the answer to it does not show us *how* to do away with poverty, disease, and injustice in particular situations.

Closely connected with this focus on specific problems is the belief that intellectual activity is justified to the extent to which its results are translated into action. Ideas that make a difference are those upon which people act. An idea must not merely inform us or please us, but rather it must move us to action and to the changing of our ways. If an idea does neither, it is worthless and may be ignored. The "practical" orientation so often associated with American life and thought is most evident at this point; an idea is a "mere" idea unless we can see how a situation is changed through the medium of that idea. If, after having the idea, everything remains the same as it was before, then the idea makes no difference —it is without a cutting edge.

The demand that thought be directed to specific problems expresses not only the American concern for locating and overcoming immediate difficulties; it expresses as well some embarrassment in the face of speculative questions about the foundations of life and the meaning of death. If the demand reveals a high confidence in the power of thought to resolve immediate problems, it also betrays a tendency to underestimate man's nature as a reflective animal. It is not a matter of the traditional clash between theory and practice, but rather of the difference between distinct types of questions. In a complex, technological culture we encounter immediate problems stemming from a multitude of maladjustments and failures in the spheres of business, politics, economic development, education, and public health. The specific and immediate problems are largely of a "practical" sort in the sense that their solution calls for technical knowledge and the proposal of definite courses of action.

Unhappily confusion sets in at the point where "real" problems are identified with those immediate difficulties which the instrumental intelligence can handle. The fundamental question is whether the "problems of men" are all of this kind. May it not be that there are times when the most "practical" problems of all, the problems whose solutions will make the greatest difference both to individuals and the society at large, are the largely speculative questions of the kind called "useless" by the practically oriented reason? This possibility has been a constant source of uneasiness for the American mind. Even if we define man as the tool-making and problem-solving animal, the question still remains as to *which* problems he will tackle. The fact is that man is more than a technician; he is a reflective being who is concerned about himself, his nature and destiny. Not all of the problems he confronts are of the sort which the pragmatic intelligence finds congenial. James and Royce saw this most clearly, despite the divergence in their views on other topics. Each saw that man is a being for whom such questions as the meaning of responsibility, the reality of God, the place of intelligent beings in the universe, and the status of beauty, are all "practical" problems of the highest importance. And yet they are precisely of the sort which Dewey, for example, advised us to disregard. These issues differ from the sort of immediate, specific problem generally called "real" by the typical hard-headed American. They differ in their scope especially, because they refer to life and the world as a whole rather than to some special province. They may have their special import for this or that person, but they are general in character, referring to man as man and to the relatively permanent nature of things. Nevertheless they cannot be ignored nor can they be spirited away as "impractical." Since mid-century it has become increasingly clear that questions about man and his inner life—his morality, his religion, his sanity—have taken command as the "real" problems of men.

The primacy of action remains, nevertheless. Ever since the days of Jonathan Edwards action has been taken as the chief clue to the sincerity of the individual. Willingness to act upon a belief, especially one involving risk, meant that a person took seriously what he professed to believe. This often meant that the active part of man's nature overshadowed the purely intellectual, the aesthetic, and the religious. Here William James set the pattern. Ideas and beliefs reveal their true meaning when we know the conduct to which they lead. Gradually there was established the idea that thought must be limited to what has direct bearing on human conduct; the notions that cannot be translated into some course of action were to be ignored.

Whatever belongs to religious interpretation, aesthetic appreciation, and the satisfaction of speculative curiosity is finally overshadowed by overt activity aimed at control of the external environment. When James, for example, interpreted religion and theology he found it difficult to attach meaning to such theological concepts as guilt and atonement because he could not see how they might be translated into human conduct. Despite his deep understanding of religion as a living force in life, and his sympathetic description of its many forms, he did not take seriously enough man's quest for *understanding*, his need for a unified outlook on the world which takes us beyond action and striving. Job, for example, passionately hoped for the end of his troubles and sufferings, but he sought even more fervently for an understanding of the world, for a ground of belief in the basic justice of things; he sought for an answer to the question: Why do human beings suffer?

The answer to that question, if indeed an answer can be found, will not dictate a course of action; it will not tell us what to do if we want to elimnate suffering, although such an answer may well help us to face the world and its terrors with courage and resolve.

The third belief defining the American philosophic spirit strikes the note of optimism for which America has both been praised and attacked from within and without. The belief says that the environment of life can be transformed in accordance with human desires, that the face of nature can be civilized, and that major obstacles to progress can be overcome by the application of knowledge. This belief is the clearest expression of the American will; it represents what Santayana called "aggressive enterprise" and the spirit that inhabits the American skyscraper. Dewey gave to this belief its most forceful utterance. It coincides with his instrumental view of intelligence. Underneath it all is the conviction that no problems exist which are, in principle, incapable of being solved through applied knowledge. The universe presents no ultimate riddles and it sets no absolute limits to human ingenuity and skill. Wherever problems are encountered or obstacles arise, there is the place for human intelligence to demonstrate its ability to meet and master external circumstances.

Until recent years, this optimistic creed was directed largely to the external environment. The knowledge gained by the natural sciences was supposed to provide the means for meeting the obstacles to human development posed by physical nature. The knowledge and insight of the social sciences and of philosophy were to arm us against the problems arising out of historical and social life. The emphasis was objective and external in the sense that little attention was paid to the problem of subjective or internal controls. Man is the one who brings knowledge to bear upon the course of events and he is sovereign over the empire of intelligence. That man himself might prove to be the greatest problem and obstacle to progress was not, until recently, considered as a serious possibility. It is curious in the extreme that, apart from the researches of James, the problems of the human self, exposed by the work of Freud, were not taken seriously. It is not that important contributions had not been made by those working within the rapidly growing science of psychology; it is rather that throughout the years we have described as the golden period of American thought, little attention was paid to the concerns and problems most closely connected with the individual person. The tendency was to consider man as one more animal besides others, albeit more complex. If man was acknowledged to have a problematic side, the difficulty was insufficiently dedicated to the aims of science. The possibility that the ego has depths not to be apprehended by the experimental method or mastered by the instrumental intelligence was quietly passed by. Instead attention was directed to the attack upon the environment; it was believed that nature and history present the most troublesome stumbling blocks to progress and that it is they that must be conquered. The many crises which have characterized American life at mid-century have been due to an awareness that this old creed is inadequate. It is becoming clearer that controlling the external world is not enough and that more attention must be paid to the distinctively human problems of morality, of religion, and of art.

To sum up the spirit of philosophical thinking in America as it existed until mid-century, we may say that it represented a modern version of the ancient humanistic tradition which runs from ancient Greece through the Renaissance and the Enlightenment to the present day. American thinkers have been primarily "moralists" in the sense that, howsoever strong their interest in nature and in science has been, their ultimate focus has been on the uses of knowledge and the values of things for human purposes. The instrumental has been judged superior to the intrinsic and more often than not usefulness has been taken as its own final justification. . . .